THE NATIONAL BLACK DRAMA ANTHOLOGY

THE NATIONAL BLACK DRAMA ANTHOLOGY

ELEVEN PLAYS
from America's Leading
African-American Theaters

Edited by Woodie King, Jr.

APPLAUSE
NEW YORK • LONDON

An Applause Original
THE NATIONAL BLACK DRAMA ANTHOLOGY
Edited by Woodie King, Jr.

Library of Congress Cataloging-in-publication data:

The national black drama anthology : eleven plays from America's
    leading African-American theaters / edited by Woodie King, Jr.
        p.   cm.
    ISBN 1-55783-219-6
    1. American drama--Afro-American authors.   2. Afro-Americans-
-Drama.   I. King, Woodie.
PS628.N4N38   1995
812.008'896073--dc20   95-34945
                                                                    CIP

British Library Cataloging-in-publication data:
A catalogue record for this book is available from the British Library.

Applause Theatre Books, Inc.
211 West 71st Street   406 Vale Road
New York, NY 10023   Tonbridge KENT TN9 1XR
Phone: (212) 496-7511   Phone: 0732 35775
Fax: (212) 721-2856   Fax: 0732 770219

CONTENTS

Introduction

Yes, there is a series of theatres that produce predominantly new plays written by Black writers. To confound the reader even further, all of these theatres are Black controlled; all are located in the inner city sections of large metropolitan areas. Although this anthology represents only a fraction of these Black theatres; it is representative. These plays celebrate the diversity of Black voices writing for the American theatre. The playwrights cover a broad range of very basic Black concerns; observing the changing status of Black people in America and recording and defining the history of a people.

The theatres from whence these plays emerged are integral to the Black continuum. The theaters and productions are chronologically introduced by the age of the institutions. The oldest theatre is Karamu located in Cleveland, Ohio. It recently celebrated its 80th Anniversary. The first plays of Langston Hughes were first presented at Karamu. For over forty years Karamu has experimented with non-traditional color blind casting of its productions. An excellent trained group of Black actors and actresses from Karamu are now working in the professional theatre and in the motion picture industry.

In Dahomey is the restructured and adapted book by Shauneille Perry for the music of Will Marion Cook. The original book was written by Jesse B. Shipp for the 1903 Broadway and London production which starred the comedy team of Bert Williams and George Walker. The Karamu production in 1990 was a huge hit; it was the first revival of *In Dahomey* since 1903.

The Inner City Cultural Center is a multi-racial institution; using Black, Asian and Latino artists in non-traditional ways for the past thirty- one years. In 1990, Inner City Cultural Center purchased the IVAR Theatre in Hollywood where it now produces all of its plays in Hollywood. However, *IAGO*, by C. Bernard Jackson was produced prior to the IVAR Theatre purchase. It was produced in the 1978/79 season by Inner City Cultural Center at Black Theatre/USA.

Iago is frequently described as the most villainous character in all the world's literature. C. Bernard Jackson's new portrait of Iago is one to challenge all the old assumptions. This work attempts to examine to relationship between Iago and Othello from a different vantage point; through the eyes of Iago's wife, Emelia.

The Negro Ensemble Company was founded in 1967 by Douglas Turner Ward, Gerald S. Krone, and Robert Hooks. It grew out of the Group Theatre Workshop founded in 1964 by Robert Hooks. The Negro Ensemble Company was considered the premiere Black theatre company from its inception with hits like: *Song of the Luisatanian Boggy, Ceremonies in Dark Old Men, Kongi's Harvest, Dream on Monkey Mountain, The First Breeze of Summer, River Niger, Sty of the Blind Pig, The Great McCaddy,* and *A Soldier's Play* just to name of few of its hits. The Negro Ensemble Company theatre training program ranked with the best in the United States. The faculty included Paul Mann, Lloyd Richards, Ron Mack, Kristin Linklater, Louis Johnson, Lonne Elder, and Michael Schultz. In the mid-1980s, after NEC's hit "A Soldier's Play," the company's funding was severely reduced. Ten years later, as of this writing, Negro Ensemble Company is in the process of revitalizing itself.

Henrietta, by Karen Jones-Meadows is a three character play that had an excellent reception at Negro Ensemble Company. Karen Jones-Meadows is one of only a handful of women playwrights produced by the company in its 28 year history. *Henrietta* was produced in the 1985 season.

The Federal Theatre represented here with *Robert Johnson: Trick the Devil,* by Bill Harris is only one of the many hits since the theatre's founding in 1970. Other outstanding productions were *Black Girl,* by j.e. Franklin, *In New England Winters,* by Ed Bullins, *What the Wine Sellers Buy,* by Ron Milner, *The Taking of Miss Janie,* by Ed Bullins, *For Colored Girls Who Have Considered Suicide when the Rainbow is Enuf,* by Ntozake Shange, *Showdown,* by Don Evans, *When Chickens Come Home to Roost,* by Lawrence Holder, *The Dance and the Railroad,* by David Henry Hwang, *Hospice,* by Pearl Cleage, *Long Time Since Yesterday,* by Vincent Smith, and *Robert Johnson: Trick the Devil,* by Bill Harris. With all of these visible works introduced into the American mainstream, it would seem New Federal Theatre is on secure ground; it is not. In 1989 New Federal Theatre became independent of its 19 years of funding from Henry Street Settlement. In the 1992/93 season *Robert Johnson: Trick the Devil* emerged as an outstanding hit. It won six AUDELCO Awards, including best production of the season.

ETA was incorporated in Chicago in 1971 as a non-profit organization. ETA Theatre is represented here in *Love's Light in Flight,* by Charles Michael Moore. ETA owns its theatre. It's the only theatre that could sustain itself by its large subscription audience. In 1995 ETA's subscription was 93% capacity. ETA's premiere productions of *Checkmates, Stepper's Ball, Stoops* and *Good Black Don't Crack* were huge hits. Its founder and producer, Abena Joan Brown, is an individual deeply committed to Black values and the Black community.

Charles Michael Moore is a major creative writer. His plays include the award winning *The Hooch, Tatum Family Blues,* and *Love's Light in Flight.*

Kuntu Repertory Theatre in Pittsburgh, Penumbra Theatre in Minneapolis, and Jomandi Productions in Atlanta represent a new breed of Black Theatres. Each of these theatres present traditional Black plays that were originally produced in New York as well as new works developed by the company. Rob Penny is the playwright-in-residence at Kuntu Repertory Theatre. All of his plays premiered there, including his outstanding hit *Good*

Black Don't Crack. Rob Penny introduced August Wilson to the theatre.

Marion McClinton and August Wilson created works for Penumbra Theatre. It is one of the top five Black Theatres in America in budget size.

Tom Jones and Marsh Jackson are co-artistic directors of Jomandi Productions. They write as well as direct and act. Marsha Jackson's *Sisters* is one of the theatre's longest running productions, including a five-week run off-Broadway in New York City.

Crossroads Theatre in New Brunswick, New Jersey is the largest and most visible Black Theatre company in America with a mid-90s budget of three million dollars. Its producing director is Ricardo Khan. Khan is also an excellent actor and fine director. With sheer energy and excellence Crossroads Theatre moved into a modern state-of-the-art theatre facility in the heart of New Brunswick. Crossroads Theatre is represented by two plays, *Buses*, by Denise Nicholas and *Tod, the Boy, Tod*, by Talvin Wilks. Why two plays from Crossroads Theatre? In the past five years the company produces a new play development series called GENESIS. Out of that series Crossroads Theatre selects its next season of plays. Crossroads has produced an incredible number of plays, almost twice as many as any the other Black Theatre.

Crossroads National Education and Arts Center of Los Angeles, not to be confused with Crossroads Theatre of New Brunswick, is a theatre institution under the direction of Marla Gibbs. Crossroads of Los Angeles is the youngest of all the Black companies included in this anthology. It also focuses more on its training program than on its production of new plays. The phenomenal success of Jeff Stetson's *The Meeting* however, prompted its inclusion in this collection. *The Meeting* is an excellent theatre piece for Black History Month presentations. It is the only theatre piece that exists with a dramatic face to face meeting between the Rev. Dr. Martin Luther King, Jr. and "our Black Shining Prince," Malcolm X.

These theatres and these plays must be brought to the attention of a larger audience. Publication is the best way to reach this audience. Historically, when a play produced by a Black theatre closes it ends the public's consciousness of the play. Very few people outside of its immediate audience will know of its existence until now.

The plays in this anthology represent an aesthetic unparalleled in most collections. Herein are hit plays from Black theatres and Black playwrights speaking on the Black experiences and never before mass published.

WOODIE KING, JR. is founder and producing director of the New Federal Theatre in New York City. New Federal Theatre has presented over 150 productions in its 24 year history. Mr. King produced the Off-Broadway productions of A Black Quartet, Black *Girl, Behold! Cometh The Vanderkellans, Prodigal Sister,* and *Medal of Honor Rag;* on Broadway, he co-produced *For Colored Girls Who Have Considered Suicide When The Rainbow Is Enuf, Reggae,* and *What The Winesellers Buy.* His direetorial credits are extensive and include work in film as well as theater. He directed five productions of *Home* by Samm-Art Williams at Cleveland Playhouse, Stagewest, Virginia Museum Theatre, Pittsburgh Public Theatre, and Cincinnati Playhouse; *Appear and Show Cause* by Steve Taylor at New Federal Theatre, Cleveland Playhouse and Pittsburgh Public Theater; *A Raisin In The Sun* by Lorraine Hansberry at GeVa Theatre; *Cockfight* by Elaine Jackson at American Place Theater; *Daddy* by Ed Bullins at New Federal Theater; *The First Breeze of Summer* by Leslie Lee at Center Stage of Baltimore; *Sizwe Bansi Is Dead* by Athol Fugard at Pittsburgh Public Theatre, Indiana Repertory Company, and Studio Arena of Buffalo; and *What The Winesellers Buy* at New Federal Theatre and New.York Shakespeare Festival Mobile Unit National Tour. In 1985, he was nominated for a Joseph Jefferson Award for *Boesman and Lena;* in 1986, he won an Audelco Award for *Appear And Show Cause* and in. the 1987/88 season he won a NAACP Image Award for *Checkmates* at Inner City Cultural Center (Los Angeles). He directed *Checkmates* on Broadway, at ETA (Chicago), Jomandi (Atlanta), Lorraine Hansberry (San Francisco) and Arena Stage (Washington, D.C.). In 1987, he directed *Splendid Summer* at American Place Theatre, Night,Mother at the Virginia Theatre Company. In 1989, he directed *Good Black Don't Crack* at ETA, Chicago; in 1990, *God's Trombones* at the Ford's Theatre, and *Joe Turner's Come and Gone* at the Detroit Rep. In 1991, he directed a new production of *A Raisin In The Sun* and in 1992 he directed *The Member of the Wedding* both at GeVa. In 1993, he directed *Good Black Don't Crack* at The Billie Holiday Theater in Brooklyn and produced and directed *Robert Johnson: Trick the Devil* for which he won Audelco Awards as Best Director and Best Play of the Year. That year he directed *Checkmates* at the St. Louis Black Repertory Theatre. In 1994, he has directed *And The World Laughs With You* at Crossroads Theatre Company in New Brunswick, NJ.; and *Mudtracks* by Regina Taylor at Ensemble Studio Theatre. He is currently directing *A Raisin In The Sun* at The Alliance Theatre in Atlanta.

Bill Harris

ROBERT JOHNSON: TRICK THE DEVIL

New Federal Theatre

Bill Harris

Bill Harris is an Associate Professor of English at Wayne State University in Detroit. He was previously Chief Curator at Detroit's Museum of African American History. While living in New York City in the 1980s, he was Production Coordinator for JazzMobile and the New Federal Theatre. During his stay in New York Harris had three productions, including *Stories About the Old Days*, which starred Abbey Lincoln, and *Every Goodbye Ain't Gone*, starring S. Epatha Merkerson and Denzel Washington.

Awards include a Rockefeller Foundation Writer in Residence Grant for *Coda*, a comedy/drama about jazz; the Theatre Communications Collaboration Grant for Artists; and the Distinguished Arts Achievement Award from Wayne State University.

Of particular interest to Harris is giving voice to the often unheard, ignored, or misunderstood independent and creative spirit of African American males. His characters are often jazz musicians, blues singers, and others who thrive outside the so-called "norm."

Harris is currently working on a novel, several plays, and a series of narrative poems on the life of Charlie Parker.

NEW FEDERAL THEATRE

The arts have always played a unique role at Henry Street Settlement. Since 1905, the landmark "Neighborhood Playhouse" has developed promising actors, directors, and playwrights while providing theatre experiences for thousands. Growing out of a theatre training program at Mobilization for Youth, New Federal Theatre (NFT) was officially founded by Woodie King, Jr. in 1970 at Henry Street Settlement. In the summer of 1970, we held our first training workshop, the Arts for Living Program. A small grant from the New York State Council on the Arts, together with funds from the Settlement, launched the Theatre's first season in the basement of St. Augustine's Church on Henry Street.

As of 1980, the New Federal Theatre has been an independent institution. Our workshop classes consist of the Teen Drama Workshop, and we recently combined the Black and Latino acting classes into the Multi-Cultural Professional Training Workshop. We also restructured our Women's Playwriting Class, renaming it the Zora Neale Hurston Writer's Workshop. The Reading Series offers women playwrights an opportunity to have their work rehearsed with professional actors and a director and read before an invited audience, with post-play feedback moderated by the director of the workshop. Over a four year period, from 1990 to 1994, the Zora Neale Hurston Writer's Workshop has presented 64 scripts to the public.

Now in its 25th season, New Federal Theatre has carved a much admired special niche for itself in the New York area and national theatre world. Specializing in minority drama, it has brought the joy of the living stage to many minorities who live in the surrounding Lower East Side Community and greater metropolitan area. It has brought minority playwrights, actors, and directors to national attention and has sponsored a variety of ethnic theatre groups and events. Writers first presented at New Federal Theatre are now a part of the literary mainstream of American playwrights. NFT has produced 150 plays and brought attention to over 100 playwrights. Many of the plays and playwrights have reached national significance and much wider audiences through being showcased at New Federal Theatre. The productions that began at New Federal Theatre have often moved to Broadway and larger venus, receiving such acclaimed awards as the Drama Desk and Drama Critics Circle Awards, Obie Awards, AUDELCO Awards, Tony nominations, and coveted prizes such as the Richard Rogers Productions Award of the American Academy and Institute of Arts and Letters, and the Kennedy Center Fund for New American Plays.

ROBERT JOHNSON: TRICK THE DEVIL
by Bill Harris

Directed by
Woodie King, Jr.

Cast in Alphabetical Order:

Kimbrough...JAMES CURT BERGWALL

Georgia..DENISE BURSE-MICKELBURY

Robert Johnson...GUY DAVIS

Stokes...GRENOLDO FRAZIER

Lem...HERMAN LEVERN JONES

Time: Late 1920s
Place: Georgia's Colored Jook Joint

SONGS AND MUSICAL NUMBERS

CROSSROADS BLUES...by Robert Johnson

HELLHOUND ON MY TRAIL.................................by Robert Johnson

STEADY ROLLIN MAN..by Robert Johnson

C'MON I MY KITCHEN ....by Robert Johnson

SOMEONE TO WATCH OVER ME................................by Guy Davis

PREACHIN' BLUES ....by Robert Johnson

STONES IN MY PASSWAY ....by Robert Johnson

CROSSROAD BLUES..by Robert Johnson

JUDGMENT DAY ....by Robert Johnson

OTHER MUSICAL BLUES SONGS BY GUY DAVIS

SETTING
A jook joint in the deep south.

TIME
Summer, 1938

CHARACTERS
STOKES: Blind piano player. A seer.
GEORGIA: Late 30s early 40s. Her own woman.
ROBERT JOHNSON: Mid 20s. Lean. Blues singer. insecure and braggado-
cios.
KIMBROUGH: White. New England academic.
LEM: A broken man in his late 30s early 40s. Georgia's Estranged husband.

The jook area should be divisible (when necessary) into two sections by means of
lighting, in order for separate conversations to take place unheard by those in the
adjacent section. One area is around the piano, the other centers around a table
set near the stairs to GEORGIA's room.

PROLOGUE
(We hear ROBERT singing.)
(Lights up on ROBERT. He is in makeshift hotel room/recording studio, Sunday,
June 20, 1937, San Antonio, Texas. He is facing into a corner with his back to
the audience, playing and singing. The song ends. He sits intensely still.)
(Lights up on STOKES in GEORGIA MAYBERRY'S COLORED JOOK
JOINT c. 1938. A small roughhewn structure which seems to smell of funk and
fried fish. There is a bar made of a plank supported by two barrels. There is a
dance floor. STOKES is at the upright piano. It is Wednesday evening. The sun
is setting, but the moon is shining bright.)
STOKES: Robert Johnson? Yeah, I knowed him. And he was a shining star.
Met him in the flesh not too long before he died.
(We see ROBERT poised to play)
STOKES: *(cont.)* Yeah, I knowed him. And he was a shining star.
(Hold a moment on STOKES who does not acknowledge ROBERT. We hear:)
VOICE OF ENGINEER: You ready with another there, Robert?
(Robert is silent, intense.)
VOICE OF ENGINEER: Ok, now I'm going to count off and then you start—
One. Two. Three...

(Robert sings, repeating the first tune.)

STOKES: Died right over there. Now it's plenty of folks say they was here and what not. Tell you everything that happened. What all he did, how he died and everything. Lies. They wasn't here. I was.

(Lights down on ROBERT.)

STOKES: *(cont.)* Anyway he come in here like I say. On his way from doing some records. Last ones he was ever to make. But when he first come in it was me and Georgia in here. Lem hadn't got back, but he wasn't long coming.

ACT ONE

SCENE ONE

GEORGIA: I better get started cooking. Folks'll be starting to trickle in here directly.

STOKES: Ain't going be no need to cook a bunch of fish and all, Georgia. That Greyhound bus don't stop till tomorrow, y'know. Ain't going be but a couple folks coming in. Both of them going be strangers, and they ain't coming for your fish.

GEORGIA: There you go with some more your mess.

STOKES: *(Continuing.)* It's going be raining too hard.

GEORGIA: How it's going rain, Sugar, and ain't a cloud in the sky?

STOKES: *(Silent.)*

GEORGIA: This another one of them tricks you supposedly picked up from your grandmama?

STOKES: They ain't tricks.

GEORGIA: Even on Wednesday night some come in here for one of my fish sandwiches. One or two'll even sneak off from the prayer meeting, if Reverend Hatcher get to praying so hard he make a mistake and close both his eyes. Only preacher I ever seen pray with one eye open.

STOKES: Tell me he be watching the collection plate *and* that sweet smelling gal run that usher board through that one eye. And all the signs say it's going rain, so them people in the low lands better roll up their pants.

GEORGIA: You and your grandmama's signs.

STOKES: Bet you a fish sandwich.

GEORGIA: I look like a fool betting against something you say. *(At window.)* Here come somebody. Just coming 'round the bend.

STOKES: White or colored?

GEORGIA: Dressed up, but he colored.

STOKES: He early.

GEORGIA: You expecting somebody?

(Stokes is silent.)

GEORGIA: *(Looking out the window. With obvious admiration.)* This boy coming here walk like his daddy is in J.D. Rockefella's will, you hear me! And that sure is one good looking suit. And he wearing it too!

STOKES: What else?

GEORGIA: And he toting a guitar.

STOKES: *(Not surprised.)* Uh huh—

GEORGIA: You know who he is and what he want?

STOKES: We'll see.

(We hear sound of barking dogs/hellhounds.)

GEORGIA: *(With innuendo.)* Hope it do rain now. I don't think I feel like cooking no way.

(Robert enters. He is sharp)

(DOGS cease.)

(During the following Robert shyly moves to GEORGIA, conversing, getting drink, etc., in the process of hitting on each other, as:)

STOKES: *(Playing to audience)* That was about when he come in. I could see right off was something about him. See, my grandmama was a healer. Ma Ruth was her name. Had the gift and the Black Wisdom from the olden days. And I ain't just talking about motherwit when I say Black Wisdom. And ain't talking about slavery when I say olden days. Ma Ruth had it but it took me a long time; but I got it now. Had to wander off down a lot of blind alleys, but I got it now.

ROBERT: This the crossroads where the Greyhound stop at?

GEORGIA: Sure is, Sugar. It ain't till tomorrow, but you welcome to wait. You by yourself?

ROBERT: Ain't I enough?

GEORGIA: We'll see. It look like rain to you?

ROBERT: What you talking about girl?

GEORGIA: Stokes say its going to rain. *(Loud enough for STOKES to hear)* I kid him, but I been knowing Stokes long enough that if he say the hen dipped snuff all you got to do is look up under the right wing and you'll find the box. He say two more folks we ain't expecting coming too.

STOKES: Got it from my grandmama. Some used to say she didn't know what she was talking about, was full of stuff as a Christmas goose. Thought it myself before I found out better. She used to sit out there on that porch just a rocking. And if she said something, it come to pass. She was a healer. And a heap more.

ROBERT: *(Interested.)* What could she heal?

STOKES: What-ever ailed you.

ROBERT: How?

STOKES: Various of ways. Sometimes she could heal them just telling them a story. Just sit there and rock, slow and easy as a summer sunset drowning in its flames. Tell you a story and by the time she got finished...

ROBERT: And she could protect you too, couldn't she?

STOKES: *("That's right.")* She had her ways.

GEORGIA: Claim he got some of his tricks from her.

ROBERT: *(Focusing on STOKES.)* You say you did, huh? Well that's good to know.

STOKES: Now I can't stop what's got to happen...

ROBERT: *("I understand.")* But you do what you can.

STOKES: *("Yes.")* When I can.

ROBERT: They tell me time was when things was known most folks has forgotten.

STOKES: Some folks might forget, but the truth of things don't change. You play that guitar?

ROBERT: I'm particular. I don't let just anybody touch my guitar.

(ROBERT very deliberately takes the instrument from its case, moves to STOKES, kneels before him and using both hands presents it to STOKES. STOKES takes it and "senses" it with his hands before returning it. Begins to play. STOKES accompanies him as GEORGIA, moved by their music dances a little step. Tune ends.)

GEORGIA: *(To audience.)* I was always scared of that kind of old woman like he say his grandmama was. Look to me like all that went against the church. I was still in my mama's house then and she went for Christian, and all us kids too. I've kind of fell away from that some though, since I been out on my own.

ROBERT: *(Sings and plays, seducing GEORGIA. To GEORGIA.)* You work here, huh?

GEORGIA: It's my place. That's my name, Georgia, that you read above the door.

ROBERT: I missed it, what it say?

GEORGIA: Georgia Mayberry's Colored Jook Joint. I'm Georgia.

ROBERT: And I'm colored.

GEORGIA: Everyday.

ROBERT: Well, Georgia, that's something mighty fine and real impressive. Got you a place with your name over the door, and here I am sitting up in it, big as life.

GEORGIA: Big as life and twice as sharp.

ROBERT: How come you ain't married?

GEORGIA: Who said I ain't?

ROBERT: You didn't mention no Mister on the sign.

GEORGIA: That don't prove nothing.

ROBERT: Where he at then?

GEORGIA: That's for me to worry about.

ROBERT: He went off left you, didn't he?

GEORGIA: Mostly he was a hard working man, but work around here was scarce. But, *(Indicating the jook joint with pride.)* I was doing fair. He took to walking heavy and talking loud—Hadn't never been no gentle man with a tender touch—like you look to be.

ROBERT: You saying you think I ain't nothing but a cream puff man?

GEORGIA: Just yall different, as cornbread and shoe leather. And I don't want to hear a word against him.

ROBERT: Don't matter to me if he was one of Jesus' apostles or too mean to be baptized; you don't care enough to put him on the sign, I don't care nothing about him at all. Now what kind of services you got in Georgia's Colored Jook Joint, do the sign say that?

GEORGIA: *(With innuendo.)* It's early so I ain't turned on the fire yet. What you got a taste for?

ROBERT: Give me somewhere to lay my head. *(Pause as they study each other.)* Then watch over me while I take my rest.

GEORGIA: *(Intrigued.)* You ain't no little bitsy baby. Why you need somebody watch over you while you sleep?

ROBERT: I didn't say somebody, Miss Georgia with your name up over the door, I said you.

GEORGIA: Oh—That is what you said, ain't it.

(They pantomime the following: —as STOKES plays—she reaches into her bosom and gives him the key, points the direction of her room, indicating she will be there soon.)

(ROBERT exits up stairs.)

(During the following he takes off his coat and shirt, lays on the bed. He tosses and turns restively; at best napping for a few moments at a time, as:)

GEORGIA: *(to audience)* Men. Damn them all. I wouldn't care if God turned all of them into hedge hogs and run them in the deep blue sea—I got a husband all right enough. Had one. Left about a year ago. Ain't heard peep or squeak from him since. I was a fool to marry him in the first place. He was worrisome as hell, but he come in handy from time to time. But I like to see a man busy and he got to the place he stayed too drunk to even put down rat poison. Started staying drunk and ugly mean. We had some words and he went off. *(harder)* Naw, I wouldn't care if all of them was long gone—*(laughs)* Long as it didn't rain no more I'd be all right. That's my weakness. Rain. Don't ask me why. Look like rain just make my love river rise. Just let a good hard rain be falling, and a man sweating and grunting and calling my name... And then lay there with him after, and listen at the water running down off the roof. Hell, can have damn near anything Georgia got. Don't even have to leave no receipt. It rained around the time Robert come in. I remember that. And don't think it'd come down like that in a long long time. Know it ain't since.

(We hear DOGS barking.)

GEORGIA: Oh, yeah, and that white man showed up just about that same time, too, I remember that.

(Kimbrough enters.)

(DOGS cease.)

STOKES: *(to audience)* He come in here talking wild. Looking for somebody he said. A matter of life and death. Hell, everything a matter of life and death to white folks. Especially one looking for a Negro he ain't never seen, been looking for three weeks, and ain't got nothing to go on but a name and some blues records he heard, and a bunch of lies Negroes done told. Me and Georgia went to work on him trying to find out who and what he wanted without telling him a blessed thing. You'd've thought we was Butter Beans and Susie the act we was putting on.

KIMBROUGH: I'm lost. Been looking for someone three weeks.

STOKES: You ain't lost no more. We just found you, didn't we Georgia?

GEORGIA: Just like Columbus sailing the ocean blue in 14 hundred and 92. This Georgia Mayberry's Colored Jook Joint like the sign say. I'm her.

STOKES: You probably want the white place, it's...

GEORGIA: Fellah come through here looking to do some carpentry work or painting. Didn't have but one arm. I fed him two or three days had him make me that sign. I think its pretty, don't you?

STOKES: He looking for the white place, Georgia?

GEORGIA: His money green, he welcomed to spend it with me.

KIMBROUGH: I'm looking for someone. It's important.

STOKES: I don't see nobody here but Georgia and me. And we just in here signifying and passing the time away till the rain come.

GEORGIA: He swears it's going rain.

STOKES: Best be on your way before the bottom fall out.

KIMBROUGH: *(To audience, weary)*
There wasn't a cloud, but a blind, black bluesman,
in a crossroads shanty, stuck together
by tarpaper, rusted Coke-Cola plaques and
a pitiful, childishly painted sign,
was forecasting rain like MacBeth's witches.
The perfect symbol of all I'd been through
since setting out on my three week long search—
entering, a stranger, into a world
of shadows and smoke where nothing was solid.
The undisciplined world of soil tillers,
servants, idlers, roaming song singers,
childlike perpetrators of unrepentant,
potluck violence, and a mistrustful,
superstitious, incomprehensible
soul. A world so strange to me I wouldn't
be surprised to see two moons, or for ghosts
to rise up from their graves and begin dancing
waltzes to minuets in the midnight sun.
A world where it was as difficult to get
a truthful answer as an honest days work.
A world acknowledging no future and no past;
concerned only with the present moment.
My assurance that my own world, of reason,
order and certainty would be an equal
trial of their patience and sanity was
my minor but solitary solace.
(To STOKES and GEORGIA)
Maybe you can help. I'm looking for someone.

STOKES: Who?

KIMBROUGH: Robert Johnson. Do either of you know him?

STOKES: Is he somebody? Or somebody just trying to get along?

KIMBROUGH: He's a colored boy. Plays guitar and sings.

STOKES: Roads full of them.

GEORGIA: Did you say what you want him for?

KIMBROUGH: I have to talk to him. Find him. And talk.

GEORGIA: *("That ain't telling me nothing.")* Do?

KIMBROUGH: I've come a long way, and I've got to find him.
For the last three weeks I've followed highways,
black tops, back roads and wagon rutted gullies.
I've been laughed at, misdirected and lost.
I've been ignored by strapping gandy dancers
chained leg to leg by the side of a track;
threatened by stiff necked plantation foremen
who cursed my looking for a colored man;
dismissed by landowners in their shined shoes,
straw hats, hard eyes and starched white Sunday shirts;
and lied to by blank faced colored people
who wouldn't trust a white man named Jesus Christ:
listened to stories from people claiming
they were raised with him, were, in fact, his best friend;
or they'd played the blues with him or taught him how.
Women who said they'd loved or hated him
some separately some at the same time.
But for all that, none could ever produce him.

GEORGIA: These women? how many women would you say it was?

KIMBROUGH: Many too many for it all to be true.

GEORGIA: And so you just looking for him, and he ain't done nothing wrong.

KIMBROUGH: *(He has heard it before.)* Neither to me, the law nor your good
Lord.

STOKES: *(skeptical)* So you just seeking this colored boy, with nothing to go on
but a name.

KIMBROUGH: I know stories—but not what's false or true.
Blew jew's harp and harmonica as a boy,
but he wanted to master the guitar.
No matter how he tried he met with no success.
And then, the story goes, he suddenly
disappeared. Although there is a lot of speculation,
nobody knows for sure just where he went.
Some say into the Bayou, some say out west.
Some say he was only gone for two weeks,
some say it was for as long as half a year.
But, when he returned no one could out play him.
He was the best, they say, anyone had ever heard.

STOKES: That be the truth, what they say it all mean?

GEORGIA: I want to know too, where he went? and what he did while he was there.

KIMBROUGH: They say he went and dealt with the devil.
Met Satan at the crossroads late at night.
Traded something he didn't think he needed,
for what he couldn't get any other way.
He was totally different when he returned.
Say he couldn't stand to stay in one spot.
Say he couldn't let other men's women be;
and for all that he'll come to a no good end.

GEORGIA: So, he sold his soul to the devil, so he could pick the guitar and chase some tail.

STOKES: My grandmama say the white folks the one started that talk about the devil. She say wasn't no devil in Africa till the white folks took him with them in the first empty slave ships they took over there. She say white folks ended up with us, and we ended with the devil.

KIMBROUGH: He made some records. Some race records. Blues. One of you must have heard at least one of them.

STOKES: Why?

GEORGIA: All my records got broke.

KIMBROUGH: (Frustrated.)
How could somebody make records like his
and his own people not even know his name?

GEORGIA: Just because you want him don't mean we got to know him.

STOKES: You know all the white folks made records?
(Kimbrough is silent.)

STOKES: If I could hear him though I could tell you whether he from Alabama, (Demonstrates.) Texas, (demonstrates.) eastern Arkansas (Demonstrates.) or Tennessee; whether he's a rambler or ain't never left home. And if he been north? what railroad he took. And don't let him be from Mississippi!— especially the Delta. Can nail it down then to plantation and damn near who his daddy was.

KIMBROUGH: I told you, Robert Johnson is his name.

GEORGIA: (To STOKES) Can't always go on a name, can you?

STOKES: I knowed a Robert Smith one time. They called him Chicken Lips. White folks called him Uncle Chicken Lips. Knowed a woman they called Pot Luck... But no Robert Johnson.

GEORGIA: I remember a Bo-Peep, a Snooky, a Baby Boy and a woman named Barefoot. Now them some names.

STOKES: ...Mo Jo, Skeeter, Black Pearl...Zero. Every year at settling time Zero'd get mad because he'd come out in the hole again. Worked a whole 'nother year and come out owing the white man. Zero'd get drunk and run everybody out of town, white folks, dogs, everybody. Him and his family was such good workers though till the landlord couldn't afford to kill him, so he let Zero have his little fun. Happened so regular they turned it into a local holiday. Zero Day they called it. Let me see, who else?

GEORGIA: A fellow up in Hopkins, Mississippi they first named School Boy. Probably hadn't even never been near no school, so, of all the things they could have called him, they still called him School Boy. Anyway, one night he went to dreaming he was in a fight, got his pistol from under his pillow, shot his self in the foot. They called him Four Toes after that.

STOKES: Smokey Junior. He lived up by Miller County. Had some trouble about something with the Klan down there. Found him shot three times in the heart. Sheriff said he committed suicide.

GEORGIA: *(Laughs.)* Who ever heard of a Negro committing suicide anyway?

STOKES: Sheriff claimed Smokey Junior did.

GEORGIA: Naw, no Robert Johnson. But I knowed somebody one time didn't have no legs, stuttered when he talked, and kept a rattlesnake named Gertrude for a house pet. And they call that negro, Hambone Red. Now, this one time he got into it, probably behind some signifying, with another negro. Over a woman run a whore house for a Chinaman outside a turpentine camp near Morganfield Station, Alabama.

STOKES: Right there where the Black Diamond Streamline train cross the Burnett River there.

GEORGIA: That's right. Now the woman she was double sized. Weighed 500 pounds soaking wet.

STOKES: Must took a barrel of water to dampen her, and had to weigh her on cotton scales.

GEORGIA: I don't know what they weighed her on, but it come to 500 pounds when they got through.

STOKES: That's five bails! You ever picked 500 pounds of cotton?

GEORGIA: You?

STOKES: Yeah.

KIMBROUGH: But you're blind.

STOKES: They didn't care nothing about that, they just wanted that damned cotton picked. But about Hambone Red...

GEORGIA: And now the fellow Hambone Red got into it with stood six foot seven inches in his big bare feet. And was broad through the shoulder as a crossbeam in a Baptist church.

KIMBROUGH: "To have a giant's strength; but it is tyrannous
To use it like a giant." What was his name?

GEORGIA: Second Cousin. That was all anybody called him. Second Cousin. Everybody. Whether they was kin to him or no. So Second Cousin stood up there tall as the center pole in a revival tent as he threatened Hambone Red about this woman.

STOKES: Hell, she weighed 500 pounds, was enough of her for both of them.

GEORGIA: Second Cousin wanted all of her to hisself. And threatened Hambone Red about her. Now Hambone Red couldn't run...

STOKES: Because, you say, he didn't have no legs.

GEORGIA: That's right. And neither could he get his lie out good, because he got excited when Second Cousin threatened him...

STOKES: And he went to stuttering. *("Right?")*

GEORGIA: That's right.

STOKES: I don't blame him, negro that size.

GEORGIA: That's right. So wasn't nothing left for Hambone Red to do but defend his self best way he knew how.

KIMBROUGH: "But that defenses, musters, preparations
Should be maintained, assembled, and collected
As were a war inexpectation." So,
What did Hambone Red do to defend himself?

GEORGIA: Shot Second Cousin.

STOKES: Did?

GEORGIA: Five times.

STOKES: Damn.

GEORGIA: Ankle, knee, stomach, chest and head.

STOKES: Chopped him down like a pine tree.

GEORGIA: To keep that big negro from chucking his little ass off that trestle down in front of that Black Diamond Streamline barrelling south through there that evening like convicts busting out of jail.

STOKES: *(To KIMBROUGH.)* Every evening, 7:30 like clockwork. And even if that Streamline hadn't killed him, being throwed off that trestle would've.

GEORGIA: Whole thing scared Hambone Red so bad that when it was over he didn't stutter no more.

KIMBROUGH: Cut down as was Titus Andronicus.
"And hither hale that misbelieving Moor,
To be adjudg'd some direful slaughtering death,
As punishment for his most wicked life."
What happened did Hambone Red go to jail?

GEORGIA: Not yet.

STOKES: Kill a white man, next stop hell. Kill a negro, fare-thee-well.

GEORGIA: Negro steal a nickel, do some time, white man take a million, that's just fine.

KIMBROUGH: *("Amazing.")* And what was the woman's name who was the cause?

STOKES: Yeah, names is what got us going on this in the first place. What was the woman's name they was fighting over?

GEORGIA: Honeydipper.

STOKES: And what about the snake?

GEORGIA: Gertrude? What about it?

STOKES: You tell a story you got to tell it all.

GEORGIA: Well I heard what finally happened was Honeydipper was getting over in the bed with Hambone Red one night, stepped on Gertrude, killing it on the spot. And it scared big Honey dipper so bad she fell over on top of Hambone Red. Killed him too.

STOKES: Umph! Bet it crushed him like a grape.

GEORGIA: So, that's the story of Hambone Red, Honeydipper and Gertrude.

STOKES: *(To KIMBROUGH.)* See, so what all that tells you is, a name don't mean what it might where you come from.

GEORGIA: White man get a name he can keep it forever

STOKES: We ain't knowed our real name since we been here.

GEORGIA: Best we can do is you know somebody by the name they go by.

STOKES: He might be "so and so" over here, then be "such and such" over there. See. And neither one might not be what his mama named him. And I might know some stories on a fellah, but not *his* story, you see. And even if you know, like I say, it ain't etiquette to tell. It's strictly his business. And see, the way yall keep us dipping and dodging with this Jim Crow business and all, thing like leaving forwarding address can take second seat to trying to put food in your belly.

KIMBROUGH: But I *paid* them: tobacco, whiskey, money,
to deliver him to me, or tell me
where he could be found. And they'd promise me—
(In black dialect.)

"Robert, he be at such and such a place,
such and such a time." Or, "He was just here
yesterday, tomorrow he be at so
and so," and I go, and they would tell me,
"He just left yesterday," or, "We never
heard of nobody go by that name, boss."

STOKES: Like the Indian say, "A heap see, but few know."

KIMBROUGH: What Indian?

STOKES: *The* Indian.

KIMBROUGH: I'm afraid I don't understand the reference.

STOKES: *("That proves my point.")* See.

KIMBROUGH: *(With edge.)*
This is serious. You think if it wasn't
I'd be chasing after a colored boy
I know less and less about the more I ask?

STOKES: *(not intimidated)* I don't know what you'd do.

KIMBROUGH: Why do all you people take me for a fool?
(Sound of THUNDER. Pause as they react to it.)

STOKES: Well, yall ain't going worry me about looking for a guitar playing man.
(Sound of THUNDER, followed by RAIN. Pause as they react to it.)

GEORGIA: *(To STOKES.)* You know where I'll be. *(To audience.)* I think it started raining just as I was going upstairs. *(Laughs.)* I took it as a sign. *(To KIMBROUGH)* You need anything, Stokes'll get it for you. You can pay him. *(She exits.)*

SCENE 2

(GEORGIA'S room. A big, ornate brass bed dominates the space. It is her pride and joy. There is a night stand with pitcher and basin.)
(Robert is seated on the bed with his guitar. He sings and plays. Georgia softly enters and closes the door behind her. She listens, unnoticed by ROBERT. When the song ends, Georgia makes her presence known.)

ROBERT: *(Startled.)* You oughtn't sneak up on somebody like that.

GEORGIA: This is Georgia's room, Sugar, she don't sneak into her own room. You been sleep?

ROBERT: Not good if I was. I ain't slept good in I don't know how long. You know where around here I can get me a mojo hand?

GEORGIA: What's the matter, Sugar?

ROBERT: Smell trouble, and I want to be prepared.

GEORGIA: 'Cause of that white man? He the one got you so you can't sleep?

ROBERT: What white man?

GEORGIA: The one down there with Stokes.

ROBERT: What he say he want?

GEORGIA: Say he looking from somebody named Robert Johnson. Colored he say. Made some records.

ROBERT: He say what he want with him?

GEORGIA: Talk to him, he say.

ROBERT: You believe that's all?

GEORGIA: You believe a chicken can swim? Your name Robert Johnson. Ain't it?

ROBERT: I ain't told you what my name is.

GEORGIA: I knowed before he said it he was looking for you.

ROBERT: Spencer is my name.

GEORGIA: It was Robert Johnson when you made them records.

ROBERT: You know so much how come you didn't tell him who you thought I was?

GEORGIA: I don't know nothing 'bout that man.

ROBERT: You don't nothing 'bout me, neither.

GEORGIA: I know you Robert Johnson and sang on them records.

ROBERT: *(Coy)* What records?

GEORGIA: *Kind Hearted Woman, Terraplane Blues.*

ROBERT: You mean to tell me you know all them tunes, girl?

GEORGIA: *Crossroads Blues* and *Rambling On My Mind...*

ROBERT: How about *Walking Blues*, and *Preaching Blues?*

GEORGIA: I know more than that.

ROBERT: How you know it was me?

GEORGIA: It was something, I don't know, in the way you said something, some word or something—and the twitter I got like the first time I listened at your blues.

ROBERT: Did, huh?

GEORGIA: Had every one of them till somebody got mad for me playing them so much.

ROBERT: Who? What he do?

GEORGIA: Throwed them on the floor. Yeah, and stomped on them. Every last one. You know how something can be the last straw...?

Oh, I got him straight all right, he won't do that no more. But I sure did hate he did it. White fellow come through selling snake oil and records out the back of his car. Bought one of every he had. Cost me almost five dollars. But we talking about him downstairs there. And what he want with you?

ROBERT: *("I ain't sure.")* Its about something he want, not something I done.

GEORGIA: You sure?

ROBERT: All I know is he been tailing me a couple weeks I know of. Well, he may think he the fox, but I got plenty tricks to throw him off the scent. I even doubled back on him one time and bird dogged him for a few days. Couple of times was close on him as I am to you right now, but he was so busy searching, didn't have sense enough to look around.

GEORGIA: That's how white people do, can't see nothing but what they want to see. Make me mad. Think things ought to be just because they want them that way. Like if they want they can grow grapes in January, or hitch up a cotton bale and take it for a ride.

ROBERT: Think they can switch off the sun, or change the way the river run.

GEORGIA: They can be more worrisome than a tooth ache.

ROBERT: Ain't there no negroes where he come from!? Why the hell can't he just leave me in peace!

GEORGIA: He didn't come all this way to just turn and go back home.

ROBERT: Yeah, he going keep on, even if he got to wear the bottom out from under his shoes.

That Stokes down there, do he know his stuff?

GEORGIA: I ain't seen all he can do, but I know I don't want to get on his bad side. He can see more from inside then most can from out. And he told me a story how his grandmama did a white woman for slapping her: put some of that mess on her, and all I know is Miss What's her name laid there for six solid days, couldn't move nothing but her eyes. And when she did get up wasn't a hair no where on her body.

ROBERT: Well I need somebody to do something. I'm tired of ducking him.

GEORGIA: What he want you for? 'cause of something evil you done? Some deal you made at that crossroads? So you can sing and play to make the men fret and the women sweat—

ROBERT: That what you think?

GEORGIA: He say your song so powerful 'cause it's evil. Say you couldn't play for squat, just hanging about getting on everybody's nerves. Then you went off and stayed. —And when you come back, you could flat play the ticks off a yard dog.

ROBERT: More proof you can't believe half what white folks say.

GEORGIA: I heard about that before, but you the first I ever knowed done it. Tell me what happened at that crossroads, Sugar.

ROBERT: What you want to know that for?

GEORGIA: Because I want to, that's all; 'cause I want you to tell me.

ROBERT: All you got to know is I went and I come back.

GEORGIA: But what you men have to go for in the first place, that's what I don't understand.

ROBERT: *(Strums guitar throughout following.)* My daddy picked cotton, and the white man picked him. Picked him clean as a hound's tooth. When I was a child coming up, look to me like him and all the rest like him was planted so deep down they couldn't get loose to grow up toward the sun...But there was some men I seen wasn't like that. I said to myself, these some special, some hoodoo negroes here. Had them a hoodoo so strong they could escape the hell of being planted and plucked, then come back with big northern city names in their mouths: St. Louis, Chicago, New York, De-troit. Telling stories of wild women, sweet whiskey, and green back dollar bills. And them ground planted men, like my daddy, couldn't do nothing but watch. While their own womens laughed for them hoodoo men like they didn't laugh no other time. And you know what that hoodoo was them special negroes had? Singing and playing the blues. Singing and playing the blues. So, shoot yeah I hung around them, trying to learn that hoodoo they had. Now I could blow the harmonica as a little boy. But I soon put it down. To my mind if a little boy could do it, couldn't be too much hoodoo to it. Couldn't make the women wild and the men have to get drunk and want to fight you. So I put that harmonica down and got after this guitar. Till I got so I could slip that slide so to make it talk to me like a best buddy; *(Demonstrates.)* hum and howl like the wind whining across a headstone; *(Demonstrates.)* squall like a freight train flying across the midnight silver moon—*(Demonstrates.)* or moan like a woman, touched low, slow and deep down to her soul.

GEORGIA: Make her feelings come down like that rain falling down out doors.

ROBERT: *(Abstract.)* But it's two sided—

GEORGIA: What, Sugar?

ROBERT: Been times I been playing and I'll look up and there'll be one somebody, might be a man or a woman, off by their self in the midst of all the dancing and drinking and carrying on, looking at me. Just looking. Quiet and steady as a oak tree. I remember the first time. A cold chill run over me, and I had a low feeling like somebody had stepped over 'cross my unmarked grave—I had a wife and baby to die. During birthing. She wasn't nothing but 16 years old. I wasn't barely but a boy myself. That was the worse I ever felt. Worse than my mama and daddy separating, so I ain't talking low like that. But scary. Because I know that that somebody looking is getting more than just the fun and good times of what I'm doing. Something in it is touching more than their feet. It's done got inside them. And they holding me responsible for driving away their trouble or heartache. *(Shudders. Pause.)*

GEORGIA: It's what you done for me the first I heard you. Singing *Kind Hearted Woman*. Made something in me—twitter—

ROBERT: I got me something I can do good as anybody I know; something to make my name known. All I want is to be let alone to do it! What I ought to do go get in his face. Ask what the hell he think he want, and who he think he fooling with? And I don't like the answer, bust his brain out, what I ought to do.

GEORGIA: You might get some on your pretty suit, Sugar. You want to act crazy, stay up here and act crazy with me.

ROBERT: You might be in it with him all I know. How I know?

GEORGIA: *(Sharp. Not a denial or an explanation, a warning.)* You got in here without knocking and I ain't asked you to leave.

ROBERT: *(Backing down.)* He just keep on dogging me, ain't going be satisfied till I goddamn run him clean to hell and back!

GEORGIA: Stokes'll deal with him—so you just take it easy for a little while.

ROBERT: I almost wish it was a crowd of us downstairs right now. I'd go down there and sing till they stomp their feet and reel and nobody didn't give a damn. Maybe all together we could raise it up so till Georgia Mayberry's Colored Jook Joint would just break loose from the ground and float off from this old messy world, like a robin on a reefer breeze.

GEORGIA: That's the spirit, Sugar, and you got Georgia to keep you company. Don't even think about that man.

(Robert is silent.)

GEORGIA: *(cont.)* What can Georgia do, Sugar?

ROBERT: Come lay with me—then let me sleep.

GEORGIA: *(Joining him on bed.)* You just rest easy and clear your mind. Now I don't know what that white man want, but I'll tell you about me: it ain't your soul that Georgia is after.

(An action to arouse him. It does.)

(Fade to BLACK on them.)

(Lights up on KIMBROUGH and STOKES.)

KIMBROUGH: *(To audience.)*
Sometimes I'm this close and I know it, but
I blink and the clue disappears, or I
breathe and it scatters like dandelion seeds...
But I know he exists because I heard him;
1000 or more miles and a world away.
No more than a noise, at first: strange, primal;
impenetrable as Shakespeare's sonnets
would be to the wild man of Borneo—
but still, no less remote, removed, alien
to my ear, and esthetics and heart—at first!

STOKES: *(to KIMBROUGH'S back)* You still ain't dropped the other shoe and
said what you want with this boy.

KIMBROUGH: I first heard it the day my grandfather died;
*(We hear recording of ROBERT JOHNSON singing Hellhound on My Trail,
then fades, as:)*

KIMBROUGH: *(Continues.)*
from the Victrola of his colored maid.
Dear old Auntie Belle. She'd been my nanny
and my father's before me, Auntie Belle
my grandfather's maid, but really more like
a trusted member of the family.
But never during all those years, man and boy,
had I heard her play anything like that.

STOKES: *(To audience.)* Probably heard it everyday and just wasn't listening.

KIMBROUGH: I didn't know what it was, didn't know
why I heard it then but never before.

STOKES: *(To audience.)* Maybe the first time he'd had the blues. *(To KIM-
BROUGH)* Maybe its just a song. Something he made up and ain't no
more than that.

KIMBROUGH: You haven't heard it, therefore you can't know.

STOKES: I've heard the blues, I've had them and I've sung them too.

KIMBROUGH: But you haven't heard Robert Johnson's blues.
His are different from all the other ones.

STOKES: Ain't but 3 or 4 ways about the blues, and I know them all: blues to
get you a woman; to get one off your mind; or, to sing Satan from your
door. And if who singing them ain't singing to the peoples understanding
about being kicked with the same boot as them, he ain't got no business

with it. That's all to it. Now what make you think you know blues from a bird's nest?

KIMBROUGH: Once, as a child I eavesdropped outside a jook.
The room was thick with glistening dancers,
the pine floor shook beneath their stamping feet.
It was Brueghel's "Peasant Dance" in black face;
raw and raucous as Mephistoe's *bal masque*,
with two colored blues shouters singing about
water rising and their baby going down —
But it was just race music, no more than that,
only coon tunes, "...full of sound and fury
signifying nothing." Just darkie fun.
(To audience.)
But then I heard Robert Johnson sing blues.

STOKES: *(To audience.)* Seen one blossom, swear he invented spring.

KIMBROUGH: *(To audience.)*
The sound was not from the Golden light of Bach
or Brahms, was nothing like the nightingales.
It erupted from a light-strangling darkness,
yet it *flowed*, as pentameter from the Bard.

STOKES: *(To audience.)*
Nigger go to work
white man go to school
white man be the scholar
play the nigger for a fool.

KIMBROUGH: My families history goes back three hundred years.
I have no business sense, but the interest
accrued on a sizeable inheritance
allows me the leisure to teach Shakespeare
to refined co eds at an all girls school.
My days are spent in staid contemplation,
my revelations are calm, civilized,
quiet as tea poured into China cups.

STOKES: *(To audience.)*
Nigger get the leavings
white man take his ease
nigger do what he can
white man what he please.

KIMBROUGH: But hearing Robert Johnson made me question
all of the things, the rules I thought I knew.
It was too frank, too straightforward to be false,

too unselfconscious, too heartfelt, and heathen-
ugly to be a sham. It revealed man's
loss of innocence, his disobedience,
his fall, the consequence, the need to atone.
Those—themes are—Biblical, Shakespearian,
the gist, the heart and soul of my lectures.
How does he—this unschooled black Orpheus
produce songs as universal and complex
as the intellectual love of my life?

STOKES: Orpheus?

KIMBROUGH: A hero god from Greek mythology.
The greatest poet-musician of his time.
When he played rocks were moved and rivers changed course.
He descended into hell once and his
music eased the suffering of the damned.

STOKES: I can play so deep myself sometime make them want to put me in jail.
What happened to Orpheus?

KIMBROUGH: He was murdered because of a woman.

STOKES: Could make a blues about that.

KIMBROUGH: Robert Johnson exists. Someone knows him. And I will find
him, I will, don't think I won't.

STOKES: The longer you look the lost-er you get. When you first heard him
at least you knew where *you* was. Three, four weeks later you still ain't
found him and you lost too. You puts me in the mind of Brer Fox in
behind Brer Rabbit.

KIMBROUGH: My Auntie Belle told me those as a child.
Nonsense tales, anthropomorphized critter
stories with trite cautionary morals
for kids. Diversionary, but little more.

STOKES: Might've found who you think you looking for by now you'd've listened about that cunning bunny rabbit. Lives lean and tricks his way
along. Them stories, you take so light, come with us from Africa, carry the
Black wisdom like my Ma Ruth used to heal. They don't just tickle, they
teach. And you might be the fox amongst them school girls, but you in
Robert Johnson's briar patch now.

KIMBROUGH: *(Skeptical.)* And you think you can help me locate him.

STOKES: *(Ignoring this last.)* Ma Ruth was born in slavery. Seen all her kin die
or sold. But she outlived them that owned her.

KIMBROUGH: My grandfather died a multi-millionaire.

STOKES: She was the first on the plantation to spot Abe Lincoln's Unions soldiers riding up the road and bringing Emancipation. She called them Blue Bellies, Mr. Lincoln's Blue Bellies. Said she was in the big house in the main bedroom, whooping and waving one of Miss Sue Ann's Sunday best petticoats, like it wasn't nothing but a common dusting cloth. Said that night the negroes and the Blue Bellies drank elderberry wine, ate smoke house turkey, and danced juba till they dropped—and ain't once called Jesus' name. I used to love for her to rock me on her lap and tell me them tales. Long time later, I'm grown and'd been gone, and something called me back just as she was dying. They lead me in the room. Tell me she can't talk. I reached and find her hand. She said my name clear as day. And I said, "Yes'm." And felt what I first thought was a death tremor running through her to me, least that's what I thought it was at first. Run up my arm like the monkey up the flagpole. And hit me like a spooked mule kicking in its stall. I don't know how long it took me to come to. But look like I heard drumming and waves of water and people moaning. Moaning and a creaking. And them drums—like the sound of Ma Ruth's chair rocking on that porch. Rocking and drumming. And moaning and water waves—

KIMBROUGH: I received a telegram: "Come quickly.
Stop. Your grandfather is gravely ill. Stop.
Do not delay. Stop." I took the first train.
I reread "Measure For Measure," arrived
before he passed away. But I could not
go in....I could not go into that room—

STOKES: *(To audience.)* And just as I was about to get somewhere with him...
(We hear DOGS barking.)

LEM: *(Enters. Wet. Weary. To audience.)* The last thing I felt like fooling with right then was white folks. Not after what I'd been through moving that dirt.
(DOGS cease.)

STOKES: *(To audience.)* Lem come in just about then. I could tell by his foot steps he was a different man than'd left here. Lem was Georgia's husband. He'd left out of there about 6 months before. And hadn't even said goodbye or been heard from since. Said some things to me before he left I didn't appreciate, but he took his sorry tail up Highway 76 before I took the time to do anything about it.

LEM: I'd been moving dirt down to Reed County. Government building a levee, keep that water from rising up washing away them peoples living in the low lands. Till I went up there I didn't know just how bad a negro could be treated. All I knew about before that was these regular red necks

ig'ing me; and their poll taxes, and Jim Crow mess, and lynching and all—
But moving that dirt learned me how bad being black could be sure
enough. Make seven days seem like a year. Don't get me wrong, this I'm
talking about ain't no prison, I ain't talking about no prison camp. We
wasn't accused of nothing, hadn't been convicted of no crime. We was
working in a levee camp. Uncle Sam was the contractor, but Satan was the
supervisor. Had a white man straw bossing over it so mean wouldn't shave
hisself keep from cutting his own throat. He meant for that dirt to be
moved and drove them negroes like mules and them mules like negroes.
By 10 o'clock every morning so many mules was on their knees you swear
they praying, water running out their eyes like spanked babies. By noon
their hearts was busting in them like fifty cents fire crackers on the Fourth
of July. He told time by the sun, and long as it was light there was work to
be done. They say he went down to hell on vacation one time, Devil
scared to open the door to let him in. —That's why I didn't want to see no
white man right then. And he called me out my name before I got in there
good.

KIMBROUGH: *(To LEM.)* Robert?

LEM: *(Snatching his cap off.)* Say what, mister?

KIMBROUGH: Robert Johnson. You're Robert Johnson aren't you?

LEM: No, sir, I'm—No, sir. That ain't my name, no sir.

STOKES: That ain't him.

LEM: No, sir, I ain't nobody you looking for, sir.

KIMBROUGH: Do you know who I am talking about?
Robert Johnson, a colored boy. A singer.
Travels around and sings. Made some records.

LEM: Ain't that who Georgia had them records by? The ones I...?

STOKES: *(A warning.)* That you *what?*

KIMBROUGH: You say the woman, Georgia, had his records?

STOKES: *(A threat.)* Is that what you said?

lem: No, sir. I was thinking about something—somebody else. That's what.

KIMBROUGH: Are you sure? Robert Johnson. Think. *Crossroads Blues.*

LEM: *(To audience.)* Just like down there on that levee. Didn't make no difference. Dirt hauling negro same as a blues hollering one far as they concerned—

STOKES: *(To KIMBROUGH.)* Naw, he don't know nothing about him. He
don't know nothing about nothing. *(To LEM.)* I don't know what you
come back here for.

LEM: Where else I got to go? Where Georgia at? I want me a drink.

STOKES: You don't want to know where she is or what she doing, and who going pay for that drink? You?

LEM: *(Moving to whiskey.)* Pay?! You better get you some eyes, see who the hell you talking to.

STOKES: I can see good enough to see what you can't. And you might as well go on and have a drink. You going need one when you do see Georgia. You messed up when you left here, boy, and you messed up double when you come back.

LEM: You the signifyin'est—somebody I ever seen. What you think you signifying about now?

STOKES: *(Signifying)* But I'm going wait, let her tell you. And just like the Signifying Monkey, I'm going have a ringside seat from up in my tree so when she light into you won't none get on me. And when you hear it see just what you going do 'cause I know you ain't going take it, "suppose to be" bad mud dauber like you.

LEM: Old man, with what I been through I don't want to hear nothing about nothing from you, all right?

STOKES: Go on have you a drink then, let me talk to this man. You want to find Robert Johnson? Pay me what it's worth to you and I'll tell you how to find him.

LEM: *(Gets drink. To audience as he sits alone and broods.)* They claim I poisoned that boy Robert Johnson. You poison rats. Hell, that's the way a woman kills. I'm a man. I'd've wanted to kill him I'd've killed him fair. —Besides, I didn't have no reason to do nothing to him no way. He wasn't nothing special. That white man'd been looking for him all that time and couldn't find him prove he wasn't nothing. Them white folks ain't going miss him. Be just be another nigger gone. Plenty more where he come from. That's what they thought to that levee where I was working. I'd've like to've seen him up there trying to move that dirt. Shit. What could a little milky nigger like him do with my woman?

STOKES: *(With money in his hand from KIMBROUGH.)* There's two ways of hunting: the hard way and the smart way. You been doing it the hard way. You been running around behind the squirrel trying to catch him while he was looking for nuts to gather and bury. Right then he don't even know where he going and what he going do next, so that make it double tough on you. —That's the hard way. The smart way is to be where he already got a nut, or better yet be where he at while he *getting* a nut!

(Lights down on them, up on GEORGIA'S ROOM.)

SCENE THREE

GEORGIA: *(Sitting up in the bed looking at the fitfully sleeping ROBERT. To audience.)* He was a man outside, but deep down he was just a scared little boy.
(ROBERT moans and tosses.)
(GEORGIA tries to soothe him.)
(ROBERT wakes with a start. Frightened.)

GEORGIA: What is it, Sugar, what's the matter? Did you have a bad dream? That it?

ROBERT: I got to get him off me! I got to get him off me and that's all to it. On me like haints and won't let me sleep! Can't allow him to dog me no more, whether I got to do mean things or what.

GEORGIA: Okay, Sugar, okay. You going get him off you and it's going be okay. *(Rises and dresses.)* Let me go down, see what's happening. Rain seem to be letting up. He might even be gone—Even if he ain't we'll get him off you so you can sleep.
(ROBERT plays)
(Lights fade.)
(End of Act 1.)

ACT TWO

(No time has passed.)

KIMBROUGH: I am tired of being played the fool
by servile and indifferent colored men,
devious and indolent at the same time,
and women, arrogant and secretive.
Tired of poor whites, or buckras as they're called.
Tired of this supposedly idyllic
South-land. It is not peaceful nor bucolic,
but a powder keg ready to explode.
Ruled by mean old men like my grandfather—
lack logic King Lears or Old Testament
Jehovahs, blind as you, but think themselves
omniscient. With nothing to recommend
their leadership save their ruthlessness.
(To STOKES.)
I want to get on tomorrow's crossroads
Greyhound and quickly quit this backward land,

but first I want Robert Johnson. And I
know you know more than you're willing to tell,
but, "I'll have this secret from thy heart, or
rip thy heart to find it." If you work magic
conjure him, or I will set up an alarm
that there is a wild nigger on the loose;
create heinous crimes for him: murder, rape,
and unleash those mindless redneck dogs.

STOKES: A lot of folks would suffer.

KIMBROUGH: *("It's your choice.")* It's your choice. The blame will rest at your door.

STOKES: I could tell you where he's at, but I can't tell you how you can find him.

KIMBROUGH: No more now! I am tired of riddles.
Tell me something, and tell it to me straight.

STOKES: If I could snap my finger and he'd be standing here in a pin striped suit you wouldn't know no more about nothing than you do right now. And so you still wouldn't be satisfied.

KIMBROUGH: Don't worry about my satisfaction.

STOKES: If you find him, and only see what you want to see, you won't be done done nothing but wasted your time and ours too.

GEORGIA: *(Enters, sees LEM.)* I knew if somebody didn't kill you you'd be back darkening my door one day.

LEM: *(Trying to be cheerful.)* Same road took me off brought me back again.

GEORGIA: You too late, even if you changed your ways.

LEM: Somebody been in here done changed your mind? *(Indicating STOKES.)* Is it him? How come you got so much confidence in Stokes, don't believe nothing I say.

GEORGIA: You messed up.

LEM: You know things around here had me in a tangle.

GEORGIA: When things went wrong you acted like you was the only one being pushed around.

LEM: I'd done everything I could think to do. Sharecropping, hired hand nobody couldn't afford to hire. Wasn't no railroad work except for convicts. Even tried a little bootlegging and gambling, you know that. Till all that run out too.

GEORGIA: I told you before you left here whether or not I missed you I wouldn't take you back no more. So, you can bottle up and be on your merry way.

LEM: I heard they had that levee work and was looking for men. I had to go where the work was.

GEORGIA: Then that's where you should have stayed.

LEM: They wouldn't let me be no man up there.

GEORGIA: *(Almost weakens.)* Wouldn't?

LEM: Wouldn't. And they was working us to death, do you hear me, working us poor, ignorant negroes to death. Till all you feel like doing is laying your head down on the ground.

GEORGIA: *(Hard.)* I know what it is to be mistreated.

LEM: Would you at least cook me some catfish? and a batch of them drop biscuits? You'd always do that at least. Even when you was mad.

(GEORGIA is silent.)

LEM: *(cont.)* What if I still got feelings for you?

GEORGIA: You better get over them, you know what's good for you.

LEM: You saying you got another man? Is that what you saying?

GEORGIA: It's a poor dog ain't got but one bone. But what I got or going get ain't no more your business than what the mole found in the hole.

LEM: Just because luck been with you, Georgia, don't think you can always have your way. And you still my wife, you know. We said till death do us apart.

GEORGIA: You ain't said how you got away from that levee camp.

LEM: I done what I had to do—I ain't the same as I was before I was up there moving that dirt, so be careful, you don't know how much I can stand.

GEORGIA: You broke your mirror with me when you stomped on my records. You remember that, don't you? so, now, what else you think you going do?

LEM: I told you I was sorry about that.

GEORGIA: Sorry don't fix them records I paid my good money for. Now you better go on somewhere and get yourself unwound.

LEM: I thought that's what I was coming here for.

GEORGIA: I said what I got to say. Now you can start something in here you want to. But try me again, hear, and I got something I been keeping on ice for you.

LEM: You just think because this white man in here—

GEORGIA: This is 19 and 38. Slavery been over almost 75 years. I run this joint. Not no over seer, no captain, foreman or quarter boss. This is my joint. And both yall in it. And I don't care no more about him than I do you.

LEM: It's just a good thing he in here all I got to say, but he won't be always.

GEORGIA: You neither. And I'll be here when both yall gone.

(ROBERT enters)

LEM: Who is this black snake crawling from under my bed? You think this your new nigger? What you doing up there? Don't you know who I am?

ROBERT: *(To GEORGIA.)* I didn't see no ring on your finger, and neither one in your nose.

LEM: She my woman.

ROBERT: I think she *used to be* your woman.

GEORGIA: *(To ROBERT, a warning.)* He can be mean.

ROBERT: To women maybe, but he don't want to fight, even over you. I seen that look on men before. Men like my daddy that let some white men run him off from his home. Made him sneak off from his family, in a dress, in the middle of the night. With nothing between his legs but his tail.

LEM: *(To audience.)* It took a man to move that dirt, and he wouldn't've lasted 10 minutes on that levee—Ain't nobody that ain't been up in that death camp can't know what it's like. Worse than slavery up there. Least in slavery they half way tried to take care of a slave, no other reason than they'd had to pay something to get them. On that levee job they work a negro to death they come out ahead. So he couldn't tell me nothing about what it was like moving that dirt. *(To KIMBROUGH.)* And he wasn't singing about nothing but what the rest of these niggers want to hear when they come in here on a Saturday night to rub up against one another. That's all it was, something to get drunk and holler loud to. *(To GEORGIA.)* He wasn't nothing special. And didn't nobody know him, except maybe a few negroes from around where he lived. But that didn't stop him coming in there like he was some big city nigger just stepped down off the Streamline Special. *(To audience.)* They say he was in truck with the Devil—that's how come "he could play so good." Well if he did have something to do with the Devil wasn't worth it. Sure as hell didn't stop that poison from making him howl like a scalded yard dog before it killed his hicty acting ass. That's all I know.

KIMBROUGH: You, in the suit, what name do you go by?

ROBERT: Who you looking for?

KIMBROUGH: You answer my question. What is your name?

ROBERT: I got more names than some men got fingers.

KIMBROUGH: You had one at birth. What was your daddy's name?

ROBERT: Had more daddies too than some got toes. My mama's married name was Dodds. My daddy, my real daddy's name was Johnson. I was my mamas "outside" child after her husband'd got run off by some white men.

He was a Dobbs. Later my mama and us we went to live with him in
Memphis a while. By that time he'd changed his name to Spencer. So
them white men couldn't find him. Later on I had another step daddy
name of Willis. So, I been all of them one time or another.

KIMBROUGH: "...Thy kinsmen hang their heads at this disdain,
thy issue blurred with nameless bastardy:
And thou, the author of their obloquy,
shalt have thy trespass cited up in rhymes,
and sung by children in succeeding times."

ROBERT: What is that, a song?

KIMBROUGH: A quote from *The Rape of Lucrece.* It is
an incredible narrative poem
written by the bard, William Shakespeare.
Shakespeare, someone you have never heard of.

ROBERT: That who you looking for?

KIMBROUGH: As unlikely as it may seem, I may
finally have found who I was looking for.

ROBERT: *("You have.")* Pleased to make your acquittance.

KIMBROUGH: How can I know, for sure, that you are him ?
and not just yet another impostor.

(ROBERT sings and plays)

KIMBROUGH: Why have you been running away from me?

ROBERT: I been going about my business. Any running you been doing it.

KIMBROUGH: Okay then, why did you let me catch you?

ROBERT: You been at my back long enough, time to turn and let you see my
face.

KIMBROUGH: "...give me them that will face me," said Henry the Fourth.
Shakespeare, again. You don't know Shakespeare do you?

ROBERT: I don't know you neither. Somebody send you or you come on your
own?

KIMBROUGH: You are my first compulsion, Robert Johnson,
or Spencer or Dobbs or whatever you
chose to call yourself.
(To GEORGIA:)
Its as you said, "What's
in a name?" It is your music, your blues
that made me lusty blooded enough to
abandon my leisure and my routine
for this summer of my sweet discontent;
searching for the source of the intrusion

in order to explain it for myself
and set everything back to proper balance,
then return home "with unhack'd swords and helmets
all unbruise'd." Do you understand all of that?

ROBERT: What you want?

KIMBROUGH: I have to know by what alchemy you
turn the limited raw material
of this pitiful, dirt poor, dark ages...

ROBERT: This suit don't say nothing about no pitiful or dirt poor.

KIMBROUGH: *(To audience)* That is another thing I did not expect.
(To ROBERT) What did you give to get what you have?

ROBERT: I started with nothing, so I didn't have nothing to give up.

KIMBROUGH: How do you explain where your songs come from?

ROBERT: *("That's simple.")* Listen at my records. *(Alibiing.)* If somebody told
you I took something...

KIMBROUGH: I have listened to them, over and over.

ROBERT: Where was you when they told you whatever it was set you on my
trail?

KIMBROUGH: Boston, but nobody told me anything...

ROBERT: Boston?

KIMBROUGH: Yes—

ROBERT: *(Puzzled.)* I was up that way one while...

KIMBROUGH: *(Surprised.)* You?

ROBERT: Bunch of big cities. Light on every corner, 2, 3 jooks in every block.
(Bragging to LEM and GEORGIA.) Walk in them same's I walk in here. Be
white women, everything. Chicago. De-troit, New York City. St. Louis.
Even singed over the radio. Went all up in Canada. Like t've wore that
highway out.

GEORGIA: It as cold as they say?

ROBERT: Alaska ain't got nothing on it.

GEORGIA: *(Laughing.)* Oo-oo weeee!

ROBERT: When I left there had icicles long as axe handles hanging from the
trees, snow was elbow deep.

GEORGIA: I'd like to see that one time before I die.

ROBERT: See what happen how I got up there in the first place, I met this one
white man, but turned out he couldn't do me no good. But then he
knowed somebody. And so I singed a few for him and he had better sense
than the first one, and we was off to San Anton'e. And before I knowed it

I was up in there making me some recordings. Just the same as Charlie Patton...

GEORGIA: I know about him too.

ROBERT: Uh huh, me and him from the same home town. And Son House and all of them. Willie Brown too. They all got records. Just like me.

KIMBROUGH: Their's were issued before yours, weren't they?

ROBERT: *("So what?")* They just older than me, that's all.

GEORGIA: So what happened?

ROBERT: How it went was we went in what they called a studio. They had them hillbillies in there ahead of me. Then me. Mixed in between a bunch of cowboys and Mexicans and all them, see. But I was the onliest blues man in there. Not 'cause there wasn't plenty of them around. But I reckon they wanted the best's the reason he sent for me in the first place. First tune I cut was *Kind Hearted Woman.*

GEORGIA: That's one of the ones I had.

ROBERT: And if I knowed then what I do now I'd sure've dedicated it to kind hearted Georgia.

GEORGIA: *(To audience.)* He still ought'n't't've said what he did to Lem like that. It's things a woman can say to a man that another man can't. Especially not in front of other men. Look like the devil gets in 'em. Make 'em be at each other like yard dogs over a soup bone. Must've got in Robert make him *say* what he did. Got in Lem too, make him *do* what he done. Men—

ROBERT: Well, that day I put down about 7 or 8 before I told them I was tired and I quit. So they still got some they ain't even let out yet. I don't know what they waiting on. Them ones they got just as good as the one they let out, you want to know something. But you know how them white folks is...

KIMBROUGH: *(To audience.)*
I don't understand; am bewildered by it.
I may have found who I was looking for
but he was in no way what I expected.

ROBERT: *(To GEORGIA with eye on LEM.)* You want to know something, I'm thinking about forgetting them Satan songs. I done made him famous enough as it is.

KIMBROUGH: *(To audience.)*
In one breath he could speak of metaphors,
but in the next might mouth braggadocios
flimflam or spout hoodoo mumbo jumbo,
or engage in a petty domestic spat.

ROBERT: Might sing about nothing but love from now on.

KIMBROUGH: *(To audience.)*
So I still could not reconcile, absorb
nor accept the inexplicability
of his acquittance with the treatises
and themes so evident on his recordings.
And his presence did nothing to clarity
and thus render it less mystifying.

STOKES: *(To audience.)*
Can't see the forest,
can't see the trees,
can't see for looking—
that's just the way it bes.

ROBERT: *(Braggadocios. "Ain't this a bitch...")* What you say you do way up there in Boston?

KIMBROUGH: Teach.

ROBERT: Reading and writing? or arithmetic?

KIMBROUGH: Shakespeare. Boston's Garrett Girl's Academy. A college.

ROBERT: College?

KIMBROUGH: English Literature. Professor.

ROBERT: *(Surprise and relief.)* College. That's the highest school, ain't it? And you a professor, and say that's what this—? You ain't no Pinkerton, or—somebody looking to throw me in jail for some law I broke somewhere? You trucked all this way looking for Bob to ask me something about my songs? *(To others. From this point forward he performs to GEORGIA and LEM.)* Ain't that something, then. Well that sure one on me. Well, professor, you just ask away. What you want Bob to tell you?

KIMBROUGH: *(Direct)* Are they true?

ROBERT: What you mean true?

KIMBROUGH: Do they mean what they say?

ROBERT: What else they going mean but that?

KIMBROUGH: You don't understand.

ROBERT: No, reckon I don't. You got to explain better what you want.

KIMBROUGH: You make references—Talk about things: studying evil and dusting your broom—

ROBERT: *(Laughs.)* That's what you talking about? Well the most education I got is mouth to mouth, and that's just my unschooled way of telling something. Chicago ain't my home like I talk about in *Sweet Home Chicago*, and I ain't never had no Terraplane automobile to break down on me because I ain't never had no Terraplane automobile. It's just a way of helping paint a picture like—

KIMBROUGH: A metaphor—

ROBERT: *("—Okay—")* —to drive the song along.

KIMBROUGH: Where do they come from? Do you sit and write them...?

ROBERT: *("What kind of question is that.")* They just come. No one place or time. Be like a fire, they bubble and boil from inside. I take them see if they'll please the people.

LEM: *(In KIMBROUGH'S ear.)* He ain't such a much. Was, wouldn't took you so long to find him.

KIMBROUGH: *(To ROBERT.)* Do you have any idea what you've done?

ROBERT: Ain't nobody better than me at it, I know that. Do, let me hear you call their name.

KIMBROUGH: You have been able, somehow, to tap into
the themes and to connect with conflicts
that are central to the literature
of all civilization. Do you know that?

ROBERT: *(False modesty.)* They come to me and I sing them.

KIMBROUGH: *(To audience.)* The innocent ignorance—

LEM: *(To audience as he poisons whiskey.)* Didn't have no business talking to me like that, front of my woman and that white man, I know that.

KIMBROUGH: *(To ROBERT.)*
"What's to be done?"
asked Lady MacBeth—a character from
William Shakespeare, the playwright that I teach.
And her husband, the king said, "Be innocent
of the knowledge, dearest chuck" —chuck means chicken—
a term of endearment, like you say Sugar,
or Honey Chile. "Be innocent of the knowledge, dearest chuck, Till thou
     applaud the deed. Come, blindness
Scarf up the tender eye of pitiful day;
And with thy bloody and invisible hand
Cancel and tear to pieces that great bond
Which keeps me pale!—Light thickens; and the crow
Makes wing to th'rooky wood:
Good things of day begin to droop and drowse;
Whiles night's black agents to their prey do rouse.—
Thou marvell'st at my words: but hold thee still;

Things bad begun make strong themselves by ill:
So, prithee, go with me."
(MacBeth Act 3, Scene 2, line 45.)

ROBERT: *(Pause.)* Now I didn't get all of that, but parts of it did put me in the mind of some things: night falling and things coming out to do their business in the dark. *(Plays and sings.)*

(KIMBROUGH singing, following ROBERT call with a response.)

ROBERT: *(Ends playing, impressed.)* —You do that pretty good.

KIMBROUGH: In your Satan songs you sing about the crossroads. Are those tunes true, have you been there?

ROBERT: How come you don't think that's one of what you called it?

KIMBROUGH: Metaphor.

ROBERT: And ain't just "mumbo jumbo"? or another *(For the benefit of all.)* metaphor?

(He moves off to get drink.)

STOKES: *(To audience.)* A crossroad's where it all come together, what a crossroads is. Highest up and lowest down and everything that's been before. In you and all them that's yours; crisscrossing. The lightest and the darkest, the worst and the best: guaranteed good time for the body and the soul. Can be a church, a way-station where train lines intersect, or in a jook like this. That's what a crossroads is.

LEM: *(To audience.)* Crossroads or straight it's all trouble. Be danger in every step you take. And ain't just me; same for the race everywhere I been.

ROBERT: *(To GEORGIA, signifying to LEM.)* 'S why it's so good to find somebody'll let you stop and rest.

LEM: Never know what might happen, though. Rest at the wrong time could end up over in your coffin, folks looking down in your face. You know you ain't too poor to die.

ROBERT: Good looking suit to be buried in though, ain't it? But you couldn't afford it was to sell your soul.

LEM: That how you got it?

ROBERT: Wouldn't sell mine for no less that what I couldn't get no other way: peace of mind. And for everybody to know my name.

LEM: Ain't no peace in this world, not for no nigger. Ain't nothing for no nigger but dirt to move. I moved a ton of dirt myself, a shovel load at a time. All to keep that water from rising up running over them people in them low lands. Ain't no telling how many people I saved. But you think anybody know my name? And peace? Only way to get peace is to die. You better think about that.

ROBERT: Just because them people broke you up there you ain't got to take it out on me.

LEM: You ain't too slick to be cut down, and don't think you is.

ROBERT: *(taunting)* "Well, leave this morning if I have to ride the blind, Yeah, I feel mistreated, and I don't mind dying."

KIMBROUGH: *(Heart felt.)*
"And so, from hour to hour, we ripe and ripe,
And then, from hour to hour, we rot and rot;
And thereby hangs a tale." *As You Like It.*

ROBERT: *("I'll see you that one and raise you one.")* "I rolled and I tumbled and I cried the whole night long."

KIMBROUGH: *(Man to man.)* Do you sleep peacefully, Robert Johnson?

ROBERT: *(Man to man.)* Not for a long, long time.

KIMBROUGH: *(Abstract.)* I have this dream and I hear your music— *(Evasive.)* Doesn't matter—it's off the track, as you say.

ROBERT: I'll tell you what's off the track. You. It was more than some metaphors of mine drawed you to me all the way from Boston.

KIMBROUGH: The question is, how you are able to grasp
intuitively ideas my students
fail to understand with intense tutoring.
Is it because you suffered while I was
cradled in an ivied ivory tower?
The answer I want is should I footnote
your "creations" in the Book of Riddles
as the effect of a freak alignment
of the stars? and fly back to my Northeast nest.

ROBERT: *(Direct.)* You full of shit as a year old privy, and like a blind man in the light—what would help most folks ain't no good to you at all. I bet my bottom dollar you been to your crossroads and you was scared to follow through.

KIMBROUGH: *(Reerecting a wall, but with bitterness)*
I'm a careful man who's led a charmed life.
I give lectures to privileged co eds
whose highest ambition is to barter
their youth and beauty to robber baron mates
who will stifle them in the name of "love."
Debutantes, with no more use for Shakespeare
than...

ROBERT: *(Impatient.)* Than a two legged mule needs a harness.

KIMBROUGH: Exactly. *(With irony.)* And I pride myself on it.

STOKES: The way Ma Ruth would tell it, ones like Robert, their job ain't to do it for you, but to open up the way. *(Referring to LEM.)* Like that boy's job was to build up dams and levees, Robert's was to clear the path. Getting by the best way he could was the way he earned his bread and beans. And like Brer Rabbit he done it fair or foul. And you couldn't always say if he was lying or telling the truth.

ROBERT: For what you need to know you asking all the wrong questions. But since you here I'm going tell you about my trip to the crossroads, and what happened when I was there. *(He goes to get drink.)* Now I'm going tell you the story of how I tricked the Devil and learned to play this here guitar. Now I'd heard all them talk about going to the crossroads and what all so I made it up in my mind I'd go see for myself.

STOKES: *(To KIMBROUGH.)* That's the only way you can know.

ROBERT: So I tell Willie Brown, "I'm going take my guitar and go down to the crossroads, man, see what old Satan got to say." And old Willie say he would go but there was this old juicy gal had finally said what he wanted to hear. And since he could run into old Satan anytime, but this might be his only shot at this big legged brownskin he was going let me go head on by myself. Well, that was all right 'cause I'd been alone like that most of my life. And so I went on down. Got there just after midnight just like they say. And I waited. But didn't nothing happen. Way off in the distance I heard a dog howl and an old owl cut loose with a hoot, so I sat down and got out my guitar and went to picking at a little tune. And still didn't nothing happen. And so I said to myself, shoot, I look like a fool sitting out here on the edge of west Hell waiting on somebody, so I got myself on up from there and was just fixing to go on about my business, when all of a sudden I heard a laugh. And the Devil showed up. Sitting opposite of me on the stump of a tree. He wasn't no bad looking fella as far as that went, least not like I might've thought. Didn't have no faceless head with two horns swarming around with flies, big long tail and claws on his feet. He was just a ordinary white man in a suit and tie—but still he had blood in his eye. He explained the way it was supposed to go is I hand him my guitar and he play on it then hand it back, and the deal be done and I be able to play from then on like a rabbit can run. Well I thought about it and it seemed too easy to me. I hadn't never got nothing before I didn't earn, nor most of what I had; so I wondered what made me think he was about to start then? And besides, I'm particular, and I don't let just anybody handle my guitar. I'm funny like that. So I got sassy and told him my guitar was all I had and if he wanted to play he had to get his own damned guitar. He told me, "Give me that goddamn guitar here, nigger!" And I didn't move. I'm thinking that's the way they talk to you here then it ain't a bit better than where I just left, and to hell with it! I could've stayed home I wanted to be treated like a dog, fool or a child. And Satan say if I *didn't* hand it over he was going do everything but eat me, and he might do that too. Well, I was new to the place, so I didn't know if he could or no. And he told me then, "All right then, let me see what you can do." And so I hit the lick I'd learned from worrying Son House and them. And the Devil fell out laughing. Laughed so hard he almost hurt hisself. Well that hurt my little feelings, and made me mad at the same damn time. So I kept on—trying to make up something, trying to remember every music I'd heard, from the Delta through the swamps of Louisiana, 'cross the Mississippi and the Gulf on the Brazos. But that just tickled him all the more. He told me, he says, "Get on 'way from here, boy, you ain't doing nothing but wasting my time." But he was having too much fun laughing to move. And I kept on like didn't nothing matter, not a man, woman, child or plot of land. But I did quit trying to copy cat off them others playing. But still the Devil he say, "Boy, you can't play no music." Still I was whipping that guitar more ways than a skinner can whup a mule. But I could feel myself getting weaker. And I was getting scared. He wasn't laughing no more. Everything was changing and I could feel myself sinking down to the deepest places and the darkest parts—deep in hell as a hawk can fly in a week, to where 60 seconds was a day. Pigs could have puppies. And dead men dealing 5 card stud laughed at 3 headed babies as they drowned in lakes of sand. I was slipping back to the beginning of all mankind, but I kept on playing, knowing it was all stood between me and losing my soul. But I kept on playing—But then little by little, from somewhere, I don't know, from me, mostly—I thought. But maybe not. Look like something told me to walk them four corners from point to point. And I did. Then kitty corner. Then round and round. And that's what I done. And something else come to me and say, "Bob, the best way to get ahead is to go back where you started." And I reckon that's when I took the Devil by surprise. Because then it wasn't just me no more—You know how folks, the old folks, talk, when they be setting around last before bed time, taking the ease of the evening air; we little nappy heads be dozing at their knee. And their words and thoughts be drifting out, like cook smoke into the moonlight—telling about *their* old folks and their old *folk's* folk, far back as they could tell. And all what'd happen and the feelings to the time before the Devil first come to over there where they started. And following on up through their low down days and nights of sorrow: the bondage, being bid for on the block, the lash, Jim Crow, the rope, the chain gang and the Klan. And the longer I played look like the stronger it was coming out that guitar. And *that's* what got the Devil, because he couldn't call none of it a lie! The strings was so hot they was smoking and fire was coming from the box. And I handed it to him, and I say, "Now you can play it if you want to." But it was so hot till he couldn't handle it. And well—that just poured him back in the jug! He was so jealous all he could do was get out his guitar. And play. And it was the meanest, most hellish blues I ever heard. And just like I done with Willie Brown and them, I watched and saw how he done it. And *that's* how I got to know the Devil's tune! And he knew it. But right then wasn't nothing he could do. And then he say, "Get on 'way from around here, boy, I ain't got time for you now." And he got up and walked with me back to the gates of Hell. He told me, he say, "You going take some studying. But just as sure as 3 times 9 is 27, some day you bound to fall." But I had him then, and him or nobody else couldn't tell me nothing. Now that's just how it happened, and every word is true. *(Goes to get drink.)*

LEM: *(To GEORGIA.)* He lying. He got to be lying and I know it. The average one whose soul the Devil wants is so hungry their only chance to live is to try to catch the buzzard and pick him clean—make a duster from the feathers, boil the bones for soup. That's the only way they let us live. And the Devil know just when to come to you. And when he do you be so hungry you give in for the promise of a plate of hog guts and dandelion greens.

GEORGIA: *(Suspicious.)* How you know?

LEM: I don't know to this day which one of them was the devil: Mr Big John or Little Big John. Might've been both for all I know. They say the devil is two-faced. Well down there where I was moving that dirt at he had two faces, that's all I know. One black and one white. And they both come to me one night in my sleep. Shook me wake all of a sudden. I sat bolt up, looked 'em both in their eyes. They was cold black and shiny. So shiny till you look in their eyes, all you could see was a reflection of yourself.

GEORGIA: What you do, Lem?

LEM: I had to get away, from that dirt, Georgia. I had to get back to you.

GEORGIA: What you do, Lem?

LEM: That's how come I know he lying, cause he ain't no better than me. You can't trick the Devil. Satan know just what to promise to get you cheap...

GEORGIA: What you do, Lem, I asked you?

(Shift to KIMBROUGH and ROBERT.)

KIMBROUGH: You faced the Devil and you walked away.

ROBERT: Tell the truth and shame the Devil.

KIMBROUGH: All I want is the road back the way I came.

ROBERT: There's stones in your passway. You can't go back that way no more.

KIMBROUGH: And you're my metaphorical hell hound.

"And you hear me howling' in my passway,
please open your door and let me in."

ROBERT: It's you got to break back through. Face your devil, walk along with him, side by side, then go your separate ways. That's the only way. And just like me you ain't got no choice.

KIMBROUGH: I'm just me. I'm powerless to change the past.
I think about it. Since my grandfather died
I think about it. Since I heard your blues
that day I can't get it off of my mind.

ROBERT: *(Direct.)* Not for a long, long time.

KIMBROUGH: When that old man died I refused to enter
the room. I had done everything I could
to separate myself from everything
he was, and our forefathers before him.
(To AUDIENCE.)
The Kimbrough family fortune came from the
trafficking in slaves. Selling human flesh.
(To others.)
I wanted nothing to do with him, his
world—nothin —nothing except his money—
which makes me a coward and a hypocrite,
and as ineffectual as Hamlet.
I try to sleep, but have nightmares filled with blues.

ROBERT: You toss and tumble, your mind look like it be red hot.

KIMBROUGH: *("Yes.")* I was on my way somewhere...

ROBERT: Night was falling.

KIMBROUGH: *("Yes.")* I'm so tired, off course. Then I find myself—
Where? I don't know—In a terrible, black
tangled thickness...

ROBERT: Darkness all around you.

KIMBROUGH: *("Yes.")* I'm afraid.

ROBERT: Don't know which way to go.

KIMBROUGH: *("Yes.")* Death and evil everywhere around me.

ROBERT: You try to holler, but won't a word come out your mouth.

KIMBROUGH: I'm afraid.

ROBERT: You got reason, look behind you. It's a hellhound!

KIMBROUGH: No. It's a metaphor.

ROBERT: With blood dripping from its fangs.

KIMBROUGH: A metaphor!

ROBERT: Ignorance is evil.

KIMBROUGH: I'm so afraid.

ROBERT: Turn around and face it.

KIMBROUGH: *("NO!")* It's a hellhound.

ROBERT: No. It's a metaphor.

KIMBROUGH: I know. I know it.
I'm a coward and a hypocrite. I
knew the source of his money, knew his fortune
came from the lies, advantage and misery.

ROBERT: Evil depends on who talking about it.

KIMBROUGH: I circled around and around the truth,
but the deal I made was to remain silent.
Comfort and leisure to teach—for my silence.
Until he died and I heard your music
and my nightmare of the crossroads started,
and I felt everything I had denied—
I hear you playing and the Devil laughing.

ROBERT: You were there.

KIMBROUGH: I was behind you. Next in line.
And all I could do was moan and tremble.

ROBERT: You was there. Down on your knees, moaning, like a sinner on the thrashing floor.

KIMBROUGH: *("Yes.")* I hear you playing, playing to save your soul.

ROBERT: And you trembling like a leaf trembling on a tree.

KIMBROUGH: *("Yes.")* I hear you and I hear the storm gathering...

ROBERT: That red eyed dog is on your tail, and you trembling down on your knees.

KIMBROUGH: *("Yes.")* I hear you playing, playing to save your soul.
But I had to find a way to save myself.

ROBERT: Save me, save you. Quit trying to hide from that red eyed dog on your tail.

KIMBROUGH: It's a metaphor.

ROBERT: Metaphor my ass, it's the hellhound, fool.

KIMBROUGH: We're in the dream together! and I hear you,
playing, I hear every note, and the blues
is trying to get possession of my soul
but I deny it, because—I'm afraid.

ROBERT: Shame the devil, tell the truth and won't be no reason to have no fear.

KIMBROUGH: If I admit that then everything else,

everything else will have been just a lie.

ROBERT: You know who and what your granddaddy was that's why you could-n't go in that room.

KIMBROUGH: I'm not responsible for what he did.

ROBERT: You lost and down low and you want to get found and rise up. You was drawed to me by my blues, admit the truth and shame the Devil. Get out that nightmare. Quit being a coward and a hypocrite.

KIMBROUGH: *("I can't. I'm...")* Afraid it's just nigger mumbo jumbo!

ROBERT: *(Hits a dissonant chord on the guitar then moves away.)* Rather take your chances with the Devil.

KIMBROUGH: *(A confession. "Yes.")* But I've found you again. And I'm with you now.

ROBERT: You won't say the truth so you can't do me no good. You can't help me sing, I know what to sing about. You can't get me no women. I can get women for myself. You can give me money but I'll spend it before you out of sight. All you can do for me is go tell them my name. That's all you can do.

KIMBROUGH: I just want peace. I want for it to stop.

ROBERT: *(Goes to get a drink.)* Then you better go stop it. 'Cause the road you took to get here was just a tour of what you're going have to pay for in hell. Go on back and teach, professor. Go trick the Devil and tell the truth.

KIMBROUGH: The world's not my concoction or my fault.

ROBERT: *(Dismissing KIMBROUGH. To others, boastful.)* I got some stuff com-ing out on my next records going be hotter than a tamale. They going be talking about it for years. They ain't going know *where* that new stuff come from. They going be asking one another, "You hear that new stuff Bob got?" "Man, yeah! I don't know *where* he got them songs from!" That's what they going be saying. You listen and see if they don't. And when you hear it, you remember how I told you it was going come to pass. My name going to have to be wrote down right beside the likes of Son House and Willie Brown....

(He suddenly grabs his stomach and falls to his knees in pain.)

GEORGIA: *(To LEM.)* What did you do?!

LEM: *(Reveals rat poison.)* You might can trick the Devil, but he still going get you in the end.

(ROBERT is moaning as he does on a blues.)

LEM: *(cont.)* Cause he make his promises, but you got to make yours too.

(ROBERT is moaning and howling.)

STOKES: Don't nobody touch him. He got to do it. He got to break through to the other side. Go on boy! Go on! Let this world know you leaving, and the other know you on your way!

LEM: *(To GEORGIA.)* I done it for you, so I could be back with you, 'cause I still got feelings for you, baby—even if you ain't for me. That's how come I done it, for you, Georgia, so I could get back and be with you.

GEORGIA: Don't try and dump them boll weevils in my cotton patch, negro! Georgia ain't ask you to do no evil, ain't got no sympathy for you if you did—whether it was in my name or no'. So you better take your soul somewhere it can't be found, that's all I got to say.

STOKES: *(To ROBERT.)* You done your work. You done struck your lick for the people to hear.

(ROBERT dies)

STOKES: Now they got to listen, each for theyself, 'cause you sure done put it out there for them to hear.

(LEM exits)

(We hold for a moment.)

(Light fades on all but:)

EPILOGUE

KIMBROUGH: *(In spotlight.)*
Robert Johnson? My research proves that he
was in league with Satan from the age of
seventeen. They sealed their evil bargain
one midnight at a lonely country crossroads.
They would consort during thunder, lightning
and rain. And when they practiced their hurly
burly the multiplying villainies
of nature transmutated fair to foul
and foul to fair. And evil did swarm around
his lust swollen, Satan stolen soul. That
explains his unnatural insights and
musical mastery, that and that alone.

(Lights off on KIMBROUGH.)

STOKES: Robert Johnson? He be back. He just going down to hell and ease some peoples minds; maybe move some rocks around, even change the way the river run. Aw, he'll be back directly, don't you worry 'bout a thing. Just like he been here before he be back again. How I know? 'Cause it's happened before. And I seen it with my own eyes!

(He laughs and plays blues on piano as lights fade to BLACK and the end of the play.)

SHAKESPEARE QUOTATION REFERENCES
"To have a giant's…"
Measure for Measure   Act 2, line 108
Isabell's speech

"But that defenses…"
King Henry the Fifth   Act 2, Scene 4
Dauphin's first speech

"And hither hale…"
Titus Andronicus   Act 5, Scene 3, line 143
Roman's speech

Measure for Measure
because of the focus on evil - with questions of personal morality. Essentially
    you get what you give.

"I'll have this secret…"
Cymbeline   Act 3, Scene 5, line 86
Clotch's speech

"…Thy kinsmen hang…"
Rape of Lucrece   line 52

"…give me them that will…"
Henry the Fourth   Act 2, Scene 4, line 167
Falstaff's speech

"…with unhack'd swords…"
King John   Act 2, line 254

As You Like It
"And so, from hour to hour…"
Act 2, Scene 7, line 26
Jaques' speech

C. Bernard Jackson

IAGO

Inner City Cultural Center

C. Bernard Jackson

Jackson is the founding and current Director of the Inner City Cultural Center. An award winning composer, author, and stage director, Jackson has served on the faculties of UCLA, USC, Loyola-Marymount, and the City College of New York. His musical compositions, plays, and articles have been performed, produced, and published throughout the world, and he has received numerous awards and honors during his career, among which is that of having the Association of Los Angeles Playwrights' Annual Award bear his name.

INNER CITY CULTURAL CENTER

The Inner City Cultural Center was founded in 1965 immediately following the explosions which erupted in Watts and other communities around the US. Its founding premise was to explore the arts as a potential tool for bridging the communication gap existing between L.A.'s diverse communities. Since its inception, ICCC has been actively involved in training, production, and presentation activities designed to increase public awareness of the rich pool of talent available within the American community.

ICCC has served as a mechanism for introducing, literally, thousands of distinguished individual artists and artistic ensembles from around the world to Los Angeles audiences. Louis Gossett, Jr., Isabel Sanford, George Takei, George Wolfe, Glynn Turman, Pat Morita, The Dance Theater of Harlem, Twyla Tharp, Paul Taylor, The National Dance Company of Senegal, The Mimura Harp Orchestra of Tokyo, and The Negro Ensemble Company are just a few of those who were first introduced to Southern California by ICCC.

IAGO
by C. Bernard Jackson

Directed by
C. Bernard Jackson

With   Rita Browne
Gloria Calonee
J. D. Hall
Lucia Hwong
Gralin Jeralo
Sab Shimono
Cheryl Tyre-Smith

As the audience gathers outside the theatre, they are greeted by a teaching assistant. He carries a radio tuned to a jazz station, or tapes.

TEACHING ASSISTANT: Ladies and gentlemen, your attention, please. The Professor has asked me to remind you that, by today, you were supposed to have read Shakespeare's "OTHELLO." Since I am familiar with the behavior patterns of participants in these so-called "study" tours, and know for a fact most of you were out partying last night when you shoulda been up in your rooms studying, I have run off for you a synopsis of Shakespeare's tragic tale of the Blackamoor and the Venetian maiden. I will be happy to let you have a copy at no cost, since I know that when this tour comes to an end, my many kindnesses will not be considered to have been their own reward. I do accept tips if you get my meaning. I suggest you read this synopsis carefully because, as you well know, the Professor does ask questions. If you expect to get any kind of a decent grade in this course, I advise you to be prepared to come up with some answers. Now for a buck, seventy five ($1.75), I can let you have this little booklet which gives you a detailed scene breakdown. For two dollars ($2.00), I can let you have a complete copy of the play.

Some seats have been set up inside and the Professor wants you to fill up the front rows first. He don't want anybody trying to hide out in the back. He hates to shout. The bus will be back to pick us up in approximately two hours and fifteen minutes Cyprian time and the rest of the evening is yours to do with what you will. Any questions? Okay. We can go in now. Fill up the front rows first. It's kinda dark in there so watch your step. Read the synopsis. The Professor should be here any minute. Front rows first.

PROLOGUE

(The AUTHOR is dressed simply. This basic costume should be somewhat periodless, although suggesting toward the 20th century. He is carrying a bag which contains: a small tape recorder, a small notebook and pen. He is addressing the AUDIENCE as he comes down the aisle.)

AUTHOR: This is it. This is the place that we've been looking for. Everything here is of the correct point in time. This fabric was woven undoubtedly about the mid-fifteenth century, somewhere in the south of Spain. This is the precise location we have been searching for. I suggest we proceed at once. Please remember, there must be complete and absolute silence during the ceremony. I must have your concentrated attention. You will keep your eyes closed tightly until I give you permission to open them. I'm going to ask those of you who are wearing glasses to remove them. Place them somewhere where there's no danger of them being broken. Now, we may or may not succeed, but, should we, you'll have the satisfaction of knowing that something of enormous significance has been accomplished.

Are you ready? Good. Then, let us begin. All eyes closed. *(Waits until they do so.)* Cover both eyes with your left hand. *(LIGHTS fade slowly to BLACK.)* Cover your left hand with your right. Block all thoughts from your mind. There is only blackness, a total void. *(MUSIC is heard - soft, very sparse.)* In the distance, you see a pin prick of light. It is moving toward you, growing in size and intensity as it approaches. It is moving closer...closer...closer, until now it is directly in front of you. It is very bright, almost painful to look at, but, you dare not take your eyes away. *(MUSIC has been growing steadily more intense throughout.)* The light is surrounding you, enveloping you, absorbing you...Now you become aware of a sound that comes from deep inside you, ...a soft, deep hum. It is a sound you are making. It forces its way out of you, becoming louder and louder as if trying to match the intensity of the light which is absorbing you. The sound will continue until I call for silence. *(CHANTING above the hum.)*

AUTHOR: Red

ENTERTAINERS: Wind

AUTHOR: Yellow

ENTERTAINERS: Earth

AUTHOR: Black

ENTERTAINERS: Water

AUTHOR: Blue

ENTERTAINERS: Fire

AUTHOR: Orange

ENTERTAINERS: Sky!

(There is the sound of soft wind, then Moorish music which builds rapidly to a climax, a clash of cymbals.)

AUTHOR: Now, lower your hands and open your eyes.

(The WOMAN stands in the center of the stage, bathed in an intense light. There is a second cymbal crash. The ENTERTAINERS (4) appear around her. They will from this point assume roles, provide music and movement as well as function as a kind of onlooking chorus,—sometimes participating in—sometimes outside the action of the play, assisting with staged costume changes, providing props, rearranging set pieces, etc., ad infinitum.

(THE ENTERTAINERS (4) and THE WOMAN perform a dance which builds rapidly to a frenzied climax. It is an ancient dance. Moorish. Nothing we have seen before. Following the conclusion of the dance, the WOMAN Crosses Down Center to address the AUDIENCE.)

WOMAN: And now that you're here...what is it you want?

(FADE)

SCENE 1

WOMAN: No! The whole business is best forgotten.

AUTHOR: But, madam…in the interests of history, should not the story be set straight?

WOMAN: History? What is history—a dirty basement window where voyeurs bend and peep desperate to catch others in acts they themselves long secretly to commit.

AUTHOR: But the story is already out—known even to children. This Englishman has woven his version of the tale so skillfully, no one dares question its authenticity.

WOMAN: To weave is one thing, to embroider quite another.

AUTHOR: Then, tell us your version of the story.

WOMAN: Who will listen?

AUTHOR: (Indicating AUDIENCE.) We will. And faithfully transmit everything you say. (To AUDIENCE.) Tell her I speak the truth.

WOMAN: (To AUDIENCE.) Nonsense! You will listen and take what you consider important and omit the rest. I know you. Peeping Thomases. *Determined* to see what you wish the truth to be.

AUTHOR: You do them an injustice, Madam! They wouldn't be here if they weren't interested in what you have to say. (To AUDIENCE.) Right?

WOMAN: Oh, they're interested alright. Interested in peeking beneath the sheets to catch a glimpse of the naked flesh of the past. Well, history can't be seen from the outside. You're going to have to jump into bed with us under the covers, into the midst of the action. I'll tell the story if they'll be a part of it, participate fully, no holding back. They pull out, I pull out.

AUTHOR: Agreed. You have first hand knowledge of the events in question. Personally knew those who were involved.

WOMAN: By sight. By touch. By bonds of blood. (To AUDIENCE.) You see, it was my husband, my father whom they accused, whose name is now so despised that even those who know him fear to mention it except in bitter condemnation.

AUTHOR: Iago.

WOMAN: That name is fictitious! That was not my husband's name. The lie begins with a highly improper proper noun. But then perhaps I should not complain for the acts which they attribute to him are as false as the name. Perhaps it is better that false deeds bear fictitious labels.

AUTHOR: What *was* your husband's name?

WOMAN: Courage. Wisdom. Devotion. That was his name!

AUTHOR: What was he called?

WOMAN: Ostrich swift, tall giraffe, stallion's mane, quiet panther, lion's roar. (Commanding AUDIENCE.) Roar Lions!

If AUDIENCE does not participate:

WOMAN: They're not participating. You said they would participate.

AUTHOR: (To AUDIENCE.) Roar lions!

WOMAN: *(Commanding AUDIENCE.)* Cry jackals! Buzzards fly. Fly buzzards! *(She cracks up delighted by her own joke.)*

AUTHOR: *(Exasperated).* Madam, you cannot expect the audience to participate if you're going to indulge in mean trickery.

WOMAN: I am the one who has been tricked. You invite yourself into my living room, bring all your relatives with you. What is that? Bad manners, to say the least.

AUTHOR: They are not my relatives. They are students on a special study tour. Shall I ask them to leave?

WOMAN: Students? How interesting. My husband and I met at the Islamic University at Cordoba. He was studying navigation, I classical languages. The Christian barbarians destroyed everything. I'll never understand why.

AUTHOR: Then, it's alright for them to remain.

WOMAN: It's just that...there are so many of them. I wasn't prepared. If they're hungry or thirsty, they'll have to fend for themselves.

AUTHOR: We've set up a refreshment center outside. You don't have to deal with any of that.

WOMAN: What if they have to relieve themselves? Moors knew something about plumbing, but these Cypriots...

AUTHOR: All that's been taken care of.

WOMAN: I hope you're right. What a mess that would be.

AUTHOR: It's been taken care of. Now...back to Iago. Can you tell us a little about him?

(The following section is done with guitar accompaniment. A la flamenco. The ENTERTAINERS appear.)

WOMAN: *(Spoken)* He was my *husband*
My *Father (Entertainers Repeat)*
My *son.*   "   "
My *teacher*   "   "
My *friend*   "   "
He was everything to me.
I was he.
He was me.
(Sung)
He was an officer of the brave
Moorish armies.
Who distinguished himself
in the battles against
Philip and Isabella.
Twice wounded at Malaga.
(ENTERTAINERS REPEAT)

And again at *Granada*
(Spoken)
And when the Moorish
armies were finally defeated,
he helped organize the
routes of retreat.

ENTERTAINER 3: Some to Africa.

ALL: SCATTER.

ENTERTAINER 1: Some to Corsica.

ALL: SCATTER.

ALL: Where centuries before the blood of our forefathers mingled in the veins of that island's hardy inhabitants.

ALL: SCATTER.

WOMAN: To Venecia's Italia's sun-drenched city states...Where, in return for our services in their war with the Turks, and with one another, they were willing to shelter us from the terrors of the Spanish Inquisition. In a time, they were to provide the boats and supplies we would need to make the journey home to our beloved Africa. Oh, how we yearned to set foot on that glorious motherland, be reunited with family and friends not seen since the conquest of Granada by the Catholic king. The Venetians, at first, treated us well enough, since we quickly proved our worth. A handful of Moorish soldiers managed to settle in a day, a dispute with a neighboring city which had plagued the citizens of Venice for a decade or more.

SCENE 2: The Moorish Camp
(EMELIA and IAGO in masks address the AUDIENCE: which, from their point of view, is divided into MOORS, TURKS, and VENETIANS.)

EMELIA: Comrades in arms. The Turks are threatening the island of Cyprus.

IAGO: The Venetians have asked us to oppose them in battle.

EMELIA: Seeing our regiments number but a handful, we are to be given Venetian reinforcements.

IAGO: Certainly, we have no objections to this.

EMELIA: However, it should be made painfully clear...

EMELIA & IAGO: These Venetians have never been to war.

EMELIA: They are schoolboys trained in classroom warfare.

IAGO: Student soldiers with wooden swords and spitballs and stomachs that will retch at the first sight of human blood.

WOMAN: Even this would be tolerable.

IAGO: But, I am further commanded to inform you that one of these schoolboys is to be appointed to lead us in battle.

WOMAN: Having authority even over my husband, Iago, to lead us to our deaths.

IAGO: I would gladly step aside in favor of some other officer with more experience in battle, but to appoint this Michael Cassio who never set a squadron in the field is an affront to every soldier who has given his life in defense of a just cause.

EMELIA: My husband plans to oppose this choice so clearly based on political expediency. And I, for one, support him with all my heart.

Have you ever been to war?

Do you know what it is to see a man bleed from his eye?

Wet his trousers?

Loosen his bowels where he stands?

Have you heard a man cry, whimper, plead, scream?

Seen a pointed dagger driven through a man's temple break against the punctured skull?

Maggots crawling in open sores?

Leg bones bent backwards?

Intestines clutched in dying hands?

And the earth made muddy with human blood?

Would you trust one, be he Moor or Venetian,

who had never seen such sights to lead you

safely through this war with the Turks?

IAGO: There are no schoolboys on their side, I can assure you.

EMELIA: *(She chooses an AUDIENCE MEMBER.)* Will you allow this man to lead you into battle against the Turks? I will answer for you. I know him not, nor do I doubt his courage but to elevate him over one whose skill and bravery has been proven one hundred times over—that is folly. And Iago, Othello is to blame.

IAGO: Emelia.

EMELIA: I dare to call our noble General a fool. He is a fool.

(She goads the AUDIENCE into chanting FOOL with her.)

ENTERTAINERS: *(EXIT chanting.)* FOOL. FOOL. FOOL.

AUTHOR: Wait! Wait! Are you saying Othello a seasoned general, a master in the arts of war would allow simple politics to destroy his judgement...

WOMAN: *(Removes mask).* Simple politics? Politics is never simple. Politics is a complex chameleon like creature, sensitive to the slightest change in its surroundings. Now, the businessmen who rule Venice are crafty. They fear us, so they place some of their own within our ranks, insist key positions of power be assigned to men of their own choosing. All under the guise of giving *aid* to the Moors.

AUTHOR: I don't understand. Why would Othello...

WOMAN: Othello is weary! He has been given a palace, servants, velvet pillows on which to rest his greying head. Never mind that we must sleep in flea infested barracks. The General is comfortable. That is politics! Offer comfort to a weary man, add a touch of flattery to calm those insecurities which forever lurk in the hearts of warriors and athletes too long on the field. Then...let the scent of an exotically perfumed flower drift into the aging warrior's chambers.

AUTHOR: Desdemona?

WOMAN: Yes. Desdemona. Let us all say the name.

WOMAN & AUTHOR: Desdemona. *(WOMAN indicates for AUDIENCE to also say the name.)* Desdemona. Desdemona. The best of men have been swayed by such sweet politics.

AUTHOR: Madam, I must admit, this is a new interpretation of the story.

WOMAN: I was there!

AUTHOR: But...

WOMAN: I say, I was there! However, if you prefer hearsay suit yourself, although even in their distorted accounts, there is evidence of the truth of what I am saying.

AUTHOR: In Shakespeare's version...

WOMAN: The Italian Giraldi Cinthio was the first to set the story down. The Englishman is in debt to him and he, by his own admission, to me. But the Italian chose to rewrite my story to suit the tastes of his readers. The Englishman did the same and you and they *(Indicating AUDIENCE.)* will do likewise. The facts are so twisted and bent out of shape that the truth looks on open mouthed, astonished by the audacity of the shameless lie. Anyway, I will try to set the story right, but, before I try to explain any further. I must know whether or not you are willing to play the "game."

AUTHOR: Madam, I don't wish to offend you but, I do not have time to be playing games with you. Your time may be unlimited but, we happen to be on an extremely tight schedule.

WOMAN: Oh. I'm sorry. I didn't realize you were in a hurry. Goodbye.

AUTHOR: I beg your pardon?

WOMAN: Goodbye. Get out. I'd like to say it's been a pleasure but it hasn't.

AUTHOR: Now, wait a minute, Madam. There's no need to get upset. All I was trying to say was that...

WOMAN: Don't explain! You made yourself perfectly clear. You don't have time for games. Now let me make myself perfectly clear. I want you out of here, and I want you out of here now! *(To AUDIENCE.)* Get out! All of you! Out I said!

AUTHOR: Madam, will you calm down.

WOMAN: No! I will not calm down.

AUTHOR: Why can't we just sit here like two sensible people. All I'm asking is a chance to ask you a few questions, to record your remarks on this machine here then I'll be able to tell your story. You do want your version of the story to be told, don't you?

WOMAN: Yes. I do.

AUTHOR: Well then, why won't you cooperate?

WOMAN: I don't trust you.

AUTHOR: I see. Alright. Why don't you trust me?

WOMAN: You have a nervous lip.

AUTHOR: A nervous lip. Look, Madam…there's no reason I should expect you to know who I am. But let me assure you that I do have something of a reputation in academic circles. In fact, there are those who consider me to be one of the leading scholars in my field.

WOMAN: Will you play the game?

AUTHOR: Articles I've written have been translated into more than a dozen languages…

WOMAN: Will you play the game?

AUTHOR: What I'm saying is that if you blow this chance you're making a big mistake…

WOMAN: Will you play the game?

AUTHOR: *(Exasperated.)* Alright. I'll play your damn game. What is it?

WOMAN: The game of being. Of not being on the outside, but inside where the action is taking place. Come, step into the center of the arena. Over here next to me.

AUTHOR: Why not? What do I have to lose?

WOMAN: Not a great deal…although, possibly more than you might expect. Come, step into the center of the arena.

AUTHOR: Alright, I'm here in the center of the "ARENA." What do I do now?

WOMAN: Simply be.

AUTHOR: Be what?

WOMAN: In this case, not what but who. *(ENTERTAINERS ENTER. ENTERTAINER 3 plays the role of RODRIGO. ENTERTAINER 6 carries the playing card of RODRIGO. Numbers 2, 1 and 4 participate in costume changes, etc.)* My friend there will be Rodrigo, a young man desperately in love with Desdemona and with whom she has apparently carried on an impassioned correspondence. And you will be Senator Brabantio, the father of the girl with whom Othello has secretly eloped. And after that we shall see who else you will become.

AUTHOR: And how will who I become be determined?

WOMAN: By the best of all possible means…by chance. Put on the night shirt. *(THE ENTERTAINERS dress AUTHOR)* There, it is done. The perfect picture of a man whose world is about to fall apart. *(SHE pushes AUTHOR*

now BRABANTIO up the aisle through the AUDIENCE.   TO AUDIENCE.)
We shall soon see how this Italian politician responds to the news that his
household's most precious jewel, his daughter, Desdemona, lies not dreaming peacefully in her bed, but is hotly clutching to her snowy bosom a
Moorish general's woolly head. *(EXITS.)*

SCENE 3:   A STREET IN VENICE

RODRIGO: *(ENTERTAINER 3 as RODRIGO takes letter out of belt and reads.)*
Rodrigo, My Dearest Friend, I have told no one else this, but thee.
General Othello has asked me to marry him. I know my father would never
consent, so we plan to elope. By the time you receive this letter, I will be
happily wed. Loving me as I know you do, I'm sure you will understand.
(End of letter.)
'Tis monstrous. The wedding must be stopped. I love the lady and if I
should lose her, I would forthwith drown myself. Life without her would
seem empty of all meaning.   Thieves!   Thieves! *(Starts to run to
BRABANTIO's house.)* Thieves!   Thieves!   Senator Brabantio wake up!
Look to your house! Your daughter! Your purse! Wake up! Thieves!
Thieves! *(Desperately tries to awaken the sleeping household.)*

BRABANTIO: *(Appears at end of aisle through AUDIENCE.)* What is the matter
there?

RODRIGO: Signor, is all your family within?   Are your doors locked?

BRABANTIO: Why, wherefore ask you this?

RODRIGO: Oh, Signor, Signor just moments ago, a messenger did deliver unto
me this letter.   Your daughter, this very night plans to elope with the
Moorish general.

BRABANTIO: What say'st thou?   Speak up!

RODRIGO: I am robbed. Put on your gown. My heart is burst. I have lost half
my soul. Even now, now, very now, an old black ram may be topping your
white ewe. Arise, arise, awake the snoring citizens with the bell, or else the
Devil will make a grandsire of you. Arise I say!

BRABANTIO: What!   Have you lost your wits?   Who are you?

RODRIGO: My name is Rodrigo.

BRABANTIO: The worse welcome.   I have charged thee not to haunt about my
doors.   Hast thou not heard me say my daughter is not for thee?

RODRIGO: Most grave Brabantio, you'll have your daughter covered with a
Barbary horse. You'll have your nephews neigh to you. You'll have cours-
ers for cousins.

BRABANTIO: What profane wretch art thou?

RODRIGO: I am one, Sire, that comes to tell you your daughter and the Moor
may well now be making the beast with two backs.

BRABANTIO: Thou art a villain.

RODRIGO: You...a Senator.

BRABANTIO: This thou shalt answer. I know thee, Rodrigo.

RODRIGO: Sire, I will answer to anything. Do not believe that I would trifle with your reverence. Your daughter, if you have not given her leave, I say again hath made a gross revolt. Straight, satisfy yourself. If she be in her chamber, or your house let loose on me the justice of the state for thus deluding you. Here is the letter, Signor writ to me in Desdemona's own hand.

BRABANTIO: *(Goes up audience to search house.)* Strike on the tinder. Ho! Give me a taper! Call up all my people! Light! I say, light! *(ENTERS.)* Gone she is. O unhappy girl! With the Moor, say'st thou? O heaven! How got she out? O treason of the blood! Are there not charms by which youth and maidenhood may be abused? Have you not read, Rodrigo, of some such thing?

RODRIGO: Yes, Sire, I have indeed.

BRABANTIO: Oh, would you had had her! Do you know where we may apprehend her and the Moor?

RODRIGO: I think we can discover them, if you please go, along with me. But, Sire, we must hurry!

BRABANTIO: Pray you, lead on! Oh, good Rodrigo, I'll reward your pains.

RODRIGO: I pray we are not too late!

(They Exit.)

SCENE 4: OTHELLO'S PALACE

(Scene opens with wedding dance performed by ENTERTAINER 4. *And conclusion of dance* OTHELLO *played by* ENTERTAINER 1, *and DESDEMONA played by* ENTERTAINER 2 *ENTER in masks.)*

OTHELLO: And now thou art mine, fair Desdemona.

DESDEMONA: Thine, my lord. And art thou not mine as well?

OTHELLO: Absolute.

DESDEMONA: I am glad of it, my lord. For t'would be a strange bargain if I were to be thine alone and thou not mine.

OTHELLO: It would be strange though not uncommon.

DESDEMONA: But thou art not common, my husband. Thou art a general. And I a Senator's daughter, therefore, ours will be a most uncommon marriage, and that uncommonness will bind us together `till...

OTHELLO & DESDEMONA: Death do us part. *(They laugh.)*

OTHELLO: O, thou art an excellent wretch. Perdition catch my soul, but I do love thee! And when I love thee not, chaos is come again. I have a gift for thee.

(ENTERTAINER 4, Enters with strawberry covered handkerchief, and ENTERTAINER 3 with linen parchment and ostrich plume.)

DESDEMONA: A marriage gift.

OTHELLO: A wedding gift, to show that nothing do I hold back. *(Takes gift from ENTERTAINER 4, who Exits.)* Take this token, with it, I pledge my undying love.)

DESDEMONA: A handkerchief. 'Tis quite pretty.

OTHELLO: A handkerchief did an Egyptian charmer to my mother give. She told her, while she kept it, t'would subdue my father entirely to her love. My mother dying gave it me. Take heed on't. Make it a darling like your precious eye. There's magic in it. I have still another gift for thee. *(ENTERTAINER 3 gives him gifts.)*

DESDEMONA: Linen parchment.

OTHELLO: Of the finest quality.

DESDEMONA: And a pen made of ostrich plumes. Who told you of my passion for writing letters?

OTHELLO: I have the power to see through souls.

DESDEMONA: Is it possible, my lord?

OTHELLO: No. One of your servants told me.

DESDEMONA: Thank you truly, my lord.

(ENTERTAINER 4 Enters and gives OTHELLO a note. NO. 4 and 3 Exit.)

OTHELLO: I must leave thee.

DESDEMONA: Leave me, my lord?

OTHELLO: The Duke bids me come to the palace. I will return straightaway. *(He Exits.)*

(DESDEMONA Exits performing a dance with the handkerchief, putting it in her bosom.)

SCENE 5: OUTSIDE OTHELLO'S PALACE

(BRABANTIO, played by AUTHOR, Enters in mask.)

BRABANTIO: Othello! Where is Othello?

OTHELLO: *(Played by ENTERTAINER 1 Enters, in mask.)* I am here Signor Brabantio. How may I serve you?

BRABANTIO: O' thou foul thief, where hast thou stowed my daughter?

OTHELLO: She is there, inside my house. Voluntarily she came.

BRABANTIO: Voluntarily. That is a lie! Would a maid so fair incur general mockery by running to the sooty bosom of such a thing as thou? I charge thee with practicing witchcraft. In the name of my office I hereby place you under arrest. Resist. I run you through.

OTHELLO: Good Signor, you shall command more with your years than with your weapons. Where will you that I go to answer your charge?

BRABANTIO: You will be taken before the Duke of Venice.

OTHELLO: Well and good, for it is to the palace of the Duke that my steps were leading me just as you arrived. The Turks are approaching the island of Cyprus. *(They Exit.)*

SCENE 6: THE PALACE OF THE DUKE OF VENICE
(The DUKE Enters, played by WOMAN, in mask.)

DUKE: *(To AUDIENCE.)* Senators of Venice, my apologies for having summoned you so hastily to these chambers. But two hundred Turkish galleys are approaching Cyprus. The situation is grave. I have sent a messenger bidding the Moorish General, whose services we have employed for this very purpose to appear before us here. It is clear the time for action is now. The Moor will defend our interests on Cyprus.

(BRANBANTIO and OTHELLO Enter led in by a SERVANT.)

BRABANTIO: My lord Duke and honorable members of the Senate, I request permission to address the Council.

DUKE: Regarding the situation on Cyprus?

BRABANTIO: 'Tis a personal matter, Sire.

DUKE: Very well, but be brief! There are pressing matters of State which command our attention.

BRABANTIO: *(Addressing AUDIENCE.)* My lord Duke and honorable members of the Senate. A matter of grave personal concern has drawn my attention away from the affairs of State. My daughter, was this night stolen from my household, abused and foully corrupted by one in whom we have mistakenly bestowed our confidence. I accuse him, the Moor. He has used the blackest of magic to twist my daughter, Desdemona, to his evil design. May I remind you that, encamped within our city's gates are an army of his fellows who look to him continuously for example. No one in Venice is safe...

DUKE: Othello, would you speak in answer to these serious charges.

OTHELLO: Most revered signors that I have taken away this old man's daughter, it is most true. True, I have married her. She came to me willingly. If there be doubt, as doubt I see upon some faces, I do beseech you, send for the lady and let her speak of me before her father. If you do find me foul in her report, the trust, the office I do hold of you not only take away, but let your sentence even fall upon my life.

BRABANTIO: With Council's permission, I will straight to his house to fetch her here myself.

OTHELLO: If I'm not mistaken, the lady has already been sent for and awaits me in the antechamber.

DUKE: Fetch Desdemona hither.

(DUKE and BRABANTIO Exit.)

OTHELLO: She will come willingly here as she came willingly to me. And 'til she come I will a round, unvarnished tale tell of how I won her, what "charms," what "potions" I did use…
Her father oft invited me to his table…
(*Lights come up on SENATOR BRABANTIO*)

SCENE 7: BRABANTIO'S HOUSE
(*A SERVANT—played by the WOMAN—leads OTHELLO played by ENTERTAINER 1 into the house. BRABANTIO played by AUTHOR and DESDEMONA played by ENTERTAINER 2 enter. All actors wear masks.*)

BRABANTIO: Ah, good Othello, right on time. In Italy when we say 8 o'clock, we generally mean 9. I'm so glad you could come. You've met my daughter Desdemona. (*Calling SERVANT.*) Ho! bring wine. General Othello is here. Quickly, none of your sluggish ways this night. Quickly! Wine, food. Set the table here. (*SERVANT bustles about trying to look efficient, but obviously somewhat confused by BRABANTIO'S contradictory commands.*) No. No. Not there. Here. Set the table here.

DESDEMONA: (*Amused.*) Good, my father, art thou not going to offer the noble General a seat?

BRABANTIO: A seat? Of course. (*SERVANT picks up pillows to give to OTHELLO.*) Leave the pillows by the table, we plan to sup! (*To OTHELLO.*) Please do be seated General and excuse me but a moment. It would seem to be necessary that I have a private word with the household staff. They are idiots. But then, good help is hard to find in any age and any clime. (*To SERVANT.*) Come! This way.
(*BRABANTIO Exits followed by SERVANT who wrings hands nervously.*)

DESDEMONA: (*Indicates for OTHELLO to be seated.*) My father tells me thou art a very brave soldier General Othello.

OTHELLO: I am well versed in the arts of war, Mistress, but, am known to be quite cowardly when it comes to social matters.

DESDEMONA: Well, this is not a battle, General. Lower thy guard. Please, sit down.

OTHELLO: Thank you, Mistress. (*Sits.*)

DESDEMONA: And I would be pleased if thou would address me by my given name.

OTHELLO: And so I shall, …Desdemona.

DESDEMONA: Hast thou been wounded?

OTHELLO: Six times. (*Each time indicates location of wound.*) Once in Araby by desperate bandits. Once in Gaul by a knight of the cross. Three times in Spain in the battles against King Philip, and once in Africa by a maiden with sparkling black eyes whose fiery glances pierced me to the heart.

DESDEMONA: (*Sighs.*) Would that my own eyes were sparkling black.

OTHELLO: It may be that blue eyes may penetrate as deeply.

DESDEMONA: Is't true that thou hast traveled over the whole world?

OTHELLO: Oe'r much of what is presently known of it.

DESDEMONA: Wondrous things must thou have seen in thy travels. Wouldst thou speak of them to me. Little do I know of the world than what may be seen by day in the streets and shops of Venice.

OTHELLO: Some things need not be seen to be known and some things are better left unknown.

DESDEMONA: Speak to me of thy travels, of the things thou hast seen.

OTHELLO: Ragged cliffs, cloud kissed mountain ranges, waterless deserts, Teutons that feed on human flesh. Tigers and elephants and long necked giraffes, and strange religions that command men to put out their eyes for God's sake. Slave and Master have I been and know that both do suffer. One in body, one in soul. And having seen all this, little have I learned. All I know now, I knew before, for there is no such thing as innocence.

DESDEMONA: No such thing as innocence, my lord? My father thinks me innocent.

OTHELLO: That is the game fathers are expected to play.

DESDEMONA: There is a wisdom in thy words. And a sadness too. Are wisdom and sadness always so closely united?

OTHELLO: I fear that is now the case but fervently hope t'will not always be thus.

DESDEMONA: 'Tis strange. 'Tis passing strange and pitiful, wondrous pitiful. Wouldst thou had a friend who having thy same qualities of wisdom and bravery might also find to his liking a far too sheltered maiden. For such a one t'would be a simpler matter to woo me. I would give him my whole heart for all my life long.

(There is music. DESDEMONA Exits.)

SCENE 8: THE PALACE OF THE DUKE OF VENICE

DUKE: *(Enters.)* If what you have just said be true, Othello, 'tis indeed a most touching story.

OTHELLO: She loved me for the dangers I had pass'd. And I loved her that she did pity them. This only is the witchcraft I have used. But, here comes the lady. Let her speak of it herself.

(BRANBANTIO and DESDEMONA Enter.)

BRABANTIO: Come hither, gentle mistress. I wish you to speak freely. Do you perceive in this noble company, to whom you most owe obedience?

DUKE: Speak child.

DESDEMONA: My noble father, I perceive here a divided duty. To you I am bound for life and education. Both do learn me to respect you, the lord of duty. I am your daughter, but Othello's my husband. And so much duty

as my mother show'd you, preferring you before her father, so much I pro-
fess due to the Moor my now lord and loving master.

DUKE: 'Tis clear, the girl loves her new husband. What say you, Brabantio?

BRABANTIO: The marriage has my blessing. I have done.

DUKE: Othello, take thy new wife and get thee to Cyprus. The Turks are
preparing to pluck that undefended jewel.

OTHELLO: I leave tomorrow. One further thing before I go. I have reached a
decision which I know will please you. I have chosen as my second in command for this foray against the Turks, one Michael Cassio. There are
many among my own countrymen of proven loyalty, with more experience
in battle, but it seemed, to me, fitting I find a way to demonstrate my affection for that nation which gave birth and sustenance to my new wife.
Cassio will lead the Moorish garrisons into battle. Commanded only by
me.

DUKE: A wise decision. Cassio is well known to the members of this Council.
He comes of good family and can be depended upon to keep the common
soldiers in their proper place. I congratulate the General on his decision.
And wish him well on this expedition.

(DESDEMONA Exits, as OTHELLO begins to Exit he is stopped by
BRABANTIO's voice.)

BRABANTIO: Moor! If you have eyes to see, look to her. For she has deceived
her father and may thee.

(OTHELLO Exits. WOMAN removes DUKE mask, and AUTHOR removes
BRABANTIO mask.)

WOMAN: You are doing quite well.

AUTHOR: Madam, thus far your story closely parallels the Englishman's version, in fact, often relies on his words for the telling of it.

WOMAN: The Englishman writes pretty speeches. I see no reason to alter
them, except as they stray too far from the truth.

AUTHOR: But, the people, the times, the places all seem to be, essentially, the
same. I fail to see where the Englishman has strayed from what you call
"the truth."

WOMAN: My husband was an African not a Venetian.

AUTHOR: Well, I'm sure that was simply a small matter of dramatic license.

WOMAN: A small matter.

AUTHOR: I mean, it doesn't significantly alter anything.

WOMAN: It alters everything.

AUTHOR: I fail to see how.

WOMAN: If you fail to see how changing a man's race, color, nationality and
religion alters things then you are an idiot.

AUTHOR: Madam, you may call me what you like. I don't intend to allow ver-
bal insults to sway me from my basic purpose which is to simply uncover

the facts. Now you, the Italian and the Englishman all agree that Iago was bitter over Othello's appointment of Michael Cassio as his Senior Officer. Is that correct? He was bitter, wasn't he?

WOMAN: Yes. He was bitter.

AUTHOR: *(Triumphant.)* Good. We've managed to agree on something. Now, the question which I and many other scholars would like to ask is: Was this the primary cause of Iago's hatred for Othello...

WOMAN: Hatred? *(Shocked.)*

AUTHOR: Was that the reason Iago systematically set out to destroy the General. I mean, there is some indication in both Shakespeare and Cintho's accounting that Iago may have himself been interested in the fair Desdemona.

(The WOMAN knocks the AUTHOR to the ground.)

WOMAN: If words like those ever again escape from your stupid mouth, I promise that, wherever you are, I will find you and drive a dagger through your thick skull.

AUTHOR: I'm only repeating what...

WOMAN: Shut up! Destroy Othello? What perverted minds conceived of such filth. Lies. Lies. Lies! My husband loved Othello. In fact, desperately sought some means of avoiding the calamity which we believed would befall Othello if the course he chose was maintained.

AUTHOR: What calamity did you foresee?

WOMAN: Othello's abandonment by those who held him in most respect. (ENTERTAINER 1 *Enters as IAGO, sits Stage Right. WOMAN dons EMELIA mask. Faces AUDIENCE.)* Moorish soldiers would not follow Cassio to their deaths. *(EMELIA crosses to IAGO. The following scene is a flashback into the past.)*

SCENE 9: IAGO'S QUARTERS

EMELIA: I understand Othello has made his decision.

IAGO: 'Tis final. He officially announced Cassio's appointment in the Senate last night.

EMELIA: Othello has made his decision, we must make ours. The General no longer needs us. Let us away! Leave the General and the Venetians to deal with their enemies as best they may.

IAGO: 'Tis not possible. The Venetians would never voluntarily consent to our leaving, not without having first fulfilled our commitment to confront the Turks.

EMELIA: With Cassio in command such a confrontation would be suicidal. Surely Othello must understand that. I say we take by force, if necessary, the supplies and ships needed to make the journey home. To Africa!

IAGO: Wait. We must not act hastily in this matter. I have pledged I will find a way to bring Othello to his senses.

EMELIA: You have failed, Iago. Let us away.

IAGO: Would you abandon Othello when he needs us most?

EMELIA: It is we who have been abandoned.

IAGO: No, have you forgotten it was Othello, who brought us safely here? It was Othello, who nourished our courage, who bolstered our spirits, who forced us on when each of us would eagerly have surrendered to Philip, to hunger, to cold wind. Emelia, have you forgotten it was Othello, who carried me on his shoulders when I could no longer walk? Emelia, was it not Othello's cloak that warmed you that bitter cold night in the mountains while he slept naked, only his tough black hide to shield him from the wintry gale? Abandon Othello? Madness! Should he ask us to give our very lives, we dare not forget that we owe our lives to him. It was Othello that brought us together. Remember?

(OTHELLO, played by AUTHOR appears, IAGO crosses to HIM. It is a memory sequence. EMELIA remians seated.)

OTHELLO: Iago, how long have we known one another?

IAGO: When we first met, I was a young seaman. His head in the stars. The sea's uneasy balance locked between his knees.

OTHELLO: And I a horse soldier, mud on my heels...

IAGO: And the smell of manure in your cape.

OTHELLO: We almost came to blows that first time.

IAGO: O, I was arrogant in those days.

OTHELLO: It is that combination of arrogance and stubbornness which makes some men uneasy in thy presence, Iago.

IAGO: You are right, my lord.

OTHELLO: Yes. I am right. Just as I was right about the war against Philip.

IAGO: Yes. Had they listened to you, we would have been better prepared. You knew they would come by land. Our ships were useless.

OTHELLO: Yes. I was right about that and about Emelia, too. *(ENTERTAINER enters and begins playing guitar.)* I knew she loved you from the moment I saw her. Yet, you stubbornly refused to believe it.

IAGO: I still don't understand how you knew.

(EMELIA begins dancing to the music. The other ENTERTAINERS ENTER.)

OTHELLO: The eyes, Iago. You must learn to read eyes.

(The following sequence is a flashback to a party at the Moors camp. It is the moment when EMELIA and IAGO first meet.)

EMELIA: Iago, come dance with me.

IAGO: I dance poorly.

EMELIA: You're not enjoying the party. I so much wanted you to enjoy it.

IAGO: You know that I have been transferred to a calvary unit. We leave tomorrow.

EMELIA: I know. Jacinth, Othello's wife told me.

(JACINTH Enters played by ENTERTAINER 4 *and begins to dance with OTHELLO.)*

IAGO: Did she also tell you that I know nothing of horses.

EMELIA: She told me that Othello believes you will make a superb horseman. That with those bowed legs of yours, you will sit a saddle as though glued to it.

JACINTH: Iago dislikes the smell of manure, but my husband says...

JACINTH & OTHELLO: You will quickly grow accustomed to it.

IAGO: I will choke to death. I am a seaman whose lungs are accustomed to the smell of moist winds. The stench of Othello's riding boots makes me sneeze even now.

OTHELLO: What say you? You impudent young scoundrel, I'll have your head now. *(He charges toward IAGO, with JACINTH restraining him, playfully.)*

JACINTH: No. Othello wait!

OTHELLO: You will learn to ride, Iago. I will teach you, for Spain's sake.

IAGO: I am a seaman. My precious rump is too tender to be jostled about on those sacks of donkey bones which you gallop mercilessly through the city streets.

OTHELLO: Donkey bones. Donkey bones! These African steeds are the finest horses in the world.

IAGO: You'd be better off riding camels or elephants, as our forefathers did, than those pitiful ponies.

OTHELLO: Enough! I will teach you to ride. First, you will learn to play the horse, saddled, bridled and spurred a hundred paces. And then, the groom until you master the use of shovel and brush, and last, the jockey. Whip and reins in your left hand, and a naked shimmering blade...in your right. Then we shall see how well you stand up to the crusading white knights in their armored suits and metal masks. We'll soon find out what Iago is made of, when a hundred lances are aimed at your throat. Will Iago hold or, trembling, leap into the nearest mud hole and try to swim for his life.

IAGO: I will hold you up, Othello.

OTHELLO: Then I fear we shall fall together.

JACINTH: Othello, leave Iago alone. Can't you see he enjoys teasing you.

(SHE leads him away.)

OTHELLO: Arrogant upstart.

EMELIA: Iago, you are a devil. Why do you taunt Othello so?

IAGO: I like him. And I think he will teach me much about horses.

EMELIA: They say there's no finer horseman in all Moorish Spain. No more courageous soldier.

IAGO: Yes. He has a proud heart. I can see that, but his pride is easily wounded. That is his weakness.

OTHELLO: *(Laughs.)* Weakness? Othello has no weaknesses.

IAGO: *(To EMELIA.)* I must go.

EMELIA: I like you, Iago. Promise me you'll be careful. *(She is again seated on bench. End of flashback.)* You are right. We owe our lives to Othello. But for him, we would have, all of us, long ago perished. We will gladly give our lives for Othello.

IAGO: Do not misunderstand me. I do not ask that we foolishly give up our lives. What I do ask, is that we make clear to the Venetians that, however mistaken we believe Othello to be, he nonetheless, has our support. It is politics we are involved in. Venetians must know that we will never abandon Othello to their tyranny. Before we would do that, we ourselves would take his life. We will go to Cyprus, and if Othello command it, we will take orders even from Michael Cassio. Othello even in his folly is deserving of our absolute allegiance. We will go to Cyprus.

IAGO & EMELIA: To Cyprus.

(Exit.)

SCENE 10: ARRIVAL IN CYPRUS

(ENTERTAINERS 2, 3 and 4 Enter to dress the AUTHOR as CASSIO, while saying the following dialogue:)

ENTERTAINER 2: On our arrival

ENTERTAINER 3: In Cyprus. The Turkish ships

ENTERTAINER 4: Lay anchored off

ENTERTAINERS 2, 3, 4: The Cyprian coast.

ENTERTAINER 4: The General

ENTERTAINER 3: Bade us immediately make preparations

ENTERTAINER 4: For possible

ENTERTAINERS 2, 3, 4: ATTACK!

ENTERTAINER 4: Michael Cassio

ENTERTAINER 3: His newly appointed commander.

(AUTHOR Exits.)

ENTERTAINER 2: Being ordered to set

ENTERTAINERS 2, 3, 4: The watch. Responded thus.

(CASSIO Enters.)

CASSIO: Iago hath direction what to do. But, notwithstanding with my personal eye, will I look to't. *(ENTERTAINERS Exit.)* Iago. Iago.

(IAGO Enters played by ENTERTAINER 1.)

IAGO: Yes, commander.

CASSIO: We must to the watch. 'Tis early yet, but the General commands it.

IAGO: 'Tis the Moorish custom to set an early watch, when the enemy lies so close at hand.

CASSIO: They will not attack tonight. There's too much moon. I suspect our General has cast us thus early for love of his Desdemona.

IAGO: She is a most exquisite lady.

CASSIO: And, I'll warrant her full of game.

IAGO: Indeed, she's a most fresh and delicate creature.

CASSIO: Her eyes, so cat like. Provocative. Yes?

IAGO: Yes. You might say so.

CASSIO: And when she speaks, every word is like an invitation to love.

IAGO: She is indeed…lovely.

CASSIO: Well, happiness to their sheets! Come, Iago, I have a skin of wine. *(Pulls Flask.)* Sit a moment.

IAGO: Commander, we must to the watch.

CASSIO: Sit a moment. Let us drink to the health of Black Othello. I doubt not but that he will exercise the young mare well this night. In Venice, the grape is the core of all social relations. It washes down our food and warms our limbs on cold, damp nights.

IAGO: Being descendants of the desert, Moors value clear fresh water above all other forms of liquid refreshment.

CASSIO: T'would do you no harm to bend this once. Be polite.

(Offers flask to IAGO.)

IAGO: No thank you, Commander.

CASSIO: 'Tis your loss. *(Drinks wine.)*

IAGO: The Commander's arm is well practiced in the art of tippling.

CASSIO: At the Academy none was my better. *(He begins to sing.)*

(Sings.)

And let me the canakin clink, clink

And let me the canakin clink.

A soldier's a man.

And life's but a span.

Why then let a soldier drink!

IAGO: The Commander sings well. And that is an excellent song.

CASSIO: I learned it in England, where I went to study the art of fighting with sword and dagger. In England, they are indeed potent in pottling. Your Dane, your German, and your swag bellied Hollander—Drink Ho! Are nothing to your English. If you would learn facility with the flask go to England, Iago. Now the Scandinavian has some reputation for drinking but, I assure you the Englishman puts him quite to shame. He sweats not to over throw your Scot. He gives your Frenchman a vomit, 'ere the next pottle can be filled. To the health of our General, to Black Othello. And to his eager young wife. We must to our affairs, Iago. The Moor has bade the watch be set, and I have promised to o'er see it, personally.

IAGO: Perhaps, good Cassio, t'would be better if I attended to this watch. An hour's sleep might...

CASSIO: Sleep? I am not sleepy. You think, sir, that I am drunk? Is that what you think? I am not drunk. I can stand well enough and speak well enough.

IAGO: Excellent well.

CASSIO: Why very well then, you must not think that I am drunk. I will show you that I am not drunk. T'was not just to learn to pottle that I went to England, t'was to master the use of sword and dagger in combination. Are you familiar with the art, Iago?

IAGO: No, Commander. Moors fight with sword alone or dagger alone. One arm to do the cutting the other to shield the cutter.

CASSIO: You Moors are quite backwards in your fighting methods. The use of sword and dagger is the newest development in the martial art. The dagger serves as sword *and* shield thus providing one with twice the striking power. Come, I will show you how 'tis done.

IAGO: Perhaps tomorrow, good Cassio. The methods of my forefather's have stood me in good stead 'til now. Our duty tonight is to watch the sea for signs of movement in the enemy fleet.

CASSIO: You are a rascally fellow, Iago. I know my duty and have no need for you to teach it to me. I will do the teaching here. But you must show yourself a more apt pupil. I find you quite sluggish, but then perhaps the blame for that does not belong to you but to your...ancestry.

IAGO: Commander, I beg you.

CASSIO: I beg you, Iago. Try to overcome your ingraft infirmity. 'Tis difficult, I know, but I will try to help. A willingness to learn has been known to overcome a lack of natural aptitude, but reluctance locks you in the monkey's cage. Be bold, Iago come forth. The cage door is open. I offer you the best wine in all Europe, and you tell me Moors prefer water. I offer to teach you advanced methods of self defense and you say the outmoded and clumsy methods of your forefathers are sufficient to your purposes. Well, I will show you how wrong you are. Come. *(Draws sword and dagger.)* Fence with me, Iago. Be bold now. Come out of your cage little baboon.

IAGO: You are drunk, Commander.

CASSIO: Drunk, you say! Why then to touch me here *(Indicates chest.)* should be an easy matter. Draw your sword!

IAGO: I dare not...

CASSIO: More reluctance, Iago? A timid orangutang. How amusing. I order you to draw your sword.

IAGO: Sir, I dare not for, were I to draw my sword, nothing in the world would prevent me from killing you instantly.

CASSIO: Draw!

(IAGO draws sword. BOTH FREEZE WITH SWORDS CROSSING. WOMAN Enters, running beneath sword. ENTERTAINER 3 pushes IAGO Offstage Left. ENTERTAINER 4 pushes CASSIO to Stage Right. All Exit except WOMAN and CASSIO.)

WOMAN: *(To AUDIENCE.)* Cassio would have been dead had not some of our countrymen rushed to the spot to restrain Iago. Othello was sent for poste-haste. He was furious, of course. Striding up and down. *(WOMAN becomes OTHELLO.)* What now, now Ho!

OTHELLO VOICE: *(Voice Offstage done by ENTERTAINER 1.)* From whence ariseth this?

WOMAN: Are we turned Turks and to ourselves do that which the Turks would gladly do to us?

OTHELLO VOICE & WOMAN: What was it that began this?

WOMAN: Was it Iago?

OTHELLO: Was it Iago?

WOMAN: He has long opposed Cassio's appointment as my second in command. Would he stoop to murder to win his point?

OTHELLO VOICE: What!? In a time of war.

WOMAN & OTHELLO VOICE: Yet wild, the people's hearts brimful of fear, to manage private and domestic quarrels in night and on the court and guard of safety.

WOMAN: 'Tis monstrous!

OTHELLO VOICE: 'Tis monstrous! Who began it?

WOMAN: A wine skin and almost empty. I've never known Iago to be fond of wine. *(Turns to CASSIO seated Stage Right.)* Cassio, you stink of wine. It was you!

OTHELLO VOICE: It was you, Cassio.

WOMAN: That my second in command should be found drinking on watch in time of war is intolerable. Such an officer, be he Venetian or Moor, I would immediately dismiss.

WOMAN & OTHELLO VOICE: *(Overlap.)* Cassio, never more be officer of mine.

ENTERTAINERS VOICES: *(Offstage. Overlap with the above line.)* Cassio, never more be officer of mine.

(WOMAN Exits)

CASSIO: *(Stands.)* Reputation, reputation, reputation. Oh, I have lost my reputation. I have lost the immortal part of myself. O, God, that man should put an enemy in their mouths to steal away their brains! That we should, with joy, transform ourselves into beasts.

Come, Cassio, you moralize too much. I or any man living may be drunk at some time.

OFFSTAGE VOICES: Cassio, never more be officer of mine.

CASSIO: Good wine is a good familiar creature, if it be well used. Exclaim no more against it. I could heartily wish this had not befallen, but since it is, mend it for your own good. I will ask him for my place again.

OFFSTAGE VOICES: Cassio, never more be officer of mine.

CASSIO: He shall tell me I am a drunkard! And had I eight mouths such an answer would stop them all. I know what I shall do. Our General's wife is now the General. I may say so in this respect. He hath devoted himself to the contemplation of her parts and graces. We were close once, I will confess myself freely to her, importune her help to put me in my place again. This broken joint between me and her husband, I will entreat her to splinter. In the morning, I will beseech the virtuous Desdemona to speak to the General on my behalf.

(CASSIO Exits, singing "CANAKIN SONG.")

SCENE 11: A STREET IN CYPRUS

(TIME: The following morning. The WOMAN dressed in CLOWN garb, with ENTERTAINERS Enter singing with considerable gusto although rather nasally. Throughout the song they drink from CASSIO's flask which WOMAN finds.)

(REFRAIN:)
it's morning and the dew
Is thick upon the grass.
And cock - a - doodle - doo
And you can kiss my bloody...finger

WOMAN: *(Verse:)* O' you know yer belly's empty
From the way it starts to rumble.
And the way it starts to gripe.
And the way it starts to grumble.
But, if you haven't got a farthing
There's not a thing that you can do
Except to sing this bloody song
About the bloody morning dew.
Now, my noble lords and ladies
Have more food then they can eat
More wine than they can drink
Velvet slippers for their feet.
Well, my noble lords and ladies
With your fancy tailored clothes

You can take your velvet slippers
And shove'em up your...bloody nose!
(CASSIO Enters and crosses to WOMAN who turns facing him at end of song. Surprised. From CASSIO's Entrance the ENTERTAINERS *have been trying to warn the WOMAN that he is there. When she turns, they Exit scattering Offstage.*

CASSIO: Nose?

CLOWN: My nose, Sir. I was referring to a special trick of singing taught me by my dear departed father. Some sing through the mouth, my father used to say, but music made through the nose is sweeter by far than any other. I would gladly show you how 'tis done if you wish, kind and noble sir, although the noble gentleman should be forewarned that singing too lustily through the nose can, on occasion, lead to bleeding. Although, that seldom is the case once one has mastered the technique properly. Such bleeding is most likely to occur when one, foolishly, attempts to sing through one's nose on an empty stomach, which is the precise situation in which I find myself on this sunny morning, having not a single farthing with which to buy that piece of bread which would pacify my stomach and put my nose back in tune.

CASSIO: Here's money for you. I so like your music, that I desire you, for love's sake, to make no more of it.

CLOWN: Well, sir, I will not.

CASSIO: If you have any nose music that may not be heard, feel free to sing to thy heart's content.

CLOWN: We have none such, Sir, although, I have some songs which were specially writ to be sung softly through one nostril.

CASSIO: Prithee, let thy nose rest awhile. Dost thou hear my honest friend?

CLOWN: No, I hear not your honest friend. Although, I indeed hear you quite clearly.

CASSIO: Dost thou know who resides in this house?

CLOWN: Being new to Cyprus, I do not know, my lord. Tho' I have been told 'tis the Moorish General whom they have sent from Venice to defend us from the Turkish fleet and his young and beautiful wife whom they call Desdemona.

CASSIO: For one who is recently arrived you have already harvested considerable information.

CLOWN: A poor man does well to keep himself informed, my Lord. For often it is only his wits which stand between him and destruction.

CASSIO: I have another piece of gold for thee, if you will do me but one small favor.

CLOWN: And what favor might that be, my Lord?

CASSIO: If the General's wife be stirring, tell her there's one, Cassio, entreats her a little boon of speech. Wilt thou do this?

CLOWN: And what if the General himself, or one of his men should answer, good Sir?

CASSIO: Why then say that you are new to Cyprus and by accident, called at the wrong house. Dost thou understand me?

CLOWN: I understand that thou would'st prefer that the General not know that thou art conversing with his wife. Consider me discretion itself, my good Lord.

CASSIO: Do good, my friend.

CLOWN: I applaud thy audacity, noble sir. I'll not fail thee. The General's wife will come straightaway. 'Tis good as done. But take care young sir, I've seen such things as this turn bloody.

CASSIO: I fear you misinterpret my intentions sir.

CLOWN: My interpretation of your intentions matters not, my lord. It is how others might interpret them that should give you cause for concern. (CLOWN Exits.)

SCENE 12: OUTSIDE OTHELLO'S PALACE
(ENTERTAINER 2 Enters as DESDEMONA in mask.)

DESDEMONA: Good Cassio what a pleasure to see you. Why come you not within? (Attempts to draw him into the house. He declines.)

CASSIO: I come to ask a favor, Desdemona.

DESDEMONA: But, you seem so pale. Are you not well?

CASSIO: Not well at all, my lady. Last night I drank too much wine, and now, I have a pain upon my forehead, (Indicates place.) here.

DESDEMONA: (Touches place tenderly.) 'Tis a pity, but, I have often warned you that your addiction to the flask would be your undoing. Have I not warned you?

CASSIO: Many a time.

DESDEMONA: But would'st thou take heed?

CASSIO: (Shamefaced.) I would not.

DESDEMONA: Here, let me but bind it hard, within this hour it will be well. (She begins to tie handkerchief with strawberries around his head.) But Othello's wrath is less easily dismissed.

CASSIO: Then you know what has happened.

DESDEMONA: Drunk on watch? O', Cassio…t'was a most unsoldierly thing to do. Othello is quite vexed to be sure. Nevertheless, (Making him wait…) I do believe he can be softened.

CASSIO: I beg of you, Desdemona, speak to him on my behalf.

DESDEMONA: Perhaps I will, but thou needs must promise me, faithfully, that thou will drink no more.

CASSIO: Naught but water…in the Moorish fashion.

DESDEMONA: Good. I will do all I can in thy behalf. *(Secures handkerchief.)* There.

CASSIO: Bounteous Madam, whatever shall become of Michael Cassio, he's never anything but your true servant.

DESDEMONA: I know't. I thank you. And do hereby give thee warrant of thy place. Assure thee, if I do vow a friendship, I'll perform it to the last article. My lord shall never rest. I'll watch him tame and talk him out of patience. His bed shall seem a school, his board a shrift. I'll intermingle everything he does with Cassio's suit.

CASSIO: And that failing?

DESDEMONA: Why, I would then prevail upon my good and noble father to reason with him. I ought not tell you this but,…

CASSIO: Oh, please.

DESDEMONA: *(Whispers.)* I have already sent a letter informing my father of your dismissal.

CASSIO: No!

DESDEMONA: Yes! By tomorrow my father will have such information as he may need to take what action to him seems best. Be merry, Cassio, for thy solicitor shall rather die than give thy cause away. Stay and dine with us, Cassio Here me speak on thy behalf.

CASSIO: Not now, good friend. I am very ill at ease, unfit for mine own purposes.

(IAGO Enters and watches the action, unobserved.)

DESDEMONA: Farewell then for now. I'll notify thee.

(Exits.)
BLACKOUT
END OF ACT I

ACT II

(As the Lights come up, Music is heard. The AUTHOR and the WOMAN are seated on pillows. The ENTERTAINERS are seated around stage. Relaxed. As the MUSIC ends the WOMAN pours wine for the AUTHOR.)

AUTHOR: Thank you my good madam. I was much in need of some refreshment. *(Leans back obviously comfortable and a bit full.)* May I call you Emelia?

WOMAN: That is the name my mother gave me, so I must assume that is what she meant me to be called. More wine?

(She pours.)

AUTHOR: William.

ENTERTAINER 4: William?

AUTHOR: That is the name that was given to me. William Romeo Henry Macbeth. My mother was a teacher of classical literature. The Englishman's plays were her greatest passion.

WOMAN: And you inherited her passion and that passion led you all the way to Cyprus.

AUTHOR: Yes.

WOMAN: Where by these most unusual means, you hope to enhance your reputation as a scholar.

AUTHOR: Yes! Although I must admit that I did not expect the experiment to so dramatically succeed.

WOMAN: That is because you have been raised in the Christian tradition. Moorish peoples have long known that such things are possible.

AUTHOR: Yes. It was an old African woman who explained how I should go about it.

ENTERTAINER 1: *(IAGO)* Did she also warn you of the dangers?

AUTHOR: One who is in pursuit of truth can ill afford to be timid.

WOMAN: I quite agree. Now, where did we leave off?

ENTERTAINER 4: With the business of the handkerchief.

AUTHOR: Was there a handkerchief? Some scholars have felt that handkerchief was a rather flimsy device which the Englishman created to move his story forward.

ENTERTAINER 3: But remember, there was a handkerchief in the Italian's version as well.

AUTHOR: That is true.

WOMAN: O, there was a handkerchief alright. But make no mistake, tho' the handkerchief caused Othello considerable vexation, in the end, it was the letter which shattered whatever affection existed between the General and the fair Desdemona. For reasons of their own, the Italian and Englishman omitted mention of the letter entirely. *(Picks up decanter.)* More wine?

(She pours. All ENTERTAINERS *Stand showing impatience.)*

AUTHOR: Thank you. *(Sips.)* A remarkable bouquet.

WOMAN: It is very old. 1490 from the best vineyard in Spain. Now, you're quite sure you're ready to see this through to the end?

AUTHOR: Of course.

WOMAN: From this point forward, you understand...

ENTERTAINER 1: *(IAGO)* There will be no further interruption...

WOMAN: ...and no turning back?

*(*ENTERTAINER 3 *begins to remove the pillows and wine, etc.)*

AUTHOR: I'm certain you don't intend to leave us hanging at this point in the story.

WOMAN: No, definitely not, at this point. But I wanted you to be reminded that things now begin to get quite bloody. If you feel at all squeamish...

AUTHOR: Emelia, let us proceed.

(ENTERTAINER 4 *holds cards for AUTHOR to choose. AUTHOR holds card up.*

WOMAN: Be Othello.

(ENTERTAINER 3 *gives AUTHOR dagger and mask. WOMAN puts burnoose on him. As the* ENTERTAINERS *Exit they walk in a circle around the AUTHOR. WOMAN Exits.* ENTERTAINER 1 *puts on IAGO mask and remains.)*

SCENE 1: MOORISH CAMP

OTHELLO: Iago.

IAGO: You sent for me, Sire.

OTHELLO: 'Tis time we talked.

IAGO: If it concerns Michael Cassio, I would prefer you speak to him directly. As you know, I hold him not in my affection.

OTHELLO: *(Smiling.)* Thou art as stubborn as ever, Iago.

IAGO: I learned from one well versed in the art of stubbornness, my lord.

OTHELLO: No. 'Twas not to discuss Michael Cassio that I called you here. 'Twas to discover if thou art still loyal to me.

IAGO: Loyalty is like green timber. It must be oiled frequently, if it is to retain its shape.

OTHELLO: What dost thou mean?

IAGO: To answer directly my Lord—yes. Perhaps more loyal now than before. In former times, my loyalty was based on respect and admiration I held for a wise and fearless leader. 'Twas a selfish loyalty which admitted of no weaknesses in its object.

OTHELLO: Weaknesses? *(Laughs.)* Othello has no weaknesses.

IAGO: I know, my Lord.

OTHELLO: Oh, would that repute and self judgment were more often in agreement. I understand there is some restlessness in our camp. You are close to the men, Iago. Do you know what is troubling our people?

IAGO: It is a subject I have been anxious to discuss with you, General.

OTHELLO: Speak freely, old friend.

IAGO: Africa.

OTHELLO: Africa. Yes.

IAGO: Our people are anxious to be going home. Have little stomachs for this waiting game we now play with the Turks.

OTHELLO: I am sworn to defend Cyprus.

IAGO: The Turks are not our enemy, Othello.

OTHELLO: Perhaps not. But, the Venetians and Cypriots are our friends.

IAGO: They need us. That is the extent of their friendship.

OTHELLO: We have an obligation.

IAGO: I never yet liked the role of mercenary soldier. It does not suit us well. In Spain we fought for what we believed. Here I know not why we fight.

OTHELLO: To protect those who have extended their hands to us.

IAGO: Is it that you have lost your zeal for returning home? I think thou art afraid.

OTHELLO: Take care, my friend.

IAGO: "Friends" have the right to speak plainly.

OTHELLO: Take care you do not abuse that right. You think me afraid. Afraid of what?

IAGO: Of Africa. Of home. We all share that fear. We were callow youths when we set out for Spain. Now that land is lost. We are forced to return home in defeat. A thousand questions run through our minds. Who is left of those we knew. How will we live? Will we be seen as strangers come to demand a share in a community we long ago abandoned? Africa is a generous land, Othello. We are Her sons and daughters. 'Tis where we belong. Not here fighting battles for a people that hold us in contempt.

OTHELLO: No.

IAGO: You have a family waiting for you at home...a wife who loves you. What of them?

OTHELLO: That love died long ago, Iago. It had become a thing of duty between us. Nothing more. We are better off apart.

IAGO: I did not know.

OTHELLO: That is not surprising since we ourselves did not know until one day it dawned on us that no gesture of affection had been exchanged between us for several months. Neither by word, nor glance, nor touch. I have a family here now. A new wife who, loves me and is fresh as Spring. Here, I know I am needed. You are right. I do not share your enthusiasm for returning to Africa. I am not ready to retire.

IAGO: Retire? What sayst thou? Africa needs men with military skill. I think now more than ever before. Rumors come daily to our ears concerning the activities of the Portuguese.

OTHELLO: The Portuguese? Portugal is a nation of fishermen. What rumors are these?

IAGO: That they have begun to traffic in slaves.

OTHELLO: What is new in that? To force a defeated enemy to serve the victor has been a custom practiced by many tribes and nations.

IAGO: 'Tis said the Portuguese now make a business of slaves. Take women and children by the thousands to be resold. That is not a matter of punishing some affront, but of converting black flesh into gold.

OTHELLO: Thousands? Portugal is a small country. Poor. Why would they need to harvest so much human flesh?

IAGO: 'Tis said a vast new world has been discovered. The blood of Africans is to be used to fertilize the soil of this new land.

OTHELLO: Dost thou believe these fanciful stories, Iago?

IAGO: I know not what to believe, my lord. But, I am convinced we are wasting time here. We may be needed at home. Africa calls.

OTHELLO: Then, go there!

IAGO: Sire?

OTHELLO: Go, I say. Those, of you, who wish to leave have my permission to do so.

IAGO: And what then? Will you fight the Turks single handed?

OTHELLO: I have a Venetian regiment at my disposal.

IAGO: An army of theoreticians molded in the image of Michael Cassio? No! We will not leave you here to die for lack of competent support.

OTHELLO: Why do you hate Michael Cassio so?

IAGO: (Heated.) For thy sake, Othello. I hate him for thy sake. He is a fool and yet you seem blind to't. He mocks you openly, yet you seem blind to't. He seduces you with fawning speeches and further...(Stopping himself.) No. I go too far. I've said enough and will say no more.

OTHELLO: Speak what is on thy mind, good friend. 'Tis best I know all.

IAGO: Look to your new wife! Observe her well with Cassio. Look to't.

(IAGO Exits.)
(The Lights Fade slowly. Music Up.)

SCENE 2: OTHELLO'S PALACE
(AUTHOR as OTHELLO is Downstage. ENTERTAINER 1 as IAGO is on Upstage Ramp. DESDEMONA Enters with ENTERTAINERS 3 and 4 and sits on bench then begins to sing, accompaning herself. All three wear DESDE-MONA masks. The following scenes have a sense of unreality about them. Events overlap, sometimes happening simultaneously.)
(SONG: "WILLOW SONG")
The poor soul sat sighing by a sycamore tree
Sing all a green willow.
Her hand on her bosom.
Her head on her knee.
Sing willow, willow, willow.
The fresh streams ran by her.
And Mumur'd her moans.
Sing willow, willow, willow.
Her salt tears fell from her.

And soften'd the stones.
Sing all a green willow.
I called my love false love.
But what said he then?
Sing willow, willow, willow.
If you court more women,
I'll couch with more men.
Sing willow, willow, willow.

DESDEMONA: My lord, there is good food on the table. Wilt thou come to breakfast?

OTHELLO: I have no appetite. Dine without me.

3 DESDEMONAS: *(Sighing.)* Oh.

OTHELLO: *(To IAGO.)* How stand the Turks?

IAGO: The situation is unchanged, Sire.

OTHELLO: How long can they sit there I wonder. Soon they must replenish their supply of food and fresh water.

IAGO: I would think so, my lord.

DESDEMONA: Think'st thou the Turks will attack, my Lord?

OTHELLO: Only they know the answer to that question. They play a curious waiting game that strains the nerves. They neither advance nor retreat, only make their presence strongly felt. We have no choice but to maintain our defenses in good order and wait.

DESDEMONA: 'Tis a fetching problem, indeed, my lord.

OTHELLO: Many feel we should take the initiative. Your father, for example...

3 DESDEMONAS: Oh.

OTHELLO: ...feels we should strike the first blow.

3 DESDEMONAS: Oh!

IAGO: Cassio is eager for a fight.

OTHELLO: That is true. But, I have no stomach for throwing inexperienced young men into battle unless forced to't. *(Pause.)* Desdemona,...

3 DESDEMONAS: Yes, my lord.

OTHELLO: ...I thought I saw Michael departing earlier. Was't he?

DESDEMONA: Ay, and so it was, my lord.

OTHELLO: Why stole he away so guilty like?

DESDEMONA: 'Twas his discretion my lord. He came to me as a suitor, one that languishes in your displeasure. We spent a good while talking. If I have any grace or power to move you call him back. If he be not one that truly loves you, I have no judgment in an honest face.

OTHELLO: My wife pleads his cause.

IAGO: Sire?

OTHELLO: Cassio. My wife pleads his cause.

IAGO: Does she, my lord?

OTHELLO: She wishes me to reinstate him.

IAGO: So I have been told.

OTHELLO: Told already? And by whom told?

IAGO: My wife...

DESDEMONA: Emelia.

(EMELIA Enters and takes letter from DESDEMONA.)

IAGO: Desdemona's maidservant, my lord.

OTHELLO: Yes. They are oft together. And what is it your wife has told you?

IAGO: That Desdemona has written to her father concerning Cassio's dismissal.

(EMELIA Exits.)

OTHELLO: Has she now? Strange, she made no mention of it.

DESDEMONA: Good love, call him back. He is penitent. Ay, so humbled he hath left part of his grief with me. Call him back.

OTHELLO: Dost thou see something amiss between Cassio and my wife? If thou dost love me show me thy thoughts.

IAGO: My lord, you know I love you.

OTHELLO: I know thou weigh'st thy words before thou give'st them breath. Speak to me as to thy thinkest, give thy worst of thoughts the worst of words.

IAGO: You do truly love this Desdemona, Sire?

OTHELLO: I do.

IAGO: And she truly loves you?

OTHELLO: Yes. She loves me.

3 DESDEMONAS: We spent a good while together. *(Overlap 1, 2, 3.)*

IAGO: Then bring her home with us. To Africa.

DESDEMONA: No.

DESDEMONA 2 & 3: Why stole he away so guilty like?

OTHELLO: T'would be too sudden a change to be so isolated from family and friends, from things familiar.

DESDEMONA: If I have any grace or power to move you. Call him back. You'll never find a more sufficient man.

IAGO: Is she as tender as that?

OTHELLO: Yes. She is tender...to me.

DESDEMONA 2 & 3: Good love, call him back.

IAGO: That is sad then for that very tenderness could lead to her undoing.

OTHELLO: What dost thou mean?

DESDEMONA 2 & 3: Shall it be shortly?

IAGO: She is young and inexperienced. Being so tender could she not be easily led by someone with a calculating nature?

3 DESDEMONAS: Tonight at supper?

OTHELLO: Cassio.

3 DESDEMONAS: Tomorrow at dinner then?

IAGO: Yes, Cassio.

DESDEMONA: Why, this is not a boon. 'Tis as I should entreat you wear your gloves.

DESDEMONA 2: Or feed you nourishing dishes.

DESDEMONA 3: Or keep you warm.

DESDEMONA: Nay, when I have a suit wherein I mean to touch your love indeed, it shall be full of pose and difficult weight, and fearful to be granted.

IAGO: I believe him to be treacherous. Capable of using any means to achieve his ends, even unto the seduction of your wife.

DESDEMONA 3: Tomorrow night.

DESDEMONA: Or Tuesday morn.

DESDEMONA 2: Or Tuesday noon.

DESDEMONA 3: Or Wednesday morn.

3 DESDEMONAS: I pray thee name the time.

OTHELLO: Prove it!

DESDEMONA 3: Prove it!

DESDEMONA 2: Prove it!

EMELIA: Prove it!

IAGO: Have you not sometimes seen a handkerchief spotted with strawberries in your wife's hand?

OTHELLO: I gave her such a one. 'Twas my first gift.

IAGO: Such a handkerchief did I today see Cassio wipe his brow with.

EMELIA: Iago, you yourself said that to appoint Michael Cassio is an affront to every soldier who has given his life in defense of a just cause!

OTHELLO: 'Tis not possible.

DESDEMONA 2 & 3: Why stole he away so guilty like? *(To Desdemona.)*

IAGO: This I saw with my own eyes.

OTHELLO: 'Tis not possible.

DESDEMONA 2 & 3: He came to me as a suitor.

IAGO: My lord!

OTHELLO: Not possible.

DESDEMONA 2: Not possible?

EMELIA: Not possible!

OTHELLO: If it be true. If she prove false...

(Following Overlapped.)

EMELIA: Iago, I say we take, by force if necessary, the supplies and ships needed to make the journey home, to Africa.

IAGO: We owe Othello our lives. I pledge to find a way to bring him to his senses!

3 DESDEMONAS: If I have any grace or power to move you, call Cassio back.

EMELIA: You have failed, Iago.

IAGO: My lord!

(EMELIA, IAGO, DESDEMONA 2 & DESDEMONA 3 Exit.)

DESDEMONA: *(Sings part of the "Willow Song." EMELIA wearing DESDE-MONA mask, ENTERTAINER 3 and ENTERTAINER 4 in DESDE-MONA masks and IAGO all Enter for the following scene. The 3 DESDE-MONAS giggle throughout. They and IAGO represent the turmoil in OTH-ELLO'S mind.)* My lord, are you feeling better?

OTHELLO: Somewhat better.

DESDEMONA: I have written Cassio to bid him come speak with you.

OTHELLO: Indeed. Give me your hand. 'Tis a good hand, a frank one.

DESDEMONA: You may, indeed, say so. For 'twas that hand that gave away my heart. Come now your promise.

OTHELLO: What promise, chuck?

DESDEMONA: Why, that you would speak with Cassio, of course.

IAGO: Has thou not sometimes seen a handkerchief spotted with strawberries in your wife's hand?

OTHELLO: Lend me thy handkerchief.

DESDEMONA: Here, my Lord.

OTHELLO: That which I gave you.

IAGO: Cassio is treacherous.

DESDEMONA: *(Hesitates.)* I have it not about me.

OTHELLO: Not?

IAGO: Not.

DESDEMONA 2: Not.

DESDEMONA: No, indeed, my lord.

OTHELLO: 'Twas my mother's. To lose it or give it away would be a heavy offense.

IAGO: Such a handkerchief did I today see Cassio wipe his brow with.

DESDEMONA: Would to God that I had never seen it.

OTHELLO: Ha. Wherefore?

DESDEMONA: Why do you speak so startlingly and rash?

OTHELLO: Is't lost? Is't gone? Speak. Is it out o' the way?

IAGO: She is young and inexperienced.

DESDEMONA: Heaven bless us.

OTHELLO: Say you?

IAGO: Could she not be easily led by someone with a calculating nature?

DESDEMONA: It is not lost. But what and if it were?

IAGO: Such a handkerchief did I today see Cassio wipe his brow with.

OTHELLO: How?

DESDEMONA: I say it is not lost.

OTHELLO: Fetch't, let me see it.

IAGO: Africa is a generous land, Othello.

DESDEMONA: Why so I can, sir, but I will not now. This is a trick to put me from my suit. Pray you, let Cassio be received again.

3 DESDEMONAS: Call him back.

OTHELLO: Fetch me the handkerchief. My mind misgives.

DESDEMONA: Come, come, you'll never find a more sufficient man.

OTHELLO: The handkerchief.

DESDEMONA: A man that all his time hath founded his good fortunes on your love.

OTHELLO: The handkerchief.

IAGO: Such a one did I today see Cassio wipe his brow with.

DESDEMONA: I have it not!

DESDEMONA 3: Tomorrow night.

DESDEMONA 2: Or Tuesday morn, or Tuesday noon.

3 DESDEMONAS: Or Wednesday morn. I pray you, name the time.

OTHELLO: Away.

   (Exits.)

EMELIA & DESDEMONA 2: Is this man jealous?

DESDEMONA: I ne'er saw this before. Sure there's some wonder in this hand-kerchief. I am most unhappy in the loss of it. Perhaps things are as some women have declared them to be.

DESDEMONA 2: 'Tis but a year or two shows us a man.

EMELIA: (DESDEMONA.) They are all but stomachs.

DESDEMONA 2: And we, all but food. They eat us.

DESDEMONA: Hungrily.

DESDEMONA 2: And when they are full.

3 DESDEMONAS: They belch us.

   (DESDEMONA Exits. IAGO Exits. DESDEMONAS 2 and 3 and EMELIA remove masks. WOMAN begins singing toward where DESDEMONA exited.)

WOMAN: Oh, my noble lords and ladies have more food than they can eat.

   More wine than they can drink.

   Velvet slippers for their feet.

Well, my noble lords and ladies
In your fancy tailored clothes
You can take your velvet slippers and shove them up
your bloody nose.

EMELIA: Hear the trumpet? It signals that Brabantio has received his daughter's letter and now a messenger is come from Venice in swift reply.
(During the proceeding dialogue she gives ENTERTAINER 3 *the LODOVICO mask and letter.* WOMAN *and* ENTERTAINER 4 *Exit.)*

LODOVICO: *(OTHELLO Enters.)* God save the worthy General.

OTHELLO: With all my heart, sir.

LODOVICO: The Duke and Senators of Venice greet you.

OTHELLO: Welcome to Cyprus, noble Lodovico. Had I been forewarned of your coming, a fitting reception would have been prepared.

LODOVICO: I appreciate your thoughtfulness, good General, but I come only to deliver a message and must return on the morning tide.

OTHELLO: Ah, so quickly to business. No matter, let us proceed.

LODOVICO: Firstly—the Good Senator Brabantio sends greetings to his daughter, the General's wife and wishes her to know that he has received her communication and earnestly thanks her for it.

OTHELLO: I shall convey the message to my mistress.

LODOVICO: Secondly—

OTHELLO: Secondly—

LODOVICO: The Duke and Senators of Venice wish me to convey to the General their request that immediate preparations be made for an attack on the Turkish ships which have illegally intruded themselves into our coastal waters.

OTHELLO: That is folly.

LODOVICO: Thirdly—it has come to the attention of the noble Duke and his Council of Senators that one, Michael Cassio has been peremptorily dismissed from his post as commander in the service of the Venetian forces stationed at Cyprus. It is requested that he be promptly reinstated.

OTHELLO: Desdemona's letter.

LODOVICO: I am required to seek an immediate response to the aforementioned requests, my Lord.

OTHELLO: Requests...or commands?

LODOVICO: In the language of the court, they are generally regarded as synonymous, my Lord.

OTHELLO: There are times when plainess of speech would have better effect.

LODOVICO: Yes, my Lord.

OTHELLO: You may inform the Duke and his Senators that, in my opinion, an attack on the Turkish fleet, at this time, could only lead to disaster. I have sent my report explaining fully my reasons for having reached these conclusions. I urge the Council to read that report with the utmost care.

LODOVICO: I believe they have already done so, General.

OTHELLO: I see. Then, as to Cassio's dismissal, I trust they are also already aware that he was discovered drunk on watch.

LODOVICO: I believe they are aware of that, Sir, but feel that this single offense is not of sufficient gravity to warrant his dismissal. He is held in high regard by the Duke and the Senate and is considered, by them, to be most trustworthy.

OTHELLO: I see.

LODOVICO: It pains me to deliver to you the following instruction, good Sir, but, it is my duty to inform you that if, for any reason, you find it not in your power...to comply with any and all of the above requests, you are to return with me to Venice.

OTHELLO: And who then would be left in command here on Cyprus?

LODOVICO: Commander Cassio, Sir.

IAGO: *(Offstage.)* She is young and inexperienced. Could she not be easily led by someone with a calculating nature?

OTHELLO: *(After a pause.)* I will not lead these school children into an unprovoked battle which would most assuredly end in their destruction. I will not. Let Cassio do it. I will return with thee to Venice.

LODOVICO: We depart on the morning tide, good Sir. Quarters aboard the ship will be prepared for you and your mistress. Please, report here at dawn prepared to sail.

OTHELLO: *(To self.)* So, they command me home, deputing Michael Cassio to assume my position.

IAGO: *(Offstage.)* He is treacherous, capable of using any means to achieve his end, even unto the seduction of your wife.

OTHELLO: Very well, sir, I obey the mandate. Cassio shall have my place. And, sir, tonight, I do entreat that we may sup together. You are welcome, sir, to Cyprus. Goats and monkeys.

LODOVICO: Goats and monkeys, my lord?

OTHELLO: The ancient symbol of treachery, my good Sir. Goats and monkeys—they abound here in Cyprus. 'Til tonight, Sir.

LODOVICO: 'Til tonight, my Lord. *(Exits.)*

(EMELIA and IAGO Enter in masks.)

IAGO: Now does Othello see 'tis true.

EMELIA: All his fond love thus does he blow to heaven.

EMELIA & IAGO: 'Tis gone.

(EMELIA Exits.)

OTHELLO: Iago! Iago! Iago!

IAGO: *(Crossing to him.)* How now, my Lord?

OTHELLO: Iago, that handkerchief that was my mother's.

IAGO: Yes, my Lord.

OTHELLO: I would have it back.

IAGO: 'Tis done, my lord. *(Exits.)*

(ENTERTAINER 3 *Enters and takes CASSIO mask from box.* ENTERTAINER 4 *Enters and with 3 takes swords and places them on stage, crosses with mask, CASSIO in the middle. Exit laughing.*

SCENE 3: AT THE FORTIFICATIONS

(AUTHOR, in CASSIO mask, crosses to IAGO, who is standing watch.)

CASSIO: Standing the watch again tonight? 'Tis three nights in a row, is it not?

IAGO: Aye. And what of that?

CASSIO: Well, it would seem that, in General Othello's opinion, no other officer is fit to perform the awesome duty of keeping an eye on the Turkish fleet. It does not seem fair, Iago.

IAGO: Not fair to whom, Cassio?

CASSIO: To you, Iago. It is not fair to you. No officer should be required to stand watch three nights in a row.

IAGO: I do not mind, Cassio.

CASSIO: It is not a question of your minding, Iago. I mind. You deserve a rest and I intend to see that you get one.

IAGO: Your meaning escapes me, Cassio.

CASSIO: O, dear me. Perhaps you've not heard. Did not Othello inform you?

IAGO: Inform me of what?

CASSIO: Well, you see, a messenger sent by the Duke himself arrived today... bearing important news.

IAGO: And what news is that?

CASSIO: As of dawn tomorrow...someone should have told you. As of dawn tomorrow, I, Cassio, will be the new General of Cyprus. I am to be your new Commander. Othello has been ordered back to Venice for failure to take aggressive action needed to bring the present situation with the Turks under control.

IAGO: And this in consequence of Desdemona's letter to her father.

CASSIO: Desdemona's letter? What dost thou know of that?

IAGO: Only that she had requested that her father intervene on your behalf.

CASSIO: And so she did but, in doing that, she did only what would be expected of so close a friend.

IAGO: How close are you and Desdemona to one another, Cassio?

CASSIO: Where I come from, those words are considered most ungentlemanly, Iago.

IAGO: Where I come from, the acts you have committed are considered even more ungentlemanly than the words, good Cassio.

CASSIO: If I were you I would be cautious in both words and deed, Iago. Otherwise, you shall have to be quite sharply scolded.

IAGO: Dost thou think so, good Cassio? And when and where shall this scolding take place?

CASSIO: Unless, thy manners improve...why tonight. Here.

IAGO: I think I deserve that scolding, Cassio. Yes. I think I desperately need to be taught a lesson. But before we begin, my lord General Othello has asked that I secure the return of that napkin which you borrowed from the fair Desdemona. It was a gift to her.

CASSIO: More bad manners, Iago? In Italy it is the custom that what is borrowed is returned to the lender. I shall return the handkerchief to the General's wife...tomorrow.

IAGO: The General wishes that it be returned to him tonight.

CASSIO: I like not thy insolent manner, Iago.

IAGO: Then, I beg you to help me correct it, Cassio, for after all, thou art a Venetian noble and I but a rude Moorish soldier in sore need of proper instruction. In fact, when last we spoke, you promised to teach me the use of sword and dagger proclaiming we Moors to be quite backward in our fighting methods. Keep your promise, good Cassio. I would learn this new art and, as you see, I have come prepared with sword (Pulls sword.) and dagger. (Pulls dagger.) Teach me, Cassio. I long to be taught.

CASSIO: You have been fully warned.

IAGO: Teach me, Cassio. I beg you. Instruct me. I am in need of proper instruction.

CASSIO: (Taking sword and dagger.) You chose to ignore my warning, now you shall know my wrath. Defend yourself! (They fight.)

IAGO: I fly away! I run! I cry out! Save me! Save me from Cassio's sharp blades. Oh! I will be cut to pieces! Cassio was trained by Englishmen and is the finest swordsman in all Europe. But Cassio forgets that Iago is not of Europe, and Africans too know something of sword play. Strike me here, Cassio. NO! Here. Sword. Dagger. Dagger. Sword. Am I getting it right, Cassio? Am I? Am I an apt pupil? I like your teaching, but the lesson is beginning to bore me. Let us bring it to an end. (He stabs CASSIO.)

AUTHOR: (Ripping off the CASSIO mask.) Madam, I am wounded. Madam! Madam!

WOMAN: (Enters.) Emelia. My name is Emelia remember.

(ENTERTAINERS Enter carrying props. Stand around AUTHOR.)

AUTHOR: At this moment, I don't care what your name is. Can't you see I'm bleeding.

WOMAN: Tsk! Tsk! Here, sit down. *(Looks at wound.)* Oh, it's but a small puncture, barely the size of my little finger.

AUTHOR: Call a doctor!

WOMAN: Oh, come now, really! Stop behaving like a child. Here, let me have your handkerchief. *(She dabs the wound with the handkerchief.)* There, the bleeding's stopped already.

AUTHOR: Infection. It could become infected.

WOMAN: *(Pours wine into the wound.)* A little alcohol will prevent that.

AUTHOR: This is insanity.

WOMAN: Insanity. Why?

AUTHOR: Madam, you could seriously have wounded me.

WOMAN: In other words, you don't like the way we play the game. You think us too rough.

AUTHOR: I don't like the game, period. I'm a scholar, not an athlete. I don't know why I let myself become involved in this ridiculous business. Furthermore, your story lacks credulity. You've twisted everything around to suit what I'm beginning to suspect is quite a distorted vision of what actually happened.

WOMAN: In other words, you don't believe that we have been telling you the truth.

AUTHOR: Let me put it this way, Madam, based on what has just occurred, I'm beginning to doubt your ability to see the truth objectively.

WOMAN: O', I had not realized we were talking about objectivity. I was under the impression that you were sincerely interested in hearing our version of the story.

AUTHOR: That is quite true, but let me be frank, I am a scholar, and have a responsibility to separate fact from fiction.

WOMAN: I see. In other words, when you return home, you intend to record not what we see, but what you see.

AUTHOR: What I am saying, Madam, is that I am a trained observer. And that what I am obligated to do is compare the information which you have given me with other available data, and thereby, I would hope to arrive at some accurate estimate of what the facts in actuality were. I'm sure you understand that, as a scholar, I could not be expected to take everything you say at face value. You do understand, don't you?

WOMAN: I believe I do.

AUTHOR: I wanted to make that point clear before we went any further.

WOMAN: I do wish you had made it clear before we began. But no matter. I understand perfectly now.

AUTHOR: Good. *(Catching his breath.)*

WOMAN: Shall we continue? You are interested in continuing, aren't you? We're really quite near the end. It would be a shame to break the momentum of the story, at this point.

AUTHOR: Just give me a moment to catch my breath.

WOMAN: Take another card! Quickly! *(AUTHOR takes card.)* Turn it over! Look at it. *(It is the card of DESDEMONA.)*

AUTHOR: Desdemona? You don't expect me...

WOMAN: Yes! Desdemona. *(Each of the ENTERTAINERS gives him the items of dress as the WOMAN calls for them).* Her necklace. *(ENTERTAINER 3 puts it on him.)* Her nightgown. *(He starts to put it on reluctantly. WOMAN stops him.)* No! No. Take off the shirt. *(AUTHOR protests.)* Seekers after truth can afford to be neither timid nor modest! *(He takes off the shirt. Begins to take off his pants. WOMAN stops him.)* No. You can remove the trousers after you put on the nightgown. *(He dons the nightgown.)* Yes. Now, you can remove the trousers.

AUTHOR: *(He has put the nightgown on backwards.)* It's on backwards. My side, it's bleeding again. I'm getting blood on the gown.

WOMAN: It doesn't matter! Now the robe. (ENTERTAINER 5 *puts the robe on him.)* The mask. (ENTERTAINER 3 *gives him the mask.)* And finally the hair. (ENTERTAINER 3 *gives him a blond wig. WOMAN admires her handiwork.)* Fair Desdemona.

AUTHOR: And who are you?

WOMAN: I am the Black Moor.

ALL: Othello.

WOMAN: *(The ENTERTAINERS give her OTHELLO mask burnoose, and dagger.)* And these are our bed chambers. And, soon, I come to accuse you of having made a mockery of me before all the world.
(She pushes DESDEMONA, who Exits.)

SCENE 4: OTHELLO'S PALACE

(There is a fierce knocking Offstage. The WOMAN is now OTHELLO. OTHELLO indicates for ENTERTAINER 4 to go to the door.)

LODOVICO: *(LODOVICO, played by ENTERTAINER 3, is heard Offstage.)* Othello! Othello! For heavens sake quickly!

OTHELLO: *(LODOVICO Enters.)* Good Lodovico, but what is this? You are torn and bruised. What has happened?

LODOVICO: They have taken Iago.

OTHELLO: What? Who?

LODOVICO: Cassio ordered Iago arrested. Had him beaten, tortured, murdered.

OTHELLO: Ho! where! *(Begins to rush out.)*

LODOVICO: No! It is too late, Othello. He is finished. And worse news. They have attacked the barracks where your countrymen are quartered, catching the Moorish soldiers in their sleep. Most are already dead.

OTHELLO: This cannot be!

LODOVICO: It is so, Othello!

OTHELLO: How is't possible?

LODOVICO: Cassio accuses you of conspiracy. He has drawn the Italian officers together, and boldly accuses thee of conspiring with the Turks, offering as proof your refusal to attack those he calls "Your allies" in a devilish plan to overrun Cyprus and all Italy.

OTHELLO: O' that is monstrously false.

(OTHELLO and LODOVICO freeze.)

(CASSIO, played by the AUTHOR, appears on the balcony, the ENTERTAINERS Enter into the AUDIENCE and become citizens of Cyprus.)

CASSIO: This is Michael Cassio speaking.

ENTERTAINERS: Hail Cassio!

CASSIO: As you know, I am the new Military Commander of Cyprus.

ENTERTAINERS: Hail Cassio!

CASSIO: And as your new Commander, I am here to inform you that the course of events here on Cyprus are about to take a dramatic turn. *(Crowd murmurs.)* There is a black and foul smelling fragrance in the air, and those familiar with its deadly stench would recognize it as the unmistakable odor of poisonous treason.

ENTERTAINERS: Treason? How? Who?

CASSIO: For seven days the Turkish galleys lay anchored off the Cyprian coast and in seven days not a single move was made to dislodge them. Why? Why?

ENTERTAINERS: Why? Why? Why?

CASSIO: Because those who were sent here to oppose them are in fact their allies.

ENTERTAINERS: No! No! No!

CASSIO: Yes! It is so! On what do I base these charges against Pause. Othello.

ENTERTAINERS: Othello? No! No! It can't be.

CASSIO: …and his band of Moorish cut throats. Here is the evidence—contained in a letter sent to me by the General's own wife. I quote: "My husband says we have no choice but to maintain our defenses in good order and wait." *(Crowd murmurs.)* Those are the words of the man who was sent here under orders to sweep the Ottomites into the sea. Wait? For what do we wait?

ENTERTAINERS: Why do we wait?

CASSIO: For our throats to be cut in our sleep?

ENTERTAINERS: No!

CASSIO: Our daughters defiled?

ENTERTAINERS: No!

CASSIO: Our sweet sons to be impaled on the bloody lance of Moorish treachery.

ENTERTAINERS: No. No.

CASSIO: Well, we will wait no longer.

ENTERTAINERS: We will wait no longer.

CASSIO: We will show the yellow skinned Turk and the devilish Black Moor that the men of Venice can be terrible when faced with betrayal. First the Moors.

ENTERTAINERS: First we strike the Moors.

CASSIO: We will capture treason while it sleeps. Destroy them utterly.

ENTERTAINERS: Kill the Moors.

CASSIO: Then, when the dogs who lap at our hands while defecating on our sheets are dead, we will show the Turks in how little regard we hold their reputation as warriors.

ENTERTAINERS: Kill the Turks! Kill the Moors!

CASSIO: Strike now!

ENTERTAINERS: Kill the Moors!

CASSIO: But, wait. The one they call Iago. Spare him.

ENTERTAINERS: Spare Iago? Spare Iago? Why?

CASSIO: I want him brought here, alive, to me. He is deserving of special consideration. Down with traitors!

ENTERTAINERS: Destroy the traitors! Kill the Moors! *(All Exit.)*

LODOVICO: *(Picks up dialogue with OTHELLO.)* Cassio stirs up his troops and the citizenry. Prods them with drink and fans the embers of their ancient suspicions. I made attempts at opposition, but he accused me of being in thy pay, ordered me seized. I broke away, managed escape. Cassio is a madman. The mob approaches, Othello! Wilt thou come with me?

OTHELLO: My wife?

LODOVICO: I think she and Cassio to be in this together. He announces 'twas she who exposed your villainy to her father. Flee, good Othello while there is yet time.

OTHELLO: I stay.

LODOVICO: Adieu, brave General. *(He Exits.)*

(ENTERTAINER 4 Enters.)

ENTERTAINER 4: Sire! There is a mob outside. They have captured Lodovico—murdered him! Now, they're headed here!

OTHELLO: Lock the doors! *(ENTERTAINER 4 Exits.)*

(The following scene is done with the WOMAN as OTHELLO.   The ENTER-
TAINERS *Enter in a Processional.)*

OTHELLO: Was that thy plan Desdemona?

ENTERTAINER 1: Was that thy plan Desdemona?

OTHELLO: To plot my undoing even unto murder?

ENTERTAINER 1: To plot my undoing even unto murder?

OTHELLO: But why?

ENTERTAINER 1: But why?

OTHELLO: If thou didst prefer Cassio.

ENTERTAINER 1: If thou didst prefer Cassio.

OTHELLO: Why chose then me?

ENTERTAINER 1: Why chose then me? Or was it that having chosen...

OTHELLO: Or was it that having chosen...

ENTERTAINER 1: Thou didst repent of thy choice.

OTHELLO: Thou didst repent of thy choice.

ENTERTAINER 1: Yet lacked means to undo what was done.

OTHELLO: Yet lacked means to undo what was done.

ENTERTAINER 4: In Catholic Venetia, a marriage vow once taken sticks forever.

OTHELLO: But I would have set thee free.

ENTERTAINER 1: But I would have set thee free.

OTHELLO: To couple Cassio.

ENTERTAINER 1: To couple Cassio.

OTHELLO: Or what ere thou wouldst.

ALL: Or what ere thou wouldst. *(Overlap.)*

ENTERTAINER 1: Would willingly have borne the pain of thy loss.

OTHELLO: Would willingly have borne the pain of thy loss.

ENTERTAINER 2: But to stoop to such deception as this.

ALL: It plucks at mine eyes, turns them crimson with rancid hate.

ENTERTAINER 1: It is the cause *(To OTHELLO.)*

ENTERTAINER 2: It is the cause, my soul.

OTHELLO: Let me not name it to you, you chaste start!

ALL: It is the cause.

ENTERTAINER 1: Yet, I'll not shed her blood.

OTHELLO: Nor scar that whiter skin of hers than snow.

ENTERTAINER 2: And smooth as monumental alabaster.

ENTERTAINER 4: She must die.

(AUTHOR, as DESDEMONA, Enters and begins to write a letter.)

ENTERTAINER 1: She must die!

OTHELLO: Put out the light.

ALL: And then.

ENTERTAINER 1: Put out the light.

ALL: Put out the light.

OTHELLO: And then.

ALL: Put out the light.

OTHELLO: Once we have pluck'd the rose, we cannot give it vital growth again.

ALL: It must needs wither.

(DESDEMONA, played by the AUTHOR, begins to read letter she has written to RODRIGO. ENTERTAINERS 1, 2, and 3 all Exit. OTHELLO removes mask and dagger and gives them to ENTERTAINER 4 who Exits. WOMAN begins to walk toward DESDEMONA.)

DESDEMONA: Dearest Rodrigo, My husband has been recalled from Cyprus. So I will soon be at home. I am glad for I have not been happy here. But, all this will I explain when you come to visit me after I am once again happily settled in the beloved city of my birth. I an uncommonly sad tonight. I know not why..... Who's there?

WOMAN: Have you pray'd tonight, Desdemona?

DESDEMONA: Ay.

(ENTERTAINERS Enter wearing death masks, and gather around DESDEMONA.)

ENTERTAINER 1: If you bethink yourself of any crime unreconciled as yet to heaven and grace...

WOMAN: Solicit for it straight.

ENTERTAINER 4: Think on thy sins.

WOMAN: That letter which thou didst send to thy father, what didst thou tell?

ALL: What didst thou tell?

DESDEMONA: Only news.

ENTERTAINER 1: And that handkerchief which Othello so loved and gave thee, thou gavest to Cassio.

DESDEMONA: No, by my love and soul!

ENTERTAINER 2: Take heed...

WOMAN: Take heed of perjury.

ENTERTAINER 1: Thou art on thy death bed.

DESDEMONA: Lord have mercy on me!

WOMAN: I say...

ALL: Amen.

DESDEMONA: I never loved Cassio, never gave him token.

ENTERTAINER 1: Enough!

ALL: Enough!

DESDEMONA: Send for Cassio...let him confess the truth.

ALL: Too late!

DESDEMONA: What—is he dead? Alas, he is betray'd. And I undone!

ENTERTAINER 4: She weeps for Cassio!

ENTERTAINER 1: Weep not, my sweet.

WOMAN: Cassio lives.

ENTERTAINER 2: And now seeks Othello's destruction!

WOMAN: Iago dead...

ENTERTAINER 1: Lodovico dead!

ALL: All Othello's brave followers dead!

ENTERTAINER 1: And now...

WOMAN: Thou dies't, Desdemona!

DESDEMONA: O, kill me not!

ALL: Desdemona must die!

(ENTERTAINER 4 *Forces pillow over DESDEMONA'S face.*)

AUTHOR: Breaking away. I'm not (*Ripping off mask.*) Desdemona. I'm William. I'm a teacher of English literature, who came here to seek information and to interview you. This is all just a game!

WOMAN: Then the "game" is not yet over. (*Roaring.*) Who are you?

AUTHOR: (*Hoping to evade her fixation on DESDEMONA.*) I am Rodrigo. Yes. I am Rodrigo

WOMAN: Rodrigo? Rodrigo is dead!

AUTHOR: How did he die?

WOMAN: He drowned himself for thy love, Desdemona.

AUTHOR: Mercy madam!

ALL: Who are you?

AUTHOR: I am William, a teacher of English lit...

WOMAN: No! You are Cassio! Commanding General of Cyprus in Othello's place. Put on the mask. (*Starts to give him CASSIO mask.*) Put it on. (*AUTHOR starts to accept mask. WOMAN takes it back.*) Wait! Cassio is dead.

AUTHOR: No. Only wounded. Iago wounded him in the side.

WOMAN: The Turks killed him.

(ENTERTAINER 1 *stabs AUTHOR with a dagger.*)

ALL: Who are you!?

WOMAN: What too weak to answer? No matter, I will answer for you. You are that child woman, whom Othello did choke unto death.

(ENTERTAINER 1 *chokes AUTHOR.*)

ALL: Who are you!?

AUTHOR: You are mad.

WOMAN: Mad? Angry? Bitter as lemons, full of gall? Yes. I am mad! And you will now be Othello and you will take your own life, otherwise they will torture you until your body ruptures as they did my poor husband, who did his best to save you.

Yes. Iago died for your sake. Hurry! Cassio's men are at the door. The strong oak will soon give away. *(There is the sound of a battering ram.)* Do you wish to know what they did to my husband? What they will do to you if they find you still alive? You will beg for death. Kill yourself now, Othello. Make it quick, one thrust at the heart, it is done. Do not let them do to you what they did to Iago, my good husband, whom they seized and tortured. First, they blinded him, then tore the nails from his fingers, piled rocks upon his chest until his ribs broke, beat him with heavy sticks between his legs held wide apart til the blood flowed in rivulets through the creases of his thighs. They hated that part of him more than any other. Why? Why? Are men of Africa so awesome in this aspect? When they were done they cast his ruptured and dying body at my door. They will do worse to you, Othello. Dost thou doubt that? It is you they fear, and they will punish you pitilessly for having made them afraid. They will crucify you. Save yourself. *(She forces him to stab himself.) (*ENTERTAINERS *carry* AUTHOR *Offstage.)*

Who am I? Othello? No, Othello is dead. Iago? No, Iago is dead. I…am Emelia. Yes. Emelia. Wife of Iago. I am a Moorish woman who fled from Spain by the side of a noble warrior. And was forced to watch him risk his life, then die for his loyalty. And it is I, who send the message to the Turks that the General is dead and that Africans no longer fight on the side of Europe. The Turkish ships move closer to shore. Their fierce warriors scramble over the fortifications of this tiny island, and the schoolboy commander, Michael Cassio, seeing their fierce and terrible eyes that burn like hot coals in their deep sockets, turns on his heel and runs, screaming for his pitiful life.

The Turks do set the city aflame and everyone within is burning. See the smoke curl along the ceiling? The flames licking at the walls. Feel the heat. Hear the timbers crackle. Smell the roasting flesh. Hear the screams of children trapped. Of fists pounding against jammed doors. Of glass breaking. Of old men leaping from windows. Flesh thudding against cobblestoned earth. The Turks are in the city, and the city is in ruins. And all are dead, save me.

They came and asked me what had happened. *(*AUTHOR *Enters from the* AUDIENCE *and stands Downstage looking at the* WOMAN *and Cinthio wrote it all down.)* And though I told him exactly what I'm telling you, he changed the facts as he saw fit, so I vowed to squat, wait here in this house which I had built over my husband's grave and will not leave nor let my spirit rest until what truly happened here is known and the story is set right, for I would clear his good name.

Good name in man and woman is the immediate jewel of our souls:
"Who steals my purse steals trash;
'tis something, nothing; 'Twas
mine, 'tis his, and has been slave
to thousands. But he that filches
from me my good name robs me of
that which not enriches him and
makes me poor indeed."
Iago was an honest man. I speak his name with pride. IAGO. IAGO.
ALL: IAGO. IAGO.
BLACKOUT

Marsha A. Jackson

SISTERS

Jomandi Productions

Marsha A. Jackson

MARSHA A. JACKSON began her professional training at Houston's High School for the Performing and Visual Arts, where she completed with honors a program in Drama and advanced academics and was selected by the faculty as the Outstanding Drama Student, among other academic awards. She is an honors graduate of Smith College with two degrees, one of which is in Theatre. She attributes her college abilities as a performing artist to training with persons including Tina Packer of the London Academy of Dramatic Arts, Edward S. Hill, Linda Shuler and Cigdem Akkurt. During her development as a writer, she emulated the spirit of her mentor, internationally renown artist, Sonia Sanchez. In addition to her role as co-founder and Co-Artistic Director for Jomandi, Marsha has taught at Spelman College, offered workshops and consultancies in Houston, Atlanta, Philadelphia, and Bermuda.

Her career credits include work in film and extensive achievements in the theatre as director, playwright, and actress. She has directed numerous productions for Jomandi including *Hip 2: Birth of the Boom, Zooman and the Sign, El Hajj Malik, Cane, Witchbird,* and *That Serious He-Man Ball.* Marsha was the writer of the Jomandi productions *Sisters, Witchbird, Josephine Live, Savannah,* and *Dunbar Fantasy;* she collaborated with Co-Artisitic Director Tom Jones in the writing of the plays *Le Corps N'est Pas Mort, Voices in the Rain, Dream Street Blues,* and *Medley.* The artist has toured extensively both nationally and abroad. Among her favorite roles are Mama E. in *The Fishermen,* Lena in Fugard's *Roseman and Lena,* a schizophrenic jazz/blues singer in the world premiere of *Black When I'm Singing and Blue When I Ain't,* and Olivia in her own play, *Sisters.* She made her Broadway debut in 1988 opposite Denzel Washington in *Checkmates,* which also starred Ruby Dee and Paul Winfield. Marsha has been recognized with numerous professional awards; they include:

Fulton County Arts Council Individual Artist Award (1988)

Atlanta Business League/Black Women Entrepreneur—Entertainer of the Year Award (1986)

Clark College Role Model Award (1983)

Bronze Jubilee Award Nominee (1982-80)

Semi-finalist for the Kool Achiever Award (1989)

Artist of the Year/CPE Chapter, Delta Sigma Theta

Artist of the Year Award, Pan Hellenic Council of Greek Organizations, and numerous other citations from the city and county.

"SISTERS"

From the Playwright

These are pieces of my life woven into a tapestry of two lives. I believe that we are all similarly born from one source and thereafter grow or stumble into disparate lives, until what we have become supercedes the tie that binds. We tread relationships which move against the very current that remembers the force of our movement as one. We are parented by preoccupations that obscure understanding. I embrace the faith that love passeth understanding; while it is not necessary to understand to love, it is necessary to love to understand. "*Sisters,*" then, is a treatise on love. It is my sincerest hope that understanding will follow.

Thank you Tom and Andrea for lending your vision to this treatise of hope; and thank you to my dear friend (CBC) who kept believing and who first whispered the story of aborted love in my ear. My "Sisters" is dedicated to my sister, Pamela, and to each of the women in whom I have discovered a "Sister"— including those whose struggle is their name.

"... and are we not one daughter of the same dark mother's child breathing one breath from a multitude of mouths. . ."
- from the *Sisterhood Song of the Yenga Nation*

- Blest be the tie that binds.
Marsha A. Jackson

JOMANDI PRODUCTIONS

JOMANDI PRODUCTIONS is the State of Georgia's oldest and largest Black owned and produced professional theatre company. The theatre has developed and mounted 40 world premieres in its first 16 years, which have included work written or adapted for the stage by the company's artistic directors. Since 1979, Jomandi has mounted national tours of several works: *Voices in the Rain, Do Lord Remember Me, She'll Find Her Way Home, Sisters* (by Artistic Directory Masha A. Jackson), *The Wizard of Hip* (by Artistic Director Thomas W. Jones, II), and *Bessie's Blues*. Both *Sisters* and *The Wizard of Hip* enjoyed successful Off-Broadway runs.

Jomandi has the most extensive tour program of any professional company in the southeast. The Company has been honored by inclusion on numerous tour rosters; has featured in performance for three years by invitation at New York's prestigious Lincoln Center Festival Out-of-Doors, and was featured among an invited group of nationally renowned artists in the ONLY IN AMERICA National Bicentennial Festival.

The Theatre is one of a select group of theatres to have received two major grants from the National Broadcasting Company (NBC), as part of its "New Voices Program" which recognizes achievement in the development of new work in the field of the American Theatre. In 1990, the theatre received the Governor's Award in the Arts, and in 1992, Jomandi was one of eight theatres in the country to receive a grant from the Lila Wallace Readers Digest Fund Theatre for New Audiences Program. Jomandi was the first African American institution invited to appear in the Joyce Theatre American Theatre Exchange where the play *Sisters* was presented in an extended run in New York in 1990. It was one of nine companies to receive a major grant from AT&T through its AT&T: OnStage sponsorship program for the world premiere of the play *Today*, by Valetta Anderson. Other acknowledgements and awards received by the company's Artistic Directors include 5 AUDELCO Nominations, 3 Bronze Jubilee Nominations or Awards, the San Diego Drama Critics Award, and service on advisory panels for numerous foundations and public agencies.

Jomandi's presence beyond the theatre proper and into the community-at-large in cities around the country has been established through its innovative Community Without Walls Program, which includes an annual JUNTEENTH FESTIVAL which reached an audience of 100,000 people in its second year.

"Sisters"
by Marsha A. Jackson

Directed by
Thomas W. Jones, II

Cast

OLIVIA WILLIAMS ....Marsha A. Jackson
CASSIE CHARLES ....Andrea Frye

"SISTERS"

CHARACTERS:
OLIVIA Williams (OLIV), thirtyish. Both women are African American. Olivia must be dark complexioned. Although her grandparents were perhaps working class, all she has ever known intimately is the nouveau   riche class of her parents. She is something fragile kept in a glass case to long. We first see her impeccably outfitted in a tailored business suit and pumps. Although she tries to hold herself together emotionally, she shows signs of withering.

CASSIE CHARLES (CASS), Late 30's to mid forties, her age is not as clear. In her day she was "fine & (high) yellow." There is yet energy and vitality in her attack, yet age in her dialect and insight. She is a "pussycat" at heart, though one would not immediately know it. She is a survivor.

BOTH CHARACTERS are intentionally broadly drawn in Act I such that the laughter is the medium of entre into the complexity of each character and situation. "Mugging" is not appropriate, playing against the obvious is desired. If the two women appear "stereotypical" at anytime, it is purely a defense—a means to find a "comfort zone" in an awkward situation. However, as each drops her defense or is caught off guard, each woman should be uniquely and genuinely defined beyond the limitations of "her type".

TIME/PLACE: The late eighties to early nineties, NEW YEARS EVE, about dusk, 7:30 p.m. A metropolitan city, preferably Atlanta, and probably the South. Note: There are numerous references specific to Georgia and Atlanta.

SETTING: OLIVIA's OFFICE is on the twentieth floor of a major corporate building, Peat, Montgrief and Simon. The office is conservative and modern, furniture "swank" even plush, cool tones.

THERE ARE SIX PLAYING AREAS DEFINED THUSLY: A sunken floor which makes up 3/4 of the DS playing area, a raised platform with a window USL defining the back wall of the office, a hallway US of the platform area with an elevator UC, the "exterior" front of the building, which may be simply defined by a vacant 4'x4' playing area DSR, and finally, (optionally) a descending/ascending staircase (or platform) hidden until use by a scrim US of the elevator. On the Platform level there is a bookcase USR and a chair USL next to the large glass window overlooking the downtown section of a large major city. DSC of the platform is a drafting table (optional).

OLIVIA's desk and chair are DSL with as necessary, desk, files, floor lamp, and a TAPE/CASSETTE PLAYER. SR is the door with a NAME PLATE which leads to the hallway & elevator.

IT IS EARLY EVENING, NEW YEAR'S EVE. IN THE DARK AS THE PLAY OPENS, against the actions of OLIVIA and CASSIE defined below, we should hear against THE TAPED SOUND OF CHILDREN PLAYING:

PROLOGUE: (PRE-RECORDED)

OLIVIA: I was my daddy's little princess.

CASSIE: Me and M'dear used to walk down the street of hardknocks.

OLIVIA: I admit it was a sheltered life.

CASSIE: She kept a roof over my head.

OLIVIA: My sister? She was my best friend. There were these other kids in the "old neighborhood"—

CASSIE: The Alley Children—

OLIVIA: The Alley Children, we didn't play with them.

CASSIE: The "Alley Children" is what they called us.

OLIVIA: They would never amount to anything my Daddy said...

CASSIE: *(sing-song, as children do playing)* "Don't play with the Alley Children."

OLIVIA: We couldn't play with them.

CASSIE:: Kids could be so mean; I couldn't wait to grow up; just to not hear that no more.

(THE PROLOGUE CONCLUDES WITH THE FOLLOWING "SIS-TERS" THEME:)

(sung)

WOMENS VOICES:

Blest be the tie that binds

Our hearts in kindred love

A fellowship of Kindred minds

Is like to that above.

(THE PRECEDING DIALOGUE BEGINS IN THE DARK. By the time it concludes lights are up dimly, in the hallway and in Oliv's Office. There are boxes of various sizes scattered all over Oliv's office. She has brought them to pack her things. Only a picture or two remains on the walls. Items have been taken out of the bookcase, but most books still remain. Oversize cardboard, "storyboards" rest on top of and against the drawing board. There should be a general sense of disorder, throughout the room.)

(IN THE NEAR DARK, AS WE HEAR THE "VOICE OVERS OF OLIVIA AND CASSIE," OLIVIA removes her NAMEPLATE from her door and enters the room. SHE takes the nameplate to her desk, removes her "spike heels" from her feet replacing them with "sneakers" (typical of the "downtown" sneaker crew). She puts on the headset of her cassette player, and absently, oblivious to the entrance of CASSIE in the hallway, she begins the chore of packing.)

(AT THE CONCLUSION OF THE "SISTER'S" theme, the lights are up and we see the women for the first time clearly.)

(CASSIE, is also wearing her HEADSETS, with her BEAT BOX strapped to her hip. She MAKES HER WAY down the the hall (if visible at all) toward OLIV's OFFICE.)

CASSIE: *(she sings along without reserve in full crescendo)*
I'm every woman....
It's all in me. Anything you want done baby,
I'll do it naturally.
I'm every woman, it's all in me.
Woa, woa, woa. Woa, woa, woa.

OLIV removes her headset and turns from her desk. She is startled by indistinguishable "moaning" from the hall. Cautiously, with a paperweight raised above her head ready to strike, she crosses to the door.
She opens the door just as Cass turns to enter the room.

CASSIE:	OLIVIA:
Woa!! *(ad lib surprise, etc....)*	Oh my God! oh—
aagh, got—to be more careful.	it's just you. You scared me.

OLIV stands stolidly in the doorway.

CASSIE: Sorry.
OLIVIA S'alright. I didn't realize anyone else was here besides security.
CASSIE: They left long time ago.
OLIVIA Do you need to get in here?
CASSIE: I'll wait on you.
OLIVIA I may be a while. *(CASS turns away)* No, come on in.
(CASS SHOUTS FROM THE HALLWAY, as she gathers her things. THE FOLLOWING LINES OVERLAP.)
CASSIE: Do you know what time it is? People have gon' home. It is New Year's Eve.

OLIVIA: Yes I know. I'll come back after you've finished, I won't hold you up; I didn't expect anyone but security to be here today anyway.

CASSIE: All I know is I gotta get your office 'fore I can go home.

OLIVIA: Go ahead. But I have to—I mean, I need to—

CASSIE: You'll have to leave when I do...when I turn the system on.

OLIVIA: Fine. I guess I'll go get a Coke or something.

(OLIVIA EXITS.)

CASSIE: Don't she have a home? A man? Something?! I'll be damned if I come back here on Saturday just to do her office. *(Begins to drag her vacuum and other cleaning things into the office)* 'Like other people don't have work to do. She can work around me, if she wants. I got things to do.

(CASS opens the door to OLIV'S OFFICE seeing the total disorder and mounds of boxes for the first time.)

CASSIE: Uhn—uhn. Not the kid. What I look like, Hazel? I could be here til next week. Me and Miss Sadit' gon' have a talk.

(CASS ENTERS the room and stumbles over a box.)

CASSIE: Wonder why she have all these boxes? Uhn-uhn, we gon' talk. We got labor laws, Ya know! *(She picks up a dust rag and futilely tries to tidy the desk)* Got to make room for the damn dust.

(CASS notices OLIV's headset on the desk. She removes her own headset and puts on OLIV's.)

CASSIE: Wonder what kinda music Miss Olivia De Haviland be listening at while she tossing these boxes aroun' the room. (She punches the button and listens. *(The MUSIC SHOULD BE AUDIBLE TO THE AUDIENCE. The music is UNMISTAKEABLY MUZAK, Johnny Mann repetoire with strings.)* Eww! *(she does a quick double take)* Ew-no. *(cutting it off)* Lawd, that chile done lost all her color. *(wincing)* MU-ZAK! Now where did she have this thing? *(She fumbles papers to return it to the proper place. OLIVIA noticeably watches outside the door)* Better re-wind...

(OLIV re-enters the room. CASS is startled this time.)

OLIVIA: Something wrong?

CASSIE: Oh! No, nothing wrong. I—I—just was wondering why you had all these boxes...that's all!

(CASS quickly xes away from the desk. OLIV tries to watch her unnoticed. OLIV hurries to the desk and tries affecting calmness to retrieve her purse left on the desk. She checks for something missing. LIGHTS flicker. THERE IS A LOUD CLAP OF THUNDER. She realizes that it was the tape player that has been tampered with...)

OLIVIA: Uh-hm,...boxes. *(said surreptiously to get a reaction from CASS.)* Would we like to hear a little music?

CASSIE: *(quickly, to avoid the Muzak)* I carry my own, thank you.

(MUSIC CUE: OLIV hums throughout.)

(OLIV changes the subject to continue to inspect the office.)

OLIVIA Has it been raining all day? *(XES to window)* It is bad out there. The streets look awfully glazed—

CASSIE: Uhm-hm, "glazed."

OLIVIA: I come in here sometimes and lose track of time. *(really noticing the dark sky)* It really does look bad out there, if I didn't know better, I'd—

CASSIE: You know you're going to have to leave when I do.

OLIVIA: Yes. I guess this will still be here Monday.

CASSIE: You need ALL these boxes?

OLIVIA: *(affronted)* You can move them if they're in your way.

CASSIE: *(equally affronted)* It's your office.

(CASS EXITS to empty a trash receptacle.)

OLIVIA: I know it's my office. It's my desk, my chair, my name on this name plate. *(Under her breath)* Mine! At least I won't have to put up with that anymore. *(Inspects her desk)* I guess everything's here. She really hacks me off. *(Searches her desk)* What was she doing if she didn't take anything?

(CASS re-enters.)

(OLIV affects nonchalance. She is overly efficient.)

OLIVIA: You will have to work around me. I need to finish up, as much as I can.

(OLIV continues packing and discarding.)

CASSIE: Whatever, but this is New Years Eve, I have things to do. I won't be here long.

(CASS puts on her headsets. She cannot hear OLIV's question.)

OLIVIA: Fine. Will you people be back here on Saturday? *(repeats shouting)* I said—WILL YOU PEOPLE BE BACK HERE ON SATURDAY?

CASSIE: *(almost indignant)* Who people?

OLIVIA: You people—maintenance…security.

(THE LIGHTS FLICKER)

CASSIE: I won't be here.

OLIVIA: But they will? *(no answer)* Look, I really want to finish this up before Monday.

(CASS is at the end of her tolerance. She ignores the question.)

CASSIE: *(turning on the vacuum)* You mind?? *(she doesn't wait for an answer.)*

OLIVIA: No. Go ahead.

(CASS vacuums around the corners of the boxes.)

(OLIV begins to take books out of bookshelf.)

(THE LIGHTS FLICKER. Vacuum stops.)

CASSIE: Musta pulled the damn plug…I mean,..er, uh, I musta displugged the electrical cord.

(she exits to the outer reception office)
(OLIV continues to work. THE LIGHTS flicker to BLACK.)

OLIVIA: Hello? You still out there? HELLO!? *(Trying to make her way past boxes to the door)* Ouch…Are you still *(trips)* damn it! Hello? IS ANY-BODY ELSE STILL IN HERE !!

(CASS re-enters standing calmly over the frantic OLIV. She turns her flashlight on OLIV sprawled on the floor.)

CASSIE: The lights went out, we didn't go deaf.

OLIVIA: I didn't know you heard me….

(CASS gives her a hand to her feet)

CASSIE: Don't mention it.

OLIVIA: …Why didn't you answer me? What happened?

CASSIE: The lights went out.

OLIVIA: I can see that.

CASSIE: Then you're better than me.

OLIVIA: I mean why did they go out?

CASSIE: Do I look like Georgia Power to you? I don't know. *(looking out window)* The whole city's black.

OLIVIA: The whole city?

CASSIE: I just said that. And Jesus, look at that expressway, headlights strung out for miles. Look there! Don't that look like snow?

OLIVIA: The weather man said nothing about snow.

CASSIE: *(she crosses to phone and dials)* I don't think they had to have his permission.

OLIVIA: Snow! In Atlanta! You know this city. That's why traffic is backed up. Can't you dial out?

CASSIE: No. *(she begins to gather her things)*

OLIVIA: If the temperature is dropping, this mess could freeze up. We got to get outta here.

CASSIE: We got to get out of here.

OLIVIA: I just said that. Where are you going?

CASSIE: If the temperature is dropping, this mess could freeze up.

OLIVIA: I just said that.

CASSIE: We got to get out of here.

OLIVIA: I just said that! Wait! The traffic is already backed up. We should just wait in here.

(LIGHTS FLICKER)

CASSIE: Wait for what? At best this is a snow storm. No telling what it will be an hour from now. Take me at least an hour to get home. Come on!

OLIVIA: The power just went out. It's not even safe to think about taking the elevator.

CASSIE: There's a backup generator.

OLIVIA: We're on the 20th floor. Couldn't the back up generator go out?

CASSIE: Are you coming?

OLIVIA: Maybe we could take the stairs.

CASSIE: What? You can walk twenty flights of stairs by yourself!

OLIVIA: But what if the generator goes out? We could be stuck.

CASSIE: Get your coat....

OLIVIA: My coat? Why am I getting my coat?...

CASSIE: GET YOUR COAT!

OLIVIA: Are we taking the stairs?

CASSIE: GET YOUR DAMN COAT!!!

OLIVIA: I got it...I got it; so are we taking the stairs?

CASSIE: Get in.

OLIVIA: I can't, the doors are closed.

CASSIE: Push the button.

OLIVIA: I don't want to push the button. I thought we were taking the stairs. I'm not getting in there. I was content to wait in my office.

CASSIE: I told you before, when I leave, you leave. Now, get in.

OLIVIA: I can't, the doors are closed.

CASSIE: Don't start no mess with me.

OLIVIA: But I told you, I don't want to get stuck in an elevator til God knows when...

CASSIE: We won't get stuck if you shut your—

OLIVIA: I'm claustrophobic.

CASSIE: I don't care what kind of closet freak you is—get in the friggin' elevator!

OLIVIA: I AM NOT PUTTING my body in a glorified pine box.

CASSIE: What pine? What box? (she pushes the button, nothing happens) Alright. (quietly) We'll take the stairs...

OLIVIA: One of us should use a little common sense. That's all I'm saying—

CASSIE: Shut up. We're taking the stairs shut up.
    (THERE IS THE SLAM OF A DOOR. THE WOMEN CONTINUE DOWN THE STAIRS WITH DIALOGUE.)

OLIVIA: I always thought these doors locked between floors. Do you have some kind of pass key to open them on the way back? Wait a minute, have you tried this before? What if your pass key doesn't work on—

CASSIE: Don't talk to me? Okay? We're taking the stairs. Don't talk.
    (OLIVIA begins to SING.)

OLIVIA: "When you walk through a storm..."

CASSIE: DON'T SING.

OLIVIA: Fine. Could you please keep the light so I can see my feet.

CASSIE: If I shine the lamp on your pretty little feet, I might trip over you and break your pretty little neck.

OLIVIA: Ow! Would you stop stepping on my heels.

CASSIE: Say what?

OLIVIA: You get in front. You lead—this is your turf anyway; you know how to deal in the dark.

CASSIE: If you had a man, you would, too.

OLIVIA: I know you didn't mean that the way it sounded. I'll pretend I didn't hear that.

CASSIE: If you don't mind, I'd like to get home before I'm forty.

OLIVIA: Well it's a little late for that.

CASSIE: Move it!

OLIVIA: I'm doing the best I can to keep up with you. Lest you forget, I fell. I'm wounded!

(THE TWO WOMEN enter the "BUILDING EXTERIOR" playing area.)

CASSIE: Oh Jesus—

OLIVIA: Mary—

BOTH: Holy Father!

OLIVIA: I told you it was snow. It looks like a ghost town out here. You're not still planning to go out in this mess, are you?

CASSIE: If there's a bus out there I'm leaving.

OLIVIA: There's not bus out there. Nothing's moving out there.

CASSIE: Shit, it's cold.

OLIVIA: I'd take you home if I had my keys.

CASSIE: What do you mean, IF you had your keys?

OLIVIA: You said "Get my coat." You didn't say anything about car keys. *(silence)* You didn't!

CASSIE: Slap me.

OLIVIA: Excuse me.

CASSIE: Slap me. If this ain't a dream, I want a good excuse to kill you. *(quietly)* Stuck out on the damn perimeter and not a bus in sight.

OLIVIA: Wait upstairs with me, and I'll take you home when this stuff melts. How's about it? How're you going to get anywhere now? Let's wait upstairs.

CASSIE: We just walked twenty flights of stairs. I'm not going all the way back up there. I got keys to the building.

OLIVIA: And I will not wait in somebody else's office when I have my own office. Who knows how long we'll be stuck?

CASSIE: Fine. Walk to twenty. I'm waiting in the lobby.

OLIVIA: Oh no, no. You said the doors lock going the other way; you have to see me back to twenty. You're the only one with any ole' pass key.

CASSIE: I'M THE ONLY ONE WITH ANY KEYS! Girlfriend, you are tap dancing on my last nerve.

OLIVIA: Does this mean we're taking the stairs?

(THEY BEGIN TO WALK BACK UP THE STAIRS.)

OLIVIA: A little tip—if you breathe out through your mouth and try not to think about how tired you are, you won't be tired. *(beat)* Are you alright?

(CASS' panting builds to gasping throughout OLIV's bantering.)

OLIVIA: One more thing, since I'm driving, I insist that we wait until we know it's safe to go. Maybe when we can see the line on the expressway moving again. Are you alright? *(no answer)* Just stop. Will you at least try it? Think of something pleasant!

CASSIE: I is—but you' still here.

OLIVIA: I know you didn't mean that the way it sounded either. I'll pretend I didn't hear that. Do you realize we're the only one's left in this entire building? *(silence)* Don't you suppose security could have at least checked back to see if you made it home? You should report them on Monday.

(THE TWO WOMEN RE-ENTER the office from the hallway.)

OLIVIA: *(Oliv is invigorated, Cass near death)* Are you coming? *(No answer)* Are you— *(Cass nearly knocks her down entering)* You know, under the circumstances you're being very unagreeable. How much does it hurt you to answer a simple question?

CASSIE: Do your mouth run by battery, remote, or what?

(CASS enters the office and Xes immediately to the phone. She attempts to dial and is unable to get a dialtone. The two remain in silence for a beat. LIGHTS flicker to BLACK.)

OLIVIA: Well we survived 20 floors, I suppose we can survive anything now.

CASSIE: Look, I don't know why it is that you don't want to get out of here. Maybe you don't have no family or nothing. But I got a little boy at home by hisself for all I know; so soon as you ready, I'm ready. But the minute I see a train out there moving, anything moving, I'm gone. And if you can see around the corner of your nose, you'll leave when I do, so I don't lose my job.

OLIVIA: I hope you understand, I can't drive in this mess; I live on the other side of 285.

CASSIE: This ain't gon' work. *(rises)* I'll be next door.

OLIVIA: What? Staying in here with me has got to be better than waiting in an empty room all by yourself. *(CASS lunges for the door)* Please?! Can we just try to get along?

CASSIE: Alright. But, this is as good as it's gon' get 'tween you and me. "Hi" and "Bye." Let's get that straight.

OLIVIA: Okay, fine.

CASSIE: *(a competition for the last word)* Good.

OLIVIA: Fine.

CASSIE: *(after a pause)* Good.

OLIVIA: *(silently mouths, "Fine.")*

CASSIE: *(after a beat, resoundedly)* GOOD.

(CASS xes to the phone and tries to dial out again. She cannot dial out and sits anxiously. She rummages her pockets for a cigarette.)

(OLIV xes to an opposite side of the room, trying not to speak.)

OLIVIA: Do you have to smoke? *(draping her face)*

CASSIE: *(quietly)* Aw shit.

OLIVIA: Thank you.

(LIGHTS FLICKER TO BLACK.)

OLIVIA: Thank you. People don't realize. It travels. Smoke. That's how it gets in your clothes. And the latest report from the Surgeon General—

CASSIE: "Hi" and "bye."

(CASS TURNS OFF the flashlight.)

OLIVIA: You know, I used to be afraid of the dark as a child.

(CASS turns the LIGHT BACK ON.)

OLIVIA: Thank you.

(OLIV digs in her purse and finds the crumpled remains of a bag of chips.)

(CASS watches her eat them with ladylike precision.)

(OLIV silently offers her one, which CASS declines. When she has finished…)

CASSIE: *(matter of factly)* We might be here for days. You should have saved that til you was really hungry.

OLIVIA: *(miffed)* I was hungry. *(she crumples the bag and moves to put it in the trash.)*

(THE FOLLOWING LINES OVERLAP:)

CASSIE: Look, you can mess up if you want to, but I'm not coming back here Saturday just to do your office.

OLIVIA: It's just a bag of—

CASSIE: When I'm through, I'm through.

OLIVIA: Fine. *(she puts bag in trash)*

CASSIE: Good.

OLIVIA: I said FINE!

(CASS rises abruptly to empty the trash and finish her work.)

CASSIE: And another thing, all this chit, chat ain't even necessary.

OLIVIA: We can at least try and be civil to one another.

CASSIE: Who said I was a civilian? Do I look like a civilian to you? DO I??!

OLIVIA: *(quietly)* No. Not at all.

CASSIE: Well then!

(LIGHTS begin to flicker.)

(LIGHTS COME BACK ON with a HUM.)

OLIVIA: Thank God Lights! That the back up generator?

CASSIE: Gotta use the phone again.

OLIVIA: Who are you calling now?

CASSIE: S'personal, ya mind?

OLIVIA: Excuse me.

(CASS fails to get a dial tone. She sits impatiently. OLIV paces then quietly resumes packing.)

OLIVIA: Did you see a box with some pictures in it?

CASSIE: Somewhere.

OLIVIA: Did you move it?

CASSIE: It should be there somewhere under your desk.

OLIVIA: Well why didn't you tell me you moved it?

CASSIE: Why didn't you ask me nice?

OLIVIA: Excuse me?

CASSIE: You heard me. *(shouting)* WHY DIDN'T YOU ASK ME NICE? You know, you oughta learn how to talk to people. It's not what you say, it's how you say it.

OLIVIA: And you people ought to learn not to touch things that aren't yours. Things on my desk that belong to me!

CASSIE: Look, you told me I could move the doggone box. And where do you get off with this "you people" crap!?

OLIVIA: "You people!"—

CASSIE: Do you see "people" standing here? If you do, then, you need to tap me on the shoulder so I know to leave the room. *(indignant)* You "people"! And if you don't want "people" to smoke, then you need to move the damn ashtray.

OLIVIA: It's not a damn ashtray, it's quartz!

CASSIE: Say what?

OLIVIA: This is my quartz conversation piece you put your butt out in!

CASSIE: I don't need this job. You think my feet and my feelings ain't hurting bad enough already?

OLIVIA: I didn't make your feet hurt.

CASSIE: Well somebody did—making me walk up twenty-one flights of stairs. TWICE!

OLIVIA: I shouldn't have to listen to this—

CASSIE: And I shouldn't have the headache of trying to be polite to some Miss Somebody who don't give a damn about somebody she can't see over her blue-brown nose— "you people."

OLIVIA: I'm sorry.

CASSIE: Naw, I'ma tell you about yourself Miss Ann. I wasn't trying to steal nothing off your desk either.

OLIVIA: I didn't say—

CASSIE: Didn't have to. I saw the way you peeped the desk when you came back in here. I picked up the tape to hear what kinda music you blue noses be listening to, but I wasn't tryin' to steal the thang. I got my own. It's a SAN-SUI, and that's Jap-o-nese, in case you did not know it. And that music you was listenin' to, it was awful!

OLIVIA: I like it.

CASSIE: Awful! I don't need this grief. *(steps over boxes to her things)* And another thing, I don't want you to take me nowhere in your car. No-where!

(CASS BEGINS WRAPPING HER VACUUM CORD LIKE A NOOSE AROUND THE APPLIANCE.)

OLIVIA: Then iceskate home and be happy!

CASSIE: I don't have to listen to no accusations from a rookie. I have had it up to here with you, girlfriend. How do YOU spell "pissed"?

(OLIV breaks down crying. The dam burst now. CASS waits for the crying to subside before she can leave.)

CASSIE: *(quietly)* Talk to people nice is all I'm saying.

(OLIV continues crying.)

CASSIE: People got feelings. And don't one person's feelings cost more than anybody else's. *(Olivia boo-hoos)* Alright. *(softening)* Now, now....

(OLIV lets out a long squeal reminiscent of a hit dog.)

CASSIE: Now don't do that. Come on. You alright now?

OLIVIA: Yeah. *(too cheery)* Fine! *(breaks down)*

CASSIE: It ain't natural is what it is. Full moon, blizzard outside, you and me in the same room for more than a minute. Ain't none of this mess natural. You alright?

(BOTH OVERLAP, consumed by the emotions of the moment.

OLIVIA: I'm Fine. It wasn't just you anway. It's ...it's...(crying uncontrollably)

CASSIE: Told you we shouldn't've said nothing. Wouldn't have been talking like that in the first place, if the city hadn't blown a damn fuse. That ain't changed nothing in here.

(CASS picks up phone receiver.   Listens.   Puts it down.   Hands OLIV a Handi-wipe to dry her tears.)

OLIVIA: Thank you. *(about to blow her nose until she realizes what she has been given)* OH, no thank you.

CASSIE: I should've stuck to my first feeling and got out of here. The horse is dead now. Damn, what my head wouldn't give for a drink. Kool-aid, anything.

OLIVIA: *(composing herself)* Did you say drink? I think I can be accomodating. It's in one of these boxes. Probably the one you moved.

(OLIV produces a bottle of Grand Marnier, or other liquer.)

OLIVIA: It was an office warming gift. Would you like some?

CASSIE: I was just talkin'; sure, if you buying.

OLIVIA: Now, if I could find my coffee mugs.

CASSIE: I saw something that looked like a mug in that box over there, *(under her breath)* but in this office what it looks like and what is ain't necessarily the same thing.

OLIVIA: What did you say? Oh, here they are. I knew I was saving this for something. I hope it's okay. *(CASS OPENS THE BOTTLE)* It's a little warm.

CASSIE: Work faster. *(takes a cup)* Happy New Year.

OLIVIA: Oh yeah! Really, it's about three hours away...New Years.

CASSIE: Three long hours. *(She pours herself another drink)* Aren't you going to have some?

OLIVIA: I was hoping to save some for later. But, since WE are going to drink it all up. Maybe I'll have a little. Just a little.

(CASS pours a drink for OLIV.)

CASSIE: *(out of habit)* Cheers.

OLIVIA: Right, cheers. *(beat, it is obvious OLIV does not drink)* I don't know what I meant by the "your people" comment. In fact, I didn't mean anything—

CASSIE: No matter, guess you had to be there.

OLIVIA: Guess so. Anyway, I didn't mean to offend you.

CASSIE: Sorry a'ready. You and me both. You know, all the years I been cleaning your office, I never looked out this window before. I really don't do windows. You got a nice view. Postcard pretty. It's so still out there...like the city took the holiday and left nobody but you and me...in here... alone...*(the two drink.)* You know, they say the way you spend New Year's Eve is the way you'll spend the whole rest of the year.

CASSIE:	OLIVIA:
(quietly) God!	*(quietly)* Oh, really?

OLIVIA: I suppose this will only make matters worse. Here I am stuck in my office with a woman who doesn't even know my name, whose name I don't know.

CASSIE: Oh, I know your name.

OLIVIA: You do?

CASSIE: You think I come in a room and don't read the name on the door?

OLIVIA: Right. So what is...I'm sorry I don't know your name.

CASSIE: Didn't suppose you would. I ain't got no door to put it on. Cassie Charles. MIZ Cassie Charles.

OLIVIA: Nice name Cassie Charles.

CASSIE: My momma liked it. It's not there.

OLIVIA: What's not where?

CASSIE: Your name. It's not on the door.

OLIVIA: No. I took it down.

CASSIE: You leaving? That's what this is about?

OLIVIA: Yes, I'm changing offices.

CASSIE: Oh...yeah? You know I used to do your office when you were on sixteen.

OLIVIA: *(BEGINS to pack up things)* No, I didn't know that.

CASSIE: So where you going now?

OLIVIA: I don't know. I don't know. Aw-well, all this talk is nice, but I really do need to get back to work.

CASSIE: Why are you in such a hurry to get this finished up by Monday?

OLIVIA: Guess I wanna start the New Year with a clean slate.

CASSIE: You lost me.

OLIVIA: I feel cramped, disordered, when my space is out of order like this. It's kind of cathartic. If I can make sense out of this—find a raison d'etre, then maybe I can see my way clear again. Don't try to figure it out.

CASSIE: I won't. I guess Kevin's had his dinner.

OLIVIA: Kevin? That your little boy?

CASSIE: My little man. He should be asleep by now.

OLIVIA: How old is he?

CASSIE: Nine, going on forty Saturday. First New Year's Eve we been apart since he was born. You know I went into labor on New Year's Eve...right on the wire. I heard the first gun shot and felt the first pain. Guess that's why I'm all sentimental. *(sings)* Gonna take a sentimental—*(stops song)* He's alright.

OLIVIA: I'm sure he is.

CASSIE: Sure he is. You got kids?

OLIVIA: No.

CASSIE: Didn't think so. Your hips too tight. *(Olivia's reaction begs for a response)* I ain't funny, I just notice things like that. You want help with some of this? *(refering to packing)*

OLIVIA: If you like. Over there. *(refering to the desk area)*

CASSIE: *(picks up Oliv's name plate from the top of a box)* So what the "D" stand for in your name?

OLIVIA: "D"? Oh, Delphine—Olivia Delphine Williams.

CASSIE: "Del-phine"?

OLIVIA: Funny huh?

CASSIE: Guess your momma liked it. You got family living?

OLIVIA: Yes?

CASSIE: Just wondered; you ain't tried to call nobody.

(OLIV takes the name plate and securely places it back in the box. She works away from CASS again.)

CASSIE: You know there must be thirty doors with Account Executive on it. I always wondered do ya'll do the same thing.

OLIVIA: Not exactly.

CASSIE: What you be doing behind your door?

OLIVIA: I'm responsible for ad concepts, sometimes the actual design or copy.

CASSIE: Which one got you this new office?

OLIVIA: A campaign I did for Ford Motors.

CASSIE: Oh yeah?

OLIVIA: Yes.

CASSIE: So what was this great idea that got you moved upstairs?

OLIVIA: I don't even have the roughs of the story boards.

CASSIE: "Storyboards"? You mean them cartoon looking things I see around here in some of these offices?

OLIVIA: Yes. It would be easier to show you.

CASSIE: Then show me!

OLIVIA: I couldn't.

CASSIE: Go ahead.

OLIVIA: No. I really couldn't.

CASSIE: Suit your—

OLIVIA: If you insist. Ford Motors has a new line of pick-ups called the Romper.

CASSIE: Never heard of it.

OLIVIA: No one has yet except in test markets. I originated the idea of the national ad campaign. That's how I got this office.

CASSIE: Just like that hunh?

OLIVIA: Well you have to use your imagination; but the commercial goes like this. There's this truck, see? "The Romper"—cuts across the rugged terrain, against a dusky sky—then over a man-made obstacle course; I can't do this—

CASSIE: Alright, if—

OLIVIA: The Romper— stops, in the middle of the course. The camera zooms—it moves in—on the figure of a man standing with a staff in his hand. *(She demonstrates)* As he approaches the cabin the announcer, this James Earl Jones voice says: "We make 'em tough enough to withstand all tests". The camera pans inside the cabin and there's this little kid inside *romping*, having the time of his life "honk, honk, beep, beep". Then, "the hook"—

CASSIE: "The hook"?

OLIVIA: "The hook"—the camera zooms in for a close up on the face of the man—Father Time. He has this pained look on his face and he's trying to pry the cabin door open with his staff, but he can't; just as the announcer says again: "We make 'em tough enough to withstand all tests—EVEN THE TEST OF TIME—THE ROMPER." The camera pulls out to this picture of Father Time climbing all over the cabin, and the little kid inside is still just romping, when the audio comes up on this jazzy version of *(sings)* "Should old acquaintance be forgot and never brought to nigh—" *(song crescendos with the image of Olivia flooring the Romper into the sunset)* That's it!

CASSIE: Uhm-hm.

OLIVIA: So? Tell me what you like?

CASSIE: I like James Earl Jones.

OLIVIA: I mean, tell me how you like it?

CASSIE: Haven't seen that one yet.

OLIVIA: You won't for another couple of months until it goes into national release. But, go on, tell me. What do you think?

CASSIE: And that got you this office?

OLIVIA: The agency made a lot of money on that account.

CASSIE: I bet. What were you doing to come up with somethin like that?

OLIVIA: What was I—DOING?

CASSIE: Beats me how somebody like you can come up with something like that.

OLIVIA: Someone like me?

CASSIE: Yeah, how did you do it?

OLIVIA: What do you mean—

CASSIE: I won't go out and apply for your job tomorrow.

OLIVIA: —someone like me?

CASSIE: Well, I never figured you and a pick-up for one.

OLIVIA: That's all you meant?

CASSIE: So, you went to school for that?

OLIVIA: I can't say I learned it all in school, no.

CASSIE: That's what I figured. They weren't teaching us how to hustle pick-ups when I went to school. Although I will admit to a few years 'tween you and me. So how does somebody like you learn how to do that?

OLIVIA: You said it again. "Somebody like me"; "like me"? What am I like?

CASSIE: Miss Priss, Miss Hi-Si'ety. You know as much about a pick up as I know 'bout a quartz conversation piece what look like a ashtray.

OLIVIA: Oh. That's what you mean.

CASSIE: *(looking around)* So you got here in a pick-up.

OLIVIA: It really is more difficult than it sounds. You have to study a client's product, their market; you have to know the image they're trying to build. You know, people always try to discount the artistic process as easy, because it's so difficult to explain. You have to have an imagination—or rather, a gift for free association to be able to create a hook—a public signature that will sell.

CASSIE: You talk real textbook; that's one reason I couldn't do your job. But I figure I got imagination, and I'm clever enough. What you mean by that "free 'sociation"?

OLIVIA: "AS-sociation." For example, "ROMPER" made me think of babies; but rather than "baby soft," the client wants to be associated with "baby tough"; To be honest with you, New Year's was coming up, and that made me think of Father Time. So you might say, one thought led to another and—

CASSIE: That's how you came up with that mess? Amazing! "Free 'ssociation," huh? Oh, don't get your feelings hurt; I'm not buying a truck. I suppose it's good if you're buying a truck; real good I suppose. Got you this office, anyway.

OLIVIA: It's not always cut and dried. Sometimes ideas come easily, and other times it requires you to summon all your intellect, your training, your imagination—

CASSIE: Right. So, what you tellin' me you do behind your door is figure up ways to make people like me want something we probably don't need...

OLIVIA: No, no, no. What WE DO is create a demand for something the public doesn't—know that it needs.

CASSIE: Free 'sociation.

OLIVIA: As-sociation.

CASSIE: What do you AS-sociate me with?

OLIVIA: You?

CASSIE: Yeah. I know you never thought twice about me before, but what do you associate me with?

OLIVIA: Cassie, free association doesn't work with people; it's more an association of words and concepts—like moon and june, night and day, light and dark—not people.

CASSIE: But I bet you could do me. Cass and what? How does that mind of yours fix me up?

OLIVIA: I don't know.

CASSIE: Sure you do.

OLIVIA: No. Really.

CASSIE: Yes you can.

OLIVIA: I really can't.

CASSIE: I could do you.

OLIVIA: Please don't!

CASSIE: YES!

OLIVIA: NO!

CASSIE: OOOOlivia!—sounds like a—goddess or something. Like the ones in those Greek stories who was always getting hung up on their mamas and daddies and cutting their eyes out and stuff. Yes! Yes! Olivia, Goddess of... Mu-zak! Yea. *(chanting)* Oli-vi-a, then I think of that skinny chick in Popeye.

OLIVIA: That was Olive Oyle.

CASSIE: Same dif'. Anyway, this is my free 'sociation. Then, I think of green—olives is green ain't they? Then there's mint green like the kind in that dark chocolate candy—the kind that's always too sweet. Know what I mean? Sure you do. Then, I 'sociate you with a office—like this. *(Indicates picture on wall)* And a picture like that. And your car? Something with four doors even though it's probably just you. But blue—a blue car, cause a green car would be too much green even for you. A blue car that's it. Four doors, reliable, and dependable. That's you. And I think of you in pumps, *(Olivia discretely tosses her pumps in a box)* *(CASSIE amuses herself)* Tight pumps that hurt by the end of the day. So, we wear sneakers on our lunch hour. Or maybe, it's just my feet hurtin'. So, how'd I do? That you?

OLIVIA: I drive a red Porche.

CASSIE: O-kay. Your turn now. So what do you associate me with?

OLIVIA: I don't think Porche. I don't know. I haven't thought about it.

CASSIE: What's there to think about? "Work," for one. Don't you look at me and think of work?

OLIVIA: I work.

CASSIE: Not the kind of work that I do.

OLIVIA: Work is work.

CASSIE: If you believed that you'd have my job. You brought this free association up, anyway; why don't you want to play?

OLIVIA: Because it doesn't go like this. You don't use it to categorize people.

CASSIE: Who says? People do it everyday. You just gave it a name. Look, don't you want to clear the air? A new year is on the way. 'xactly what did you expect would happen when you asked me to stay in here with you?

OLIVIA: Conversation.

CASSIE: Oh, conversation. "How about this weather we havin ?" "Bad ain't it?" Next.

OLIVIA: What do you expect? We don't know each other. And I don't like the idea of someone guessing and second guessing my every move, and what I like and dislike. I just don't like it.

CASSIE: That's what you do for a living. That really bother you?

OLIVIA: Wouldn't it bother you?

CASSIE: Somebody taking the time to think about me—no. If you mean tipping around what's real—yes. I'm not afraid of saying what's on my mind.

OLIVIA: Obviously not.

CASSIE: If you were expecting me just to sit here in your office and talk to you about your name on your door, WHICH AIN'T ON YOUR DOOR NO MORE, you made a mistake.

OLIVIA: WHAT I EXPECT is a certain amount of courtesy from someone I have invited into my home.

CASSIE: YOUR HOME?

OLIVIA: (final) MY Home!

CASSIE: Your "home"??! There I go again. Here I thought this was an office, just cause it looked like an office. I know from 4:00 til 8:30 I've got nine more that look just like it to clean, and I call them offices; but this is your "home," well excuse me. (Talking to her ever-present Grandmother) M'dear you was right about another thing. You put two opposites together and all you get is two people who do not belong. (CASS picks up phone; tries for dial tone and this time gets one.) Hello? Hello? Can you hear me? Yes? Hi, baby— (talks uninterrupted)

OLIVIA: You got through?

CASSIE: —The phones and power went out. How's it over there? You alright? ... Good. Good. Did Miss Campbell stay with you? ... I'm okay, it's just a mess over here; it might take me most of the night to get to you, but I'm coming, ya hear? ... You eat dinner? ... Good. You go to sleep now ... Sure you can. I love you baby .... Happy New Year to you, too. Now, let me talk to Ms. Campbell. ... Yes M'am, I'm alright. I don't know what's running, but I'll get there how I can. It might take a while... uhm-hm, I will. ... Thanks for giving him his dinner and staying. ... Happy New Year to you. ... uhm-hm, bye. (Hangs up)

OLIVIA: Your little boy is alright?

CASSIE: Yeah. (dials again)

OLIVIA: Who are you calling now?

CASSIE: The Negro Mover. Hello, Rapid Transit? Hello—? (slams phone receiver down) I dunno what I was thinking, they close at three-thirty when the weather is clear.

OLIVIA: Why are you calling public transportation? I told you I'd take you home.

CASSIE: On your flying carpet what look' like a car? No thank you, I want to go home now.

OLIVIA: You want to be stranded in that mess that's still out there? Then you go right ahead.

CASSIE: Naw. I don't make no mistake three times...foolish, if you ask me.

OLIVIA: I didn't.

CASSIE: You wouldn't. You think I ain't got sense enough to know what's going on here.

OLIVIA: I couldn't care less about what you think you know.

CASSIE: Well, that's the first honest thing you said all night. It don't take no genius to figure out that you ain't too happy about leaving this office.

OLIVIA: Yes, I'm leaving. I said that.

CASSIE: But I ain't supposed to have sense enough to figure out that you lost your job. That's why you in a rush to get out of here by Monday. Not cause you want to, cause you have to.

OLIVIA: Who are you? Dr. Joyce Brothers of Buildings and Grounds?! I didn't ask for your prognosis. I didn't ask your opinion five minutes ago when you volunteered it, or two weeks ago when I quit. I QUIT! Do you mind? I didn't ask you first. I finally got tired of being treated by every-damn body in this building—including you—like I had PALSY or something.

CASSIE: Palsy! Palsy! What's Palsy got to do with it? Honey, half of what you thinking people feeling about you—me anyway—is in your mind. "Free association" is the constant state of yo' mind. Here, I am thinking it's just me. You strung out cause your name ain't on the door no more. Big deal on the door!

OLIVIA: IT IS A BIG DEAL TO ME!

CASSIE: Big damn deal. You'll just leave here and go stick it on some other door. THE COMPANY STILL OWN THE FRONT DOOR and everything behind it. So until your name on the front door, your name might as well be mine.

OLIVIA: Oh No No No! My Name—Olivia DELPHINE Williams—spells four years under-grad, TWO YEARS grad school, TWO YEARS as an apprentice, THREE YEARS as a production artist and over a year HERE! Nooo, I haven't been in the basement for over twenty years like you—

CASSIE: I'm not that old—

OLIVIA: But I landed the biggest account the company got this year.

CASSIE: You mean the truck?

OLIVIA: YES, DAMNIT I MEAN THE TRUCK! Carlyle made the presentation, but I did the work; that was my idea! Nobody else eats, sleeps and drinks Peat, Montgriff and Simon. This place was work. This place was play. This place was sex!

CASSIE: Sex?

OLIVIA: Yes, sex. Seven years, I have been married to this place; and the the worst thing I ever did was to give up everything I knew of a personal life. And why? 'Cause if I did, Peat, Montgriff and Simon were going to be good to me in my old age. And do you know why I'm losing my job? Do you want to know why?

CASSIE: Cause they didn't like the sex?

OLIVIA: Is that what you want to hear?!!

CASSIE: What I want to hear? Girlfriend, give me a break.

OLIVIA: Let's get one thing straight. I'm not your girl; I'm not your friend. WE aren't anything. (She escapes to her boxes stuffing them with files for emphasis. CASS gathers her things to leave) Twenty-eight other people around here trying to do half the job I'm doing; and I'm supposed to be satisfied witha coupla bonuses, a new office, and a title on the door that doesn't mean anything. And this is as good as it's going to get!??

CASSIE: What the hell is wrong with that?

OLIVIA: 'Cause that bastard did everything, but to come right out and to tell me to stop dreaming! He makes my presentation and he's V.P. now. So he gives one of his "good ole boys" his old job; and then, this—this clown— that I trained—he makes my supervisor, "Art Director." That should have been me, at least! "Olivia," he says to me, "your evaluations are wonder- ful. It's just for this company—your image—"

CASSIE: "Image"? What did he mean by that?

OLIVIA: He meant that I'm the one concept this company can't sell; no, they won't sell. "Maybe," he said to me, "when things change." His hands are tied now, "because these reverse discrimination suits have gotten manage- ment all tensed up. Maybe in ten years—." He said that as if it was noth- ing. Do you know, I'll be forty one years old in ten years?

CASSIE: That ain't exactly ancient, ya' know.

OLIVIA: No. But ten years, what kind of pay off is that for the seven years I've already put in this place? Hell, I'm a woman. I want a family. Is that going to wait for ten years? I want a man in my life; I think. I don't know. It's been so long! I have locked myself away in this office and forgotten every- thing else. What it feels like to laugh, to cry, to say "Go to hell!" Go to hell (tosses a box on each name) Peat, Montcriff, AND Simon, for reneging on seven years of my life! I gave you 24 hours a day for seven years and all you gave me were these got damn BOXES!

CASSIE: Let me know, if you want to be alone now.

OLIVIA: Oh yeah. This will give you a little juicy piece of gossip to keep alive after I'm gone, won't it??!

CASSIE: You' doing pretty good.

OLIVIA: Good. Then you be sure to tell them how I tried to tear the frigging walls down. *(OLIV looks for something to strike at and futiley tosses a stack of her books.)* Tell them how Olivia stuck it to them, like they stuck it to me! Oh, damn.

(After the emotional volcano, OLIVIA stops herself and looks at the office, a reflection of her pain. She cries softly. CASS stands stunned.in silence for a beat.)

CASSIE: Do this mean we can go home now?

(LIGHTS BLACK).

END ACT I.

ACT II.

(THE LIGHTS FLICKER TO BRIGHT. OLIVIA sleeps on the sofa in the office. CASS watches her sleep. She puffs a cigarette and fans the smoke in the opposite direction.)

CASSIE: *(a la Rod Serling, she puffs on a cigarette throughout a la Bette Davis for dramatic emphasis.)* Meet—Cassie Charles. Single. Afro-American. Cleaning lady. Thought—it was a regular day at work. Thought this woman was going to drive her home in a red Porsche—which probably ain't no red Porsche. Thought she'd be home for New Years Eve with her little boy. Instead, she here babysitting Miss Olivia Del-phine—yes, I said Delphine. Miss fugitive from the Pepsi generation—Williams. We stranded here in her home—what only looks like an office. Here in the Twilight Zone. *(She mimics the "Twighlight-zone" theme)* Do-do, do-do, ... *(repeats)*

OLIVIA: Oh my head.

CASSIE: *(OLIV stirs)* Welcome back to the Twilight Zone DELPHINE.

(OLIV wakes herself. CASS discretely savors a last few puffs on the cigarette before she puts it out.)

OLIVIA: Have I been asleep long?

CASSIE: Yeah...it's been so peaceful. I started to pick up this mess, but I left some for you...since you did it.

OLIVIA: Do I smell smoke?

CASSIE: Damn! Girlfriend, you know what you need?

OLIVIA: Valium.

CASSIE: No. I know what you really need.

OLIVIA: Oh please.

CASSIE: Oh don't blush. I couldn't see it no way. Really! You need a good hot, sweaty, non-involved x-rated fling. What I call you before? Miss Priss— Uptight? Holler if you hear your name.

OLIVIA: Spare me, okay.

CASSIE: Well if throwing boxes your thang…right on.

(OLIV xes to window.)

OLIVIA: Is something sitting on my head?

CASSIE: *("Twilight" theme)* DO-DO-DO-DO-DO-DO-DO-DO

OLIVIA: Nothing is moving out there?

CASSIE: That's why I'm still sitting here.

OLIVIA: You know, a man is not the answer to every woman's problem.

CASSIE: Oh, but the right one can make you forget you got problems.

OLIVIA: A matter of opinion. You married?

CASSIE: No…no.

OLIVIA: Then why don't you solve your problems with a man?

CASSIE: Cause we was talking bout you.

OLIVIA: Were we?

CASSIE: You doggone right. You was cursing and throwing boxes cause you lost your job; you coulda accidentally hit me. You called me old—

OLIVIA: I called you old?

CASSIE: THEN, you took your marbles in your corner and went to sleep.

OLIVIA: I called you old?

CASSIE: In forty languages…

OLIVIA: Sorry…

CASSIE: I let you slide. But don't do it no mo'. So, why did you lose your job? For real now.

OLIVIA: I told you. I didn't lose my job. I quit. For Real!

CASSIE: You quit your job.

OLIVIA: Didn't I just say that?

CASSIE: Different folks, different strokes. I ain't gon' leave my job just over gettin my feelings hurt. My floors get stepped on every day, and I still come back the next day to clean 'em. It's a job.

OLIVIA: That's the difference between a job and a career.

CASSIE: Eww! Then explain to me why you leaving your "career"? Don't know, huh? What I thought. I hope not behind your boss. You gonna meet a thousand more like him.

OLIVIA: I know why I'm leaving.

CASSIE: Why?

OLIVIA: Because I don't know what I'm up against anymore.

CASSIE: Say what?

OLIVIA: It's very clear to me that I should leave just on G.P.! The ethics have all changed up here, I don't know. Maybe it's always been this way—

CASSIE: Wait a minute—wait a minute.

OLIVIA: Staying here rubs against the grain of the way I was brought up.

CASSIE: I know what I said, I can hear myself talking. I ask a simple question and I get a textbook. Okay. So you was brought up.

OLIVIA: Really, it goes back to when I was in college. That was a time when everything I ever believed in was put to a test.

CASSIE: *(talks to M'dear)* No, I'ma ask her. *(to OLIVIA)* So what happened?

OLIVIA: It didn't even happen to me directly. I went to a predominantly white college.

CASSIE: No!

OLIVIA: There was this girl who lived across the hall. She was Black too, but you never would have known it to look at her. I can't even remember her name—just that she was a second semester freshman from Upper Montclair, New Jersey; anyway, from the moment I arrived, she took me under wing.

CASSIE: I suppose that's nice.

OLIVIA: —where to be seen? Who to be seen with? The "sisters" in the BSA—especially those with afro's deep enough to hide a pick in—

CASSIE: I had an afro— *(Defines a humongous afro.)*

OLIVIA: —they were in the "not to be seen with" category.

CASSIE: Mine was small.

OLIVIA: Montclair didn't understand their passion to be Black in a "lily pond", and I guess she didn't want me to understand it either. She was thrilled, no—proud, that at another time in her life she had actually passed for White. I found myself pulling away from her and still she tried to be my friend.

CASSIE: Why was she so anxious to be friends with you?

OLIVIA: I don't know.

CASSIE: If she was hoping to pass, you kinda woulda been a dead give away. Don't you think?

OLIVIA: Maybe I didn't pose a threat to her because I didn't spend much time with the other Black students either.

CASSIE: Oh, you mean you didn't "hang"?

OLIVIA: No, I was scared for one. It was my first time away from home... alone...a freshman on scholarship, afraid of failing. No. I didn't—I couldn't "HANG." But she did convince me once to go with her to a mixer —the dances the white kids threw. It was part of a whole way of life she was trying to get into—mixers, earth shoes and tofu; you know, real "preppie"-like. That's what puzzled me most about her. This girl was smart. But she never used that to impress these girls she wanted to be her friends. Instead this very articulate girl struggled with her own memories like they were some kind of foreign language. She was always trying to relate to them and their stories. She wasn't trying to be like them; she wanted to be them; and I could see that they resented it. I guess it is kind of hard to like somebody who doesn't even like themselves.

CASSIE: *(under her breath)* That's true.

OLIVIA: Finally, this one Saturday night, I had been up late studying, when I heard this pounding. It was Montclair struggling with the key to her door. She was trying to get in her room. She must've awakened the whole floor; they were already standing in the hall when I finally opened my door. She sat like an abandoned child at the closed door her key still in her hand. With all of us staring, she looked up at me and said, "I can't get in Olivia; why can't I get in?" Her parents came for her the next day. I joined the BSA within the week. I also started calling my sister every week. She was a music major about to finish up at Fisk. I think she was going through her own kind of culture shock too. That year, we must have swapped boxes of Black novels and the names of hundreds of Black writers, Fanon, Ellison, Toni Morrison, Margaret Walker—

CASSIE: *The Color Purple*, right? Good movie.

OLIVIA: —that was Alice Walker. Gwen Brooks, Sonia Sanchez, Maya Angelou, any and every book, we could get our hands on. It was almost like when we were back at home; we were still trying to "fix our heads" in a way…thumbing through those books hoping we'd stumble across whatever we needed to know to "make it."

CASSIE: So what's this girl's story got to do with you now?

OLIVIA: Don't you see? I got my Phi Beta Kappa key and thought I had it made. I thought I had the key to open any door, to get in any place I wanted —even here, to the top of the tower.

CASSIE: What tower?

OLIVIA: The tower—the twenty first floor—

CASSIE: The executive floor—?

OLIVIA: That's it. In this company that's the top of the tower. The key to making it couldn't be color; that didn't get her into the world she wanted so badly. So it had to be something else—like my Daddy always taught me. "Just be respected for the knowledge you command," he would say, "Olivia that will open all kinds of doors for you." It should be that simple.

CASSIE: Oh. That mean you ain't supposed to be respected if you didn't go to school?

OLIVIA: No, you can be respected for hard work, *too*.

CASSIE: Oh, "too." Well knowing is one thing. Doing is another.

OLIVIA: That's exactly what I'm saying. On a history teacher's salary, my Daddy laid the world at our feet; he brought up me and my sister to believe that if we worked for something, it should be ours. But just in case there was something he couldn't tell us—about being women in particular, about what we needed to hold on to—we read our books.

CASSIE: So what did them books tell you bout being women—in partic'lar?

OLIVIA: There was this one book—SULA. She was a woman whose fire— whose passion—could have been a thing of beauty, if it had found the proper channel. But it didn't. So she destroyed herself, and perhaps the only person who ever really loved her, her best friend, Nel. In fact, that's the thing about all of the women in all of those books; they were either tragically unrestrained like Sula; or, they were like Nel with this amazing—sometimes numbing capacity to just keep holding on. They were holding on to some belief inside themselves as profound as God and known only to themselves.

CASSIE: So, which one of them women is you?

OLIVIA: Nel.

CASSIE: Well damn. Now I see why you throwing them books all over the room. They ain't done you no good—You ain't holding on to nothing. You giving up.

OLIVIA: What else can I do? I don't feel like God creating things anymore. I feel like the Invisible Man. And I'm fighting a losing battle around here just tyring to be seen and to be heard.

CASSIE: No wonder. God is a man. It's a man's world, honey. I feel invisible round here too. And you'd be surprised who be doing it to me.

OLIVIA: "God is a man?" "It's a *man's world*." That kind of mindwashing is ingrained with you isn't it? You don't even hear it. We are living in a technicolor age, but we want to keep seeing seeing the world in black and white. Or maybe it's me. Maybe things haven't changed. What could I have been thinkin? I've been killing myself for a promtion I can never have, because I came out looking like the shadow of my Daddy instead of looking like you.

CASSIE: Looking like me ? *(sizing here up)* You mean my Addidas? You mean color? If I had your job, I could have had that promotion because of my color?

OLIVIA: It crossed my mind.

CASSIE: Then honey, you are the one seeing the world in black and white.

OLIVIA: What else could it be? I dress the part. I talk the part. I give my 110% better than everybody else the part.

CASSIE: I don't believe we having this conversation. Cause of my color, I could have had your job and the promotion?!! C'mon honey, let's pack up these boxes and get you out of here.

(THE TWO WOMEN BEGIN CLEANING THE RUMMAGE AND PACKING.)

OLIVIA: What's left but color? Advertising is my business. I hear my clients. After the "Black is beautiful" 60's, the 70's almost made this dark child an extinct breed.

CASSIE: And you getting scarcer round here by the minute.

OLIVIA: Tell me the last time you saw a major ad campaign with someone who looked like me? If it's not an ad to "come back to Jamaica...where what's old is what's new, they better have green eyes and thin lips, or some other acceptable variation on an all-American theme. *(thumbing professional magazines at Cassie)* Where are the women who look like me?

CASSIE: Oh hell, they still Black. I remember a time we didn't have no Black models. Light, dark, nor otherwise.

OLIVIA: Oh great. How does that sound? We got kept out so long, we just glad to be here!

CASSIE: You just bein' petty now.

OLIVIA: I am not being petty. Just like I did, thousands of little girls still need to see themselves in magazines, in boardrooms, in the media. And they need to see themselves with dark skin, round noses and full hips too—

CASSIE: Well you a little slack in the hips sugar. But what's the point you trying to get to?

OLIVIA: Growing up, the only place I ever found someone who looked like me was in books. You know why? Because I could paint the picture in my mind. Nancy Drew did not have blonde hair and blue eyes; she had kinky hair, and brown eyes just like me.   Growing up you have to see yourself, or you don't imagine even having a place in the world. I didn't get into advertising to be a "role model." Hell, I wanted to get in here and create NEW models.

CASSIE: Maybe they just showing what is. Except for *Essence*, you don't see too many career magazines with women with braids and afro's either.

OLIVIA: Career women's magazines. They know what time it is. Do you know I can't wear braids here?

CASSIE: Can't!

OLIVIA: Can't.

CASSIE: So what you doing back in this lily pond?

OLIVIA: 'Cause this is the world I live in. My world is from Madison Avenue and out there to McDonalds!

CASSIE: How McDonald's get in your nightmare?

OLIVIA: Right up there with Mc-Apple pie.

CASSIE: You right about that. McDonald's is the American way. I got my first job pushing burgers at Mickey Dee.

(THE WOMEN CONTINUE REPACKING; the act of packing and cleaning is now second nature to both. They should incorporate the action of packing to punctuate the conversation.)

OLIVIA: And what did you do at McDonald's?

CASSIE: Do? Brain surgery. —I bussed tables, then I worked the register. Why?

OLIVIA: *(laughs)* That figures.

CASSIE: Why does that "figure"?

OLIVIA: Just figures you'd be behind the register; where were all the real dark children? —in the back at the grill?

CASSIE: Now you getting down right silly.

OLOVIA: Naw, THEY thought WE couldn't handle the language at the register. *(pretending to be "so-called typical/stereotypical" black street kid)* "What kinda cheese you want on your burger? America or switch? *(american or swiss/ cheese)*

CASSIE: Now stop! I was good with numbers; this fore they got the little machines that could talk back and count the change for you. THAT'S how I got to the register, darling.

OLIVIA: Maybe. But there were some of us who are good—JUST MAYBE—who don't get the chance, cause we don't look like somebody corporate America wants sitting in their front office.

CASSIE: Then say that!

OLIVIA: Don't get mad at me Cass; if I'm confused, it's cause we even do it to ourselves.

CASSIE: I didn't ask to be included in your "we."

OLIVIA: Whether you asked or not, WE ARE. YOU ARE. Everyone of us! Especially if we're over thirty, we have some memory of "good hair," and wive's tales like marry light" and "fair" skin? Does that make dark skin un-fair? See the contradictions in that kind of language? You'd think that we would remember how we got this way in the first place. But no, we accept that crap and keep on trying to get over, "If you're brown, stick around. If you're yellow it's mellow. If you're Black, get back." I don't even go to clubs anymore, because I can't psyche myself up to sitting there watching all the men single file past me to the "fair-skinned sister" who just walked in the door.

CASSIE: That may have been true when I was still out there, but, naw...that rap done all changed up now. That color don't make no nevermind, once the negro come and ask me, "Yo' sugar! what's yo' sign? And, uh, like what yo' name is? Uhm-hm. And what do you *do?*..Uh-*huh*." He's gon' get right out of my line and ride home with you in a *red Porsche.*

OLIVIA: Look...maybe. I'm not even saying all men are like that. I certainly don't think in those terms.

CASSIE: Then, what are you saying ?

OLIVIA: I'm saying it's a constant struggle to know what you're up against.

CASSIE: Remind me never to ask you to explain anything really complicated to me.

OLIVIA: How do you think I feel? I think I have this thing figured out—

CASSIE: —Just remind me not to.

(OLIVIA continues talking to herself, CASSIE continues working).

OLIVIA: It's not as black and white as color. It really is achievement; Montclaire was wrong. Daddy was right. Then it goes back to color and quotas. Affirmative action—we gonna' let "the spook" get a little bit closer to "the door." And I was so close, I could touch it, even see it. The door to opportunity right here with my name on it *(SHE flings open her OFFICE DOOR to reveal the "missing" NAME PLATE)* Now that's out! *(closes door)* The "Good ole boys" have decided they don't have to have a conscience; I must have a complex! If I can't get my foot in the door, "Then damn girl, you must need a new pair of shoes." A new pair of shoes! Next it will be something as arbitrary as a Brooks Brothers suit, blue eyes, and hair on my chest. Where will I be then—?

CASSIE: Remind me never to ask…You know what your problem is? You think the world supposed to be fair.

OLIVIA: My problem is I don't have a job.

CASSIE: You did that to yourself. Naw, I know what your problem is. You ain't got nobody to talk to but yourself, and we both know what them conversations must be like.

OLIVIA: Let's drop it.

CASSIE: Ain't you got nobody to talk to? What about that Phi Beta Kap or that BSA? Don't you still see none of them?

OLIVIA: No.

CASSIE: Ain't that like a sorority?

OLIVIA: Oh, no…the BSA, was more a political action group.

CASSIE: Like the Rainbow Coalition.

OLIVIA: Sort of. There were sororities, but I didn't join.

CASSIE: OOhh, I thought that's what college was all about. Them sorority things. Like in Gidget—well no, I don't suppose you could call no beach no sorority. But like this movie I saw on the late show, "The Group". Murphy Brown was in it. She was one of these women who took this oath and called one another,.. uhm…, something.

OLIVIA: Soror?

CASSIE: Naw, that wasn't it. Well maybe they wasn't a sorority. But don't you have no soror sisters?

OLIVIA: No.

CASSIE: Well, your real sister then…somebody! Who you talk to 'fore you talk to me today?

OLIVIA: My sister, but we haven't talked in years.

CASSIE: Kinda hard to figure a person like you having a sister anyway. Everybody gotta have a mother and father to get here, but sisters' not so much a fact of life. I didn't have one.

OLIVIA: *(to herself)* We were very close.

CASSIE: Don't you think—what's her name?

OLIVIA: *(she remembers Cass is in the room)* Diana.

CASSIE: Uhm, another princess name. So, don't you think Diana—

OLIVIA: No. I don't.

CASSIE: Excuse me.

OLIVIA: I mean, I don't think—

CASSIE: Hey, not my sister. You can bet, if I had a mainline to M'dear, I'd call her.

OLIVIA: Who?

CASSIE: M'dear. My grandmother, I used to call her M'dear, that's southern short for—

OLIVIA: Mother dear. Yes, I know.

CASSIE: Well some people don't. They look at you crazy like you can't talk…like you have a problem saying "mother" *(mimics)* Mu-duh. Anyway, me and M'dear used to talk, I guess, the way you and your sister used to talk.

OLIVIA: You talked to your grandmother about everything?

CASSIE: Yeah! M'dear was old, but she was awake! Had to be, she raised me.

OLIVIA: Why's that?

CASSIE: My momma left when I was little. I left school in the tenth grade to do M'dears work for some people she had been working for for thirty-five years. She's the one taught me bout people…she made no put-ons bout who she was, and what she did for a living. That's why I don't. If it's honest; it's a respectable living.

OLIVIA: Like my Father taught me.

CASSIE: She said, you gotta be able to live with what you doing. That don't necessarily mean be happy either, just that what you do at night comes to light in the day. She'd say, "the eyes the mirror of the soul." Oh, she tole me a lot of things. After twenty-one years, some of her had to rub off on me.

OLIVIA: How could you just leave school like that?

CASSIE: I couldn't not leave school; three people couldn't make it off no welfare check. I had this little cousin Mikey lived with us.

OLIVIA: But how could you just not go?

CASSIE: Easy. First I took some days off from school, and worked week-ends. By the time I got to the 'leventh grade, I just stopped going.

OLIVIA: Why did you have to be the one?

CASSIE: I never knew my daddy. Like I tole ya my mama was gone. She and M'dear never did see eye to eye on how I was being raised. When she left, wasn't no question on who I was gonna stay with. M'dear run herself ragged waiting on us. This one day she was cooking breakfast for Mikey screamin' his head off, when she slipped in some grease and broke her hip.

She was crippled for the rest of her life. She couldn't do no mo' days' work, so I did it for her.

OLIVIA: Why don't you go to school now?

CASSIE: Honey, you the wrong one to be cheerleading on that one.

OLIVIA: Why? Don't you want things better for yourself?

CASSIE: Better as compared to what?! I use to see them people on "Dynasty." They kept psychiatrists and them valium doctors in business. 'Po folks take a fifteen cents "Goody Powder" and keep right on stepping.

OLIVIA: People don't just stop dreaming.

CASSIE: Dreaming. M'dear usta say, "Never have a dream, never have a dream come true."

OLIVIA: Right!

CASSIE: I say dreaming is God's curse.

OLIVIA: Dreaming is a curse?

CASSIE: Being ungrateful for what you got, and wishing for things you can't have. If that ain't a curse, I ain't seen one. You do what you gotta do.

OLIVIA: That's a cop out.

CASSIE: To work? To hustle? That's a cop out? I got the hardest job of you and me both; and that's putting my son to bed and making sure he don't ever see me wishing him away—hmph, dreaming! He don't see nothing but Cass his momma, not somebody who was gon' finally have things for myself before he came. And he don't care that I ain't got no letters behind my name. "C-a-s-s," no dash, no dots, no letters; that's all she got.

OLIVIA: Maybe that is all he sees. But what about him? Don't you want him to go to college?

CASSIE: Yes, but that ain't no end all.

OLIVIA: No, it's a place for him to begin. And what if you get sick? Is he going to have to quit school in the fourth grade to take care of you?

CASSIE: No.

OLIVIA: So how is he supposed to make it? College must be— twelve, fifteen thousand dollars—

CASSIE: I could—

OLIVIA: —a year! How's he going to make it if—

CASSIE: I can't worry about that now! Maybe that's where me and my mama were alike. You get by from day to day. That's how you deal with the curse. I don't have time to think of no dreams, cause I'm too busy working. Maybe if I had a daddy promising me there was something on the other end—I'd dream too. But I deal with what is, and whatever happen, happen cause it meant to be.

OLIVIA: Doesn't that scare you?

CASSIE: Hell yeah. Life is meant to be scary. That's why they call it "life" and not "play." Being scared keeps you moving. Sent you packing, didn't it?

Didn't it? *(beat)* Life got you scared to call home… Your family mad at you or somethin'?

OLIVIA: No.

CASSIE: You mad at them? Shame? God chile, what you do rob a bank? Your momma still love you.

OLIVIA: My parents aren't living.

CASSIE: Excuse me. Well you being all secretive—it's just you and your sister then?

OLIVIA: Yes.

CASSIE: You mean you got one family on this earth and you ain't talking to her?

OLIVIA: We talk.

CASSIE: I hope not like you talk to me.

OLIVIA: A conversation works two ways.

CASSIE: Uhm-hm, sure do. So when was the last time you talked to her?

OLIVIA: It's been a few years.

CASSIE: Years! I talk to M'dear three times a day, and she been dead for fifteen years ! I guess family don't mean that much to some people.

OLIVIA: Just cause you don't pick up a phone, doesn't mean you don't care. I SAID IT DOESN'T MEAN YOU DON'T CARE.

CASSIE: You ain't gotta shout, I'm in the room.

OLIVIA: I know what you're thinking.

CASSIE: Uhm-hm, where you want these boxes?

OLIVIA: I KNOW WHAT YOU'RE THINKING. It's the same indictment I heard from her. I put on a suit and all of a sudden I have balls where I used to have feelings? People change. They grow together, they can grow apart. After five years, it's possible. We had a disagreement.

CASSIE: Five years ain't no disagreement, it's a feud.

OLIVIA: Toss your family into the ring and see if you come back perfect.

CASSIE: I left school for M'dear. Took care of a third cousin…and I'm taking care of Kevin by myself now.

OLIVIA: You made your choice and I made mine! All I have left of a family now is in these boxes—and in a blue car with four doors downstairs. Doesn't that count for anything?!

CASSIE: It's a matter of what you can't live with. Ain't my place to judge.

OLIVIA: But that's what you're doing. Just like she did. I couldn't explain to her, it was because of Daddy that I stayed here and I worked. That's how he brought us up; she heard him differently. I couldn't do anything at home but hold his hand—or hers. But here— all of this was going to be my legacy to him. To make it here. He was so proud of me when I got this job. I hadn't even been here a year, when she called me to "come home"; when I was hired, they made it clear to me "this place is your home—this is your family." That's why they like young, single people, because there is no home, no family ties. So, how do I tell her now, that I have lost everything that she thought meant anything to me then. Don't you think I wanted to go home? Don't you think I know, he was my father too?! *(beat of realization)* Oh my God.

CASSIE: If I was scared as you to go home, I'd throw my hat in first to see if she tossed it back. Why don't you call her?

OLIVIA: She could call me—

CASSIE: Just like you could her. Life is too short to go through it alone. Thank God, I have Kevin—and you have your sister.

OLIVIA: No, not on the phone.

CASSIE: Next best thing to being there.

OLIVIA: No...I need to see her. It's just got to be in person.

CASSIE: Damn you stubborn.

OLIVIA: If I could see her, I'd know if it was alright. Maybe, if she could see me she'd under—. What's that your grandmother said, " the soul being the eyes"—?

CASSIE: The eyes being "the mirror of the soul," yeah.

OLIVIA: What do you know about my soul by looking into my eyes?

CASSIE: I don't even have to look in your eyes. You put all these things in here, so people be too busy to look in the direction of your soul. All I gotta do is look at these walls in this place you call "home" to know what your soul is like.

OLIVIA: And?

(THEY BOTH LOOK AT THE BARE WALLS.)

CASSIE: Scary ain't it? Life—hard to swallow without something to wash it down. *(Cass crosses to the Grand Marnier)* You want some? Help your headache. *(silence is the answer)* You know, this talk getting awfully heavy on my tongue. Don't your head feel heavy?

OLIVIA: It's not just the talk....

CASSIE: Oh girlfriend, we haven't even put a dent in this bottle. Give yourself a shot. *(She gives Olivia a re-fill of her mug)* Know what I'm afraid of?...if I start crying now, I'll be crying all year long.

(THE DAMN BURSTS WITH THEIR SHARED LAUGHTER.)

CASSIE: Can you get something sides beach music on this box of yours? *(CASS fiddles with the tape/radio player.)* Shoot, I'm missing Dick Clark's Rockin' New Year's Eve. I know you' use' to Lombardo, but we gon' dance tonight. Can you get radio on this thang?

(THE WOMEN RESPOND AS CASSIE SEARCHES THE RADIO.)

RADIO: *(Acid rock)*

(CASSIE cringes; OLIVIA jumps with a start to her feet and races to turn the dial. CASSIE changes the station.)

RADIO: *(Calypso)*

(OLIVIA releases a squeal of excitement and moves to the beat.)

CASSIE: No. *(turns dial)*

RADIO: "Day 352 of America held hostage this is Rush Limbaugh."

CASSIE/OLIVIA: Hell no. *(turns dial)*

RADIO: *(MUSIC CUE: AN OLDIE BUT GOODY SLOW DRAGGY kind of song. Suggested, "Stay in My Corner" or "Oo-Baby, Baby.")*

CASSIE: *(squeals)* Eww!- baby, baby.

OLIVIA: *(amused)* ooo-baby.

CASSIE: Naw honey, you been suited up too long. Read my hips, it's EEWWW-baby, baby! *(CASSIE remembers the basement "grind" with her body)*

OLIVIA: *(letting loose)* EEWWW! *(failing miserably)* Baby, baby. *(trying to mimick CASS down to the "grind")* Eww baby, baby baby.

CASSIE: Work with it sugar. Before the night is over, I want to see some color in those cheeks. All four of em.

(THE TWO DANCE TO THE MUSIC RELEASING THE TENSION OF THE EVENING.)

CASSIE: You know what this makes me think of?

OLIVIA: What's that?

CASSIE: Jughead's back seat.

OLIVIA: Jughead?

CASSIE: Well, that's what I called him. Luscious was his name. *(pronounced, "loo-shuhs")*

OLIVIA: Luscious Loo-scious, huh?

CASSIE: Oh yeah. He was my BEST boyfriend. 'Fact, he was my first real boy-anything. He was the first one I let get into any serious petting. Didn't neither one of us know what the hell we was doing. But we must of done something right this one night; cause, we turned the sound off at the drive-in and this song was playing. And he was leaning over me…and, I must have moved against him in the right direction—you know what I mean. Well, I didn't realize how serious it was; 'til he dropped me off at home, and I looked down at the front of my new skirt and saw where he left this spot to remember him by. I didn't tell him cause he woulda been embarrassed. But I took the skirt to school the next day and showed it to my best friend Brenda Scott.

OLIVIA: How did he do that through his clothes and everything?

CASSIE: I think the boy musta been sick. I ain't never seen nothing like it. And I didn't know, I thought I wasn't a virgin no' more.

(THE MUSIC AND THE LATENESS OF THE HOUR MAKE THE TWO ALMOST HYSTERICAL WITH LAUGHTER. AS THE EVENING PRO-

*GRESSES THEY BECOME HIGH ON THE INTIMACY OF LAUGH-
TER.)*

CASSIE: Tell me something? You remember the best time?

OLIVIA: You mean the first time?

CASSIE: Honey, the first time is never the best time. You scared and that shit hurts. No, no, no. Let's talk about the freakiest time.

OLIVIA: Don't you think its kind of gauche to compare?

CASSIE: I didn't ask for his vital 'tatistics; I just asked if you remembered. Like doing it on a football field at midnight. TOUCHDOWN!!

OLIVIA: My school didn't have outdoor sports.

CASSIE: Aw, you can tell me.

OLIVIA: No. Alright.

CASSIE: Yes?

OLIVIA: Well, there was this one guy—right after college—Herman.

CASSIE: "Herman." Ooo, this is getting good and freaky.

OLIVIA: He was an accountant.

CASSIE: OOOoo, an accountant. So what he do? He do it by the numbers?

OLIVIA: This is awful.

CASSIE: Yes!!

OLIVIA: Alright. I remember him because the whole time—you know what I mean "the whole time"? *(Cassie enthralled, nods)* The whole time, he kept his glasses on. *(Cassie waits)* Wait a minute, wait a minute. He kept his glasses on, and they got all steamed up, and he couldn't see. Wasn't that freaky? *(OLIVIA falls out laughing, then realizes she's laughing alone)*

CASSIE: That's as good as it's got? You need a man.

OLIVIA: He was just one. I've known men.

   (MUSIC CONTINUES underneath scene. Suggested, segue into jazz instrumental set, suggested jazz flute or piano.)

CASSIE: YOU EVER BEEN IN LOVE?

OLIVIA: I've been in love with the idea, I just didn't have a person in mind.

CASSIE: It's just another concept with you ain't it? Well 'pacifically, what kind of man would you be in love with—IF you had a person in mind?

OLIVIA: Well, specifically…he'd have to be well-educated, a family man, and owning his own business would be nice.

CASSIE: Barbie, so far you describing Ken.

OLIVIA: What d'ya expect? I don't have a particular person—Ok. He'd be gentle. I know. My best friend. He'd have to be. I believe that's what most women are looking for, someone to laugh with, and to cry with—

CASSIE: That's the one thing we agree on. He'd have to keep me laughing. I like to laugh, and I don't too much on my own. *(OLIV tries to re-enter the conversation)* Were you finished?

OLIVIA: *(surrendering)* Cry with me— You go right ahead.

CASSIE: He'd have to take care of me, cause I can be po' by myself. And Kevin would have to like him—a lot. And he'd have to be good when and where he supposed to be good. And if he gon' be good as much as I want him to be, he probably gon' have to be younger than me—bout five or ten years. I don't want no baby. And it be real nice if he had big hands and big feet.

OLIVIA: Why is that?

CASSIE: Sugar. Didn't you and your sister ever talk about men?

OLIVIA: Of course we talked about men.

CASSIE: Well what she tell you about a man's feet?

OLIVIA: His feet? Oh, yes, yes. She used to say,—wait, let me do it. *(hand on hips, finger swinging)* "If he doesn't have clean shoes, then he better not even come to pick me up."

CASSIE: But what about the feet in the shoes.

OLIVIA: The feet?

CASSIE: Didn't she tell you that you could tell the size of—. By looking at the size of a man's hands, and his feet—I'm losing you fast ain't I? Well, I hope your man has clean shoes. And I hope mine has nice big feet. Now, Kevin's Daddy—

(CASSIE amuses herself mimicking his big feet. During this, OLIVIA catches on to the innuendo.)

OLIVIA: I was wondering about him? Kevin's daddy?

CASSIE: What was you wondering?

OLIVIA: Right now, I'm wondering—*(mimicking big feet)* why aren't you with him?

CASSIE: Cause he's Kevin' Daddy, and not my husband.

OLIVIA: Yes, but, didn't you love him?

CASSIE: Oh, I felt a lot of things for him—lust—and lust— and lust. But not love until he was long gone. At first, the thought of him made my heart beat fast—made me nauseous. But that, like the thrill of morning sickness got played out real quick. I had been taking care of somebody all my life it seemed. After M'dear and Mikey, baby was one thing—but husband—that was another. Kevin was five months when his daddy left. I remember cause I was feeding him and he was beginning to teethe. He kept pulling on my breasts hard to make me look at him. And one day I did; all my ugly empty feelings had passed through me and made something beautiful. I figured what me and his daddy had couldn't've been all bad. He in Connecticuit now with a family of his own. He ain't rich, but he send me something for Kevin now and again. He trying.

OLIVIA: That's what I feel I'm missing...motherhood, family.

CASSIE: In due time. Don't be in no rush to give it up.

OLIVIA: Give what up?

CASSIE: To give up part of yourself. That's the only way you gon' love somebody.

OLIVIA: I don't think you have to give up anything—

CASSIE: Shh—, don't try to think while grown folks is talking. What you say M'dear? *(Oliv gets ready to speak)* Sh-sh, she's talking. *(listens)* Uhm-hm., uhm, hm. Got it. *(To OLIV)* Like she say, women, we go through phases. And we ain't just talking 'bout menopause; it's more than that.

OLIVIA: What does she mean then?

CASSIE: First there's birth. Then after that, it's from one half life to another. We always trying to hold on to half cause at every turn a woman is always giving something up.

OLIVIA: I haven't lost anything in becoming a woman.

CASSIE: Sure you have. We all do. Why you think they call it "losing your virginity." Before that you lose your innocence.

OLIVIA: How is "innocence" any different?

CASSIE: 'Cause once you been hurt you know you can be hurt again. And even that virginity is a tricky thing. You walk around your nose wide open and think you can't lose it again. But since your blossom first been picked, ain't you never felt like there's a man out there who could re-arrange your stems?

OLIVIA: But I still don't think of falling in love as a loss. You gain a new perspective on your life. You discover new sides—

CASSIE: Gain how? You start thinking of yourself, as "somebody's girlfriend," "Somebody's lover," "Somebody's wife." And that's what you become— "somebody who got to be attached to somebody to be a woman."

OLIVIA: I surely would argue with that.

CASSIE: Argue all you want. It's true. Then, you become "somebody's mama." *(Twilight Zone theme)* Do-do-do-do. Now, I love Kevin. But once you have a kid, you lose control of seventeen, eighteen years of your life. That's if you a good mother. What you need becomes second. See what I mean, holding on to half a life?

OLIVIA: There you're wrong! Not allowing your child to run your life is as much a part of being a good mother—

CASSIE: Look, you talking that Mr. Spock mess; I'm talking the way it be. See M'dear, I told you she wouldn't listen. Then, you hit forty—almost half a century. Damn that sound old. Anyway, you think you should have it all together, but you don't; cause all your life, you been operating with half a deck.

OLIVIA: I'm not forty, I wouldn't know.

CASSIE: You close enough to feel the chill. And THEN, and I only know this cause M'dear told me, you hit menopause. The mind is willing but the body cain't. And I don't even have to say no more 'bout that. From there on, you operating with spares. Spare teeth, spare hair—looking for that miracle cream to turn back the clock.

OLIVIA: It's funny if it's not true.

CASSIE: It's funny to you now!

OLIVIA: Sounds like it's all down hill from birth.

CASSIE: I suppose it would be, except for the half your innocence that remains. It keep you believing in the rightness of things. So you figure, if things gon' be what they will, somewhere, somehow, I'll be whole again!. I just hope it ain't when I'm in a hole six feet under.

(THEY LAUGH.)

CASSIE: I make up a lot off that off the top of my head; but M'dear knows when I'm lying and she quiet now, cause I'm telling the truth.

OLIVIA: If it's not true, it's something to think about.

CASSIE: Thank you. Yeah it is. I got a lot up here thinking about. I always figured I'd do something important with it too. When I was a kid doing days work? Now remember, I was just a kid. I'd sit in them fancy rooms on them plush sofas conducting interviews with my vacuum hose microphone. See, I figured I'd be somebody important—like Oprah Winfrey. *(a la Oprah)* "Today we talk with 'Men who don't like women who like women who like men." What you think girlfriend?" Or I was I was gon' be a reporter like Jackie Onassis. She was a reporter. You didn't know that did you?

OLIVIA: No.

CASSIE: Yeah. That's how she met Jack. Going around reporting and taking pictures with her Kodak, "click, click." I figured I'd meet me somebody like that too.

OLIVIA: A president?

CASSIE: Naaw, he didn't have to be no president. I would prefer someone with steady work. Four to eight years, I don't call that steady. Maybe a doctor or lawyer...I had a good prospect too, once.

OLIVIA: Really? What happened?

CASSIE: He said, "Cass, I be the last one to let you down." —OH! Swept me off my feet. Then I found out the Negro was an undertaker. With my luck, they'd find a cure for death. Lord, my mouth drowning out the music. Come on Miss Ann! Get yourself up on this dance floor, and let me sit you back down. Don't you ever get loose girlfriend?

OLIVIA: Yes, I get loose when I go to the islands!

(SHE DANCES. CASSIE JOINS HER IN A SHOW-OFF.)

CASSIE: Your mind may be in some island, but your body's in Georgia without a basic bone in it. Pitiful.

(THEY DANCE A WHILE.)

CASSIE: See, I told you, you can't hang.

OLIVIA: Can't hang? I hang so tough, coat hanger is my middle name.

CASSIE: Coat hanger! Lord chile, save the comedy for them what invented it.

OLIVIA: Oh I know comedy honey. *(picks up imaginary "walkman" imitating Cassie from Act I encounter)* "I carry my own, and its a San-Suee; and that's Jap-o-nese, in case you did not know it."

CASSIE: *(still laughing, the drinking begins to take over)* Oh finally, I get my free association.

OLIVIA: You got it.

CASSIE: You think you the only one what can play dress up? *(she now affects her sense of "highbrow")* Boulez, vous coujay a bic moi?

(OLIVIA continues laughing.)

CASSIE: *(cont.)* If I want your opinion I'll give it to you, damn it. If I could figure out where it is. Probably in the damn box you moved.

OLIVIA: *(continuing the "free association")* You tole me I could move the dog-gone boxes.

CASSIE: *(fakes a Mary Tyler Moore tantrum)* Mr. Grant, make them stop laughing. I swear by Pat Boone I'm hip.

(OLIV laughs again.)

(THE TWO ARE NOW OBVIOUSLY HIGH FROM THE DRINK. THEY TALK without REALLY hearing one another.)

OLIVIA: Oops, one of us has had too much Nick At Night.

CASSIE: Are we talking without permission again? *(fakes German accent)* You vill not listen. You must be punished.

OLIVIA: *(Holding the bottle of liquer, pouring as she speaks)* I'm working on that.

CASSIE: *(She is brimming with liquor and the emotions of the day. She crosses to the office door and begins to take in the evening)* Ain't this a picture Delphine? You and me ringing out the old and ringing out the old— Who would believe it? Three, four hours ago, you didn't even know my name.

(The truth of what she is saying begins to resonate for her.)

OLIVIA: *(lost in her drink)* Right now, I don't even know my name. *(Olivia fiddles with the dial)* This music is too mellow, too sentimental, let's pump it up—

CASSIE: You didn't even know my name. Alley Children didn't have no names. Still don't do they? *(Shouts out door)* IT'S CASSIE CHARLES!

(OLIVIA is jolted into sobriety by CASSIE's shout and sudden change of mood. OLIVIA TURNS THE RADIO "OFF.")

(MUSIC CUE OUT).

CASSIE: Let's close the door and keep the Alley children outta of your office. Sorry, your "home." *(whispers)* When I was a kid—I used to hear the kids a coupla blocks over singing, " We don't play with the Alley children." Did you think we didn't have ears? *(OLIV watches silently)* Yeah, and dreams! But only made your stomach hurt more when you thought about what you didn't have. The Good Humour man wouldn't even come down my block. Hell, I wouldn't have gone down there, if I didn't have to.

Alright, alright, I'll 'fess up. Since I been here, I had one dream that made me feel good. I was down on my knees like this, polishing my floors slick. Then I'd see you coming around the corner in them $100 spikes you call "shoes" and slip, fall flat on your perfect behind and finally, we would be eye to eye! And today it happened. What'd ya know? Dreams do come true.

You know, I figure it takes about as many years to make a good cleaning lady; I mean one that can play free association with you, as it takes a good account executive to get her name on the door. Only difference tween you and me is time and a title.

OLIVIA: I'm sorry Cassie. I didn't mean to—

CASSIE: Don't be sorry, ain't nothin' been said. Tommorow you won't remember nothing but the hang-over. 'Nothing but New Year's Eve and that bottle over there talking. So keep your sorry for yourself. See, that's another difference tween you and me; I got my pride, but you sugar, you just going through the motions.

OLIVIA: Why are you so hard, Cassie—?

CASSIE: Cause I have to be, can't count on you. You talk about being a role model for somebody, but you booking and leaving Carlyle to mess with somebody else's mind. I'd be a sad case if I was looking for you to cover my back—

OLIVIA: Cassie, you can't expect me to stay here. I don't owe you anything.

CASSIE: The hell you don't. Do you think you woulda made it to the top floor, if you didn't have thousand of Cassie's with "no names" to remind you of what you was running from? I DON'T CARE HOW MANY LETTERS YOU GOT BEHIND YOUR NAME, Carlyle ain't gon' let you think you nobody, if I don't. Why you get an office and think you any different, any better than me? Just cause you can use big words don't mean you dealing, sugar. Just mean you got a vocabulary. Shit, I can buy a dictionary!

OLIVIA: I don't have to answer to you for all the years I have put in this place that I won't ever see again.

CASSIE: Naw, you don't. But tell that to your sister. Tell that to your daddy. That po' man is probably turning over in his grave!

OLIVIA: You leave my family out of this!

CASSIE: You the one brought 'em in here. That wasn't just your name on the door, Olivia Williams. Isn't that your sister's name, "WILLIAMS"? Your daddy's name? When you took your name off that door, their's came down right along with it. This office cost you your family. I sure as hell would fight for it if it was mine.

OLIVIA: Then get off my back and fight for your family. You, fight for Kevin.

CASSIE: I've been fighting for him all his life!

OLIVIA: Fighting for him how? Is he going to have to quit school in the fourth grade to take care of you?

CASSIE: Back off.

OLIVIA: If you die tomorrow, Cassie, all you're going to leave him is a mop and a vacuum.

CASSIE: I can take care of my son.

OLIVIA: Right. Your son. I'm sorry. I forgot that's who you are "somebody who's always taking care of somebody;" and now it's your son. Who's taking care of you, Cassie? You've been so busy working, trying to convince yourself you don't deserve a life, you didn't even feel it when you gave up! You didn't even feel it when you just stopped living your own life.

CASSIE: I'm forty-one years old.

OLIVIA: I'm thirty-one.

CASSIE: I got a little boy.

OLIVIA: I have—this office.

CASSIE: I ain't got no daddy holding my hand telling me everything is gon' be'—

OLIVIA: Neither do I.

CASSIE: I don't have no degree.

OLIVIA: I don't own this company.

CASSIE: Starting over?

OLIVIA: Yes. No difference Cass.

CASSIE: Then you tell me how?

OLIVIA: I don't know. *(beat)* I never joined those sororities in school, because I didn't know what to expect going over on line. But look at where we are now. You're on one side and I'm on the other; I don't suppose either side of the line is easy.

CASSIE: I'm forty-one years old.

OLIVIA: That's not exactly ancient, you know.

(THE TWO SIT IN THE SILENCE.)

OLIVIA: *(cont.)* You believe in New Year's Resolutions?

CASSIE: I don't put no stock in such things.

OLIVIA: Maybe cause you never had anyone to keep you honest. You have your lighter?

CASSIE: What we gon do "resolve"—to burn the building down?

OLIVIA: *(giving Cassie a pad and pen)* You are going to write your resolutions, and I'll write mine.

CASSIE: I don't know what to write. You ain't doing so good either. Can't we just sing happy birthday and call it a night? *(beat)* Just suppose I quit my job.

OLIVIA: Just suppose, hum,hm. *(OLIV begins to write)*

CASSIE: What else could I do? I don't know anything else, and Mickey Dee's out of the question.

OLIVIA: Just suppose.

CASSIE: I'm not thinking of nothing; cleaning is all I know.

OLIVIA: Then stop thinking so hard, and open your eyes.

CASSIE: Meaning?

OLIVIA: Meaning, doesn't this firm hire you through some kind of maintenance service?

CASSIE: And?

OLIVIA: And, why couldn't you have your own maintenance service?

CASSIE: I couldn't do that.

OLIVIA: Right, you couldn't do that.

CASSIE: Why couldn't I do that? I could do that. This fairy tale mess has gone to both of our heads.

OLIVIA: Cass, you gotta start somewhere. Maybe this year, you get your GED. Maybe next year you could start supervising some of the crews around here.

CASSIE: Why I gotta wait until next year? Next year. I may as well be runnin' it now.

OLIVIA: Okay, Okay. Before next year.

CASSIE: Who says I HAVE to have a GED? I'm good with numbers. Long as I get them right on a page, I can have my business.

OLIVIA: Okay. Okay.

CASSIE: I'll go to school, if I have to—

OLIVIA: Whatever you say, just right it down.

CASSIE: How many years can I put on this paper?

OLIVIA: As many as you want, this is our ceremony.

CASSIE: Ceremony? La-dee-dah .

OLIVIA: *(foldings her resolution)* Hurry. Fold yours up and meet me at the quartz conversation piece that looks like an ashtray. You have your lighter? *(CASS STANDS beside OLIV sitting on the floor)* I suppose the sorors said something official sounding before they went over on line.

CASSIE: Sorors? You and me? Well pinch me hard. *(She sits beside her)*

OLIVIA: You first. *(CASS hesitates)* Just say what ever comes to mind. *(OLIVIA begins to burn her resolutions CASS follows suit, speaking:)*

CASSIE: This is for the sisters on the other end of the line. Those here and far away, too. I suppose you had to say something official sounding?

OLIVIA: Yes.

CASSIE: Well?

OLIVIA: Sometimes—sometimes, I still need so badly to look into a face that isn't mine and feel eyes like mine—or to hear a voice that could touch—

CASSIE: like mine—

OLIVIA: Like mine.

CASSIE: Sometimes, I need somebody to hold me back, when my arms are tired.

OLIVIA: And tell me everything is going to be alright.

CASSIE: And what's not right has a place, too.

OLIVIA: That's the part that's hard.

CASSIE: Sometimes, I wish you could look at me as if I was your sister coming through that door after all these years.

OLIVIA: The last time I saw my sister, I almost didn't recognize the face that looked like mine staring back at me; there were so many things we both wanted to say to each other. Daddy taught us a lot of things but that, we didn't know how. It's not just you Cassie. *(beat)* Cass, what you said before?

CASSIE: Which I said before?

OLIVIA: We couldn't be bound to walk around with just half a life—

CASSIE: You mean a man? That better half nonsense?

OLIVIA: No I don't mean that. A man does complement you. But the other "half" has got be another "half." It's sort of like looking in that mirror your grandmother talked about and seeing yourself made whole again. Like me looking at you.

CASSIE: Maybe so...maybe so. How did the "going over" end?

OLIVIA: I think they must have said a final word of some sort.

CASSIE: We used to say a benediction at the end of church...let's see..."Blest be the tie—

OLIVIA/CASSIE: *(joining in)*—the tie that binds.

CASSIE: Amen, I guess.

OLIVIA: Yes, Amen.

CASSIE: No, party...no having fun?

OLIVIA: Yes, I suppose there was a party.

CASSIE: Well tell me the good stuff too.

OLIVIA: So now we party.

CASSIE: One thing?

OLIVIA: Yes?

CASSIE: What did you write down on that piece of paper, your resolutions?

OLIVIA: I had ten.

CASSIE: Can't you tell me one, or does that jinx it?

OLIVIA: I suppose not, if I don't have to speak it out aloud.

CASSIE: Well?

(OLIV pretends to lean in to whisper to CASS.)

(Then, mimicking the "big foot" scene from earlier, she proceeds to take gargantuan strides around CASS.)

OLIVIA: Ooo-Baby, baby.

CASSIE: Why you little tramp! Shoot, I didn't know we could promise to have fun too.

OLIVIA: How bout a little music for our party.

(OLIV XES to desk and reaching for the tape player/radio; she reaches instead for the telephone.)

CASSIE: Oh sure, you'll be having fun, while I'm working my butt off for some maintenance service. I'm going to own. That's dirty pool from a rookie *(she sees fireworks for the first time)* Hmph, pi-ti-ful. Fools shooting fireworks in all this mess.

(THE LIGHT FROM FIREWORKS PAINT HER FACE.)

CASSIE: *(looking at fireworks)* I don't get into that Patrick Henry stuff, but ain't that the fourth of July or what?

(OLIV has dialed and now observed by CASS talks on the phone.)

OLIVIA: This is Olivia. Happy New Year. I guess you're out. I'm out too. It's been a long night. I know you're surprised to here from me, but I'll call you tomorrow. Bye. Diana, We need to —*(hangs up)*—talk. *(acknowledging Cassie's presence)* Answering machines are taking over the world!

CASSIE: Yeah. Get your coat. *(she crosses to the door)*

OLIVIA: My coat? Why?

CASSIE: You were doing so good. Don't get silly on me now.

(OLIV XES to window.)

OLIVIA: Oh, the fireworks. How Pretty! Happy New Y—oh, the traffic is moving! Cass, the traffic—

CASSIE: I KNOW. Get your coat!

OLIVIA: Oh, my coat. Yes. *(Cass EXITS into hallway)* I got my coat...I got my coat.

(THEY MOVE TOWARD THE DOOR.)

CASSIE: AND GET YOUR KEYS!

OLIVIA: Oh, of course, my keys *(she crosses to retrieve her purse)*

(THEY BEGIN TO EXIT. OLIV stops in doorway staring into office.)

CASSIE: You got to have duckets to start a business.

OLIVIA: Wait a minute.

(OLIV returns to her desk and pulls out an object, yet undetectable to the audience. The night and the years come back to her. Almost sacredly. OLIVIA returns her name plate to the door.)

(Then, as if shorning a shroud, she takes off her straight haired "wig" and her braids fall around her shoulders. She places the wig in a packed box.)

OLIVIA: Now we can go home, "sister." *(she begins to sing as they X to the elevator).*

CASSIE: Well, how about it? The duckets? After tonight, you know where I live?

OLIVIA: *(Sings.)* I'm every woman, it's all in me.

(OLIVIA keeps singing in answer.)

CASSIE: I mean with your promotion and everything.

(THEY REACH THE ELEVATOR. Push the button.)

OLIVIA/CASSIE: *(sings)* Anything you want done baby, I'll do it naturally. I'm every woman, it's all in me

(THE ELEVATOR LIGHT POINTING "UP" COMES ON. The women respond with laughter.)

(BLACK OUT.)

(SUGGESTED CURTAIN CALL, "I'm Every Woman" sung by Whitney Houston or Chaka Kahn; Suggested post performance, "Let's All Live Together" sung by Patti Austin.)

Nubia Kai

HARVEST THE FROST

Penumbra Theatre Company

Nubia Kai

Nubia Kai is a poet, playwright, and novelist who has been published in *Black World, Journal of Black Poetry, Black Scholar, Solid Ground, Obsidian, Black American Literature Forum, Quilt Catalyst, Black Books Bulletin, City Arts Quarterly*, and numerous other magazines, journals, and anthologies. Some of her plays have been published in *New Plays From the Black Theatre*, edited by Woodie King, Jr., and *Roots and Blossoms*, edited by Daphnew Williams-Ntiri. She has also published two books of poetry, *Peace of My Mind* and *Solos*, and a collection of fables and folktales for children, *The Sweetest Berry on the Bush*. Ms. Kai has received several writing awards, including two NEA (National Endowment for the Arts) awards, three Michigan Council for the Arts awards, three D.C. Commission for the Arts awards, three Tompkins awards, and two McCree Theatre awards. She has traveled widely in Africa doing research for a new book on the sacred history of African-Americans.

Her play *Parting* was first produced by Woodie King, Jr. at the New Federal Theatre in the summer of 1983. *Parting* also toured Michigan with Aldyanna Theatre Co. in 1988 and was produced at the Howard University Theatre Festival in the summer of 1992. *Harvest The Frost* was first produced by Penumbra Theatre in Minneapolis-St. Paul in October, 1984, and Woodie King directed the play in the summer of 1992 at ETA Theatre in Chicago.

PENUMBRA THEATRE COMPANY

The Penumbra Theatre Company was founded in 1976 by Artistic Director Lou Bellamy as the resident theatre company of the Hallie Q. Brown Community Center in Saint Paul.

Balancing the pursuit of artistic excellence in productions with the African American interests of Penumbra and the surrounding community has presented some unique challenges. The solution has been a mix of entertainment and educational opportunity presented in the community and for the community-at-large. Penumbra takes deliberate risks in choosing the plays for production. The subject matter of this work is often about the immediate community. Penumbra's commitment is vividly illustrated through the work produced on our mainstage, as well as such programs as the Understudy and Training Program and Summer Institute (programs for high school and college-age members of the community to study and work with company members), as well as the Cornerstone Dramaturgy and Development Project (an original play development project).

As a forum for the playwrights who strive to present alternatives to the majority view, Penumbra's Cornerstone Dramaturgy and Development Project provides the perfect blend of exciting talent and artistic support found in few places across the nation. The project participant, selected by committee, is awarded an in-residence workshop of the participant's piece with company members, the Playwrights' Center, and production of the original piece as part of the mainstage season. This process allows the playwright and company to further explore the depth and dimension of the new play. The first Cornerstone participant was Pulitzer Prize winner August Wilson.

Penumbra's goals are: to increase public awareness of the significant contributions that African Americans have made in creating a diversified American theatrical tradition; to encourage and facilitate a culturally diverse and all-inclusive America by using theatre to teach, criticize, comment, and model; to use theatre to create an American mythology that includes African Americans and other people of color in every thread of the fabric of our society; to redefine and expand the consciousness of our audiences and our theatrical communities to include a sympathetic and realistic portrayal of people of color; to encourage and facilitate a proactive approach toward the staging of plays that address the African American experience.; to increase the opportunities for audiences to view drama that falls within our raison d'etre by providing the only consistent professional platform for the illumination of the African American experience in drama in this region; to continue to maintain and stabilize a black performing arts community.

HARVEST THE FROST
An original script by
Nubia Kai

Directed by
Lou Bellamy

Cast in the Order of Appearance

Renson Blackman ....Claude Purdy
Grandpa Early ....Abdul Razzac
John Blackman ....Sherman Woods
Tracey Blackman ....Estelene Bell
Rayford Blackman ....Terry Bellamy
Kwame Hakimu Kemit Mtu
  (s.n. Renson Blackman, Jr.) ....James A. Williams
Amelia Grice ....Charlotte McGregor
Nancy Blackman ....Tia Mann-Evans

Act I
The Blackman Home early Saturday evening.

INTERMISSION

Act II
Scene 1: One week later.
Scene 2: 2 days later.

HARVEST THE FROST

Troublin is seasonin. "Simmons ain good til the frost hit em."—Plantation
  Proverb

CHARACTERS:

RENSON BLACKMAN: Early fifties. Master auto mechanic and business-
  man. Intelligent, honest, generous, compassionalte.

NANCY BLACKMAN: Forty nine. The estranged wife. Very attractive,
  medium height, affectionate.

KWAME KAKIMU KEMIT MTU (s.n. Renson Blackman Jr.) Thirty.
  Oldest child of Renson and Nancy. Tall, handsome, wears dreadlocks or
  Afro, earing and African clothes. Very culturally and politically con-
  scious.

GRANDPA EARLY: Renson's father. Mid-seventies. Tall, slim, well-
  dressed, street wise, stubborn.

RAYFORD BLACKMAN: Twenty-nine. Slight build, self-pitying, bitter,
  obnoxious, alcoholic, highly dramatic.

TRACEY BLACKMAN: Twenty four. Confused, defensive, slightly selfish
  but open minded enough to mature.

JOHN BLACKMAN: Eighteen. Athletic build, liveley, kind-heated, gentle.

AMELIA GRICE: Mid-forties. Attractive divorsee looking for love.

TWO MOVING MEN.

ACT I

Set in 1982, the home of the Blackman family. Center stage is a large living
  room with a long couch, matching leather chairs, glass top cocktail table
  and lamptables. Magazine rack sits next to the couch. Telephone sits on
  large lamp table between the two sofa chairs. Small bar covered with
  bottles of liquor and glasses is four or five feet behind living room and
  divides the living room from the dining room area.

To the right of the living room is the front door, next to it, the front closet
  and dining area. At the rear of the dining room is a stairway leading
  upstairs.

Two steps lead from the left of the living room into a modern kitchen. Wood
  paneled cabinets surround the walls; round table; matching chairs are in
  the center of the kitchen' counter and sink are to the left of the two steps;
  refridgerator to the left of the stove.

Between the bar and the kitchen is a long panel or wall dividing the living
  area from the downstairs bedrooms and bathroom.

SCENE I

*(Early Saturday evening during the first week in November, Detroit. The liv-
ingroom. Grandpa Early stuffs his pipe, sitting in the chair closest to the bar.
Renson, sitting in the chair on the other side of the lamptable thumbs through
the sports section of the newspaper.)*

RENSON: Look like the frost comin tonight.

GRANDPA EARLY: *(Lighting his pipe casually, crossing legs.)* Frost come every
  night round here. Frost don't come cause do temperatute drop. Frost
  come to make the persimmons sweet.

RENSON: *(Looks baffled, ponders, putting down paper.)* Your wisdom whips
  around my head like a boomerang. You too swift for me. What kinda
  frost are you talking about, the bitter or the sweet?

GRANDPA EARLY: Don't see why you can't fit it in yo maind that it's both.
  Ever see persimmons grew? Sho, don't you member? We had a tree
  right out in the yard in Prairieview. After do frost come in dey wasn't
  ripe dey was bitter.

RENSON: That was so long ago I can barely remember.

GRANDPA EARLY: Well I'm here to remind you.

RENSON: *(Smiling.)* Yes suh, wise father.

GRANDPA EARLY: *(Pointing his finger.)* Looka dere, you ain't broke do frost
  from your face like that in a long time.

RENSON: Aww cmon, we be crackin jokes and signifying all day busting my
  ribs—

GRANDPA EARLY: *(Cutting him off.)* Ye-ah but bustin yo ribs ain't the same as
  a smile. Laughs might come from a joke but a smile come from joy, from

down in the heart. Nah I ain't knockin laughin. Laughin food fo de soul and it flush out de tightness in your limbs and muscles, but—

RENSON: *(Finishing his sentence.)* It don't mean that a man's happy.

GRANDPA EARLY: Right.

RENSON: And smiling does?

GRANDPA EARLY: Umm, I think so, if he smile a lot. Seem to me the man that smile a lot is happy, while the man that laugh a lot really ain't.

RENSON: I see your point.

GRANDPA EARLY: You been mopein and carryin the frost since Nancy left. It's good to see you smile now and then.

RENSON: Does that mean I'm getting better?

GRANDPA EARLY: I hope so for yo sake.

RENSON: Didn't know I was lookin that bad.

GRANDPA EARLY: Didn't know? You make this house shiver so many dead ghosts comin outta you. The woman's been gone almost a year and you still mopein.

RENSON: *(Depressed, gets up, paces the floor.)* Hasn't exactly been the best year of my life. It's been one of the hardest.

GRANDPA EARLY: Been hard fo everybody. My arthritis been botherin me more than ever.

RENSON: Junior...I mean Kwame said if—

GRANDPA EARLY: *(Angrily.)* You said it right the first time—Junior. Named after his own daddy and then go and change it to some funny soundin African name.

RENSON: I been thinkin about changing my name to Kwame Sr. since I was born on Saturday too.

GRANDPA EARLY: *(Standing up, indignant, fist balled at his side.)* I know you done lost yo fool mind. Over my dead body you'll change your name.

RENSON: *(Looking back over his shoulder.)* Sure will. The pride in a man don't count when his head is cold.

GRANDPA EARLY: Man better have pride bout somethin.

RENSON: Maybe that's the same way Kwame feels about havin a slave name. What's that to be proud of? When I thought about it I realized I felt the same way myself. A man's name oughta say who he is, what he is, his character, his nationality and clan and special gifts and all that. Look at how we came by the name Blackman. Wasn't that—

GRANDPA EARLY: *(Fixes a drink at the bar.)* I know how we came by de name Blackman *(Narrowing his eyes)*, you ain't gotta remind me bout family pride and none a dat. You need to remind yourself to respect your father and your father's name. You know what it means for a man to have sons to carry on his name and he go and change it?

RENSON: *(Passionate, plaintive.)* Change is necessary. Change is motion. Change is life. Everyday you live you change. And what you sayin ain't true cause I have a son named after me and I don't feel that way.

GRANDPA EARLY: *(Sipping drink.)* Naw, you gone up and change yours and break yo old Daddy's heart.

RENSON: Your wisdom whips around your head like a boomerang too or you're just being stubborn.

GRANDPA EARLY: Don't tell me I'm stubborn like I'm yo child.

RENSON: *(Apologetic.)* I'm sorry. I guess my philosphy is simple. I call a man what he wants me to call him. That's paying him his respects, givin him his propers. If he wants me to call him by a crazy nickname that's what I'll call him. If Kwame don't wanna be called by his slave name—

RENSON: Slave names...slave names...Yuh sound like you just come out de fields. Don't much know what slavery is. I use to split rails fo twenty-five cents a day from sun-up to sundown when we first move to Arkansas. Befo dat we pick cotton all day and part the night down in the Delta and come up owing the boss every year and even that was a vacation compare to what my grandpa had to do. I don't 'preciate you callin my name a slave name cause I done told you a thousand times Blackman ain't no slave name.

Grandpa's master name was Elmer Kayes White, the dirtiest dog in Mississippi. Grandpa Joseph change his name to Blackman soon as de war come, and he run off and join de union army. He say, "what he look like black coal callin hisself Mr. White after a man lower that a suck egg dog. So he call hisself 'Blackman' cause he was proud to be a Black man and proud to be free. Whole lots of Black men that runaway change dey names tight dere in de camps to 'Freeman' and 'Mr. Brown,' 'Mr. Black.' 'Mr. Smith' come from lots a dem blacksmiths. Most smiths was Black slaves den so they take de name 'Smith.' And Jounson come from John de Conqueror and John who give de Book of Revelation. Folks back then say dey was de same spirit.

RENSON: *(Amazed.)* No kiddin? *(Pause, expressive.)* Now you ain't never told me that part of the history. But don't you see that's exactly the same idea Kwame's expressing four generations later. And check it out, Kwame Kakimu Kemit Mtu still means Black man—wise Black man, born on Saturday. I dig that, man.

GRANDPA EARLY: *(Swallowing drink.)* I don't give a damn what it mean.

RENSON: *(Admonishing gently.)* That's a selfish attitude.

GRANDPA EARLY: *(Whips around, snaps back.)* Don't tell me it's a selfish attitude. You de one ain't got no pride. No wonder Nancy slip off—

RENSON: *(Taking a step towards Grandpa Early, furious, raws his hands.)* Quiet! Be quiet! *(Grandpa Early rears up, straightens his shoulders and glares at his* *son.) (Frustrated.)* Hey, look, I'm sorry for hollerin ar you, but how much you think I can take?

GRANDPA EARLY: *(Apologetic, lowering his gaze, releasing his shoulders.)* I shouldn't of said that...It just come out—should think befo I speak...and well you know how my tongue gits loose once I go tuh drinkin.

RENSON: *(Turns away from Grandpa, sad, annoyed, hurt; stands with back to him.)* You said what you felt.

GRANDPA EARLY: *(Apologetic, puts down his drink.)* Look...ah...ah ain mean to git you upset, son. I'm just an old fool with a bag full of wiseacreing tricks. A wise man ain't got much to say, let 'lone put his foot in it. I want you to know I can feel what you goin through. Why I member when yo Mama and me got in a fight and she went and took yall to Aunt Jessica's house. Member? Wasn't gone longer than a month but I thought I was gonna lose my mind. Lawd, if that woman hadn't come back to me I dunno what I would a done. Probably end up on the corner wid de rest of dem winoes. She was a good woman to put up with me all dem years.

RENSON: *(Half-bitter, glances over his shoulder.)* That's all a good woman is to you—one who puts up with you? *(Turns around.)* She was good cause she was sweet, kind, and gentle and full of love. She deserved to get some of it back, not to be patted on the head and told she a good woman cause she put up with yo shit!

(Grandpa Early stares shockingly at Renson. Renson sits on the edge of the couch, picks up a pack of cigarettes and lights up.)

GRANDPA EARLY: *(Insulted, hurt.)* Whadda you mean she deserved to get some of it back, hard as I worked to keep food on de table and make a good home—

RENSON: You were a good provider but you could have provided more love.

GRANDPA EARLY: *(Resentful.)* What the hell do you think love is?

RENSON: It's not money, Daddy. It's not *(Pulls coin from his pocket and slams it on the cocktail table.)* handin somebody some money. You know that.

GRANDPA EARLY: *(Proud, head held high, defensive.)* I loved your mother more than you'll ever know. *(Firm.)* She knew that. She knew I loved her and needed her and she swore when she came back from Aunt Jessica's that time that she'd never leave me agian.

RENSON: What you do, make her swear?

GRANDPA EARLY: *(Very angry.)* What de hell you mean did I make her!—

RENSON: You gave the orders. She obeyed you just like a servant.

GRANDPA EARLY: Woman spose to obey her husband. She was a good woman. She wouldn't—

RENSON: Obey you? Why she gotta obey you?

GRANDPA EARLY: Gawd say in de Bible de woman spose—

RENSON: *(Waving his hand no.)* Uh-unh, naw, God ain't said that. That's some of King James' stuff. God is right here *(Points to his heart.)* and he hasn't said that to me.

GRANDPA EARLY: *(Pours another drink.)* Must not be listening good. If you hadda listened you might not be cryin de blues now.

RENSON: So what are you sayin, that Nancy slipped around on me cause I didn't put a harness on her, like you put on Mama? I don't need that—

GRANDPA EARLY: *(Hostile, angry, loud.)* You've got no right to speak to me about how I treated my wife!!

RENSON: She was my mother.

GRANDPA EARLY: *(Bitter.)* I don't care if she was your mother. She was my wife and I was a good man to her. Don't know why you wanna tear into my marriage like a ravin wolf. Just cause yours didn't work don't give you no license to take vengeance on me!

RENSON: I don't agree with your philosophy on women. And I never like the way you ordered Mama around and never wanted her to go out, even with you.

GRANDPA EARLY: You yo Mama's child alright.

RENSON: You've always said that.

GRANDPA EARLY: Give a woman too much rope and she hang herself. Look at what happen to Nancy. Just look at these young wild gals today.

RENSON: You think that's why she started seein that guy? Cause she wasn't chained to the house like a dog, like a bitch? Nancy is a mature woman. She's forty-nine years old. Been married thirty years and has five grown children. She knew what she was doing; that was her choice.

GRANDPA EARLY: *(Sits down, drinks.)* Yeah, and it sure was a bad one. Woman is a whole lot different these days. I'd never believed Nancy' do somethin like that. She was a good woman, a good mother and good looking too. Had a beautiful marriage. Why she go and hang herself? And look, just look at the dead ghost lurking in the curtains and hurt and sufferin she done caused.

RENSON: *(Sad.)* She realizes that...more than any of us.

GRANDPA EARLY: Now that it's too late. Now that de home is wrecked. Good thing Tracey move back to cook de meals and clean up. This place was startin to feel like a burnt out shanty. Where is Tracey and the children? I ain't seen em all day.

RENSON: She ran away. As a matter of fact she said she's tired of cooking and cleanin up behind grown men and gotta take care of her kids and study for classes, so she took Jomo and Ebody up to Shay Lake to a friend's cottage for the weekend. And I don't blame her.

GRANDPA EARLY: She's your only girl, I expect you to spoil her.

RENSON: Spoil her?

GRANDPA EARLY: She...And you act like you tryin to make up to her for that lousy husband she got. Workin overtime to feed dem children and put her through school. Her old man oughta be doin that.

RENSON: The point is, he's not doing it. He didn't half support em while they were together. Whadda you think he's gonna do now?

GRANDPA EARLY: What makes you think she ain't seein him? I wouldn't be surprised if she with him right now. De way she carried on after you flattened him on the porch that day, I wouldn't be a bit surprised. She still loves that man. And long as she feel like that bout him, you can look for her to go runnin away—right back to him.

RENSON: I'm her old man now. As long as she's here or in need I gotta help her and my grandchildren. I don't mind helping her finish her education. I always thought she should have finished college before she got married and started her family. The way these young dudes are nowadays you can't tell what's gonna happen in a marriage.

GRANDPA EARLY: It's the times we livin in. (*Lights pipe.*) Everything's fallin apart. Who woulda thought you and Nancy's break up after thirty years of one of the happiest marriages I ever seen. Seem like Gawd just cut yall from the same silk-cotton tree. How she could do that to you I'll never understand. You been gooder than gold to that woman.

RENSON: She's been gooder than gold to me.

GRANDPA EARLY: Sho she have. I ain't sayin she hasn't. That's why I can't understand why she go and take up with another man. I know that woman loved you. She been good to you.

RENSON: Maybe it's not meant for you to understand.

GRANDPA EARLY: Gettin saucy with me ain't gonna change it.

RENSON: (*Serious.*) I'm serious. I don't think you should try to understand; just accept it, like I've had to accept it.

GRANDPA EARLY: But you didn't accept it. That's why you gettin a divorce.

RENSON: (*Looking squarely at Grandpa, serious.*) I'm not sure about that.

GRANDPA EARLY: (*Puffs on his pipe, scoots to the edge of chair, curious.*) What you mean, you ain't so sure?

RENSON: (*Soft.*) Just what I said. I want her back. I don't want a divorce. I want a marriage. I want my woman back. (*Pause.*) I asked her to come back two months ago. I asked her again last week.

GRANDPA EARLY: You mean you goin through that again? How many times you gotta forgive her to find out you can forgive her but you can't forget, and there's where the union goes sour.

RENSON: (*Slowly, contemplative.*) I can forget. I have forgotten. I want her back.

GRANDPA EARLY: You said that before. You say that with your mind and your mouth but your body says somethin different. Your body speak how you really feel. The proof of the puddin's in de tastin.

RENSON: She can taste me now. I been made sweeter by the frost, just like you say. She can taste this fruit.

GRANDPA EARLY: *(Narrowing his eyes.)* How you know she ain taken up with somebody else, or that she ain with…*(hesitant)*…him.

RENSON: You always think the worse. Frankly, I don't care if she is seein somebody else. I doubt if she's seein Malone cause I saw him a few weeks ago.

GRANDPA EARLY: Oh ye-ah? Where at?

RENSON: He came by the shop. Needed a new exhaust system.

GRANDPA EARLY: You mean that snake had de nerve to come to your place of business for you to wait on him after fuckin yo wife. I'd a taken a wrench and crowned him fool of de year. He taken you for a chump. A negger askin for a ass kickin when he go that far.

RENSON: He seemed surprised to see me since I'm usually at the bump shop. Besides, he knew he'd git quality work without getting cheated and that's a big drawing card in the auto mechanic business.

GRANDPA EARLY: Rationalize all you want. That man is messin with you, challengin yo manhod.

RENSON: *(Gets up, pours a drink.)* I'm not worried about Dr. Malone.

GRANDPA EARLY: *(Sarcastic, bitter.)* Doctor? That's a fart. Skunk don't make near as much money as you. Didn't make no more than Nancy. Cause he got a Ph. D he spose to be somebody special and don't make enough to send his own children to college. And this nigger spose to be so intelligent but ain intelligent enough to hook up his own exhaust or build his own business. Naw, he can talk about money and business but he ain't got de sense to put his hand in de dirt and build him somethin like you. What Nancy think, you wasn't good enough for her cause you sweat and get your hands greasy when your businesses are secure enough where you don't even have to do that?

RENSON: I don't think it was that. *(Leans against the bar, drinks.)*

GRANDPA EARLY: *(Intense, desparately wanting to know.)* Well, what was it? Was it because he was a younger man?

RENSON: *(Solemn.)* No. He was in love with her. She was attracted to him. I think it was the adventure of it…that made her…*(Pause.)* curious. After all, I was the first and only man she ever had.

GRANDPA EARLY: *(Embittered.)* So she decide she gone try somebody different—a man who just happen to be younger with a doctor's degree in Economics but can't make no money. Next you'll be tellin me it's alright for her to experiment with other men. What's to keep her from deciding she wanna experiment again?

RENSON: You throw stones pretty hard for somebody who didn't see nothin wrong with experimentin with other woman yourself.

GRANDPA EARLY: That was child's play. And I'm a man—

RENSON: And that's suppose to make it alright for you to run around but not her?

GRANDPA EARLY: *(Looking baffled but answering candidly.)* Yeah!

RENSON: You got a weird sense of justice. Believe they call it a double standard.

GRANDPA EARLY: Call it whatever you want. It ain't de same when a woman run around. She kill de home.

RENSON: Distrust and disloyalty kill the home whether it's a man or a woman. It ain't the same cause a woman is more inclined to forgive when a man won't. Just like I couldn't cause of my false pride. But I'm the one hurtin cause I love her and I want her back.

GRANDPA EARLY: Hogwash. You ain forget. You can forgive, but you can't forget. You ain't the first man I know that didn't have no more feelin for his wife after he caught her cheatin.

RENSON: I can forget! It's you that can't forget! And you sure didn't make it no better not speaking and glaring at her like she had on a scarlet letter.

GRANDPA EARLY: I didn't speak cause I din't have nothin to say.

RENSON: Naw, you so full of resentment for something you did yourself without a second thought. *(Grandpa Early cuts his eyes at him.)* You should be the most sympathetic.

GRANDPA EARLY: *(Angry.)* Well I'm not and I'm too old to pretend I am. Look at how she hurt you and all of us.

RENSON: I believe you're more concerned about your home cooked meals than anything.

GRANDPA EARLY: Buck me all you want. It was you couldn't get no fire in de poker, not me. Oughta quit lyin to yo'self. When a woman cheat on a man it ain't de same. Yo dick know what yo mind refuse to accept. Let bygones be bygones. I say you oughta go on wid de divorce. Stop torturin yo'self. Amelia's a nice lady, a fine lady. You a family man and you need a wife.

RENSON: Amelia's a nice lady, but she's not Nancy. And if she comes back I want you to respect her. However you feel about what she did, I want you to respect her just like you always did.

GRANDPA EARLY: *(Stands up.)* That's askin lots more than—

RENSON: *(Furious, shouting.)* I don't give a damn what you say! *(Demanding, stern.)* I'm sayin you have to respect her. I'm tellin *you*, you *have* to *respect* her, or you can move down on the corner with the winoes.

GRANDPA EARLY: *(Looks dry, stunned, shaken.)* Never thought I'd hear such disrespect comin from you. You act like I'm some kinda animal stead of your father. You scolding me bout other women—What about you? You ain't never took up with no other woman on the side? Most men have.

RENSON: *(Paces room.)* That doesn't make it justice cause everybody doing it.

GRANDPA EARLY: You ain't answered my question.

RENSON: (*Very serious.*) You may not believe this, but in the thirty years we've been together I've never been intimate with another woman.

GRANDPA EARLY: (*Throws head back.*) Ohh Jesus. (*Takes a seat.*)

RENSON: Does that make me a square, a chump? Hunh? Cause I don't chase women like other men when I don't even want to. Why should I pursue hamburgers when I got the choiciest steak? I never wanted another woman and I never felt less than a man cause I didn't. I don't have to chase skirts to prove something to myself. Lots of men chase women just for that—so they can feel like they're men based on popular definitions but never his own. Otherwise he shouldn't have to *feel* like a man. He'd be a man.

(*A key is heard turning in the front door. John, eighteen, muscular, energetic, ebullient comes in carrying a football helmet and sportsbag. Puts bag and helmet down by the door.*)

JOHN: (*Big smile.*) Hi!

RENSON: Hey John. How'd the game go? (*Smiles.*) Looks like you did okay.

JOHN: (*Boyishly ashamed but still cheerful.*) Naah—We lost. Plus I fumbled a pass on our ten yard line in the last four minutes of the game; their fullback intercepted and got a touch down. Up unitl then we were winnin 10-7. So the coach and everybody is pissed off at me. Lose one more and we blow the finals. It's tight. (*Comes in while talking and sits on the couch.*) So I'm laughin to keep from cryin. (*Raises Black power fist.*) Smilin to keep the spirit up. How you doin Grandpa Early?

GRANDPA EARLY: I'm doin. (*Sips drink.*) Congratulations!

JOHN: (*Surprised.*) Congratulations? (*Smiling.*) But we lost.

GRANDPA EARLY: I ain't congratulatin you for losing the game. I'm congratulatin you for comin in here lookin like a winner even when you fumbled the ball that caused yall to lose. Nah that's what I call havin the right spirit. (*Holds up glass.*) Here's to de Conqueror—my grandson. Yuh can't keep a good man down.

JOHN: (*Jokingly.*) Can I drink to that?

GRANDPA EARLY: Sho, I don't see why you can't. But I ain't yo Pa. I'm yo grandpa. You gotta ask him. (*Points to Renson.*)

JOHN: Naah, I was just kiddin. I want somethin cold. Any ice tea or pop in the refrigerator?

RENSON: I doubt if there's ice tea unless one of yall made some. Tracey went up to Shay Lake for the weekend.

JOHN: Aww, no fried chicken tomorrow.

RENSON: (*Chuckles.*) No woman, no fried chicken. Look at this mess. Three generations of Black men and none if us ever learned how to cook.

GRANDPA EARLY: Fried chicken ain't nothin to cook. All you gotta do is wash it off, cut it up, put some salt and pepper on it and fry it.

RENSON: *(Putting out a welcoming arm to Grandpa.)* There's your Sunday cook, John.

GRANDPA EARLY: Oh-no, not me. I didn't say I was gonna fry no chicken just cause I know how. I'm ah goin to the racetrack tomorrow. I ain't got time to be tied up in no kitchen. What bout you, Renson, you know how to fry chicken?

JOHN: Yeah, but can he make dressing, fried corn, greens, cornbread and sweet potato pie? I can go to Churches and get some fried chicken.

RENSON: Good idea!

GRANDPA EARLY: Yeah yall fo to Churches chicken for dinner. I'm goin to the races, and if I get lucky I'll take yall out to dinner next Sunday over at Mom's kitchen. Nah that's where we can get some sho nuff down home soul food.

RENSON: That still doesn't solve the problem we have of not knowin how to cook ourselves.

JOHN: You got a good point. What if a man decides he doesn't wanna get married or live with a woman. He's got to live out of restuarants the rest of his life? That food isn't good...not everyday.

RENSON: *(Steps into kitchen.)* I'm gonna learn how to cook somethin besides grits and eggs and fried chicken. *(Takes apple from fruit basket on table.)*

JOHN: When Tracey comin back? *(Drinks pop, then picks up sports magazine and thumbs through it, leg thrown across arm of couch.)*

RENSON: Sunday night I believe. She has a class Monday. You haven't seen Ray have you? *(Bites apple.)*

JOHN: No—Why? He hasn't come home yet?

RENSON: I haven't seen him in about three days.

GRANDPA EARLY: Me neither but I ain gon grow no gray hairs over it. The man is grown.

JOHN: With the mind of a child.

GRANDPA EARLY: Look who's talkin—The baby emself.

JOHN: Ray's my big brother and I love him, but he's got a problem.

RENSON: *(Pensive.)* We've got a problem—Ray.

GRANDPA EARLY: Depends on how much we try and carry his burden. We can't do it so ain no sense I tryin.

(Grandpa goes to closet, takes out stetson hat and overcoat.)

RENSON: Where you goin?

GRANDPA EARLY: *(Straightening his collar in the mirror inside the closet door; turns back.)* Who are you—my Daddy? I gotta report to you fo I leave de house?

RENSON: Cmon Daddy, just tryin tuh keep up with you. We a family.

GRANDPA EARLY: We a family but you ain't my Mama. I don't ask you where you goin.

RENSON: *(Pouting in jest.)* Maybe you don't love me no more.

GRANDPA EARLY: *(Firm but jokingly.)* Who said I ever loved you? Just cause I put food on yo table don't mean I love you, right? *(Grins.)*
(John looks at them and laughs.)

RENSON: Funny, ya know, while Nancy was here you use to let her know where you were goin without being asked.

JOHN: *(Abrupt, excited.)* I forgot to tell you, Daddy. Mama called last night. We talked for about two hours. I hadn't talked to her in a month. She wanted to talk to you but you hadn't come in. She said to call her.

RENSON: *(Surprised, excitement and joy subtly show in his expression.)* Wh... What time did she call?
(Grandpa stares with suspicion and disdain.)

JOHN: Round eight-thirty. *(Studies his father's expression.)*

GRANDPA EARLY: *(Clears his throat.)* Krrr-umph...I'm goin on down de road. If you just gotta know, Ma I'll be down at Sidney's house.

RENSON: *(Mimicing woman's voice.)* You be good son, and don't stay out too late and don't drink too much and please leave dem young gals alone. *(Grandpa Early rolls his eys at Renson and exits. Renson turns to John, chuckles.)* I don't think he liked that.

JOHN: *(Laughs.)* I don't either. *(Browses thorugh magazine, drinks pop.)*

RENSON: *(Hesitant, nervous, paces room.)* So...uh, how's your mother?

JOHN: *(Looks up from magazine, shrugs shoulders.)* Oh man, she's cool. Sounded wonderful to me. Maybe it's something about the air in Anchorage. Her voice just...went all through me. *(Gradually grows sadder, tears come in his eyes.)*

RENSON: *(Noticing John's discomfort.)* She say anything about...coming back to visit?

JOHN: Ye-ah...in fact, she said she was coming back for Kwame's graduation. Sure will be good to see her again. She's so far. *(Gloomy.)* Why she have to move so far? *(Breaks down crying.)*

RENSON: *(Watches sympathetically.)* You want her to come back, don't you? *(John nod, gets up, exits into bedroom on the left side of panel.)* John. John! *(John comes out of bedroom.)* *(Strong passion, gentle.)* It's alright. I understand.

JOHN: *(Gazing, blank-faced.)* If you understand...why you gettin a divorce?

RENSON: *(Walks towards John.)* What if I told you we may not be getting a divorce.

JOHN: Would it be a true statement?

RENSON: I hope so...it's up to your mother. I'm glad you feel the way you do about her coming back. That'll make it easier for her. Grandpa Early and Ray don't feel the same as you do.

JOHN: They got their own minds.

RENSON: I'm glad you've forgiven her.

JOHN: (Matter-of-factly.) Forgive her for what?

(Renson is stunned, visibly embarrassed at his patronizing attitude his son exposes; stares wide-eyed, motionless. John exits into bedroom. Renson takes seat and presses his hands against his forehead, disgustedly.)

(Suddenly loud arguing and cursing between a man and woman is heard outside the front door. Renson stands up; agitated to a fever pitch; paces area near the door.)

JOHN: (Looking up at Renson.) She'll be okay. Just a slight bruise over the left eye. If she was a football player it'd be minor. (Pause.) Guess that's not the best analogy...

TRACEY: (Spewing bitterly.) You're close. That's what he thinks I am, a damn football to be kicked around.

RENSON: (Whirling around, enraged.) Then why in the hell do you go back to him?! You like gettin kicked around?! You like gettin slapped upside the head?! I feel like a damn fool chasin that niggah when you (Points to Tracey) brought him to the door.

TRACEY: (Gets up shouting.) Well you don't have to chase him!! You don't have to chase him!!

RENSON: (Loud.) I'm not going to!! Why don't you just go back to him. You're not a teenager. You don't have to sneak around lying to me about going to spend the weekend at your girlfriend's.

TRACEY: (Spiteful.) No, I souldn't have to sneak if you didn't treat me like some teenager. You don't own me! I'm a grown woman and I see who I wanna see when I wanna see them. If I had told you I was going to spend the weekend with Cecil you would have bitched like hell! (Bold, forceful.) I don't like being put under pressure to where I have to lie.

RENSON: You're lying to yourself, Tracey.

TRACEY: Then let me lie to myself, if that's what I wanna do! Let me do it without having to answer to you.

RENSON: Where are the children?

TRACEY: Is that all you care about—the children? What about me?

RENSON: I care about them because they're not responsible for themselves.

TRACEY: (Desparate, emotional.) What about me?

RENSON: You're not responsible for yourself either, but you son't seem to recognize that, or else you don't care.

TRACEY: That's not what I mean.

RENSON: You think I don't care about you? That's the problem—I care too much, and it hurts me to see you waste your life on a stupid punk like that.

TRACEY: (*Defensive.*) You call him a punk?! One think Cecil isn't is a "punk." When he makes love to me better—

RENSON: (*Frowning, agitated.*) Makes love to you? Is that what you call makin love? Rammin your head in the fuckin door!

JOHN: (*Pleading.*) Hey, Daddy, she's already upset.

RENSON: (*Ignores John, raging.*) Is that makin love?! Hunh? You're not gonna answer me? Naw sweetheart, makin love is done twenty-four hours a day or he's fuckin you, babee! Fuckin yo mind!

TRACEY: (*Vengeful, seething.*) How can you of all people talk about somebody not making love? When you couldn't give Mama as much as an hour (*Hinkty.*) of your love making,...or she'd be here right now.

(*Renson stares at her as if immune to her insults. Tracey exits into bathroom. Renson goes and stares out of front window, somber, pensive. John stands in the middle of the room baffled, confused.*)

JOHN: (*Disturbed.*) Everything's going crazy ever since Mama's been gone. Ray never drunk this much before. And I never heard you...you talk to Tracey like that. (*Renson fidgets, but doesn't answer.*) Tell you the truth, I lost the ball today cause I was thinkin about Mama on that cold ass island.

RENSON: Peninsula.

JOHN: What did Tracey mean when she said you...you didn't give Mama an hour of your love making?

RENSON: (*Not turning around.*) Why don't you ask her.

JOHN: Okay...I will.

RENSON: (*Turns back, blurting.*) I didn't mean that.

JOHN: You don't want me to ask her?

RENSON: (*Walking back to living room.*) Not really. She meant what she said. After I found out about her relationship I sort of rejected her in that way.

JOHN: (*Reflecting.*) Then...you ran her away.

RENSON: (*Ashamed.*) I didn't mean to.

JOHN: But you did...

RENSON: (*Sincere.*) Can you forgive me?

JOHN: Forgive you for what?

RENSON: Will you do me a favor then?

JOHN: Run it.

RENSON: Tell your mother I love her and I want her to come home.

JOHN: (*Smiles.*) Sho will. (*John exits into bedroom.*)

(*Tracey stomps out of bathroom and goes to telephone; angry, cuts hateful glances at Renson.*)

RENSON: *(Compassionate.)* Are you alright?

TRACEY: *(Ear to receiver, shrugs soulders, flits eyebrows.)* Who me? Why I'm as tough as a football.

RENSON: Are the children with him?

TRACEY: *(Hangs up phone.)* No. They're not with him if that makes you feel any better. They're over Aunt Minna's house.

RENSON: So she's in on this too?

TRACEY: In on what? Cause I asked her to watch the kids for a few days so me and Cecil could be alone. *(Harsh.)* We can't be alone here since you hate him so much can't stand to see him in your house.

RENSON: I never said he couldn't come here until I heard him call you a "hoe" out on my front porch.

TRACEY: You didn't have to knock his tooth out. *(Dials phone.)*

RENSON: Act like he want some more knocked out. I mean, what kinda cat is he to come here again and do the same thing? *(Pause.)* What were you fighting about?

TRACEY: Oh you'll never understand. *(Speaks into phone.)* Hello, Bill, yeh, Tracey. How are you? Havin a few problems right now. Can you do me a favor? I want you to come by and pick me up. I need a ride. Okay. Bout twenty-minutes. That's fine. Thanks. See you then. *(Hangs up phone.)*

RENSON: You want me to pick up the children?

TRACEY: Bill's coming by. I wanna talk to him about something, then we'll pick them up on the way home.

RENSON: I could keep the kids tonight if you wanna go out with Bill.

TRACEY: *(Suspicious of his motive.)* Bill, Bill—What are you tring to do, push me off on Bill? I'm not interested in Bill. He's just a friend.

RENSON: I'm just trying to be helpful. Everything I say to you...you think I'm against you. You and Cecil. It's like he's become something between us that's tearing us apart.

TRACEY: He is something between us! He's my husband and I'm not your little girl anymore.

RENSON: Try and understand my position. I'm not in love with him, therefore, I don't see all the hidden beauty in him that you see. All I see is how he's hurt you and I don't like the man.

TRACEY: *(Calming down.)* Maybe you should try and see him the way I see him.

RENSON: How can I?

TRACEY: You can if you try.

RENSON: I don't think you're seeing yourself clearly. That's why you can't make up your mind what you wanna do.

TRACEY: Well I've made up my mind about one thing: I'm not staying here.

RENSON: *(Surprised.)* What? You're just moving out because of—

TRACEY: Cecil wants me to come back. I'd been thinking about it. I figure I might as well be a slave to one man as to be a slave for four. I went with him this weekend so we could talk about it. When I decided not to he wanted to fight.

RENSON: *(Sorrowful.)* I know we've been actin like spoiled boys since you've been here but that shits gotta stop. I'm gonna learn how to cook and clean this house right.

TRACEY: You're gonna have to if you wanna eat cause I'm gone.

RENSON: Where?

TRACEY: Bill's got a vacant flat upstairs. I'm gonna see if he'll put me up until I can get a job.

RENSON: And what about school?

TRACEY: I'll have to go part-time.

RENSON: I can still pay your tuition.

TRACEY: You don't have to.

RENSON: I want to. I can help with your other expenses if you want to stay in school full time.

TRACEY: I appreciate your offer, but I don't want to be tied to you like—

RENSON: You don't have to be tied to me. I just wanna help. How you gonna work and go to school and take care of two babies? Oh I know lots of women do it, but it's not easy.

TRACEY: *(Thoughtful.)* Nothing you really want ever is.

RENSON: *(Sadly.)* So I'm runnin you away too?

TRACEY: *(Looks at her father seriously; no resentment.)* No-oo...not really. *(Empathetic.)* I know you mean well and I'm sorry for what I said about you and Mama.

RENSON: *(Sympathetic, soft.)* I'm sorry for what I said. You don't pour water on a drownin baby. *(Comes closer.)* I'd wish you reconsider making a move.

TRACEY: *(Sighs.)* It's nothing to reconsider. I think this is best. I just can't make the adjustment. I feel smothered here. Ray is drunk all the time and Grandpa Early is naggin, and I wanna blast my music and paint the walls lavendar or sleep with a man or blow some coke and I can't do that here. I gotta have my own crib.

RENSON: You think if your mother were here things would be different.

TRACEY: Yeah, they'd be different. But I'd still need my own place.

RENSON: You think it would be better if she was here?

TRACEY: I think so. I wouldn't be expected to take her place.

RENSON: *(Surprised.)* Is that what you think you're doing?

TRACEY: Yes. It's really—I can't explain it...but I get the feeling sometimes you—*(Pause.)*

(Renson looks ghastly, mouth open.)

RENSON: I'm what?

TRACEY: *(Slow.)* That you think I'm Nancy instead of Tracey. That's why you practically begged me to come back when Cecil and I first separated. *(Pause.)* I became somebody you could look to on the rebound. Someone close enough to you to love but not close enough to touch.

RENSON: *(Shakes head not wanting to believe her.)* No—no...

TRACEY: You asked me. I feel too dependent on you and I wanna be independent.

RENSON: Have I mistreated you?

TRACEY: No...Daddy...you don't understand. You've given me everything. You've showered me with money, gifts. You've cared for the children. You've been sweeter than honey. If I was your wife I'd be thrilled but I'm not your wife and I feel smothered.

RENSON: I don't understand you. And since you're not a woman who appreciates good treatment, I can't fully accept your view as right.

TRACEY: *(Loud, angry.)* Well why you ask me then?!

RENSON: Cause I wanna know.

TRACEY: Not you. You already know.

RENSON: I don't understand women who despise good treatment, who disrespect and misuse men who would do anything for them. Then waste themselves on a man who dogs em. It's crazy. And I always find that these women are selfish and they get what they deserve. They're looking for what they deserve—selfish men.

TRACEY: *(Firm, intense.)* I'm not you're woman.

RENSON: You're my daughter. You come from my loins and I care about you.

TRACEY: *(Sarcastic.)* Maybe I'm not worthy of your valiant love.

RENSON: *(Serious.)* Maybe you're not.

TRACEY: Ha! That's a laugh. Your love is like a glass of ice water thrown in my face. Your love is the reason I'm gettin out.

RENSON: You just said I've been sweeter than honey.

TRACEY: I forgot, and colder than ice water.

RENSON: Which is it?

TRACEY: Both.

RENSON: *(Paces room, inquisitive.)* Tell me...truthfully. Have I always been that way?

TRACEY: No...You changed after you and Mama first broke up.

RENSON: *(Contemplative, mumbling to himself.)* Must have been like that all the time and just didn't know it until now. *(Turns to Tracey.)* I was put to the test and I failed. Just like an engine, after I build one I have to test it and see if it'll run.

TRACEY: If you want Mama to come back, why don't you ask her. You all had a good relationship. Least I thought so. If my marriage was one-tenth as good I'd hang in there.

RENSON: I've asked her to come back.

TRACEY: So what she say?

RENSON: She said no the first time I asked. I asked her again, recently. I'm still waiting for an answer.

TRACEY: Good luck. You deserve the best.

RENSON: Then why...why do you think she started seeing that professor? You're a woman—

TRACEY: *(Disgusted.)* Oh God, you still worried about that. That's the trouble right there. You can't forget and it's ruining you.

RENSON: *(Slow.)* That's the same thing Grandpa Early says, the same thing Nancy says. I thought she mighta told you something she didn't tell me.

TRACEY: What are you saying, you don't trust her? Did you ask her?

RENSON: Yes I asked her.

TRACEY: What did she say?

RENSON: She swore there was never any cause...that I never did anything to her to make her want another man.

TRACEY: Dere it is!

RENSON: It's not that I don't trust her. I keep thinking I must have done something and whatever it was I don't wanna do it again.

TRACEY: Did you hear what I said? She told you. It was for nothing. You've punished her enough.

RENSON: *(Fiery.)* I wasn't trying to punish her!

TRACEY: Whether you were trying or not, you did. Oh, I'm sure I did my part. I sure ain't no angel but I expected Mama to be one. Cecil do his thang and go actin a fool and I go fuck other men, but I sure never thought my sweet innocent Mama would do nothin like that.

RENSON: *(Stunned at her confession about seeing other men.)* You mean...you go around with other men besides your husband?

TRACEY: Oh no. I shouldn't have told you that. I'll have to listen to it the rest of my—

RENSON: Please Tracey. I was just wonderin if I heard you right.

TRACEY: *(Staunch, unashamed.)* You heard me right.

RENSON: And you wonder why Cecil goes upside your head?

TRACEY: *(Loud, defensive.)* So that gives him the right to beat me while he fuck anybody he please?

RENSON: That don't make it right.

TRACEY: That don't make it wrong either, far as I'm concerned.

RENSON: I admit I'm old fashioned. I don't understand this "New morality." All I know is how it's destroying the Black family.

TRACEY: So is the "old" morality.

RENSON: *(Guilty, embarrassed.)* I know I was wrong. *(Pause.)* Maybe you're right about me wanting you to take your mother's place. When a man doesn't have a woman seems like he searches for one to share his wealth with. Otherwise what am I working for? For Ray to go drink it up? For Grandpa Early to lose it playin poker? You're the one with the greatest need.

TRACEY: I can't take her place. And I can't take the place I had when I was growing up either.

RENSON: Do what you feel is best. And since behind all of my altruism is some kind of hidden selfishness I suppose—

TRACEY: I could never call you a selfish man.

RENSON: *(Apologetic, frustrated.)* I shouldn't have shouted at you the way I did. When I thought about it I realized Nancy would have handled it entirely different. She never would have gone off on you like that, not while you were upset. I look at Ray and know your mother could deal with him in a way—I don't have the patience. It's like...havin to learn how to be a mother and a father. I've gotta learn how to love without conditions. If I could have done that while your mother was here I never would have lost her.

TRACEY: Are you ready for it now?

RENSON: I'm ready to try.

TRACEY: Trying is not enough.

RENSON: *(Perturbed.)* You don't think I can do it?
(Car horn blows.)

TRACEY: *(Glances at door.)* There goes my ride. *(Picks up jacket, hurrys towards front door.)* I gotta go. I should be back in a few hours.

RENSON: Tracey, you didn't—

(Tracey exits quickly. Renson turns around, wanders to the bar. Lights cigarette, nervously, then puts it out. Goes to closet, gets coat and storms out of the house.)
(Lights.)

(ACT II)
(SCENE I)
(A few hours later Ray comes in drunk, staggering, piddling around in the dark. Sings the blues, laughing between lines, trips, stumbles on his knees and tries to pull up on the kitchen counter. Doorbell rings. Kwame, the oldest brother wearing a loud dashiki, akbada coat, rasta crown and earring finds the door open;

comes in and turns on the light. Takes off wool akbada and notices Ray kneeling on the floor by the kitchen counter.)

KWAME: Ray! What's the matter, man?

RAY: *(Slurring words drunkingly.)* Whatchu mean...mean what de matter? I'm prayin muthafucka. Ain't you eber seen a nigger pray befo?

KWAME: *(Chuckles.)* Prayin...Look like you squashin roaches. Man you need some prayer. *(Coming towards Ray.)* I got just the right herbs for you, Ray.

RAY: *(Harsh.)* Fuck you and yo sisters, sissy!

KWAME: Cmon man. Brother brought back some fresh spirolina straight from the Cameroons. Known to take out the fire-spirits of any animal. I'm gonna get some of that stuff in you if I have to force it down your throat with a jaw opener.

RAY: Jaw open mah mouth and...and yo jaw open lak volcano...

KWAME: That's alright too, long as you get better. *(Looks in refrigerator and takes out two lemons.)* Where's everybody? *(Ray looks around blank.)* *(Pause.)* Ain't no sense asking you nothin.

RAY: *(Rancid, cutting.)* What you expect...a welcome home party like you always get?! Kwame—the great hero who went to jail rather than go to the Nam. I know is was cause you was scardt, chicken...a yellow-hearted cheat!

KWAME: *(Squeezes lemons, mixes it with red pepper and distilled water.)* Is that why you went, Ray, to prove that you weren't?

RAY: I din't have to prove nothin!

KWAME: Then why did you go?

RAY: *(Stands up, wobbling, then steadies himself.)* Cause I didn't have no reason not to.

KWAME: That's a lie. You knew better.

RAY: Why? Cause you said so?! You and your party punks pushing confusion like they was beans.

KWAME: We were clear on that issue.

RAY: Wasn't clear on nothin if you ask me.

KWAME: Is it clear to you now? Now, that you've come back with Agent Orange and can't get one dime of disability. Can't even get the government to get a doctor to look at you.

RAY: Fuck you, son-of-a-bitch!

(Ray swings at Kwame. Kwame dodges him, grabs his arms from behind and strectches them in a karate lock. Ray groans.)

KWAME: *(Firm.)* Alright man, cool out! You hear me? I don't wanna have to hurt you.

(Kwame lets go of Ray; Ray turns back punching Kwame hard; Kwame flips him backwards on the floor.)

RAY: Lemme go punk!!

KWAME: *(Balls up fist.)* I'm gon sink my fist in yo mouth if you don't shut up!
(John rushes in sleepy eyed, wearing pajamas and robe.)

JOHN: *(Groggy.)* What happened?

KWAME: Ray's drunk and tryna fight me.

RAY: *(Mimics woman's soft, high-pitched voice.)* Ray's drunk and tryna fight me.
(Own voice.) Sissy muthafucka!

JOHN: Is it Sunday yet? Where's Daddy and Tracey?

KWAME: I just came in, man. The door was left open. Ray was kneeling over
there at the counter.

RAY: *(Shouting.)* I was prayin nigger!

JOHN: Ain nobody seen you in three days. *(To Kwame.)* This has been a weird
night.

KWAME: I want you to drink this juice I hooked up. Get some of that shit
out of your system.

RAY: *(Protesting, angry.)* I ain't drinkin none of that poison. You think I'm
crazy?!

KWAME: It can just sit here then til you get ready for it.

RAY: Yuh, you can thow it in de damn toilet cause I ain't drinkin nothin you
got to gib...me.
(Ray gets up and comes at Kwame again.)

JOHN: Look out Kwame!
*(Kwame turns, blocks Ray's blow and lands two karate chops across Ray's neck.
Ray falls backwards on the floor, groaning. Passes out.)*

JOHN: *(Goes towards Ray.)* He's out.

KWAME: He'll be okay. I just tapped him. I thinks it's more the alcohol than
the blow. Everytime I see him he's getting worse. *(Shakes head, piteously.)*
If he don't quit at his age, man, he ain't gon make it to fifty, if he make it
that far. He's killin himself everyday.

JOHN: Yeh, I know what you mean. I hate to say this but I think he's got
some mental problems.

KWAME: Course he does. You may not remember when he first came home
from the war. His nervous system was shot. Lots of brothers came back
from the Nam with Agent Orange and all kinda other disorders and don't
even know it.

JOHN: He needs to see a psychariatrist.

KWAME: Naw, not a psychiatrist. They'll just put him on some medication
that'll make him worse. Lots of clinics use natural remedies and that's
better. AA is better that the shrinks. But he needs something that'll cure
the Agent Orange. There's this bad naturopath in Ann Arbor who says
he can help him. If I can just get him to go.

JOHN: Howya gonna do that?

KWAME: That's the whole key right there. I can't. He's gotta wanna get well himself.

JOHN: Is it Sunday yet?

KWAME: Saturday night.

JOHN: That figures. Black folks on Saturday night. Cecil and Tracey was at it again. And that was only a little while ago, then I went back to sleep and hear all that noise and you and Ray duking.

KWAME: Cecil was over here?

JOHN: Yeah man, they was fightin. He hit her out on the porch.

KWAME: *(Dubious.)* You mean he came back here again after Daddy knocked out his tooth? What did Daddy do?

(Kwame takes an apple from the basket.)

JOHN: Chased him, I think. Then Daddy got mad at Tracey and they started arguing. Man, this whole night's been *crazy*.

KWAME: *(Enters livingroom.)* Didn't you have a game today?

JOHN: Yeah…we lost. *(Pause.)* Mama called last night. *(Takes seat.)*

KWAME: Oh yeah? How is she?

JOHN: Fine.

KWAME: I'm gonna call her. I haven't talked to her in three weeks and I haven't even aswered her last letter.

JOHN: She said she was coming back in December for your graduation.

KWAME: Aww man, that'll be a treat. Hope she'll stay for Kwanzaa. We got a lot of festivities planned this year.

JOHN: Hope she'll stay for good.

KWAME: Now that would be even better.

JOHN: Daddy wants her to come back.

KWAME: I don't think he ever really wanted her to leave.

JOHN: *(Pensive, slow.)* You believe in prayin, Kwame?

KWAME: Sure do. I pray every morning and evening just like Mama and Daddy taught us. Just like the birds. *(Holds up apple.)* This is pure food for the body. Prayer is pure food for the soul. Why you ask?

JOHN: Just wonderin if it might help. *(Pause.)* How long you stayin in town?

KWAME: Til tomorrow night. We doin this gig over at the Musician's Inn tomorrow.

JOHN: Which group?

KWAME: *Kuumba.*

JOHN: Don't think I've heard that one.

KWAME: We play some of everything but all in a sort of uninterrupted musical mosaic.

JOHN: I'd like to see it, man.

KWAME: Come on through. I'll get you in. You don't have to worry bout the bread. I don't know if I can pick you up, but maybe Daddy'll let you use the car. Or he might come himself. He needs to get our more and enjoy himself.

JOHN: Who knows? Maybe he just needs to be alone.

KWAME: Hey man, why don't you sit in with us? You still playin trumpet?

JOHN: Not since football season's been in. Sports keeps me kinda tied up. I'll be playin basketball soon as the football season's up.

KWAME: You should come on and sit in so you won't get rusty. And man, *(Expressive)* you shouldn't put down yo axe cause you got a tone quality on that cow horn that's rare.

JOHN: You think so?

KWAME: I know so. And I'm not just sayin that cause I'm your brother. Lots of musicians who've heard you have said that. The band would love to have you sit in on the jam session.

JOHN: *(Undecided.)* I dunno man.

KWAME: Think about it. You got til tomorrow.

(Renson unlocks the front door, enters solemn, absentminded. For a moment he doesn't notice Kwame and John. Kwame goes over to greet him.)

KWAME: Daddy?

RENSON: Kwame! When'd you get in?

(They embrace, give a black power handshake.)

KWAME: Came in tonight for rehearsal. Got a hit tomorrow afternoon over at the Musician's Inn. Why don't you come on and check it out? John wants to go too.

RENSON: Afternoon? What time?

KWAME: Doin a matinee at four.

RENSON: *(Hangs up coat.)* Aww...I'm not gon be able to make it, man. I promised this guy I'd finish workin on his truck tomorrow at two. I'll be tied up at least four or five hours.

JOHN: Wow, if it's at four I can't go either. I gotta go to football practice at three o'clock.

KWAME: *(Shrugs, sighs.)* I tried. Maybe next time. In fact, mark this on your busy calendars. *Kuumba* will be playing on "Kuumba" night of Kwanza: December 31, at the Kuumba Playhouse. Dig that action: Trible Kuumbas. You know it's gon be some powerful creativity happenin.

JOHN: *(Shakes his head.)* I kinda hate to miss that too.

KWAME: Just don't miss Kuumba night.

JOHN: I won't. I'm gonna mark that.

RENSON: *(Touching Kwame's shoulder.)* It's good to see you. You look great.

KWAME: *(Teasing.)* You don't look bad yourself for an old man. *(Looks in his eyes.)* Even losin some of them worry rings around the eyeballs.

RENSON: *(Smiles.)* Been drinkin my gingseng tea.

KWAME: That'll do it. With a little lovin in the cup you'll be alright. How you and Miss Amelia doin?

JOHN: *(Cutting eyes and tone.)* Miss Amelia?

RENSON: *(Glances at John)* I haven't talked to her in a while.

JOHN: Did you call Mama?

RENSON: *(Sits down.)* Yeah. *(Face drops, sullen, weak-voiced.)* I talked to her. *(Heavy silence fills the room. John studies his father's eyes. Kwame watches both of them.)* Did Tracey come back?

JOHN: I'm not sure 'less she went to bed. I'll go look. *(Goes and peeks into bedroom.)* Naw, she's not here.

KWAME: *(Sits down.)* What's this I hear about her and Cecil?

RENSON: *(Disgust.)* Shh-eet, that husband of hers is a Fool with a capital F.

KWAME: You mean he actually hit her on the porch?

RENSON: *(Nods.)* And I got upset with Tracey cause she went to spend the weekend with him and he jumped on her. She ain't swallowed enough of him yet to vomit him out.

KWAME: Don't worry, she'll get tired of it sooner or later. Might be sooner than we think. I know Bill—the brother she's seein now. He really digs her, man. He told me when I saw him up in Ypsilanti last weekend. He's a good brother too. And a hell of a photographer. He's very conscious.

JOHN: Sure are on a matchmakin mission tonight.

RENSON: Speaking of matchmakin, how's Yaza and the baby?

KWAME: *(Big smile.)* Nzauri—beautiful! Kumasi's growing like a little tree. *(Ray moans. Renson turns around.)*

RENSON: What's that?

KWAME: Ray—

RENSON: Where? *(Gets up.)* I see em. Drunk?

KWAME: Drunk and fightin mad.
(Renson goes into kitchen, runs cold water into a pot; John covers his eyes. Renson pitches the water in Ray's face.)

RAY: *(Sputters, howls, kicks.)* Gotdammit!

RENSON: Come on back to life. You too heavy to carry to bed.

RAY: Leave...me 'lone.

RENSON: You not gonna use the kitchen for your bedroom. We gotta eat in here.

RAY: Eat in the bathroom with natural food!

RENSON: *(Bold.)* Just get up and go to bed.

JOHN: Want me to help?

RENSON: He's a big man. He can walk.

RAY: *(Getting up.)* Walk? He can fly like a bird, like the wren's son. But his wings are crippled by the salty sea. *(Dramatic.)* He haunts the house of the golden stool. *(loud.)* Where is your throne, Osei?! Why do the Sansibangi spirits torture you?

RENSON: *(Steps in front of him, poseing as actor.)* My son is possessed with rotten jinn. My blood was never disconnected from his. His spirit haunts my blood.

RAY: *(Empty, cold stare.)* That is…sad, Osei. Perhaps…you should *kill* yourself.

RENSON: *(Stares back.)* Life is not that bad to me. Not even you can make it that bad.

RAY: But you can make it that bad for me without even tryin. How's that for a man whose spose to be the family man extradonnaire?

KWAME: That's your opinion. And a foolish one at that.

JOHN: Yeah man, you gotta bomb Daddy.

RAY: *(Turns on John.)* Who asked you, shithead?

JOHN: *(Snaps back.)* Nobody. I don't have to have nobody to ask me to speak.

RAY: But I do. I gotta ask for my turn!

JOHN: That ain't true. You take everybody's bat.

RAY: *(Pointing.)* I'm gon take yo ball and yo bat, sweetie.

RENSON: Ray, it's getting late and we're tired.

RAY: I'm tired too. *(Ambles around the room.)* Sick and tired!!

KWAME: Why don't you let me take you to this naturopathist—

RAY: *(Fierce.)* Why don't you kiss my ass bitch.

(Kwame stands up, belligerent.)

RENSON: Hold on Kwame.

KWAME: He the one better hold on to his tongue. He ain't so drunk he don't know what he talking about.

RAY: Bitch! Bitch!! Hoe!!

(Kwame tries to ignore Ray. Ray staggers pass him and plops on the sofa.)

KWAME: I planned to spend the night here, but I can't deal with this.

RAY: Nobody asked you to deal with it. Who you think you are, the Messiah? Yeh, Mr. Buster Brown, the biggest clown in town—that's what you think. Think you a goddam prince cause the castle was always put around you. Renson's oldest son, spittin image of his father cause he jacked off first, ha ha. Wanted a son created in his image. The second son, born in haste didn't come out so good. Least not good enough for the Blackman tribe. *(Silly.)* They were under the illusion they were warriors. The second born was little like his little ol mammy and couldn't compete with the bigger bucks on the basketball courts. So they put books in front of his nose and told him he could play girly games if he wanted to. Didn't tell him about jockeys and welterweights or Kung Fu masters. Had to find out about that on TV that they claim Black folks shouldn't watch. Ha! I see why not. So you can have full reins on your own brainwashing methods.

KWAME: You gotta warped imagination. They gave you books cause they thought you'd make a great writer.

RAY: Didn't ask me what I thought.

RENSON: We did. Remember, you said you wanted to be a writer.

KWAME: I remember that.

RAY: *(Wild-eyed.)* Then how come I don't remember?

RENSON: You don't wanna remember.

KWAME: Or else you can't.

RAY: *(Cutting eyes at Kwame.)* The hell I can't. I wanted to be a football player, a track star!

KWAME: That was your fantasy. You hated football practice and you couldn't run ten miles without falling out, but you had the mind of a razor and could write your butt off.

RENSON: You wanted to do everything Kwame did instead of what you were naturally gifted to do.

RAY: *(Mocking, vicious.)* Commies…Commies—What are you Communist Negroes? You gonna tell me what I'm suited to be, what I'm gifted for. Bullshit! Just some more brainwashin bastards.

RENSON: What do you want to be now? That's the most important thing? What do you wanna do?

RAY: I wanna drink.

JOHN: You gotta be kiddin.

(Ray goes towards the bar. Renson steps in front of him.)

RENSON: Oh no. No more tonight.

RAY: *(Defiant.)* What am I, a prisoner?

RENSON: Yeah, you're a prisoner. You're locked in the bottle. So you just take a breath of fresh air.

RAY: You ask me what I wan now, right?

RENSON: What do you wanna be? What kind of man do you wanna be? You wanna be a bottle of whiskey?

RAY: *(Nods head quickly.)* Yeah, yeh…Dat's what I wanna be.

KWAME: A geni locked in the bottle, instead of a genius sharing his gift with his people.

RAY: Who asked you anything?!

RENSON: Is that all? A bottle of whiskey. That's the choice you've made?

RAY: Ye-ah, yeh—

RENSON: Well don't blame me for your choice. Whatever mistakes I've made, whatever I've done to hurt you in the past is past.

RAY: *(Mimicing.)* It's past. You walk away nobly from your bowels you left on the floor and tell me—it's past. I've passed my bowels now. Hey, I'm just bein myself. I'm just bein what you always wanted me to be—myself.

RENSON: I never took you for a geni in the bottle.

RAY: *(Embittered.)* You never took the time to see what I was. So busy with your business. Didn't have time for Mama neither, did you?

KWAME: *(Getting angry.)* Why don't you go to bed.

RAY: Didn't have time for her neither? That's why she started gettin her action somewhere else.

RENSON: *(Angry.)* Alright niggah, you done said enough!

KWAME: *(Grabs Ray by the collar.)* Damn right he done said enough!

RAY: *(Vicious, defiant.)* I ain't said nothin yet. You don't know how long she been doin it. Dat professor wasn't the only one. There was more than one, more than five!

(Renson rushes to Ray, hits him, knocks him down.)

RENSON: Liar!

KWAME: Shut up Liar!

RAY: You wish I was lyin. Beat me all you want! Big, black bubble eyed bucks!

RENSON: *(Enraged.)* You a damn lie! And I'll beat you to death if you don't quit lyin on yo Mama.

KWAME: *(At same time as Renson.)* Insane fool!

RAY: I knew! I knew all the time. I knew about all her men!

RENSON: *(Furious, grabs Ray's collar, slaps him.)* Liar!! What's the matter with you?! Have you lost yo mind?!!

JOHN: Don't pay no attention to him, he's drunk.

KWAME: He ain't that damn drunk!

RENSON: He's crazy!

RAY: She did…she did! I say her!

RENSON: *(Shoves Ray back on the floor.)* You a lie! Take it back muthafucka or I'll stomp you so help me!!

RAY: Go ahead! Stomp me! I'm tellin the truth and you hate the truth.

(Renson stomps him twice in the back; Ray groans. Renson pulls him by the collar and punches him in the neck.)

RENSON: You lyin and you gon fess up, punk!

KWAME: *(Loud, threatening.)* Take it back, chump!

RAY: I ain't takin shit back!

(Renson slaps his face repeatedly.)

RENSON: The hell you ain't! *(He yanks Ray by the collar, shakes him hard. Ray bleeds from the nose and mouth.)* You a bottle of bad whiskey that's goin in the garbarge can.

(Renson pulls Ray up from his armpits and starts dragging him towards the back door. Kwame grabs his legs and together they step into the kitchen.)

JOHN: *(excited.)* Yall not really gon put him in the garbage can are you?

RENSON: You think I ain't? You can be a witness.

RAY: *(Hollers, screams.)* No-oo...! No! No! I take it back! I take it back! I was lyin. I was just foolin...*(Cries.)*

KWAME: You a fool alright! *(Drops his legs.)*

RENSON: *(Let's Ray down.)* Anything to get attention. *(Breathes hard.)* Call yo own Mama a hoe just to get attention. You're sick! And you're gonna get some help or you gettin out. I'm not gon let you stay here and make everybody else miserable just cause you miserable.

JOHN: Misery loves company.

KWAME: Company don't necessarily love misery. I don't.

(Grandpa Early unlocks the front door, enters tipsy but not drunk, croons an old tune: "Ain Misbehavin" or one of Duke's tunes.)

GRANDPA EARLY: *(Raises his hat in a greeting.)* Mornin.

JOHN: It's mornin already?

GRANDPA EARLY: *(Glancing at his watch.)* Twelve-thirty.

KWAME: Hi, Grandpa Early. You early tonight.

GRANDPA EARLY: Sidney whipped the pants off me tonight. I had to come home. *(Hears Ray crying, peeks around in the kitchen.)* What's ailin him? He get in a fight?

(Kwame glances at Renson; Renson looks back at Kwame. John watches Grandpa Early.)

RENSON: We had to get rough with him. *(Flops down in big chair, leans head back, disturbed.)*

GRANDPA EARLY: Damn. He bawlin like a baby.

KWAME: He's drunk. On the nut.

GRANDPA EARLY: *(Goes into kitchen.)* Why ain't yall git somethin for his nose and mouth. *(Grandpa exits into bathroom, comes out with wet towel, wipes Ray's nose and mouth. Ray snatches the towel from him.)* Cmon I'll take you to bed.

RAY: *(Mumbling.)* I don need you to take me to bed.

RENSON: Take yourself then. *(Harsh.)* Now!

(Ray struggles to his feet, stumbles through living room, dining room, up the back stairs.)

GRANDPA EARLY: Smart alick. Wipe a wretch's nose and he give you his snot rag.

JOHN: What a night. *(Vexed.)* Feel like gettin outta here. This house is haunted. *(Exits into bedroom.)*

RENSON: *(Hands covering face, distressed.)* Haunted. Seems like it doesn't it? Just like you was saying earlier.

KWAME: I'm not scared of ghosts...but I don't like bein around negative energy. I think I'll go stay over my mother-in-law's tonight. *(Grandpa Early hangs up his coat.)*

RENSON: You not lettin no bad spirits chase you away?

KWAME: Naw, just given 'em space, and givin myself some too. Ray's had this thing against me ever since he came back from the Nam. Like I said before, I think he has Agent Orange.

RENSON: *(Worried.)* We've got to do something for he ends up in a mental institution.

KWAME: I was just tellin John, I know this naturopath in Ann Arbor who can treat him. But I can't make him go.

GRANDPA EARLY: Sho can't. Yall forget drinkin just a symptom. His sickness ain't got nothin to do with no alocohol or no Orange Agent. His Orange Agent ain't nothin but de fires of envy burning his insides. Been jealous of his big brother since he was a toddler, not since he come from the war. That's his real affliction. *(Kwame and Renson stare at Grandpa Early, remaining silent.)* I'm goin to bed. *(Grandpa starts towards backstairs.)*

KWAME: Goodnight Grandpa Early.

GRANDPA EARLY: Goodnight. *(Exits upstairs.)*

(John comes out of bedroom wearing jacket and cap, track pants and track shoes.)

RENSON: You goin out this late?

JOHN: Yeah, been sleepin all night, thought I'd get some air, maybe catch a late show at the all night movie.

RENSON: Vacating the haunted house, hunh?

JOHN: For awhile.

KWAME: I'm going that way, you need a lift?

JOHN: Naw, think I'll jog downtown.

KWAME: I gotta go too for my mother-in-law goes to bed. I don't have a key.

RENSON: *(Disappointed.)* There's an extra room upstairs. You don't have to go.

KWAME: I wanna go.

RENSON: Might as well...everybody else is abondoning me.

KWAME: Aww, don't feel like that. *(Compassionate.)* Hey, I'm sorry about this whole thing. I'll come by tomorrow before I go back to Ann Arbor. *(Clasping Renson's arm.)* Try and get some rest.

(Kwame exits. John goes to the front door.)

JOHN: *(Curious.)* You said you called Mama?

RENSON: *(Hurt, gloomy.)* Yeah, I called her.

JOHN: *(Hesitant.)* Did...did she say she was coming back?

RENSON: *(Dry.)* No...she's not coming back.

(John stares off, brokenhearted, turns and exits. Renson hangs head.)

ACT III

SCENE I

(A week later at the Blackman house, two moving men are taking large boxes, some small tables, some small tables, a lamp, etc. out of the front door. Tracey is busy taking food from the cabinets and refrigerator. Renson enters the front door wearing mechanic suit, cap and jacket. Hangs up jacket and hat, enters living room.)

RENSON: I see I'm just in time.

TRACEY: You're home early.

RENSON: I left the shop so I could see yall off.

TRACEY: Did you see Ebony and Jomo out in the car with Bill?

RENSON: *(Smiles.)* Ye-ah, I'm gon miss those rascals. *(Slow.)* And you too.

TRACEY: Don't worry I'll be back to visit. Probably get sick of me.

RENSON: Call me if you need a babysitter.

TRACEY: *(Tender, soft.)* Thanks. Thanks for everything, Daddy. I'm really sorry about the things I said to you last week.

RENSON: We were both upset, and you didn't say anything that wasn't true. I needed that.

TRACEY: *(Thoughtful.)* You know this'll be the first time I've actually been on my own—

RENSON: I spose it's time.

TRACEY: I called Mama last night and told her I was moving.

RENSON: How is she. *(Takes out check book, writes check.)*

TRACEY: Okay. Least she sounded okay. She was disappointed about me moving. Guess she'll think you'll starve to death if I'm not here to cook. I told her since she was so concerned she oughta come back. I think she wants to. She was complaining about Anchorage not having enough Black people. She could deal with the snow if thee were enough Black folks to keep it warm. I better be gettin on. They're waiting for me. *(Picks up shopping bag.)* I took a few things for us to eat.

RENSON: I wanted to give you this. *(Hands her the check.)*

TRACEY: *(Looks at check, surprised.)* A thousand dollars?! You don't have to do that. Bill was gonna let me slide on the—

RENSON: Have something of your own. Please take it. No back talk.

(Tracey embraces Renson; they hug.)

TRACEY: Thank you, Daddy. *(Renson kisses her forehead.)* I'll call you in a few days, let you know how I'm doing. *(Renson's arm around her shoulder, they walk to the door.)* Good-bye.

RENSON: Good-bye.

(Closes door, ambles through living room. Music up. Renson goes to the telephone, dials. Ray comes downstairs slovenly dressed, hair uncombed, hungover. Renson hangs up phone.)

RENSON: *(Turning around.)* Ray—I didn't know you were here.

RAY: *(Wryly.)* Yeah, I'm here. *(Stretches, yawns, walks into the kitchen and opens the refrigerator.)* What time is it?

RENSON: Quarter to three. You just wakin up?

RAY: Guess so.

RENSON: You don't know?

RAY: Don't you? Seem like a crazy question to me.

RENSON: *(Annoyed.)* Know somethin, Ray, you not leaving me much choice but to pack your bags and send you on your way. I'm not gonna let you walk on me, man. Son or not. *(Ray takes a beer from refrigerator, opens it and starts drinking.)* The first thing you gonna put on your stomach is beer?

RAY: Ain nothin else in here to drink.

RENSON: It's some spring water in there. What about that stuff Kwame brought you?

RAY: She-eet...why I gotta drink spring water and that green slime while everybody else boozin it?

RENSON: Cause you can't drink. *(Pause.)* I let you move back here for one reason. You started working at the shop and said you were trying to get yourself together. You worked one month and Ben had to fire you. You went to the clinic six weeks and got busted. I'm startin to believe you was fakin all along. You just needed someplace to rest your head and had run out of women to lay on. The game is up. You gettin outta here.

RAY: *(Slamming beer can on the counter.)* You just gonna put me in the streets? I ain't got no money—

RENSON: There's the Billie Holiday Clinic, the Elmhurst Clinic. You know em better than I do.

RAY: *(Enters living room.)* They want you to go cold turkey overnight.

RENSON: Good.

RAY: *(Disturbed.)* Why...why you wan do me like that? I ain done nothin. I ain botherin nobody. Why everybody—

RENSON: I don't even wanna hear that. I told you last weekend when you slandered your mother to get your act together or get out.

RAY: *(Resentful, bitter, defiant.)* You just mad cause Tracey got sick a yo ass and Mama left, and now you want me to leave. Takin yo shit out on me, that's what you doin. Give Tracey all the money she want, send her to school, take care of her brats just cause she a broad. If I was a broad—If I was a broad, *(Guestures like a woman or sissy.)* with tits and hair like *(Italian accent.)* Diana Ross or Rick James, an ass like Gina Lollabridgida I'd be the Queen Bee round here.

RENSON: Thinkin bout havin your sex changed?

RAY: Thinkin bout startin a men's liberation movement. It's badly needed.

RENSON: *(Looks hard at Ray.)* I've already started mine.

RAY: *(Angry, vindictive, vicious.)* The broads! Just cause they broads they got special priviliges. Tracey take yo money and buy cocaine and snort all night while you stay home and take care of her bastards. Won't even lend me two dollars. Just cause she a broad. You ain gon set no bitch out in the streets without a dime cause you weak for dim—

RENSON: *(Moving pugnaciously towards Ray, firm.)* You a *bitch*. And I'm settin you in the streets without a dime. Maybe without a head.

(Ray moves around the room away from Renson.)

RAY: Whatcha go do, man? De big man gon cut me down? Cut me down, hunh? *(Points finger.)* You did that when you dropped the seed. Member? You gave me the lil biddy seed. *(Dramatic.)* Was that fair? Billy—You gon cut me down some more?

(Ray backs quickly into the kitchen and pulls a long butcher knife from knife rack.)

RAY: *(Belligerent.)* Bause I get drunk don't mean I'm a punk! *(Loud.)* Ain't you or no other bitch lovin muthafucka gon slap me around like I'm a broad!

(Renson starts to take a step into the kitchen, looks hard at Ray but is also thinking. He turns away, heads for the front door and opens it wide.)

RENSON: *(Intrepid.)* I don't play with knives. Get out!

(Ray is taken aback. Stares mouth open at Renson, then at knife. Suddenly hurls the blade on the kitchen floor and storms out of the house. Renson closes the door behind him. /Music up./ Renson walks slowly to the telephone, picks up receiver, pauses, then puts receiver down. Doorbell rings. Renson hurries back to the door, swings door open to Amelia.)

RENSON: Take—Oh? Amelia, come in. I thought you were somebody else.

(Amelia, early forties, dressed in business suit enters.)

AMELIA: You were expecting somebody?

RENSON: No-oo, not really. Can I take your coat?

AMELIA: I'm not stayin long. I had just come from a meeting and I was close by so I thought I'd stop and say hello, and also invite you out to dinner.

RENSON: *(Shies away, thinks.)* I...uh...appreciate your offer but I promised Daddy and John I was gonna cook this evening.

AMELIA: *(Amused.)* You? Cooking?

RENSON: *(Smiles.)* I'm learning. Figure fixin a meal can't be much different than fixin cars. Just gotta learn. Fact I took a roast out this mornin to thaw out.

AMELIA: *(Joking.)* After you get through with that you can come over and have a real meal.

RENSON: So you think I can't get down. You wait. After I get good at it I'm gonna have you over for dinner. I won't use you for a guinea pig tonight.

AMELIA: Now that'll be something to look forward to since I don't see you very much these days.

RENSON: I know. I've really been busy. Workin overtime—

AMELIA: Why?

RENSON: A man don't stop workin cause he's makin money. Work is part of living.

AMELIA: That's not what I'm talkin about. I haven't heard from you in over a month. And you haven't returned my calls. What's wrong, honey?

RENSON: Been havin a bad case of the blues. Family problems.

AMELIA: I saw Ray leave as I drove up. He looked pretty distraught. No coat or anything.

RENSON: Yeah, I thought you were Ray coming back for his coat. *(Pause.)* Tracey moved today.

AMELIA: Oh did she? Where?

RENSON: She's got a flat over on the East side.

AMELIA: I can sort of understand…being the only woman in a house full of men can be…uh. Well I had four brothers and it was rough. By the time my sister was born all I could do was be a second mother.

RENSON: As long as she's satisfied, so am I.

AMELIA: If you can't make it to dinner how about checkin out Dakota Staton over at Dummy George's tonight?

RENSON: That should be nice. *(Thinking hard.)* I guess I'm just not in the mood to go out tonight.

AMELIA: *(Disappointed, sad.)* I see. And you don't wanna see me anymore either?

RENSON: I didn't say that.

AMELIA: You didn't have to. You've already let me know that in so many ways.

RENSON: It's not that I don't wanna see you anymore. I like you a lot. I like you for a friend.

AMELIA: But not a lover.

RENSON: *(Honest, pensive.)* No. Not a lover. If that's what you want it to be Amelia, I'm sorry I can't be that. I'd only be playing games, lying to you and me.

AMELIA: I suppose that's why I love you, Renson. Cause you're good and honest. *(Amelia comes up to him, kisses him lightly on the lips while touching his face.)* Good-bye. *(Turns and exits.)*

(Renson goes ino kitchen, puts roast into a pot, cuts onions, prepares meat, etc. Doorbell rings. Answers door; Ray comes in shivering.)

RAY: It's cold. *(Shivers, clasps his arms.)* I'm freezing man. It's freezing out there!

(Renson takes Ray's coat from the front closet.)

RENSON: Here's your coat.

RAY: *(Takes coat, puts it on.)* Can I warm up some? *(Rubs hands, vigorously.)* Can I get a drink of...somethin to warm my insides. That hawk was whippin all through my bones.

RENSON: *(Calm, dispassionate.)* Should I give a drink of water to a man that tries to kill me?

RAY: Naw, naw I didn't do that. You was comin at me and I was just trying to defend myself. *(Whines, upset.)* Hey, I'm sorry...I'm...mmm just... fucked man. Fucked! *(Pause.)* Daddy, I'm hungry. I haven't eaten in two days. I ain't got no money—

(Renson goes to kitchen, looks in the refrigerator. Ray eases over to the bartable and slips a fifth of whiskey under his coat. Renson takes out a loaf of bread, lung meat, cheese, apples, oranges, etc. puts them in a bag.)

RENSON: *(Hands Ray the bag.)* This oughtta hold you for today. Now give me back that fifth.

RAY: *(Shocked.)* I just wanted a drink. *(Gives back bottle.)* Somethin to warm my insides.

(Telephone rings. Renson answers it.)

RENSON: Hello? No, John's not here. Can I take a message? Tyesha. Okay, I'll tell him you called. Ohh, if he comes straight home from the game around seven. Call back then. Bye. *(While Renson is talking on the phone Ray eases a pint of vodka from the bar, slips it into large coat pocket and heads for the front door. He is leaving when Renson hangs up. He notices the vodka is gone and goes after him.) (Disgusted, pulls Ray inside by coat collar.)* What de hell is wrong with you?! Give a man bread and you steal from him?

RAY: *(Pulling away, aggravated, intense.)* Stealin! Shit! Cause you won't offer me a gotdamn drink when my insides is freezin.

RENSON: Your brain is frozen.

RAY: Want me to beg for it? That's what you want. *(Mimic, high voice.)* Please Daddy...*(Falls on knees, supplicates.)* Please can I have my bottle. I'm over twenty-one.

RENSON: You are sick.

RAY: Damn right, I'm sick. *(Grips stomach, painfully.)*

RENSON: Then get some help, Ray. You're not hopeless. Nothing is hope—

RAY: *(Screams.)* Help! Help! Help!

RENSON: Shut up!

RAY: Help! I'm beggin you for help now. You won even help me.

RENSON: *(Holds out hand.)* Gimme back the bottle.

RAY: *(Pouts, looks around crazy, mimics baby.)* Don't take my bottle, Daddy. You don't even wanna help me. You don't wanna help me. *(Renson pulls Ray up from his knees, takes bottle from his coat pocket.)* Can I take my clothes with me or does that become your property too?

RENSON: You can take anything you wanna take that's yours.

RAY: Where I mo put it, in the alley?

RENSON: That's your problem. That's where you've chosen to put yourself.

RAY: Not in November. It ain't fair.

RENSON: You're a grown man. I'm not responsible for you anymore.

RAY: *(Mimics.)* Get some help. Get some help! *(Serious.)* Has it ever occurred to you I don't want any help? Not yours or Kwame's or that funky clinic or anybody else's.

RENSON: It's accurred to me quite a few times. You just want hand-outs.

RAY: Right. Give me a hand-out. *(Thrust out hand.)* You wanna know the truth? If you wanna help me, give me a hand-out. Give me some bread and butter and jelly and wine. That's what God does—provide. You wanna play God, give me some bread—the way God gives me bread. And don't tell me bout no conditions cause he ain't got no conditions for lovin. And til God reach his hand out to help me *(Very loud, wild-eyed, passionate.)* can't nobody help me! Ain't nobody, no medication, therapy, health food, counseling bullshit, nothin gonna change me. That's who gon change me—God! And nobody else. I get sick or hearin that shit.

RENSON: And who's gonna change God? What did you think God is?

RAY: He ain't you. He's in me. When he gets ready to change me, he will.

RENSON: No-oo, It's when you get ready to change him—your idea of him. God gives rain and sun and seed but you have to go out and plant and sow if you want fruit, if you want results. God doesn't change your condition until you change it yourself. *(Holy Quran.)*

RAY: What if I can't change my condition? If I could change it, don't you think I would?

RENSON: I believe you spoke the truth the first time. You don't wanna change. You wanna blame it on God and waddle in self-pity cause that's the easy way.

RAY: I'll take a hand-out. Just like I was handed out. Niggers handed out like welfare cheese for Viet Cong. That's all niggers are anyway—hand-outs gettin hand-outs. Niggers gettin head, arms, nuts blown off and can't even get a wheelchair from the muthafuckas when they come back.

RENSON: You didn't have to go. You handed out yourself—for what?

RAY: *(In tears, enraged.)* For what? I din't do it for the honkie! I didn't give a damn about them! Any damn thing Kwame does is the gospel. Cause he went to jail, I was spose to go to jail too. *(Cries.)* For once, for once...just once I wanted *you* to be proud of me cause I did something different. Cause I went to war like a man. But no...you were ashamed of me. Anything Kwame did you were proud of, even if it was sitting on his behind in jail reading books rather than going to fight.

RENSON: *(Thoughtful, concerned, intense.)* That's why you went to war?

RAY: *(Wide-eyed, anxious.)* Yes—You went to war. Was proud of your medals. Remember the stories you would tell us about the war?

RENSON: *(Gloomy, paces room.)* That was a long time ago. I was ignorant. I didn't understand what I was fighting for. I was brainwashed. A fool! We were actually protesting, raisin hell for the right to fight. To prove to the white man we were brave too. Our blood could spill too, long as it wasn't for Black folks. Thank God things have changed. We've made a transition. I'm not the same man I was in 1945. I'm not the same man I was a few days ago.

RAY: *(Ashamed.)* Cause Kwame changed.

RENSON: Cause change is inevitable. *(Reflective, sympathetic.)* And that's... that's the reason you went in the army—to please me? *(Tears in eyes.)* Oh Ray—I'm sorry you had that impression. Fighting in itself doesn't make a man. Any fool can fight. That's all I was doing in Germany. A fool fighting and didn't know what I was fighting for. We have to learn to fight for the right things: for our families, and our livelihood and our self-respect. *(Puts hands on Ray's shoulders, looks straight into his eyes.)* We've made the same mistake—being pawns and gladiators for white men. But we don't have to hate ourselves of feel sorry for ourselves. All we have to do is *change.* *(Makes pistol shape, points at Ray.)* And point the gun to the real enemy. *(Passionately embraces Ray; Ray cries softly.)*

SCENE II

(Ten days later. Thanksgiving Day. Renson, John, and Grandpa Early are getting ready to go to dinner over Tracey's house. Renson is wrapping packages in the kitchen. John enters living room carrying tie.)

JOHN: Do I have to wear this monkey suit? I have trouble with this tie.

RENSON: You don't have to wear a tie or a suit coat. Long as you're not looking like a bum.

JOHN: Made me think of Ray. You heard from him?

RENSON: Not in almost two weeks, and I'm worried. Ain nobody seen him. He hasn't been at his usual hangouts. He hasn't come back for his clothes or nothin.

(Grandpa Early comes downstairs in a biege 3-piece mohair suit, silk tie, brown alligator shoes. Dressed to kill.)

JOHN: *(Amazed.)* Wow, looka here. Who you getting ready to slay, Grandpa?

GRANDPA EARLY: Only that what's slain already. Turkey, dressing, white bass, rump roast, rice and gravy, collard greens, okra soup and fresh rolls. De vegetarians can have the salad and the beets.

RENSON: Big Daddy Early! You done quit cuttin up and gone to carryin on! *(Grandpa Early profiles and poses.)*

GRANDPA EARLY: Well it ain't everyday we get invited out to Thanksgiving dinner.

JOHN: Was nice of Tracey to invite us over. Must have felt sorry for us.

GRANDPA EARLY: Whatchu doin Renson? It ain't Christmas yet. It's just Thanksgiving.

RENSON: Somethin wrong with giving my grandchildren some gifts on Thanksgiving, or any day?

GRANDPA EARLY: Naw, but you ain gotta wrap em.

RENSON: Why not? You gift wrapped.

JOHN: *(Testing.)* Yeah, and Grandpa's already warned us: to beware of Greeks bearing gifts. *(Doorbell rings.)* I'll get it.

(John opens the door for Kwame, dressed in a djellaba, fela, slacks and long overcoat.

KWAME: *(Takes John's hand, gives Black power handshake.)* Hey John—What it is?

JOHN: You got it, man.

KWAME: *(Looking tired, nervous.)* You on your way over to Tracey's?

RENSON: Hey hey man. We was just headin out. You?

KWAME: Hey Grandpa Early. Mighty sharp. *(Touches Grandpa's shoulder, affectionately. Speaks to Renson.)* We came down early. Yaza's helping Tracey with some of the food.

RENSON: *(Brings packages out of kitchen.)* So you're already over there. *(Looks closely at Kwame.)* What's the matter? You look kinda blue.

KWAME: You haven't seen Ray have you?

RENSON: *(Concerned, with much attention.)* No. You? *(Kwame shakes his head.)* Been lookin for him a week. I've checked the bars, clinics, corners where he hangs out. Ain nobody seen em.

KWAME: Cecil just called over to Tracey's with some bad news.

GRANDPA EARLY: *(Surprised.)* Cecil? What else could it be but bad news?

KWAME: It's about Ray. Or could be about Ray.

(John puts on his coat.)

RENSON: What about Ray?

KWAME: Some friend of Cecil is down in the county jail and said they gang raped and beat this cat the other night for rapin some teen-age girl. He thought he looked like Ray so he got word to Cecil. I just came by to tell you. I'm on my way down to the county jail to see.

RENSON: *(Holds head in anguish.)* Ohh noo!

KWAME: He ain't sure it's Ray cause he's only seen him a few times. But he thinks it's him.

RENSON: *(Disconcerted.)* All the places I've looked, I never thought of checkin the county jail.

GRANDPA EARLY: *(Shakes head.)* Lawd have mercy...dat boy...

JOHN: *(Worried.)* Hope it ain't him.

RENSON: I'm goin with you. *(Hands the car keys to John.)* Here, you and Grandpa Early go and have a good time. Take these presents for the kids.

GRANDPA EARLY: How you spec we gonna have a good time? What's this about somebody gettin raped?

KWAME: That's the way they test a new man in the Joint. And if he's accused of rapin somebody, he can just get his behind ready.

(Renson and Kwame exit. John paces the floor, worried.)

GRANDPA EARLY: Pacin de floor ain't gon fed us. Might as well eat.

JOHN: *(Very sad.)* I ain't hungry.

GRANDPA EARLY: *(Depressed.)* Me either. *(Sits down.)* Was starvin a minute ago. But ah ain hungry atall now. How Renson speck we gon have a good time worryin to death bout dat boy. Dat kinda stuff ain't happen too much when I was comin long. Man tear anodder man barehanded fo he let dat happen.

JOHN: *(Annoyed.)* How he gonna whip fifteen men?

GRANDPA EARLY: *(Piteous, shakes head.)* Dat's one of de low downest doggish mess I ever heard of. When men fall that low, hell ain't wide 'nough for em.

JOHN: *(Unbelieving, hurt.)* Jus couldn't do nothin like that to my brother.

GRANDPA EARLY: Brother? When he was here, he was a winehead, a bum.

JOHN: He's that too, but I don't wanna see him hurt.

GRANDPA EARLY: My how we cry when the dodo bird fly.

JOHN: A dodo bird with the golden eggs.

GRANDPA EARLY: You notice the value when they away from you. That boy got brains. Shame he don't use them.

JOHN: Make you never wanna take a drink.

GRANDPA EARLY: A man gotta be moderate. *(Pause.)* Ever tell you the story about Vaughn Manley? He was an old friend of mine back in Arkansas. Had twenty-five acres a land and twenty-five children. He was a hard-working family man, but he had one problem—de jug. Didn't know when to cut it loose, so it took hold of him instead. *(John takes coat from rack.)* Well, he had all these children to take care of so one day dey cide to play a trick on em. *(John exits. Grandpa hears the door slam and stops immediately.)* I be damn.

(Grandpa Early fixes a drink; sits back on the sofa, nods off to sleep. Lights dim. telephone rings. Grandpa opens eyes but continues to sleep. Telephone rings again. A little later Renson and Kwame enter, distress, dazed, hurt.)

GRANDPA EARLY: *(Wakes up.)* What happen?

RENSON: *(Very sad.)* He's dead.

GRANDPA EARLY: *(Shocked, grieved.)* No-oo.

KWAME: That was him who was gang raped. He jumped out the fifth floor window of the hospital this morning.

GRANDPA EARLY: *(Stunned.)* Yuh mean he?—

KWAME: *(Nods.)* He killed himself. *(Pause.)* I can't believe it. I always thought he would get better. *(Cries.)* I really did. What a waste of Black manhood. He was so brilliant...How could he...? Couldn't he see that? *(Hot.)* Did he have to jump out that goddamn window and kill his ass?

RENSON: Are you ashamed of him, Kwame? Are you ashamed that he took his own life?

KWAME: *(Reflects.)* No. I'm not ashamed. I believe a man leaves here when his time comes.

GRANDPA EARLY: *(Grieved, hurt.)* Why it have to come like this?

RENSON: Don't make no difference. I believe he died a long time ago—in Vietnam. He's free now. He's really free.

GRANDPA EARLY: God have mercy on his soul.

RENSON: I saw it coming. I dreamed about him falling out of a window.

KWAME: *(Gloomy.)* After gettin beaten and raped by fifteen dudes he just didn't wanna live. Somehow they get us believin that our manhood can be taken away that easily—that's it's some caked up shit in your ass instead of the strength of your soul. *(Grandpa Early leans over, cries.)* *(Excited.)* Grandpa, you alright?

GRANDPA EARLY: *(Distraught, cries.)* Think I go lie down on John's bed. *(Renson comforts him.)*

RENSON: Yeh, you do that.

KWAME: *(Goes to telephone.)* I'll start callin the family. You got Tracey's number?

RENSON: Let them eat their food.

KWAME: I'll call Mama. *(Dials number, waits.)* Hello Mama. Happy Thanksgiving to you too. Were you busy? I wish I could. No good news today. Yeah, Ray. He's dead. Died this morning. *(Painful.)* Mama, it's real ugly. Daddy been dreamin about him too. He was picked up for loitering and some girl who had been raped identified him as the man who raped her. So the inmates raped him and beat him pretty bad. We didn't even know he was in jail. He didn't call nobody. Anyway, this morning he jumped from the fifth floor window at the hospital. I know. I know, Mama. Broken up. His neck and limbs was broken, but he's not mutilated. We recognize him. He's here. You're the first person we've told. *(Renson, looking blank, goes upstairs.)* Yes...yes it has. I hate that you're all alone at a time like this. Okay...yeah. Call us before your plane leaves, we'll pick you up from the airport. *(Hangs up phone.)* Mama said she'd be in on the first flight in the morning. *(Notices Renson is gone.)* Daddy...Daddy.

(He dials telephone. Loud knocking at the door. Kwame answers it; Tracey rushes in.)

TRACEY: *(Loud, excited.)* What happened? I been calling the house. Nobody answered. *(Notices Kwame's distress.)* What happened? *(Weak.)* Was that him they beat up?

KWAME: *(Nods slowly, sad.)* He's dead.

TRACEY: *(Covers her face, screaming.)* No-oo!

(Tracey brreaks down and cries. Kwame comforts her. She cries on his shoulder.)

SCENE III

(Eight days later. Three days after Ray's funeral. House is a showcase of flowers left from the funeral. Nancy Blackman, a young looking, very attractive woman of forty-nine is packing up cakes, pies, potato salad, chicken, etc. Tracey enters from her old bedroom.)

TRACEY: You look beautiful, Mama.

NANCY: *(Big smile.)* Packing up all this food, Gabby Hayes would look beautiful.

TRACEY: I'm serious. You don't look a day over thirty-five and you're almost fifty.

NANCY: Ssshhh...don't say that so loud.

TRACEY: Why? Everybody around here knows it.

NANCY: It's me. I don't wanna hear it. *(Pause.)* I packed up some of that chicken and potato salad. It's enough food here to last til next Thanksgiving.

TRACEY: *(Scanning her mother, admiringly.)* Food or not—and you know Daddy's been trying to cook—you look like you belong here.

NANCY: After all Tracey this has been my home for twenty-two years. I even picked the house.

TRACEY: Yeah, but you look like you're in the right place, at the right time.

NANCY: Did you think I wasn't going to come back and bury my son?

TRACEY: Cmon Mama don't be so glib. You know what I'm talking about.

NANCY: I hate to have to come back for Ray's funeral, but it's good to be home. *(Looks around.)* It still feels like home.

TRACEY: Mind if I ask you a personal question?

NANCY: Depends on what it is.

TRACEY: You goin back to Alaska?

NANCY: Nobody's asked me to stay.

TRACEY: I want you to stay and so does everybody else. I believe you took that assignment in Alaska cause if you had stayed in Detroit or Chicago or even down South you wouldn't have been able to stay apart.
(John enters room.)

JOHN: And I want you to stay.

NANCY: *(Smiling at John.)* How are you, hon?

JOHN: Haven't felt this good in months. Guess it's cause my Mama's home. *(Puts his arm around her, kisses her forehead.)*

NANCY: For a little while. I gotta go back to work Monday.

JOHN: *(Disappointed.)* Monday? Aww Mama—

TRACEY: Ever heard of quitting?

NANCY: On a day's notice?

TRACEY: Well, I've done it lots of times. But I know—your generation is a little more polite.

NANCY: *(To John.)* You hungry? There's plenty of food.

JOHN: No I gotta go to practice. I don't want anything heavy on my stomach. *(Pause.)* Think you'll make it to the game, Tracey?

TRACEY: I don't know. Uhh, I might have to work.

JOHN: You comin Mama?

NANCY: I wouldn't miss it for anything. Even though it is kinda cold.

TRACEY: Very cold.

NANCY: I gotta see what my star half-back is doing.

JOHN: I haven't been doing too good this season. But I promise you the best game they've seen the whole year.

NANCY: *(Looks skeptical, teasing.)* How can you promise that? How do you know which way the ball is going to fall?

JOHN: I don't. *(Smiles.)* But...ya know, I gotta show off for my Mama.

NANCY: You don't have to show off for me. You're fine just like you are.

TRACEY: You look better to her off that field than on it.

JOHN: *(Disappointed.)* Yall never liked football anyway.

NANCY: Football is so rough. I don't like seein you get hurt.

JOHN: I've been offered a football scholarship to Ohio State.

TRACEY: *(Surprised, delighted.)* Ohh, that's great John! I mean, football's not my favorite sport—but a full scholarship is wonderful! Congratulations!

NANCY: *(Calm, unimpressed.)* You going?

JOHN: I was thinking about it.

NANCY: Is that what you really wanna do?

JOHN: *(Reflective, slow.)* I'm not sure. I'm still undecided.

NANCY: Know what I'd like to see you do?

JOHN: *(Curious.)* What?

NANCY: *(Sincere.)* Keep studying your horn. You have a gift that can be shared with millions. Share it. You'll find fulfillment in that, that I don't believe you'll ever get playing football.

TRACEY: *(Faint smile.)* I'm kinda surprised to hear you say that—The way you use to leave the house whenever John startin practicing. *(Laughs.)* And leave me here to babysit. *(They both laugh.)*

NANCY: *(Amused.)* Things have changed now. *(Serious.)* One of the things I miss most in Anchorage is our music. I see what a healing, what a comfort it is more than ever. You should see the collection I've gotten since I've been there. Everything Miles, Dizzy, Billie and Bird ever did.

JOHN: Wow! gotta come up and see you.

NANCY: You're welcome to come stay with me anytime.

JOHN: Rather you come here.

NANCY: If it'll encourage you to keep playing I can send you my records. We need musicians. We need them like we need doctors. Study engineering if you want, but don't forget your *roots*. That lives...far outlives the machines.

JOHN: I figured if I took the scholarship Daddy wouldn't have to pay.

TRACEY: That's why I say, go ahead. It's a free education.

NANCY: Yes, but look what you're giving up—your body, your mind. That's all you've got. Your father wouldn't mind paying for it out of his pocket if you turned down the scholarship. Then you can go to the school you want to without worrying about the labor and time you owe to ol mastuh on the football field. Don't sell yourself into slavery with a football contract.

JOHN: *(Curious, thinking.)* You think that's what I'm doing?

NANCY: Sure that's what you're doing. You risk your life and limbs for a carrot and an oversized ego while white men stand by and bet on you like horses and get rich. *(Intense.)* I don't like seeing you used that way. *(John roams the room, pensive.)* Think about it.

JOHN: I will. Fact, I put my trumpet in the shop a few weeks ago. Just haven't had the money to get it out yet.

NANCY: Did you ask your father?

JOHN: No.

TRACEY: You know he didn't ask him.

NANCY: Why? He would have given it to you.

JOHN: Yeh, I know. I didn't wanna bother him since I'm working part-time. I just needed to save up some more money.

TRACEY: *(Shakes head, smiling.)* You're so much like Daddy it's amusing sometimes.

NANCY: If you want I can give you the money to get it out or *lend* you the money, whichever you prefer.

(Tracey picks up grocery bag.)

TRACEY: I gotta get back.

(Nancy and Tracey walk towards the door; they kiss.)

NANCY: I'll come by and see you before I leave. Kiss Jomo and Ebony for me.

JOHN: Which was you goin?

TRACEY: The East side. You need a lift?

JOHN: I'm goin in a different direction.

TRACEY: *(Smiles.)* That's okay. Cmon, I'll drop you.

JOHN: *(Puts on coat, picks up sportsbag.)* Thanks. See ya later, Mama.

NANCY: Good-bye.

TRACEY: Thanks for the food. *(Exits.)*

(John embraces and kisses Nancy.)

JOHN: *(Gentle.)* Don't forget your roots…We love you— *(Exits.)*

(Grandpa Early comes into livingroom, nods coldly at Nancy. Goes to bar and pours a drink.)

NANCY: *(Smiles.)* That's all you going to eat?

GRANDPA EARLY: *(Hurt.)* It's my life. I live it the way I want to. *(Rolls eyes at Nancy.)* You live yours the way you want to.

NANCY: My my Grandpa, what big eyes you have—

GRANDPA EARLY: All the better to see you with, my dear.

NANCY: And what big teeth you have Grandpa— *(Grandpa turns and growls at her.)* *(Stern.)* All the better to eat me with? Go ahead, I'm not afraid of the big bad wolf.

GRANDPA EARLY: *(Harsh.)* Yeah, and you ain't little red riding hood neither.

NANCY: *(Firm.)* You better believe it. You've been chasing me like a wolf ever since me and Renson first got separated—

GRANDPA EARLY: *(Bitter, spiteful.)* Ever since you took up with that two-legged computer.

(Nancy turns back to him.)

NANCY: *(Stern, sarcastic.)* Here's my back, Mr. Wolf, you wanna give me a hundred stripes?

GRANDPA EARLY: *(Sharp, emphatic.)* My name is *Mr. Blackman!*

NANCY: *(Faces Grandpa.)* Then why don't you act like a *Black man* instead of an executioner?!

GRANDPA EARLY: *(Forceful. loud.)* You lucky woman. Back in ancient times they use to kill adultresses— *(Nancy slaps him hard. Grandpa stands up, furious.)* *(Wide-eyed, angry.)* If you wasn't a woman I'd break you in half!

NANCY: *(Soft.)* And what else? Cause you love me and don't wanna admit how hurt you are? *(Grandpa stares at her hard.)* I'm not sorry. *(Smiles, sighs.)* I feel good. I should have done that a long time ago.

(Grandpa gradually breaks down, sits at the bar, emotionally staggered.)

GRANDPA EARLY: *(Pouting, hurt.)* Bet not do it no more.

NANCY: *(Angry.)* Who are you of all people to accuse me? If I'm an adulteress, what does that make you? You sure ain't no saint. And of all the women I've known you to have—women you could care less about—I never accused or condemned you. *(Pause.)* One thing I can say about your opposition. It's helped me to grow. It's helped me to face myself and say I'm a *good woman.* I'm the woman I always was, not the woman you wanna make me out to be. Thanks Grandpa for that.

(Grandpa finishes drink, goes to the door and puts on overcoat.)

GRANDPA EARLY: *(Soft, reflective.)* Maybe that's what I was here for. *(Turns back putting on hat, wry.)* Welcome home, Mama.

(Renson comes downstairs. Grandpa exits.)

NANCY: Hi. How do you feel?

RENSON: Alright. How about you?

NANCY: Much better. This is the first day I haven't thought much about Ray. I pray he's at peace now. He didn't have much while he was here.

RENSON: We can't worry about that. We did all we could for him.

NANCY: *(Cold, questioning.)* Did we?

RENSON: I think so...Uh—I did—least I did the best I knew how. Might not have been much, but I'm not blamin myself. *(Pause.)* Found out I didn't know much about raising a family at all, since you been gone. Funny ain't it. Thought I had it all together.

NANCY: I know the feelin. Sometimes I feel like a child learning all over again.

RENSON: That's good. It's good to feel like a child, sometimes, isn't it? That's how I've been feelin. I've just been fighting it.

NANCY: *(Contemplative.)* A child who learns the meaning of failure, of pain.

RENSON: It's no disgrace to fall; it's a disgrace not to get up.

NANCY: *(Somber.)* Ray won't get up.

RENSON: He doesn't have to anymore.

NANCY: *(Gloomy, guilty.)* Did we do the best we could? I wonder—I've been wondering ever since he passed—what did I do wrong?

RENSON: You can't fault yourself for another person's...person's life. The life they choose to live.

NANCY: We planted to tree. We did it go crooked? Why didn't we straighten it out before it was too late.

RENSON: *(Frustrated, complaining.)* What good is it to blame ourselves?

NANCY: *(Pensive, intense.)* I need to know…how much,…how much *(painful)* I really hurt him.

RENSON: Yunne Ray—He blamed everybody for his problems. Our only fault was we couldn't reach him.

NANCY: *(Pleading tone.)* But why? Why couldn't we? I mean…if we had done something,…something together—Something that could have—

RENSON: Ray wasn't open to listening.

NANCY: *(Cries.)* I hadn't talked to Ray since I left. He wouldn't talk to me…no more, yunno. Wouldn't…answer my letters.

RENSON: *(Irritated.)* Ray was sick.

NANCY: *(Mournful.)* He hated me.

RENSON: No, he didn't hate you. He loved you. He didn't do anything to you that he didn't do to anybody else. He didn't speak to me either. Why you driving these nails into yourself?

NANCY: *(Upset.)* They drivin me, just like they drove Ray.

RENSON: *(Stares at her, sympathetic.)* I didn't know you felt this way. *(Soft, guilty.)* We been drivin these nails into you.

NANCY: *(Hesitant, ashamed.)* What…what about…that girl? I dunno why it's bothering me. Do you think he really raped that girl?

RENSON: *(Disturbed.)* That's not important. Case closed.

NANCY: *(Sad.)* It's out of the courts; it's not out of my mind.

RENSON: Why are you keeping it there?

NANCY: What do you think? I don't wanna believe it…I don't believe it. *(Curious.)* Do you?

RENSON: *(Emphatic.)* Ray is dead and buried, so let's bury his past with him!

NANCY: How long does the soul take to leave the body?

RENSON: *(Paces the room, agitated.)* What's that got to do with Ray? Would that make his death more logical if he did rape the girl?

NANCY: No! *(Pause.)* I…ah don't believe he would do that…but—

RENSON: You have doubts about.

NANCY: *(Confused.)* I dunno. I keep thinking about that girl. I feel we should talk to her.

RENSON: *(Hot, snappy.)* For what?! What's it gonna do but bring up a lot of bad feelings? She swore it was him. You're gonna tell a raped woman your son didn't rape her just because he's your son? You weren't there.

NANCY: *(Desperate, demanding.)* Do you think he did it? I wanna know.

RENSON: I don't think about it.

NANCY: *(Accusing, curious.)* Why? You believe he did it—don't you? *(Pause.)*

RENSON: *(Sullen, ashamed.)* I hate to tell you this…it's what you're asking for. They claim they found a lot of evidence: Ray's fingerprints, Ray's blood-type and skin under her nails—I was curious too. I went to see her. She remembered the scar under his breast and the burns on his right shoulder. She even told me some of the things he said while he raped her. It was him. You can save her the trouble of recounting that experience. *(Nancy cries.)* He was sick. He wouldn't even talk to you—his own mother. He turned against the one who brought him into this world. Can't you see—all his defiance of you was taken out on that girl? Is his death more logical now? He earned the curse of the gods for that.

NANCY: *(Crying.)* I never realized how sensitive and fragile men could be.

RENSON: Trouble is, sometimes, we afraid to show it. *(Renson embraces Nancy.)* Don't let none of those ghosts around here trouble you. When you smile the house smiles and the bad spirits go away. It's been like that since you've been home. *(Looks at her.)* Don't spoil it.

NANCY: Ray ain't gon go away.

RENSON: Don't let it be a thorn. Let it be a wild black rose. Let's build a memorial for him. *(Soft, sad.)* A hunting ground for displaced warriors.

NANCY: *(Confesses, tearful.)* We should have never let him go to that damn war!

RENSON: He had his reasons. They weren't...all wrong.

NANCY: *(Pulls away from him.)* How can you justify him getting his brains mangled—

RENSON: I'm not. He had his reasons. We couldn'tstop him.

NANCY: Not with force. *(Convinced.)* But with words we could have.

RENSON: Let's build a memorial for him. *(Tender, loving.)* Let's rebuild our family.

NANCY: You won't forget what I did.

RENSON: I've already forgotten.

NANCY: I've already forgotten.

NANCY: I've had ten months to think about what happened. I was wrong... *(Sorry.)* I had to pay, I had to realize that.

RENSON: So you've paid...and I paid and we've all paid. Why do you want more bloody sacrifice? *(Pause.)* What happened is my fault. I drove you away. You had a reason. You must have had a reason.

NANCY: *(Frustrated, annoyed.)* Would it make you feel better if I did? I've told you before I didn't have a reason. I wasn't even in love with him, and I was happily married to you.

RENSON: You still are married to me.

NANCY: You want me to make up a reason for you? I had no reason.

RENSON: Did you hear what I said? You're still my wife.

NANCY: ...and Ray's still your son, but he's not with you. *(Solicitous.)* What about the victims? What about the victims of this sewage system?

RENSON: We're not sewage cleaners.

NANCY: *(Very sincere, intense.)* We have to be. We live here. The memorial has to grow beyond these walls. And it has to be for the living. We walk down these streets and pass young men like Ray everyday. We gotta *do* something for them. We *live here. (Pause.)* I'm serious.

RENSON: I know you are. *(Soft smile.)* And I'm proud of you. I really am. Whatever you do, I'm with you. *(Comes close to her, bends down turning his back and offers his shoulders.)* Let me be your striking arm of lightning... The will that goes forth at the sound of your voice.

NANCY: *(Smiles.)* You'd promise me the Canary Islands.

RENSON: *(Grins.)* Hey! *(Unfolds her.)* Let's go to the Canary Islands. We can go right now without even leaving the house.

(They kiss, hug.)

NANCY: I know you'll do it. You're a man of your word. *(Loving.)*

RENSON: *(Passionate, loving.)* How long has it been?...A century it seems since I've held you like this.

NANCY: *(Sighs.)* Too long.

(Passionate kissing.)

RENSON: We've harvested the frost this year. Love oughta be better and sweeter than ever. Stay with me...Don't go back to snow man's land.

NANCY: I have to go back to work Monday. *(Kisses between phrases.)* I hate to quit in mid-air. I'll come back when—

RENSON: Fuck them polar bears. *(Kisses her cheek, neck, lips.)* Do I have to lock you in here and throw away the key? This is your house. Without you it's a house full of ghosts that moan all day and all night.

NANCY: Ghosts—I see them everytime I look at that landscape of ice and snow. *(Pause.)* And I've always loved you...

(They kiss; Renson puts his arm around Nancy, they walk off towards the bedroom.)

CURTAIN

Karen Jones Meadows

HENRIETTA

Negro Ensemble Company

Karen Jones Meadows

Karen Jones Meadows is a writer working in the mediums of stage, film, and television. She writes for adult and young audiences with an emphasis on creating works that are specific in character and universal in theme, passion, and resolution. Her full length stage plays for adults include *Henrietta*, *Tapman*, and *Major Changes*. Her young audience plays include *Private Conversations*, *Everybody's Secret*, *Sala Cinderella*, and *Harriet Returns for Us*. She has worked in various capacities with The Negro Ensemble Company, Hudson Guild Theatre, The Women's Project, New Federal Theatre, Houston Ensemble Company, Indiana Repertory Company, Penumbra Theatre, Frederick Douglass Creative Arts Center, and Luna Stage Company. Karen is a recipient of a Drama League of New York Playwright Award, The Cornerstone Award from Penumbra Theatre, and an Emerging Artist Fellowship. Currently she is Visiting McGee Professor of Writing at Davidson College in N.C., and is working on projects with Blackground Entertainment, Onyx Media Group, and A.R.M. Productions. Also an actress and producer, Karen has performed in feature and television films and commercials, and co-produced short films for Fox Television and Comedy Central. Karen has one perfectly delightful, strong, and wise son, Jayson.

THE NEGRO ENSEMBLE COMPANY

Nearly three decades after its establishment, The Negro Ensemble Company has achieved an American cultural miracle. In the past 28 years, over 400 plays have been produced and developed, 300 Black American writers and directors have been given opportunities, and over 4,000 actors, actresses, designers, technicians, and administrators have produced theatre. Over the years millions of theatre-goers nationally and internationally have seen NEC-originated plays about the Black experience in America. It is now widely recognized that the NEC has led in changing the face of American theatre. Our impact has been universally felt. Theatres such as the Goodman in Chicago, Guthrie in Minnesota, Mark Taper in Los Angeles, the Alliance in Atlanta, Walnut in Philadelphia, Alley in Houston, the Arena Stage in Washington, D.C., as well as the Cincinnati Playhouse all look to the NEC to enrich the program they offer their residents.

Internationally, NEC performed in Italy, Australia, and as part of the 1976 Olympic Games in Munich, West Germany. NEC performed to enthusiastic audiences at the Dublin Theatre Festival (1982), the Olympic Games in Los Angeles, California (1984), the Edinburgh Arts Festival (1984), the American Theatre Festival in London, England (1984), and, under the sponsorship of the United States Information Agency, toured southeast Asia extensively from Kuala Lumpur to Manila, Hong Kong, Bangkok, and Singapore (1987). NEC premiered Charles Fuller's *We*, a work about the Reconstruction era, at the National Black Arts Festival in Atlanta, Georgia (1988) and performed for "sell out" crowds at the National Black Theatre Festival in Winston-Salem, North Carolina (1989).

At home, in New York City, NEC has taken three plays to Broadway and has been nominated for as many Tony awards. In 1982, our production of Charles Fuller's *A Soldier's Play* won a Pulitzer Prize for best new American play.

The television documentary on PBS' American Masters Series profiled NEC's unparalleled body of talented artists, many of whom have successfully crossed over into the mainstream of TV and film. From *Fences* to "The Cosby Show", from *A Soldier's Story* to *The Color Purple* and *Pulp Fiction*, we are proud of our alumni and their successes since their original NEC days.

The roster of artists who have distinguished the productions of the NEC include Adolph Caeser, Barbara Montgomery, Frances Foster, Charles Brown, L. Scott Caldwell, Denise Nicholas, Eugene Lee, Michelle Shay, Graham Brown, Moses Gunn, Clevon Little, Denzel Washington, Roscoe Lee Brown, Rosalind Cash, Roxie Roker, Sherman Hemsley, Godfreid Cambridge, Ester Rolle, Phelicia Rashad, Jackee Harry, Debbie Morgan, Hattie Winston, and last but not least, Samuel L. Jackson.

HENRIETTA
by Karen Jones-Meadows

Directed by
Samuel P. Barton

CAST

HENRIETTA	Frances Foster
SHELEEAH	Elain Graham
THOMAS	William Jay

TIME: Fall. Present day.
PLACE: New York City

CHARACTERS

HENRIETTA	50-60 year old woman
SHELEEAH	28 year old woman
THOMAS	37-47 year old man

The play takes place in New York. Henrietta sits outside of a
brownstone apartment building. The set can be simple or elaborate
according to the means of the theatre.

(Act One, Scene I—It is late September, a weekday morning in New York City. At curtain rise, Henrietta is seated on a crate yelling at the passers-by and blowing up paper bags and busting them. She is tattered, but not dirty. The sounds of the street can be heard.)

HENRIETTA: Politics is a dirty business. Have mercy, I'm glad I'm me. Keep walking, don't hurt my feelings—don't hurt them a bit. *(Blows up paper bag.)* Humph. *(Motions to move on.)* I don't talk to nobody that listens. Get you in trouble. Look at Malcolm...how they shot him down. Know why don't you?—Cause he talked too much. To be smart, he wasa ignorant sucker. Now me...I don't talk to nobody that listens. *(Gets another paper bag and is blowing it up. Takes a lot out of her and she sits to bust it.)* Won't shoot me. *(Enter SHELEEAH.)* I don't talk to them folks. Listening people are a dangerous lot. —What's that you got on—

SHELEEAH: Don't you yell at me today old lady. I had enough of you— *(Walking up to Henrietta menacingly.)*

HENRIETTA: *(Looking up from the crate, Sheleeah standing over her.)* What's that you got on? Looking like an art carnival. All them colors. You a painter sweetie? *(She laughs.)* You do that yourself? *(Sheleeah starts to leave.)* Somebody help me! There's a nut over here—can't get no help. These streets are dangerous. You trying to intimidate me girl? Cause you cain't.

SHELEEAH: I just want to know why you think it's your duty to bother me every time I come past here, I'm getting tired of it. You embarrass me.

HENRIETTA: Cause I feel like it. You feel like showing off. You wearing all them colors, figured you must want to be seen. I was only trying to help. For real. I'm a teacher, I teach people what they need to know. Don't look at me like that, I'm a teacher and I command respect. *(Sheleeah walks away, Henrietta blows up a bag)* Well, I use to command respect. *(She pops bag.)* *(Lights fade out.)*

(Scene II—It is now Saturday evening. Lights rise. Henrietta is dressed the same and reading a newspaper and cutting out pictures and articles.)

HENRIETTA: Gold's gone up—better run down to Tiffany's and put a bracelet on laysway while I can...but then again, I don't need it. People get so envious. *(Enter Sheleeah—Henrietta peers through a hole in her paper as Sheleeah walks straight by ignoring her.)* You in mourning girl? Black don't do a thing for you...Hey... hey...Hey, lady in black. *(Lights fade out.)*

(Scene III—The time is now Sunday, in the morning. Lights rise up on Henrietta dressed the same. She has a bag of fruit beside her and a plastic bowl wedged between her legs. She begins cutting up the fruit into the bowl. She is quiet. There's a crate next to her. Sheleeah enters dressed very nicely.)

HENRIETTA: You look a sight better than you did yesterday. Black don't do a thing for you. I don't like you in no black clothes. *(Sheleeah walks over to her.)* I like you in that lavender and yellow you wear. The scarf gives it a nice touch. I had a lavender outfit one time, but I wore orange with it. I must a looked like the devil, lavender and orange...that don't go together. Is this going to be real deep or what, cause I'm not in a deep mood. This is one of my happy go lucky days—

SHELEEAH: I want to talk to you. Why do you pay so much attention to what I wear?

HENRIETTA: That's it? That's what you had to talk to me about?

SHELEEAH: No I'm leading to something.

HENRIETTA: Oh, that's our get acquainted lead in...I get it. Well...cause you one of my steadies. I look out for my steadies. You in a hurry?

SHELEEAH: No.

HENRIETTA: Well, sit down. Here. *(She picks up the crate beside her and pulls it up closer to her.)*

SHELEEAH: I'm not going to stay long, but I decided to take some time and just uhh, talk to you.

HENRIETTA: Lucky me. Did I look lonely or something? I don't want to go around looking like I need someone to talk to, cause I don't. I talk to myself just fine.

SHELEEAH: Yeah, you do a pretty good amount of talking to other folks too. Aa a matter of fact, most of them would prefer if you didn't.

HENRIETTA: I just knew somebody would be by today. That's why I brought the other chair. Somebody always comes on Sunday. People not so much in a hurry on Sunday, generally speaking. *(She peels a grapefruit—Peels it whole then the under skin, then the casing aroumd each section.)*

SHELEEAH: Yeah, I guess you're right.

HENRIETTA: Oh yeah, I'm right, I excel at being right...Seeds don't bother me, but the skin gets caught in my teeth. Seeds are good for your teeth and skin. Let me see your face. *(She rests her hands on Sheleeah's lap, Sheleeah flinches)* Yeah, you could use quite a few seeds. You been trying to bleach your skin?

SHELEEAH: No, I haven't.

HENRIETTA: Sure looks like it. People don't admit that so readily these days.

SHELEEAH: I don't bleach my—

HENRIETTA: What's your name?

SHELEEAH: Sheleeah.

HENRIETTA: Sheila?

SHELEEAH: No, Sheleeah.

HENRIETTA: Spell it. *(Henrietta drops peels on the ground—Sheleeah looks at her scornfully)* I'll pick it up. I'll get it, go on spell it.

SHELEEAH: S-H-E-L-E-E-A-H.

HENRIETTA: Probably your mother wanted to name you Sheila and couldn't spell it. That's all right, that's all right. Plenty folks can't spell. Where you work?

SHELEEAH: I'm an accountant.

HENRIETTA: No, not what you do, where you work?

SHELEEAH: At Parker, Parker and Westmore.

HENRIETTA: You ain't listening girl. Where: Like what street. Not who or what, but WHERE!

SHELEEAH: Fifty-second and Third.

HENRIETTA: Thank you, thank you, thank you. Now...now, what do you do?

SHELEEAH: I told you, I'm an accountant.

HENRIETTA: Oh, well now don't get huffy. You're not dealing with a regular person here so you can't expect me to absorb all these facts in a normal manner. Anyway, don't matter cause you work too far downtown and I usually don't go that far—was gonna meet you for lunch, but that's out now.

SHELEEAH: That's too bad. I've got to—

HENRIETTA: No, we'll work some other arrangement out. *(She stirs the fruit in the bowl)* Let me see...Want some?

(Pulling spoon out of paper bag and taking a mouthful, then offering some to Sheleeah.)

SHELEEAH: No, no thank you. I have to go.

HENRIETTA: Your boyfriend coming over today? He spent the night last night didn't he?

SHELEEAH: Excuse me?

HENRIETTA: Your boyfriend coming over today? You know, the one with the car. That is a baad car. Reminds me of Harry's when—

SHELEEAH: I don't discuss my private business with strangers.

HENRIETTA: Everybody else is talking about it, you may as well.

SHELEEAH: Been nice meeting you.

HENRIETTA: Henrietta Mabeline Barthalamew. Everybody calls me Miss Effie though. Now you've met me.

SHELEEAH: Okay, well, nice meeting you, take care and I'll, uhh, see you again.

HENRIETTA: Where you runnin' off to? I ain't offended you have I, cause if I did, it means you too sensitive. Don't like no tempermental women. Gets on my nerves.

SHELEEAH: No, I'm not tempermental, I just have to go.

HENRIETTA: You the one came up here talkin' to me. Now you gotta run. I hope that creep with the car ain't the reason. His car is nice, but I don't like his face, not one bit, though I try not to judge people. But he's a tad flamboyant. Like a girl, if you get my drift.

SHELEEAH: You think he's flamboyant? *(She sits)*

HENRIETTA: I sure do.

SHELEEAH: I don't. He's rugged...and masculine, he's sweet, but he's manly. I've known him a long time, and—

HENRIETTA: Don't have to convince me. You the one gotta—I like that other guy. The dufis looking one.

SHELEEAH: I know just who you're talking about. He's boring. I mean really boring. How do you manage to see who comes and goes?

HENRIETTA: I'll admit, he don't look like much, but you could work with him. You know, get him to trust you, teach him to dress and how to stand so he wasn't such a drip.

SHELEEAH: Umm-umm, no way. He's hopeless. Anyway I have to—

HENRIETTA: If he's hopeless what'd you go out with him for?

SHELEEAH: Cause I wanted to.

HENRIETTA: That's okay, that's what I'm here for, the problems of the world. What's that guy with the car's name?

SHELEEAH: Marcus.

HENRIETTA: La dee dah. Got money huh?

SHELEEAH: Yeah, enough.

HENRIETTA: How about the other one?

SHELEEAH: Yeah, he' s got money too.

HENRIETTA: Well you got it made. Dirty money?

SHELEEAH: You'll never know. *(She walks away)*

HENRIETTA: Better stay with the drip. He's more your speed. Best to know your own limitations and he's yours. Believe me—You got any mayonnaise jars, or pickle jars?

SHELEEAH: I don't know, I don't think so.

HENRIETTA: Well, see what you can do about rounding some up.

SHELEEAH: I can't do anything about rounding up—

HENRIETTA: I've used up all my sources and I need some for my business. Quart size are good.

SHELEEAH: I don't know where to find any jars and—

HENRIETTA: If you'll drop them off, let me see, Thursday, yeah, Thursday's good. I'd appreciate it. I'll be here in the morning, but I have an appointment at three, can't tell you where, but if you miss me, I'll stop by your place in the evening.

SHELEEAH: Miss Effie...

HENRIETTA: Please don't call me that. It hurts my feelings.

SHELEAAH: *(indignant)* I'm sorry I forgot your other name. You said everybody calls you...

HENRIETTA: Shelra is it?

SHELEEAH: Sheleeah...

HENRIETTA: Henrietta Mabeline Barthalamw. Say the whole name, come on together *(Henrietta orchestrates—both say the name together.)* Hen-ri-et-ta-Ma-bel-ine-Bar-thal-a-mew. That was good.

SHELEEAH: Henrietta, you can't drop by my house.

HENRIETTA: Oh, well excuse me for living and breathing... *(She starts putting away the fruit mixture)* You're so high and mighty. Too good for my company.

SHELEEAH: I didn't mean to imply that. I don't like company, period. I—

HENRIETTA: Oh, I see, what's them men stuck up in your house called? No, no forget it. Don't answer me, cause it ain't none of my business in the first place, so goodbye and see ya 'round.

SHELEEAH: Don't get mad.

HENRIETTA: I'm not. I'll get my jars somewheres else. I've had my business for twelve years, so don't think a Miss Priss like you will shut me down. It's been a pleasure talking to you, but I don't think it's going to happen again. Have a lovely day, Miss Priss.

SHELEEAH: I'll try to find you some jars and bring them Thursday, and please don't call me Miss Priss.

HENRIETTA: I wouldn't use them jars. I hope you marry Mr. Car. You two are perfect for each other.

SHELEEAH: *(Walking away)* See you later.

HENRIETTA: No, you won't be seeing me. Maybe in your dreams. You need to be going to church with your sinner self. Sleeping with two men. Your supposed to love people, and do all in your power to help them, but not you. You learned young didn't you! Didn't you! Hurt my feelings like that, well... *(wiping her face)* I don't need you. I never did. Never. I was pretty too, I had boyfriends too, and they did nice things for me. So see, I don't need you. Or anybody else either *(After everything's packed she puts one crate inside the other and heads off stage.)* I'm through being nice to people. I know better. Uhh ohh, maybe I got a new screw loose. Highly irrational, highly!

(End Scene III)

(Scene IV—Mid-morning, Sunday, one week later. Sheleeah enters from S.L. carrying a big bag of jars. Henrietta is seated on her crate leaning forward hands clasped and dangling over her knees.)

HENRIETTA: Well, it's about time. You're three days late.

SHELEEAH: Here are the jars.

HENRIETTA: Put em down. Got quart size didn't you? Larger's okay, but nothing smaller. Spoils the blend. There's an art to making—

SHELEEAH: I brought these jars so you'd stop hollering obsenities at me. What's wrong with you, screaming at me like a maniac? *(Takes a jar out for Henrietta's approval)* You'd think you'd act better with someone who's doing you a favor.

HENRIETTA: I needed them jars. Had to get them. I know how, little girl. I use incentive training, works everytime. I wish you hadn't a come till next week. Had a heap of things to call you—

SHELEEAH: I believe you too. I don't know how you think of half the things you call people.

HENRIETTA: And you actin' like you didn't hear me. I knew you were listening.

SHELEEAH: Yeah, the whole world was listening. You got a lot of nerve. Somebody one day will hurt you for messing with them.

HENRIETTA: No they won't, I been doing it for years—some people you can't bother, rolls off their back and some will knock your head off—I can spot them and I don't mess with 'em—but you, you are a prime target if there ever was one. You want respect. Good game. Just itching for it.

SHELEEAH: Really? I look like somebody who ought to have a dere-uhh—dere—

HENRIETTA: Go head honey, spit it out, DERELICT. Don't bother me a bit that's what you think I am. Been called worse when it was true, so go right on ahead.

SHELEEAH: If you can holler in the street, I can sure speak my mind and you are a derelict of sorts. That's not to say—

HENRIETTA: You're hot now, keep talking.

SHELEEAH: Don't tell me you can't take what you dish out?

HENRIETTA: I'm not dirty, I don't stink. I don't eat filth or live in the gutter or vomit on myself or...What do you think a derelict is?

SHELEEAH: I think it's uhh, a person who doesn't take care of themselves...and doesn't have the guts to face life...uh, is weak and preys on the emotions of others. I think it's someone like you.

HENRIETTA: *(Looking up at Sheleeah from her crate)* Well you're right. I am a derelict. But you're wrong in your definition. A derelict is anything— including people—who've been casted out or thrown out by society, not necessarily by any fault of their own, mind you. Just down on luck. It's you folks who make derelicts. It's people like you, who call yourself better or whatever you do in your ivory towers, who make derelicts like me. Little girl, you're nothing but a child and until you learn better you ought to keep your mouth shut and listen and learn. That's your only function, to listen and learn.

SHELEEAH: I'm just trying to have an upfront conversation with you. You're a bag lady right? Right? Just take the jars. *(Henrietta doesn't answer)* Would you like a paper? I'm... going over there, and I don't mind getting two.

HENRIETTA: I read it this morning. How much does it cost?

SHELEEAH: Dollar-twenty-five.

HENRIETTA: Okay, get me one-dollar and twenty-five cents worth of pickled eggs. Include the tax if you will. And bring me a receipt. *(Sheleeah looks at her in disbelief)* You don't need it. You were going to buy a paper anyway— what's the difference?

SHELEEAH: There is one, but it's not worth explaining to you. I'll be right back.

HENRIETTA: How come you only get the Sunday paper?

SHELEEAH: If you must know, I read the daily paper at work and I don't read the Saturday paper at all.

HENRIETTA: You tight with money, ain't you? Guess it's an honor you even volunteering to buy me a paper.

SHELEEAH: I'll be right back. *(She starts to leave)*

HENRIETTA: Don't take too long, cause I'm hungry. And don't stop to what with none of them degenerates, that's what you were describing, those men on the corner, degenerates. Bunch a bums. Me I'm a derelict. *(Still looking after Sheleeah, she yells)* Your skirt's hiked up in the back—your butt's showing. Fooled you. *(She laughs)* I love pickled eggs, love em, love em. Pickled eggs and cornflakes. Should a told her to get me some cornflakes. Wouldn't a done it, snootie broad. She got sly ways.

(THOMAS enters S.R. carrying the Sunday paper)

THOMAS: Here you go Miss Effie.

HENRIETTA: Thank you Thomas. *(She takes paper and puts it aside off-handedly.)*

THOMAS: *(Aware of her disinterest)* Got to run, I'm going to church this morning.

HENRIETTA: Nobody asked you to stay. What they giving away in church?

THOMAS: Nothing. What's wrong with you, what's the matter?

HENRIETTA: Nothing.

THOMAS: Come on tell me.

HENRIETTA: My back hurts. And my teeth hurt. My gums is swole.

THOMAS: Why don't you see a dentist?

HENRIETTA: You got a good heart, but your brain ain't all it could be. But when you go to church, ask God to help you see the light. He'll tell you. Listen. It'll come to you.

THOMAS: Something else is bothering you.

HENRIETTA: No just my back and my teeth and there's a pain in my behind. *(Sheleeah enters.)*

THOMAS: Hope you feel better.

HENRIETTA: I don't even think he got it. Pitiful.

SHELEEAH: Here you go. Three pickled eggs and a receipt.

THOMAS: Miss Effie don't have no manners, I'm Thomas Bost—

HENRIETTA: I do too have manners.

THOMAS: Miss Effie's not feeling well, what's your— *(extending his hand)*

HENRIETTA: I'm fine.

SHELEEAH: *(Switches bag from right hand to left so she can shake hands)* Sheleeah Hampton.

THOMAS: Thomas Boston.

HENRIETTA: Or call him TB, you know like in tuberculosis.

SHELEEAH: Nice to meet you Mr. Boston.

THOMAS: Thomas.

SHELEEAH: Thomas.

HENRIETTA: Shelra...Shelra...Miss Effie...Miss Effie. Hey, anybody got any mint julips for us to sip, eh Thomas...Thomas.

THOMAS: I'll be seeing you both. Nice to meet you. Miss Effie I'll check on you later.

HENRIETTA: I'm gonna be doing good. *(Sheleeah starts away.)* No, wait! Not you. Thomas, go on about your business. Shelra I want to talk to you. Sit down.

SHELEEAH: I have to go.

HENRIETTA: You always have to go. I don't want you to go. I want you to stay here and talk with me for awhile. Okay? A few minutes. There I said it. I begged you.

SHELEEAH: You didn't beg me. I'll stay for a few minutes.

HENRIETTA: I did too beg you, but I'm learning to be humble. Makes me want to throw up.

SHELEEAH: Where'd you get the paper from?

HENRIETTA: *(Sarcastically)* TB. Sorry, Thomas.

SHELEEAH: Thought you read it already.

HENRIETTA: I did, I read the man down the streets paper every Sunday before he even gets up. Don't get up til about eleven, 'cept one time when he was sick or something and then he was up all night.

SHELEEAH: Well doesn't Thomas know that.

HENRIETTA: No, I don't tell him. Bringing me the paper is a big deal for Thomas see, he steals it from different places and makes him feel like he's accomplished something. You know how it is.

SHELEEAH: No I don't.

HENRIETTA: You just act like you don't. But you do know. Now don't you? Humm? *(Pause)* Thank you for the eggs. *(She takes the bag)*

SHELEEAH: You're welcome. I didn't know whether or not you liked hot ones.

HENRIETTA: No, I don't. *(Checking the eggs)*

SHELEEAH: I got mild. I understand you being hungry. Go on and eat.

HENRIETTA: No I can't eat and talk at the same time. Want to come to my house?

SHELEEAH: Where?

HENRIETTA: Where I live. Do you want to?

SHELEEAH: Henrietta, I don't think you have.

HENRIETTA: Nothing will get you. I have a room and nothing lives there but me. Dracula left a few weeks ago and wolfman is mad so he ran off to the woods.

SHELEEAH: Very funny.

HENRIETTA: Want to come to my house for lunch?

SHELEEAH: Thought you didn't have any food?

HENRIETTA: I don't, you'll have to bring it.

SHELEEAH: I can't today.

HENRIETTA: Well, you want me to come to your house?

SHELEEAH: Uhh, uhhh—

HENRIETTA: Just say no and be done with it.

SHELEEAH: Henrietta, I'm probably never going to invite you to my house. We don't even know each other.

HENRIETTA: Well, how are we supposed to get to know each other if you're afraid. You have nothing to fear from me. I'm harmless. Do I look like a murderer or something? *(Throws hands in the air)* Just don't understand. We were getting on so well. I thought we could have a good friendship and then—

SHELEEAH: I'm leaving.

HENRIETTA: Oh, you're just plain mean. Anybody who doesn't respond to that plea is sick. I'm screaming out for...How about dinner on Thursday? I'll cook. You don't even have to bring the food. Okay? How about it? I'm practicing being humble.

SHELEEAH: Can I tell you during the week?

HENRIETTA: *(Rising from crate)* Don't make me have to curse you in the street!

SHELEEAH: No, I will, I'll think about it. I have a lot to do this week, but if I can—

HENRIETTA: *(Crossing back to sit crate)* You'll do me a favor and come? I'll take it that way.

SHELEEAH: Where *do* you live?

HENRIETTA: I'll tell you, after you tell me. You didn't pick up any salt at the store did you!

SHELEEAH: How can you eat salt on pickled eggs?

HENRIETTA: Easy. I sprinkle it on, and shove it in. Easy as I'll see you during the week. Bye, bye. *(She exits S.L.)* I certainly hope you can make it. *(Picks up paper and begins reading)* A new committee has been formed to study the actions of the previous committee. According to the new committee there are questions about the old committee for the new committee to answer. That's a fine bit of journalism.

END SCENE IV

(Scene V—Inside Henrietta's apartment, there is a small table with a hot plate on it. The room is cluttered with many things resembling an attic. The rear and side walls are covered with banners, newspaper clippings, cards, photos, and other momentos. On the walls in the adjoining corner are three nicely framed pictures, two men on either side of a woman. There's a clothesline hanging across the room. Henrietta is downstage stirring a pot of beans. Sheleeah is discovered looking around the array of junk as the lights rise.)

HENRIETTA: We got say, two, three more hours on these beans.

SHELEEAH: What do you mean two or three hours? It's eight o'clock.

HENRIETTA: I knew better than to buy these old beans at Max's. Probably been there since they opened in nineteen hundred.

SHELEEAH: What else can we eat?

HENRIETTA: I went out of my way to buy something you'd like and I could cook on this thing. There's rice and chili made with my own hands, from scratch, so if you'll be patient one minute I'll be through and we can talk while it cooks. You're just as jumpy as I don't know what.

SHELEEAH: *(Walks over to the wall and examines pictures)* You've got a lot of stuff Henrietta. Lota stuff.

HENRIETTA: Not stuff. Momentos. My memories.

SHELEEAH: Who's that?

HENRIETTA: *(Turning to see.)* My daughter.

SHELEEAH: You have a daughter?

HENRIETTA: Ummhumm.

SHELEEAH: Where is she?

HENRIETTA: I'm not in position to say.

SHELEEAH: What do you mean?

HENRIETTA: I'm not in a position to say.

SHELEEAH: Well, did you lose touch or what?

HENRIETTA: SHELRA, I'M NOT IN A POSITION TO SAY!!!

SHELEEAH: Okay, okay. Who's that?
   (Walking along the wall.)

HENRIETTA: That's my son.

SHELEEAH: Oh, come on.

HENRIETTA: And do what?

SHELEEAH: You really have children? You're joking, right?

HENRIETTA: I have three children...Know why I left my mind? Had to go. Too much in there. Wasn't enough room in there for me and all those thoughts floating around, you can separate your mind, you know that. Anyway I left, couldn't stay where I wasn't needed. I'm not crazy, just out of my mind.

SHELEEAH: Come on tell me about them Henrietta.

HENRIETTA: Nothing to tell. Leave me alone. Keep picture hunting and leave me be.

SHELEEAH: (Gets Henrietta and drags her to the wall) Put down the spoon and come here and tell me about...

HENRIETTA: They're dead. Every last one is dead...All three. Now you're uncomfortable, right? Shoulda left well enough alone. I had me two boys and one girl, they were...

SHELEEAH: I'm sorry, I wouldn't have pushed you had I known that. I'm really...

HENRIETTA: Shut up and listen girl. See, my boys was born first. Keith and Fraizer. Fraizer was named after his great-grandpa. Fraizer was hell on wheels, and fine he'd a broken many a heart if a lived. Now Keith, Keith was sickly the whole time. But I never thought he was gonna die. Never did, and they never told me either. In fact I don't even know how I found out must be something caught in my mind. Can't get a handle on that stuff. I told you about that.

SHELEEAH: Oh God: I'm sorry, I'm really sorry...

HENRIETTA: Now, something I DON'T allow is God talk.

SHELEEAH: What?

HENRIETTA: Nope. See, most people don't know what they're talking about, and I can't allow it in my house. I mean room.

SHELEEAH: I said something about God?

HENRIETTA: That's what I'm talking about, you don't even remember it. You're a funny lady. (Pointing to a picture of her sister on the dresser.) You haven't met my sister yet, have you? You wouldn't like her. She's got age spots on her hands—she's not that old either. Comes from being hateful, I think. But her babies are alive don't you know? They sure are. And she's a child abuser and her husband's a child molester, sure as I'm sitting here and stirring these beans.

SHELEEAH: Where was this one taken?

HENRIETTA: That's another thing, too. Her husband, the child molester, is still alive. See those men? Are you paying any attention at all? See those men here... (Showing her the pictures.) These are my husbands. Henry and Laney. Guess which one's which.

SHELEEAH: I can't I...

HENRIETTA: Oh, go on, let's have some fun.

SHELEEAH: This one's Henry and that one's...

HENRIETTA: Right. They look like their names, don't they? Ummhumm, they sure do. Henry was kind of firm and stiff, and Laney was a good time man.

SHELEEAH: Yeah. How are the beans coming...

HENRIETTA: I visit the graves. All of them, the children's and Laney and Henry...I buried Lane right next to Henry. Henry is probably fit to be tied. But we're all family the way I see it.

SHELEEAH: Henrietta, maybe I can take you out for dinner since...

HENRIETTA: I visit the graves you know, and sometimes I can feel the spirits entering me. I sit on top of graves and eat breakfast and sing and...

SHELEEAH: Henrietta please enough of grave stories! (Apologetically) I'm sorry but it gives me the creeps. How about...

HENRIETTA: Tell me about your people. Your people must be alive or dead folks wouldn't give you the creeps.

SHELEEAH: Yes, my family is, well the immediate family at least are all alive and doing quite well.

HENRIETTA: You know we have the opposite problem.

SHELEEAH: What's that?

HENRIETTA: Dead people give you the creeps and live people give me the creeps.

SHELEEAH: Nobody's died in my family for ten years or so. I'm not familiar with death.

HENRIETTA: Well, you will before it's over.

SHELEEAH: I don't think about my family very much. We aren't close.

HENRIETTA: You should be. Mother's should see to that. It's their job. It's their duty.

SHELEEAH: What are the jars for?

HENRIETTA: Fruit salad.I make fruit salad and sell it.

SHELEEAH: Oh.

HENRIETTA: First and fifteenth. People tend to be more generous around then. I'm no bum you know. I earn my keep. I'm respectable and I have to maintain the standard of living to which I have become accustomed. That's a joke. Can't you tell? Don't you have a sense of humor? Hello, are you alive in there?

SHELEEAH: I have two brothers myself.

HENRIETTA: My daughter's name was Tootie. That's what I called her. So see, she had two brothers too, just like you.

SHELEEAH: I haven't seen my brothers in a long time though. I had to leave home when I was sixteen.

HENRIETTA: Same thing happened to Tootie.

SHELEEAH: My father and I didn't see eye to eye at all. So, I had to go. I was like you in a way. Kinda just out there, know what I mean?

HENRIETTA: Tootie's father was mean to her too. Couldn't understand it. He was a good man, but he and Tootie, just didn't hit it off. And she was a girl. Girls are usually the apple of...

SHELEEAH: I'd meet my mother. Sneaking you know. Weird. She should have stood up to him. She knew he was wrong. She should...

HENRIETTA: Some men fancy boys better.

SHELEEAH: I don't know what it was. I guess it still is, since I don't hear from either one of them anymore, or my brothers. But I know they're okay, cause people tell me.

HENRIETTA: Don't rely on people to tell you nothing. People told me Tootie was alright. AND SHE WASN'T. SHE SURE WASN'T... I was like your mother. I should have spoken up in the first place. Laney died the year after she left. See Tootie was Henry's child, they all were. Laney was a good time man...then he died of meanness, I say. Henry just died. Quick. Laney threw up blood and wouldn't go to the hospital, it was his insides rotting of meanness, but Henry was gentle and he just was sitting down talking and then Buump. Out dead as a doornail. He was clean though. You know he didn't leak from nowhere or anything.

SHELEEAH: I had enough about death and dying and please change the subject.

HENRIETTA: *(Out to Audience)* I'll never go back back there now, so forget it....I'm going to the funeral home. I TOLD YOU TO FORGET

SHELEEAH: What's wrong? What's...

HENRIETTA: I DID IT!!! I SHOULD HAVE GOTTEN HER AND I DID-N'T, I SHOULD HAVE...

SHELEEAH: HENRIETTA! This is upsetting you. I can't help you...

HENRIETTA: *(Yelling at Sheleeah)* I don't need your help!!!! What makes you think I need your help? HENRIETTA MABELINE BARTHALAMEW DON'T NEED YOU NOW! WHERE WERE YOU WHEN I DID? HUH? WHERE WERE YOU WHEN...see Laney was my second husband and he raised those children like they were his, and then...I don't know where Henry went I don't...What's your father do to you when he's mad?

SHELEEAH: *(Indredulous and cautious)* Nothing. He doesn't—

HENRIETTA: Oh, I see. That's the secret. Do nothing. *(Pause)* How do you know you don't like them?

SHELEEAH: What?

HENRIETTA: Graves.

SHELEEAH: I just know, look Henrietta, it's getting late and...

HENRIETTA: We'll plan a pinic. I'll bring fruit salad and you bring sandwiches, cornbeef with mustard, that's good, that's real good. And we can watch the souls rise up in the morning, like the sun, every morning.

SHELEEAH: NO, I don't go to graves. Instead of making fruit salad, why don't you get a regular job. Isn't it illegal or at least dangerous? Do you sterilize the jars?

HENRIETTA: Nope. Maybe I'll poison somebody and they'll electricute me. See I'm only here waiting to die. It's as simple as that. Just waiting. Biding my time. It ain't so hot to be normal. I been normal. As a matter of fact I was normal longer than I've been touched. So, see I have compared the two. You have nothing to compare. You're so normal it's a shame. It's a disgusting shame. That's why I...

SHELEEAH: I've done some weird things. You make me sound boring.

HENRIETTA: Oh, now you want to compare idiosyncrasies. You can't win. *(Pause)* You want some sherry?

SHELEEAH: Yeah, yeah, I'd like that. Sherry. You've got sherry?

HENRIETTA: *(Pulling sherry bottle from behind sofa cushion)* I've got class my dear. And a lot of it. Notice how I do everything with style.

SHELEEAH: Ummhumm. Doesn't the rest of your family, wonder where you are?

HENRIETTA: I hope they do. But I know they don't. They don't care about me. And my family is all dead. I thought I told you about that.

SHELEEAH: You did. I mean like your sister and nieces and...

HENRIETTA: My sister found me one time. I won't tell you what called her, but it got people to coming around and looking, cause they thought we were going to fight. She wouldn't fight, cause she knows I been waiting to kill her for fifteen years. She was at Fraizer's funeral and Toot's too. Talking about, "that girl was on drugs" and I had to knock two of her teeth out. It's safe to say I hate her stinking guts.

(ENTER THOMAS)

THOMAS: *(Speaking from outside her door)* Got any garbage to go Miss Effie?

HENRIETTA: No:

THOMAS: You all right in there? Miss Effie?

HENRIETTA: Yes, I'm fine. Mind your business.

SHELEEAH: Who's that?

HENRIETTA: Thomas.

SHELEEAH: Thomas, the man from Sunday, the papers?

HENRIETTA: Yeah. He's my landlord.

SHELEEAH: Oh.

HENRIETTA: Anyway where was I? Umm, umm, I don't know. I'm not hungry. Let's not eat these beans, don't trust them. Come here look at them.

SHELEEAH: *(Crosses to look at beans)* Yeah, they're darker than they're supposed to be aren't they?

HENRIETTA: Something's wrong with them, I don't know what, but...

SHELEEAH: I wouldn't mind filling up on this sherry. It's good. I've never had it before. Isn't it expensive?

HENRIETTA: Of course it is. I don't buy no cheap...

SHELEEAH: I don't mean to be personal but...how'd you manage to afford...

HENRIETTA: Yes you do. I got it from an antique store. I love antique stores. I have a special one and look out for me. They had this case that was fifteen or sixteen years old, something like that. Had a skim of some kind on top, but I took that off. Taste fine to me.

SHELEEAH: *(Looking into her glass)* A skim? Like film?

HENRIETTA: Bout that thick. This is my first time drinking it. Seems all right to me. *(She drinks it down)* Want some more?

SHELEEAH: I...I guess so...what the heck, if I'm gonna die from it, I may as well be happy.

HENRIETTA: You won't die. It's good. *(Pours more into both glasses)*

THOMAS: *(From outside the door)* Miss Effie I'm back.

HENRIETTA: Congratulations.

THOMAS: You got any company in there?

HENRIETTA: No, I'm just talking to myself.

THOMAS: Okay. Well, good night.

HENRIETTA: Good night, Thomas. *(She whispers)* He's supposed to be doing me a favor or so he thinks. I pay him five dollars a month rent and he thinks he owns me. I take care of his needs too.

SHELEEAH: You mean he makes you sleep with him?

HENRIETTA: Not that kind stupid. I wash his clothes and pick up food. Things like that. And he lets me use his bathroom and store my fruit in his refrigerator. He steals my salad you know, but I steal stuff from him too. Not really stealing, but...

SHELEEAH: I'm glad he doesn't make you sleep with him. I hate sleeping with men I don't like.

HENRIETTA: Why do you do it?

SHELEEAH: I have to, or at least I did at one time.

HENRIETTA: Why?

SHELEEAH: Because I didn't have anything, and it was a way to get it.

HENRIETTA: Your mother didn't raise you right. Now that's not fair, I don't even know your mother. I'm sorry, cause people said the same thing about me when Tootie died. My sister was right. She was a junkie, but it wasn't my fault. I helped her all I knew how. My sister's the one whose kids should have kicked the bucket. At least one would have been more fair. I'm jealous. That's it. I'm a jealous horror. So are you.

SHELEEAH: What?

HENRIETTA: Sure you are or you wouldn't sleep with those men. You want what they have, just like I want what she has. We are terrible people. Let's pray. *(She gets down on her knees grabbing Shelleah's hands on the way down. Sheleeah pulls away.)* My circulation is poor. That's why my hands are cold. Feel them. *(She reaches out to touch Sheleeah's face. Sheleeah withdraws again.)* You sure don't like to be touched.

SHELEEAH: Not my face. I don't like my face touched.

HENRIETTA: *(Rising)* I can't stay down here, plus I don't pray. Not too much.

SHELEEAH: Could I have some more sherry?

HENRIETTA: You're not going to sit around here getting drunk all night. And I only got three bottles of this.

SHELEEAH: Considering you are starving me to death.

HENRIETTA: You ain't starving girl. You need activity. Let me see. Do you play games?

SHELEEAH: NO.

HENRIETTA: I thought not. But I know we must have something in common. How about puzzles? You like puzzles?

SHELEEAH: How come *they* call you Effie?

HENRIETTA: Cause of F words.I use F words a lot like...

SHELEEAH: I get your point.

HENRIETTA: Jigsaw puzzles, you like them?

SHELEEAH: Yeah. I like them.

HENRIETTA: Okay then, that's what we'll do.

(Effie bends down slowly, holding back and reaches under Sheleeah's legs to get puzzle box. Then moves over to the hot plate on table and takes hot plate off to sit it on floor.)

SHELEEAH: Not on the floor!

HENRIETTA: Oh, shut up, no dirt gonna get in there. Might help anyway.

SHELEEAH: Please, not on the floor.

HENRIETTA: *(Puts the pot on floor)* Help me with this.

SHELEEAH: *(Crosses to table puts hot plate on floor then puts pot on hot plate as Effie clears the rest of the table.)* This isn't heavy. You could have done this yourself.

HENRIETTA: Mean and selfish, never helpful or...

SHELEEAH: Save it.

(They sit with puzzle)

HENRIETTA: I've done this one about five times.

SHELEEAH: It looks complicated.

HENRIETTA: Take out the corners first.

SHELEEAH: I don't do it that way.

HENRIETTA: Only one way to do a puzzle and that's corners first.

SHELEEAH: Why'd you start acting insane?

HENRIETTA: I beg your pardon?

SHELEEAH: I want to know for me. I could make great progress at work.

HENRIETTA: Want to act nuts hunh?

SHELEEAH: It's the control I want.

HENRIETTA: Try and take control is a sure way to go nuts.

SHELEEAH: You know how to control people. You make them go around you, scared to death you'll say something, or hit them...curse them, anything.

HENRIETTA: That's what you want me to teach you to be...

SHELEEAH: I don't want anything from you. I just enjoy your freedom. (She snaps a puzzle piece together) Got one.

HENRIETTA: Good. But you're supposed to be taking out corners.

SHELEEAH: I told you I don't do it that way.

HENRIETTA: Gotta learn to listen.

SHELEEAH: My grandmother had these framed in her bedroom. I always thought it was so ugly, cause the pictures looked cracked and broken and she had them in cheap frames so there'd be a glare. Like a cracked up world and she had a wrinkly cracked up face and...

HENRIETTA: I believe you're getting drunk. Must not of had enough to do, do all them puzzles and hang 'em up for pictures. I always had a lot to do. I did, and now I don't. Why is that? You know why?

SHELEEAH: No.

HENRIETTA: Me either. I don't understand it. I used to be a good person. Maybe I did something to somebody by accident and I'm being punished.

SHELEEAH: You're still a good person.

HENRIETTA: No, I'm not. Or why would I be here? I like it. Maybe that's why. It's not bad. Different. An alternative lifestyle. And I like it, I really do.

SHELEEAH: You can talk yourself into anything. You know that don't you?

HENRIETTA: Of course I do. I excel in being correct.

SHELEEAH: Then what do you think you did wrong?

HENRIETTA: I didn't mean to do whatever it was. I helped my children and my husbands. I even asked Henry if I could marry Laney, and he said yes. He sure did. So why's everybody so mad at me? Hunh? Why I am I being punished, huh? WHAT'S THE MATTER WITH EVERYBODY???... You ask too many questions. You don't know me.

SHELEEAH: I'm trying to get to know you though. You're a different kind of person, and...

HENRIETTA: I ain't no different kind of person.

SHELEEAH: I didn't mean it like that...

HENRIETTA: Put on your listening ears...Remember when they used to tell you that in school? I was a school teacher. Know what? I was an aide really. But they fired me. I didn't need them. They were brats and hoods, just like Tootie. Tootie was, I loved her, but she was a thug. A girl thug, with a knife and everything. I shoulda beat the crap out of her.

SHELEEAH: Maybe it wouldn't of made a difference. You said you did the best you could.

HENRIETTA: No, the best I knew how. I was telling you to listen to something...Umm, umm, uhh, oh yeah. Don't get to know people. That's my advice. Face values the best deal. Don't try to get to know anybody. Know as little as possible and don't form no expectations. Then they can't let you down, cause you never got up.

SHELEEAH: You don't belong in the street. You ought to be...

HENRIETTA: Dead.

SHELEEAH: NO.

HENRIETTA: Don't worry. It won't happen. One time two people got shot and killed with me in the middle and I was fine. Bet if I tied myself to a train track no train would come for three days. I'm meant to be here. That's it. Gonna be here. If I could, I'd float right outta here though.

SHELEEAH: That's an awful way to feel about life. You hold on a bit though. Like keeping this apartment and eating. You could starve yourself to death, or kill yourself.

HENRIETTA: Are you crazy?

SHELEEAH: You just need a specific purpose. A reason to...

HENRIETTA: I don't like serious talking and we been doing a lot of...

SHELEEAH: Something could come and make it all worthwhile, know what I mean?

HENRIETTA: You taking psychology or something? Don't practice on me.

SHELEEAH: I just want to be your friend. I don't have many and neither do you.

HENRIETTA: And I want you to. What am I saying? No I don't. I DON'T WANT FRIENDS. I have to go. I...I...have to check on the food and serve it so you can go on home. *(She checks the pot on the floor and then drops the lid feeling very uncomfortable.)* It's not done, it's not Shelra.

SHELEEAH: Sheleeah.

HENRIETTA: I'm sorry, I'm sorry. That's right, I messed up your name. And we can't eat. I have a headache, don't you, I do. *(Henrietta takes puzzle away)* Can I hold your hand I'm cold. Can I? I won't hurt you I promise. I'm tired, I have to go now.

SHELEEAH: *(Snatching hand away)* Why are you saying that? If you don't want to be serious we don't have to.

HENRIETTA: Gotta go, gotta go, gotta go...

SHELEEAH: What's wrong with you? I know you're not crazy, so don't pull that stunt with me!

HENRIETTA: Don't speak to me like that. I don't have to take it. Don't make me angry cause I'm not used to this and...

SHELEEAH: I'm not used to no mess like this either, I'm leaving if you are going...

HENRIETTA: Well, leave then! I've had my company anyway. They've been here all the time checking you out! So there, fooled you, didn't I. We've all been checking you out.

SHELEEAH: Bye, Henrietta.

HENRIETTA: You can't go, cause I didn't dismiss you yet. I am your hostess. Unless you're a dog-face cow or something? Huh? Miss Priss...*(Sheleeah starting for the door)* WAIT!! WAIT!! I'm sorry...Shelra.

SHELEEAH: SHELEEAH!

HENRIETTA: Okay, okay. I'm sorry. I'm sorry. Please don't go, Please!

SHELEEAH: It's late and you're pretending this, that and the other and I don't have time for any of it.

HENRIETTA: But please don't go. Stay and keep me company. I'm lonely...

SHELEEAH: You are not. You love it like that. By yourself.

HENRIETTA: No, I don't. I'm so lonely I could die.

SHELEEAH: Good! That's what you want anyway. I'm gone.

HENRIETTA: Well, then go on FOOL. Go yourself right out the door, cause don't nobody need you, anyway. I'm tired of begging you dog.

SHELEEAH: You're right. You are crazy.

HENRIETTA: Well, I told you that! You're an idot if you didn't believe me. You can't go nowhere. 'Cause you didn't eat these beans I cooked. And I cooked them especially for you. And if you don't eat them, Miss Priss...

SHELEEAH: I TOLD YOU ABOUT CALLING ME THAT!!

HENRIETTA: OH, YEAH, WHAT YOU GONNA DO ABOUT IT? MISS PRISS??

SHELEEAH: PLENTY IF YOU DON'T STOP CALLING ME THAT!!!

HENRIETTA: MISS PRISS!! MISS PRISS!! MISS PRISS!!

SHELEEAH: I FEEL RIDICULOUS STANDING HERE FIGHTING WITH A CRAZY WOMAN!

HENRIETTA: YOU JUST OUGHT TO!

SHELEEAH: WELL I DO! *(Pause)* I'll see you later.

HENRIETTA: You mad?

SHELEEAH: No.

HENRIETTA: You sure?

SHELEEAH: Yes.

HENRIETTA: You know why?

SHELEEAH: What?

HENRIETTA: You know why, don't you?

SHELEEAH: No, why?

HENRIETTA: Cause I'm a perfectly adorable person, once you get to know me.

SHELEEAH: You warned me against getting to know you.

HENRIETTA: But you are getting to know me right?

SHELEEAH: Yeah, I'm getting to know you all right.

HENRIETTA: And you're rather taken with me, right?

SHELEEAH: Ummhumm, you're interesting.

HENRIETTA: Probably we can be the best of friends and you will love me, right?

SHELEEAH: We'll see.

HENRIETTA: Of course you will. Everybody loves me if I let them. Except Tootie. Till she died. Know why I called her that?

SHELEEAH: No, why?

HENRIETTA: Because she'd lay in her bed and toot. She'd go toot...toot...toot, and I started calling her Tootie. Isn't that funny? Names are funny, how they start.

SHELEEAH: Yes, I guess they are.

HENRIETTA: It's funny how I want to call you that. I want to call you Tootie.

SHELEEAH: Ummhumm.

HENRIETTA: Is it okay? I know you aren't, I know that. You have to believe me. I'm aware, I know things. Can I call you that?

SHELEEAH: Yes.

HENRIETTA: And we'll go on picnics, right?

SHELEEAH: Yes.

HENRIETTA: And maybe you'll love me. No rush, take your time.

SHELEEAH: Maybe in time...I'll love you.

HENRIETTA: Okay, Tootie. Thank you—Thank you. This time I'll be better. I'll be so much better.

(End Act One)

(Act Two, Scene I—It is late October on a weekday morning, several weeks later. The scene takes place outside the Brownstone and inside the one-room flat. The scene opens with Sheleeah and Thomas seated on the stoop. Henrietta's crate is there by the stoop. LIGHTS RISE)

THOMAS: Anyway, it was the biggest boat I ever saw. It had about a hundred sails and all kinds of equipment and—

SHELEEAH: You have no idea when she'll be back?

THOMAS: No. And then they had three Admirals and—

SHELEEAH: Well, look, tell Henrietta, I'll be back.

THOMAS: The dock was—

SHELEEAH: Could you tell me when I come back?

THOMAS: I'm almost finished.

SHELEEAH: Thomas, just tell her please. I'm in a hurry or I'd listen to your story. *(Sheleeah Exits.)*

THOMAS: No you wouldn't.

HENRIETTA: *(Walking on from street carrying a bag full of fruit. Her hair is nicely combed and she has on a fancy hat.)* Oh, Thomas, I'm so tired.

THOMAS: I told you to let me go for you. Here, I'll take that, you sit down right here.

HENRIETTA: I gotta get ready for Tootie.

THOMAS: She was just here.

HENRIETTA: I missed her?

THOMAS: Had to go to work or someplace, cause she was in an awful big hurry. Why're you all dressed up?

HENRIETTA: She's always in a hurry.

THOMAS: I've been painting.

HENRIETTA: That's good. You need to keep in practice.

THOMAS: I decided to invite Sheleeah to my church picnic.

HENRIETTA: You just ain't the kind of man she dates.

THOMAS: No, not a date. Like a sister, or a cousin or something.

HENRIETTA: You're gonna get your feelings hurt, TB. These women are mean, trust me, I used to be one.

THOMAS: Want me to fix your clothesline?

HENRIETTA: No, I took it down. Tootie says it makes my room look cluttered.

THOMAS: I think it makes it look good. Lived in.

HENRIETTA: I put it back when she's not around.

THOMAS: Holding out on her, huh? Not like you and me—we trust each other.

HENRIETTA: Now pick these things up and take them in for me. I need to think, sleep, one or the other. Can't figure out which though. I don't hardly know where to put things to keep my room from being a clutter. *(Sheleeah enters.)*

SHELEEAH: Hellooo!!! Anybody… *(Walking into the apt.)* Oh, hi, Thomas. *(Crosses to Henrietta.)* Well, I did it, I pretended to be a little off. *(Henrietta and Thomas look at each other.)* Not too crazy, just a tad. Enough to make people unsure. It's great. I've been watching your every move.

THOMAS: Miss Effie ain't off.

HENRIETTA: That's all right Thomas.

THOMAS: Well she ain't!

SHELEEAH: OFF was probably a poor choice of words, FREE. I was free instead of appropriate.

HENRIETTA: What are we going to do, now that you finally got here.

SHELEEAH: We've got some paper work to do.

THOMAS: If you want, I could...

SHELEEAH: No, thanks, Thomas.

THOMAS: But you don't even know what I was going to say.

SHELEEAH: I know I don't want to do it. Henrietta did you take care of your little business?

THOMAS: What little business?

SHELEEAH: I'm speaking to Henrietta.

THOMAS: I know, but what business?

HENRIETTA: Not yet. And we can't talk in front of Thomas, if we're not going to include him.

SHELEEAH: Alright. *(Turns facing Thomas while Henrietta signs the papers. Sheleeah makes sure Thomas' view is obstructed. Henrietta hands her the papers and Sheleeah checks them.)* I'll see you later.

HENRIETTA: See you Tuesday, right?

(Sheleeah EXITS)

THOMAS: I don't think I'm going to invite her to the picnic. Is she nice to you?

HENRIETTA: She's real nice to me. Tootie's just trying to fit in, that's all. I'm going to take my nap now Thomas. *(She immediately curls up on her couch.)*

THOMAS: Well, I'll be here. Maybe I can help you make some fruit salad later.

(LIGHTS FADE OUT)

(Scene II—It is November, a month later. It is evening and the street light shines over the stoop outside Henrietta's stoop area. Thomas is leaning against the fence, blocking the entrance way. He's in conversation with Sheleeah as the LIGHTS RISE.)

THOMAS: Evening. Looking mighty pretty as always.

SHELEEAH: Thank you, excuse me.

THOMAS: You, uhh, uhh, still showing up here, uhh, pretty regular. You and Miss Effie still in business, huh?

SHELEEAH: We are and will be, so get use to it. Thomas please move.

THOMAS: NO. What was that in that blue box the other day? Day before yesterday?

SHELEEAH: Thomas, please, you are irratating me to no end, now, MOVE.

THOMAS: You're going to get in trouble. What was it? I don't take no stuff. I been known to hurt people for—

SHELEEAH: A dress! A dress for Henrietta. THOMAS, PLEASE LET ME PASS, I'M IN A HURRY AND I DON'T—

THOMAS: Was it pretty? Was it expensive? It was, wasn't it.

SHELEEAH: Yes. (*She jerks at gate*)

THOMAS: Effie's on to you, girl.

SHELEEAH: Oh, yeah?

THOMAS: Yeah. (*Thomas steps aside*)

SHELEEAH: Thank you.

THOMAS: Miss Effie's expecting you. That's the only reason I moved. Didn't move for you, WOULDN'T DO NOTHING FOR YOU. GOT YOUR BUTT UP ON YOUR SHOULDERS,   THINKING YOU CUTE, YOU—

SHELEEAH: LOOK, LET ME TELL YOU SOMETHING HERE, DON'T START THAT SCREAMING IN THE STREET AT ME, I'M—

THOMAS: (*He changes back to his boyish manner proud of himself*) Sound like Miss Effie don't I? She do it good. I do it pretty good, don't I?

SHELEEAH: Look Thomas, see if you can understand this, I know you don't like me, but see, I haven't done anything to you for you not to like me.

THOMAS: Yes you did, you're trying to take Miss—

SHELEEAH: (*Patronizing*) Wait a minute and let me finish. Now, it doesn't matter, we're just never going to get along too well, so, why don't you leave me alone. Act like I'm not here, and after awhile you'll forget you're even mad at me, and we can just be civilized. Okay?

THOMAS: My reputation's been getting around, hasn't it? You scared of me now, ain't you?

SHELEEAH: You have no reputation, Thomas.

THOMAS: I DO TOO HAVE ONE. I BEEN IN JAIL YOU KNOW I WAS A KILLER?

SHELEEAH: Great, Thomas. Write about it. (*She starts to walk away.*)

THOMAS: YOU WON'T TAKE NOTHING FROM ME. NEVER. NEVER.

SHELEEAH: Bye Thomas. (*She walks into Henrietta's house, leaving Thomas sitting on the stoop alone.*)

(*INSIDE THE FLAT*)

HENRIETTA: What you doing talking to him?

SHELEEAH: How'd you know we were talking?

HENRIETTA: I was peeking though the door and your lips were moving. Course you both could be kind of weird.

SHELEEAH: Well, if you saw him, why didn't you rescue me?

HENRIETTA: Cause it looked so fascinating. What was it?

SHELEEAH: Just shooting the breeze.

HENRIETTA: Thomas don't shoot no breeze.

SHELEEAH: Well, he did tonight. Listen, I got the license. See here, and we can—get our business together...

HENRIETTA: This ain't no we project is it, cause I don't do group nothing.

SHELEEAH: When I say we, I mean you. Anyhow, you can be in business within a month.

HENRIETTA: I don't know about this.

SHELEEAH: Don't worry.

HENRIETTA: I do worry. This isn't for me. I'm not supposed to—

SHELEEAH: Suppose is going to have to come out of your vocabulary.

HENRIETTA: You sure don't have to get dressed and go—

SHELEEAH: Did you tell Thomas you were moving yet?

HENRIETTA: No, I'm not sure about that either.

SHELEEAH: You have to.

HENRIETTA: Why?

SHELEEAH: Because, look at this place. You can't stay here.

HENRIETTA: I can't leave either. I can't go no place like that.

SHELEEAH: Yes you can. It's a much better place.

HENRIETTA: Yeah, I know, I know. But it's not home, and Thomas—well Thomas needs me here. I take care of him.

SHELEEAH: He's a grown man, he can take care of himself.

HENRIETTA: I'm a grown woman, you won't let me take care of myself.

SHELEEAH: Cause you were doing a lousy job.

HENRIETTA: No I wasn't.

SHELEEAH: Yes you were.

HENRIETTA: No I wasn't.

SHELEEAH: Yes you were. Did you do the recipe yet?

HENRIETTA: No, been working on it though. There is no set recipe. I just cut and mix and add a little sugar and cinnamon and—

SHELEEAH: Whatever you do, write it down, so people can understand it. These are serious business folk you have to—

HENRIETTA: I just just want to go out and sit on my crate.

SHELEEAH: Well, you can at night.

HENRIETTA: And get my head knocked off?

SHELEEAH: Come on, Henrietta, write.

(Thomas crosses into hallway and sits on floor doodling.)

(Sheleeah walks Henrietta over to the table and gets paper and pencil and forces her to start writing.)

SHELEEAH: Went to Bear Mountain, Sunday with Roger...and his kids. I hate kids.

HENRIETTA: Oh, come on.

SHELEEAH: I told you, and you won't listen. Ready made families is a drag. You'll end up a babysitter.

HENRIETTA: Naw, it's not like that.

SHELEEAH: Okay, you say so...The stores won't give me anymore food once they find out I'm in business...you know that don't you? Don't worry about it, you'll have money.

HENRIETTA: I don't want money. You know, I had to study months to learn how to get things free. I had an apprenticeship, you know, so I could learn how to survive in the street. No matter what you do, *(SHELEEAH is studying the wall of pictures again.)* you have to study with the masters. I had me three teachers.

SHELEEAH: Ummhumm. *(Picks up old magazine and begins reading)*

HENRIETTA: I learned a lot too.

SHELEEAH: Like what?

HENRIETTA: Like how to walk so I look broke down, but helpless so I wouldn't get arrested. How to talk, which was easy, since broken English is easier than good grammar. And ah, ah, I don't know, how to beg if you have to, but see—I wasn't good at the nitty gritty kinds of street life, like eating behind people and stealing and sleeping in the street and doorways, that's why I got me a gig and an apartment. Plus I helped Thomas.

SHELEEAH: Thomas needs to help himself. Are you writing?

HENRIETTA: Yes. Don't let him upset you. I know he's jealous. He wants to be bad. He'd a been a hood, if he hadn't a been so stupid.

SHELEEAH: How'd he buy this building?

HENRIETTA: He inherited it. His mother and I were aquaintances. It's a long story. His brother and Fraizer were friends, they both got killed together, I told you about that funeral didn't I?

SHELEEAH: Yes, several times. I'm going to have to leave soon.

HENRIETTA: Why?

SHELEEAH: Cause I found three grey hairs, right up in here, and this stuff gets dyed, tonight. What you going to do, when your hair starts looking like mine? I plan to keep it dyed. Gotta keep the men coming.

HENRIETTA: You know any men?

SHELEEAH: Do I know men? Are you kidding?

HENRIETTA: For me.

SHELEEAH: Henrietta!

HENRIETTA: Yeah, bout fifty, no make that forty-five—between forty-five and sixty.

SHELEEAH: Some range.

HENRIETTA: I'm desperate.

SHELEEAH: It sounds stupid, but I never thought of you being lonely for a man.

HENRIETTA: Those pangs hit hard sometimes...I want one with a brown pin striped suit, and a pocket watch.

SHELEEAH: That's not in style.

HENRIETTA: For the fifty, sixty gang it is.

SHELEEAH: I'm not hip to the fifty, sixty crowd yet.

HENRIETTA: And I want hit to wear a Stetson and strut... (she prances) me around on his arm. But most of all, I want him to know where some good restaurants are...A man would be nice.

(Sheleeah moves to Henrietta and gives her a kiss and a hug.)

HENRIETTA: What's that for?

SHELEEAH: Because you're a wonderful person, and I enjoy your company and I felt like it.

HENRIETTA: Look over there in that draw and get me the thing wrapped in—

SHELEEAH: I know just the guy. George. George Murray.

HENRIETTA: I never met a George I liked yet.

SHELEEAH: He works with me. He's in the fifty, sixty set and...Henrietta, how old are you? (Simply gives her a discouraging look) Come on, tell me! Anyway, he seems pretty nice. Has an old car, but well kept. Like an antique. A uh, 'bout a fifty-nine Chevy or something.

HENRIETTA: Got all his teeth?

SHELEEAH: I haven't the slightest idea.

HENRIETTA: I've heard, heard mind you, not experienced, that dentures bite you when you kiss, and if I get the chance to pucker up, I don't want nothin' to spoil it.

SHELEEAH: Well, I'll check it out. I'll say, Mr. Murray, I want you to go out with my friend, if you have all your teeth, but if—

HENRIETTA: How much does he make?

SHELEEAH: I don't know.

HENRIETTA: Check that out too, and if he has a pension, and where he lives, and—

SHELEEAH: You're getting a little carried away, a little too soon, don't—

HENRIETTA: See if you could arrange it for about two weeks from now. If your hair comes out looking good, I might go get mine done too.

SHELEEAH: You're too much.

HENRIETTA: I'm happy—Go over there to that draw and bring me the wrapped up tissue. First draw.

SHELEEAH: Here?

HENRIETTA: Yeah. Top draw.

SHELEEAH: This?

HENRIETTA: Yeah, yeah, that's it. Open it up.

SHELEEAH: *(Looks at Cameo Broach)* Oh, that's beautiful. That's georgous. Where'd you get it.

HENRIETTA: Never mind that, just remember where you got it.

SHELEEAH: I can't take this.

HENRIETTA: Why not?

SHELEEAH: Because...it's too valuable.

HENRIETTA: Not more than you. Come here, so I can put it on you. *(She places cameo around Sheleeah's neck.)* That's pretty.

SHELEEAH: *(Looking in hand mirror)* That's fabulous. I look like class now.

HENRIETTA: You look like class anyway. I was going to give it to Fraizer's fiancee but she married somebody else. So let him give her one...Fraizer had fifty more days in active duty, then he would have been home. I've got the flag in the draw.

SHELEEAH: I know. Please, write, Henrietta.

HENRIETTA: I'm think, I'm thinking.

SHELEEAH: No, you're not, you're talking.

HENRIETTA: You're going to distribute this right? And those people—Right. Well, what am I going to do? I don't get to do anything.

SHELEEAH: Yes you do. *(Puts her arm around Henrietta.)* You get to take the money.

HENRIETTA: That's no fun.

SHELEEAH: I know several people who'd differ with you on that point.

HENRIETTA: What else do I get to do?

SHELEEAH: Well, if you're lucky—

HENRIETTA: No chance of that—

SHELEEAH: You'll get famous. Like Famous Amos Cookies or something.

HENRIETTA: Yeah, FAMOUS HENRIETTA FRUIT SALAD.

SHELEEAH: Or something like that. You go ahead and finish, I've got to—
    (Thomas knocks on the door.)

THOMAS: Can I come in?

HENRIETTA: Come on Thomas. Let him think he's a part of this, okay?

THOMAS: Miss Effie...

SHELEEAH: She doesn't like to be called that—

THOMAS: I came to ask you not to move. I came to ask you not to leave me... and to be a part of this building some more..

HENRIETTA: Thomas...

THOMAS: No, wait. I've been your friend for a long time now, and I took real good care of you before she ever showed up, and I want some respect as being almost family.

HENRIETTA: I respect you, Thomas. And I know it took a lot for you to come here like this in front of Tootie and say these...

THOMAS: And she's not Tootie! —She's an intruder!

HENRIETTA: Oh, yes she is. She's my Tootie now.

THOMAS: Tootie comes, but not through Sheleeah.

HENRIETTA: Yes she does.

THOMAS: No she don't.

HENRIETTA: Yes she does.

THOMAS: No, uhh, uhh, no she—

HENRIETTA: Yes! Yes! Yes, she is too my daughter!

SHELEEAH: Wait a minute here, we're all getting a little carried away, don't you think?

HENRIETTA: You, sit down! Me and Thomas will handle this!

SHELEEAH: We have to stop playing these games now, I'm serious. Enough is enough.

HENRIETTA: But, it's not a game. It's for real. Isn't it Thomas?

THOMAS: I guess so. Yeah.

SHELEEAH: Henrietta, come on now. You've been sitting here talking to me just as normal as can be, and I know you're not going to flip out on me now.

THOMAS: See! Somebody ought to off her, cause she's rude! That's all there is to that! She say any trash to anybody, any old kinda way and think people should take that stuff, don't she, don't she do that?!!!

SHELEEAH: Henrietta, be confident. Everything is going to work out fine and—

HENRIETTA: STOP IT! YOU ARE CONFUSING ME!

THOMAS: SHE'S THE ONE DOING IT! SHE THE ONE! I AIN'T DID NOTHING!!

SHELEEAH: You're right about that! You ain't did nothing. You didn't do nothing for about forty years, far as I can see and probably won't—

THOMAS: OH YEAH, OH YEAH. COME UPSTAIRS SISTER! I'LL SHOW YOU. YOU CAN SEE FOR YOURSELF! I GOT PICTURES I DREW! I GOT THINGS I MADE. I WAS HONORABLE MENTION IN KINGSBRIDGE CENTER!! THAT'S RIGHT—

HENRIETTA: WHY ARE YOU TWO FIGHTING! PLEASE!

SHELEEAH: You made honorable mention. Whoopie doo—Thomas, you're like a child!!

THOMAS: YOU GET OUT!

HENRIETTA: Stop screaming in my house! Right now, right this minute, or I'm gonna—

THOMAS: YOU LEAVE US ALONE!!!

SHELEEAH: I'm not leaving her along with you! You're a moron!

THOMAS: I AM NOT!

HENRIETTA: TOOTIE!! Don't talk to him like that!! Don't treat him like that!

SHELEEAH: WHY ARE YOU DEFENDING HIM? He's hopeless—

HENRIETTA: He's a *man*.

SHELEEAH: He's no man, He's—You said yourself—

HENRIETTA: DON'T YOU SAY IT. DON'T YOU EVER REPEAT FAMILY SECRETS I TELL YOU! HEAR ME?!! ANSWER ME WHEN I'M TALKING TO YOU!! TOOTIE, YOU HEAR ME TALKING TO YOU, DON'T MAKE ME HAVE TO—

THOMAS: I KNOW WHAT YOU'RE SAYING ABOUT ME. DON'T THINK I DON'T KNOW YOU TWO SIT IN HERE AND TALK ABOUT ME AT NIGHT AND LAUGH AT ME.

HENRIETTA: No. We don't Thomas.

SHELEEAH: YES WE DO, THOMAS—HENRIETTA...We have to make a decision here.

THOMAS: She wants you TO CHOOSE. TO CHOOSE BETWEEN ME, OR HER—

HENRIETTA: I can't do that Thomas, I WON'T DO THAT! DON'T WORRY!

THOMAS: THAT'S WHAT SHE WANTS!!

HENRIETTA: Well, she can't have it. I won't leave you. We can't leave each other—we're a family.

SHELEEAH: What are you saying!!? You're going to give up your life for a— a—a—

HENRIETTA: You think you're better than me. You want me to rise to your level. That's it! But I won't. It ain't up! It's even! Thomas and you and me, are all even.

SHELEEAH: You don't understand.

HENRIETTA: No, you don't understand.

THOMAS: I don't understand.

HENRIETTA: Yes, you do—good as any of us.

SHELEEAH: He's dependent on you. Why do you put up with—?

HENRIETTA: So—You're dependent on me too. You get off feeding your ego on taking care of pitiful me.

SHELEEAH: Are you serious?

HENRIETTA: Of course I'm serious. I'm a very serious minded person. Both of you get something from me, just like I get something from you—As a matter of fact, I'm the only one coming up short.

SHELEEAH: I've got nothing else to say.

THOMAS: Good.

HENRIETTA: There's something else you can say. We're going to have to sit down and work this all out.

SHELEEAH: Not me. THE MAN STEALS NEWSPAPERS!! I'm not sacrificing myself—

THOMAS: I'd do it for you. I'll be friends with HER, if you stay.

SHELEEAH: *(to Effie)* But you've got nothing to lose! I'm trying to tell you, I have a career, I have plans—

HENRIETTA: Of course I do! I'll lose everything I have. Can't you see we're family again—

SHELEEAH: But that's nothing. This place is nothing. I won' t say Thomas is—Henrietta, you'll meet new people and be able to lead a reasonably normal life. Henrietta, you want to date, don't you?

HENRIETTA: FOR WHAT!!

SHELEEAH: Don't you want to have fun again and socialize and gain respect? How about owning your own business?

HENRIETTA: I've got my own business. You want that business. Power and money, that's you, not ME!

SHELEEAH: This isn't mine, this is yours!

HENRIETTA: Be for real, Tootie, this is not for me. I'm happy the way things are NOW!

SHELEEAH: HENRIETTA!! YOU BE FOR REAL. I'M NOT TOOTIE!! WHO'S HE SUPPOSED TO BE, KEITH OR FRAIZER.

THOMAS: I'm always Thomas, she likes ME, that way.

HENRIETTA: STOP IT!!!!!!!!! DON'T TAKE MY FAMILY!!!!! DON'T TAKE MY FAMILY!!!!!!!!!
(All fade.)

(Scene III—Late afternoon, two weeks later. Thomas is inside the building, knocking on Henrietta's door. He exits and stands against the fence before Henreitta's arrival.

THOMAS: *(Knocks)* Miss Effie! *(knocks again)* *(Thomas exits outside.)* Miss Effie! You all right, Miss Effie? I been looking all over for you.

HENRIETTA: You can see, I wasn't on the fence. I can't find Tootie. I been in my spot for two days and she ain't been around.

THOMAS: I know.

HENRIETTA: Think if I go up to her apartment, she'll get mad? She might be sick. She picked up my money and I need it.

THOMAS: She ain't there. Let's go inside, Miss Effie.

HENRIETTA: No. I'm going down to her job. Soon as I remember where it is. Maybe she's there. Sheleeah, came by—

THOMAS: No, the truth is, I went there.

HENRIETTA: You went to her house?

THOMAS: Yes. While you was gone.

HENRIETTA: Did you scare her?

THOMAS: No. She almost scared me.

HENRIETTA: She explain to you about our deal? Ain't she smart. Smart as a whip. Put herself through college and everything—

THOMAS: She didn't tell me bout no deal. Well, really, she didn't say much a nothing at all. I saw her at the uhh, uhh, store, at first. And we just talked there. But she said she was gonna come by, but she didn't. And I know you was looking for her, so I went up there. Let's go inside.

HENRIETTA: No. Why? You got a fear of air?

THOMAS: Cause, you're going to be upset with me—

HENRIETTA: Why what'd you do? What'd you do to her? You hurt her, Thomas?

THOMAS: No. No, I didn't. I just stood there listening and she said she was gonna move away and that she was tired of the madness and that—

HENRIETTA: No she didn't. Tootie wouldn't say that and she wouldn't leave and not tell me. She wouldn't go nowhere without me. We're a team. She told me—We worked it all out.

THOMAS: And I saw the truck men, when they came to count the stuff. I started helping her pack.

HENRIETTA: LIAR!!!! YOU'RE A LIAR!!! SHE WOULDN'T DO THAT TO ME!!! YOU DID SOMETHING TO HER, DIDN'T YOU?!!!

THOMAS: No, no, I just helped her pack and—I don't know when she's moving. Not today—

THOMAS: YOU CAN'T STAND ME HAVING A FRIEND *(She attacks him)* CAN YOU? CAN YOU?.

THOMAS: Yes, I can, cause you didn't move. That's all. PLEASE, DON'T HIT ME, MISS EFFIE.

HENRIETTA: WHAT'D YOU DO WITH—

THOMAS: STOP IT *(He drags her into the house)* STOP IT! I DIDN'T DO NOTHING! EVERYBODY'S STARING AT US—

HENRIETTA: YOU'RE SLIME! SLIME! TAKE YOUR HANDS OFF ME THOMAS. WHERE'S MY TOOTIE??? WHERE IS SHE?? OH, THOMAS PLEASE, I NEED HER. I NEED TO—

THOMAS: I KNEW IT WOULDN'T WORK. I KNEW SOMETHING. I KNEW THIS WOULD NEVER WORK OUT. DIDN'T I? DIDN'T I? (*He pulls Henrietta into the flat and throws her on the couch.*)

HENRIETTA: I HATE YOU! GET OUTTA HERE!! GET OUT OF MY ROOM!!

THOMAS: You got to clam down.

HENRIETTA: YOU TOOK HER AWAY FROM ME!! WHERE'VE YOU GOT HER, WITH YOUR CRAZY SELF? HUH?

THOMAS: YOU STAY THERE. YOU STAY RIGHT THERE. DON'T GET UP, OR, I'LL—I'LL DO SOMETHING TO YOU.

HENRIETTA: DON'T YOU THREATEN ME. I'LL KILL YOU UP IN HERE. GIVE HER BACK!! THOMAS, THOMAS YOU HEAR ME? WHERE YOU GOING????

THOMAS: I GOTTA GET SOMETHING!!

HENRIETTA: THOMAS, PLEASE, PLEASE. I'M BEGGIN YOU! GIVE HER BACK. I'LL DO WHATERVER YOU WANT. I'LL NEVER LEAVE, I'LL LIVE HERE FOREVER, ONLY, PLEASE—

THOMAS: I don't have her. She just left. She just left us here.

HENRIETTA: She couldn't go nowhere that fast. Thomas, Thomas, please.

THOMAS: Well, she did. I guess she did. I don't know. She said she was. She said—

HENRIETTA: Tell me, just what she said.

THOMAS: She said that it was hard, but she had to cut, uhh, uhh...

HENRIETTA: Come on Thomas, remember. Remember, this one—

THOMAS: I'm trying, but I can't.

HENRIETTA: You think she really left?

THOMAS: I know she did. I helped her packing, I saw the men.

(*Thomas starts to leave.*)

HENRIETTA: Where are you going?

THOMAS: I gotta wash your face is all. That's all. Stay there. I'll be right back.

(*Thomas exits to his apartment to get washcloth*)

HENRIETTA: Don't leave me. (*Rocking herself*) What'd you come here for? WHY? What'd you come here for bothering me? I wasn't bothering you. I WASN'T HURTING ANYBODY. NOBODY!! NOBODY!!! NOOOBOOODYYYY!!! OH, THOMAS PLEASE, DON'T LEAVE ME!!! THOMAS PLEASE, please, please...Where you going, I GOT TO SEE YOU!!

(*She starts to get up when Thomas enters with washcloth.*)

THOMAS: Here you go Miss Effie. (*Pushing her back down. Places cloth on her forehead*) I saw this in a movie one time. Does it feel good?

HENRIETTA: No. (*She tries to rise.*) I gotta go to Tootie. She needs me. She needs—

THOMAS: She don't want you Miss Effie. I do.

HENRIETTA: How come she didn't tell me? She should have told me.

THOMAS: She gets scared too. She gets scared. She's afraid. She's more afraid than us? Don't you think so?

HENRIETTA: But I need her.

THOMAS: Know what? She said, we had each other. And she didn't have nobody. Said we could take good care of—

HENRIETTA: We talked about it. We made a deal. Didn't she tell you about it?

THOMAS: I don't know.

HENRIETTA: But, see, Thomas, I picked her. I picked her and she wasn't supposed to do this to me. SHE KNOWS THE STORY!!!

THOMAS: We have to stay away from the people.

HENRIETTA: Yes. We do. We have to. But not her. I'm going to see her. I was good this time and she shouldn't have left me.

THOMAS: Shhhh, shhhh. You were doing fine, till, she came messing with you. People torturing you.

HENRIETTA: SHUT UP THOMAS, CAUSE YOU DON'T KNOW ABOUT IT! ABOUT HOW IT IS. As a matter of fact, get out!!! I don't need you here. I don't want you here with me—I got her to go home, you know? Then maybe that's it.

THOMAS: No.

HENRIETTA: Yes I did. And they're a family again. Maybe that's why. Maybe she just doesn't need me anymore. I did my part. I have to figure it out. I solved her problems, I believe—

THOMAS: I don't want you thinking I did nothing to her. I know my reputation is—bad.

HENRIETTA: Only a lunatic would care about your reputation, Thomas. (*She sits up with wash cloth still on her head.*) Go away, cause I'm sad. I'm real sad. Low-life stays where they're not wanted. Are you such a low-life, that—

THOMAS: I'll be right here.

HENRIETTA: Kinda like death, Thomas. Death all over again. I've got to find her.

THOMAS: Call me if you need me. Keep that on your head.

HENRIETTA: Won't need you. Won't need nobody, for this one. I'm seasoned. (*Thomas exits to sit on stoop outside.*) It's my fault for trying to be her friend. Tootie!! Sheleeah!!! Ugly name...I always could say it! Hear me? Sheleeah!! I always could!!! Huh? Won't you come back and be my child?

I want to teach you…I've got to go there…I've got to go to the graves…I haven't visited the graves.

(ALL FADE.)

(Scene IV—Same evening…Lights up on Henrietta outside on her crate, in the usual place. She has the blue box beside her.)

HENRIETTA: Good morning…Hey there, hey how you doing? What's heppenin' fella. Looking good, sweet thing…Your glasses get thicker everyday. I believe you lying to yourself. You can't see out them things. I'm taking bets this man can't see nothin'. Any takers—There's a shadow following me. Shhh. See it? See it? *(Dodges and ducks as though pursued.)* I see her, but I keep my distance. She's attached like—you need that paper? Can I have—? Boy I tell you…That girl tried to get me. Her sense of reality was off. Calling me things I wasn't. Attachments, lots of expectations and attachments. That's what messes you up. You better listen good, I know. I know…because I excel in being…correct. *(Quiet thought. Lights fading.)* This is the kissing booth and I'm the Queen Mother and for five cents, you can, no make that four cents, we're running a special today—

THE END

Charles Michael Moore

LOVE'S LIGHT IN FLIGHT

ETA Creative Arts Foundation

Charles Michael Moore

Charles Michael Moore has worked as an actor, writer, director, and teacher. His play, *The Hooch*, has been performed in New York and Chicago at ETA. He has won numerous awards in his field, among them the ACTF Award for playwriting in 1976. He has worked in many school systems across the Midwest in the field of creative writing and playwriting, which he is now teaching at ETA. As an actor, he was last seen in Chicago as the "Blind Man" in *Muddy Waters*. In 1987, Mr. Moore received the AKA "Monarch Award" for playwriting. In 1987, Mr Moore's production, *Love's Light in Flight* at ETA was chosen as the theatre's "Pick of the Season." He recently conducted an acting camp in Piney Woods, Mississippi. Mr. Moore served as acting coach for ETA's production, *Strange Fruit*. Mr. Moore and the ETA cast of *Love's Light in Flight* had a highly successful run at the Walker Theatre in Indianapolis. Mr. Moore is just returning from the Coronet Theatre in Los Angeles where the production enjoyed a successful run.

ETA Creative Arts Foundation

ETA Creative Arts Foundation was incorporated in April, 1971, as a non-profit, tax-exempt organization to provide training for performance opportunities for youth and adults on Chicago's South Side. In the past 19 years, the organization has become one of Chicago's leading performing arts organization in the Black community, with a commitment to the production of new works and the development of individual artists. The foundation emphasizes and gives a sense of direction and hope as reinforcement that Black people can control their own destinies within the context of community.

After years of "vagabonding", ETA took the first step in establishing a permanent center when it purchased the 15,656 sq. ft. facility at 7558 South Chicago Avenue. Newly renovated, the facility has a 200-seat theatre, a theatre library, a lounge, an art gallery, a student studio theatre, a cabaret theatre, workshop space, and offices.

In addition to housing ETA's varied programs, the facility also accommodates the physical needs of other arts groups which have not had a place to stage their productions, and thus it contributes to the overall cultural life of the community.

At the same time, this facility provides jobs…for staff and faculty, for budding performers, for professionals in varied disciplines of the arts, for technicians in the arts.

For 19 years, ETA has conducted a full schedule of classes in the performing and technical aspects of the arts–drama, music, dance, directing, lighting, stage management–training over 100 students each year. Many of ETA students have gone on to college for further study. Over the same period, ETA has mounted over 60 mainstage productions and has for seven years conducted a Reader's Theatre program to assist developing playwrights.

LOVE'S LIGHT IN FLIGHT
by Charles Michael Moore

Directed by
Charles Michael Moore

CAST

Burnetta	Martice Edge
Venus	Dalvalie Friend
Lannette, Lady, Waitress	Lori Clovetta Watson
Imani	Renee Lockett-Lawson
Earl, Man	Askia Bantu
Arthur, Mike	Dennis Allen
Green, Thug, Voice	Andre T. Teamer
Halsted	Darryl Reed
Leonard	Cliff Frazier

Time: The 1980's
Place: A town called Beecher Heights, Michigan
Cast in Order of Appearance (Some Multiple Roles):
HALSTED BRIDGES, age 40
EARL KEITH, Age 42, MAN IN CHICKEN CHARLIES, age 60's
LEONARD HAYES, age 35
BURNETTA HAYES, age 32
VENUS STRATTFORD, age 32, VOICE IN EARL'S ROOM, age 20's
MIKE, age 40's, ARTHUR STRATTFORD, age 32
LANNETTE, age 23, BUS STOP LADY, age 20's, RESTUARANT WAIT-
RESS, age 18
IMANI (SANDRA), age 38, VOICE IN EARL'S ROOM, age 20's

ACT I
Scene 1

*The set is separated into three sections. The mainstage area represents the home
of BURNETTA HAYES. Visible are part of the living room and kitchen. A
couch, phone stand and cordless phone are in the living room. In the kitchen are
a table with three chairs, a stove, and refrigerator. The kitchen has a back door
and an exit to the back rooms. The living room has a front door and an exit to
the upstairs. The two other sections of the stage are portable and skimpy in detail.
Down stage left represents the home of EARL KEITH. Visible is a love seat, coffee table, and night stand. There is a front door and an exit to the back rooms.
At this time, the down stage right area represents a Greyhound Bus Terminal.
Visible are a bench, a pay phone, and a neon sign reading, "BUS." Later, this
area will be converted into a Tire and Auto Shop office with a desk, two chairs and
a phone. A neon sign reading, "Tire and Auto," will be all for this scene.
AT RISE: The Bus Terminal is lit. HALSTED BRIDGES, age around 40, sits
on the bench listening to his cassette tape player with headset, and writing, and/or
reading in his notebook of poetry. Beside him are two travel bags. The music
HALSTED hears is "LOVE'S LIGHT IN FLIGHT," by Stevie Wonder. The
audience also hears the music. The music is interrupted by the voice of the bus
attendant over the loud speaker.*

VOICE: Final call, gate six, bus now leaving for Owosso, Durand, Lansing,
Battle Creek, Kalamazoo, Grand Rapids, Niles and Chicago. Making
connections for all points west. All aboard, please.

*(EARL KEITH, age 42, enters from the "loading zone" waving good-bye to
someone on the bus. EARL is a bit flashy in his dress as he fights to stay young.)*

EARL: *(Backing in)* Bye...Bye, have a good trip...Bye...! Good riddance! *(He
spots the phone sign and heads for it as he searches in his pocket for a quarter. On
phone.)* Hello...good morning...Yes it is I. The Earl is back together...
hey, I told you. Just put her on the bus not more than a minute ago. I do

not play. You ready for some company...? You what? Wake that clown up and tell him I said go home...! Okay now, don't mess up. I only got three days and you know the thangs I can do to you in three days...Cool, later, baby.

(He hangs up in disappointment. He then takes out his phone book and looks up another name.) Beatrice, Beatrice, here we go... *(He takes out a quarter but fumbles it in his excitement. While looking for it, he spots Halsted, an old friend.)* HALSTED?

HALSTED: *(Looking up from his paper, surprised.)* Earl?! *(They laugh, hug and shake hands.)* Well, I'll be...

EARL: Will you look at this? Boy, I ain't seen you since, "...19 what?" So, what in the world brings you back here to Beecher Heights, Michigan, no, no, Why?

HALSTED: Good question. Been sitting here trying to figure the same thing out for the past hour.

EARL: You waiting for somebody? Somebody coming to pick you up?

HALSTED: Not really. I'm just here reading the paper.

EARL: When you get here?

HALSTED: Came in on the 5:15 that arrived at 7:20. This man and woman got into a fight in the back of the bus. I mean a fist fight. She knocked out two of his teeth, and he bit her on the leg with the rest of them. Bus driver had to take them both to the hospital.

EARL: For real?

HALSTED: And you know what it was all about? Who was going to use that funky bathroom first.

EARL: They must of been married.

HALSTED: Had to be. Acted like it.

EARL: Damn. You aint gone crazy and got married again, have you?

HALSTED: No, not since I left here. No, I'm...well...*(Searching for words.)*

EARL: Yeah, I know what you mean. This chick I'm hooked up with now...You remember Cheryl Switzer?

HALSTED: Who in the...?

EARL: Yes you do. She grew up with us in the "Sticks." I took her to the junior Couple Dance with me...

HALSTED: That was more than 20 years ago, Earl. What is she, your lady, or something?

EARL: Be for real. You must of really forgot me. Hey, this is still Earl Keith you're talking to. The only thing THAT old I keep around me, is pennies! No, hell naw. Me and Cheryl's daughter been kicking it around for about the past year, or so.

HALSTED: Her daughter?

EARL: Her 23 year old daughter.

HALSTED: Oh!

(*EARL slaps his hand.*)

EARL: Yeah, a stone nut if I ever saw one. Halsted, when I first met her, a strung out junkie.

HALSTED: A junkie?

EARL: Chocolate candy junkie. Five pounds of chocolate a day. Face broke out, teeth all rotten in the front, skinny as a rail because she wouldn't eat nothing else. I took her in, got her off the fudge, bought her twelve hundred dollars worth of new teeth, and put some weight on that tight little frame.

HALSTED: Is that right?

EARL: Oh, she's cool now. Nice round boody girl, you know what I mean? If she wasn't such a crybaby I wouldn't mind being worried with her.

HALSTED: Crybaby?

EARL: Hell yeah. She cried everytime she thought I was screwing around on her.

HALSTED: Then she must of went through a box of Kleenex a day.

EARL: I ain't married to the girl, I just called myself taking her in and helping her out.

HALSTED: Out of her dress, out of her draws...

EARL: What can I say? I wasn't charging her any money for rent. She's the one that fell in love. I got tired of the mess myself. Sent her butt back to her Mama. Cheryl lives over in Kalamazoo. Told Lannette to get herself together and get back with me in a week.

HALSTED: Then what?

EARL: Aw, she ain't coming back. I doubt it seriously.

HALSTED: (*Feels the silence.*) So, uh, what else has been happening?

EARL: Nothing much. How long you here for?

HALSTED: (*Shrugs shoulders.*) Don't know.

EARL: Where you staying?

HALSTED: With my sister.

EARL: Burnetta? Boy, I haven't seen your sister in...She still live over on Prinston?

HALSTED: Sure does.

EARL: Still married to, uh...

HALSTED: Leonard.

EARL: Right, yeah. So, how you getting over there? Need a ride?

HALSTED: I could use one.

EARL: Yeah. I'll take you by there, be glad to...I just thought of something. What are you doing riding a bus anyway? Ain't you still an auto mechanic?

HALSTED: Sure am.

EARL: Yeah, you used to be one of the best auto mechanics here in Ingrain County.

HALSTED: I'm not a slouch now.

EARL: Always had the baddest souped up ride in the Sticks. I know you ain't walking.

HALSTED: You see these two "Feetwoods," don't you? That's it!

EARL: Damn, life's a blip, ain't lt?

HALSTED: A blip blip.

EARL: For real. *(Grabs a bag, HALSTED grabs the other.)* You still drinking beer?

(Exiting.)

HALSTED: Beer for breakfast? Cool!

(LIGHTS FADE OUT)

ACT I
Scene 2
BURNETTA'S house. She and her Husband LEONARD are in the middle of an argument as she fixes his lunch for work. LEONARD is 35, BURNETTA is 32.

LEONARD: *(Still getting dressed for his factory job.)* Runnin' around here, doing things behind my back, ignorin' me like I don't even live here no more. Where the hell is he goin' to sleep?

BURNETTA: Your family comes by here like it's the Holiday Inn. Your doggone sister's kids eat more food here than ours do, and you have the nerve to throw this mess up in my face...

LEONARD: If you think I'm gonna let that fat butt brother of yours break this couch down, you got another think comin'! I ain't even got the damn thing paid for yet.

BURNETTA: Your mama comes up here from Mississippi, every year, laying all over this couch and don't nobody say a word...

LEONARD: Good for nothin', no good bum! Runnin' up and down all over this country like he's God's gift to the U.S.A. Don't half work, still owes me $15.00 from ten years ago...

BURNETTA: And yeah, this couch wasn't too good when your old drunk brother Leroy laid up here and peed all over it. I don't care what you say. Halsted is my brother, and he can stay here as long as he likes.

LEONARD: Yeah well, the first time I see his face stuck up in my refrigerator, I'm throwin' him out, because I aint feedin' him! *(Snatches his lunch pall, his work cap, and keys. Exits through the side door. BURNETTA runs to the door behind him.)*

BURNETTA: And I know you been getting off work at two o'clock in the morning instead of four o'clock like you been claiming! *(The phone rings. She rushes to)* Hello! Oh, hi girl... no, that fool had the nerve to jump all over me about Halsted coming here to stay a few days...

LEONARD: *(Enters looking for his cigarettes, he claims.)* Can't even get out the door good before she jumps on that phone. *(Loud.)* That's why ain't no work ever did around here.

BURNETTA: *(Ignores him.)* No he hasn't come in yet...thought he was gonna be in this morning...

LEONARD: Where did you put my cigarettes?

BURNETTA: Told me he was coming, in on the Greyhound...

LEONARD: *(Heads for door.)* I'll buy me another pack.

BURNETTA: *(Cups phone.)* You keep bringing your behind in here at five or six in the morning, you want to.

LEONARD: I told you we've been working overtime.

BURNETTA: Funny nobody else gets any overtime.

LEONARD: We got a special government contract.

BURNETTA: Government contract. Let me find another heffers lipstick in my back seat.

LEONARD: That was them kids lipstick. Crazy talking woman. *(Exiting.)*

BURNETTA: You remember what I said.

LEONARD: And you remember what I said about your brother. *(Exits.)*

BURNETTA: *(Back on phone.)* Did you hear him? Dirty dog...six or seven o'clock in the morning everyday...Overtime my foot. His money ain't been overtime...oh no, that either. Especially that. Got so now he won't even get in the bed until I get out of it....*(The side doorbell rings.)* What did he forget now...? Hold on...uh...I'll tell you everything...*(She goes to the door and screams for joy when she sees HALSTED. Hugs, kisses, greetings.)* Come on in here with your good-looking self. Lost all that weight and everything.

HALSTED: Yeah, I see who found it for me, too.

BURNETTA: Ooh, you got that right. I can't walk by a refrigerator without gaining five pounds.

EARL: *(Enters closing door.)* Then you better sit down somewhere before you go through the floor.

BURNETTA: Earl! Look what the cat drug in. *(They hug and laugh.)* Where did Hall find you? *(HALSTED signals he has to go to the Bathroom.)* You remember where it is...

(HALSTED exits.)

EARL: Found me? I found him...Dude was sitting on a bench in the bus station.

BURNETTA: You working at the bus station, now?

EARL: Work? What's that? I ain't worked in almost a year. They laid me from the foundry way last December.

BURNETTA: Ain't it funny how the shops are giving away so much overtime work, with all these other people still laid off?

EARL: Overtime? Whose getting overtime? Bull...

BURNETTA: That's what my husband claims. Says he has to work over every night.

EARL: Oh, yeah, well, maybe he might.

BURNETTA: Sit down somewhere, Earl. You men love to take up for each other.

EARL: No, it depends on what plantation, I mean, plant they got you working at.

HALSTED: *(Enters with a sigh of relief.)* Almost didn't make it. Me and Earl been drinking beer all morning. Where's Leonard?

BURNETTA: Gone to work. You just missed him.

HALSTED: The kids, what? Still in school? *(Checks watch.)*

BURNETTA: They'll be here soon enough. I'd better start cooking dinner. You hungry?

(EARL is. He clears a space at the table.)

HALSTED: What you cooking?

BURNETTA: Pork chops.

(EARL makes a bigger space.)

HALSTED: Well, no thanks.

BURNETTA: You still don't eat pork?

HALSTED: Naw...

BURNETTA: I forgot all about that.

HALSTED: Don't worry about it.

BURNETTA: I got a chicken in the freezer...

HALSTED: That's okay.

BURNETTA: It won't take too long to thaw out.

HALSTED: Hey, don't put yourself through so much trouble, sis. I'll pick up something to eat later.

EARL: Man, what are you talking about? All the bar-b-que ribs and hot links you and me both have gone through? Since when did you stop eating pork?

HALSTED: Had to be at least twelve, fifteen years.

EARL: Yeah okay. I remember I quit one time. Didn't eat pork for three months. Who was that chick? Anyway, one day I was, had just finished shooting a game of hoop with my son Kenyetta, boy Hal, you wouldn't recognize Kenny now...

HALSTED: I bet I wouldn't. What is he, 15, 16?

EARL: Seventeen years old, six feet three, 195 pounds, looks almost as good as his old man. Yeah we were shooting some hoop, see, running up and down the court for three hours. Hey Burnetta, I has to keep myself in shape for the ladies, you know? So, uh, we finished our little one on one and I dropped him back off at his Mama's house...I need to take you by there, too. Drucilla would love to see you again...*(Halsted nor Burnetta remember her.)* Yeah so, she was back in the kitchen cooking, and hey, the girl can cook, Drucilla can burn. I be wondering sometimes why I got rid of her in the first place. She was cooking some pork chops, some stuffed pork chops. I don't know what she stuffed them with, but man, I could smell them cooking when me and Kenny pulled up in the driveway! Meat smelled so good, my toes curled up and my eyes started watering. Kenny said, "Daddy, you better stop all that crying and come on in here and eat." You think he had to tell me twice? ZOOM! Yall should of seen me. The woman had me crawling all over the kitchen floor on my knees, begging... "Drucilla please, let me just lick the skillet, or something." And here she goes... "I thought you and that new girlfriend of yours quit eating pork." Suddenly I remembered why I left her in the first place. Cruel, mean woman! Made me stay down there and beg for fifteen more minutes for a damn pork chop sandwich...and I did, too. Shoot, I don't care what you say, a niggah's hungry enough, he'll eat anything that ain't moving.

BURNETTA: I know that's right. *(Earl and Burnetta slap hands.)* Oh lord, the phone! *(She rushes to the phone.)* Hello! Mildred, I'm sorry girl, we got to talking...You hear him? Yeah, it sure is. Doesn't look like he's almost 41 at all...Yes you did. You heard Earl's voice, too...

EARL: Oh, oh...

BURNETTA: *(To EARL)* Mildred said to tell you you can come by to see your daughter anytime you're in the neighborhood...

EARL: I knew that was coming. Look here, you alright?

HALSTED: Yeah I'm alright.

EARL: You got my number. Give me a call so we can hook up. *(Heads for the side door.)*

HALSTED: Okay Earl, thanks for the ride.

EARL: Call me tonight. *(Exits.)*

BURNETTA: *(On phone)* Yeah, he's gone. Ran out the door like the house was on fire. You shoulda did like your Mother told you and took his behind to court. *(To HALSTED.)* Did you know about your friend?

HALSTED: Know what?

BURNETTA: Mr. Babymaker...what you say, Mildred? Mr. Sperm Bank? Shame on you, but it's true. Had the nerve to be standing here talking about some other chick of his...Yeah! "When I got rid of her." Like he's so, ooh. I can't stand it...

HALSTED: Uh, where do you want me to put these bags?

BURNETTA: Girl, will you let me get off this phone and help my brother out...? Okay, I will...bye. *(Hangs up.)* Oh, that Mildred. Talk your head off. Come on. *(HALSTED grabs his bag.)* Yeah, she said be sure and ask you to stop by for dinner sometimes.

HALSTED: That's nice.

BURNETTA: If you want to get raped, it is. I hate to say this about my best friend, but Mildred Toles is one of the hoe-in-est women in BeecherHeights, Michigan. I don't even trust her around Leonard. She's screwed around with every man I've ever introduced her to.

HALSTED: Oh yeah? What did you say that number was?

BURNETTA: You can do better than that.

HALSTED: I was just joking...I guess.

BURNETTA: *(At overcrowded hall closet.)* Your clothes can go in here. Sorry we ain't got that much room, but with four kids in a three bedroom house...*(Shrugs her shoulders.)*

HALSTED: Heard that.

BURNETTA: You can sleep on this couch. Might be a little lumpy.

HALSTED: Believe me, the Hyatt Regency never looked as good as this does, now.

(He slaps the back of the couch and raises a cloud of dust.)

BURNETTA: Good, let me find you a couple sheets. *(She exits. HALSTED can finally relax. He plops down onto the couch and bounces back up. A child's toy was in the groove. He tries to relax, again. BURNETTA enters with the sheets.)* You look tired. Want to lay down now?

HALSTED: No, I'll be alright...This town has changed quite a bit, hasn't it? Earl and I drove around all morning long and I couldn't find a single house I grew up in. And you know we lived all over this town. I mean, entire neighborhoods uprooted, replaced with freeways, parking lots, fast food chains. Then, when you go into the grocery store around here, you'd better know how to speak Arab to get what you want.

BURNETTA: Or Korean if you want some clothes.

HALSTED: Hey, don't we own anything anymore?

BURNETTA: Liquor store down on Church Street. Chicken Charlies is colored owned.

HALSTED: Oh yeah, and the rib joint.

BURNETTA: Lord yes.

HALSTED: Damn. That's why I'm back here. This is why I had to come back home. I've got to get myself together. Got to have something of my own.

BURNETTA: What more do you want?

HALSTED: What in the world do I have? Don't have a home. Haven't had a wife in 18 years. The only son I have is off somewhere in the Navy...

BURNETTA: You get up and go whenever you want to. You travel all over the country. You know how to fix cars so good you can get work wherever you please...

HALSTED: Work? Where? And since when has work ever been enough, anyway?

BURNETTA: *(She feels his frustration, goes to prepare dinner.)* So, how is, uh, what's her name?

HALSTED: Imani.

BURNETTA: Yeah, her.

HALSTED: She's cool.

BURNETTA: You two still together?

HALSTED: Not really.

BURNETTA: Never got married, huh?

HALSTED: Nope.

BURNETTA: Wasn't she some kind of a lawyer?

HALSTED: Something like that...

BURNETTA: Well, doggone big Brother, tell me something. You ain't catching no hints. What's the deal? Yall was together a long time.

HALSTED: Over five years.

BURNETTA: She came here with you to Mama's funeral. Has it been that long?

HALSTED: Mama's funeral. We had just gotten together about a month before then. I called it destiny, then. Here I was on my way to Cleveland for the first time in my life...

BURNETTA: You were living in Atlanta, right?

HALSTED: Yeah. While I was down in Atlanta, I had hooked up on this good job in Cleveland teaching auto mechanics at the Auto Doctors Institute. So, like I said, I was on my way into the city, got off at the downtown exit looking for a hotel, and there she was.

BURNETTA: At the hotel?

HALSTED: No, on the highway. Standing in front of her car. Had a busted radiator hose. Steam was flying twenty feet ln the air. Poor girl must of thought the car was on fire. *(A deep sigh.)* Then...you should of seen her then at that moment. A living sculpture of African perfection. I damn near ran into a garbage truck trying to pull over to help her...Wow...

BURNETTA: Sounds like somebody still cares.

HALSTED: Shoot, like I said, that was then. Before those lovely, long fingernails turned out to be claws. Before those deep, piercing eyes started shooting daggers. Before that sweet, loving voice cussed me out a time or two. No, that was then.

BURNETTA: That's right, ain't she a Scorpio?

HALSTED: How you remember that?

BURNETTA: Because she reminded me so much of one when I met her.

HALSTED: Aw, that sign stuff...

BURNETTA: What was Mama? What was Mama?

HALSTED: Uh, Scorpio...?

BURNETTA: And you know what a hell raiser she was.

HALSTED: She did shoot Daddy in the leg that time.

BURNETTA: And meant to kill him if he ever hit her again, too.

HALSTED: I had forgotten about that.

BURNETTA: Shoot, you're lucky. I made the mistake of coming up pregnant while still living at home with her. Hal, she set my clothes on fire. Every dress, blouse, brassier she bought me, she burned. And then kicked me out of the house.

HALSTED: Really?

BURNETTA: And I mean KICKED me out. I thought she was gonna kill me. Leonard had to pull her off of me, and then she jumped on him. Busted his lip...

HALSTED: Mama?!

BURNETTA: I knew what it was, though. Doctor said she acted that way because of the tumor.

HALSTED: Oh Yeah...

BURNETTA: But my behind wasn't thinking about no tumor at the moment.

HALSTED: She had that brain tumor for years and refused to get it checked.

BURNETTA: Poor Mama. I miss her no matter what.

HALSTED: (Recalls.) Imani burned up a few of my things one time. Talk about jealous, swore up and down one day that she saw some lipstick on, well, a pair of my underwear, took all the clothes she could find that she bought me, plus all my poems and short stories that I had been playing around with, carried them out to the backyard and torched them.

BURNETTA: What? Not your poems...

HALSTED: That's where the change began. I lost the urge to write and to be with her.

BURNETTA: I hear you. But you know what? It could of been you in that back-yard. You see that movie on television about that woman who bar-b-qued her husband? Couple months ago. Leonard didn't sleep good for four weeks after that...I lit up a cigarette in bed one night and the man damn near peed on himself.

HALSTED: Started checking on his fire insurance, huh?

BURNETTA: Hey Hal, bought himself a pair of rubber P.J.'s.

HALSTED: Rubber pajamas...

BURNETTA: Oh, let me quit...But you know Hal, it's really not funny at all, if you want to know the truth about it. The way these husbands and wives are killing each other off in this town now-a-days...

HALSTED: Hey, everywhere you go—Domestic disputes.

BURNETTA: Murder.

HALSTED: In the name of love.

BURNETTA: Or whatever. Oh, I may as well tell you, that fool is acting up already about you staying here.

HALSTED: Leonard? I thought you said everything was cool.

BURNETTA: It is. He just acts like a fool whenever he gets a chance to. Nothing to be worried about. Claims he don't want his couch messed up.

HALSTED: I can sleep on the floor.

BURNETTA: You must be crazy...

HALSTED: Yeah, Earl was saying I could stay...

BURNETTA: You are staying right here. Leonard better not say anything to me. I ain't but a inch off of him, anyway.

HALSTED: I hope you aren't falling out because of me.

BURNETTA: Are you kidding? We have been fighting since the day of our wedding. The very day! It seems his Mama didn't like the idea of me holding my baby during the marriage vows.

HALSTED: Well, that was sort of strange, and in a church, too...

BURNETTA: No it wasn't. Not after all I went through. All the time I was pregnant with junior, my Mama beating me up, putting me out, calling me all kinds of names, all then, Leonard's Mama swore up and down that he wasn't the Daddy. I was trying to trick him into marrying me. And that old weak-livered mama's boy listened to her, too. But then, then when the baby came out, looking like Leonard spit him out, you should of heard his Mama, then. (*Imitates MAMA with a mouth full of snuff.*) "Yeah, that's my Grandbaby alright. That's my boy's child. Don't look like you had a thing to do with having him at all." Bitch. Excuse me, Hal. And then she had the nerve to give notice to all concerned that the baby was sitting on her side of the family during the wedding. Humph! Guess I showed her old behind...Where you going, Hal?

HALSTED: (*Needing to get away.*) Uh, I'm going to find some food. Be back in a few.

BURNETTA: Okay. I'll thaw that chicken out for you tomorrow. You be careful out there. It's dangerous.

HALSTED: Alright. (*Exits.*)

BURNETTA: (*Crosses to side door.*) And don't worry about that old fool of mine... I'll take care of him. (*Closes door as Lights fade out.*)
END ACT I, Scene 2

ACT I
Scene 3
The fore-stage area lights up and becomes a street corner in the afternoon. At the moment, music is heard as Halsted enters. He has on his earphones and the song that is playing is the song the audience hears as Halsted "walks down the street." He fades the music out as he looks up the street for a bus. Street traffic sounds fade in as Halsted speaks.

HALSTED: Damn, where is the bus...? It sure is funny how so much can change, without really changing at all....This is what you came running back home to, huh? You're going to find yourself here, huh? Can't even find a bus...

(He stands on the corner looking up the street. Enters a young lady, early 20's. Her dress is tight and modernish. She seems to be in a hurry as she walks around towards Halsted. Another character, a man that appears to be jogging, runs past the lady and Halsted. The lady looks upstage and speaks.)

LADY: Quit following me, boy. I told you to go on back over to your Grandmama's. I ain't got time. Got thangs to do...(*She stands on the other side of the stage from Halsted looking up the street. Halsted likes what he sees. When she walks toward him, he prepares himself to speak to her. The lady smiles as she walks towards him because she sees a cab. Halsted mistakes the smile for a come on. He walks towards her, extending his hand.)* TAXI! TAXI!

(She runs past him so quickly, he can't keep up.)

HALSTED: How are you doing, Miss...? Miss...Miss, wait...Doggone...

(As he looks in her direction, the jogger, wearing a ski mask, steps up behind Halsted.)

THUG: I want your wallet and all your pockets emptied out, right now.

(Halsted is shaken for a second, but decides to fight. He swirls around and the thug is knocked back to reveal he has no weapon in his hand.)

HALSTED: Uh huh. Come on with it...

THUG: You bad, ain't you? So, now we sorta play this dangerous. Check this out...

(He pulls out a big pistol.)

HALSTED: (*Very cooperative.*) That was my wallet, my pockets...

THUG: Your watch, that fancy cassette player...

HALSTED: Not my Walkman...

THUG: Say what?! (*Takes the things. Sees notebook.*) And give me this, too.

HALSTED: It's just a notebook...

THUG: (*Puts pistol to his head.*) You know, I don't like your attitude. I think I ought to...

(He aims the pistol at HALSTED'S crotch. In reflex, HALSTED covers himself and yells out. In this time, the THUG runs off quickly. Lights fade out.)

END ACT ONE Scene 3

ACT I

Scene 4

(Burnetta's house, a few hours later. She's on the phone, in her housecoat and peering out the kitchen window in search of Halsted.)

BURNETTA: ...And she was saying to me that he told her that he liked what he saw...yeah girl...and all I had on was an old faded out house dress, my hair was in rollers...no she didn't. At the Motor City Lounge? We must go by there...Here he comes. Here comes my big brother...You on your way? See you in five minutes...okay, five minutes. Bye... *(The doorbell rings as she opens the door.)* Doggone Halsted, where did you go to get some food, Detriot?

HALSTED: Damn! Food! I knew it was something I forgot.

BURNETTA: You mean you been gone all this long time and haven't eaten yet? What did you do, get lost?

HALSTED: No, I got robbed.

BURNETTA: *(Serious fear.)* No you didn't.

HALSTED: Yes I did. Some young punk put a pistol up in my face and told me to give it up.

BURNETTA: My God! Where?

HALSTED: St. John and Massachusettes.

BURNETTA: St. John and Mass...? What were you doing way over there?

HALSTED: Walking. Bus took so long to come, I decided to walk, get some fresh air. I mean, it happened so quick, I was standing on the corner, broad daylight, getting ready to say something to this big boody girl before she ran across the street when, boom...

BURNETTA: Beecher Heights has changed, Halsted. I told you it was dangerous. There are some parts of town the police don't even go in.

HALSTED: Hey, tell me about it.

BURNETTA: It's a good thing you didn't get hurt or killed. Don't you be walking up and down these streets anymore like you know where you're going.

HALSTED: Yes Mother.

BURNETTA: I'm serious.

HALSTED: I am, too. That boy stuck his pistol up in my face so deliberately, it would have been nothing for him to squeeze the trigger.

BURNETTA: They do it everyday. Killing each other everyday! Over nothing...Me, I'm ready for their behinds. You may take all my money, but buddy, when you turn to get away, your ass is grass... *(Pulls out a long pistol.)* and here's the lawnmower.

HALSTED: *(Surprised. Rolls over couch.)* You carry a gun?

BURNETTA: Hal, this is a factory town. We're surrounded by another factory town. They said on the news the other night that 82% of the money generated from this whole area of the State is factory generated money. The shops close down, or even slow down, everybody suffers. It's been a lot of suffering around here, big Brother. People moving back down south, families splitting up, gangs, robberies, murders, crack cocaine, you name it. And that ain't the half of it. What did you call it?

HALSTED: What?

BURNETTA: Husbands and wives, or boyfriends and girlfriends...

HALSTED: Oh, domestic disputes...

BURNETTA: Right. More people getting killed in bed than in the street.

HALSTED: What are the police doing?

BURNETTA: Police? They don't care about Black folks shooting each other. Long as they don't shoot them. And you got the nerve to say something to me about carrying a gun?

HALSTED: I'm not saying a word...Where is everybody?

BURNETTA: *(She goes through the finishing touches of getting ready to go out.)* Junior, Tish and Nita are spending the night over their Uncle Leroy's. They all said hi. Collette is upstairs asleep. She's on punishment for being kicked out of school again for fighting.

HALSTED: Little Collette?

BURNETTA: Fifth grade. Been set back once and heading for a second time. I don't know what to do. Which brings me up to now. You weren't planning on going anywhere tonight, were you?

HALSTED: No, why?

BURNETTA: See, my husband doesn't seem to know where he lives when he gets off of work anymore. So, tonight I'm going to see how lost I can get. *(Takes off her robe to reveal an evening dress.)*

HALSTED: Look out, now. I don't want to be pulling old boy off of you.

BURNETTA: Sh...*(Doesn't finish the word.)* I put that chicken in the refrigerator. Might be thawed out by now.

HALSTED: Okay. *(Plops down on couch.)*

BURNETTA: How much did they take? You broke?

HALSTED: He got $25.00, my watch, my walkman and my notebook! That's what really made me mad. Why my notebook? I was just beginning to start writing again. Anyway, luckily though...

(He pulls up his pant leg, removes money from sock.)

BURNETTA: Good idea.

HALSTED: I still have $125.00 left.

BURNETTA: $125.00?! This is gonna be a short visit.

HALSTED: Gotta find some work, that's all.

BURNETTA: So, you are moving back...*(She hears a car pull up and runs to the side door.)* There's the car. Okay Halsted...That's not Mildred...Oh yeah, Earl called and said he was coming by, and guess what...? *(She hears a car horn out the front way and runs to the front door.)* It's about time, girl. See you later, Hal. PARRRTAY!

(She exits quickly.)

HALSTED: Have a good time.

(The side door bell rings. Tired, hungry and with a headache, Halsted goes to the door. Earl enters laughing. He carries a six pack of beer in a bag.)

EARL: Was that Burnetta? She jumped over that clump of bushes like Jackie Joyner what's her name. Leonard better hurry up and get back on first shift. What's up Main?

HALSTED: Hey, Earl.

EARL: *(He signals out the door to his car.)* Come on in, he's here.

HALSTED: Who's out in the car?

EARL: Little cousin of mine.

HALSTED: Cousin?

EARL: You don't know her. Grew up in Tennessee.

HALSTED: How little is she? *(Enters VENUS STRATTFORD, age 32. Professional, but not stuffy. Physically beautiful, but not conceited.)* My goodness...

(There is an attraction between the two. HALSTED more so.)

EARL: Venus, Halsted...Halsted, Venus.

HALSTED: Venus...

VENUS: How do you do?

HALSTED: Venus...Uh, have a seat...

VENUS: Excuse me, but, do you mind if I use your restroom, first?

HALSTED: Of course, I mean, go ahead. It's back that way, second door.

VENUS: Thank you...*(Exits.)*

HALSTED: My goodness...

(Tries to straighten up the house and finds plenty of things to pick up.)

EARL: Put your horns back in, Maryland-Farmer. That's my cousin...

HALSTED: So?

EARL: My married cousin.

HALSTED: Don't tell me that.

EARL: Been married to the same man for nine hundred years.

HALSTED: Doggone. This is not my day.

EARL: I think you're wrong there, Brother. Think you're mighty, mighty wrong. *(Pulls out a can of beer.)* Have a cold one. *(HALSTED takes the can and rubs it across his forehead.)* Yeah, you never know what can happen in the length of a day.

HALSTED: That's for damn sure. Do you know why my head is hurting me?

EARL: From what? Eating them pork chops?

HALSTED: Man, forget you. *(Punches his arm.)* See, I'm-walking down the street...

(VENUS enters relieved and somewhat embarrassed.)

VENUS: I don't know why I let you do this to me Earl. Embarrass me like this.

EARL: What did I do?

VENUS: Keeping me away from my job, pouring beer down my throat, making me have to run into peoples houses to use their restrooms. Shame on you.

HALSTED: He did the same thing to me this morning.

VENUS: He did? You are terrible.

EARL: That's right, blame me.

HALSTED: Come on pretty lady, have a seat. You ready for another beer?

VENUS: No thank you. I've got to be sober enough to dodge those punches my husband's going to be throwing at me for sneaking out with Earl.

EARL: Bob and weave, baby, bob and weave.

HALSTED: Well, I for one am glad that Earl did sneak you out so that I could have the opportunity to meet such a lovely young lady with so appropriate a name. Venus, Star of the morning. Light of a new day.

VENUS: Oh please, tell me more.

EARL: Alright you two, don't start no stuff up in here. Thought you said you had a headache.

HALSTED: I have been cured...Let me stop. Pardon me, Ms. Venus. After the day I've had, for me to see such a lovely, excuse me, married lady, I guess I got a little carried away.

VENUS: Flirtatious, huh?

HALSTED: Can't help myself. Heredity. Blame it on my genes. Better yet, yours.

EARL: I gonna need a whip and a chair in a minute.

HALSTED: Did I do it again?

EARL: Look, Venus Strattford, Mrs. Venus Strattford, is supposed to be here to talk to you about business, not BS. Now, I got to thinking about what we were talking about this morning about you wanting to move back here to this hole in the wall, which breaks my heart because I just knew you escaped, and well, how you needed to hook up with some work. And listen, hey Venus, I ain't lying, this boy here is the greatest automobile mechanic since Andy Granitelli. What was that old played out saying you had painted over your garage? "Halsted under your hood, makes your car run good."

VENUS: Oh, an English major...

HALSTED: Poetic license.

EARL: Whatever. Anyway, Venus here, and her husband, Arthur, own a couple tire and auto centers...

VENUS: We don't own them, we manage them.

HALSTED: What, like a franchise?

VENUS: Right.

HALSTED: Very enterprising.

VENUS: Thank you. And what we need, what I nees at my store is an experienced mechanic to fill in for a few weeks.

HALSTED: Temporary work.

VENUS: My head man had to go into the hospital for an operation and is scheduled to be back in six weeks.

HALSTED: Six weeks?

EARL: *(While looking through his phone book.)* Enough time to find some permanent work around town.

HALSTED: If there is some.

EARL: Right.

VENUS: If you're as good as Earl says you are, I can use you.

HALSTED: I work hard. I do my best.

VENUS: Tell me about yourself. Earl already told me you like to write poetry.

HALSTED: Big mouth...

VENUS: I think that's very admirable. A sensitive man? Now-a-days...? So, did you have your own shop in...?

HALSTED: Cleveland. No, I didn't. I was teaching auto mechanics at a trade school.

VENUS: Interesting.

HALSTED: Yeah, while it lasted. Government contract. When Reaganomics said...*(He gestures cutting his throat.)* ...the job said...*(Same gesture.)* Been out of work for over a year.

VENUS: Are you married? *(Earl clears his throat.)* I mean, do you have a family you have to send for?

HALSTED: No.

VENUS: Oh, that's too bad. How soon can you start working?

HALSTED: How soon do you need me?

VENUS: Yesterday.

HALSTED: Tomorrow morning?

VENUS: Nine a.m.?

HALSTED: Cool.

   (The moment they shake hands, EARL is up.)

EARL: So, is everything settled?

VENUS: Hold your horses, Earl. Dang, is she that tough?

EARL: *(Throwing hint to HALSTED.)* Both of them are.

HALSTED: Both of them?

EARL: Yeah, one for me and one for you.

HALSTED: *(Not wanting to look like a dog.)* Is that right?

EARL: I got hold to a couple of, frea...*(Doesn't say freaks.)* uh, friends who said they are part of the local welcome wagon and want to uh, give you a tour.

HALSTED: Oh wow, Earl, I really appreciate that, but, uh...

EARL: But what? How come here, come here...*(Whispers.)* Man, these two chicks...

HALSTED: *(Somewhat surprised.)* Together?!

EARL: I'm telling you.

(Raises up to slap HALSTED'S hand, but he walks away.)

HALSTED: Let me take a rain check, Earl. I'm beat.

VENUS: *(Relieved.)* Right Earl, come on. At least give the man time to get settled in good before you go corrupting him.

EARL: Corrupting? Him?

HALSTED: No, seriously man, my head's hurting. I haven't eaten all day...

VENUS: See there, that's what you can do for him. Let's take him somewhere and feed him, then you can take him home.

EARL: Chicken Charlies still open?

HALSTED: I could use some food.

EARL: Then come on and eat so you can start thinking straight. These chicks are hotter than...

HALSTED: *(Remembers Collette.)* Oh man! I can't go anywhere. My niece is upstairs sleeping.

EARL: Oh no, Halsted. What about the chicks...?

VENUS: Oh well, such a shame. *(She gives him her business card.)* Here's the address and number in case there's any problem.

HALSTED: Thank you.

VENUS: Nine a.m.?

HALSTED: Eight thirty!

VENUS: Pleasure meeting you, Mr...?

HALSTED: Halsted.

VENUS: Halsted Halsted?

HALSTED: Uh no, Bridges. Halsted Bridges. Pleasure meeting you.

(EARL leads her out then pushes her out the door.)

EARL: Easy, greasy.

HALSTED: Is she happily married?

EARL: Two brats, a $90,000.00 house, two cars, a boat and a snowmobile.

HALSTED: Oh well.

EARL: Don't worry, blood. Me and you together? We can run these chicks for days. Later.

(He exits. HALSTED waves bye to VENUS.)

HALSTED: Now, that is a lovely young lady. *(The phone rings.)* Hello...*(He recognizes IMANI'S voice and changes his voice to a foreign language.)* No, so sorry, wrong number...okay, goodbye...*(Hangs up quickly.)* Imani?! *(Llghts fade out.)*

END ACT I, Scene 4

ACT I

Scene 5

Downstage Right lights up representing the lunch room of the tire and auto center. Two male employees stand to the right of the table and two chairs they brought in in the darkness. Mike eats his lunch while Green complains.

GREEN: Naw, naw, he done made me mad already. Three damn tune-ups. Three electronic tune-ups, one of them he had to replace the spark plug wires. Two grease jobs, two oil changes, and here it is just now lunch time. Full days work and you know it.

MIKE: Heard that.

GREEN: What I want to know is, who he think he is? What's he trying to prove?

MIKE: Maybe he likes to work.

GREEN: I mean, he already got the job. Strattford told him that already.

MIKE: Maybe that's the way they work in Cleveland.

GREEN: I'll tell you what it is. I think he thinks that if he rubs up to the boss lady good enough, he might get to stay on permanent!

MIKE: Permanent? You mean even after Barfield gets out the hospital?

GREEN: A good job is hard to find. That's all I'm saying.

(Hal and Venus enter and take seats to eat.)

MIKE: Yeah, I see what you mean.

GREEN: Look at him over there. Too good to eat with us. *(Pretends like he's yelling.)* Naw dude, you ain't slick. We're hip to your game...he don't know he's sitting up there with one of the coldest broads in North America. She can sit up there and listen to you rap all day and not hear a word.

MIKE: She ain't nothing but a tease.

GREEN: Oh yeah, she laughs and jokes but don't even play...with her fine lookin' self. Baby, if you wasn't so cold, and I could be so bold...

MIKE: *(They slap hands.)* Heard that.

(The lights build on Hal and Venus.)

HALSTED: ...So I turned around and boom, there it was. I thought I was in Vietnam, or something. The boy was ready to blow my head off if I blinked wrong.

VENUS: That must have been horrible.

HALSTED: Hey, it's a good thing I didn't have to go to the bathroom, or…
(*They laugh. Green sneers as he and Mike exit.*)

VENUS: You'd better talk to my cousin Earl about using one of his pistols.

HALSTED: I may have to.

VENUS: We even have to keep a gun here in the office.

HALSTED: Beecher Heights, Michigan, the wild, wild Mid-west.

VENUS: That's about it. Anyway, how do you like this so far?

HALSTED: Love it. And the job, too.

VENUS: Do you really?

HALSTED: Yes.

VENUS: You work so fast, so easy. It doesn't seem to be a challenge to you.

HALSTED: I'm not messing up, am I? Something wrong?

VENUS: No, no there's nothing wrong with your work. I'm very pleased with
it. You're a highly professional mechanic.

HALSTED: But…

VENUS: No buts. What I'm trying to say is, you should have people working
for you instead of the other way around.

HALSTED: Thank you. One of these days I will too, if I ever get it together.

VENUS: Oh, you wlll.

HALSTED: See, that's my problem and I know it is. I never took the time to
deal with the business end. So, like you said, I've always been working for
somebody else. When I did open my own garage back here a few years
ago, I didn't make any real money, because I didn't know how to.

VENUS: All you needed was a good business manager.

HALSTED: There you go. (*Sings out the line.*) Where were you when I needed
you, Miss Business Manager?

VENUS: How do you know it was me that you needed?

HALSTED: (*He chuckles.*) There's a lot of ways I can answer that, married lady.

VENUS: (*Playing.*) Tell me about it, baby.

HALSTED: Alright now.

VENUS: Oh, I can't joke with you, right?

HALSTED: No ma'am. There's something about you that has me very nervous.
Any jokes, glances, or innuendos will be taken quite seriously.

VENUS: I see. I'll keep it in mind.

HALSTED: I know you're the boss and it's against company policy to flirt with
the boss.

VENUS: Especially since the boss' husband could easily walk in at any time.

HALSTED: Good point. Well. I guess I'll mosy on back to the motor pool
Enjoyed my lunch break.

VENUS: So did I. By the way, you're doing a great job out there.

HALSTED: I tries, Mama.

(He exits. Lights fade out.)

END ACT I, Scene 5

ACT I

Scene 6

Burnetta's house, pre-dawn hours. The lights come up slowly as Burnetta moves across the forestage area. She is rather tipsy from another night of partying. She moves around to the kitchen entrance, trying not to be too loud. She hears Halsted on the couch talking in his sleep. She chuckles as she walks past on her way upstairs.

HALSTED: No, No! I've got to get myself together, Imani. You're wrong, there is a problem. I want my own. You're not being fair Imani...Imani!

(He bolts up and Burnetta has to rush upstairs. Hal notices his sweating brow and tries to gather himself together. He goes to the kitchen table, sees some cards and begins playing solitaire. He hears a noise at the side door. He tip-toes to investigate. Enters Leonard who is also tip-toeing to avoid Burnetta. Both men startle each other. Cards fly in the air.)

LEONARD: Lord a mercy!

HALSTED: Leonard! Oh, man! You scared the mess out of me.

LEONARD: Me?! You! What you doing up so early?

HALSTED: *(Picking up cards.)* Good question. What time you got?

LEONARD: *(Checking watch.)* Damn! Damn near six o'clock! *(Lowers his voice.)* Burnetta ain't been up, has she?

HALSTED: *(Thinks she's still out with Mildred.)* Her and Mil...uh, hey man, dog-gone. You know this is the first time I've had a chance to talk with you since I've been here. What's been up with you?

LEONARD: *(Anything to keep from going to bed.)* Same old thang. Work every-day. Too early in the morning to have ourselves a beer?

HALSTED: Man I gotta go to work in two hours.

LEONARD: Anybody sit up six o'clock in the morning playing solitaire can't be worried about a little beer putting him to sleep.

HALSTED: Well...

LEONARD: Yeah, okay then. Let me go to bed.

HALSTED: *(Has to stop him.)* Uh, why not? Pop a top, again.

LEONARD: *(Gladly sings a drinking song.)* "Pop a top again, I just got time for one more round, another one, my friend..." *(Hands him a beer.)* Yes sir, they got you working already, huh?

HALSTED: *(Sits beer down.)* Temporarily, but it's right on time.

LEONARD: Good...How's that couch doing you?

HALSTED: It's alright. Not bad.

LEONARD: Really?

HALSTED: Yeah. Hope I'm not messing it up.

LEONARD: That old thing? I was just telllng Burnetta the other day we need to be getting a new one. She's the one who's crazy about it. Acted like she didn't even want you sleep on it.

HALSTED: Oh yeah?

LEONARD: Shoot. You might not know this about your sister, but she got some funny ways. Then she tries to make it look like it's me. Ain't no telling what she done told you about me...

HALSTED: Whoosh! You dig? In one ear, out the other.

LEONARD: Yeah, 'cause it's rough out here, you know? It's tough! You work hard everyday of your life, overtime, double time, sneaking in second jobs, having a little fun, just to try to pay for what you haven't even gone out to buy yet... And it's still not enough...What do you do?

HALSTED: Yeah, what do you do...?

LEONARD: You say, "Fuck it." That's what you do. What Richard Pryor say? "Fuck It!!" Then you fuck up. Wind up being lost and looking....(*Downs beer.*) Maybe it is too early in the morning for this beer.

BURNETTA: (*Enters from upstairs surprising both men.*) Well now, ain't this nothing.

(*She is dressed in housecoat and slippers.*)

LEONARD: (*Regroups quickly.*) There you are. What did you do, fall asleep with the kids?

BURNETTA: Don't even try it, Leonard. I ain't been upstairs checking on them kids no more than fifteen minutes.

(*Both are trying to cover their tracks.*)

LEONARD: Had to be at least a half hour, 'cause we been sitting up here..,

(*Tries to get Hal to agree.*)

BURNETTA: I know how long I been up there. What time is it? Why you just now coming in?

LEONARD: I must of just now got off of work if I'm just now getting in.

BURNETTA: Whoever she is, she better have a whole bunch of money, because by the time I finish with you and these four kids, you'd better pray for super overtime!

LEONARD: You ain't gonna worry me this morning. (*Heads for upstairs.*) Skip my breakfast. I'm going to bed.

BURNETTA: (*Sarcastically.*) I'll be there shortly, dear.

(*Leonard shudders to himself as he exits.*)

HALSTED: (*Whispers.*) When did you come in?

BURNETTA: About a half hour ago.

HALSTED: I didn't hear you come in.

BURNETTA: I know you didn't.

HALSTED: But I usually do.

BURNETTA: It's only been three times.

HALSTED: Four.

BURNETTA: Oh yeah, counting tonight. It's more fun when you have to sneak to do it, ain't it?

HALSTED: You are a mess. A mess! But how did you get past me this time?

BURNETTA: The way you was laying up there talking in your sleep? I know you didn't hear me.

HALSTED: Talking in my sleep?

BURNETTA: "Oh Imani, Imani..."

HALSTED: Imani? Aw man, now she even haunts my sleep.

BURNETTA: Sounds like true love to me...Let me go to bed. Them kids will be up in no time. *(The phone rings. BURNETTA answers it quickly.)* Hello... *(She cups the receiver and yells up the steps.)* I've got it, Leonard! What's your big rush? *(To caller.)* Hello... Who...? Just a minute...*(To HALSTED)* It's for you.

HALSTED: Imani?

BURNETTA: I couldn't catch her voice. *(Hands him the phone, but doesn't go too far.)*

HALSTED: *(Expecting the worst.)* Hello...well, hello there. Good morning...no, you didn't wake me up...*(BURNETTA becomes more nosy.)* Why, that would be very nice of you. Appreciate that...7:30...? I'll be waiting...goodbye. *(Hangs up as BURNETTA gives him a sly look.)* Aw now, it was only my boss.

BURNETTA: Earl's cousin.

HALSTED: Yeah. She wanted to see if I needed a ride to work since she knows I'm taking the bus, and all.

BURNETTA: You don't have to be there until nine.

HALSTED: Well, you know, we may need to stop and pick up some coffee, or something.

BURNETTA: Right. Sure. Now, tell me again, big Brother; who's a mess? *(She laughs as he grabs his clothes and chases her out.)*

END ACT I, Scene 6

ACT I

Scene 7

(VENUS' office later that morning. HALSTED and VENUS enter, laughing. HALSTED has a bag with coffee and rolls inside. They make themselves comfortable.)

VENUS: So, Arthur picks up the book again, looks back at the figures and can't do anything but shake his head. I said, "What was that again, Arthur? My store took in more money this week than yours did? We actually doubled our volume? Why, isn't that wonderful?" He wanted to crawl through the floor. The man hates to say anything nice to me, and can't stand the idea of me doing something better than him. Halsted, every Saturday morning, every Saturday morning we have to go through this ritual. Arthur gets up at 6 a.m. to go over the receipts of both stores to record in his little book. Then he makes it a point to wake me up and inform me of how much better his store did over mine. And how I don't know how to manage this or organize that. And, to top it off, why I shouldn't be out here calling myself working in the first place. Then he takes the time to explain to me why my store does not and cannot operate as well as his. "You hire too many niggers, simple as that." See, at his store, over on the Northside, he doesn't hire Black mechanics. Refuses to. "I won't be bothered with shade tree mechanics." He irks me about that. We live in all white neighborhood, our kids are the only little Black kids at the school, we're constantly being invited to Rotary Club functions that are pathetically boring. The only Black person I've ever seen Arthur hang around with is Earl and I still haven't figured that out. So, when you came along and caught us up with all our back orders and in two weeks time, totally reorganized the shop to the point where we actually took in more receipts that the Northside store well, I'm so happy I could kiss you.

HALSTED: Be my guest.

VENUS: I should be ashamed of myself.

HALSTED: About what?

VENUS: I like being around you. When I'm around you, I find myself wondering.

HALSTED: Wondering?

VENUS: *(Joan Rivers)* Can we talk?

HALSTED: Sure.

VENUS: I've been married nine years now. My husband was the first man I was ever with and I've never cheated on him. He's the only man I know. Lately, especially lately, I've been kind of *wondering*...

HALSTED: If there's anything you're missing.

VENUS: Yes.

HALSTED: Probably not.

VENUS: You think so? *(HALSTED shrugs his shoulders.)* I just know there's got to be a lot more affection than...well...

HALSTED: You have been married nine years. Maybe the romance is a little...

VENUS: Romance? What is that?

HALSTED: Aw, now...

VENUS: I'm serious. Some men, from what I understand, are simply not romantically inclined.

HALSTED: What about before you got married?

VENUS: I was the romantic. I was the one waiting for a knight in shining armor to swoop by and save me from my grandmother, and her 9 p.m. curfew. Arthur fit the bill. He had a car, a job, and desire to marry me. He always was a good provider. Gave me everything I wanted.

HALSTED: But not what you needed?

VENUS: That's what made me start wondering. Was there something more that I needed? Why did I feel something was missing? I thought maybe if I had a job of my own and showed a little independence, my life would be more complete and I wouldn't need so much of what I thought I wasn't getting. And even maybe with me working, there would be less pressure on Arthur, so he'd spend more time with me.

HALSTED: And...?

VENUS: A situation came up. Arthur was forced to replace the manager he had here all of a sudden. Seems as though the man—a Caucasian by the way— was convicted of operating an auto theft chop shop and using this shop as a pick up point. Arthur was caught off guard, desperate, and forced to hire me right away...On a temporary basis, of course. That's been almost two years now.

HALSTED: Good. Didn't it help?

VENUS: No. Things got worse. Arthur began to look at me as competition instead of his wife. Hence, our Saturday morning lectures. But Halsted, oh my God, working in public, the men, the propositions, the daily encounters of...oh the things I can do to you Mama! It was terrible, and beautiful. I guess all women need to know they're attractive to men.

HALSTED: Helps the ego.

VENUS: Right. I even found myself acting a little flirtatious just to make sure I was attractive. But all it was was curiosity. The men would say something, I would sort of listen, and that was as far as it went, although, according to Arthur, well...No matter how hard they tried, no man could get to me.

HALSTED: So, in other words, what you're saying to me is don't even try.

VENUS: No, I didn't say that. You, I'm scared of you.

HALSTED: Me? Why?

VENUS: I don't know.

HALSTED: Don t do me like that. 'Splain to me.

VENUS: 'Splain to you? Let me put it like this, no, let me put it another way. I find you to be a very interestng person, you're traveled, experienced, you take pride in your work. And, if you tilt your head to the side like this, and the light is right, you're even sort of cute.

HALSTED: Gee thanks, I like you, too.

VENUS: You do?

HALSTED: In all seriousness, yes. Star of the morning. Light of Dawn. This is the first real enjoyment I have experienced in centuries.

VENUS: *(This is funny.)* Centuries...

HALSTED: Seems like it. However, just like your namesake the planet Venus, I have resigned myself to only worship you from afar.

VENUS: *(Disappointed)* Aw...

HALSTED: That's what I say.

VENUS: Why me? What's so special about me?

HALSTED: I don't know. I have felt so alone for so long...I don't know. The very moment I saw you, there was something so irresistible, so powerful...

VENUS: Even though I belong to another.

HALSTED: Do you? I know you do...Forgive me.

VENUS: *(They stare at each other.)* I am scared of you.

HALSTED: Me too.

(ENTER the two employees, GREEN and MIKE.)

GREEN: Man, them sweet rolls sure are looking good. Any extra?

VENUS: *(Nervous.)* Oh, sure, help yourself. *(She grabs her purse to go freshen up.)* Excuse me.

(She EXITS.)

HALSTED: *(Also nervous.)* Well, let me go check on the shop.

(He EXITS)

GREEN: Did you see all them googily eyes?

MIKE: Googilly eyes?

GREEN: The way they were staring at each other. Man, Barfield better hurry. up and get out of that hospital. This dude is serious about keeping him some work.

MIKE: Even you got to admit how good a job Halsted is doing around here.

GREEN: Sheet. I ain't admitting nothing, hard as I gotta work now. I'm tired of the mess. And after what I just saw, I know somebody else who might be getting a little tired too if they knew what what was going on.

MIKE: Who?

GREEN: Who you think? Her husband, fool.

MIKE: Her husband? Hey now...

GREEN: Hey now, what? I didn't say I was going to say anything...*(He bites his sweet roll)* yet, anyway.

(MIKE looks at him warily.)

(LIGHTS FADE OUT)

END ACT I, Scene 7

ACT II

Scene 1

(At a corner of the stage is EARL'S house. A small couch and chair are present. It is late at night. Someone is heard knocking at the door. BY the third series of knocks, EARL enters adjusting his robe. He has on little else.)

EARL: Okay, okay, I'm here. *(Spies clock.)* 12:45. Who the...*(He opens the door and is surprised by LANNETTE, the girl he puts on the bus.)* Lannette!

LANNETTE: *(She steps in, drops her bags and gives him a big kiss.)* Oh, Earl, I love you so much.

EARL: Lannette...*(Is all he can say.)*

LANNETTE: I was scared to death. I thought you moved. Tried to call you, your number's out of service. Couldn't remember your Mother's number...

EARL: I thought you were still in Kalamazoo.

LANNETTE: I just got back. The bus came in half hour ago.

EARL: But, but...

LANNETTE: I tried to call. I even sent you a letter last week saying I was ready to come back.

EARL: Last week? Early last week? Somebody broke into my mailbox last monday looking for my check, stole all my letters, bills.

LANNETTE: Really?

EARL: That's why the phone is off because I didn't get the final notice.

LANNETTE: Oh Earl, I've missed you so much. I dreamed about you every night. This has been the longest month of my life.

EARL: A month? Is that all it's been?

LANNETTE: Four weeks, two days, fifteen hours, and 26 minutes.

EARL: Well uh, so uh, how's your Mother, Cheryl?

LANNETTE: Mean as ever. Talked about me like a dog everyday. Told me I was a fool to come running back to you. But, I couldn't help myself. Earl I love you so much, and I've changed, too. I understand so much more. You'll never have to worry about me being jealous again, or crying, or not understanding about you and your children. Especially now. We can make it, Earl. I know we can.

EARL: You were gone so long. I didn't think you were coming back.

LANNETTE: You told me to take my time and get it together. You told me I still had some growing up to do and you were so right, but now, now I'm ready. Earl let's settle down, raise ourselves a family.

EARL: Lannette, Lannette, Lannette it's one o'clock in the morning.

LANNETTE: I stole my Mother's old recipe book. It's full of all the things you love. First thing tomorrow...

EARL: Listen to me...

LANNETTE: You hungry now? What?

EARL: Look...

VOICE: *(Female voice from the bedroom.)* Earl sugar, hurry back now. These sheets are getting cold.

LANNETTE: I guess you're not.

(She steps away.)

EARL: Listen to me, baby. I didn't know...I

LANNETTE: Don't touch me. Please don't touch me.

(She gathers her belongings.)

EARL: Where are you going? Do yo have somewhere to go? You need any money?

LANNETTE: *(At the exit.)* And to think I swore my Mama was wrong about you.

EARL: I'm sorry.

LANNETTE: You sure are.

(She exits.)

EARL: Damn!!

VOICES: *(TWO sexy female voices.)* EARRRLL...

EARL: Shheeet...I don't know what these women be wanting, but I'm gonna find out.

(He exits quickly. Lights Fade Out.)

END ACT II, Scene 1

ACT II
Scene 2
BURNETTA'S *house. A little later in the night.* BURNETTA *comes sneaking in the front door, feels safe, tip-toes to the bedroom door and peeks in. She relaxes. She walks to the kitchen, notices* HALSTED'S *bed is empty, and heads for the refrigerator. The lights come up suddenly and* LEONARD *stands by the switch.*

LEONARD: Computer malfunction. The robots on the assembly line were shut down at 10:15. They let us leave at 10:30, I been here since eleven. Your brother left at 11:30...Where you been?

BURNETTA: I was over to Mildred's. She had a few problems.

LEONARD: You do, too.

BURNETTA: Don't you start nothing with me, Leonard. Probably been getting off of work at 10:30 every night anyway.

LEONARD: You don't know, do you?

BURNETTA: Where's Halsted?

LEONARD: He ain't here, is he?

BURNETTA: I can go out if I want to. I ain't your prisoner.

LEONARD: Here, *(Picks up phone book.)* take this phone book and, *(throws it, at her.)* call the undertaker.

BURNETTA: *(Dodges shot.)* Call the undertaker? You a lie. There's a whole bunch of people in this book I can call to have you looking for an undertaker.

LEONARD: Then you better call them because I'm about to kick your...

BURNETTA: *(Picks up her purse and waves it at him before he leaps.)* Hit me if you want to. Hit me, if you dare.

LEONARD: You think I'm worried about that little cap pistol? *(He has stopped.)* I'll go get my shotgun and...

BURNETTA: Mighty funny ain't nothing getting kicked around here.

LEONARD: *(As he toughly backs off.)* You about a evil old woman.

BURNETTA: Yeah, evil enough not to let you jump on me anytime you feel like it. *(They both stare at each other, then turn away, not knowing what else to say to each other. LEONARD sits. BURNETTA flops up against the wall.)* Where's the kids?

LEONARD: They're alright. Some woman come by and got your brother.

BURNETTA: The woman he works for?

LEONARD: I don't know.

BURNETTA: You see your dinner in the oven?

LEONARD: Yeah...Beans needed a little salt.

BURNETTA: You eat too much salt.

LEONARD: You just don't season your food enough.

BURNETTA: Who you comparing it to?

LEONARD: *(In frustration, he reflects.)* Computers broke down, the robots couldn't work, and we were sent home. Don't make sense at all. Five years ago, I was the robot. Did the same things they do now. Reach over, pick up material, place material on machine, press spot weld button, watch smoke, remove material, place on conveyour belt, reach over, pick up material, place material on machine, press spot weld button, watch smoke, remove material, place on conveyor belt, reach...

BURNETTA: I get your point.

LEONARD: Three hours straight, two hours straight, eight hours straight. Time and a half, double time on Sunday. Reach over pick up material, place material up your...hell yeah, them computers broke down and I know why. Felt like breaking down too many times myself.

BURNETTA: But you didn't. Too damn onry.

LEONARD: You made me that way.

BURNETTA: You was born that way.

LEONARD: I hate your black butt...

BURNETTA: Except when it's laying up against your black butt...

(Their moods change.)

LEONARD: You ready to go to bed?

BURNETTA: You the one that better be ready.

LEONARD: Sheeet...

(They EXIT.)
(LIGHTS FADE OUT)
END ACT II, Scene 2

ACT II

Scene 3

Lights rise on the other corner where a table with two chairs have been set. On the table are a wine carafe, two glasses and a lit candle. Soft love music heard, HALSTED and VENUS stand dancing close together. They fit like hand and glove. Both are lost in each other. The song ends yet they continue to dance.

VENUS: *(Relaxed.)* You know what?

HALSTED: *(In a few seoonds.)* What?

VENUS: *(Another pause.)* The music's stopped.

HALSTED: Um hmm.

(They stop and she leads him to the table.)

VENUS: Do you know what time it is?

HALSTED: *(Checks his watch but it is not there.)* Uh, around 2:30, I guess.

VENUS: 2:30? Let me get myself out of here. *(No real rush.)* In a minute.

HALSTED: More wine?

VENUS: A little.

(He pours for them both.)

HALSTED: So, when are you going to tell me?

VENUS: What? Why I'm out here?

HALSTED: Yes.

VENUS: To be with you, of course...It was a threat, actually. Arthur has been promising to take me dancing for over a year and hasn't yet. I've been threatening to go out by myself for the past six months, and tonight I finally did. Thanks to you.

HALSTED: Thanks to me. It's my fault you're out here.

VENUS: I'm not blaming you. You didn't call and ask me to go out. This is something I wanted to do. So lf anybody's wrong...

HALSTED: No, I didn't say anything about wrong. I could have just as easily stayed at home tonight myself. I just don't want to get you into any trouble.

VENUS: Don't worry about me.

HALSTED: How can I not worry about you? Do you know how you make me feel?

VENUS: No, tell me.

HALSTED: Have you ever been caught outside in the cold? I mean, cold. Bone chilling freezingness, you know? No coat, no hat, no gloves. Nothing between you and that ten below zero air, but a twenty mile an hour wind.

VENUS: Is that how I make you feel?

HALSTED: No. My grandmama used to iron our sheets in the winter time before we got in the bed. Then she'd throw this huge patch quilt over us to hold in the heat. And I would curl up inside that bed and before my head would settle into the pillow good, I would be asleep. You are that warmth to me. You are the fire of my desire that warms me up in this cold, cold world.

VENUS: Um, um, um, um, um. Tell me some more.

HALSTED: *(This makes him laugh.)* Lady you are something else. Oh I feel so good around you.

VENUS: And verse visa.

HALSTED: Say what?

VENUS: Vice versa. Oh, oh, I think I've had enough wine. You may have to drive me back to town.

HALSTED: I'll drive you wherever you want to be driven.

VENUS: Is that right? Automatic or stick shift?

HALSTED: Five speed overdrive. Brown on brown in brown with a, *(Rubs his hair.)* black fur top. Want to see my twin scoop bucket seats?

VENUS: Another time.

HALSTED: Or Indy fuel injection passion?

VENUS: Alright Stevie Wonder.

HALSTED: Or my drive sha…*(shaft)*

VENUS: Halsted! Shame on you.

HALSTED: Oh, guess I got a little carried away. Good wine.

VENUS: My virgin ears can't take all that. There's something I want to ask you about, anyway. Let's change the subject.

HALSTED: Okay, what?

VENUS: Tell me about that lady in Cleveland.

HALSTED: Talking about changing the subject…

VENUS: What was so bad about her that made you leave her?

HALSTED: Venus…

VENUS: Come on, now. I told you about me and Arthur.

HALSTED: True.

VENUS: She's not going to run in here and shoot me for being with you, is she?

HALSTED: I doubt it.

VENUS: Well?

HALSTED: Well, I didn't say there was so much bad about her. Nice lady. Very professional. Helped me out a lot of times financially, and stuff. It's more of me. I got tired of being out of work, or not having enough work and being forced to be dependent on her. I began to resent the fact that I had to ask her for bus fare so I could go out and look for work. Knowing all the time that when I was out hustling up some work, she wasn't even believing me. Her daily thing was that whenever I stepped out the door, I was running to some other woman. And I wasn't. I was true and faithful and honest for five years. It got to be the only way I could keep peace was to stay my behind home and play housewife. Pretending that I'm happy making her happy. I couldn't take it. No work, no money, no pride. A prisoner of economics, a prisoner of love. It was too much. I began to lose weight because I refused to eat. Started stealing change from her purse to ride the bus. Put cardboard in my shoes and kept on stepping. Lucked up. Did a three hundred dollar valve job on a lady's car for 175.00, took the money and ran. I had to. I had to get away! (*VENUS puts her finger to his lips to quiet him. "Loves Light In Flight" by Stevie Wonder is heard.*)

VENUS: Listen.

(*The music had come up during his speech. He relaxes, takes her fingers and kisses them.*)

HALSTED: Thank you.

VENUS: Thank you

(*They kiss long and tender.*)
(*LIGHTS FADE OUT*)
END ACT II, Scene 3

ACT II
Scene 4
A spot in a remote corner of the stage. EMPLOYEE ONE, GREEN, is on the phone.

GREEN: Hello, Mr. Strattford? Green here, from over at the southside office...Yes sir, how you doing?...That's nice...no, what I was calling you for is because of Barfield...Yes sir, he's out of the hospital now. Got out early...yes sir, I did come in to speak to Mrs. Strattford about it, but her and that new guy left out to lunch before I could catch them...oh, no sir they haven't been gone long, it's just all this week I've missed them before they left out...I don't know where they be going, but, Barfield was telling me how good he feels and how he'd like to hurry on back to work...said he could be ready next week...Okay, I'll tell Mrs. Strattford to give you a call whenever they get back...Oh yes, uh, Halsted's doing a good job around here...Him and your wife get along real good...yes sir, I'll do that. Bye.

(THE LIGHTS FADE OUT on his grin.)
END ACT II, Scene 4

ACT II
Scene 5
BURNETTA'S house. Car horn is heard. Daylight. The kids are out in the car waiting for BURNETTA to go shopping. She is on stage searching for her checkbook. The kids play with the horn again. BURNETTA runs to the side door.

BURNETTA: If you don't get off of that damned horn, I'm gonna kill you all... I'll be there in a minute. *(Mumbling to herself as she continues searching.)* Soon as I find that doggone checkbook...*(Front doorbell rings)* Who is it?!

IMANI: Burnetta?

(BURNETTA opens the door.)

BURNETTA: Yes?

IMANI: *(She is wearing a permanent in her hair, dressed in a businesswoman's suit, and carries a briefcase purse.)* Hi, remember me?

BURNETTA: No, should I?

IMANI: I'm Halsted's friend, Sandra, well, Imani.

BURNETTA: Imani? Is that you? Girl come on in here. You sure do look different.

IMANI: I guess I have changed since that last time you saw me.

BURNETTA: I know that's right. Last time I saw you, you was looking like the Queen of Sheba. Hair all corn rowed, African dress...

IMANI: I've had this perm for over two years, now. Didn't Hal tell you?

BURNETTA: Not a word. What did you say your name was, now?

IMANI: Sandra. That is my name. Hal's the only person in Cleveland who still calls me Imani. Is he here?

BURNETTA: *(The car horn honks.)* Them damn kids. Halsted's in the bathroom. I'm trying to rush and get outa here to do some shopping before that old fool, my husband comes back here looking for the car. *(She bams on the bathroom door.)* Big brother, you got company... *(To Imani.)* Go on, make yourself at home. *(Feels her jacket pocket and screams...)* I've been looking all over for this checkbook. Look, make yourself at home. I'll see you when we get back. *(Before she can get to the door, the horn honks.)* I'ma kill them. Every last one of them.

(She exits. IMANI sits on the couch. She takes her compact and smoothes her face. HALSTED ENTERS wiping shaving cream from his face. Expecting to see VENUS, he is surprised.)

HALSTED: Imani!

IMANI: Why Hal, you've lost weight.

HALSTED: Where did you come from?

IMANI: May I have a kiss? (*A quick smack.*) You are eating enough, aren't you?

HALSTED: I'm doing alright. You?

IMANI: Adequate. I've missed you.

HALSTED: You have?

IMANI: You sound surprised.

HALSTED: What are you doing here, Imani?

IMAIN: It was a nice day and I thought I'd take a drive. Oh, that Ohio Turnpike. And then they expect you to pay to drive on it? Sit down, please. Are you in a hurry?

HALSTED: I've got some things to do.

IMANI: Maybe I can drive you.

HALSTED: Imani, Sandra. It's good to see you again, and I suppose we hav needed to talk, but...

IMANI: I've come to give you a ride back home.

HALSTED: I don't have a home.

IMANI: That's not true.

HALSTED: It's your home. Your name is on the lease.

IMANI: What's mine is yours. You know that.

HALSTED: Bullshit.

IMANI: Why are you being to hostile towards me? You leave out of the door in the middle of the night without so much as a good-bye. You don't call or write for more than a month. You know how I worry about you, yet you leave me high and dry as if what we had all those years meant nothing at all. I thought I deserved more than that.

HALSTED: How short the memory can be. Now, all of a sudden, you can't recall how the day before I left town, you kicked me out of your place, again...

IMANI: We had an argument...

HALSTED: ...for the nineteenth time in the five years I stayed with you...

IMANI: We both said things we didn't mean.

HALSTED: ...and how I had to sleep in my old raggedy piece of Pontiac, because there was no place else to sleep.

IMANI: You could of come upstairs. You had your keys.

HALSTED: To do what? Argue and fight some more over your imagination?

IMANI: What specifically were we arguing about? I don't recall.

HALSTED: Which woman was it that time? Or was it a phone call...?

IMANI: Oh, the jealousy argument. Alright, so I'm possessive. You've known that all along...

HALSTED: Yeah, justify...

IMANI: So what made that moment so different? We are both argumentative people...

HALSTED: Because I got tired of it. Because the only reason you can accuse me and harrass me anything you feel like it, is because you have no respect for me. And the reason you don't respect me is because I don't have a damned thing of my own. And everytime I walked out the door trying to get myself together, you took it all wrong.

IMANI: Well, you have to admit ….

HALSTED: I don't have to admit anything. I wasn't doing anything to admit.

IMANI: Perhaps not. Perhaps it was just coincidence that the waitress down the street kept calling you.

HALSTED: Can't I get calls from people? You do.

IMANI: So you saying you didn't have an affair with her?

HALSTED: Stop with the leading questions, counsellor. I'm not under cross-examination.

IMANI: Then answer me.

HALSTED: For the thousandth time, no. No to her, no to the the lady across the hall, no to the receptionist at the trade school, no to your cousin, no, no, no!

IMANI: Halsted, you stopped wanting to be with me, go out with me, make love to me…You are not a priest…

HALSTED: Here we go again. *(They pause)* When I first met you, I thought you were the epitomy of an African Princess transplanted to America. Your hair, your clothes, your name everything was together.

IMANI: Yes, everything but my bank account. I'm sorry, Halsted. I know I don't look the way I did when we first met, but it was a change I had to make. We're talking economics here. My native pride was not putting food in my, our mouths, so I had to make a choice.

HALSTED: And you chose the White man.

IMANI: I chose the money. I'm still Black. If I didn't have this permanent, hair would still go back when I sweat. I still mail my donations to the NAACP, in fact, now, I can afford to send even more to them. Things have not changed.

HALSTED: You have.

IMANI: Havn't we all? Hal, you've got to be realistic. These rich White corporate leaders feel threatened by a Black person acting too black. The last thing I need when I'm arguing a case is unnecessary prejudice.

HALSTED: Sho' you right.

IMANI: It's true. I may not be crazy about this image I'm projecting now, but I'll tell you one thing. When I was Imani, I was making $15,000 a year. Sandra makes 75.

HALSTED: I wonder what you'd do for one hundred. That really trips me out. Go downtown now a days all you see working down there is White men and Black women. If that ain't planned…

IMANI: I'll put it this way, it doesn't mean a thing to me. You, I want. Why? I'm still trying to figure it out. But, it is you that I want.

HALSTED: Humph, the only time you show it is after I leave.

IMANI: You never miss your water...

HALSTED: That gets old, Imani. You can't play "after whist" with love all the time. All I hear is what you will do, what you're going to do as soon as you finish this brief, that deposition or this client or whatever...listen to me, damn. The whole role system has reversed. When I get around you, I turn into a damn housewife complaining about attention. (*Gathers himself together.*)

IMANI: (*Tries a little tenderness.*) You know, the other day I was cleaning out a closet, and I found some of your old notebooks. Remember how you used to write me a new poem everyday? What happened to all that?

HALSTED: Well, for one thing, you burned up most of my notebooks...Like you said, we all change.

IMANI: Come on back home with me, Halsted.

HALSTED: I have to get myself together.

IMANI: How long that going to take?

HALSTED: I don't know.

IMANI: How long do you expect...let me rephrase that. Do you expect me to wait?

HALSTED: Not really.

IMANI: Beecher Heights, Michigan is a hell of a place to get oneself together. (*She hands him some papers.*) Your mail.

HALSTED: You opened it? (*Reads.*)

IMANI: Just in case of emergency.

HALSTED: They're calling me back at the Institute...Teaching three days a week...

IMANI: Three days is a good start.

HALSTED: Beginning in two weeks...(*He's not enthused.*)

IMANI: (*Writing on business card.*) That should be enough time to get yourself together. Right...? I'm staying in Detroit at the Renaissance. It's a short drive. Give me a call, we'll have dinner. My treat of course. (*She hands him the card and prepares to exit.*)

HALSTED: (*All he can do is watch her walk out the door.*) Damn...

(*He slams the card to the floor as Lights fade out.*)

END ACT II, Scene 5

ACT II
Scene 6
(*The shop. VENUS and her husband ARTHUR age 32, are present.*)

VENUS: What do you mean he's got to go?

ARTHUR: I believe I made myself clear.

VENUS: Shouldn't that be my decision since it is my shop?

ARTHUR: I have been very patient with you, Venus. It wasn't my idea to hire this guy in the first place. I could have just as easily sent one of my men over to replace Barfield, and you know that.

VENUS: Arthur, look at the quality of work Halsted is producing. Look how many orders we've filled. Go back there and see how organized...

ARTHUR: For Christ's sake, Venus. Why is it that every guy you meet you have to act silly over?

VENUS: I am not acting silly.

ARTHUR: You don't need to be out here in public, period.

VENUS: And what is that supposed to mean?

ARTHUR: You are so gullible, so silly about the ways of this world. These guys come up and throw you their fancy lines about all the things they've done and all the places they've been, and you fall for it.

VENUS: Arthur...

ARTHUR: And all these guys are doing is ego tripping. Trying to see how many women they can get to fall in love with them. I tried to tell you this in the beginning. Tried to get you to see this before you came out here calling yourself being independent. But no, you think you know so much.

VENUS: I'm so sick and tired of you cutting me down. According to you, I'm a lousy cook, a lousy housewife, mother, bill payer, store manager, what else? We can't say lousy lover because I do believe you've forgotten.

ARTHUR: See there. There you go again. Going off on me for nothing. It wasn't like this before. Not until you became Ms. Store Manager. Or should I say not until this, Halsted came along.

VENUS: You have been cutting me down for a long time, long before Halsted or any of the last three men we've argued about.

ARTHUR: Me? What about you? I can't even come home anymore from a hard days work and find a decent meal prepared for me.

VENUS: I cook, everyday, and I'm just as tired as you.

ARTHUR: That's what you call cooking? Pot pies T.V. dinners, boil it up in a plastic bag?

VENUS: Well, I'll just be...Why don't you cook then? Or pick up the kids?

ARTHUR: That's your job. You're the one that wants to do mine.

VENUS: Excuse me. I forgot my place.

ARTHUR: Look at you. You should be ashamed of yourself...How much do you know about this guy? I heard about him from a couple people. Your cousin Earl for one. Yeah, he told me about the guy not too long ago. You know he's been married before.

VENUS: He told me.

ARTHUR: Oh he did, huh? Did he tell you how he left his wife for another woman? Left his wife and three year old son, broke up his family because of his thing about women? Did he tell you that?

VENUS: You have a lot of nerve telling me something Earl Keith had to say about as many women as he runs through.

ARTHUR: Yeah, that's right, protect the guy, why don't you?

VENUS: I'm not trying...Arthur, that three year old son you're referring to is now 20 and in the service. What in the world does that have to do with Halsted's work performance, now?

ARTHUR: Just going to walk all over me, huh? Forget about me and the kids baby, you got yourself a man. Don't even have to worry about us an more, at all. Huh! Yeah, I got your number. Break up your whole family over some no good for nothing drifter whispering sweet lies in your ear. I thought you had better sense than that. Obviously I was wrong. Barfield reports back to work next week. You have flipped your behind around here long enough.

VENUS: Arthur you are wrong!

ARTHUR: Get this through you silly head, Venus. You've gone too far. Running off at the mouth about this guy, defending him, sneaking off to lunch with him, everyday...

VENUS: Lunch?

ARTHUR: Yes! I know about that too. I'm fed up with him, and you, and I want his ass out of this shop immediately. *(Exiting.)* And if you don't pull your- self together right away, I'll have your behind in divorce court so fast it'll make your head swim.

(Storms OUT.)

VENUS: Don't do me any favors! *(Her frustration swells.)* Damn...

(BLACKOUT)

END ACT II, Scene 6

ACT II

Scene 7

BURNETTA'S house. Later that evening. She and LEONARD sit on the couch watching television and necking. LEONARD whispers something interesting to BURNETTA.

BURNETTA: Ooh Leonard. Can you still do that?

LEONARD: Might be worth a try. Why don't you climb out of that dress?

BURNETTA: The kids will be back from the show, soon.

LEONARD: They got at least another hour. Come on...

BURNETTA: Let's go to the bedroom.

LEONARD: I want to do it out here.

BURNETTA: Halsted might walk in.

LEONARD: Hell with him…it's time we had some privacy.
  (He kisses her neck)

BURNETTA: Oh yes…

LEONARD: If it wasn't for so many interruptions…no telling what we can get into…

BURNETTA: Umm hmm…what has got into you tonight?

LEONARD: You wanna see…?

BURNETTA: Don't write a check you can't cash.

LEONARD: Tonight I got cash overflow.

BURNETTA: Talk to me, daddy…

LEONARD: *(Sits up quietly.)* Was that the door?

BURNETTA: Door?

LEONARD: I thought I heard your brother coming in.

BURNETTA: Oh no, please, not now…

LEONARD: Be our luck if he did, huh?

BURNETTA: Let's go to the bedroom.

LEONARD: This my house, my couch, I can mess around anywhere I want to.
  (He rubs her the right way.) Right?

BURNETTA: Yes, yes, yes…*(They neck some more. LEONARD stops again.)*
  What's wrong now?

LEONARD: Can't concentrate. I keep expecting that door to come flying open.

BURNETTA: Forget that door, darling…

LEONARD: We gotta do something about this Bernie, I'm serious.

BURNETTA: About what?

LEONARD: I'm getting tired of your brother being here.

BURNETTA: He's hardly ever here.

LEONARD: He's here enough. Blocking my action on this couch.

BURNETTA: Why the couch?

LEONARD: You know how we get sometimes. Get these wild urges…

BURNETTA: You mean like the whip cream and honey?

LEONARD: Oh yeah. I forgot that one. Well, I got this wild urge right now
  to…*(He whispers something.)*

BURNETTA: Please, be my guest…
  (LEONARD makes a move and stops abruptly.)

LEONARD: No, not when I know old Hal is gonna come walking in that door
  any minute now.

BURNETTA: Damm it. He does need to start looking for a place.

LEONARD: That's what I'm saying. Getting tired of him blocking my action.

BURNETTA: Said he was only gonna be here a couple weeks.

LEONARD: Look to me like he moved in.

BURNETTA: Aw, Leonard...

LEONARD: Seems like it.

BURNETTA: *(She tries to get him back into the mood, but he resists.)* Alright, alright I'll talk to him.

LEONARD: I don't mean to put him out on the street, or nothing.

BURNETTA: No, no. He can afford a place. I'll give him time to find one.

LEONARD: As long as it's not too much time.

BURNETTA: I heard that.

(They kiss again)

LEONARD: Umm...you seen the T.V. guide?

BURNETTA: What?

LEONARD: I hear there's a good western on tonight. *(He breaks the mood and goes to change channels.)* The kids will be back soon, anyway. Why don't you pop some Popcorn?

(LIGHTS FADE OUT)

END ACT II, Scene 7

ACT II

Scene 8

(Chicken Charlies order counter. One side of the stage is lit. There's a bench for people waiting to get their order. There's the sound of "ding, ding," as a car enters the drive thru.)

WAITRESS: Welcome to Chicken Charlies. May I take your order?

VOICE: *(Young male)* Yeah, I want, no let me get uh, yall got any, no here they go, I want six wings...*(To his girlfriend.)* You want the dinner, baby? *(To WAITRESS.)* No, we just want the six wings, and uh, two strawberry...*(to friend)* What? French fries? *(To WAITRESS.)* Do the wings come with fries?

WAITRESS: Yes sir. French fries and two slices of bread.

VOICE: *(To friend)* You hungry tonight, ain't you baby? *(To WAITRESS.)* Okay, two orders of six wings, mild sauce, two strawberry...

WAITRESS: Sir we don't carry sauces. This is not a rib joint.

VOICE: No sauce? *(To friend)* They ain't got no sauce.

WAITRESS: Would you repeat your order, please?

VOICE: Say what?

WAITRESS: That was two orders of six wings, two strawberry shakes...

VOICE: Naw, I said two vanilla shakes.

WAITRESS: You said strawberry.

VOICE: I meant vanilla. And two ears of corn...

WAITRESS: No corn.

VOICE: No corn neither? *(To friend.)* What you say, baby? Naw, we ain't gotta stay here. Cool. *(To WAITRESS)* Say lady, nevermind, skip it. We're going to the rib joint.

("DING, DING")

WAITRESS: Your daddy. *(During this time HALSTED has ENTERED and waits to place his order. On the bench sits an old man who has been waiting for his order for some time. He mutters to himself about the inconvenience.)* Welcome to Chicken Charlie's. May I take your order?

HALSTED: Yeah, uh, I'd like...

(The old man butts in.)

MAN: What the hell is taking so long with my order?

WAITRESS: Just a few more minutes, sir.

MAN: You said that five minutes ago.

WAITRESS: May I take your order, please?

HALSTED: I'll have the Number Seven.,

WAITRESS: Number Seven. Anything to drink?

HALSTED: Yeah, a strawberry shake.

WAITRESS: For here or to go?

HALSTED: Here.

WAITRESS: Thank you, sir. There will be about a five minute wait for the chicken, if you don't mind.

HALSTED: Five minutes?

WAITRESS: Yes sir.

HALSTED: Alright

(She gives him his ticket.)

MAN: I should of remembered what I learned a long time ago. If you're hungry and in a hurry, don't come to no colored restaurant. *(To HALSTED:)* You know what I mean? Colored people can't do nothing right. Fast food, humph! Been waiting for fifteen minutes for some fast food. They just don't care, don't give a damn. Act like I'm doing them a favor to come in here and spend my money...Look at him back there cooking. Moving like he got all the time in the world. Scared he's gonna mess up his hair. *(Yells out.)* You better not drip none of that jeri Curl mess on my chicken...If he was my kid, I'd beat all that junk out of his head. *(To HALSTED.)* You got any kids?

HALSTED: Yeah, but he's grown.

(ARTHUR ENTERS and gives his order.)

MAN: Grown and gone. That's what mine did, too. Ungrateful bastards. Old lady, too. Run out the door chasing after some other man. Didn't have a penny to his name. Damn fool woman. Up and gone and run out. Now,

I gotta come here to eat. Work hard all day long and gotta come here to get fed. Twenty three years together for nothing. What kind of man is that that would take another man's wife away from him? Huh? All them damn woman out there and he gotta go chasing after mine. What the hell he see in her, anyway? Lost her looks fifteen years ago. Never did keep the house clean. Raised all the kids up against me...What he take my wife for? Why he mess with me?

(He sulks in silence.)

ARTHUR: Old guy is loud, but...

HALSTED: Yeah, you talk that much, you're bound to say something that makes sense.

ARTHUR: I know what he means about these women. They get out there, start making a little bit of money, and the hell with you. You know what I mean?

HALSTED: I hear you. Try dealing with one when she makes more money than you.

ARTHUR: Oh my God.

MAN: Now see! I knew it was going to happen. There goes the damned bus! Be another half hour before another one comes around here. *(He gives the counter a dirty look and sits back down.)*

HALSTED: That man is upset.

ARTHUR: Aw, there's always somebody like that around this place. I try not to frequent the place myself. What bugs me is these young thugs around here at night. I wish one of them would mess with me. *(Pats his jacket)* I've got something for them. Can't play around out here anymore...How long you been waiting?

HALSTED: About five minutes.

ARTHUR: They do take their time.

HALSTED: I don't mind. The food's pretty good.

ARTHUR: Better than home cooking sometimes, huh?

HALSTED: Shoot, I love to cook.

ARTHUR: Looks like I need to learn how.

HALSTED: Hey, as active as women are now-a-days, you better know how to. Be done starved to death waiting.

ARTHUR: That's what I mean. What is wrong with these women today? Why can't they act like they're supposed to?

HALSTED: Like they're supposed to? I know a couple women that would cut your throat for saying that.

ARTHUR: I don't care. These modern women, they just...You know what I mean?

(Makes a "poot" sound with his mouth. HALSTED is surprised to himself, at himself, because he now hears how this kind of thinking sounds.)

ARTHUR: *(con't)* I'm beginning to understand my father a lot better as I get older. He laid down the law. I used to think he was overbearing on my Mother, but...*(HALSTED shrugs his shoulders)* You don't agree?

HALSTED: No, I was just thinking, your father wouldn't of lasted too long around my house. My Mother *(He laughs to himself.)*

ARTHUR: She was tough, huh?

HALSTED: Shot my old man in the leg with his own pistol.

ARTHUR: Killed him?

HALSTED: No, barely scraped the skin. I think she scared ten years out of his life, though. No, I believe if men and women all started out on an equal basis, they'd get along a hellofa lot better.

ARTHUR: Hey, bullshit. First of all, who determines what "equal" is? Like friend of mine says rather crudely, "treat these broads too nice, and they'll walk all'over you."

MAN: That's right, brother. I know what you mean. I agree with you 100%. *(Is heading toward the counter and is right in the girl's face as she turns to announce his order.)*

WAITRESS: Number *(Surprise)* 53.

MAN: You put some ketchup in there?

WAITRESS: Yes sir.

MAN: More than one napkin? *(She gives him extra napkins. He exits.)* Now I gotta walk a whole damn twelve blocks before the food gets cold. Dirty rotten...

WAITRESS: *(Has another order.)* Number 55.

ARTHUR: That's me. *(He steps forward and pays for his food. Then, trying to flirt, he gives the WAITRESS a tip)*

HALSTED: Well, hang on in there, Brother.

ARTHUR: You, too. Good rapping with you. *(Offers his hand.)* Art.

HALSTED: *(Shakes his hand.)* Hal.

WAITRESS: Number 54.

(HALSTED steps forward to pay for his food to exit. as ARTHUR starts door)

ARTHUR: Hal?

HALSTED: Art? *(They turn, look at each other.)*

ARTHUR AND HALSTED: Naw.

(They wave it off as ARTHUR exits, and HALSTED pays for his food.)
END ACT II, Scene 8

ACT II

Scene 9

(The stage is converted into EARL'S house. He stands in front of his kitchen window, eating a chicken leg and taunting someone out the window. It is LANNETTE, who cannot be seen. She has been in EARLS' backyard all night long.)

EARL: Umm um, this chicken sure is good. Better come on and get some, I know you're hungry by now...*(Bites again.)* Alright, be that way...crazy... *(Knock at door, EARL goes to the door.)* Who is it?

HALSTED: Halsted, *(EARL opens the door with a mouthful of chicken.)* Earl I'm glad you're home, I need to talk to somebody,

EARL: Well, if it's trouble you wanna talk about you're gonna have to wait in line. I need your help right now. *(Leads him to the window.)* Look.

HALSTED: Who is that?

EARL: Lannette.

HALSTED: Who? Oh. Kalamazoo?

EARL: Been standing out there all night long.

HALSTED: What is she doing in your backyard?

EARL: Acting crazy.

HALSTED: What have you done to that girl?

EARL: I ain't did nothing. She come barging in here last night, one o'clock in the morning, saw a few things she wasn't ready to see.

HALSTED: Busted your butt, huh?

EARL: Ain't no ring on her finger. Hell...

HALSTED: So, now she won't come in.

EARL: Said she was gonna stand out there and starve herself to death because of me.

HALSTED: What are you going to do?

EARL: I was gonna finish this chicken and wait for you.

HALSTED: Wait for me?

EARL: Yeah, go out there and talk to her for me.

HALSTED: Me!

EARL: You know how to talk to chicks and not make them mad at you.

HALSTED: Earl...

EARL: Come on Halsted...

HALSTED: Man, I came over here to talk to you about my problems.

EARL: At least find out what she wants me to do. *(Escorting him out, front door-bell rings)* She won't tell me a thing.

HALSTED: Man...

EARL: Thanks pal.

(Pushes him out and goes to answer door. ARTHUR ENTERS.)

ARTHUR: *(Upset)* Well, I hope you're happy, now.

EARL: What's up Art?

ARTHUR: You really want to know? Do you really want to know?

EARL: Man, I ain't got time for no games...

ARTHUR: Evidently your friend does. Guess whose been messing around with my wife?

EARL: Aw, who this time?

ARTHUR: No, no it's not like that. No not at all. Now it's not merely a matter of suspicion, we're talking confession. Venus told me what she was doing. Told me who she was doing it with.

EARL: Arthur I really don't have time for you and my cousins problems.

ARTHUR: Your friend Halsted does.

EARL: Halsted?

ARTHUR: Yes, Halsted. Venus told me they've been hanging out, going out and God knows what else.

EARL: Halsted?

(He breaks out laughing.)

ARTHUR: It's not funny, Earl.

EARL: You're right, I know it's not, I'm not laughing about that.

(He continues to laugh.)

ARTHUR: Yeah, we'll see how funny it is when I blow his ass away.

EARL: Come on now Arthur. I don't believe that at all. Halsted?

ARTHUR: I go home, a bag full of hot food, calling myself saving my wife some work, she jumps down my throat about some old argument and throws this guy's name all in my face. I confront her about the situation, and what does she do? *(Mocks her voice)* "Yes we've gone out together, yes, we care about each other, so what?" I mean, like, who the hell am I to ask? I'm killing him. That's all there is to it.

EARL: How do you know Venus was telling the truth?

ARTHUR: Why would she lie about someting like

EARL: She might have been trying to make you mad.

ARTHUR: Mad!? Mad?! You tell me where this guy lives, and I'll show you mad.

EARL: Calm down, Arthur. Killing Halsted won't do nothing but get you in trouble.

ARTHUR: I don't care, Earl, I do not care. If he has that much nerve to disrespect me, then I've got enough nerve to kill him.

EARL: Speaking on confessions, what about that little chick you brought up here the other night? Sounds like you and Venus both...

ARTHUR: Oh, I SEE. I see where you're coming from. You're gonna be on their side, huh?

EARL: No, I just want you to start thinking straight.

ARTHUR: I need a beer. You got anything to drink?

EARL: No, uh, why don't you run to the store for me, and pick up a six pack.

ARTHUR: *(Sees a cognac bottle. Pours himself a glass and downs it.)* This'll do.

EARL: *(Takes bottle.)* Slow down on my Cognac. This is for the ladies.

ARTHUR: Where's the store? I left my car.

EARL: Up on the corner. Two liquor stores.

ARTHUR: Alright. Let me run to the bathroom first.

EARL: *(ART EXITS. EARL starts for the back door when the front door flies open ENTER VENUS. She is furious.)* Now what?

VENUS: Earl, where is your gun? Where is your gun?

(EARL tries to quiet her down, because of ARTHUR.)

EARL: Hey cuz, chill out. We got company.

VENUS: Look at my face. Is there a bruise? Arthur's Mother claims she didn't see one. I swear if there is...

EARL: Your face is red. What happened?

VENUS: I've been hit, that's what happened. Beat up, slapped around like a child, that's 'what happened.

ARTHUR: *(ENTERS)* Now tell him why. Tell him what you did.

VENUS: So, here you are, you dirty...*(EARL has to hold her back.)* Let me go, Earl.

EARL: Now look Venus. I ain't gonna have all this stuff in my house, now.

ARTHUR: Where the hell are the kids?

VENUS: Don't you worry about it.

ARTHUR: Where are my children?

VENUS: Your children are at your Mothers.

ARTHUR: What did you do? Go over there and tell her some more lies?

VENUS: What are you doing over here?

EARL: Now look you two, I got enough problems...

ARTHUR: Tell him what you told me. Tell him how you destroyed our marriage..

VENUS: You tell him. You're doing all the talking.

EARL: How do I always get in the-middle...

(Doorbell rings. EARL groans in agony as he goes to the door.)

BURNETTA: *(She ENTERS followed by IMANI.)* Earl, where is my brother? You seen him?

EARL: Hey, Burnetta...

BURNETTA: Hi. He said he might run by here. I need to catch him before he gets back to the house.

EARL: Looks like you been in a hellofa fight. Whats happening?

BURNETTA: Aw, that old fool husband of mine jumped all over me tonight for nothing.

EARL: What? *(Sees IMANI.)* Oh, good evening.

BURNETTA: Earl this is uh, Sandra, Halsted's friend. If she hadn't a come along and pulled that fool off of me...

IMANI: Looks to me more like I was pulling you off of him.

BURNETTA: Oh, he had me all set up. Hid my purse from me, poured some cheap wine in me, talking all those lies to me...

EARL: Burnetta you better sit down somewhere, cool out.

BURNETTA: I ain't got time, Earl. I gotta find Halsted and make sure he don't go around Leonard.

IMANI: I've got his clothes out in my car. We can go back to Cleveland, tonight.

BURNETTA: Yeah, Leonard took all his clothes and threw them out the door acted like a complete *fool...(Notices VENUS and ARTHUR for the fisrt time)* Oh, I'm sorry. I didn't know you had...*(To VENUS.)* Hi, girl. Don't I know you? Yeah, Halsted's boss.

VENUS: Hi.

ARTHUR: Halsted's ex-boss. He doesn't work there anymore.

BURNETTA: Who are you?

ARTHUR: I'm her boss.

VENUS: Ha!

BURNETTA: You her husband?

ARTHUR: For now.

BURNETTA: Girl, I didn't know you was married.

ARTHUR: I guess your brother didn't know, either. Or should I say, didn't care.

BURNETTA: What is your problem?

ARTHUR: Your brother is my problem. Adultery is my problem.

VENUS: Arthur...

ARTHUR: Why hide it, now? The damage has been done.

VENUS: You're not being fair...

ARTHUR: I'm not being fair?!

IMANI: What are you saying Halsted has done?

ARTHUR: Who are you?

IMANI: I'm his wife·

ARTHUR: His wife? His WIFE?! This guy is impossible.

VENUS: Halsted's not married.

IMANI AND ARTHUR: How do you know?

ARTHUR: Yeah, how do you know? You think he can't lie to you?

BURNETTA: Hey, wait a minute. What are you saying about my brother?

ARTHUR: He's a no good, dirty...

BURNETTA: Alright now. Don't forget that it is my brother you're refering to.

ARTHUR: And does that make it right for him to step into my marriage and tear it apart?

BURNETTA: If it's tearable, then tear it up. Don't come blaming my brother for your shortcomings.

ARTHUR: I'll tell you what, just let me see him, if you dare. Just let me see him.

HALSTED: *(ENTERS calling EARL.)* Earl. Man, have you got a problem.

EARL: Speak for yourself, blood.

(All eyes turn to HALSTED)

HALSTED: Well, how's everybody this evening?

ARTHUR: You?

HALSTED: You?

ARTHUR: Why you...*(He attacks HALSTED and is puiled away by EARL and BURNETTA before he can do anything.)* Let go of me...

EARL: Not here, not here.

IMANI: *(Fired up)* So, this is why you couldn't take the time to call me, huh? Finally got caught in one of your lies, huh? You dirty...*(She jumps him and he restrains her)* Play me for a fool, will you?

HALSTED: *(Has her in his arms.)* Calm yourself down.

EARL: Now look Arthur. You don't know how to act, you'll have to leave!

ARTHUR: What about him? Why can't he leave?

HALSTED: What the hell is going on around here?

ARTHUR: I know all about you and my wife?

IMANI: Now, deny that!

HALSTED: I don't know what you're talking about.

ARTHUR: You are lying...

IMANI: *(Breaks away.)* He won't admit anything. He's too much of a coward to admit anything

HALSTED: Venus what did you tell him?

IMANI: The safest thing for you to do is not say a word.

VENUS: I'll say what I please.

ARTHUR: Watch yourself woman.

VENUS: I told him that we went out a couple times. I told him that we may have feelings for each other. I told him that I cared about and...you
(ARTHUR goes after her.)

ARTHUR: Why you...
(Before he can strike, HALSTED is on him, IMANI jumps HALSTED. EARL and BURNETTA try to stop the action. There's cussing, yelling, screaming and

chaos.   HALSTED and VENUS break free.   HALSTED has gotten ARTHUR'S pistol from his shoulder holster.)

HALSTED: Alright, all of you. Back off and be cool. You want me to admit something? You want me to tell all of you the truth about how I feel? Venus is mine! I'm taking her out of here now and I don't give a damn what any of you think. Any of you!

(BURNETTA cheers.)

ARTHUR: She's my wife.

HALSTED: Not any more.

ARTHUR: Venus...

VENUS: You heard him, Arthur.

IMANI: You fool, you stupid, ignorant fool. The man has a gun!

(Her blind rage has her running at him. ARTHUR runs from the other angle. The sound of a shot stops them all. HALSTED checks the pistol. ARTHUR checks to see if he's been shot. All are still standing. Then EARL realizes what has happened.)

EARL: My 38. Lannette!

(He runs out the back. All run to the window)

VENUS: Oh my God...

(LIGHTS FADE OUT)

END ACT II, Scene 9

ACT II

Scene 10

(The Bus Station. Halsted and Venus are seated on the bench We hear the voice over the P.A. system.)

VOICE: Your attention, please. Indian Trails announces the first boarding call for express service to Cleveland and all points East, now boarding at gate number two. All aboard, please.

HALSTED: Well...

VENUS: Yeah, well...the final countdown, huh?

HALSTED: I guess so.

VENUS: You sure this is what you want...? Yes I know, we've gone over all this already... I want to go with you...aren't you going to say thing?

HALSTED: I don't know what to say.

VENUS: You sure picked a fine time for that.

HALSTED: I guess so...Venus, I'm sorry. I certainly never meant to cause you all this trouble.

VENUS: It's not so much trouble. That girl wounding herself in Earl's backyard kind of shook Arthur up. He's even willing to talk.

HALSTED: She shook me up, too. I thought I fired the shot...

VENUS: The thing is, I don't want to talk to him. Not now, anyway.

HALSTED: I thought I had killed someone, in the name of love...Venus, you have two children, you have a family. I don't want to be the one to destroy that. We both have a chance to stop this thing before it goes too far.

VENUS: But do we really want to? I'm sorry, I promised to be strong.

HALSTED: Love IS blind. I know what that phrase means, now. God, what have I done?

VENUS: What have we done? I know it's my fault, too. I realize now how dangerous flirting can be. Fooled around and fell in love.

HALSTED: We fell in love.

VENUS: I guess I'm the only one that still is.

HALSTED: I still love you. That's why I'm doing this. It's got to stop somewhere.

VENUS: But where? Is that where you're going, back to, Sandra?

HALSTED: Hell no! I can't go backwards either. No, I have a chance with this job in Cleveland to make a new start for myself. Maybe from there I can clean up some of those mistakes I made in my life.

VENUS: Mistakes? Like me?

HALSTED: You certainly weren't a mistake. If it weren't for you I wouldn't know what love is. And in the name of love, I have to say I'm sorry because I've got to go.

VENUS: I know you do.

HALSTED: I've saved enough money to get me a place and now I've got to go to work on me.

VENUS: Sounds pretty good. I just hope you're sincere.

VOICE: Your attention, please. Final boarding call for Indian Trails Express service to Cleveland and all points East now boarding at gate number two. All aboard, please.

HALSTED: Well, let me go fly away on this bus...You know what, Earl lost a quarter over there behind those lockers...

VENUS: A quarter?

HALSTED: 25 cents. Come and help me find it.

(They go behind the "lockers." They embrace and kiss. A stream of activity begins as they continue to kiss. Enter IMANI and BURNETTA.)

IMANI: *(Not seeing the couple.)* Will you look at this? Can you believe it? From a forty thousand dollar Mercedes, to a 35 dollar bus ticket...

BURNETTA: Girl, I know Earl's neighborhood was getting bad, but stealing cars?

IMANI: Oh for the peaceful mediocrity of Cleveland.

BURNETTA: *(As they exit.)* I appreciate you letting me stay with you for a couple days, but if I ever see that fool husband of mine, I'm gonna kill him!

ARTHUR: *(He and GREEN rush in.)* You sure she didn't have any suitcases with her?

GREEN: I don't know, Mr. Strattford. I just heard her checking on the Greyhound bus schedule...

ARTHUR: Oh, God...

(They also exit to the loading dock.)

EARL: *(He and LANNETTE enter. Her hands are heavily bandaged.)* Yeah, Lannette, you're really lucky. That old raggedy piece of pistol of mine could of blown your face off when you fired it.

LANNETTE: No, you the one that's lucky, Earl. Because I was aiming at you through the window.

EARL: Oh baby...

(They exit.)

LEONARD: *(Enters with his back to the audience.)* This way to the bus from Mississippi? This way? Alright, thank you. *(He turns to look for his Mother and we see his face scarred, black eye and a couple of band aids.)* Mama! Look what she did to me, Mama...

(He exits to the loading dock.)

HALSTED: *(Their kiss is ended.)* Well...

VENUS: Yeah, well...Carry your bags, sir?

HALSTED: Yeah, my whole shaving kit thanks to Imani's stolen car.

(They head for the loading zone.)

VENUS: You know this isn't over between us, don't you?

HALSTED: Maybe not. But, at least this phase has ended somewhat peacefully.

VENUS: True. Yeah, and there's no one else around...

(Just as they are about to kiss again, all the people offstage shout.)

ALL: WANNA BET...?!

(Loud argument is heard. The song "LOVE'S LIGHT IN FLIGHT," is heard)
Curtain

Denise Nicholas

BUSES

Crossroads Theatre

Denise Nicholas

Riffin' With Denise Nicholas
Excerpts from an Interview
by Synde Mahone

In the space of our dreams, the symboled dramas of the subconscious mind come to life. The encoded messages give clues to our greatest fears and deepest desires. These dreams, held in sleep, can transform our waking realities. In *Buses*, playwright Denise Nicholas explores the genre of the dream play as a means of awakening the conscious mind and freeing the human spirit.

Denise says, "We as African Americans do, or have tended to live an awful lot through our dreams. It's all of that life that we have not been allowed to live, that erupts in our daydreams and night dreams. We probably are a very dreamy people as a consequence of oppression. And that's where a lot of our cultural power comes from. It's like this thing that's constantly being pressed down and it just becomes more powerful as a consequence of being pressed down; as the character, Rosa, says in the play, 'like a volcano that never erupts.' That's the way our dreams are. It drives some of our artists absolutely mad. At the same time, it keeps a lot of us sane.

"The first treatments of the play were of a traditional format in terms of the character of Mary Ellen living in her house. I had a whole set with the Victorian house in San Francisco and characters walking around with costumes. And, oh God, did it bore me. I thought this so diminishes her impact. I went to see *The Colored Museum* a couple of times and was totally fascinated by the form; it was non-linear, non-sequential, non-traditional; it was more like an improvisation. Of all the things that we have produced as art in America, I'd say that jazz is truest to the experience I see us having. The key element in that is improvisation. It is freeing, and that has always been our need and our desire, to be free. We improvise to survive.

"I wanted to take two characters, and throw them in a context and see what happened; let them have riffs . . . The Negro Lottery is my favorite riff! There's another riff that Mary Ellen starts when she pulls out the wine and food. They start talking about flesh and money and power and food; they go off on a tangent and it becomes an argument about voting."

In jazz, the bass line provides the structure for infinite variation on the melody line. If the bass line in *Buses* is the historical truth of two characters, the melody line is the collision of their two worlds in the space of this dream play.

"The dream reality freed me to let loose of the history a bit. I was battling a thing with Mrs. Parks still living and among us; and being very sensitive to her and to her image, I did not want to cause her any apprehension about me tampering with her image. So I thought the best way to do that is to put the whole thing in a dream structure. And that way, it becomes a figment of my imagination.

"It's freeing. I didn't want the play to be weighted in history. I didn't want it to be a Black History Month lesson. It's not school time here; it's imagination time. It is about two historically real people and two historically real events—the two days that these two women were ejected from public transportation systems in their individual lifetimes; and from that moment on, it becomes a flight of fancy."

In the dream realm, the heightened consciousness permits a multi-leveled perception. We can transcend the boundaries of time and space. We can experience events and observe ourselves in them at the same time. Upon waking, upon reflection, the vivid images become distilled new truths.

"I sometimes think the characters are two sides of the same person. At least, they are two sides of me. They are metaphors for the conflict that I, as Denise, have. They are reason and passion. And in that way it i from my heart. I'm using these ladies, in a sense, to air that. Everyone has those two antitheses and we need to exorcise them, get them out there. Even though sometimes we may fall more on one side than the other.

"The play is about telling one's own story and not allowing people to write your epitaph. It's about friendship and love between people, between women. It is almost mother/daughter. Mary Ellen lived in the last century. She knows more and sees the whole thing from her vantage point. There is a theme about waiting and not waiting; putting things off and not living in the moment. The metaphor of Rosa's waiting for a bus—and allowing a bus to go finally—has to do with my abhorrence of putting one's life on hold until one dies and goes off to experience a better life in some world that we don't know about. The best of who we are and what we are needs to be expressed here with each other, and in this world, with these trees, and these flowers, and these people. God will accept what's left of us when we get there."

The journey of the artist is a lesson in living in the moment. Denise's discovery of art and theatre chronicles the African American dream of, struggle for, and realization of freedom.

"After about a year at the University of Michigan, the Civil Rights Movement was in full force, in the 60's. And I was not happy being away from the action. I wanted to be in the south. And I was very frightened of it. I also had become involved with artists at school. There was no voice for something that was inside of me. I started taking art history and feeling more attuned to artistic expression than to a political expression.

"I went to Mississippi in June of '64. The Free Southern Theatre had started up. I had met Gil Moses in New York on a break from school. In Ann Arbor, on our spring break we would all pile into cars and come to New York to be big time, meet people and see foreign films. The films, and then meeting Moses and John O'Neal had me thinking that maybe that was going to be the way for me. Gil was an artist; a musician, a writer, and an actor. I thought, 'Can black people be these things?' I left school and made arrangements to go down, and work with the Free Southern Theatre that first summer of '64.

"I didn't go back to school. I stayed down there and toured with the company and apprenticed. It was extremely exciting to be 18, 19 years old, in what really was the war zone, the trenches; it was really a guerrilla war— only they had the guns. I remember sleeping on the floor of Fannie Lou Hamer's home because they were shooting through the windows.

"I remember hearing, for the first time, very elderly black men play the guitar and play old, old, Mississippi blues. I mean real gutbucket blues. A man playing with a bottle on his finger doing slides on the guitar. I'm sitting on the porch watching this, listening to this. Learning the freedom songs and being in the places where the voter registration drives were. Freedom schools were there and there was death around. There was violence around; but there was such energy and such a positive force that it changed the south and it changed everybody that participated in it. So I stayed and I worked until September of '66. I was brought to New York by the actress Viveca Lindfors to do a show with her."

Soon thereafter Denise became a founding member of the Negro Ensemble

Company's first professional company. A year later, she went to Los Angeles to star in the television series, *Room 222*. Most recently, she co-starred with Bill Cosby in *Ghost Dad* and is often seen on the television series, *In The Heat of the Night*.

The evolution of the artist—from actress to playwright—is the dream of freedom still quaking in her heart. It reflects her ongoing process of self-definition, her pursuit of her own liberating truth.

"Writing keeps me anchored in being an artist. It exorcises my demons more than acting ever will. It gets the little demons out of their little boxes and lets them fly around. Then I have to put them back in there. When I'm acting, I have to control myself because I'm usually acting in things written by other people; and it's usually TV which means it's really not always that deep. More often than not, it's going to be kind of slight; every now and then you'll get something swell. Writing is an opportunity to create something swell.

"It's my intent to take the audience on a little bit of a trip that allows them to release laughter and tears. We're always a mixture of our laughter and our tears. I hope they take the trip with the actresses and experience their unveiling, their taking these layers off and becoming more real and more true. I hope they understand that that is for all of us to do: the truth of who we are to the world, to our loved ones, our colleagues. The gift of who we really are **is** a gift. Maybe they can do that a little better in their own lives if they see people doing that—and see that they don't fall, they're not destroyed because of it; that, in fact, the truth does set you free."

CROSSROADS THEATRE COMPANY

Crossroads was founded in October 1978 by Ricardo Khan and L. Kenneth Richardson, graduates of the Mason Gross School of the Arts at Rutgers University, who shared a vision of providing a nurturing environment for Black theater artists. Two years later, Crossroads became a nonprofit organization.

Since its founding, Crossroads has achieved national and international prominence for its groundbreaking work. *The Colored Museum*, which premiered at Crossroads in 1986, was seen by millions on national public television's "Great Performances." Also that year, Crossroads received the National Governors' Association Award for Distinguished Service in the Arts. In 1993, it became the first Actors' Equity company to perform in South Africa in at least three decades.

In 1991, the company entered a new stage when it moved from a century-old former garment factory to a new, $4 million, 264-seat facility in downtown New Brunswick. By the end of the 1993-94 season, Crossroads had produced 32 world premieres and established itself as a leader in the development of new work for African American theater.

Each season, Crossroads presents five full productions, with an emphasis on new works. The Associate Artists program provides a "home" for playwrights, actors, and technical personnel to develop new work for African American theater. Crossroads' Associate Artists include Ruby Dee, George C. Wolfe, Ntozake Shange, Avery Brooks, and Harold Scott. Audiences can witness the birth of new work by emerging and established artists during Crossroads' annual festival, *Genesis: A Celebration of New Voices in African American Theatre*, featuring a series of staged readings. Established in 1990, *Genesis* has featured such works as *Buses*, by Denise Nicholas, *Oak and Ivy* and *Mothers*, by Kathleen McGhee-Anderson, *The Love Space Demands*, by Ntozake Shange, and *The Disappearance*, by Ruby Dee, all of which became mainstage productions.

Through its touring program, NewRoads, the company has reached out to new audiences in order to enrich diverse communities with the cultural and educational experience of fine African American theater. Crossroads' productions have toured both nationally and internationally while such plays as *The Colored Museum*, *Spunk*, *The Rabbit Foot (Ground People)*, and *Further Mo'* went on to off-Broadway runs. In 1989, Crossroads brought Sandra Reaves' *The Late, Great Ladies of Blues & Jazz* to New York's Apollo Theatre.

Crossroads is committed to the future of Black theater in its artistic and educational programming. Through its African American College Initiative

Program, Crossroads works with theater arts faculty and students at seven historically black institutions. The program, fosters the development of new talent through workshops, internships, faculty exchanges, and arts advocacy. The Penelope E. Lattimer High School Internship promotes interest in the arts among young people, while the newly established Programming for Young Audiences will bring theatrical pieces to schools and organizations beginning in 1995. The company sponsors community forums and matinee youth summits to promote discourse on contemporary issues that are addressed on the stage.

BUSES
by Denise Nicholas

Directed by
Shirley Jo Finney

CAST

MARY ELLEN PLEASANT ....Iris Little
ROSA PARK..Petronia Paley

PLACE: A bus stop in a dream
TIME: Out of time

Biographical Notes
by Denise Nicholas

ROSA LOUISE PARKS (b. 1913) Rosa Parks will be 78 years old this year, 1991. A life may be memorialized for one singular event or achievement, but a life is so much more. That one event may not be separated from all other events of a life . . . There is a continuum, a river. With *Buses*, I wanted to release the living spirit of Rosa Parks, beyond the day on the bus, December 1, 1955. *Buses* is not a chronicle of her life. I humbly leave that to the historical biographers. I wanted to imagine her inner life, her dreams, realities, awakenings.

"Life is to be lived in its fullest so that death is just another chapter. Memories of our lives, our works and our deeds will continue in others."
Rosa L. Parks, *The Meaning of Life*
Life Magazine, December 1988

MARY ELLEN PLEASANT (c. 1814-1904) Mary Ellen Pleasant lived for nearly the whole of the 19th century. There isn't much known of her life previous to her arrival in San Francisco (c. 1849). What has been written is conjectural. At best, historical fantasy. It was never my concern to write her biography. It is my very deep concern to present her spirit, something of her, to this time. I believe she belongs to us. I sometimes imagine her walking the hills of San Francisco, quick step, sharp eyes. She might very well· be talking to herself: "I don't want them writin' nothin' on that stone! Who do the think they are? It's my stone! It oughta say what I want anyway! Shoot!"

IN LOVING MEMORY OF MY SISTER

Michele Darlene Burgen

12-25-53—2-25-80

THE CHARACTERS

ROSA PARKS: A quiet woman of deep religious conviction. She speaks with a soft, Southern accent. Her depth and intensity make up for the lack of noise in her character. She is attractive and takes that quality seriously. She has a rope of long hair which she wears in braids across her head. There is a point in the play when she will "let her hair down."

MARY ELLEN PLEASANT: A tall, spare woman who is strong, manipulative to the point of being hypnotic in her influence. She can be loud and boisterous; but, then she can behave well within the boundaries of Victorian decorum when necessary. She is a power person. The actress should have presence, vitality, grandness, sensuality. There are times when MARY ELLEN'S ego and vanity get in the way of her mission. The actress should be able to affect a Scottish accent.

303

AT 15 minutes, please play the following selections in this order: John Coltrane's "Naima," Curtis Mayfield's "Keep on Pushin'," Kathleen Battle's "This Little Light of Mine," and the Neville Bros., "Thank You, Sister Rosa."

Since the two characters never met in *REAL LIFE*, the lighting and scenery should reflect the *NON-REALISTIC* quality of the play.

THE SCENE: *A non-realistic representation of two bus stops, with benches.*

Signs on the ROSA PARKS "side" of the stage should include "MONT-GOMERY CITY LINE," "EMPIRE THEATER," and more prominent-ly, "ROSA PARKS BOULEVARD."

One sign on the MARY ELLEN PLEASANT "side" of the stage reads "OMNIBUS TROLLEY LINE."

The characters are out of time, out of place and out of mind.

> *AT CURTAIN: As the lights fade up.*
> *ROSA PARKS enters.*
> *(She is dressed as she was on that fateful day, December 1, 1955: Conservative suit, blouse with Peter Pan collar, working shoes, purse, sewing bag, hanky and small Bible in one of her bags.)*

SCENE ONE

(Rosa Parks stops to the side and looks at her "place," the bus stop, the signs. She walks to her bench, takes her hanky and dusts her bench, then sits.)

ROSA: Keeping my seat on that bus was just the tip of the iceberg. My life was like a pier whose underpinnings were rotting with rage. Anger and fear in a dead heat. That day, the anger finally overtook the fear. When you get that far, there's no turning back. Even in the most Christian of hearts, the anger will prevail.

MARY ELLEN PLEASANT: *(O.S.)* GIT YO' HANDS OFFA ME! YOU OL' BEAT DOWN CONFEDERATE FOOL!! THIS AIN'T ALABAMA, MAGPIE!

(Rosa is startled by this outburst as there is clearly no one there. She stands, looks all around, sees nothing.)

ROSA: Thought I heard someone? *(Rosa sits again)* As I was saying, my heart was turning to stone. I had to do something so I just sat there.

MARY ELLEN PLEASANT: *(O.S.)* I SAID, THIS AIN'T ALABAMA!! MUST BE WHERE YOU FROM!! *(a beat)* I knew it!! *(One of MARY ELLEN'S many parcels comes flying out onto the stage)* DON'T YOU TOUCH MY THINGS!!

(Other parcels fly out)

(MARY ELLEN PLEASANT backs onto the stage with gusto trying to retrieve her flying parcels.)

(One parcel comes close to hitting Rosa, who ducks, then goes to hide behind her bench, peeking out.)

(MARY ELLEN PLEASANT is wearing a long black dress in the style of the 1860's with white collar and cuffs, a white apron with pockets. Around her shoulders is a beautiful Tartan-plaid shawl. There is a ring of keys attached at her waist.)

MARY ELLEN: *(cont.)* WHY DIDN'T YOU STAY ON DOWN THERE WHERE YOU BELONG? *(Mary Ellen turns to see where her intended audience is, doesn't see her, continues gathering her things and softens her tone to a more dignified level but segueing quickly to a boisterous level.)* You onery piece of Dixie dirt. Ol' Confederate fool! *(then)* YOU STINKIN' PILE OF ROTTEN SHIT!! *(Mary Ellen sneaks a look to see if Rosa is there. No Rosa. She switches into an even higher gear, impatient now that none of her "approaches" has worked.)* YOU GOT COTTON BALLS WHERE YOU 'POSED TO HAVE—

ROSA: *(rising from her hiding place)* Stop it! Stop it! I won't have that kind of talk! There's no need for that out here in public! No need at all to say such things!! Stop it!

MARY ELLEN: Well, there you are! He'll see who gets the last word! *(Mary Ellen walks to center stage, throws her head back and with all her force and might, she yells.)* YOU'LL KNOW WHO I AM WHEN I'M FINISHED WITH YOU!!

(Rosa is stunned. She cautiously goes to her bench to gather her things.)

ROSA: There's no need to carry on like that. No need at all.

MARY ELLEN: I'm glad he done it. Got something to shout about now! He ain't never seen no "uppity nig—."

ROSA: *(to audience)* Some of our women can be so—

MARY ELLEN: *(indignant)* He threw me, Mary Ellen Pleasant, off the trolley!!

ROSA: I don't care what he put you off of. All that yelling and bad language...

MARY ELLEN: Let off some steam! War over, here they come, trampin' to California draggin' all that slavery slop with 'em!

(Rosa leaves her things on her bench, runs to her signs, looks at them, reading them carefully.)

ROSA: *(to herself)* Would be just like 'em to change the bus stop and not tell anybody! Just leave you to figure it out on your own. Make you late and all...

MARY ELLEN: Are yee daft?!! Over there talking to the air.

ROSA: Slavery slop? What war?

MARY ELLEN: You are daft! The Civil War, what do you think?

ROSA: I believe I'm lost.

MARY ELLEN: It's myself that feels lost. Been ridin' that trolley since it's very first run. I'm shopping. I board and the new driver, a dixie magpie, throws me off, saying the colored can't ride! Since when, I say? Since right now, says he. "What do you mean? We been ridin'," I say. He says, "Well, you ain't ridin' no more." He then grabs me by the arms, my parcels fall all around, and he slings me out and proceeds to pitch my parcels out behind me! Now have you ever heard of such a thing?

ROSA: (quietly) Yes, I have. It was a bus.

(She looks hard at Mary Ellen.)

MARY ELLEN: The man don't know there's no law in this town 'bout the colored ridin'!

ROSA: This town?

MARY ELLEN: San Francisco. Where else?

ROSA: But this is Montgomery, Alabama.

MARY ELLEN: You are lost, girly!

ROSA: Montgomery City Line. I got put off...

MARY ELLEN: You got put off it, whatever it was, where ever it was and you got put off cause you colored, just like me.

ROSA: Yes, but I didn't leave it at that—

MARY ELLEN: And neither did I!

ROSA: You couldn't have done very much. It just happened. (then) Didn't it?

MARY ELLEN: I took care of the Omnibus Company. Filed a suit and I won!

ROSA: You won?

MARY ELLEN: They settled.

ROSA: You got money?

MARY ELLEN: I wanted to ride the trolley without being bothered by Dixie magpies. I got that. More or less.

ROSA: I don't recall hearing—

MARY ELLEN: Nobody did! And if they have their way, nobody ever will. They're gettin' ready to mark my stone and that will be the end of it!!!

ROSA: Your stone? What kind of stone?

(Mary Ellen begins to dance around Rosa.)

MARY ELLEN: "Alabaster shrines, delicate and fine, Monuments of granite and rock. Marble memorials, markers in gold, Pyramids of block on block, Tombstones and gravel, gravestones all."

ROSA: Gravestones?

MARY ELLEN: (singing the last line) "But, epitaphs are written by the living!"

ROSA: *(very quietly)* Who's going to do this?

MARY ELLEN: Don't make no difference who! They ought to leave me alone. I have my rights! They ought to leave well enough alone.

(Rosa goes to gather her things with the purpose of getting away.)

ROSA: If your life is in order, that stone is a celebration. A marker...to let the generations know you passed through here.

MARY ELLEN: Shoot! They gon' make it a street sign to purgatory! I don't want them writin' nothin' on that stone! It's my stone!! Who do they think they are? It ought to say what I want it to say!!

ROSA: I see. Well. It's been very nice talking with you, but it's getting late. I best be getting on home.

MARY ELLEN: Later than you think. When they mark your stone, I'm telling you, it's too late.

ROSA: Too late for what?

MARY ELLEN: No more guessin'. No more this one sayin' that and that one sayin' this. No more nothin' but darkness, Rosa.

(Rosa stops cold, walks down to the edge of the stage and addresses the audience.)

ROSA: I did not tell that woman my name. She's crazy, walking around here in a dress from a hundred years ago, talking about tombstones and the Civil War. Probably somebody they let out the crazy house. Mental. Just mental. I don't want to hear another word! I just want to go on home. I wonder where did she get that dress....

MARY ELLEN: I forgot a few things is all. I don't want to be locked in the darkness, marked by a cold stone, written on by strangers...

ROSA: Are you dead?

MARY ELLEN: Depends on how you look at it.

(Rosa digs for her bible, but speaks from memory before she finds the passage.)

ROSA: "In thee, O Lord, do I put my trust: let me never be put to confusion." Lord, if this is a dream, please wake me!

MARY ELLEN: Life and dreams, swift as a good night! *(Mary Ellen walks far away from Rosa)* "Free among the dead, like the slain that lie in the grave, whom thou rememberest no more: and they are cut off from thy hand."

ROSA: Who are you?

MARY ELLEN: I have a few things to clear up is all. Then I'll be on my way.

ROSA: What's that to do with me?

MARY ELLEN: *(falling on her knees)* They want to name me in their words for all eternity. Don't let them do that to me.

ROSA: I can't stop them from doing anything. And who is "them"? Who are "they"? Who are you?!!

MARY ELLEN: *(getting up)* Now don't go gettin' beside yourself.

ROSA: I want to get out of here.

(Rosa runs upstage and around, finding no exit)

ROSA: *(cont.)* Let me out of here!! I'm just waitin' on my bus! Where is it? You did something!

MARY ELLEN: It'll be along.

ROSA: When?

MARY ELLEN: In a while.

ROSA: It's getting so chilly.

(She pulls her collar up against the cold. Slowly, she moves to her bench, sits, holding her Bible.)

ROSA: *(cont.)* Where did you get that dress?

MARY ELLEN: Ain't it grand?!

ROSA: Somebody can sure sew.

MARY ELLEN: Pure silk, imported from China!

ROSA: Now, myself, I'd do it in another color...that's too much black. Has a tendency to look like a shroud. People of color look best in brighter hues, pastels even, not too bright so that it draws attention...not red. Lord, never red!!

MARY ELLEN: What are you talkin' about? And where did you get that concoction you got on?

ROSA: Made it myself. I'm a dressmaker, you know. But I wouldn't even think of trying something like you're wearing.

MARY ELLEN: That ain't no dress you got on.

ROSA: It's a suit.

MARY ELLEN: Never seen anything like it. *(Mary Ellen circles Rosa)* It's got a waist coat like a man's suit of clothin'. But that bottom is far too short.

ROSA: It's the fashion...today.

MARY ELLEN: You look like a chicken, your legs all hangin' out!

ROSA: Do you think my bus will be along soon?

MARY ELLEN: Soon.

ROSA: Well, I suppose it's alright if I just sit here.

(She takes a skirt out of her sewing bag and prepares to work.)

ROSA: *(cont.)* *(muttering almost to herself)* I've got to get Mrs. Simms' skirt ready for her to try on tomorrow. Easter just around the corner and everybody wants a new something! Well, if you're Christian, I'm just gonna put my faith in the Lord. If you're not, I'm sure there's a meaning I can't see—

MARY ELLEN: It's too late for divine intervention!

ROSA: *(touching her Bible)* It's never too late for that.

(Mary Ellen is pacing.)

MARY ELLEN: I come to San Francisco 'cause it was wide open. Free! You know what I mean? I was doing just fine. Almost made it to the top of the heap. Then Mr. Bell had to go and die! Talk about bad timin'!

(Rosa sits quietly trying to focus on her sewing. She tries to thread a needle. Her hands shake visibly.)

ROSA: Was he your husband?

MARY ELLEN: Not exactly. Left me hangin' over a bay of the hungriest great white sharks you ever did see! You ever seen one?

ROSA: What?

MARY ELLEN: Shark.

ROSA: No.

MARY ELLEN: Lot of teeth. Anyway. He was a good man. We made beautiful music together. Money music and love music.

ROSA: *(Pricks her finger with her needle)* Ouch!!

MARY ELLEN: Watch yourself. When he died, they stripped me of everything. Property, jewelry, even my furniture. Do you know what it feels like to be put out on the streets in front of the whole wide world? Everything you own on the street?

ROSA: No.

MARY ELLEN: The little that was left went to the lawyers. By the time they got through, I didn't even have what I came here with.

ROSA: Those things weren't yours to begin with.

MARY ELLEN: They were! I paid for them!

ROSA: But you couldn't keep them unless that Mr. Bell was protecting you? Sounds to me like they were his and he was loaning them to you.

MARY ELLEN: They were mine, I tell you! You sayin' I didn't own nothin'? I owned half the town!

ROSA: *(quietly)* Until Mr. Bell died? This "Mr." Bell, as you call him...was he white? I know things were going on.

MARY ELLEN: White and charmin' to boot. We grabbed a hold of San Francisco and wrestled it to the ground!

(Rosa walks D.S. and talks to the audience.)

ROSA: Now, you see! That's the kind of thing that made us look bad. "Mr." Bell. What did he call her, I wonder? I don't care how much music they made together. It just looks bad, a Negro woman and a white man and not married!

(There is the sound of a closing door. It startles Rosa into silence as MARY ELLEN enters a small circle of light. Mary Ellen talks to an imaginary "Mr. Bell.")

MARY ELLEN: Why are you closin' the door, Thomas? ....Well, what is it, then? You know I don't like shocks. *(she chuckles)* You like to catch me unawares. The surprise warms you. What's this? *(She takes the "package" from him)* Must be a lace table cloth or something of the sort. You are a tight Scot, you are. *(She unwraps it and sees)* Why, Thomas, it's the most beautiful dress I've ever seen! I spoke too soon. Thank you, darling. *(She turns her back to "Thomas")* But, Thomas, the boarders are comfortable thinkin' of me as their servant. They won't have me wearin' fancy dresses. In a snap, they'd take their business elsewhere. *(She faces him)* But I can wear it here in my room. Or at Geneva Cottage, I can wear it in every room of the house! *(She spins with the dress)* At Geneva Cottage, I can look the owner and never play the maid! Thomas, I believe in my heart things are changin' for the colored. When the time is right, I'll put on this dress and dance in the streets!

(A bell is rung for service.)

(The circle of light fades.)

ROSA: Why, you couldn't even wear the dress he gave you!

MARY ELLEN: It was fine with some but a canker to others.

ROSA: More canker than fine, I'm sure. You might never rest.

MARY ELLEN: I don't want to rest!!

ROSA: What DO you want then?

MARY ELLEN: I want what you have. A sacred place in history!

ROSA: You are crazy!

MARY ELLEN: Nothin' wrong with wantin' it and you sure know how to get it!

ROSA: You've got it wrong. I never went after anything of the sort. I never even thought about it. A sacred place? That sounds ridiculous! No one has a sacred place in history!

MARY ELLEN: Easy for you to say now.

ROSA: You think I plotted my life? You think all I wanted was a street named for me? You're so wrong.

MARY ELLEN: No insult intended.

ROSA: I'm just a woman who tries to live a decent life. I'm quiet. Some say aloof.

MARY ELLEN: Shoot! I never woulda got nothin' done actin' like that!

ROSA: When I'm called upon to help, I'm ready. That's all. No mystery.

MARY ELLEN: I'm countin' on that, girly, to be sure.

ROSA: I do try to live my life without running roughshod over morality.

MARY ELLEN: In 1850, San Francisco didn't have no morality!!

ROSA: People don't harvest their morals where they land!

MARY ELLEN: It was a different time!

ROSA: Not that different.

MARY ELLEN: Well, I can't take it back now.

ROSA: You can't have it both ways either. If you could, everybody would raise the devil from birth to death, then leave a white-washed legacy of lies. How to explain all the evil in the world? Somebody's doing it!

MARY ELLEN: We die with our choices no matter what's in our hearts?

ROSA: I believe it's all the same thing.

MARY ELLEN: You don't even know what happened!

ROSA: You've said plenty about it.

(Mary Ellen is quiet. She looks at Rosa's signs and "place" in history. She paces, thinking about the tapestry of her long life.)

MARY ELLEN: 'Course now, I did give some money to John Brown.

ROSA: I've never seen this bus be this late. What did you say?

MARY ELLEN: I said, I give some money to John Brown...for that raid—

ROSA: You gave money to John Brown? THE John Brown?! *(Rosa looks at her)* I don't believe that! You're the kind to say anything to get what you want.

(Mary Ellen goes d.s. and addresses the audience directly.)

MARY ELLEN: Now, that's just like a colored person to not believe another colored person! Never believe, never trust! Always talkin' against one another! It ain't gon' never change!

ROSA: Why should I believe you gave John Brown money for his raid on—

MARY ELLEN: "His raid"?! It was OUR raid! You are daft!

ROSA: If you did, why are you so worried about your stone? Put that on there. Surely, that would get you a "sacred place" in somebody's history!

MARY ELLEN: John Brown sent me a message askin' for a donation to the cause.

ROSA: Why'd he send YOU a message?

MARY ELLEN: Cause I had some money. So I went all the way to Canada to meet with ol' John Brown. He told me his plans, I give him the loot. On my way back to California, I wrote askin' him to hold off for a while. I thought if the slaves was better informed of his plans they could rise as a mass and back him. He didn't heed my advice.

ROSA: Maybe he didn't get it.

(Rosa looks at Mary Ellen.)

MARY ELLEN: Never felt too comfortable away from California. Any ol' broke white man could grab you up and sell you for a slave.

ROSA: That's a very entertaining story.

MARY ELLEN: They tried to make out ol' John Brown was a mad dog 'cause he sided with the colored.

ROSA: Today, he'd be a communist.

(Mary Ellen becomes the soldier)

MARY ELLEN: Been white folks he was sidin' with, he'd a been up there with George Washington, a saint, leadin' the stragglin' masses into battle! What's a communist?

ROSA: Anybody these white folks disagree with.

MARY ELLEN: He'd a been one then cause they sure disagreed with him.

ROSA: You, too.

MARY ELLEN: Yea, but I ain't white!

ROSA: Makes no difference.

MARY ELLEN: I'm wastin' my time!

ROSA: I've been thinking here. The wandering spirits are fine. But, we need a certain type of spirit... We need flawless wonders! Uplifting parables! We need Florence Nightingales with brown faces...

MARY ELLEN: I'm never gon' be a flawless wonder. It's too late for that. That's not fair! Nobody's a flawless wonder!

ROSA: We need monuments! That's it!! People need to be looking up!

MARY ELLEN: A piece of marble frozen in place and time, much as Joan of Arc! I would rather be free!

(Mary Ellen goes to gather her things to leave.)

ROSA: When they etch your life on that stone, you won't be free.

(Mary starts to walk away. Rosa stops her.)

ROSA: *(cont.)* I'm sorry. I didn't mean to be like a monument. It's just that in my whole life, people ask me one question. The bus! It's always about that bus. I have other things.

MARY ELLEN: *(pouting)* It's your own fault.

ROSA: No, it's not!

MARY ELLEN: Forget it. You served well, monument or not.

ROSA: I'm a seamstress and a worker in the cause of human rights. That's all.

MARY ELLEN: Better to be in the business of selling something.

ROSA: We weren't selling anything. We rode the buses back and forth to work, standing on tired feet, day in, day out.

MARY ELLEN: Cheap labor.

ROSA: The women fired the starting pistol then almost got run off the track.

MARY ELLEN: They went to the back pew.

ROSA: Didn't you ever get called on your womanness?

MARY ELLEN: Every now and then. But I went on anyway. I was alone. San Francisco was wild and full of promise.

ROSA: I'd like to shake this monument thing off. I'd like to—

MARY ELLEN: There's not a soul here but us!

ROSA: *(laughing)* You're the only soul here. *(then)* So far. *(Mary Ellen smiles at her)* What should I do?

MARY ELLEN: Try dancin' it out. Or, yellin' it out. Works for me.

ROSA: I'd only make a fool of myself.

MARY ELLEN: Anybody who did what you did on that bus ought not to be afraid of nothin'!

ROSA: I didn't say I was afraid.

MARY ELLEN: You strong as a railroad track from where I stand.

ROSA: Never thought of it that way.

MARY ELLEN: Well, we know what goes on your stone! "Here lies Rosa Parks, she refused to give up her seat to a white man on the bus."

ROSA: You make it sound so thin. A lot came from that.

MARY ELLEN: Oh, I know it did. You're gon' be a monument, like it or not. For me, I always wanted my stone to say, "Here lies Mary Ellen Pleasant, astute businesswoman who helped tame San Francisco, bearer of the Freedom torch and a Dear friend of John Brown." That says it nicely.

ROSA: What about "Mr." Bell? Don't forget him. "Here lies Mary Ellen Pleasant, etc., etc., friend of John Brown who laid down with "Mr." Bell."

MARY ELLEN: You're mocking me!

ROSA: I'm sorry. All this talk of stones and markers. It's makin' me...makin' me—

MARY ELLEN: Think.

(Rosa goes back to her bench and quietly takes up her sewing.)

(Mary Ellen doesn't want to "lose" Rosa. She decides to do something big, noisy, and attention getting. She twirls and spins around, dress and shawl flying.)

MARY ELLEN: *(cont.)* I WAS SO GRAND, FOR A WHILE!

ROSA: I'm sure you were. Still are.

MARY ELLEN: *(Painting pictures in the air)* I had a place out on the old San Jose Road. Called it Geneva Cottage. Orchards of plums, apricots, peaches, and grapes on the vine. Trellises of roses, wild flowers all around, birds of every sort—

ROSA: Sounds like the Garden of Eden.

MARY ELLEN: In a way of speakin', it was. I made some of the best wine in San Francisco! Oh, the sunsets, such as you have never seen! It was a secret hideaway place for my best customers. Away from the coming and going of the boarding houses in town—

ROSA:: Why was it a secret?

MARY ELLEN: Because MY customers needed a place to enjoy the pure pleasures of life without anybody lookin' over their shoulder.

ROSA: What kind of pure pleasures?

MARY ELLEN: STOP INTERRUPTING ME!!

ROSA: *(no longer sewing)* You didn't anwer my question.

MARY ELLEN: The pure pleasures of wine and song!

ROSA: You can enjoy those pleasures anywhere. What kind of pleasures had to be so secret?

MARY ELLEN: Wine and song. General good times. *(She stops and looks at Rosa)* Oh, nothin'!!

ROSA: Well, Miss Pleasant, I can't help you with your stone if you don't tell the whole truth.

MARY ELLEN: As if anyone cared about the truth.

ROSA: Don't change the subject. Now, what kind of pleasures had to be so secret?

MARY ELLEN: *(Quickly)* Wine and song. Women and men. *(Mary Ellen walks briskly to her bench)* Lord, I'm hungry!
(Mary Ellen digs around in her parcels and comes out with a bottle of wine, bread and a hunk of cheese. She plows into the food with gusto.)

ROSA: It was a glorified cat house!!

MARY ELLEN: *(Eating)* Call it what you will, it was beautiful. You weren't anybody at all if you didn't get an invitation to an evening at Geneva Cottage. I set a real fine table.

ROSA: Are you going to drink that wine right out here in public?

MARY ELLEN: Indeed, I am. Won't you have some?

ROSA: I don't drink. I know Negroes weren't involved at that Geneva Cottage.

MARY ELLEN: "Negroes" always sounds like vegetables to me! Give me a pound of potatoes, half pound of squash and a few of those Negroes please. We're colored!

ROSA: For your information, we haven't been colored for some time.

MARY ELLEN: We're colored for my money!

ROSA: And Negro for mine!

MARY ELLEN: Didn't know you had any!

ROSA: No need to be cruel.

MARY ELLEN: Yes, they were at Geneva Cottage. Doing everything.

ROSA: Lord.

MARY ELLEN: You look a little peaked. You better come on and have some of this food. A little wine wouldn't hurt you none either. Bring your color up!

ROSA: My color is fine, thank you. *(Rosa watches Mary Ellen eating with such gusto)* Maybe a little bread and cheese. *(Rosa moves to Mary Ellen's bench and sits.)*

MARY ELLEN: You see, Rosie—
(Rosa looks hard at her.)

MARY ELLEN: *(cont.)* Rosa. People who work hard need to play hard!

ROSA: They need to pray hard.
(Rosa eats.)

MARY ELLEN: One or two of 'em did call on the Lord! Yes, they did! One time, Ol' Judge Coffey let out a hallelujah whoop that nearly swayed the chandelier—

ROSA: You were a disgrace before God!

MARY ELLEN: I give 'em what they wanted and took a little for myself is all. Life is in the body and the purse!

ROSA: You say. So what happened to this Geneva Cottage?

MARY ELLEN: *(Taking a swig of wine)* Had to close it down.

ROSA: I can't imagine why.

MARY ELLEN: One of my girls got hurt.

ROSA: Another cathouse tale coming up.

MARY ELLEN: Her name was Cora.

ROSA: Pretty name. Don't hear it much.

MARY ELLEN: She was pretty, too. She come to San Francisco to find gold— in the form of a husband. As many others did. Couldn't read or write. She was my best student.

ROSA: And just what kind of teacher were you?

MARY ELLEN: A teacher of refinement. Taught them how to talk, how to walk, how to dress and how to rest.

ROSA: You taught them to live the life you never lived yourself.

MARY ELLEN: I didn't want to live like that!

ROSA: Mighta been nice for a change...instead of running after the sound of the bell. *(Rosa giggles) (then)* I can't believe I said that!
(Mary Ellen is not amused.)

MARY ELLEN: Every bachelor in town had his eye on Cora. She was gon' be my ticket...a kind of annuity for my waning years. You see, there were women I was groomin' to be wives and there were women who would never be wives, nobody's wives. I never mixed the two. One night out at Geneva Cottage, I readied Cora to meet the man who would be her husband. The right gown, the right jewels, all mine.

ROSA: That you couldn't wear.

MARY ELLEN: The cigar smoke was thick as orchard fog. Cora went out to get some air. Two of my guests followed her. You can imagine the horrible thing they did. *(she paces)* I didn't allow that kind of behavior in my house! They put me in jeopardy! They nearly ruined me!

ROSA: What about Cora?

MARY ELLEN: I needed those men! They were the pillars of the town. They could do as they pleased, but I couldn't. I had to sweep the thing under the rug. I had to protect my clients!

ROSA: What happened to Cora!

MARY ELLEN: She ended her life in Denver. That's the last I heard. Broken and broke.

ROSA: No one was ever charged?

MARY ELLEN: As far as the world knew, nothin' ever happened!

ROSA: Nobody said anything? You just all kept the dirty secret?

MARY ELLEN: Sometimes truth is dust, and you have to sweat and strain to find a itty-bitty little speck. Most people don't have the time.

ROSA: But you knew the truth! Others knew it!

MARY ELLEN: Someone offered me a bushel of money to tell what really happened at Geneva Cottage. He said, "You might as well take some money and go off somewheres and be Queen of the Niggers." I didn't need HIS money.

ROSA: I guess they wanted you out of their business.

MARY ELLEN: I suppose so. But I had 'em. I knew too much. It was all the same to me.

ROSA: Money and flesh. Free means so much more than that.

MARY ELLEN: A damned good start to being free. Money and flesh.

ROSA:: I don't believe that.

MARY ELLEN: Don't matter what you believe! Look at history, Rosa. You can't do nothin' without money. And wherever you find money, you sure gon' find a goodly amount of flesh!

ROSA: It's in the vote!

MARY ELLEN: You crazy if you believe that mess! To the victor goes the spoils. That means money and flesh! You can't win, you can't rule. You can't rule, you ain't free. And you can't do none of it without M-O-N-E-Y!

ROSA: Then what's the point of voting?

MARY ELLEN: I can't answer that one. You can't even get the vote without money!

ROSA: How do you know so much? Negroes weren't even voting in your day. Of course, you were busy with "Mr." Bell and his friends. Now, they could vote.

MARY ELLEN: Shoot! Wasn't nobody in my boardin' houses who couldn't vote.

ROSA: I get the picture, clear as day! Flesh and money! That's all you believe in. That's why you can't rest!

MARY ELLEN: Don't set yourself above me!

ROSA: The problem is where you set yourself.

MARY ELLEN: I know I'm right about money. Nothin's free! Not even the vote! Power is in the dollar. That's the truth!

ROSA: It's empty.

MARY ELLEN: What do you have against money?

ROSA: It's the greed that bothers me. Money, greed, power, slavery. It's all in the same mind set.

MARY ELLEN: That water done passed under the bridge. Ol' Newton Booth used to say, "Mary Ellen, now, that water done passed under the bridge!"

ROSA: Never heard of him.

MARY ELLEN: Governor of California, long before your time.

ROSA: Another one of your white men?

MARY ELLEN: He was governor. He talked sense.

ROSA: Did he give you some money?

MARY ELLEN: He ran his campaign out of my boardin' house. It wasn't free.

ROSA: Did you sleep with him, too?

(Mary Ellen cannot face this)

MARY ELLEN: *(Pulling her shawl around her shoulders)* The fog always rolls in, like a cold, damp quilt.

ROSA: *(Pulling her collar up)* There is a chill.

(The women walk to their respective benches, sit.)

(Lights dim.)

SCENE TWO

(Rosa and Mary Ellen are D.S. right and left in small circles of light.)

ROSA: *(to audience)* There was enough room for that man to sit. He didn't need my seat. He didn't have to touch my coat, my shopping bag or me!

MARY ELLEN: *(to audience)* Back when I had my places, sometimes one of 'em come in there thinkin' he was back down in Dixie. Actin' like he owned the place!

ROSA: *(to audience)* I didn't get on the bus with all that in mind.

MARY ELLEN: *(to Rosa)* Soon as my feet hit the docks, a bunch a men begun biddin' for my services as a cook! Mind you, they never asked me WHAT my business was. They seen a colored woman and BLAM, just like that, I had to be a cook!

(Mary Ellen re-enacts the auction for her services as a cook. It becomes too much a slave auction.)

(All bidding voices are male.)

VOICE: $100 a month plus a room!

VOICE: $150 with light housework!

VOICE: $200 over here! No work outside the kitchen!

VOICE: You want to hire her or marry her!!

VOICE: I wouldn't marry a coon? Not me!!

VOICE: Take her but never marry her! I'll be her master, alright!

VOICE: I'll pay $300! Haven't had a decent meal in—

VOICE: You're not a decent man!!

(The men laugh.)

VOICE: $400 and cook what you like!

VOICE: Good teeth! Now turn around and show the rest!

VOICE: $500 is my last bid!

ALL VOICES: SOLD!!

(Lights to black.)

(Mary Ellen resumes her seat.)

(Lights to full.)

MARY ELLEN: I give a piece of my heart to see once again the looks on their faces when they come in my first boarding house and seen me—the cook AND the owner! *(Mary Ellen runs to Rosa)* They cannot roll that stone! You have to stop them, Rosa, you must!

ROSA: *(sadly)* All I have to do is pay taxes and die.

MARY ELLEN: Is that all you want on your marker? "Here lies Rosa Parks. She refused to give up her seat to a white man on a bus, she paid her taxes and she died." Slim pickins for the obit writers.

ROSA: I don't know what it is I'm supposed to do!?

MARY ELLEN: Hear me! He asked me to pick a wife for him!

ROSA: Who?

MARY ELLEN: Mr. Bell.

ROSA: Will you please stop calling him "MR." Bell?

MARY ELLEN: I'll try. Did you hear me?

ROSA: I did. But I truly don't understand.

MARY ELLEN: I tried to put my pride away!

ROSA: Pride?

MARY ELLEN: You're not hearin' me!

ROSA: I don't like what I'm hearing!!

MARY ELLEN: I got to thinkin', if he had to have a wife, I'd better be the one to pick her.

ROSA: I don't like this.

MARY ELLEN: He needed a white wife for the world...for business.

ROSA: Ah. The white wife. I don't see how you can separate a heart like that.

MARY ELLEN: You think too much.

ROSA: And thank God, I do. So here you are pickin' a wife for the man you say you loved. *(then)* What was she like?

MARY ELLEN: She wasn't unpleasin' to the eye. After I cleaned her up. On the lazy side.

ROSA: Now I've heard everything.

MARY ELLEN: I saved her! Cleaned her up! Taught her how to behave in good company and she thanked me by throwing me out of my own house!

ROSA: Why does this all sound familiar? Your house?

MARY ELLEN: I built it. It was mine. We lived in it.

ROSA: All of you?

MARY ELLEN: Folks started callin' it the House of Mystery.

ROSA: Once he married her, you stayed around there?

MARY ELLEN: It was my house.

ROSA: What did you do?

MARY ELLEN: I headed the household. *(she jangles her keys)* I had control of the keys and the money. I could do as I pleased....

ROSA: You call that "as you pleased"?! You made yourself the housekeeper in your own house? No love would have me sufferin' through that kind of nonsense.

MARY ELLEN: You never allowed it is all.

ROSA: Somebody to just walk all over me? Rather be by myself.

MARY ELLEN: You never met a man and knew there was something between you that went beyond marriage love, children love, father love and mother love?

ROSA: Never happened!

MARY ELLEN: I bet it happened in your mind.

ROSA: A lot of things happen in my mind.

MARY ELLEN: Be true to yourself!

ROSA: We can imagine plenty that we can't do. Better not do!

MARY ELLEN: You mean won't do.

(Rosa gets far away from Mary Ellen.)

ROSA: I never experienced anything like you describe!

MARY ELLEN: Worse things went on. I bet you dreamed it.

ROSA: What?

MARY ELLEN: Dreamed so hard about passion—

ROSA: That's enough!

MARY ELLEN: I knew it!

ROSA: Knew what? Stop digging around in my dreams!

MARY ELLEN: Stop lying!

ROSA: There's no sense in discussing it! Dreams are for the night!

MARY ELLEN: Shoot! I was always scuffling to keep up with my dreams! Day or night!

ROSA: *(quietly)* My real dreams never had the strength to get up off the pillow. Sometimes they tried so hard...maybe they'd get up and sit beside the bed. I'd be so happy to see them facing me, awake. But soon they'd tire and lay back down. My dreams would sleep. I'd close my eyes and pray they'd come back and sit there again. My dreams weren't about your kind of passion. They were dreams of a different sort. Dreams of freedom, dignity—

MARY ELLEN: There you go with that Joan of Arc stuff again! That's fine but I believe that's not all there is.

ROSA: Who cares what you believe! My husband and I shared the same dream. We used to talk to the children, tell them about self-respect, about not fighting against one another...

MARY ELLEN: When you stop swoonin' over that, you might get down to what it takes to carry on. Just make sure you leave something so folks know you were here!

ROSA: EVERY LIFE'S NOT WORTH A STORY!

MARY ELLEN: MINE IS!

ROSA: That's a matter of opinion! I'm too tired to fool with your story and your stone, too!

MARY ELLEN: I never heard of such foolishness! You can't sit down yet cause your spirit is too strong!

ROSA: I'm a Christian woman and my spirit will rest in the kingdom of Heaven. And you will have nothing to do with it!

MARY ELLEN: Your spirit will walk the earth!

ROSA: How can you control my spirit? Who gives you the right? I don't even know you! You were dead before I was even born! You're tugging at me like a nightmare!

MARY ELLEN: Nightmares are lessons, too!

ROSA: You weren't in my life!

MARY ELLEN: Oh? Calm down and listen...cause I'm truly runnin' out of time.

ROSA: I don't want to hear anymore!

MARY ELLEN: I believe she killed Mr. Bell to get him out of the way!

ROSA: You're making it all up to confuse me! Stop it! Maybe you killed him!

MARY ELLEN: I loved him! I was only free with him!

ROSA: I feel sorry for you.

MARY ELLEN: It was 1892. Bell had been ailin' for some time. Seems like the sicker he got, the stronger she got.

ROSA: How old was he?

MARY ELLEN: 70.

ROSA: He was going to die anyway, woman. Now leave me alone and let me go on home.

(In this telling, Mary Ellen cries, blows her nose, behaves like a lovesick school girl. Some of it is real and some just for Rosa's benefit.)

MARY ELLEN: On that night, I was resting in my room, the door slightly cracked so I could hear all comings and goings. Mr. Bell—

ROSA: What was his given name?

MARY ELLEN: Thomas.

ROSA: Use it. Please.

MARY ELLEN: Thomas left his room. I had been nursing him back and he could walk around inside the house comfortably. I thought nothing of it. Then a few short minutes later I heard him scream, then a loud thump. I went runnin' but it was too late. He was in a heap at the bottom of the stairs in the House of Mystery!

ROSA: Maybe he fell.

MARY ELLEN: I could smell her perfume all around his body like a ghost.

ROSA: Did you call the police?

MARY ELLEN: I did. She was no where to be found in the house. When she arrived the next morning, she fainted with the news of her dear husband's death. She put on quite a show.

ROSA: You taught her well.

MARY ELLEN: Did you have to say that?

ROSA: Yes.

MARY ELLEN: As long as he was alive, I was goin' to be right there with him. Without him, I found I was a naked child in a storm. That's when my troubles began.

ROSA: Her's were sure over!

MARY ELLEN: She didn't have no troubles! She got just what she wanted! If I hadn't married her off to him, she woulda ended up makin' $5.00 every 20 minutes between two shacks in the mud!

ROSA: Did you ever have one quiet, dull, normal day in your entire life?

MARY ELLEN: Not that I can recall.

   (*Rosa walks a bit*)

ROSA: She sure had a motive.

MARY ELLEN: They tried to say I killed him! She put me out and took everything!

ROSA: She was his wife.

MARY ELLEN: She didn't do nothing but spend money.

ROSA: That's all she had to do. What else was she supposed to do?

MARY ELLEN: Something! Die! She was supposed to die! Not him!

ROSA: I don't want you to say that! Don't say that...don't even think it!

MARY ELLEN: In the end, it was her story. She won.

ROSA: Some victory. She suffered years watching you two.

MARY ELLEN: She didn't suffer for love cause she never loved him.

ROSA: Not for love. It must have twisted her soul that you had the keys to the kingdom...his kingdom anyway.

MARY ELLEN: That was his choice.

ROSA: He must have been the happiest man on earth. Playing musical beds in the House of Mystery! Lord!

MARY ELLEN: He did. He was.

ROSA: But he loved you.

MARY ELLEN: He did. (*then not so sure*) I think he did.

ROSA: You have worn me out!

MARY ELLEN: What are you goin' to do now?

ROSA: I don't know.

MARY ELLEN: Good way to run a life.

ROSA: Why didn't you see to your own truth? Why did—

MARY ELLEN: Time just slipped away is all.

ROSA: It does that.

MARY ELLEN: I was so busy livin'. Well, I should have taken the time.

ROSA: Yes.

MARY ELLEN: You still got time.

ROSA: Me? I wouldn't know where to begin.

MARY ELLEN: With the anger. The anger that never spoke.

ROSA: It was everywhere. In everyone. A plague of angers so hideous you could cut your own heart out for a moment of peace.

MARY ELLEN: I'm talking about yours.

ROSA: My arms were angry. My legs. My stomach. My heart.

MARY ELLEN: Let go of it!

ROSA: I don't know how!

MARY ELLEN: Oh, just let your hair down!

ROSA: Out here in public!

MARY ELLEN: Ain't nobody here but us!

> (*Rosa looks at Mary Ellen. Makes a decision to proceed and starts to take her hair down, then stops abruptly.*)

ROSA: One thing. In that house. What did you do when he went to her?

MARY ELLEN: Walked the floor...

ROSA: A woman would walk the floor tearing at her hair and cleaning out closets.

MARY ELLEN: Yes.

ROSA: Alright then. (*Rosa paces as she continues taking pins out of her hair.*) My name is Rosa Louise Parks...(*she looks to Mary Ellen*) It's a good place to start...with my name. (*she looks to the heavens*) Oh, Lord, my rock, be not silent to me!

MARY ELLEN: It ain't in heaven, Rosa!

ROSA: Can't you see I'm trying to find it!

MARY ELLEN: Put more in it! I thought you said it was all over you? Can't be that hard to find!

ROSA: (*starting again*) My name is Rosa Louise Parks. I'd like to...Oh what good is it?

MARY ELLEN: It's at the bottom. It's the thread! It's the part you never show!

ROSA: But it wasn't just anger!

MARY ELLEN: Then what? Let it fly! Let your spirit free!

ROSA: *(caught up in Mary Ellen's pushing and pulling pins out fast as her hair falls down her face and back)* I bet you thought I was shy! Well, I'm not! I'm more what you call reserved. That's different. I came up in the South. I was taught to be a lady in the old way. Being shy means you feel like you don't have anything to say..that would interest anyone. Now, I always had plenty to say—

MARY ELLEN: Hurry on to the point now! It's gettin' late!

ROSA: Alright! Alright! *(she clears her throat)* That unfortunate, nameless man who wanted my seat on the bus in 1955, didn't know that I, Rosa Parks, had been put off the bus by the same driver over 10 years earlier—

(Mary Ellen dances around.)

MARY ELLEN: I knew it! I knew it!

ROSA: Please, control yourself. Now, that was back in 19 and 43. In those days, Negroes...

MARY ELLEN: *(In a groaning stage whisper)* The colored!

ROSA: NEGROES had to board the bus at the front, pay the fare, then get off and re-board through the back door. Sometimes the driver would drive off before you got to the back door. Just leave you standing there on the curb after you'd already paid the fare!

MARY ELLEN: They wouldn'a drove off and left me! Shoot!

ROSA: Yes, they would, too! Now, hush! Now then, one day back in '43, I boarded the bus by the front door, paid the fare and proceeded to look for a seat. Just like those of the opposite race. If looks could kill, I wouldn't be here to tell it. The bus driver, James Blake, stopped the bus, came down the aisle and put me off. I'll never forget his face. Well, guess who was sitting in the driver's seat, Thursday, December 1, 1955? The same man, old James Blake!

VOICE OF JAMES BLAKE: Next stop, Empire Theater!

(Rosa is "seated on the bus.")

ROSA: *(to herself)* I don't know what he's looking at. He must think this seat's got his name on it.

VOICE OF JAMES BLAKE: Y'all git up now, so that gentleman can sit down.

ROSA: *(to herself)* I'm not getting up today.

VOICE OF JAMES BLAKE: Go on, now! Y'all better make it light on yo-selves and let me have all those seats!

(JAMES BLAKE comes down the aisle and stands over Rosa.)

JAMES BLAKE: You gon' git out that seat?

ROSA: I'm sitting in no-man's land. I don't have to get up.

VOICE OF JAMES BLAKE: Then, I'm gon' have to call the police.

ROSA: You may do that.

VOICE OF JAMES BLAKE: You under arrest, charged with violatin' the segregation laws of the City of Montgomery, the Sovereign State of Alabama!

(Sound of jail door closing, locking.)

ROSA: I'm here to tell you that unless I talked about that day on the bus, nobody cared what was in my mind. Nobody asked me what came before the bus or what came after. As if on that day, December 1, 1955, everything else in my heart just stopped. Nobody wants to be a one note song, with no call to do nothing. I was a woman with a pillow full of dreams. Back when I was a little girl in the country...The things you learn out in the country. *(she pauses)* Mr. Price lived down the road. One day, he went walking and never came back. That first day, his sister, Miss Driggs, came to our door looking for him. There were times when Mr. Price would come sit on our screened porch and talk with my daddy. But not this time. We hadn't seen Mr. Price in quite a while. On a day so hot the flies stopped flying, a bunch of us children ran to the lake. Really wasn't nothing but a pond. It was our favorite summertime thing to do. Little Lincoln was the best swimmer. He went all the way to the middle and just like a ol' fish, he went under. All of sudden, he flew straight up in the air, screaming at the top of his lungs. We thought maybe he came face to face with a water mocasin so we cleared out. Lincoln made it to the bank, choking and crying. "Mr. Price's down there, all tied up with a rock on his feet!" At first we thought he was kidding around trying to scare us. But little Lincoln was crying so we knew that he was telling the truth. We dragged our wet little bodies home talking quietly about poor Mr. Price and how did he get that rock on his feet? Did he get tangled up in a rope and fall in? Did he tie it on his own feet and jump in? At home, we told our parents who looked away, got busy with some chore. When we pressed and pushed about Mr. Price, my daddy said somebody would need some special equipment to get him out and we didn't have none of that. I lay there in my bed that night listening to them talking in anxious tones. Mr. Price's family insisted he had gone to Detroit. I heard my daddy say something about the white folks being mad at Mr. Price for something he owed them. I only knew I would never go swimming again. And that was the beginning of my fear. Alabama was a dreamy, thick place where even the movement of the trees was a command to shrink ever smaller. Those signs everywhere, "white entrance, colored entrance," "white drinking fountain, colored drinking fountain," "white school, colored school." And the colored was never close to equal. *(Freedom songs very low under the following, i.e. Sweet Honey and the Rock singing "Jacob's Ladder" or a slow version of "Ain't Gonna Let Nobody Turn Me Around")* I started working with children trying to put my heart between them and all the hatred swirling around them. I saw their eyes when busdrivers told them to get up so white children could sit down. I was with them when store clerks told them they couldn't use the restrooms. And I saw the spark of life grow dim in their eyes as they began to believe they were inferior. And when we tried to register to vote, there was the shout, "Niggers don't know nothin' 'bout no votin'!!" "You can't vote!" Lord, I pushed up against Alabama

every day of my life! It was my dreams that freed me. I dreamed of leading great hordes of people through the long corridors of death that criss
crossed the South! I studied it like a soldier! We would march through
the swamps, tearing at the strangling Spanish moss, crushing dead bones
in "Kill-a-Nigger Creek," Alabama. And we slept beneath the trees hud-
dled in small groups, whispering slogans, mapping strategies and singing
songs of freedom! *(Rosa stops)* Dear Lord, I don't know what got into me!

MARY ELLEN: I don't know.

ROSA: It's getting late!

MARY ELLEN: It is.

ROSA: *(slowly starting again)* The night was black as pitch. I was walking down
a road, then running. I was running for my life, with the ghost of Mr. Price
on my heels. It seemed he was calling for help but I could only feel terror.
When I stopped, there was no one there. I was alone. Fear had embod-
ied itself in my mind. I rested in the May grass, smelling night jasmine
around me like a sweet veil. I took off my clothes and stood still in the
moonlight. NO fear. Free. Finally free.

MARY ELLEN: I spend my whole life making history and you spent one day.
Half the world knows you and I'm not even a memory!

ROSA: You are cruel! It wasn't just one day. And it wasn't just me! It was a
lifetime that took me to that day on the bus. It was every dream of freedom, every ugly slight, every name called. Jigaboo, nigger, tar baby,
mammy, coon! It was all those who went before and those who're still
coming!

MARY ELLEN: Me! I went before!

ROSA: Yes, you. Now, can I go home!

MARY ELLEN: No!

ROSA: I'll come back.

MARY ELLEN: I'll be gone.

(Blackout.)

SCENE THREE

(Lights Up.)

(The two women have retreated to their benches.)

ROSA: Lord, being a Negro is sure a white water run! Never know where
you're going, how long it's going to take to get there or how many spills
you'll have along the way!

MARY ELLEN: Boat better be built for rough water.

ROSA: And hurricanes!

MARY ELLEN: Rosie!!

(Rosa looks hard at her.)

MARY ELLEN: *(cont.)* Rosa. Just supposin' being colored was the thing most desirous! What if, in all the world, it was the thing most precious?

ROSA: I can't even imagine it!

MARY ELLEN: Try!

ROSA: Wouldn't that be something!

MARY ELLEN: Put some money on it! That would do the trick!

ROSA: The Negro Lottery! It's the Negro Lottery!!

(The following is an exaggerated spin on the old "coon" show, both women exaggerating gestures and words.)

MARY ELLEN: If you make it mean money, everybody be tryin' to be colored!!

ROSA: You can win up to 10 million dollars in the Negro Lottery!!!

MARY ELLEN: AND YOU CAN'T EVEN PLAY 'LESS YOU CAN PROVE YOU'RE COLORED!!

ROSA: White people would go plumb crazy tryin' to prove they were really Negro!

MARY ELLEN: A lot of us been passin' would be comin' home, too!

ROSA: They would, they would, you know they would!!!

MARY ELLEN: We'd have classes in walkin', talkin' and actin' Negro!

ROSA: You'd be teaching in the other direction!!!!

MARY ELLEN: White folks would dig up all those long lost wood pile relatives and march them home for supper.

ROSA: With a stop in the kitchen to cook up some greens, ham hocks and some black eye peas!

MARY ELLEN: I could teach classes in carryin' baskets and pots on your head!

ROSA: I might take that myself! Classes in being Aunt Jemimas, Uncle Toms and Mammies!

(The word Mammy stops Mary Ellen.)

MARY ELLEN: We still do that?

ROSA: Sometimes. Classes in hip swinging, gum cracking and dressing people down!

MARY ELLEN: *(No longer in the moment)* In goin' to church and doin' it right!

ROSA: IN NEVER BEING ON TIME!!!

MARY ELLEN: It would be a hoot and a howl.

(Rosa walks off to the side.)

ROSA: Classes in pain and suffering.

MARY ELLEN: And singing about it.

ROSA: In dreams that never get up off the pillow.

MARY ELLEN: So many dead and dying dreams. That's why you need to get this thing straight. About me, I mean!

ROSA: Why didn't your own children see to your stone? And how long have you been dead, anyway? That dress is styled over 100 years ago. How come they're just getting to your stone now? And whose doing it?

MARY ELLEN: No money, no stone! No stone, no story. They been plucking at my remains for years making me what they want me to be.

ROSA: No children?

MARY ELLEN: A daughter. Lizzie. I raised her, give her a real fine weddin' and sent her on her way.

ROSA: I never heard of such a thing!

MARY ELLEN: It wasn't my fault!

ROSA: To hear you tell it, nothin' is ever your fault!

MARY ELLEN: I didn't want her to leave! I just wanted her to leave me alone about my comin's and goin's. She could have stayed right there with me. I had so much. It would have been hers. Only she didn't want it.

ROSA: Maybe she didn't like the way you got it. Poor Lizzie!

MARY ELLEN: She was poor by choice.

ROSA: It's done now. Your truth. Mine. I don't know what it is anymore.

MARY ELLEN: Cause it's buried so deep.

ROSA: I can't help you.

MARY ELLEN: I just want people to know who I really am!

ROSA: You mean, "were."

MARY ELLEN: I want you to oversee the legacy of my life.

ROSA: Why me?

MARY ELLEN: Who better?

ROSA: We're so different! I've tried to live my life like a good Christian. You—

MARY ELLEN: Livin' a good Christian life is like dyin'!

ROSA: Listen to you! You can't help yourself! You wake up and let me out of this nightmare right now!!! *(She goes to her bench to collect her things)* Some victories aren't worth what we give up to win them.

(Mary Ellen digs around in her parcels for her newspaper clippings.)

MARY ELLEN: Newspapers wrote 'bout me, plenty of times!

ROSA: Newspapers would follow a mule over a cliff.

MARY ELLEN: *(Trying to give clippings to her)* Here. You read them. Might surprise you how popular I was.

ROSA: Nothing would surprise me now.

MARY ELLEN: Go ahead. Read them.

(Rosa takes the clippings.)

ROSA: I can't read nothing without my glasses.

MARY ELLEN: Hurry now. It's getting late.

ROSA: Stop rushing me! Let me get these glasses on.

MARY ELLEN: Gettin' mighty uppity, Miss Rosa!

ROSA: Been uppity! *(Rosa selects a clipping and reads half to herself, half aloud)* "Sunday, July 9, 1899. The San Francisco Chronicle The Queen of the Voodoos!" *(Rosa looks at Mary Ellen)* Guess they had you pegged.

MARY ELLEN: If brains is colored, they call 'em "voodoo." If brains is white, they call 'em smart. Keep readin'.

ROSA: Never thought of it—

MARY ELLEN: *(pacing)* Read, woman!

ROSA: *(reading)* "The remarkable career of Mammy Pleasant, and her wonderful influence over men and women. Mammy Pleasant, the mild-mannered"—Lord, who wrote this?

MARY ELLEN: It's not joke!

ROSA: "...mild-mannered old Southern Mammy, with her spotless apron, neckerchief and her clanking bunch of keys—*(Mary Ellen clanks her keys)* "has been for many years the most discussed woman in San Francisco."

MARY ELLEN: Ain't I something?!!

ROSA: *(dryly)* You are, indeed. Or, were.

MARY ELLEN: Keep reading!

ROSA: *(selecting a clipping)* "THE CALL, Friday, December 18, 1901. Mammy Pleasant lays claim to real estate and jewels owned by Mr. Theresa Bell."

MARY ELLEN: They were not her jewels! They were mine!

ROSA: *(selecting another clipping)* "Dark Skinned Lion Tamer in the House of Mystery. Mammy Pleasant: In Whose Heart Lie Buried the Secrets of the Bell Family." No wonder they want to roll your stone! *(Rosa selects another clipping)* "Angel or Arch Fiend in the House of Mystery, Occult Power of Mammy over widow of millionaire." "THE ELEVATOR, October 26, 1866, refers to the suit of Mrs. Mary Ellen Pleasant against the Omnibus Company for ejecting her from the cars."

MARY ELLEN: You didn't believe me, did you? You thought I made the whole thing up! And I won! Just like you, I won!!

(Rosa is flipping back through the clippings.)

(Mary Ellen tries to take the clippings back.)

MARY ELLEN: That's enough, now! Give them back!

ROSA: What are you doing? I'm not finished yet!!

MARY ELLEN: Yes, you are!

ROSA: Wait a minute, now! *(She has the clippings)* What I want to know is who is this "Mammy" person they wrote about in these clippings?

MARY ELLEN: That's what they called me sometimes.

ROSA: Looks like all the time to me. They called you "Mammy"? They called you out of your name like that?

MARY ELLEN: Ain't that something!

ROSA: Well, how did they come to call you that?

MARY ELLEN: It started in the boardin' houses. You know, it made some of the customers feel right at home, havin' someone walkin' around wearin' a big apron—

ROSA: Someone? You! A bunch of white men being served by a Negro woman and they start callin' you "Mammy"?!!!

MARY ELLEN: It just caught on!

ROSA: Did you tell them to call you "Mammy"?

MARY ELLEN: I DIDN'T GIVE A GOOD GOD DAMN WHAT THEY CALLED ME AS LONG AS THEY PAID FOR WHAT THEY GOT!!!

ROSA: That's the very kind of thing we need to be free of!

MARY ELLEN: And that's why you don't have a pot to piss in or a window to throw it out of! Too damned grand!

ROSA: Grand or not, I am master of my own soul and you running around here trying to find yours.

MARY ELLEN: You can't spend it! Take it to the bank, throw it up on the counter and say, "Can I have some money for my good soul?" They'll throw YOU in the the Stockton Insane Asylum!

ROSA: Put that on your old stone! "HERE LIES MAMMY PLEASANT, SERVANT OF WHITE MEN!" Oh, no, you won't maneuver your way to dignity through me, lady!

MARY ELLEN: Nobody cares anyway!

ROSA: I care.

MARY ELLEN: Names don't mean nothin' anyway!!

ROSA: Did "Mr." Bell call you "Mammy," too?

MARY ELLEN: No.

ROSA: Tell the truth, for once!

MARY ELLEN: He had to! That's how I made my money! In front of the guests in the boardin' houses, he had to!

ROSA: "MR." Bell and "MAMMY" Pleasant! If that don't beat all. (she stops dead) Did he call you "Mammy" behind closed doors? (Mary Ellen is gathering her things, afraid, ready to depart her own dream) Was it like that? ANSWER ME, WOMAN!!

MARY ELLEN: It doesn't matter now. It's over. My dream has become my nightmare.

ROSA: You're not going anywhere until we get this straight! That's why you can't rest!

MARY ELLEN: I'm Mary Ellen Pleasant. And Mammy Pleasant. Just like every colored woman.

ROSA: No, not every colored woman.

MARY ELLEN: I don't know how to NOT be both.

ROSA: Who do you see when you look in the mirror?

MARY ELLEN: Depends on the day.

ROSA: You are a mess. What do you feel? What's in your heart?

MARY ELLEN: I DON'T KNOW ANYMORE!

ROSA: FIND IT, THEN!

(Mary Ellen paces frantically.)

MARY ELLEN: I come to San Francisco during the Gold Rush time...to get as far away from slavery as I could get...and to make some M-O-N-E-Y. There's some folks who think I come up from slavery. But I was never no slave. NEVER!

ROSA: You probably told people that lie yourself!

MARY ELLEN: No, I did not! Let me see, now. Did I tell anyone I come up from slavery? It was a long time ago. No, I don't remember any such tellin'. They just thought it.

ROSA: Maybe, just maybe, it's that get up you're wearing.

MARY ELLEN: I was raised up in Nantucket, by some Quakers. I guess that didn't sound helpless enough to suit folks. If you was colored, you had to come from slavery. I fancied myself with a good head for business. Good as any man walkin'. I was a free woman in a time when bein' a woman meant you had chains on your life. San Francisco was wide open! Shoot! I could see real quick what would sell to those white folks! Wasn't nothin' there but a lot of mud and wild men runnin' 'round half crazy over gold! Wasn't nothin' a man wouldn't do for some gold!

ROSA: A woman either, it seems.

MARY ELLEN: *(into telling the story of her life with gusto)* I set out to make my boardin' houses the most sought after in the city. To be a public servant and a private millionaire. This Mammy apron was my armor. They begun callin' me that and I didn't tell them not to. Kept my mouth shut and went straight to the bank! Pretty soon, it was "Mammy Pleasant" this and "Mammy Plesant" that!

ROSA: *(stage whisper)* Mammies suckled the men who grew up to choke us!

(Mary Ellen looks at Rosa)

MARY ELLEN: Now, did you have to say that?

ROSA: YES!

MARY ELLEN: It wasn't the same as in Dixie! It wasn't like that!

ROSA: I'd sure like to know how it was different. You gave them comfort and they gave us misery.

MARY ELLEN: But they paid for what they got. That made it different!

ROSA: Did it?

MARY ELLEN: I used that money well, Rosa! I did! I give people jobs in my places...runaways...freedmen comin' to San Francisco with not a farthin'!

ROSA: There's hope for you yet.

MARY ELLEN: I was havin' the time of my life entertaining the wealthiest men in the city! They all come to me! First, they brought their gold, then they brought their troubles. My ears were big but my lips were tight. I kept their secrets close. It was a kind of power—this knowing the worst and the best. I used it for Bell, and I used it for myself. They talked at table and I listened well. "Put your gold in railroad stock, buy that land over there." A roll of the dice, and we were winning! Then everything began to change. The big hotels come and I had to close my places down. They commenced to actin' like they just dropped from the sky like spankin' brand new angels! They shut me out! When Mr. Bell died, they scrambled around diggin' up ways to get rid of me. Didn't matter that I knew where the bodies were buried. Didn't matter that I knew where they really come from. Oh, how they hated me. They wanted to erase me, to bury me and mark me for all time in some throw away name like "Mammy"! I never was no mammy to no one! You hear me?! I saw my heights with Mr. Bell, and when he was gone, I saw the darkness. I was alone. When it was over, they didn't name no streets for me, no buildings, no bridges. I helped build it, give it a glow. Everybody loved San Francisco!

(Mary Ellen leaves all her things and slowly exits talking herself out as she talked herself in.)

MARY ELLEN: *(cont.)* They wanted it to be like I never really knew them. Like I never walked these hills knowin' them. But I knew them! When it was all said and done, I was just another niggerwoman with a throwaway name like "Mammy." I was supposed to be something special.

(Mary Ellen is gone.)

SILENCE.

(Rosa walks to the pile of things left by Mary Ellen. She packs them with love and care. She looks one last time for the bus.)

ROSA: I can walk.

(Lights to black.)

(In the black, the gospel version of "This Little Light of Mine.")

Rob Penny

GOOD BLACK DON'T CRACK

Kuntu Repertory Theatre

Rob Penny

Rob Penny was born in Opelika, Alabama and raised in the Hill District of Pittsburgh, Pennsylvania. He is an Afrocentric poet and playwright. He began teaching in the formerly named Department of Black Studies, later named Department of Black Community Education Research and Development, now named Department of Africana Studies, University of Pittsburgh in 1969. He was the chairman of the department from 1978 through 1984. Presently, he is an associate professor, conducting course offerings in Afrikan American poetry and theatre. He is married to Timamu ("She who completes my life and makes it perfect") Betty Penny since 1959. Asante Sana. Hotep and Long Live Pan-Afrikanism.

Kuntu Repertory Theatre

Kuntu Repertory Theatre is part of the Department of Africana Studies of the University of Pittsburgh. It was founded in 1974 by Dr. Vernell A. Lillie. Kuntu usually stages three major productions a year.

Kuntu is a Bantu word meaning way or mode. Central to a Kuntu play/event as defined by Paul Carter Harrison is that "time/space, spirit/corpus, and social/moral exist within a forced field of reality." This forced field of reality is designed to move participants within the theatre to action for change or for retention of that which is productive.

As the only ongoing African American Theatre group in Pittsburgh, Kuntu provides African American actors, writers, and technicians a developmental outlet not generally available elsewhere. Perhaps more importantly, Kuntu provides the Pittsburgh community with a cultural voice which speaks to the African American experience throughout the diaspora which would otherwise be unheard. During a given year, through Kuntu's efforts, approximately 25,000 persons are exposed to contemporary as well as historical African American drama. While Kuntu encourages all persons to attend its presentations, special efforts are made to ensure that members of minority groups with low and limited incomes are included in the audiences. A certain percentage of complimentary tickets are always reserved for inner-city schools, drug abuse and other enabling programs, homes for the aged, and other dependent groups.

Kuntu has produced more than 60 plays since its inception. A notable performance was the 25th Anniversary Celebration of the Broadway production of Lorraine Hansberry's *A Raisin in the Sun* directed by Elizabeth Van Dyke. The celebration included a one-woman show on Hansberry by Elizabeth Van Dyke, a seminar Master Class and 13 performances of *A Raisin in the Sun* featuring Esther Rolle. Kuntu has also sponsored many productions and workshops by women artists. A recent production was the premiere of *Union Station*, which won a Lorraine Hansberry Playwriting award for Kuntu member Marta Effinger. Kuntu also creates special works for specific groups and organizations, utilizing theatrical and psychodramatic techniques to educate and inform. For its 1990 season, KRT designed an eight week workshop for the Lemington Home for the Aged which included its preschool program, its senior adults, Kuntu members, and two young children from Holy Rosary Catholic School. The oldest member of the group was Ms. Georgia Brown, who was 104 years old. Through use of a psychodramatic approach to the theatre, participants produced an hour and a half show and a great baseball player in the Negro National League with Parkinson disease began to speak. Kuntu celebrated its 20th anniversary of its existence in 1994.

GOOD BLACK—DON'T CRACK
by Rob Penny

Cast in Order of Appearance

Phyllis	Karen Abercrombie
James, Jr	Norman C. Manuel
Janet	Ethel Parris
Dalejean	Sylvia J. Jelks
Rip	Terrance Calhoun
Kim	Gwendolyn Briley
Jimbo	Larry Tolbert
Jake	Ron Pitts
Valerie	Brenda Dunlap
Ernestine	Renee Berry
Sister Louise	Cheryl Pasteur
Snake	Billy Parker
Customer	Charles Coker
Customers	Pattie Banks, Joseph Cole, Yusef Ben Israel, Billy Parker

CHARACTERS:

DALEJEAN HARRIS: (42) *Uncompromising. Retains southern accent.*
JAMES HARRIS, JR: (17) *Black Cultural Nationalist neophyte.*
PHYLLIS HARRIS: (16) *More interested in boys. Discovery stage.*
JANET HARRIS: (13) *Loves to read.*
RIP MORTON: (34) *Easy going. Enjoys reading and music.*
JAKE: (47) *Sexually-aggressive. Workaholic. "Sophisticated."*
KIM: (20) *College student. Imposing, impulsive and intelligent.*
SISTER LOUISE: (51) *Religious. Humorous on the serious side.*

SETTINGS:

Dalejean's House (Living Room): Arcena Street
Rip's Apartment: Centre Avenue
Jake's Restaurant: Wylie Avenue
PLACE: Hill District, Pittsburgh, Pennsylvania
TIME: 1972
MUSIC:

Clyde McPhatter and The Drifters' version of "White Christmas"; Charles Brown's "Merry Christmas Baby"; Bull Moose Jackson's "I'll Be Home For Christmas."

ACT ONE PULSE ONE
(AT RISE: HARRIS' FRONT ROOM)

PHYLLIS: Well, it's me! You don't tell me what to do or what to wear. You're not my father.

JAMES JR.: Phyllis, if you knew how you looked in...

PHYLLIS: How I look is my business.

JAMES JR.: Yeah, ok, you got that.

PHYLLIS: Doggone right, I got it.

JAMES JR.: But how you look...how you dress...

PHYLLIS: Go on.

JAMES JR.: I will—if you stop running off at the lip and listen.

PHYLLIS: Listen to you. Humph. I know what you're going to say before you open your mouth, brother.

JAMES JR.: Sure, Phyllis, sure. But how you dress tells something about you. Let's everyone know what's on your mind.

JANET: Leave her alone, James Jr.

PHYLLIS: Now, Janet, don't tell him nothing. *(TO JAMES JR.)* What is on my mind, mind reader?

JAMES JR.: You don't have a mind.

PHYLLIS: Bet-bet.

JAMES JR.: Miniskirts and dresses above your knees.

PHYLLIS: So. It's me.

JAMES JR.: People can see, Phyllis. Then they form ideas about you based upon what they perceive. Overexposure removes the mystery of womanhood and leaves you a dull, uninteresting person. An object.

PHYLLIS: Boy, you're so smart, you know that. Maybe I have something worth looking at.

JAMES JR.: Get outta my face, Phyllis.

JANET: Why don't you two stop it.

PHYLLIS: Well, you tell old blacker-than-thou to get out of my life. He's your brother.

JAMES JR.: Jan, you'd better get her.

JANET: Phyllis, you're acting crazy too.

PHYLLIS: Have to get your lil half-sister to hold you, huh? I thought you were suppose to be so black and bad.

JAMES JR.: Forget it, Phyllis.

PHYLLIS: Naw, I want to know what's on my mind when I wear my clothes above my knees, no, as you say, above my navel. Anyway, why are you looking, brother, what's on your mind?

JAMES JR.: Go on, Phyllis, mind your own business.

PHYLLIS: I was—

JAMES JR.: Keep on keeping on then.

JANET: Both of you—stop it.

PHYLLIS: Bet you know what's on Joanne Wilson's mind.

JAMES JR.: The devil's got your mind sowed-up backwards.

PHYLLIS: Sheed.

JANET: I'm going to tell Mom you cussed.

PHYLLIS: Tell.

JANET: I will too.

PHYLLIS: Who cares.

JAMES JR.: You negroes need to get your heads relined with some black values.

PHYLLIS: Ok, James Jr..., we know you're black black. But so what? So what?

JAMES JR.: So. Is that the only intelligent comment you can make?

PHYLLIS: Bet I'm intelligent enough to know a hypocrite when I see one, and you take the cake, blackie. But I'm not going for it. Trying to get me—and Janet—into one them long, ugly dresses. African garb.

JAMES JR.: See, you don't know what you're speaking on. Garb is short for garbage. That's what you wear...scraps and leftovers from...

PHYLLIS: Humph, is that right? Now what you should be doing, that is, if you can take some advice—from a negro—is to get Joanne Wilson out of her minis and into an African dress. Hell, she wears the shortest dress in Schenley. But you're getting some of her, that's why you don't say nothing to her.

JANET: Oooooo.

JAMES JR.: Phyllis, you know what, you eat too much pork. Boy, are you sick.

PHYLLIS: Sick! Me? Sick of you, yeah. Nobody can say a word to you unless you jumping down their throats. Just to prove how black you are and how much you think you know. Nobody can tell you nothing.

JAMES JR.: You can't. You don't have the ability. I hate to say this, Phyllis, but one of these nights somebody's going to snatch yo lil behind into an alley or—

PHYLLIS: Bet I won't call for you, brother. I can take care of myself. Don't you worry about me, hear?

JAMES JR.: I do.

PHYLLIS: Don't.

JAMES JR.: And I worry about your values, too.

PHYLLIS: Like, I said—don't.

JAMES JR.: Ok, forget it. Look, I got to go to a meeting. *(PICKS UP HIS SNEAKERS)* But, I'm worried about you, Phyllis.

PHYLLIS: Aw, you're going to make me cry. Boo-hoo.

JAMES JR.: Remember; Mom's going to catch you one of these nights down here with Snake or when you come tipping in the crib just ahead of her.

PHYLLIS: That's what you hope. But it'll never happen.

JAMES JR.: Ok, Miss Slick with the snake.

PHYLLIS: His name is not snake.

(DALEJEAN IS SEEN WALKING DOWN THE STAIRS: SHE STOPS.)

JAMES JR.: He is a snake.

PHYLLIS: At least he's not as ugly as you.

JANET: I'm going upstairs and tell Mom on you two. You know she gets up and goes to work around this time.

PHYLLIS: Dag, Jan, you know Mom doesn't go straight to work; she goes to see that man who calls here...

JANET: I'm still going to tell.

PHYLLIS: You what? If you make a move, I'll beat your black you-know-what too.

JAMES JR.: Look how you talk to your lil sistuh.

PHYLLIS: Half-sister.

JANET: Phyllis, you making me mad now.

JAMES JR.: Been made me mad.

PHYLLIS: All of us is half. *(POINTING)* Half. Half. and Half.

JAMES JR.: We family.

JANET: That's right. Phyllis, sometimes you act-like a knuckle head.

PHYLLIS: *(GRABS JANET)* I told you never to call me out of my name, did-n't I?

JANET: Let me go. I'm going to tell Mom.

PHYLLIS: Over me, huh?

JANET: And I'm going to tell Mom how you leave me in this house by myself too.

JAMES JR.: Let her go, Phyllis.

PHYLLIS: You lil book-reader, you make me—

(JANET BREAKS AWAY AND RUNS TOWARDS THE STAIRS.)

JANET: *(SURPRISED)* Mom.

DALEJEAN What's going on down here?

(SHE GRABS JANET BY THE HAND.)

PHYLLIS: Nothing. Mom. We were just…playing.

DALEJEAN Play—I could hear yall in Alabama. What's all this talk about half? I didn't tell youns you was half anything, did I? Well did I?

ALL THREE: No ma'am.

DALEJEAN: *(TO PHYLLIS)* You started this, didn't you?

PHYLLIS: Me?

JANET: She didn't mean it like that, Mom.

DALEJEAN: Oh…how did she mean it, Janet? *(PAUSE)* Well? You got no answer, huh? I didn't thank so. Let me tell yall something. I had all three of youns—the same way too. There was no half pain and no half love about it. No half nothing. And if I ever smell youns talking about each other that way again, I'll break each of yo necks and thank nothing of it. I don't care what you hear out in the streets, just don't bring no mess in my house. Hear me?

ALL THREE: Yes ma'am.

DALEJEAN: *(TO PHYLLIS)* Now what's all this talk about you staying out all night until three in the morning and just beating me in the house?

PHYLLIS: I didn't stay out that late, Mom.

DALEJEAN: So it's true, huh?

PHYLLIS: Mom…

DALEJEAN: How long…how many times have you stayed out later than I told you too?

PHYLLIS: Just—just a few times.

DALEJEAN: James Jr., is that true?

JAMES JR.: I oun't—I guess so, Mom..

DALEJEAN: Girl, where was you at 4 o'clock in the morning?

PHYLLIS: It wasn't 4—

DALEJEAN: Don't you try to correct me. You know what I means. What was you doing? What could a sixteen year old girl be doing out at that time. Answer me.

PHYLLIS: Nothing...Mom...please...

DALEJEAN: Where?

PHYLLIS: In the projects.

DALEJEAN: What projects?

PHYLLIS: On Whiteside Road.

DALEJEAN: Now what mother would have a girl yo age in her house that...I'm—I'm not going to put the blame on her whoever she is. I put the blame on me. For having to work the evenings until two in the morning. For slaving like a mule to bring food into this house. For keeping a roof over your heads. *(PHYLLIS IS MAKING NOISES UNDER HER BREATH.)* Keep it up, hear? Getting so smart 'round here, the next thing you'll be smoking reefer in the bathroom.

JANET: Naw, Mom, Phyllis don't mess with that stuff.

JAMES JR.: That's right, Mom.

DALEJEAN: Well—Oh before I forget, whoever this boy is you been sneaking around with—just you pop up with a baby...see if you can mumble up a carton of Similac or a box of Pampers. *(NOTICING HOW IMPATIENT JAMES JR. IS)* and what's wrong with you, where you itching to get to?

JAMES JR.: Down to the Afro-American Cultural Center. You are coming to our Community Series Program tomorrow, Mom?

DALEJEAN: I don't know. But I'll try. *(SHE TURNS HER ATTENTION TO JANET.)* No wonder my baby's become a jumping rabbit around here every time the wind touches this house. Leaving her alone by herself. Phyllis, you should be ashamed of yourself. And talking about whipping somebody's hiney. Girl you ain't hardly birthed no babies in this world to...

PHYLLIS: *(LEAPS UP. ALMOST IN TEARS)* Why you picking on me?

JANET: *(BURSTING OUT BEFORE DALEJEAN CAN SPEAK)* James Jr. started it. He started it. He always says something to make Phyllis mad.

DALEJEAN: Oh he does, does he?

JANET: Yes ma'am. Just because we wanted a Christmas tree and we asked him to get one for us—so we could surprise you, Mom. But he doesn't believe in celebrating Christmas.

PHYLLIS: And we had to hear about that.

JANET: Then he gets mad at us because we won't call him by his African name.

DALEJEAN: Boy, yo father didn't give you no African name.

JANET: No ma'am, Kasisi Taifa gave it to him.

DALEJEAN: That true?

JAMES JR.: Yes ma'am. Mom, I—

DALEJEAN: Girl you know more than I do. Go on.

JANET: Well, he's always calling us niggaroes and-and pig-eaters. Mom, he be saying some nasty things when we're eating bacon in the morning.

DALEJEAN: He does. Like what?

JANET: How bacon shrivels up like a snake. That the pig'll eat a poisonous snake and won't die. That none of the different parts of the pig taste the same and yet they come from the same pig. Mom, I'm not making this up.

DALEJEAN: I believe you, honey. Just take yo time. Don't go so fast.

JANET: Well, he says the pig is one part rat, one part cat and one part dog.
(THE TELEPHONE RINGS. PHYLLIS STARTS FOR IT.)

DALEJEAN: Let it rang.

PHYLLIS: But it's for me.

DALEJEAN: How do you know it's for you? You're not the only one who gets phone calls around here. I said, let it rang, sistuh. *(PAUSE)* That boy sure doesn't give up—

PHYLLIS: Bet it's Carol.

DALEJEAN: Girl, I'll smack the taste outta yo mouth. Just keep that tone in yo head, hear? I ain't but a gnat's eyelash off you. *(PHONE STOPS RING-ING.)* I got to go. But...nobody goes outta this house until I finish my reading.

JAMES JR.: But Mom.

DALEJEAN: What?

JAMES JR.: I got a meeting at the Cultural Center. Then the Simbas, we have to pass out leaflets in the community. Then we have play rehearsal. Then...

DALEJEAN: You too old to be picking on these girls, you hear? They yo sistuhs.

JAMES JR.: Yes ma'am. Phyllis...Jan...I'm sorry. Mom, we're performing our first play Sunday at our Soul Session.

DALEJEAN: I'll be calling back here every...better yet, every time I feels like it. And I expect to speak to each one of youns too.

JAMES JR.: Mom, my meeting...?

DALEJEAN: James Jr., you be home no latter than, say, 10:30. And Phyllis...

PHYLLIS: Yes ma'am.

JANET: Oh Mom, Mrs. Nelson was by this morning.

DALEJEAN: Oh Lawd, what did that woman want now?

JANET: She didn't say.

DALEJEAN: If I have time I'll holler at her before I... *(HOLDING HER NOSE...TO JAMES JR.)* Boy, those tennis shoes...I know you can smell, can't you?

JAMES JR.: What, Mom?

DALEJEAN: Yo feet, that's what. At seventeen, you should have more get up and go about yourself. Wash them socks. A dog will sniff them and fall out dead.

JANET: *(LAUGHING)* I told you.

DALEJEAN: And you're going to catch the walking pneumonia in the snow with them tennis shoes on.

(LIGHTS FADE OUT AND COME UP ON)

ACT ONE PULSE TWO
(RIP'S APARTMENT. KIM KNOCKS ON THE DOOR.)

RIP: It's open.

KIM: Hi, Rip, it's me.

RIP: Lil Bit. How you doing?

KIM: I'm great. Got any cocoa?

RIP: I was just fixing me a cup. Want to drink a cup with me?

KIM: You know I do. Oh here's your key. You like the way I rearranged the place?

RIP: I like it. Thanks. But you know I'm not helpless.

KIM: I know that. I asked to do it, didn't I? So I must've wanted to—on the real side.

RIP: *(BRINGING CUPS OF COCOA)* Here you are, Lil Bit.

KIM: I'm not all that little.

RIP: *(TOASTING)* To our world. OK?

KIM: Our world.

RIP: So how's your finals coming?

KIM: I lunched on one. Got three due next week. Then I'll be finished for the semester.

RIP: Blew the Dean's list?

KIM: No. I'll still make it. I wouldn't disappoint my parents; they've worked too hard for me to mess up.

RIP: Going home for Christmas?

KIM: I hate going back to the infamous Richard Allen Projects.

RIP: And the flow of infamous money orders.

KIM: Oh my parents don't send that much money. Times are too hard in Philly for that. No, my part time job pays my rent and buys a few groceries.

RIP: Never been to Philly. Heard you all still have gangs up there.

KIM: Not like it used to be when my father was growing up. The Black Muslims are taking over now.

Rip. Saving lives, you mean?

KIM: Yep. The last time I was home—for Thanksgiving—it seems as though a number of my high school friends had turnt Muslim. Got a cigarette?

RIP: My lungs are as pure as the day I was born, Lil Bit.

KIM: Oh that's right, you don't smoke. Or get high. What do you do, Rip? Drink?

RIP: Can't drink either, Lil Bit. Guess I don't do much of anything. Vietnam made me want to live as long as I can.

KIM: Everybody does something. Don't you commit any sins?

RIP: I like my Jazz albums. I do Ornette Coleman…Bill Dixon…

KIM: I like some Jazz. But not your kind. Rip, don't you have any fun? Aren't you adventurous?

RIP: Young people are adventurous.

KIM: You're not that old.

RIP: Kicking thirty-five. I'm cool enough to let people live as long as they let me live.

KIM: Well you're cool—Kool and the Gang. But you're right, though.

RIP: How's that?

KIM: Young people—I'm adventurous. I'd like to be a bright, shining apple rolling down the longest hill in the world. With the ability to stop whenever I want to and to do whatever I want to—right then and there. Get it over with. Out of my system Then keep stepping. Right now I'm more than old enough and you better not lunch on that, Rip.

RIP: Well, Lil Bit, you're still a sweet-milk drinker and a teddy bear hugger to me.

KIM: Don't try it. Hmmm, I just made up my mind about something.

RIP: What's that Lil Bit?

KIM: You. Before I go home for Christmas, I'm going to prove something to you.

RIP: Kim, you've proved to me that you're an intelligent young girl. You take that, melt it and pour it all over your body. Then you'll be a peace maker in the world.

KIM: I don't understand that.

RIP: You will. But don't let it bother you though.

KIM: Okay, I won't.

RIP: And for cleaning up my crib, here's a whole can of cocoa just for you.

KIM: Thanks, Rip. You're a kind man. Good too.

RIP: Well, I don't know about all that.

Kim. I do. I still think you'll make a nice hookup for me.

RIP: Now I don't know what you mean.

    (THE TELEPHONE RINGS.)

RIP: Hello. *(PAUSE)* Hey, Jimbo, what's happening. *(PAUSE)* I can't, Jimbo. Dalejean will be here. *(PAUSE)* In about twenty minutes. *(PAUSE)* Jimbo, I told you, she...*(PAUSE)* She's not leaving until about quarter to six. *(PAUSE)* Look, Jimbo...Look, you can cuz me all you want...I'm not interested in your friend's girlfriend. *(PAUSE)* Okay, Okay. You can bring them ladies by—after Dalejean leaves. But I'm not entertaining no one. *(PAUSE)* Bye. Later. *(TO HIMSELF)* That cousin of mines going to get me busted one of these days.

KIM: Well, I guess there goes my plans for this evening.

RIP: Huh? What did you say, Lil Bit?

KIM: I had planned to come back down so we could pop some popcorn together and watch T.V. But I see you'll be too tired out to be my company.

RIP: *(LOOKING AT HIS WATCH)* Maybe some other time, Lil Bit.

KIM: Sometimes you just make me so mad, I could scream. What the heck. Thanks for the cocoa, anyway.

RIP: You're welcome. I'll walk you to the door.

(LIGHTS FADE OUT AND COME UP ON)

(RIP'S APARTMENT. DALEJEAN EXITS FROM RIP'S BEDROOM; SHE IS BUTTONING UP HER WHITE UNIFORM.)

DALEJEAN: I wish I didn't have to go to work today.

(RIP IS LITERALLY CRAWLING OUT OF THE BEDROOM.)

RIP: Don't go then.

DALEJEAN: I never take off unless I have to. *(NOTICES RIP)* Stop that.

RIP: It's how you make me feel; weak in the knees. Good God, yo pussy is delicious.

DALEJEAN: Rip.

RIP: *(STRAIGHTENING UP)* You're so sensitive. I know, you don't like black men who clowns.

DALEJEAN: Nothing's funny in this world, Rip.

RIP: But there's some humor left.

DALEJEAN: Some humor.

RIP: Well. Come to think of it when are you going to spend at least one night with me?

DALEJEAN: Rip I got children. I make it my business to be home with them during sleeping hours as best I can, especially with this job. Shoot, I can't even attend PTA meetings—and I am a parent representative too. I got something to say, plenty to say, about the board's desegregation plans too.

RIP: *(HUGGING HER)* Woman, I'm crazy about you. You lay me out.

DALEJEAN: Do I, Rip? I hope so.

RIP: That's cause I love you. You're a good woman.

DALEJEAN: Don't get tired of me, Rip.

RIP: Why should I do that. Look, there's nothing you can do to make me get tired of you. In fact, you don't even know how to do that. Anyway, if I acts like I'm tired of you, just slap me upside the head.

DALEJEAN: No, Rip, I won't hit you. If you don't have sense enough to recognize what's up with me by now, slapping you upside the head won't help none. Where's my shoes?

RIP: I threw them out the window. The hawk probably done blew them all the way to Homewood by now.

DALEJEAN: Always hiding my shoes. Where...?

RIP: Keep 'em barefooted. That's how you keep 'em.

DALEJEAN: Well, how do you keep a man?

RIP: Good lovin'.

DALEJEAN: No. You men ain't hardly ready for that yet.

RIP: What men?

DALEJEAN: You member those wooden match boxes?

RIP: Yeah.

DALEJEAN: Well, a woman should be able to keep yalls sugar cane in a lil container in her refrigerator. So the only time she'd give it back to you mens is when she needs some sugar in her bowl of cereal.

RIP: Sounds like a good idea to me. Tomorrow when I get off from work, I'll see if I can find some wooden matches. If not, will one of these Tupperware...?

DALEJEAN: Rip, we has to talk about...us.

RIP: *(LOOKING DEEPLY INTO HER EYES)* You are serious, aren't you?

DALEJEAN: About you, yes. Sometimes I think I'm a lil...

RIP: A little what?

DALEJEAN: You know, man.

RIP: I know it's snowing outside.

DALEJEAN: My left eye keeps jumping.

RIP: So?

DALEJEAN: It's a warning. Something's bad going to happen. And I feel it's going to interfere with us.

RIP: Nothing's going to do that—unless we let it.

DALEJEAN: I'm so much older than you, Rip, I...

RIP: So that's it, huh? So you've had more sun on your face than I have, so what?

DALEJEAN: I got to be sure, that's all.

RIP: Of? Of what?

DALEJEAN: Us. What's good...

RIP: Dalejean, baby, you're good from the bottom of your feet to the top of your head.

DALEJEAN: And there are my children...

RIP: Okay. One thing at a time. First, you know what Satchell Page said...

DALEJEAN: Oh no, uh-huh, I done heard all the nasty jokes about balls and bats and gloves I can take in a life time.

RIP: You haven't heard this one, I can tell. Ol' Satchell said, "Age is a question of mind over matter. If you don't mind, it doesn't matter." That's how I feel about us.

DALEJEAN: Rip, I gots to know. In here. I gots to know we are right for each other.

RIP: As long as we trust each other and endure the craziness with love, hey...Look, your stuff's so good it'll make a hound dog walk up and shake a rabbit's hand and kiss him goodnight. It'll make a dead man come.

DALEJEAN: Oh, and I thought is was all about my mind.

RIP: Want some mo' sugah in yo bowl, momma?

DALEJEAN: Yes-no. Stop it, Rip. I gots to go to work.

(THERE IS A KNOCK AT THE DOOR.)

RIP: Damn. Who could that be. I hope like hell it's not Jimbo.

DALEJEAN: Me too. The way he stares at me Like I'm someone from another planet.

RIP: Jimbo's all right—sometimes. Hell, maybe never.

DALEJEAN: Go 'head. Get the door. I has to call home and check on my children. They probably hoping I would forget to call them like I promised.

RIP: *(OPENING THE DOOR)* Lil Bit, what is it now?

KIM: You don't have to bite my head off, Rip Morton.

RIP: Yeah, I might swallow some kooties.

KIM: I know you have company.

RIP: Kim, what is it?

KIM: My pilot light went out again and I don't have any matches.

RIP: Aw...Dalejean, you have any matches?

DALEJEAN: *(ON THE TELEPHONE)* Jan, hold on a.minute *(TO RIP)* Rip, what did you say?

RIP: Matches. You have any?

DALEJEAN: Look in my purse. Jake had a batch of um made for his Christmas advertisement.

(RIP SEARCHES THRU DALEJEAN'S PURSE, FINDS A BOOK OF MATCHES, HANDS THEM TO KIM, EDGING HER OUT OF THE APARTMENT.)

RIP: *(TO KIM)* See all you want to see?

(KIM LICKS HER TONGUE OUT AT RIP IN VIEW OF DALEJEAN.)

DALEJEAN: What was that all about?

RIP: Say, this is a nice purse..

DALEJEAN: Who was that? Giving me the twice over?

RIP: Oh her. Just the kid who lives upstairs. I think she's a college kid or something. Young blood. Young kid.

DALEJEAN: She didn't look all that kid to me.

RIP: Looks can be deceiving.

DALEJEAN: I bet.

RIP: Ment-mentally, I mean.

DALEJEAN: My left eye just jumped again.

RIP: Her mind's close to an ten year old.

DALEJEAN: Well that's more that I can say for Phyllis.

RIP: How's that? What's up with Phyllis?

DALEJEAN: Fast and boy crazy.

RIP: Wasn't you at sixteen?

DALEJEAN: But I respected my parents—and myself.

RIP: Has she or hasn't she?

DALEJEAN: I 'oun't know.

RIP: Not that mother's are the first to know.

DALEJEAN: Usually the last. She's just itchin' for trouble, I can smell it on her.

RIP: Put her on the pill.

DALEJEAN: Rip, how can you...?

RIP: Everybody's poppin' the pill, Dalejean.

DALEJEAN: I'm not.

RIP: Well you use something.

DALEJEAN: That's different.

RIP: It is. How?

DALEJEAN: I'm grown. Anyway, I don't jump in the bed with every Tom, Dick and Rip I meet either. Hell, I went without having a man for a long time. I can do it. Know darn well she can wait. The pill. I hate the idea. Anyway, I had to start using something because of you.

RIP: Don't blame it on me.

DALEJEAN: Much as you like to go...

RIP: Me? It's you, baby.

DALEJEAN: I need some kind of protection or *(SHE GESTURES)* I'll be a forty-two year-old-momma.

RIP: Well, Dalejean, if you don't, you might become a grandmother sooner...

DALEJEAN: Quit. I guess this is what mothers with daughters has to look forward to.

RIP: Nature.

DALEJEAN: Yeah nature. You know, on the way down here in the jitney, I felt a lil like my mother must've felt down home. And God knows I don't want to be like her. Not that I didn't love my mother, I did. But I promised myself that when I had children of my own, I wouldn't be so strict on them as she was on me and my sistuhs. I would give my children more freedom. More rights of their own.

RIP: Dalejean, put Phyllis on the pill and stop worrying about it.

DALEJEAN: Just like that huh?

RIP: Yes.

DALEJEAN: A lot of help you be.

RIP: The pill won't hurt her. Get her thru high school, maybe she can help herself by then.

DALEJEAN: And I thought the world was much more complicated than all this. Just get the pill...Oh God...I think the pill just gives a young girl the license to...just...be...free...with it...

RIP: If Phyllis is anything like you, that's your least worry. Look, sooner or later, with or without your permission, she's going to, do it.

DALEJEAN: I don't want to sanction it by...

RIP: Dalejean, she's going to find out about heaven. Better you tell her before some blood out in the streets do.

DALEJEAN: Yeah, I guess you right. But I'm worried about losing that cord that binds us together as mother and daughter. Her first time...after that...the knot that binds us together...will be broken. She won't simply be my daughter anymore, she'll be—

RIP: That sounds like an excuse not to talk with Phyllis about the wiener and the bun. Tell you what, marry me and I'll explain to your children the facts of life the way a man's suppose to.

DALEJEAN: Keep on talkin' like that and you going to lose this good bachelor life. Man, I'll marry you in a minute if we wasn't so wide apart...

RIP: (HUGGING HER) Nothing's between us—not even air.

DALEJEAN: You're so gentle, Rip. Now, keep this up and I just might take you home and lock you to my bed.

RIP: These arms of yours are lock enough for me. And your lips are the key.

DALEJEAN: Talk trash to me.

RIP: Everyday.

DALEJEAN: Good. Hand me the phone. (RIP MOVES TOWARDS THE PHONE.) On the other hand, I guess I shouldn't worry too much about what's natural. But I'm sure gonna watch her. You know...

RIP: Yes, Dalejean.

DALEJEAN: I overheard Phyllis calling her brother and sister half this and half that.

RIP: Now that's something to worry about. Really it is. I hate that kind of thing in a family.

DALEJEAN: Me too. And I'm not going to stand for it either. Not in mine's.

RIP: *(CLOSER TO DALEJEAN)* Hey, I know you carry a load and half yourself. You give a hundred percent already. Marry me and you'll have another hundred percent. Because, hey, it's showing in your eyes.

DALEJEAN: You and people's eyes. That's you—only you—in my eyes.

RIP: And you're in my eyes too. Believe that. And you keep me full.

DALEJEAN: They better be full with me in 'em. I'm not playin' either, Rip. Call me a jitney, please.

RIP: *(GOES NEAR THE PHONE)* Did you tell them about me yet?

DALEJEAN: No. But I will—soon. Rip, I'm going to be late for work.

RIP: Give me some mo heaven. What about a quickie?

DALEJEAN: Stop it, Rip. You going to make me late...all right now...I'm going to pop you now.
   (LIGHTS DIMMING: DRYING FUCKING DANCE)

DALEJEAN: Promise you won't make me...late...for...work.

RIP: I promise...to make...you late...for work...

DALEJEAN: You...you...Oh Jesus...I love you, Rip...

RIP: I love you, Dalejean...

DALEJEAN: Stop that...I'ma bite you...if you don't stop it...Oh Jesus...yes...take yo time, Rip...take yo time...on it...the passage for love...is so...wide open for us...
   (LIGHTS OUT AND COME UP ON)

ACT ONE PULSE 4
(HARRIS' FRONT ROOM)

PHYLLIS: *(ON THE TELEPHONE)* ...NO, she called already. No. If she doesn't call around ten...she won't call again...*(PAUSE)* Jan, what time is it?

JANET: *(READING A BOOK. SITTING ON THE COUCH.)* Quarter to ten.

PHYLLIS: *(INTO THE PHONE)* Nine forty-five. That's long enough for me. Is Darrell there yet? *(PAUSE)* Well, you just tell him I'm on my way. *(PAUSE)* Dag, Carol, I can't help it if my mother's so old fashion. *(PAUSE)* He what? *(PAUSE)* He is. Dancing with that black "b," Well, I'm ready for her tail tonight. *(PAUSE)* Okay. Bye.

JANET: Phyllis, you're not going to Carol's party, are you?

PHYLLIS: Nope.

JANET: Good. Cause I'm scared in this house by my...

PHYLLIS: Scared of what? What wants to harm you? Jan, all you have to do is...look, James Jr's., on his way home right now. And I'll check the doors and windows before I leave.

JANET: Mom told you to stay home with me.

PHYLLIS: I am with you. Now read your book and leave me alone.

JANET: Then you're not going...?

PHYLLIS: Am I?

JANET: Remember what Mom said about calling us to see if we're home.

PHYLLIS: She called once, didn't she? And you know how the old lady is: she's forgetful. (IMITATIVELY) "Oh, I forgot to call youns." Youns. Boy oh boy.

JANET: You shouldn't be making fun of the way Mom talks. You'd talk like that too if you lived down south all your life.

PHYLLIS: What the heck. Jan, you know yourself how embarrassed you felt when Mom comes to open house and she talks to the teachers in her down south dialect. I know I was embarrassed, especially when she was talking with Mr. Crawford. You know how she says "youns" and "yall" and "fuh."

JANET: Well, you say yall sometimes.

PHYLLIS: That's because everyone around me says it. I just blends in, honey chile. To be sociable. That doesn't mean I like saying it.

JANET: Well, I like it; I like the way Moms talks. I'm going to be a writer and...

PHYLLIS: Much as you read, you should be something.

JANET: Well I am. I'm going to write in Black English too.

PHYLLIS: What are you reading now?

JANET: This. A Hero Ain't Nothing But a Sandwich by Alice Childress. It's about a thirteen year old boy named Benji and...

PHYLLIS: Oh that's nice, Janet. Look if Mom calls back, don't you answer the phone, hear? In the morning, we'll just tell her we were asleep and didn't hear it ring. Whatever you do, don't let James Jr. answer it. Hear?

JANET: What if he answers it?

PHYLLIS: He won't. He's too much a big brother. He wants to protect me even if it's against the wrath of his momma.

JANET: Your momma too.

PHYLLIS: But different daddies. That makes the difference in our personalities.

JANET: No it don't.

PHYLLIS: It does, stupid.

JANET: We have the same mother and that's what counts.

PHYLLIS: Not in my book.

JANET: You haven't read a book in your whole life.

PHYLLIS: Funny. I overheard Mom talking to you about your daddy. Just as she did me. And I bet she did the same with James Jr., too. My father is a musician. He played at the Crawford Grill and the Hurricane until he made it big in New York—And Paris.

JANET: I bet you don't have none of his albums. Do you?

PHYLLIS: Shut up, will you. I'm trying to tell you something. You're becoming just like your brother. A know it all. Can't tell you...

JANET: I'm not like him; I'm like me.

PHYLLIS: I know about your father too. And James Jr.'s father. His father died in a freak accident on a construction site in Leersdale, Pennsylvania. That's how Mom got that savings account. The one she has for our college education.

JANET: Well, I don't need you to tell me nothing about my father. Where's your father?

PHYLLIS: That's my business.

JANET: Oh I know where he is.

PHYLLIS: You don't know nothing dummy, except what you read in a...

JANET: I snuck in your room and seen those returned letters from Boston.

PHYLLIS: Nosey little runt. You better stay out of my room.

JANET: Make me.

PHYLLIS: You might find something in there you don't know what it is and blow it up thinking it's a balloon.

JANET: I know about them silly things.

PHYLLIS: Think you know everything 'cause you read a lot, don't you?

JANET: Yep. What you doing with them anyway; you ain't no boy?

PHYLLIS: Forget you. Come to think of it, where is your old man? Bet you don't even know where he is.

JANET: I'm not telling you nothing about him. Now.

PHYLLIS: Well I certainly won't lose any sleep over it. My father is a big time musician. I'm proud of him.

JANET: Well I don't care nothing about my father. And I do know where he is.

PHYLLIS: (A SERIOUS TONE) You mean that, don't you, Jan?

JANET: Mean what?

PHYLLIS: About not caring anything about your father?

JANET: Sure do.

PHYLLIS: How can you? He is your father, Jan.

JANET: Any man can be a father.

PHYLLIS: Who told you that—oh you read it.

JANET: Mom told me and that ain't all she told me. Now.

PHYLLIS: I wonder why I don't feel the same way you do about it. I mean, I really want to meet my father.

JANET: Well, you just have a lot to learn about life.

PHYLLIS: I love my father.

JANET: You don't even know him.

PHYLLIS: I...think...I love him, Jan.

JANET: Well, neither your father or my father respected Mom enough to marry her. Only James Jr.'s, father; he must've been a good man.

PHYLLIS: Jan, my father couldn't tell his friends he was married to a waitress.

JANET: Why not?

PHYLLIS: He couldn't.

JANET: Something wrong with his mouth. Anyway, even if one of us had a white father we'll still be sisters. And whites take good care of their children.

PHYLLIS: No they don't all do, Jan. Sometimes you're about as dumb as a piece of wood.

JANET: Sheed.

PHYLLIS: I'm telling. You cussed.

JANET: Mom won't believe you. Now.

PHYLLIS: Aw, dry up. Oh, me, look at the time. See you later, house-warmer. *(PHYLLIS SNATCHES UP HER COAT.)* And remember what I told you. *(LIGHTS OUT AND COME UP ON)*

ACT ONE PULSE FIVE
(JAKE'S RESTAURANT.)

JAKE: *(TO DALEJEAN)* Well, Good Black, that's it. All set for the first half of next week. And it sure feels good to get a jump on the holidays for a change. Things must be trying to look up and bright for me in some ways.

DALEJEAN: Well, you shop well, Jake.

JAKE: Been in the business long enough. I should be able to manage some things right. But let my wife tell it I can't even turn a corner right. *(DALEJEAN STARTS TO BUSY HERSELF BY PICKING UP AN EMPTY BOX OR TWO)* Naw, let 'em be, Good Black. I'll get to them a lil later.

DALEJEAN: I'll just move them out of sight then.

JAKE: If there was some way I could lower my overhead. Impossible to make a profit otherwise. Wish I could just sell one of my places for a decent profit. Say, Good Black, you know anyone who'd give a nickel and a dime for a pool room or this restaurant?

DALEJEAN: I thought we was doing pretty good business here myself.

JAKE: Yeah like a yoyo. The pool rooms...at least the one down on Wylie...it's those young bloods...they got a death wish or something...killing one another over four bits...drinking wine...and smoking that marijuana like it's going outta style...I don't know how parents be raising their kids these days. Raising them for prison and a coffin, it seems to me. Raising kids for the white man to punish...and trying to get me busted on a humbug too. *(PAUSE)* But thank God for you, Good black. You the best that could've happened to me.

(JAKE CHECKS TO SEE IF ANYONE IS COMING INTO THE RESTAURANT. AT THE SAME TIME, HE STALKS DALEJEAN. HE GRABS HER AROUND THE WAIST. DALEJEAN RESISTS.)

DALEJEAN: No, Jake, please. This ain't right.

JAKE: This is Jake.

DALEJEAN: Suppose yo wife comes in and catches—Oh, my God, there she is!

JAKE: *(WITHOUT TURNING)* Oh hi, Tub of lard. *(HE TRIES TO KISS DALEJEAN)* How did that feel, Good Black?

DALEJEAN: Stop it. *(TWISTS OUT OF HIS GRASP)* And I didn't feel nothing.

JAKE: *(LAUGHS)* Yes you did. Admit it.

DALEJEAN: I don't like to kiss that much.

JAKE: Good Black, you know I'm crazy about you.

DALEJEAN: I don't like crazy mens.

JAKE: *(BOASTING)* This is Jake, Good…

DALEJEAN: I know you, mistah. Jake, you got to stop this fooling around with me.

JAKE: We got to stop—

DALEJEAN: No. You! *(JAKE ADVANCES TOWARD HER.)* Look, Jake, I'll smack the cowboy shit outta…stay away from me…stop it *(STOMPS HER FOOT)* right now.

JAKE: Okay I'll stop it—if you let me find out if you a man or a woman.

DALEJEAN: I ain't nothing. And you got no right messing around with me when I don't want you to.

JAKE: It's the law of the ghetto.

DALEJEAN: Yeah. I don't want to challenge yo so-called law of the ghetto. But I will.

JAKE: Good Black…

DALEJEAN: You can't have me, Jake. And that final. You can't be grabbin' on me every time you feel like it. Like I'm some kind of—

JAKE: I'm man enough.

DALEJEAN: *(POINTING)* Not with that on.

JAKE: What? Oh my wedding band. I can take this thing off. *(HE DOES.)* Better?

DALEJEAN: That's not what I mean. And you know it too.

JAKE: Naw, woman, I don't know what the hell you mean. In this world, you got to say exactly what you mean. Where's your ring, Good Black?

DALEJEAN: When I got married other things was more important than a ring.

JAKE: Tell you what, I'll buy you one…for Christmas. How about that?

DALEJEAN: Not fuh what you want. You can't buy…

JAKE: I'll get you one for your birthday. In January, right?

DALEJEAN: It don't mean a pile a beans to you...

JAKE: Naw, my wife ain't meant—

DALEJEAN: I ain't talking about yo wife.

JAKE: My ol' lady's more like a...

DALEJEAN: I don't want to hear about your wife.

JAKE: Good Black, it'll bring me much peace to take care of you.

DALEJEAN: Not my flavor. I takes care of me. Good care too.

JAKE: I want you so bad I can taste it.

DALEJEAN: You gets nothing here but vinegar.

JAKE: I ll do anything just to get a whiff of it.

DALEJEAN: Jake, hush yo mouth now. I'm not listening to you.

JAKE: It'll work out for us.

DALEJEAN: Can't you understand that, Jake?

JAKE: I understand my feelings.

DALEJEAN: Jake, I'm not good that way.

JAKE: Woman, you built like a...

DALEJEAN: Jake, you should have something else on yo mind. Like this restaurant or...

JAKE: You look like something a man loves to eat twice on a Sunday.

DALEJEAN: You might thank I look like that. But, believe me, I ain't into that.

JAKE: Gimme some, Good Black.

DALEJEAN: No, Jake. You gets nothing here but what you pays me for.

JAKE: I'll do that too.

DALEJEAN: I didn't mean it that way.

JAKE: I'm going to get what I want.

DALEJEAN: Why don't you just leave the cold alone; I don't feel it down there no mo.

JAKE: *(LAUGHS)* You a killa, Good Black. Bet you don't keep your big thighs closed on that young punk you joogin' around with.

DALEJEAN: Now you really don't know what you talking about. You just mad 'cause I won't give you none.

JAKE: Damn right I'm mad about that, jack. Madder than a man who'd just got busted on a humble. *(PAUSE)* Good Black, I'm not trying to hurt you.

DALEJEAN: You do, Jake, you really do.

JAKE: No, I wouldn't do that for all the joints in the world.

DALEJEAN: Stop fooling around with me then. I'm cross-legged to you, Jake.

JAKE: Okay, I heard that. But tell me something...

DALEJEAN: No thanks.

JAKE: What do you expect to get out of it in the long run?

DALEJEAN: Out of what?

JAKE: You know. You and that young punk. A husband? A husband's who's not much older than your oldest kid. What do you want with a...?

DALEJEAN: I sure don't want somebody else's husband.

JAKE: How long do you expect for him to continue to fuck...?

DALEJEAN: Dirty mouth.

JAKE: Well the truth will come to light sooner or later.

DALEJEAN: What truth you got, Jake?

JAKE: The truth that's going to be beating you in the face every morning you get up, it'll be whipping on you every night when you go to bed, and it'll make you cry every time you undress and look into the mirror. But me, I don't mind a few bulges myself.

DALEJEAN: Why I'm I listening to this man.

JAKE: Don't listen to me then.

DALEJEAN: I'm not.

JAKE: But rain and thunder do come sooner or later, Good Black, you're going to have to face your relationship with him and see it for what it really is.

DALEJEAN: And what is that? No, don't answer that.

JAKE: Okay. But you just mark my words.

DALEJEAN: I marked your words with a X minutes ago.

JAKE: Suit yourself. But there are none so blind as those with eyes who will not see.

DALEJEAN: I see how ugly you talk and act.

JAKE: I tells it like I see it in my heart.

DALEJEAN: Jake, I understand the heart. A lil light in a dark place can serve a large purpose. That's all I want. A lil light to shine on me and brighten up my soul.

JAKE: But, Good Black, you can't remake the world. Or re-live your twenties by going with him. Not with him in your arms, Good Black.

DALEJEAN: You'll never understand what I'm feeling, I see that now.

JAKE: One thing, sister...

DALEJEAN: I'm not yo sistuh.

JAKE: ...At your age your thang won't outlast his.

DALEJEAN: That's enough. That did it, Jake. I quit. Damn it, I quit.

JAKE: Go right ahead, quit. Run and hide. Cry the truth of my words in your hands. Because you know I'm fanning you in the face with reality.

DALEJEAN: I don't know nothing of the sort.

JAKE: Good Black, Good Black, you situation ain't unique. It happens to the best of us. I'm just trying to keep you from getting your heart broken.

DALEJEAN: Don't do me any favors.

JAKE: You can't remake the world so you can fit in it. You pass that, Good Black.

DALEJEAN: Well maybe I can't remake the world—as you puts it. But I know I got a place in it. See I gots the will to put myself where I want to be and be with who I want to be with too. I'm not going to let you put me in a box, Jake. Never. It all started with a man and a woman. And age didn't have a thang to do with it either.

JAKE: You too old for him, Good Black.

DALEJEAN: Age. Ha. Well what about you?

JAKE: I fit on you like these gloves fit my hands.

DALEJEAN: That ain't what I'm talking about.

JAKE: Don't play hop-scotch with me, woman, spit the seeds out.

DALEJEAN: You ask for it. Age don't attract nobody. Age don't keep you ole mens from slobbering at the mouth over them young girls, do it? Naw it don't. You ole men…in yo baggy pants…smelling like wet wood…you be paying them young girls rent, their car notes, Pampers, and making groceries for them. With a big ole silly grin on yo faces. Just for a sniff of that young pooter. Slobbering at the mouth Jake. You ole men ain't nobody's sugar daddies. Got too much salt and chitlings in yo blood to plow somebody's field somebody else turned over before you. I seen you slobber. When them girls come in here with them jeans diggin' up the crack of their behinds. And miniskirts so tight 'round their hips…make yo eyes nearly pop outta yo head and you know, you can slobber good, Jake.

JAKE: Are you finished?

DALEJEAN: You a good slobbering nigga.

JAKE: Finish?

DALEJEAN: No. You just ain't gettin' none a me. And that's what's really bugging the hell outta you, ain't it, Jake?

JAKE: Cold weather's the only thing bugging me. Anyway, you quit, remember?

DALEJEAN: Why should I quit? I don't have to. You don't want to fire me. This ole chippie, as they useta say, can really do good here. Because as long as you can sneak a feel and rub against me, you won't get rid of me. Yeah, I want you to want to this ole middle-age black Alabama countrified stuff. I want you to want it, like you said, so bad you can taste it. And furthermore, Jake, you be absolutely right about me.

JAKE: How's that, Good Black?

DALEJEAN: I'm so good I can churn a man's milk into butter with one stroke. I can milk a sugar cane stalk so good it'll produce a bucket full of pure protein. Jake, I got blackberries in my jellyroll and that's the best breakfast and late night snack you'd ever wanna have in yo life.

JAKE: Yeah you can talk that talk. But it's not going to help you with that young punk. Especially when he gets tired of you and starts roaming.

DALEJEAN: That's how much you know, mistah. I can't keep the young man from climbing between my legs. My bushes stay wet.

JAKE: Ah Good Black you can't make me mad. My time will come. Just you wait and see.

DALEJEAN: Humph.

JAKE: *(PUTTING ON HIS COAT)* Yeaah, I've heard that talk on Bourbon Street. I've tamed them all. See, I got liquid gold. Just you be ready when a man comes to plow your field.

DALEJEAN: You ain't no competition. Jake, you a good man in yo own way. But my water has already been drawn and I'm drinking it. And only one man can hold my cup.

JAKE: See you later, Good Black.

DALEJEAN: Only because I works here.

(LIGHTS FADE OUT AND COME UP ON)

ACT ONE PULSE 6
(HARRIS' FRONT ROOM. JANET IS ON THE COUCH READING. THE DOORBELL RINGS.)

JANET: I'll get it. *(SHE GOES TO THE DOOR.)*

DALEJEAN: *(OFF-STAGE)* Get the mail, honey.

JANET: Good morning, Ant Louise.

LOUISE: Moaning.

JANET: Mom's in the kitchen. *(HOLLERS OUT)* Mom, it's Ant Louise.

DALEJEAN: *(O.S.)* Good morning, Lou. Be with you in a minute. Have a seat.

LOUISE: *(TO JANET)* My you're growing mighty fast.
(JANET HAS STEPPED OUT ON THE PORCH TO GET THE MAIL.)

JANET: *(RETURNING, SHIVERING FROM THE COLD)* What did you say, Ant Louise?

LOUISE: I said, are you getting ready for Christmas?

JANET: Yes ma'am.

LOUISE: Remember the Lord knows if you be naughty or nice.

DALEJEAN: *(IN BULBOUS JAPANESE HOUSE COAT)* Morning, Lou.

LOUISE: Moanin' Sister Dalejean.

DALEJEAN: Care for something to eat?

LOUISE: A good Christian woman never refuses the rewards of the Lord's breath and back, hello.

DALEJEAN: You mean my breath and back.

JANET: Mom!

DALEJEAN: *(TO JANET)* Mind yo manners, girl. Then again, ain't you got some housework to do around here. Instead of standing around looking down grown folk throats.

JANET: Yes ma'am. Here's some more Christmas cards.

DALEJEAN: Put 'em on the mantle. Ain't got time to read such things on a work day. And for heaven's sake, wake up yo sister. Unless she wants me to come up there and wake her up. I hope ain't nothing wrong with that girl. Sleeping late like this on a Saturday too.

(*JANET RUNS UP THE STAIRS.*)

LOUISE: Out of a child's mouth—"Mom!"—in a single word, can flow the truth sometimes.

DALEJEAN: What's the truth for today, Lou?

LOUISE: Take Sister Janet, she knows you were mocking me and the Lord.

(*DALEJEAN, WHILE TALKING WITH LOUISE, IS BUSY GOING AND RETURNING FROM THE KITCHEN WITH THINGS FOR LOUISE AND HERSELF.*)

DALEJEAN: Lou, you know darn well I was not mocking you or the Lord; I was simply stating a fact.

LOUISE: Yes, you was. Make fun of the Lord, ol' evil Dalejean Harris and He'll take back his breath with one inhale and flatten your back permanently with one exhale.

DALEJEAN: Oh Lou. Here put some strawberry preserves on your toast. I gotta figure out my numbers.

LOUISE: 144,000's the holy number, sister. Pray that you're in that count. I sure hate to get to heaven and ask the Lord: where is my Sister Dalejean Roberta Harris, Lord? And he say, Who? Sister Dalejean, I say, she used to live on Arcena Street, couple of doors from the old incline that used to go down into Lawrenceville. He jest shake his white wooly head.

DALEJEAN: Okay, Lou, I'll be Christianly—if you stop trying to get in my house before noon on Mondays. Hear?

LOUISE: Superstitions don't follow the ways of some of God's Children.

DALEJEAN: A man's suppose to bring good luck on Mondays, Lou, not a woman. And stop trying to save me.

LOUISE: Just trying to enter Fellowship with you, sister. My duty.

DALEJEAN: Well I'm sanctified and holy enough as it is.—Women's—or have you—forgotten—are not supposed to be preaching. That's what the old folk useta say.

(*TELEPHONE RINGS.*)

LOUISE: Well, they are. Mighty good preachers too. Not like you Sister Dale—

DALEJEAN: And I'm not like them either. Hold on a second, Lou. If it's that boy again. Been calling all morning for Phyllis. (*PICKS UP THE PHONE.*) Hello. (*PAUSE*) Hi. (*BIG SMILE ON HER FACE.*) Oh stop it. (*PAUSE*) Me too. (*PAUSE*) I can't say that, I got company. (*PAUSE*) No. They upstairs. (*PAUSE*) No, she's a she. Oh Rip, don't forget you having dinner with me at the restaurant tonight. *(PAUSE)* Me too. I look forward to it. Bye-bye. *(SHE KISSES INTO THE PHONE.)*

LOUISE: Yes. You're certainly not like them. The first thing you want to see in the morning is a man.

DALEJEAN: Reckon you right, Lou. Partly anyway. The first thang in the morning and the last thang at night.

LOUISE: Hush your mouth.

DALEJEAN: Keeps a woman in good luck with life.

LOUISE: A woman your age too. I declare.

DALEJEAN: And what's wrong with a woman.my age?

LOUISE: Don't get hincty now, sister.

DALEJEAN: Ain't nothing wrong with a woman my age that I can see *(MUM-BLING UNDER BREATH)* Age...Age...Age...that's all I hear about is somebody's age.

LOUISE: I declare the way you acting around here...

DALEJEAN: I'm sorry, Lou. How's the weather outside? Cold huh?

LOUISE: Jesus is resting his earth, hello.

DALEJEAN: Nice cold weather for the arms of a man. Wouldn't you agree with that, Sistuh Lou?

LOUISE: Hush your mouth before your tongue touches your toes.

DALEJEAN: Now we both know that's impossible.

LOUISE: Impossible: that's what they said about the King of Kings and his Resurrection—from the dead, hello.

DALEJEAN: You know, if someone was standing in this room listening to use they would thank we were nuts or on something: carrying at one another the way we do. They wouldn't understand we was the best of enemies, er, I mean friends. Just kidding. Sometimes I think of all the crazy words we say to each other and they make me laugh.

LOUISE: The words of Satan or the words of the Lord, hello.

DALEJEAN: Here are you eggs and bacon, Sister Lou.

LOUISE: Wh-what about my homefries?

DALEJEAN: Oh excuse me I forgot to take yo order, ma'am.

LOUISE: Yes you did.

DALEJEAN: Well I'm sorry, Lou, I didn't peel any potatoes this morning.

LOUISE: Now don't get me wrong, Sister Dalejean; this a do just fine.

DALEJEAN: Guess I got too much on my mind lately.

LOUISE: Yeah what's this world coming to. I say, nothing but Armedgeedon.

DALEJEAN: I 'oun't know, Lou. Guess I don't really believe in all that.

LOUISE: You don't believe in the Bible!

DALEJEAN: Sort of I was raised a Christian...

LOUISE: Hello.

DALEJEAN: James, my husband, was a great influence on me. He didn't go to church. And I swear to this day, some of his friends was communists.

LOUISE: Oh Sister Dalejean...no wonder...you...po' woman...Communist don't believe in Jesus or God. Did you know that?

DALEJEAN: But they sure believe in po' hard working folk like my James and me. My James was a union man...

LOUISE: The union of man with Jesus is our divine work, hello.

DALEJEAN: What about the union of man and woman and their children, Lou? What about that as divine work?

LOUISE: The Lord moves in...oh but you know that. *(PAUSE)* Sister Dalejean, you never told me why you stopped attending church.

DALEJEAN: I never thought about it. Must've been right after, yes not too long after James died. I used to take James Jr. to church with me. But my James never went. And he never tried to stop me from going either. After he dies so young, so strong, so full of like, so good...Guess I just stopped too. I wanted God to strike me dead for not going to church.

LOUISE: Sister, you can't die with the dead.

DALEJEAN: I'm not, Lou. But I thought I needed James with me or I couldn't go on being a woman.

LOUISE: God is who you need. You need his spiritual graces, hello. Now go ahead and tell God what you want.

DALEJEAN: Lou I know what I want.

LOUISE: Well hello.

DALEJEAN: I want to carry my own weight...Pick it up and tote it the best I can. Some people like themselves and the situation they made for themselves. I want to feel that way too. And I want to walk in the sunshine and in the snow and feel good about where I'm going and who I'm with. I'm no fool or a teenager—something folk been trying to remind me of lately. See too many things and already been set into practice before I could have my say-so about how and where I fit in. As long as I fit in without forcing it, well, that's what I want.

LOUISE: It's that man.

DALEJEAN: What man?

LOUISE: That young man...got you all twisted and turned inside out at yourself.

DALEJEAN: In that case it's a good feeling, I tell you that.

LOUISE: If you could just listen at yourself. You don't even make sense anymore.

DALEJEAN: Shouldn't have mentioned him to you. I can see that now.

LOUISE: Didn't have to. It's written all over you.

DALEJEAN: Oh I told you, woman.

LOUISE: The Lord keeps telling me every morning time. He say: Sister Louise, you go across the street and have fellowship with your sister. Console your sister, Sister Dalejean Roberta Harris...He knows your full name.

DALEJEAN: I told you that too.

LOUISE: Never you mind. He says to console you before your life is torn asunder my pleasures weakening her soul astray from some of God's children—the flock of his chosen few.

DALEJEAN: He says all that every morning?

LOUISE: Well in so many words.

DALEJEAN: Sister Lou, I lives what I believe to be a good life. Don't hurt nobody. Raises my children the best I knows how.

LOUISE: I knows that, sister.

DALEJEAN: Feeds my sparrows and pigeons in the winter. My robins in the early spring. I don't drink, smoke or stay out all hours of the night running the streets and leaving my children to run wild and raise themselves. I never let them sleep in this house unless I was here with them. Except for the few times I spent in the hospital.

LOUISE: I know, sister.

DALEJEAN: I tends to my personal business the way I feels it's best for me. But if personal doesn't fit in with my children, then I don't force it. I lets it go its way and I go mine.

LOUISE: No one is condemning you, Sister Dalejean. Surely you don't think I am?

DALEJEAN: No, I know you wouldn't, Lou. It's just that...this strange feeling keep coming over me. I can't really explain it. It's more like a dream—in this dream, there's a clock. The second hand's ticking loud...tick-tock...tick-tock...the big hands starts running real fast. Then I see myself...running...running...running...faster and faster...the big hands...running after me...until I'm outta breath. I'm scared, Lou. I don't know what it means. I look up time and clock in the dream books and I plays them numbers for weeks. But I never hits off any. Last night the dream didn't come. Then I realized...

LOUISE: A revelation?

DALEJEAN: Could be, Lou. But not the kind you thanking about.

LOUISE: Oh.

DALEJEAN: The one thang in my dreams I been fearful of looking up—death. This morning when I looked outta my bedroom at the snow, I said to myself I gots a future until it's over. And I have needs. And personal right too. And I'm not talking about you, Lou. Cross my heart. But I don't like for no one to meddle in my private life. And right now someone keep meddling with me. Not you, Lou. You too good a woman to meddle. So I'm not placing you in the same category with...

LOUISE: Get the burden off your chest, Sister DaleJean. Get it off.

DALEJEAN: Yes. But I gots to say it my way. You know I had three mens in my life. And the first one, sometimes, he don't count none much. My grandmother she always talked about rights. Rights this and rights that. Well, my rights lie hanging all the time. After James died, my rights changed. After Phyllis' daddy up and left me with his no account band and that dizzy gal who couldn't sang her way outta a hole in the ground, my rights changed again. My life—and my rights—changed when Janet's father couldn't stop beating on me, drinking and chasing fast-tailed floozies. My rights keep changing. But my rights to happiness, peace a mind and body don't change. I still need them. Because they still with me. And they mines. And I love um. I want um. If my happiness and peace is out there...wherever...then no one has a right to stand in my way...and I has the right to go out there and get un and fight like hell for them. Ain't that my responsibility, Lou?

LOUISE: Sister Dalejean, there is many a slip between the cup and the lip.

DALEJEAN: My grip is too firm now, Lou. I'm being very careful from here on out.

LOUISE: Don't let yourself go, sister. That's all I can say.

DALEJEAN: I won't. I've been hurt because of just that. But I ain't hurting nobody on account of what has happened to me. I want to lie down in my happiness with a smile on my face before I die. Wake up in peace with a new smile. In between that I want my children to climb like vines toward their own peace and happiness. People, some people, got no right in my business, especially if I don't invite them. Especially if it feels this good to me. Much as I respect you, Lou, you live your way and that makes you you. A beautiful and a good you. I lives my life my way and that makes me me. Together we bunch up. That makes the world go round like a spinning top. Our generation know life and love. But it's ours, not our children. When they and their children grow up, what will they be saying about life and love. What we told um and thought was the truth may not be the truth for them. May not have any connection whatsoever to their reality. All I'm trying to be is me. Trying hard as I can to make my statement on life and love.

(LIGHTS FADE OUT AND COME UP ON)

ACT ONE PULSE 7

(RIP'S APARTMENT. HE IS STRAIGHTENING UP. HIS TOPCOAT IS OVER THE BACK OF THE COUCH. HIS FRONT DOOR IS OPEN.)

KIM: *(APPEARING IN DOORWAY.)* Aren't we busy?

RIP: Hay, Lil Bit.

KIM: What are you looking for?

RIP: Nothing. Just trying to tidy up a little.

KIM: Why do you have the door open; it's cold in here.

RIP: Airing out what's left of wine and beer odors, Lil Bit. I hate the smell of alcohol.

KIM: *(SNIFFING)* I don't smell anything.

RIP: You don't. *(SNIFFS)* Good. Jimbo's going to ruin my life one of these days. I wish he'd find another place to take his women.

KIM: Well at least he brought one for you. So why you complaining.

RIP: Lil Bit I don't know no more about that lady today than I knew last night.

KIM: Not even her name. That's cold, super stud. *(PICKS UP LIPSTICK.)* Somebody left you a souvenir.

RIP: Jesus Christ. If Dalejean had found this I'd be...Damn that Jimbo.

KIM: Yeah put it all on your cousin.

RIP: Here Lil Bit, you can have it. Merry Christmas.

KIM: I don't want it. No telling where she puts her lips.

RIP: Shame on you. I ought to wash your mouth out with—

KIM: Oh you can use your tongue to do that.

RIP: Lil Bit, please.

KIM: Rip, stop lunchin' on me.

RIP: You going out?

KIM: Downtown. Do a little Christmas shopping in Kaufmann's.

RIP: Wait a minute. I'm going out too.

KIM: With me?

RIP: Lil Bit, I have a dinner date with Dalejean. Sorry.

KIM: Not as sorry as I am. Come on, the 82 Lincoln's due in five minutes.
   (LIGHTS FADE OUT AND COME UP ON)

ACT ONE PULSE 8
(HARRIS' FRONT ROOM. JANET AND JAMES, JR.)

JAMES JR.: *(SEATED ARMS FOLDED)* Go ahead, Jan. I'm ready.

JANET: First I call you by your free name...Damu...Simba Damu, right?

JAMES JR.: That's Seem-bah. Seem-bah.

JANET: You only have to tell me once.

JAMES JR.: I know, Jan.

JANET: Ready?

JAMES JR.: Yebo!

JANET: That's yes in Zulu. I remember that. Okay. Simba Damu !

JAMES JR.: *(LEAPS UP IN MILITARY-STYLE) Hapa! (HE STRIKES HIS CHEST JUST ABOVE HIS HEART, REFOLDS HIS ARMS)* Appreciate what's been said and if I understand it correctly, the Seven Principles are, One, Umoja (Unity)—To strive for and maintain unity in the family, community, nation and race; Two, Kujichagulia (Self-determination)—To name, define and speak for ourselves instead of being defined and spoken for by others; Three, Ujima (Collective Work and Responsibility) —To build and maintain our community together and to make our brothers and sisters problems our problems and to solve them together; Four, Ujamaa (Cooperative Economics) —To build and maintain our own stores, shops, and other businesses and to profit together from the; Five, Nia (Purpose) —To make as our collective vocation the building and developing of our community in order to restore our people to their traditional greatness; Six, Kuumba (Creativity) —To do always as much as we can in the way we can in order to leave our community more beautiful and beneficial that we inherited it; Seven, Imani (Faith) —To believe with all our hearts in our parents, our teachers, our leaders, our people and the righteousness and victory of our struggle. If I've said anything of value and worth, all praises are due Kawaida and Maulana Karenga and all the mistakes have been mine.

JANET: You got em all right. Word for word.

JAMES JR.: Asante.

JANET: Boy, it took you a long time to memorize them. I did it in no time.

JAMES JR.: I know you did, Jan. I can remember when you were in McKelvy. They put you two grades ahead of your age. Mom was so happy she cried.

JANET: Do you understand Mom?

JAMES JR.: Not really. I don't understand Phyllis at all. I wish I could talk with her like we can.

JANET: Me too.

JAMES JR.: If we could stop fighting each other.

JANET: Maybe the three of us should do more things together like brother and sisters. Ujima.

JAMES JR.: Jan you're smart. Boy. If Phyllis, you and Mom were to join the National Involvement for Africans...

JANET: James Jr. I'll think about it. I promise.

JAMES JR.: Okay. Good. Now where's my script. I got to go over my lines for the play. You know I'm playing Shaka Zulu. I hope I don't mess up.

JANET: You won't—if you concentrate. I think I'm going to write a play one day.

JAMES JR.: Jan, you can do anything you want to, you know that. I'm so glad you're my sister.

JANET: And Phyllis?

JAMES JR.: Phyllis too. But she don't listen.

JANET: I know. She doesn't even listen to Mom anymore.

JAMES JR.: Man, I sure hate to see her get strung out in the blood world.

JANET: Phyllis said for us not to answer the phone again. Just in case it's Mom.

JAMES JR.: She's giving out orders now.

JANET: What are you going to do if it rings...?

JAMES JR.: I'm going to my room. If it rings I'm pretending sleep.

JANET: I'm not staying down here by myself.

JAMES JR.: Don't be scared. I locked all the doors and windows. Ah, I'll put a chair under the doorknobs in the kitchen and the front door.

JANET: Then Phyllis won't be able to get in.

JAMES JR.: Good thinking. Yeah and I sleep heavy too.

JANET: I don't. I hear Mom every night when she comes in from work. James Jr., Mom walks real heavy.

JAMES JR.: Probably because she's tired. On her feet eight hours.

JANET: But Phyllis walks like a cat thru this house. Sometimes I can hear her sneaking pass my room.

JAMES JR.: Where do she be going? To the bathroom?

JANET: Promise you won't tell.

JAMES JR.: I promise.

JANET: To let Darrell in the house.

JAMES JR.: Stupid stupid.

JANET: James Jr., when Mom talks to herself, does that mean she's going crazy?

JAMES JR.: What do you mean?

JANET: You know how often I have to go to the toilet during the night. Well sometimes when I walk pass Mom's room, I can hear her talking to herself. Out loud. And I know she's in there alone.

JAMES JR.: Yeah, I've caught Mom talking to herself in the kitchen or just walking down the hall upstairs. But I guess she's lonely. All we can do is try and not make her cry anymore than she does. We can't live Mom's life; we don't know how it was for her when she was growing up in Alabama.

JANET: Guess you're right. Maybe she needs an adult around here with her. I'll be glad when I become an adult.

JAMES JR.: Why?

JANET: So I can make enough money to take care of Mom.

JAMES JR.: Look, you go ahead up to your room. I'll double check things down here.

JANET: Can-can I wait for you?

JAMES JR.: Sure.

   (JAMES JR. AND JANET FACING IN OPPOSITE DIRECTIONS)

JANET: They say a cat has nine lives...

JAMES JR.: Mom is a good woman...

JANET: God, please don't let Phyllis get in any trouble...

JAMES JR.: I hope Phyllis grows up to be like Mom...

JANET: Watch out for my sister...

JAMES JR.: I'm going to stop calling Phyllis a negro...

JANET: I love my sister...

JAMES JR.: I sure wish Phyllis was home...

JANET: Phyllis, please come home.

JAMES JR.: My fear is for you, Phyllis.

(LIGHT FADE OUT AND COME UP ON)

ACT ONE PULSE NINE
(JAKE'S RESTAURANT.)

RIP: (PATTING HIS STOMACH.) I can't budge a lick.

DALEJEAN: Eat that sweet potato pie. I baked that one especially for you.

RIP: Put it in a doggie bag. I can't swallow air. You know, I've always wanted to marry a woman who could burn like you.

DALEJEAN: Ole fashion cooking, you mean.

RIP: I'm not going to fall into that one, I'm just going to play pass it.

DALEJEAN: Avoiding it won't help either.

RIP: The only thing I want to avoid is bringing unhappiness into your life.

DALEJEAN: Nigga talk a lot of stuff when his stomach's full.

RIP: That's not stuff. You're the weight I choose to carry.

DALEJEAN: You know you can make a better choice.

RIP: No such happenings.

DALEJEAN: A younger choice even.

RIP: This is the last time I'm going to respond to your idiotic paranoia. And that's all it is. If I wanted to mess around with, say, a twenty...or...a nineteen year old, I could—if that's what I wanted. I mean, look, I got you. I love you. Tell the truth, I grows with you everyday. And you make me grow bigger. When John Coltrane plays "I Wanna Talk About You," that's how I feel about you. Naw, I'm serious. I don't like quick grits; I loves me some thirty minute grits. When Marvin Gaye sings "Pride and Joy," I be holding what you got in my hands. Hell, what I look like crying with two loaves of bread in my hands.

DALEJEAN: (SMILING AND GRINNING ALL OVER HERSELF.) You a mess, you know that. But I love it. Good trash-talking man. (CUPS HER BREASTS.) Two loaves...of what? Pride...and...Joy. You a mess.

(JAKE ENTERS.)

DALEJEAN: The Boss.

(JAKE GLARES AT THEM. HE HURRIES PASS THEM TO HIS CASH REGISTER.)

RIP: Tell him you're taking a break.

DALEJEAN: It's ok. Let me clean off the table. See if he wants me to do anything. Be right back. Don't you dare go anywhere.

(DALEJEAN APPROACHES JAKE.)

JAKE: What's the hell going on here?

DALEJEAN: Nothing. What's wrong...?

JAKE: You know damn well what's wrong? What's going on, Good Black?

DALEJEAN: I told you—nothing.

(RIP GETS UP.)

JAKE: What the hell is this then—a picnic? This is my place of business. Not
Kennywood Park or some...*(JAKE SPIES RIP.)* Hey, buster, hold it right
there.

RIP: Me?

JAKE: Yeah you.

RIP: I got to use the latrine. Be with you—

JAKE: Be nothing. You just get the hell outta here.

RIP: Excuse me, man, unless you want a bath.

JAKE: *(PUSHING AT RIP.)* Out!

RIP: Hey, man.

DALEJEAN: Jake

JAKE: Do I have to throw you out?

RIP: You and what army?

JAKE: Just me.

RIP: What the fuck...

DALEJEAN: Jake, what's gotten into you?

RIP: What do I have to do, go thru a civil rights struggle to piss in...?

JAKE: Piss in the Biltmore Bar across the street.

RIP: You crazy or some—

JAKE: Look, you stay outta my place or you'll see just how crazy I can be.

RIP: Man I got to piss...

DALEJEAN: Rip maybe you should...

JAKE: And make this your last free meal in here.

RIP: Hey, man, you got to come better than this.

JAKE: I ain't gots to do nothing but stay black, pay taxes and die.

RIP: Dalejean, what's wrong with this cat?

JAKE: Keep her outta this. This is between me and you.

RIP: What's between you and me?

DALEJEAN: Jake, why don't you leave him alone; he ain't done nothing to you.

RIP: But I'm about to do something to him if he don't—

DALEJEAN: Rip, please just leave.

JAKE: Do that, punk.

RIP: Hey, I don't understand this shit you pulling.

DALEJEAN: Rip, he owns the place.

JAKE: And don't you forget it, punk.

RIP: Hey look I'm not going to be a bunch a punks for...

JAKE: Beat it, boy.

RIP: I got to piss and I'm going to piss.

(JAKE PUSHES AT RIP, BUT RIP SIDESTEPS IT.)

RIP: Look, fool-ass ole man...don't make me hurt you...

(THE TWO MEN TUSSLE; RIP GETS THE BEST OF JAKE. DALE-JEAN YELLS OVER AND OVER AGAIN, TRYING TO BREAK THEM APART: "I'M GOING TO CALL THE POLICE..." JAKE FINALLY BREAKS AWAY FROM RIP.)

DALEJEAN: Jake you done lost your mind.

JAKE: *(SHAKING HIS FINGER AT RIP.)* Be here when I come back, mother...

DALEJEAN: Oh, honey. Rip Rip, he has a shotgun back there.

(RIP STARES IN DISBELIEF AND CONFUSION INTO DALEJEAN'S EYES.)

DALEJEAN: Oh Rip.

(RIP SHAKES HIS HEAD, INHALES DEEPLY, THEN EXITS.)

DALEJEAN: Oh honey.

(JAKE APPEARS WITH THE SHOTGUN.)

(LIGHTS FADE OUT AND COME UP ON DALEJEAN WHO IS LOOK-ING OUT THE WINDOW OF THE RESTAURANT. JAKE IS IN THE BACKGROUND. HE STILL HAS THE GUN IN HIS HANDS.)

JAKE: Good Black. *(BEAT.)* Good Black. *(1/2 BEAT)* Good Black.

Dalejean. Don't say nothing to me. I'm not responsible for what I might say to you.

JAKE: I could beg.

DALEJEAN: Beg. Get down on your knees and beg. I hate a beggin' man.

JAKE: Got me wrong, Good Black. I'm not a begging man. Not even an apologizing one; naw, I'm not made that way. Got too much a man in me for that.

DALEJEAN: Yeah. I seen how much man you got in you all right.

Jake. I got more than that to put in you.

DALEJEAN: That's what you hope. But I ain't no thimble.

JAKE: Good Black. I've been on my own since I was thirteen. A kid out of Lil Rock. When white folks had more respect for dogs and cats then they had for Negroes like us. I learned how to carry the stick early in my life. I've judi-popped with low-life and high-life. I done did Kansas City, Chicago,

Memphis, Detroit, Mississippi, New Orleans, Kentucky, Cleveland and God knows where else. I did all there was to do. Did it to men and women. And had it done to me. I've sang all of Jimmy Reed's songs in women's ears in every juke joint on Centre Avenue, Wylie Avenue, and this side of West Hell.

DALEJEAN: Jake, I'm not interested in your history.

JAKE: God and I...

DALEJEAN: God ain't in this—and you know it.

JAKE: God and I both know I did you a favor getting rid of that young punk.

DALEJEAN: Did nothing for me.

JAKE: A real man can make you forget a boy any day of the week. I know what a woman like you need...done to her and for her. I got the power to do a lot for you. (BEAT) Good Black. (1/2 BEAT) Talk to me, Good Black. I know you don't love that young—

DALEJEAN: Ain't nothing punkish about him.

JAKE: Don't fool yourself.

DALEJEAN: I'm not.

JAKE: Are you crying?

DALEJEAN: You can't see my tears. They too deep for your eyes.

JAKE: Turn around and look at me, Good Black.

DALEJEAN: For what?

JAKE: And tell me what you see in my eyes.

DALEJEAN: Hate. Hate.

JAKE: I want to be happy for once in my life. With someone who I know will make my life worthwhile.

DALEJEAN: You gotta stop hating for that for that to happen, Jake. Why do you hate?

JAKE: I don't. Ever since I was thirteen, I've gone thru life seeing things that I wanted: cars, clothes, houses, dogs, shoes, and yes, oh yes, women. Boo-coo women. Nothing can be without the right woman. And I guess a man wants every fine woman he takes a liking to. But there're so many of them. So many he can't get.

DALEJEAN: Well you shouldn't let your eyes get bigger than your stomach.

JAKE: Only someone like you can fill me, Good Black. I got these big ol' hands. But they empty. I use to get up every morning, look at the size of my hands, and say, Jake you got hands that could hold water like they can hold a woman's breasts. You think I'm kidding, huh? I really did that. Swear to God.

DALEJEAN: I wish you'd leave God outta your mouth.

JAKE: Yeah I thought I was so bad I could wring water dry. Because there was nothing which I haven't done and done it well.

DALEJEAN: Jake, I'm fed up with you messin' in my life, hear?

JAKE: Hell I'm fed up too. Fed up with not getting what I want. Busting my behind over forty years, eating beans and leftovers...and all those bastards who ain't paid no dues...not one bow dollar...not even one red cent of dues...those who come up after the war's over...who don't know what it be like eating beans without meat...to wear dirty, raggedy, outta style clothes...bastards...who eat fresh vegetables and drink fruit juices...and sleep on waterbeds...with tender hands like some broads...bastards...who don't even wash diapers anymore...they the ones who wound up getting all the goodies in life...Yeah I'm fed up to my limit.

DALEJEAN: Jake...

JAKE: I didn't say that for pity.

DALEJEAN: Jake, people have struggled and died so that their children would- n't have to pay dues like us.

JAKE: But why do I have to keep paying dues. Can't get ahead. Keep falling flat on my face. I see who I want and I can't get her. Why is that, Good Black, why is that?

DALEJEAN: I don't want you, Jake. You don't have any rights to interfere with my life.

JAKE: Rights. I have to take my rights—out of necessity. I learnt that the hard way. No one is making rights for me. Young folks can't have all the rights. They can't just claim everything and everyone as their own personal plea- sures. And you...you robbing my cash register.

DALEJEAN: That's a barefaced lie and you know it. I never robbed...I ain't never stole nothing in my life.

JAKE: You know what I mean. You know darn well I been paddin' your salary every week.

DALEJEAN: I didn't ask you.

JAKE: You didn't refuse it either.

DALEJEAN: Jake, you a tall man when it comes to fumblin' on me. But you had no right to abuse Rip like you did. He ain't never hurt nobody but yellow people in Vietnam. Rip could've popped you in two pieces if he'd wanted to.

JAKE: Don't make me laugh.

DALEJEAN: I should of told him to beat the slop outta you, Jake. But I ain't that kinda woman. Now, for the last time, I ain't gonna do nothing with you. I'd rather sit on it the rest of my life before I do that. (*DALEJEAN REMOVES HER APRON.*) Things has to change around here between us.

JAKE: You quitting again?

DALEJEAN: I've got a headache; I'm going home.

JAKE: Just like that, huh?

DALEJEAN: Dock me.

JAKE: Oh, I know, you're going to see...what's his name...?

DALEJEAN: None of your business.

JAKE: Flip?

DALEJEAN: Forget you, Jake.

JAKE: Oh Rip, yeah. You're going to see Rip and play big momma, huh?

DALEJEAN: Go to hell.

JAKE: What you going to do, Good Black, nurse baby boy on your big riddles?

DALEJEAN: I didn't know you could be so foul mouthed.

JAKE: That's the way you make me act.

DALEJEAN: Don't put it on me. You was raised that way, remember?

JAKE: Yeah you going to give baby boy a lil nookey.

DALEJEAN: If there's a hell you going straight to it.

JAKE: You better pray that he's not too scared...

DALEJEAN: I seen how scared he was of you.

JAKE: Yeah well he might be so scared he might not be able to get it up.

DALEJEAN: That's what he has me for.

(LIGHTS FADE OUT AND COME UP ON RIP AS HE ENTERS HIS APARTMENT. HE IS SO DEJECTED THAT HE LEAVES HIS DOOR OPEN. AS HE CLUMPS DOWN ON THE SOFA, KIM APPEARS IN THE DOOR WAY. AS SHE CLOSES THE DOOR AND APPROACHES HIM, LIGHTS DIM.)

(LIGHTS COME UP DIM ON DALEJEAN AS SHE ENTERS THRU HER FRONT DOOR. THERE IS NOISE AND COMMOTION FROM THE FRONT ROOM. THERE ARE INDISTINGUISHABLE VOICES AND THE SOUNDS OF SOMEONE RUNNING TOWARDS THE KITCHEN. DALEJEAN IS FRIGHTENED. BUT SHE MANAGES TO TURN ON THE LIGHTS. DALEJEAN CATCHES A GLIMPSE OF PHYLLIS AS SHE RUNS UP THE STAIRS.)

DALEJEAN: Phyllis! Come down here. You hear me, girl, bring yo lil behind back down these stairs this minute.

(AS PHYLLIS CREEPS SLOWLY BACK DOWN THE STAIRS, KIM LIFTS RIP'S HEAD UP. SHE HOLDS IT IN HER HANDS.)

DALEJEAN: *(TO PHYLLIS)* What was you doing down here in the dark? Who was with you...?

PHYLLIS: No-nobody, Mom.

DALEJEAN: Don't lie to me. Who was he? Who was that, that flew outta my back door?

(JAMES JR. AND JANET APPEAR IN THEIR NIGHT CLOTHES)

DALEJEAN: Girl, I'll kill you...

(DALEJEAN STARTS HITTING PHYLLIS WITH HER HANDS. JAMES JR. AND JANET TRY TO HELP PHYLLIS.)

DALEJEAN: Let go of me. Who yall grabbin' on, huh? Yall forgot who I am? *(JAMES JR. AND JANET STEP BACK)*

DALEJEAN: James Jr., check that back door. Janet go upstairs and look in my room and get me a belt. *(TO PHYLLIS.)* Somebody's going to tell me something tonight or Jesus ain't in heaven. Tell me the truth or so help me you going to wish you wasn't born for a skirt.

PHYLLIS: We didn't do nothing, Mom, honest.

DALEJEAN: So you admit it.

PHYLLIS: I was watching T.V.

DALEJEAN: Is the T.V. on? Lying lil thang. Think I was born yesterday?

PHYLLIS: No ma'am.

DALEJEAN: Look at you...in your pajamas too. Think you too grown for me to whip, huh?

PHYLLIS: No ma'am.

(JANET APPEARS WITH A FLIMSY BELT)

DALEJEAN: *(TO JANET)* And what is this for? This thang won't kill a fly. *(TO PHYLLIS)* Did you do it? *(TO JANET)* What you standing around here for? Go to your room. *(TO PHYLLIS)* Did you?

PHYLLIS: Mom, I can't talk to you that way.

DALEJEAN: But you can do...

PHYLLIS: I didn't do nothing!

DALEJEAN: Who you raisin' your voice to?

PHYLLIS: I-I was too scared.

(JAMES JR. RETURNS)

DALEJEAN: You locked that door?

JAMES JR.: Yes ma'am.

DALEJEAN: *(AFTER A PAUSE)* Good night, James Jr.

(HE GOES UPSTAIRS)

DALEJEAN: Boy must've been doing a lot of feeling on you; look at your clothes.

PHYLLIS: Mom...

DALEJEAN: Fix your clothes, honey.

PHYLLIS: Mom, I...

DALEJEAN: No need, honey. If you didn't make at this time...But you should be ashamed of yourself. With you lil sister and your brother in the same house too.

PHYLLIS: I'm sorry, Mom.

DALEJEAN: Oh Jesus. Can't trust you after this.

PHYLLIS: I...Yes ma'am.

DALEJEAN: Talk to you tomorrow. I feel like I'm dying.

PHYLLIS: Mom, I'm sorry.

DALEJEAN: Dying...I'm dying...

PHYLLIS: Mom, don't talk about dying. Please.

DALEJEAN: Go to bed, Phyllis. No. Don't fix a lie on your face, honey. I can't live like this.

(PHYLLIS STARTS UP THE STAIRS.)

DALEJEAN: I hope that boy uses protection.

PHYLLIS: Mom, we never done anything.

(ALONE DALEJEAN PACES THE FLOOR.)

DALEJEAN: When it rains it pours...well...I was sixteen once...back in 1939...Mobile, Alabama...back then things never get better for us...for none of our folk...sharecroppers...never had too much to share...just work...and more work....slavery what it was...when you get right down to it...

I was sixteen once...yes I was...and my mother was strict on her four daughters...I looks a lot like my mother...more so than my other sistuhs...so the folk around home useta say...Momma was tall as a tulip tree...and strict...Momma you sure was strict...She didn't allow no boys sniffin' around her daughters. She useta say that if we do anything with boys like Blanche Thomas, we'd grow up looking just like Blanche. And Blanche was ugly as forty miles of ugliness...but she was built...so the mens said...and there was plenty mens after big tail Blanche Tomas...

Folk say you never forget the first one who done climbed yo tree...guess some of it true...Course he don't count much in my life since the first time...but sometimes I remember ole Rufus Lee Newsome from Opelika, Alabama, Lyin' boy you ever want to meet...told me he'd get the blue balls if I wouldn't giggle with him...

Rufus Lee and his folk moved back to Opelika...then James Harris come sniffin around me...like he knows I was a budding peach tree...Daddy died six months after Momma...Kandijean, my youngest sistuh, she married first. After her first baby was born and she didn't become as ugly as Blanche, me and my other sistuhs decided marriage must be the antidote to ugliness. 'Course I always knew better. But I never was one to confide in folk about my personal business.

James Harris and I was the last to get married. By then all my sistuhs was married too. We moved to Tennessee, then to Pittsburgh...

Phyllis, honey, I was sixteen once...and I understand... *(KIM KISSES RIP)* I know how it is...one day it's for peeing and the next day it's beggin' for discovery...and you hardly know what's happening to you...when the calling comes...you got to answer it... *(DIALS RIP'S NUMBER.)* Ain't nothing I can do about it now...if you made up your mind, come hell or high water, ain't nothing or no one's going to you...when you got to say hello... you got to... *(KIM TAKES RIP'S HAND AND HEADS INTO HIS BED-*

ROOM) ...It's a good feeling but it's such a painful break with your mother.

(LIGHTS OUT ON RIP'S APARTMENT AND THE RINGING TELE-PHONE.) Where are you, Rip? *(LIGHTS FADING ON DALEJEAN)* Rip, I need you. *(LIGHTS FADING)* Where are you?

(END OF ACT ONE)

ACT TWO PULSE ONE
(THE NEXT DAY. SUNDAY. DALEJEAN ENTERS RIP'S APART-MENT. HE IS SEATED ON THE COUCH.)

DALEJEAN: *(UNBUTTONING HER COAT.)* Good morning, honey.

RIP: What's between you and that Jake dude?

DALEJEAN: *(AFTER A PAUSE.)* Can I remove my coat first?

RIP: Naw. Leave it on. Answer my question.

DALEJEAN: What...was...the question again?

RIP: You heard me!

DALEJEAN: Nothing is between us.

RIP: Could've fooled the hell out of me.

DALEJEAN: With that tone in your voice, I 'oun't know if I should stay or not.

RIP: Suit yourself. You been messing around with him.

DALEJEAN: With...? Jake? He doesn't mean nothing to me. Not that way.

RIP: Why was the fool going to kill me?

DALEJEAN: Rip...

RIP: Rip nothing. Over what? I never done nothing to him in my whole life. Never touched nothing of his—that I knew about.

DALEJEAN: You still haven't.

RIP: Yeah, sure.

DALEJEAN: *(HANDS ON HIPS.)* That's what I said, man. You can't make something out of nothing.

RIP: What does a nigger want to kill another nigger over, huh?

DALEJEAN: How would I know.

RIP: Over his money. His food. His clothes. His car. And his pussy.

DALEJEAN: What? You accusing me and—and Jake?

RIP: Dalejean, what does it sound like to you? Hell, no wonder you wouldn't take off from work to spend one night with me. You got a good thing going and—

DALEJEAN: I told you why I couldn't. And that was the truth. I'll fight those words back down your throat.

RIP: Don't yell at me.

DALEJEAN: You accuse me. And then you got the nerve to tell me not to yell. Are you...?

RIP: Yeah. We can discuss this without—

DALEJEAN: Discuss! This ain't no discussion.

RIP: Not with you yelling.

DALEJEAN: This is a trial.

RIP: Oh? Who's on trial?

DALEJEAN: Me. You. Both of us. I called you last night and you wasn't in.

RIP: I was in.

DALEJEAN: Well, you didn't answer your phone.

RIP: So?

DALEJEAN: So? So I needed you last night.

RIP: I was ah busy.

DALEJEAN: Where are you Black men when we need you, huh?

RIP: Hell, don't start talking about no fucken Black men when...

DALEJEAN: No. I know you don't want to hear the truth. Right now, I don't know what you want to hear. I can't even get a hello out of you. Or how do you feel this Sunday morning, honey. *(VOICE CRACKING IN HURT.)* Look at me! Still got my coat on like I'm outside of you. Outside in the cold. *(TAKES TWO STEPS CLOSER TO HIM, THEN HALTS.)* This morning's the first time the sun's been out in weeks. In spite of everything that's happened to me, to us, since last night, I felt real good, Rip. I would see you and be comforted by you.

RIP: Look, Dalejean...

DALEJEAN: *(OPENING HER COAT.)* See, I thought I'd wear this new dress I made. Just for you. One time you told me that you bet I'd look nice in blue. And I asked you what shade of blue. You pointed to-to something that-that escapes me now. But I kept that blue in my eyes until I found it. How do I look, Rip? And I beautiful? Is it the right shade of blue? It's not too long, is it? Cut too low here for you? *(SHE WAITS FOR HIS RESPONSE. INSTEAD OF RESPONDING, HE LOOKS AWAY FROM HER.)* All right. All right. Yes, Jake wants me. And he's tried to...to force himself on me. I don't want him. I haven't given in to his harrassment either. I'm not made that way. Rip, I wouldn't fool around with no other man if I'm in love with someone, you, and I'm giving you my favors.

RIP: Oh, so it's favors now?

DALEJEAN: You know what I mean.

RIP: I only know what I see with my own two eyes. Not through walls.

DALEJEAN: Why you doing this to me? I haven't done what you think. Many times, in this very apartment, in our bed, in your arms, I lay there being very open and honest to you about me. Told you things about me, most women wouldn't dream of telling their husbands. I didn't sugar-coat them either. My relationship with you has been open like cotton in a field. How you can sit there and pick at my feelings and accuse me of laying around with some other man. I can't understand this. And I certainly don't appreciate it. Not from you, Rip. I don't.

RIP: You think I appreciated almost getting killed by a turkey I don't know from a hole in the ground.

DALEJEAN: You can't put his actions on me. It's unfair.

RIP: You just said he wanted you. Harassing...

DALEJEAN: But his actions are his own actions. Not mine. I didn't lead him on. You wrong, Rip. You wrong. Can't you—

RIP: You didn't let him?

DALEJEAN: I don't believe you.

RIP: You did or you didn't?

DALEJEAN: Not once!

RIP: No?

DALEJEAN: Hell no!

RIP: Every woman'll give up a lil leg if she thinks she can get away with it.

DALEJEAN: What?

RIP: You hear me.

DALEJEAN: You don't believe that mess.

RIP: I really do.

DALEJEAN: Well, brother, I'm one woman who wouldn't and haven't.

RIP: *(LEAPS UP ANGRILY.)* Gaddamn this! *(HE POINTS HIS FINGER IN HER FACE, APPROACHING HER MENACINGLY.)* You my woman!

DALEJEAN: I am. *(SHE BACKS AWAY FROM HIM.)*

RIP: *(WITH HIS INSISTENCE FINGER.)* YOU be my woman!

DALEJEAN: *(CIRCLES AROUND HIM.)* I love you.
(THE TELEPHONE RINGS.)

RIP: You be my woman, you act like my woman.

DALEJEAN: *(Emphatically.)* I am! *(IN A DEMANDING TONE.)* Rip, stop this. I haven't done nothing. I haven't. I haven't.

RIP: Don't lie to me.

DALEJEAN: *(NEAR THE TELEPHONE.)* I'm not. I don't deserve this from you.

RIP: *(TAKES A JERKY STEP TOWARDS HER.)* You might deserve more than this.

DALEJEAN: Don't—don't you hit me.

RIP: *(STOPS AND JUST STARES AT HER.)*

DALEJEAN: Damn this phone. *(DALEJEAN YANKS IT UP. THE SECOND SHE DOES, A LIGHT COMES UP ON KIM WITH THE PHONE TO*

HER EAR.) Hello. *(DALEJEAN REMOVES THE PHONE SLIGHTLY FROM HER EAR AND LOOKS AT RIP; HE TURNS HIS BACK ON HER.)* Hello. *(PAUSE.)* Who? *(PAUSE.)* Rip who? You have the wrong number. *(DALEJEAN SLAMS THE PHONE ON ITS CRADLE.)* Cow! *(LONG PAUSE AS RIP SLIDES ONTO THE COUCH.)*

DALEJEAN: Cow. *(PAUSE.)* Cow. *(PAUSE.)* You have them around the corner just waiting by the phone for something like this to happen, huh?

RIP: I don't know what you're fat-mouthing about.

DALEJEAN: Bet you got a cute explanation...men always do.

RIP: Change the subject. Go ahead.

DALEJEAN: Don't worry. I'm not going to accuse you. Of that cow whoever she was. I'm bigger than that. I trust you.

RIP: Fuck some trust. You been messing around with—

DALEJEAN: For heaven's sake, man.

RIP: You're going to tell the truth before you leave here.

(PAUSE.)

DALEJEAN: I've done that already, Rip. Over and over again. What can I do to prove...?

RIP: I don't think you can prove anything to me now. Not the way I feel.

DALEJEAN: What about my feelings? Okay, I didn't mean to say prove. I meant...

RIP: Nothing.

DALEJEAN: Trust me.

RIP: How do you think you can prove something like this to me?

DALEJEAN: The proof is right here in my eyes.

RIP: There is no proof.

DALEJEAN: Why we keep talking about proof? Why?

RIP: Well, I can't look down there and see if he stretched it, can—

(DALEJEAN HAULS OFF AND SLAPS HIM GOOD AND HARD.)

DALEJEAN: Rip...you just a man of your times. Carrying your ego and masculinity around in your pants. Much like Jake. And you think that if some other man's getting some of your ego...that that somehow belittles you. Makes you less than a full man or some such mess. You think now you've lost your power over your woman. But it ain't about power over anyone. You see, us women, we know about these things. We know how and what you feel. But you never learnt how to cope with your ego. I know you wrong to feel this way. And Rip, you absolutely wrong. I don't know how to convince you otherwise. If that was possible, if women know who to do that, then we would all be able to keep our mens warm for us. I'm not bluing you, Rip. You just a man of your times, baby. *(DALEJEAN OPENS HER COAT WIDE FOR HIM)* See, baby. It is a lovely dress, ain't it? I know I look good in it. Rip, tell me how good I look in this dress to you.

(DALEJEAN BUTTONS HER COAT. AT THE DOOR SHE TURNS.) Rip, you stretched me. Stretched me wide open for your love. Only one other man ever done that to me. And he's dead and buried. With you I wanted us to happen so bad so very bad that I engulfed you whole. I allowed you to penetrate the box of my treasure. I liked the way you touched me. How gentle you was. You got strong shoulders, man, that has carried some life over hills and valleys. You were like spring water to me. After you started coming into the restaurant frequently I felt like I could touch the ceiling without standing on my tippy toes. I could kiss the sky. And I liked how slow we was with each other. How we appreciated one another over dinner—after you got off from work. Our relationship grew. A beautiful one too. Now you've pushed my happiness and my peace further away from me. I slapped you because I wanted to slap the ugliness outta your mouth. There are no slaps of love.

Rip...See you can't even look at me. I can't even fight for you no more. Because I'oun't know what you might say next. And I can't take no more ugliness from you. It's not your accusations driving me away from you, Rip. I want you to understand that I'd leap over a hundred Mr. Black America's just to get to your lips, man. But it's your silence, your mistrust, your...

(KIM APPEARS IN THE DOORWAY. KIM WALKS PASS DALEJEAN. THE THREE OF THEM STARE FROM ONE TO THE OTHER. DALE-JEAN EXITS. KIM WALKS TOWARD RIP'S BEDROOM.)

KIM: *(TO RIP)* Coming?

(LIGHTS FADE OUT AND COME UP ON)

ACT TWO PULSE TWO

(HARRIS' HOME. JAMES JR., JANET, AND PHYLLIS ENTER THE HOUSE. THEY HAVE SHOPPING BAGS FILLED WITH CHRISTMAS GIFTS.)

JAMES JR.: Boy I'm glad to be home.

JANET: Me too.

PHYLLIS: Who's going to tell Mom?

JAMES JR.: Not me.

JANET: Not me either.

PHYLLIS: I'll tell her.

JAMES JR.: No I'll tell. I'm the oldest.

PHYLLIS: Okay. Here I'll take these gifts and hide them in my room.

JANET: Hide 'em in mines. Mom never looks in my room.

(DALEJEAN WALKS DOWN THE STAIRS IN A BULBOUS ROBE.)

DALEJEAN: Hi.

JANET: *(RUNNING TO DALEJEAN.)* Mom, you should've been there.

DALEJEAN: Where?

JAMES JR.: *(NUDGING PHYLLIS)* Phyllis.

JANET: We were in Kaufmann's. When we were leaving out...on the fifth Avenue side...this security guard walked up to James Jr., and demanded to look in his shopping bags.

DALEJEAN: What?

JANET: James Jr., stood straight...straight as this house...

PHYLLIS: Jan's writing her first book.

JANET: James Jr., looked that white man dead in his eyes and said: "What do you mean what I got in my bags. I paid for what's in here and it's personal and none of your business."

DALEJEAN: *(TO JAMES JR.)* James Jr., what happened next? Did you call him outta his name?

JANET: No ma'am. People started crowding around us. The whole store. Everybody was watching.

PHYLLIS: Janet's exaggerating now.

JANET: It was too. The guard said that James Jr. had stole...

DALEJEAN: I know he was lying.

JANET: ...And he was going to take us to see the manager. Dalejean. What did the manager do?

JANET: Wait a minute, Mom. You missing the best part. The security guard snatched James Jr.'s, arm. "Man, don't be manhandling me," James Jr. said. "My mother don't grab on me."

DALEJEAN: Oh.

JAMES JR.: I didn't mean it like that, Mom.

JANET: James Jr., demanded that he be put in jail. So he could sue them. For false arrest, right?

DALEJEAN: Wait a minute. James Jr., you had my charge card, didn't you? And I told yall to always get you receipts.

PHYLLIS: Yes ma'am, we had everything. We showed them to him. Matching each receipt with each Christmas present.

JAMES JR.: I had Kwanzaa gifts. You two had X-mas...

DALEJEAN: Stop that, boy. Remember what you told me.

JANET: Mom you should've heard Phyllis. When the security guard threatened to go upside James Jr.'s head because he wouldn't let the man manhandle him, Phyllis got all hyper: "Leave my brother alone...he ain't..." when Phyllis gets real made, she says "ain't...

PHYLLIS: No I don't.

DALEJEAN: I'm confused now.

JAMES JR.: Janet's not telling it right. The man thought I hit him on a sly, I think.

PHYLLIS: Mom, I swear to God...

DALEJEAN: Don't swear. You ain't got nobody to swear to but yourself.

PHYLLIS: I swear James Jr. didn't hit that ole white man.

JANET: Phyllis did.

DALEJEAN: So why didn't you tell the man that?

JANET: I wouldn't squeal on my own sister, Mom.

DALEJEAN: Well, it's over. Whatever comes I'll handle it. Don't yall worry about it. Ain't nobody going to run over my children and stand on two legs.

JAMES JR.: Mom, can I go down to the Afro-American Cultural Center?

JANET: Me too?

DALEJEAN: Go on. Don't yall take nothing outta this house that doesn't belong out of it.

JANET: I won't.

(JAMES JR. AND JANET EXIT.)

DALEJEAN: *(TO PHYLLIS.)* What you doing mopen around this house for the past four days?

PHYLLIS: I'm on punishment and you didn't say...

DALEJEAN: Girl you better get outta my sight. My house ain't no prison.

PHYLLIS: Mom...

DALEJEAN: Honey, don't smear it if it's not messy.

PHYLLIS: It's not. I want to say I love you and I'm sorry.

DALEJEAN: Well don't be sorry...

PHYLLIS & DALEJEAN: Just be careful.

PHYLLIS: I will.

DALEJEAN: And make sure that sneaky boy uses some protection—if you can't wait until we see Dr. Greenlee next week. Tell him to buy one of them whatchamacallits?

PHYLLIS: Mom I know.

DALEJEAN: Guess you do. Everybody else does too. Limit yourself, honey, hear?

PHYLLIS: I'm not doing anything Mom—for a long time.

DALEJEAN: If you say so. I want college for all three of youns. Anyway I'm too young to be a built-in babysitter and a grandmother. But you not too young to be a mother.

PHYLLIS: I'm not ready for anything like that.

DALEJEAN: Anytime after college graduation will suit me just fine.

PHYLLIS: Me too. Bet you'll make the best grandmother in the world.

DALEJEAN: I know that. Oh, honey, bring that boy around sometimes. I want to read him.

(LIGHTS FADE OUT AND COME UP ON HARRIS' FRONT ROOM. SISTER LOUISE IS SITTING ON THE COUCH DRINKING THE LAST OF HER COFFEE. DALEJEAN ENTERS WITH A FRESH POT OF COFFEE.)

LOUISE: The chicken has come home to roost.

DALEJEAN: My roosting days are over. I'm a flying lark. And I ain't got no salt on my wings.

LOUISE: Well like I was saying, you just thought you were in love with this boy.

DALEJEAN: Man.

LOUISE: Well I'm just outdone.

DALEJEAN: *(POURING COFFEE.)* Watch your hand, Lou.

LOUISE: You probably gave the poor boy worms.

DALEJEAN: Enough coffee for you?

LOUISE: A plenty—if you're going to be stingy with your delicious coffee. *(PAUSE.)* Now there's no room for my cream.

DALEJEAN: I'm sorry, Lou. Just ain't my week to tell the truth.

LOUISE: Come sit down. Let's thrash this thing out together.

DALEJEAN: Nothing to thrash out.

LOUISE: Is too. Bad as you been looking around here. Looking like a sick hen. And down right inhospitable too. In II Peter, Verse 2, it says...

DALEJEAN: Things like this happen to the best of us, Lou.

LOUISE: Hello to that. Tried to tell you about these younger mens.

DALEJEAN: What ah younger mens?

LOUISE: Don't get salty now, sister. You can't play wife without the Lord's blessing, hello. And expect to be rewarded too. Outlaw sex, I call it.

DALEJEAN: As long as we been friends I still can't tell what goes on in your mind. It's surprising to me that you has seven children.

LOUISE: Not to me. With the Lord's blessing, hello. Not foolish love.

DALEJEAN: I didn't tell you I was in love with no one.

LOUISE: You don't have to. You acts it. And you sure looks it. Like you lost your best...

DALEJEAN: I don't feel like I've lost...

LOUISE: Well pray tell, what is it then?

DALEJEAN: None of your nebby business.

LOUISE: Well shut my mouth. I'm old and I knows my place.

Dalejean : Well I'm not old. But I know my place now.

LOUISE: Half truths. I can read them a mile away—blindfolded.

DALEJEAN: Keep talking, Lou. I got all afternoon.

LOUISE: As you know I'm not one to put down or low rate the women of our race. Or any race for that matter. Race is like sand in the desert thru the Eyes of Jesus, hello. Now there is them that is and them that is not.

DALEJEAN: That so.

LOUISE: In the chosen flock, that is. The children of Jesus comes in many shades, sizes and colors with different temperaments, of course. The onliest power is the power of Jesus' salvation. To be born again. God knows we need salvation. No superstitions. God knows we need redemption. The love of Jesus, hello. Not the lust of man's flesh.

DALEJEAN: Lou, I want Rip.

LOUISE: Sister Dalejean, don't be a slave to the flesh of man. It leads you down into the briar patch of the sooper pitchfork. Look at yourself, sister. You're letting yourself go. You got man-whipped written all over you. Reach out for the true Man of men, He'll lighten your burdens for you. *(DALEJEAN OPENS HER MOUTH.)* Don't say the wrong name again, my sistuh. Look at it this way. Look around at the conditions of the world today. What do you see? Great disorders. Old men and young gals laying up together. In the grit of the body. Against the gravy of the soul. Flesh lovers. And flesh seekers of adulterous undertakings...as sure as I'm in this house built on sand and communism. And drinking this awful...awful black coffee.

DALEJEAN: I ran outta cream, Lou.

LOUISE: That's a sign of the times. A sign of the great disorders. We're running out of time, sister. Heads cut off from the Body of Jesus Christ, hello. Women and women laying up together. Freaking out. Yes that's what they calling it these days...freaking out. Sodom and Gomorrah relived...down the street...Wylie Avenue...Homewood...in the red bricks of the projects...Herron Avenue...Schenley Heights...East Liberty...Northview Heights...

DALEJEAN: In Fox Chapel. Mt. Lebanon...

Louise. Get away, Satan. Get away from my sister, Sister Dalejean Roberts Harris.

DALEJEAN: You could use some good Satan yourself, Lou.

LOUISE: I hears you, Satan. Knocking at the lips of my sister. Get off her back, Satan. Riding my sister like she's a swine devoid of a soul. Get. Before the water hose of my Jesus drowns you like you're an ant in the ocean of Armageddon. Get out of those poor blind foolish seekers of the flesh. The bareback flesh. The fleshy part of the flesh. The hidden parts of the flesh. *(TO DALEJEAN.)* Can you feel the spirit, Sister Dalejean?

DALEJEAN: Yes.

LOUISE: Hello. Look around at the conditions of the world. Gays ain't gay. They bad and sad. Look around at the conditions of the world...over there, sister. See. Womens and younger mens. Middle age womens and younger mens. Younger mens and middle age womens, I say, laying up together.

DALEJEAN: Hello!

LOUISE: I knows my Jesus hasn't forsaken you, my sister.

DALEJEAN: Rip has, Lou.

LOUISE: See that's it. The Lord hasn't. Listen to me, Sister Dalejean. I come to you out of duty as a friend, a neighbor and a Christian.

DALEJEAN: I know, Lou. But I need some milk in my bowl sometimes.

LOUISE: Come here, sister. Stand with me before the Almighty.

DALEJEAN: Lou...

Louise. A younger man can be mighty pleasing to a woman your age, can't he, sister?

DALEJEAN: Yes he can.

LOUISE: He can satisfy your physical needs.

DALEJEAN: Yes he can.

LOUISE: He can get into the deepest parts of you, can't he, sister?

DALEJEAN: Oh yes, the deepest...

LOUISE: He can make you feel mighty proud to be a woman?

DALEJEAN: Who you tellin'.

LOUISE: He can raise you up to emotional pinnacles unknown before?

DALEJEAN: Yes, yes.

LOUISE: He can burn you up with fever?

DALEJEAN: What you say.

LOUISE: He filled you, hasn't he, sister?

DALEJEAN: To the brim.

LOUISE: He...

DALEJEAN: He put dazzling stars on my nipples.

LOUISE: He did?

DALEJEAN: He brought gladness to my soul.

LOUISE: You say dazzling stars on your...

DALEJEAN: He worked with me real slow...

LOUISE: Did he, sister?

DALEJEAN: Yes.

LOUISE: How slow?

DALEJEAN: Molasses slow. Blackstrap molasses at that.

LOUISE: Did he now?

DALEJEAN: And tender like a feather.

LOUISE: Do tell.

DALEJEAN: All around...here and there...

LOUISE: He put dazzling stars on my...

DALEJEAN: All around the world.

LOUISE: Oh all around the world.

DALEJEAN: And gentle.

LOUISE: Oh gentleness.

DALEJEAN: Climbing...climbing together...the fire coming...burning...

LOUISE: I feel it, sister...

DALEJEAN: The milk churning...

LOUISE: Churn milk, Churn...

DALEJEAN: Flooding my insides...

LOUISE: Churn...

DALEJEAN: Faster...

Louis: Harder...

DALEJEAN: More...

LOUISE: Lots more...

DALEJEAN: I can't breath.

LOUISE: Help me, Jesus, it's coming.

DALEJEAN: Yes. Yes.

LOUISE: Jesus, have mercy.

(DALEJEAN AND LOUISE CATCH THEMSELVES.)

LOUISE: But did he fill the spiritual vacuum in you, sister?

DALEJEAN: He did, Lou.

LOUISE: Jesus can do it better.

DALEJEAN: Last night, I woke up screaming Rip's name, Lou.

LOUISE: Should've called on Jesus, sister Dalejean.

DALEJEAN: I love him, Lou.

LOUISE: Try Jesus before it's too late. Don't make another mistake.

DALEJEAN: Mistake. You think I don't have any sense, don't you?

LOUISE: I never said you didn't have any sense.

DALEJEAN: Well what do you think. You think I just rushed into this man's life without foresight. I thought about it a thousand times over backwards, frontways and sideways. I talked it over with myself until I was blue in the face.

LOUISE: Did you talk it over with Jesus first?

DALEJEAN: No. Just myself.

LOUISE: Well look at that. No wonder. Should've conferred directly with Him, hello.

DALEJEAN: I want Rip.

LOUISE: Poor Sister Dalejean, how you must've endured with that young man.

DALEJEAN: Endured? I loved every blessed moment of it and then some.

LOUISE: I know. I know. Now you have Jesus to turn to. You need Him more now than before. You need Him to carry you the rest of the way. Say it, sister.

DALEJEAN: Say what, Lou?

LOUISE: Say I need Jesus. I need Jesus. Call on Him, sister. Call His Holy name. He'll come into you. He'll come into your heart and soul. He'll cleanse it white as snow. Say it sister: I needs my Jesus.

DALEJEAN: Lou, please...

LOUISE: I needs my Jesus. Say...

DALEJEAN: Don't make me, Lou.

LOUISE: Say it before it's too late.

DALEJEAN: I—I...

LOUISE: Go on. Tell the truth and shame the devil.

DALEJEAN: I need Rip. Lou, I need him. And he needs me too. He ain't going to be full without my arms, my lips...

LOUISE: Reckon I don't understand what you're going through. And it's not my place to butt into your private affairs.

DALEJEAN: That's not so. You just keep buttin' in, hear? I mean that too. And I promise I'm never going to run outta cream again. Soon as one of them children come in I'm sending down to the corner store and get us some cream, hear?

LOUISE: Hello.

DALEJEAN: Wait a minute. I'm turning this television on. One of them spooky stories comes on around this time. You watch it while I fix us a real nice lunch.

LOUISE: Well hello. Ah sistuh Dalejean, I believe it's your Christian duty to confide in me directly. Now...about those dazzling strawberries on your...

ACT TWO PULSE THREE

(RIP'S APARTMENT. KIM HAS PREPARED DINNER FOR HER AND RIP. THEY ARE EATING ON THE COFFEE TABLE.)

KIM: *(CALLING OUT TO RIP.)* Come and get it.

RIP: *(ENTERING FROM THE BEDROOM.)* Button up yourself.

KIM: Aw baby.

RIP: Do it. *(1/2 BEAT.)* Now.

KIM: All right.

RIP: And stop acting like a little kid.

KIM: I'm not. But that's the way you want to treat me.

RIP: I don't.

KIM: I do something wrong again?

RIP: No.

KIM: The last few days you've been jumping down my throat for nothing.

RIP: I have?

KIM: Yep. At every little thing I say or do. If you're getting tired of me, tell me. You don't have to hurt me with an attitude.

RIP: Are you going to sit down and eat or not?

KIM: See. See what I mean. There you go again. Snapping out over nothing.

RIP: *(LOOKING AT THE FOOD.)* Looks good.

KIM: Thanks. I wish we could eat at the kitchen table like...

RIP: This is fine with me. What's this?

KIM: Cabbage.

RIP: What are these red...and green things?

KIM: Peppers, silly. Eat. *(PAUSE.)* Rip, I was thinking...

RIP: Thinking about what?

KIM: I was wondering maybe I should move down here with you.

RIP: Come again.

KIM: Well I spend more time down here than I do up—

RIP: Kim, I have to think about that.

KIM: You have lots of time.

Rip. I thought you were going home for Christmas.

KIM: Changed my mind. A woman's prerogative. Nope I'm going to stay right here with you. Keep my eyes on you. You know, Rip, you're a very spiritual man.

RIP: Me? You must be kidding.

KIM: Special too.

RIP: Both?

KIM: Both. I can't get over it. Me and you. I'm so lucky.

RIP: Kim, I have to talk to you about something.

KIM: Not now, Rip. Let's eat first. *(PAUSE.)* Rip, give me an equal chance, hear?

RIP: At what, Kim?

KIM: You know. Against...them. You see, I"m learning a lot from you. Not that I need a man to become a woman. But you make me feel special.

RIP: Kim...Hell I feel like a capon.

KIM: Rip, can't nothing come between us, can it?

RIP: I wouldn't be too sure of that, Kim.

KIM: My guards up. Oh, guess what?

RIP: I really don't feel like guessing .

KIM: I came last night. The first time in my whole life. It was wonderful. What a Christmas present. Boy.
(LIGHTS OUT AND COME UP ON)

ACT TWO PULSE FOUR
(JAKE'S RESTAURANT ON CHRISTMAS EVE. DALEJEAN BEHIND THE COUNTER. JAKE ENTERS WITH A BOTTLE OF WHISKEY IN A BROWN STATE STORE BAG.)

JAKE: See your ready and rearing to go.

DALEJEAN: *(REMOVING HER APRON.)* Everything's in order here.

JAKE: *(EYING HER UP AND DOWN.)* Don't we look nice.

DALEJEAN: *(MODELING.)* You like it?

JAKE: What's to like. Outside don't mean nothing. It's snowing outside, don't mean we ain't alive.

DALEJEAN: We alive, Jake and doing good business this holiday week too.

JAKE: We? We. We on speaking terms again?

DALEJEAN: I never stopped speaking to you, Jake.

JAKE: Oh no. What do you call it?

DALEJEAN: I stopped letting you feel all over me.

JAKE: No, I stopped. On my own accord too. It hurts to be whupped at every turn in your life, Good Black. But at least I'm man enough to frown and bear it.

DALEJEAN: Jake, you don't have anything to frown about. You can't be a thief and a man too.

JAKE: *(RIPPING UP THE BAG.)* Yeah. I'm probably the only man in the world who can put salt and pepper on disappointment and eat it.

DALEJEAN: Don't be so hard on yourself. And Jake...

JAKE: What's that, Good Black.

DALEJEAN: Thanks for letting me off early tonight. I need this. I need this.

JAKE: What the hell. You be back to work the day after Christmas, hear? And you're off ten o'clock New Year's Eve. I'm closing this joint down for New Year.

DALEJEAN: I got it, boss.
(DALEJEAN PICKS UP HER COAT.)

JAKE: You look...you look great, Good Black. Inside, you look even better. Good Black, you a great lady.

DALEJEAN: Thanks, Jake. That's real sweet.
(DALEJEAN PICKS UP TWO GIFT-WRAPPED PACKAGES, SEPA-RATES THEM, THEN HANDS ONE TO JAKE.)

DALEJEAN: Merry Christmas.

JAKE: Never had a merry one. Thanks.

(DALEJEAN STARTS FOR THE DOOR.)

JAKE: Oh, Good Black.

(DALEJEAN STOPS AND TURNS.)

JAKE: Good Black, don't crack, hear?

DALEJEAN: I won't, Jake. I won't. Ever.

(DALEJEAN EXITS. JAKE TAKES A DRINK FROM HIS HALF EMPTY BOTTLE.)

JAKE: There goes a great lady. What is she doing in a jungle. The Hill's a messed up place for a lady. Man who can explain why a person or themselves are placed right here...right now...in this place...in this time....Hay a great lady works right in here...she just walked through that door...fine as she wants to be...You can't force nothing on her, world. If she doesn't want it, you can't make her drink it. Great old black lady. She got two suns under her armpits. She taught me something about women. And a hell of a lot about myself. Yall want a hit. Yall want a hit. I'm talking out loud... the top of my lungs...cause it's my joint...it's my good gin...it's snowing outside...and I'm celebrating my first Christmas...

(LIGHTS FADE OUT AND COME UP ON)

ACT TWO PULSE FIVE

(RIP'S APARTMENT. KIM AND RIP ARE SEATED AT OPPOSITE ENDS OF THE COUCH. THERE IS A KNOCK ON THE DOOR. KIM OPENS IT. DALEJEAN ENTERS. ALTHOUGH SHE NOTICES KIM, DALEJEAN ACTS AS IF SHE IS NOT THERE. DALEJEAN WALKS OVER AND PUTS A RECORD ALBUM ON THE RECORD PLAYER. SHE THEN SITS DOWN IN A CHAIR WITH HER COAT ON AND HER GIFT-WRAPPED PACKAGE ON HER LAP. KIM LOOKS AT RIP WHO DOESN'T DO ANYTHING. HE JUST SITS THERE, SOMETIME STANDING, STARING AT DALEJEAN.)

(KIM REALIZING THAT RIP IS MORE INTERESTED IN DALEJEAN LEAPS UP AND RUNS OUT OF THE APARTMENT. AFTER KIM LEAVES, DALEJEAN TAKES OFF HER COAT. RIP GETS UP TO HELP HER. BUT SHE WAVES HIM OFF. SHE REMOVES IT HERSELF, PLACING IT OVER THE BACK OF THE COUCH.)

(SHE HANDS RIP THE GIFT. HE TAKES IT, NODS, PLACES IT ON THE COFFEE TABLE AND GOES TO KISS DALEJEAN. SHE WAVES HIM OFF AGAIN.)

(RIP SITS ON THE COFFEE TABLE. DALEJEAN STRUTS BEFORE HIM IN HIS FACE, TOUCHING HIS EARS, THE NAPE OF HIS NECK, CHIN...THEN FINALLY SHE TAKES HIM BY THE HAND AND LEADS HIM INTO THE BEDROOM.)

(LIGHTS OUT BLACK AND COME UP ON)

ACT TWO PULSE SIX
(HARRIS' HOME. JAMES JR., JANET AND PHYLLIS.)

JANET: What she want to talk to us about?

PHYLLIS: All I know is Mom said for us not to go nowhere until she comes down stairs.

JAMES JR.: Hope it's not bad news. I heard Snake—

PHYLLIS: Darrell.

JAMES JR.: I Heard he was coming by on this unholy day.

PHYLLIS: He is. To bring my present.

JANET. And to meet Mom.

JAMES JR.: If he ain't right, I hate to be in his shoes when Mom gets thru with him.

PHYLLIS: He's right.

JAMES JR.: Really Phyllis?

PHYLLIS: No it's not right. Darrell and I were coming to the first day of Kwanzaa tomorrow at the Afro-American Cultural Center...

JAMES JR.: My man Darrell. Anyway if you dig him, Phyllis...well you got pretty good taste sometimes.

(Dalejean comes down the stairs. Bulbous robe again.)

DALEJEAN: Why the long faces? *(Beat.)* Santa Claus was good to yall this year, huh? *(Beat.)* OK. What...what if I told yall I was thanking about getting married. *(Beat.)*

JANET: I think it's nice, Mom.

JAMES JR.: It's a shock to me.

DALEJEAN: How long its going to take you to come outta this shock you in?

JANET: Mom, if that's what you want, then I think it's great.

DALEJEAN: OK, Janet, we heard from you. Anyone else?

JAMES JR.: Is he going to live with us?

(The girls laugh.)

DALEJEAN: James Jr., please.

JANET: Boys are silly, ain't they Mom?

JAMES JR.: I guess it's okay.

DALEJEAN: Phyllis?

PHYLLIS: I'm happy for you, Mom. He's got the best woman in the whole world going for him.

JANET: Who is he?

PHYLLIS: Yeah, what's his name? Bet he's cute?

JANET: Of course he is; Mom wouldn't marry no scab...

DALEJEAN: Wait a minute. Don't yall get carried away with all this. I said I'm thinking. Thinking, I said.

JANET: You mean, thanking, Mom.

DALEJEAN: Yeah, thanking. That's when it's real serious when you thanking, right?

JANET: Right.

PHYLLIS: Boy oh boy, Mom's been sneaking around.

DALEJEAN: The difference between me and you is that I'm grown and you're not yet.

PHYLLIS: Well, a father is a father.

DALEJEAN: I never said I was trying to get youns a father. You have fathers. Decent fathers—in their own rights. I never spoke evil about yo fathers to you. I done help shape yall with these two arms and this brain in my head. It took a lot of Alabama wit. But I did it. Now you going to have to make whatever you want of this—if it happens. But what I want is not a father for youns, I want a husband for me—and a few extras on the side.

JANET: We don't mind having another grown person around the house, do we James Jr.?

JAMES JR.: Three against one. I'm sure we can make him into a father. Right?

DALEJEAN: Oh, one more thing. He's a wee bit younger than me.

PHYLLIS: So?

JAMES JR.: Yeah, Mom, so what. You don't need an old man. Ain't nothing wrong with you.

DALEJEAN: You ain't said nothing.

JANET: Yep, Good Black don't crack.

DALEJEAN: Girl, where did you hear that?

PHYLLIS: She read it.

JANET: I read it.

PHYLLIS: Told you.

JAMES JR.: Well one thing for sure when he gets in this family, he'll get old fast.

DALEJEAN: Let's not start rushing old on him yet. I gots plenty a work for him to do. I sure hope yall like him. Well yall certainly surprised me. Fooled me. But I like it. Yall keep fooling me like this, hear?

PHYLLIS: Mom he can't help for being crazy about you. You're a tough-looking momma. Isn't she James Jr.?

JAMES JR.: She's all right.

JANET, PHYLLIS, DALEJEAN: All right!

PHYLLIS: Let's beat him.

(LIGHTS OUT AND COME UP ON)

(ACT TWO, PULSE SEVEN)
(RIP'S APARTMENT. HE IS ON HIS WAY OUT THE DOOR WITH HIS OVERCOAT ON AND PACKAGES UNDER HIS ARM. WHEN HE OPENS THE DOOR KIM IS STANDING THERE WITH A WHITE ENVELOPE IN HER HAND.)

RIP: Kim. Hi.

KIM: Rip.

RIP: Looks like you're cutting out.

KIM: Yep. Home to Philly.

RIP: Well you have a Merry Christmas and a Happy New Year, hear?

KIM: Yeah, sure, Rip. One very special one. You understand, don't you?

KIM: I understand.

RIP: What you got there?

KIM: Just a card and a note. For you.

RIP: Thanks. Very nice of you.

KIM: You good people, Rip. It was for more than you think.

RIP: I hope so.

KIM: Sorry about that Christmas dinner I promised you.

RIP: Me too.

KIM: For real?

RIP: On the black hand side.

KIM: Kool and the Gang. Some things go on forever. Can I walk with you?

KIM: Sure. I'm going down here on Centre and Catch the 82 Lincoln downtown to the ole faithful Greyhound.

RIP: I would like to talk with you a few minutes. Maybe it'll help both of us to keep our heads together.

KIM: Oh I'll be all right, Rip. Philly's home. It's my sanctuary.

RIP: Well you keep looking for your tomorrows, hear? *(RIP TAKES HER SUITCASE.)* It's going to be a long wait on that 82.

KIM: Waiting is what I have to carry. And it goes on forever.

(LIGHTS OUT AND COME UP ON)

ACT TWO PULSE SEVEN
(HARRIS' HOME. DALEJEAN, JAMES JR., PHYLLIS AND JANET ARE OPENING CHRISTMAS GIFTS. WHEN THE FRONT DOOR BELL RINGS.)

JANET: I'll get it.

(JANET RETURNS WITH RIP. DALEJEAN KISSES RIP ON THE CHEEK. SHE THEN INTRODUCES RIP TO HER CHILDREN.)

(RIP HANDS HIS GIFTS OUT: FIRST TO JANET, THEN TO PHYLLIS. JAMES JR. IS RELUCTANT AT FIRST TO ACCEPT HIS BUT WITH JANET AND PHYLLIS NUDGING HIM, HE ACCEPTS IT.)

(RIP AND JAMES JR. SHAKE HANDS. RIP THEN HANDS DALE-JEAN HER PACKAGE.)

(THE DOORBELL RINGS AGAIN.)

JANET: I'll get it.

(JANET RETURNS WITH SISTER LOUISE.)
(SLOW FADE, THEN ABRUPT BLACKNESS.)

Shauneille Perry

IN DAHOMEY

Karamu House

In Dahomey by Shauneille Perry.
Copyright© 1990 by Shauneille Perry. All rights reserved.

Shauneille Perry & Will Marion Cook

SHAUNEILLE PERRY (Author of Book) works as a director, writer, and teacher in New York. A theatre graduate of Howard University, she was a member of the original Howard Players. She holds an M.F.A. in Directing from the Goodman Theatre in Chicago and was a Fulbright Scholar in Classical Theatre at the Royal Academy of Dramatic Art in London. She has directed over 100 plays, regionally and abroad, most recently the critically acclaimed *Williams & Walker*, starring Ben Harvey and Vondie Curtis Hall.

Ms. Perry is the author of six plays for young people, the book of the musical *Daddy Goodness*, the radio soap *Sounds of the City* (which aired in 30 cities for two years), *A Holiday Celebration* (with Ossie Davis and Ruby Dee), and numerous other radio and television scripts, articles, and essays. She has two Cebas for writing, and is a "Distinguished Howard Player" and "Distinguished Howard Theatre Alumna." She is staff writer for *Black Masks* magazine and is Director of Theatre at Lehman College of the City University of New York.

WILL MARION COOK (Composer, 1869-1944) in 1898 directed a musical-comedy sketch, *Clorindy, the Origin of the Cakewalk*, that created a sensation on Broadway. He had composed the music to lyrics written by Paul Laurence Dunbar, rehearsed for weeks a hastily gathered group of twenty-six Black performers, and finally wrangled the opportunity to have it produced at the Casino Roof Garden after much travail.

Cook was well-equipped to present New York with its first Negro musical-comedy sketch. Born in Washington, DC, he achieved distinction as a composer, conductor, and violinist. His parents were both graduates of Oberlin College; his father went on to become a law professor at Howard University. The boy early revealed musical talent and at the age of thirteen was sent to Oberlin Conservatory to study violin.

KARAMU HOUSE

Founded in 1915, Karamu House quickly became a model of integration and cooperative artistic expression. Since its inception, Karamu has provided people of all backgrounds opportunities for personal development and the achievement of artistic excellence. Today, in addition to offering a fine Theatre season, Karamu offers a wide variety of programming designed to facilitate opportunities through the pursuit of education and of excellence in the arts. Karamu offers settings focused on artistic tasks, common ventures and positive social interaction in a multi-cultural, multi-racial context. We are proud to be celebrating Karamu's 75th Anniversary this year.

It was 1903 when the original *In Dahomey* became the first all-Black show to run on Broadway. Starring the famous comedy team of Bert Williams and George Walker, the entire musical was written, directed, and produced by Blacks. For nearly a decade following this, the William and Walker Company produced other such shows. *In Dahomey* also ran for seven months in London, introducing the Cakewalk dance to Royalty and London Society.

The present incarnation was launched by New York Producer Woodie King, Jr., who, after a long search, uncovered the original music. The music, composed by Will Marion Cook, has lyrics by Paul Laurence Dunbar, James Weldon Johnson, Alex Rogers, and others. A new book has been created for the production by Shauneille Perry.

Known for its wealth, natural resources, powerful kings, and history of slave trading, Dahomey, West Africa, fell to French occupation in the late 1800s. After "independence" it was renamed the Republic of Benin in 1975.

IN DAHOMEY
A Musical Comedy in Two Acts

Book by Shauneille Perry
inspired by characters of Jesse A. Shipp

Music by Will Marion Cook
Paul Laurence Dunbar
Alex Rogers
Bert Williams
and others

Directed and Choreographed by
Dianne McIntyre

Cast in Order of Appearance

Hamilton Lightfoot	John Fleming
Rosetta Light foot	Barbara Finley
Mr. Singh	Michael Bell
Ada	Kelly Goler
Henry Stampfield	Miguel Osborne
Minnie	Regenia Williams
George Reeder	George Bruce
Shylock Homestead	W. Walker Gibson
Cecelia Lightfoot	Bobette Hurst-Sudduth
Rareback Pinkerton	Reggie Kelly
Akanji	Roderick Williams

ACT ONE

Time: 1903
Place: Gatorville, Florida
    Scene 1 Post Office
    Scene 2 Detective Office
    Scene 3 Post Office

Musical Numbers

Overture

"Swing Along" ....The Company
"I Want To Be A Actor Lady ....Rosetta Lightfoot
"Molly Green"..George Reeder
"The Cakewalk Jig" ....Shylock Homestead, Rareback Pinkerton
"Swing Along" Reprise....................................The Company
"Brown Skin Baby Mine" ....Rareback Pinkerton
"Jonah Man" ....Shylock Homestead
"Colored Aristocracy" ....Cecelia Lightfoot
                 with Ada, Minnie, and Rosetta Lightfoot
"Emancipation Day" ....Hamilton Lightfoot and The Company
"The Caboceers" ....The Company
"Chocolate Drop"...Rareback Pinkerton
"Happy Jim"...Shylock Homestead
"Cakewalk".................Rareback Pinkerton and Shylock Homestead
"The Czar"............................Henry Stampfield and The Company
"My Dahomian Queen" ....Hamilton Lightfoot
"Brown Skin Baby Mine" Reprise.....................Rareback Pinkerton
"African Aristocracy" ....Cecilia Lightfoot
                        with Ada and Minnie
"Actor Lady" Reprise......................................Ada
"Just The Same"...Akanji
"A Story"........................Cecelia Lightfoot and Minnie
"That's How The Cakewalk's Done" ....Mr. Singh
"Emancipation Day" Reprise................................The Company
"The Czar" Reprise..The Company
"Every Negro Is A King"............Shylock Homestead and Rareback
                                 Pinkerton
"Broadway In Dahomey Bye and Bye".......................The Company
"That's How the Cakewalk's Done" ....The Company

The play takes place in America and Africa in Two Acts
Time: 1900's
Places: Florida, USA   Dahomey, West Africa

All actors play double roles.
In America The Characters Are: *In Africa They Become:*
Rosetta - Young Woman (Black)   Princess Assadou
Hamilton Lightfoot - Her father (Black)   King Menuki
Mr. Singh - Shopkeeper (East Indian)   Mr. Singh
Minnie - Young Woman (Black)   Mandisa
Mr. Reeder- Postman (White)   Father George O'Reeder,
                                                a Missionary

Henry Stampfield - His assistant (Black)   Henri
Cecelia Lightfoot - Rosetta's Mother (Black)   Queen Ayat
Shylock Homestead - A young detective (Black) Himself
       (Also a Song and Dance Man)
Rareback Pinkerton - A young detective (Black) Himself
       (Also a Song and Dance Man)
Ada - A young woman (Black)   Aduke
Akanji - A young African Prince (Black)   Mutu - Akanji's Cousin

ACT I
Scene 1

> *The Overture is played. As it begins to fade an actor walks past with a sign say-*
> *ing "1903" (The sign may be flown in or dropped).*
> *The chorus, led by Rosetta, dances a rousing production of "Swing Along"*
> *Watching in the corner approvingly is Hamilton Lightfoot. The number ends,*
> *and the chorus disperses talking among themselves...*

ROSETTA: How do we look, Daddy?

MR. SINGH: Think we're good enough for New York, boss?

ADA: Personally, I think Rosetta's solo is too long.

MINNIE: What you think is that yours is too short!

HAMILTON: Folks...ladies and gentlemen, please...we'll never get to New York
    or any other place this way...besides, have we forgotten our original pur-
    pose?

ADA: How could we? (*as if by rote*) "The Dahomey Preservation Society was
    founded specifically to raise and forward funds to our brethren-

MINNIE: And sisteren...

ADA: on the far away shores of Africa to help them...

(Everyone is mouthing the speech now as Lightfoot listens)

HAMILTON: ...in their constant struggle to throw-off the shackles of colonialism." Splendid! And, as we all know, this show, appropriately called, "In Dahomey" will afford us the funds for our next major shipment of shoes to our brethren.

MINNIE: And sisteren...

MR. SINGH: Mr. Lightfoot...no woman's shoes in last package. I know. I pack only for men.

ROSETTA: Why are the women always last Daddy?

HAMILTON: I...I don't recall now...but let's get back to the point. This show is for Africa, not Broadway!

REEDER: Yep, get to it Hamilton...Can't rehearse all night...it'll be delivery time before you know it, this is still a post office, remember.

STAMPFIELD: Whoever heard of rehearsing in a post office anyway? It's not yours to close.

REEDER: Now that's between me and Uncle Sam. He rents it from eight to five. After that, its my space and I do what I darn well please.

HAMILTON: And he darn well pleases to let us hold meetings and rehearse shows rent-free, and for that we are grateful. Thanks again Mr. Reeder.

MR. SINGH: Why you do it, boss?

REEDER: Oh...just my way of saying "thank you" to this country. It's been mighty good to me since I sailed from Ireland's shores, those many years ago.

STAMPFIELD: That sure wasn't the same ship that dragged my pappy here! How'd you get here Mr. Singh?

MR. SINGH: With my Uncle...by train from San Francisco.

(The cast begins quietly rehearsing in the background as Rosetta goes over to Minnie, taking her aside.)

ROSETTA: Miss Minnie, do you know when Mr. Shylock is coming? I do want him to hear my song. I did hope he would get here before Mama...since she doesn't...uh...doesn't—

MINNIE: Approve of him? Oh, go on and say it girl, everybody knows your mother has her nose in the air and her head in the clouds...she'll never think anyone's good enough for you unless they make front page headlines in the New York Age.

ROSETTA: ...I'm so ashamed...

MINNIE: No need to be...she just wants the best for you. And Rosie, I've got to say it, even if Shylock Homestead is my brother, he's...he's an entertainer! Now who would want their daughter to marry...a performer?

ROSIE: But he's a detective...And a performer...I mean a performing detective.

MINNIE: Shoot! That detective office ain't nothing but a front for booking out of work actors into odd jobs. Why, he and Rareback wouldn't know a robber if they saw one.

ROSIE: But we are all performers, Minnie. All of us here...Mr. Reeder, Mr. Singh, you, me...even Daddy.

MINNIE: For fun honey...and for funds, Rosie, like your Daddy says, to help our relatives across the water. Say, what does Mr. Hamilton think about you and my brother?

ROSETTA: Oh he's all for it...but he knows we've got to make Shylock acceptable to Mother somehow...

REEDER: Hamilton...I told you, I've got to shut down soon...we open up early.

HAMILTON: O.K. O.K.! uh...Rosie, are you ready?

SINGH: Mr. Hamilton...you wanna see my dance now?...I gotta get back to store.

ADA: Your store open this late?

MINNIE: Yeah...he's still trying to find all them shoes supposed to be in Africa.

REEDER: Hamilton!

HAMILTON: Rosetta!

ROSETTA: *(Jumping up to sing) (Sings "I Wants To Be An Actor Lady")*
(As she sings, Ada gestures to Minnie her displeasure indicating she would like to be singing. At the same time Shylock Homestead comes in and listens to Rosetta's song admiringly while Cecelia Lightfoot, Rosetta's mother, enters after him and watches them both.)
(When Rosetta finishes, Hamilton rushes up to her and they embrace, as everyone looks on with approval...except Cecelia.)
(Cecelia goes to Rosetta and gently but firmly takes her aside as the following people speak overlapping.)

ROSETTA: Mama...please...you have got to understand that I...

CECELIA: Rosetta my dear, I wish you would find another song that can express...

REEDER: Locking up everybody!...Locking up!...

SHYLOCK: Wait! Wait! Ham, you can't stop now...I'm waiting for my partner...me and Rareback gotta show you the new Cake-walk...

SINGH: Yes Boss...and I got a new dance too...I have to show everybody.

HAMILTON: Well...I don't know...Mr. Reeder, what do you say? Can we stay?

SHYLOCK: *(Jumping in)*...He says yes, cause we haven't heard his song yet, right Mr. Reeder?

HAMILTON: What's this Reeder...a song? For Africa??

REEDER: Africa? No...for Broadway! I mean of course for Africa...by way of Broadway...and Ireland. I mean it's my thanks to the country; my new country...by way of my...old country...in honor of my—

MINNIE: Don't tell me...

REEDER: ...adopted country...

SHYLOCK: Africa???...

REEDER: Precisely!

HAMILTON: Sing, Mr. Reeder.

(*Mr. Reeder sings "Molly Malone." At the end, they break into applause.*)

(*Rareback Pinkerton enters with a young African man dressed in a business suit and carrying a briefcase.*)

RAREBACK: Bravo! Bravo! Mr. Reeder...I can't think of a finer tribute to Mother Africa, by way of Ireland than your heartfelt rendition of that tender tune. Now, as a dazzling climax to what promises to be the most successful effort ever...I've brought to this august group two surprises...one is the presence of this gen-u-ine-bon-a-fide African brother who is here in our midst as a student but is also in need of our services to help him out of a jam...and my second surprise, before we hear the brother's story, is a presentation by my partner and me of the newest, latest gen-u-ine version of...The Cakewalk Jig! Hit it Shylock!

(*The two dance a short jig. Rareback and Shylock beckon for the others to join in. There is a reprise of the beginning number "Swing Along" with Shylock, Rareback and Rosetta taking the dancing leads. Only Cecelia and the African student look on.*)

SINGH: (*Jumping in to do the dance he's wanted to do all along.*) And now my time!

HAMILTON: That's it! That's it! Just what we needed to pick that number up!

(*As dancing builds in exuberance, Mr. Reeder calls out—*)

REEDER: Closing time, closing time! Time to close so I can open up!

ACT I

Scene 2

(*The office of Shylock Homestead and Rareback Pinkerton...It is small, bare and neat with a table and two or three chairs. Rareback enters with Akanji, the African student.*)

RAREBACK: Come on in Kanji, this here is the place me and my partner Shylock operate out of. It ain't big, but it's ours.

AKANJI: Very nice...very nice. And you are in the business of lost persons, Mr. Pinkerton?

RAREBACK: Well...yes...if they ain't too far gone...I mean if they ain't gone too far...lost...yes...we probably can find them.

AKANJI: Good! Then you must help me. Now I am in this country from Africa only six months and...

RAREBACK: Hold up Kanji...wait till my partner gets here so we can hear the whole story...he's on his way.

AKANJI: Oh...Well I can tell you ...

RAREBACK: How did you like the number you saw last night? Of course, you only saw a short rehearsal...

AKANJI: Ah yes...I thought it to be very...

RAREBACK: Bet you never saw any fancy footwork like that back in...your country did you?

AKANJI: Well, we have ...

RAREBACK: And that ain't nothing compared to them big-time Broadway boys and girls.

AKANJI: Yes...I've been to—

RAREBACK: Don't worry, one day you'll get to the big city too, my boy.

AKANJI: Mr. Pinkerton, I think I should tell you...

RAREBACK: One more thing Kanji...did you see that beautiful brown skin doing the solo turn last night?

AKANJI: I did...she is your wife?

RAREBACK: No, brother...and that's the saddest tale of all...I love that little gal, though she don't know it, but she loves my partner Shylock.

AKANJI: Does he know it?

RAREBACK: He knows it, she knows it, and her mama knows it, but her mama won't have it, cause she thinks old Shylock ain't good enough. Of course you don't know nothing about that society stuff where you come from...just one big happy family, I expect.

AKANJI: Well...my father is a ...

RAREBACK: (Sadly) Rosie's my heart, Kanji, if only she was mine...I'd give anything for that sweet woman...or someone just like her.

AKANJI: You know, Rareback...Miss Rosetta has a great likeness to someone that I...

RAREBACK: Hey listen to this, man...I wrote it about her.

(Sings "Brown Skin Baby of Mine.")

(Song finishes.)

AKANJI: Beautiful Mr. Rareback...just—

(Homestead enters with Hamilton.)

HOMESTEAD: Say Rareback, what are you doing rehearsing during office hours? (to Akanji) and how are you my brother, sorry I didn't get to meet you formally last night.

HAMILTON: (Proudly) And let me express how truly delighted I am to make the acquaintance at long last of a true citizen of our ancient and honored civilization. What part of Africa are you from young man?

AKANJI: Dahomey.

HAMILTON: My Lord! Did you get the last shipment of shoes we sent?

(Akanji looks perplexed.)

RAREBACK: Kanji wants to hire us Shy...to find somebody for him.

AKANJI: And something. Let me explain...

HAMILTON: I think you boys ought to let Mr. Kanji get a word in.

SHYLOCK: Right...right...right. Go ahead brother.

AKANJI: Well...Thank you. I am greatly in need of your help.

HAMILTON: *(with humility)* I know son, that's exactly why I started the Preservation society. To help save you folks over there from them European invaders.

AKANJI: No...no, that is not the kind of help I am in need of at the moment sir. You see, there was this neck chain, you would call it a necklace I suppose, a jewelry piece.

RAREBACK: Oh Lord...you got yourself mixed up with some gal already?

AKANJI: No...no...no...not a girl, a brother.

SHYLOCK:

RAREBACK: OH???

AKANJI: By brothers I mean he is a fellow-tribesman...he is in fact, a relative, a distant cousin...but he has behaved like an enemy.

HAMILTON: Mr. Kanji, you'd better start from the beginning.

SHYLOCK: The very beginning. Who are you brother?

AKANJI: *(Proudly)* I am Prince Akanji Ukala Omara Ekwuanzi Fatoba Samuel Tomoloju of Tuma, a small village outside of Kandi, Dahomey.

RAREBACK: Hot damn! Can we just call you Sam?

HAMILTON: Excuse these ignorant fools, your majesty...their experience with royalty is rather limited...go on with your story....

AKANJI: My father, Chief Menuki has many acres of land in the village which he rules. We grow maize and yams and other things but we also have many animals—

SHYLOCK: We know about them lions and tigers and elephants.

AKANJI: No, no we have cattle and goats. Because we do not know well how to administer to their sicknesses, Father has sent me to your Tuskegee Institute to learn such things...

RAREBACK: But why are you here in Florida?

AKANJI: To find you...The famous detectives Sherlock Holmes and Dr. Watson...all the texts from England speak highly of you....

SHYLOCK: But we're Shylock Homestead and Rareback Pinkerton!

AKANJI: I assumed something got lost in the translation.

RAREBACK: No, lost in the water when them slave ships was crossing over.

HAMILTON: You've found the right men, Prince, but what have you lost?

AKANJI: A neckchain...which bears the ancient seal of Chionga Ulara Omojola. It was given me by Father the King to identify the next ruler of our Kingdom. I fear it was stolen by my Cousin Mutu, who has long been my rival.

RAREBACK: How'd he get it?

SHYLOCK: Don't ask so many questions, man!

AKANJI: I think he took it even before I left...I didn't really notice until I got here and unpacked...it is never worn except for ceremonial occasions...

SHYLOCK: Well hell, s'cuse me Prince, but it could be anywhere now. I mean The United States is a big place–

AKANJI: No...no...he's in Africa.

RAREBACK: Well that's even bigger.

HAMILTON: No...no...no...he has to be in Candy.

AKANJI: *(correcting)* KAN-DI.

HAMILTON: Yeah...he has to be right there in the village because that necklace won't do him any good anywhere else.

AKANJI: Precisely! And I have got to find him and get it back and expose him to my father and the villagers.

RAREBACK: But if your Daddy gave the thing to you, won't he know this other guy stole it?

AKANJI: Maybe...but it is custom. I lose face to have allowed him to take it. That is why you must come with me to Dahomey and help me to find him.

RAREBACK & PINKERTON: Go to Dahomey? Us?

HAMILTON: Go to Dahomey! Yes, you! What a challenge! What an opportunity I can see the headlines in the Afro-American, The New York Age, The Crisis, The Pittsburgh Courier...American Negroes journey to Africa to help their brother reclaim a kingdom...Why...it will be like another emancipation! And The African Preservation Society will be your official sponsor! You'll be heroes!

RAREBACK: Mr. Hamilton...you've got a powerful imagination.

SHYLOCK: I don't even know where Dahomey is!

RAREBACK: I don't even know where Africa is!

AKANJI: I'll be your guide of course!

HAMILTON: Let me go tell Cecelia and Rosie and the others...we must prepare some gifts...I wonder if Singh found the other shoe shipment...Back in a while fellows!

RAREBACK: Oh Lord Shylock, how did we get into this?

SHYLOCK: I don't know! We don't know nothing about detecting...

RAREBACK: And we sure don't know nothing about Africa!

SHYLOCK: We ain't got a penny...and I got a girl I can't marry because I'm nobody in her Mama's eyes...

RAREBACK: *(To himself)* And I love a girl who don't even see me...

SHYLOCK: Yeah...Who's that?

RAREBACK: *(Looking at Akanji)* Oh just somebody...*(whistles or hums Brown Skin Baby.)*

(Shylock sings Jonah Man uptempo—not sadly.)
(At the end of the song Akanji says...)

AKANJI: Brothers! I have the answer to all your troubles...by helping me in Africa...I can help you here...trust me!

SHYLOCK: How can that be?

RAREBACK: You ain't dealing in voo-doo is you?

AKANJI: No...but I do have ancient powers you know...starting with this... *(shows a roll of dollars)*

RAREBACK: Ain't nothing ancient about them greenbacks...

AKANJI: Come with me to Africa...you may find many answers that you seek...

SHYLOCK: I don't see how going away will...
   (Door opens. Hamilton and Cecelia and Rosetta enter with chorus ladies.)

HAMILTON: Prince Akanji *(fumbles with name)*...uh...

AKANJI: I'm Prince Akanji Ukala Omara Ekwuanzi Fatoba Samuel Tomoloju of Tuma Dahomey.

HAMILTON: May I present my wife Cecelia and my daughter Rosetta?
   (Rosetta bows)

CECELIA: *(extends hand)* I am so happy to make your acquaintance, Prince and to welcome you to our Colored Aristocracy here in America.
   (Cecelia, Rosetta and two ladies sing Colored Aristocracy as Shylock grimaces.)
   (The song finishes.)

AKANJI: I am honored Madam. And your lovely daughter reminds me of someone I know back home.

ROSETTA: Really?
   (Mr. Reeder enters with Mr. Singh.)

REEDER: The boxes are all outside ready to go.

SINGH: I pack socks this time Boss, and hats. Shoes I never find. But socks fit women too...no difference.
   (The chorus goes in and out bringing suitcases, Safari hats, pith helmets for Pinkerton and Homestead as Hamilton takes center and proclaims...)

HAMILTON: Farewell to our dear detective friends who are off to conduct a reverse emancipation for our blood bothers in the far off Motherland. We wish them Godspeed and a safe return. Then we can truly proclaim that the Africa Preservation Society has fulfilled its mission! Wait until Dr. DuBois hears about this!
   (There is a big flurry of activity as they parade, march and sing, "Emancipation Day.")
   End of Act I

ACT II

Scene 1

(A wooded terrain in Dahomey just on the outskirts of the village of Tuma. It is twilight, and the local residents are completing their various daytime activities. The production number is "The Caboceers Entrance.")

(When the number finishes and the residents are quiet, there are voices offstage. It is Shylock, Rareback and Akanji. By now, darkness is setting in.)

(Offstage)

SHYLOCK: Man, where are we?

AKANJI: The distance is not long now.

RAREBACK: That's what you said an hour ago!

(The Dahomians scatter, though nearby are Aduke [Ada], Mandisa [Minnie], King Menuki [Hamilton], Queen Ayat [Celelia], Singh [Mr. Singh], Henri [Henry Stampfield]).

AKANJI: *(Entering)* I think we must go further that way...

(His voice moves him further offstage.)

(The Dahomians are now offstage.) (It is dark.)

RAREBACK: *(Stumbling Onstage)* Akanji...wait a minute...don't go so fast... wait...I can't see nothing...

SHYLOCK: Why do you think they call it the dark continent, stupid?

AKANJI: Ah, there you are!...Now listen, I'm going to forge ahead. Although it's dark, I know my way and I can move faster if I'm alone...The village is just a few kilometers on the other side of the hill and I will go there first.

RAREBACK: Oh no...you ain't leaving us here...with all the lions and tigers... and elephants and things.

AKANJI: I told you that was in East Africa! There are no lions and tigers here.

(There is a noise. Rareback jumps.)

RAREBACK: Oowweu! What's that!

SHYLOCK: Shut up fool! You want the whole village to welcome us even before we get there? Akanji wants to sneak up on this father, The King, before that evil guy Mutu sneaks up on him!

AKANJI: Precisely! I must reach my father and explain everything to him alone before anyone knows that I am there...otherwise he will believe the lies of my wicked cousin, Mutu.

RAREBACK: Fine!...And now we got you over here my man...why don't you just take care of your business, and we'll get on back home and take care of ours! *(he starts to leave)*

SHYLOCK: *(Pulling him back)* Hold on Rareback! You know our part of the deal...we got to help Akanji get this necklace thing back so he can claim his rightful heritage.

RAREBACK: Damn his heritage! He knows more about his than we know about ours!

SHYLOCK: ...But our mission is to guard him.

RAREBACK: My mission is to guard me! Besides, I think he's as lost as we are!

AKANJI: I am not. Trust me! But I must go...while there is darkness.

RAREBACK: No! That's the reason to stay! Can't you deal with your Daddy in the daytime?

AKANJI: I will be back for you by the first cock crow of dawn...do not be afraid...you are surrounded by the spirits of my ancestors...and yours
(He exits)

RAREBACK: That's what I'm afraid of...

SHYLOCK: *(settling in)* Relax, Rareback...settle down man, Akanji knows what he's doing. He'll be back soon.

(As this conversation proceeds; The Dahomey residents, except the King and Queen are quietly re-appearing very stylized around the stage. Whenever the detectives look around; the people stop and assume a pose...as an animal, a tree, a leaf, etc.)

RAREBACK: Oh yeah? What makes you so confident? Here we are in the middle of no-where with no-body, and worse, we don't know why. You a Jonah man alright...and now we are both "Jonah-men."

SHYLOCK: I know why I'm here Rareback. When brother Akanji hits me with those georgous greenbacks for helping him regain his title, and my name is in capital letters across the New York Age newspaper on Broadway USA, where we'll be headlining prior to our London engagement before the Prince of Wales; I will be a proud strutting, happy rich somebody with pretty Miss Rosetta Lightfoot on my arm, so rich that when Miss Rosetta's mama sings about The Colored Aristocracy, it will be me she's talking about!

RAREBACK: Lord...I thought I was with one crazy African, now I see it's two!

(An animal-person moves/or makes a slight noise...)

RAREBACK: Shylock...did you hear...something?

SHYLOCK: *(scared)* No man...and if I did...I ain't saying so.

(A figure moves.)

RAREBACK: Shylock...did you see—

SHYLOCK: Man I said don't even ask me!

RAREBACK: *(Loudly)* AKANJI!

(At that call, all the figures start to move slowly almost as shadows in a rhythmic pulsating fashion with drums underneath. The Caboceers refrain plays softly.)

RAREBACK: *(shaking)* I gotta say it Shylock...them things is moving...trees... ghosts and I don't know what all...

SHYLOCK: It's...spirits...Akanji's ancestors man...moving around to protect us, that's what he said.

RAREBACK: How they going to protect us?...they don't even know us!

SHYLOCK: So...So what do we do?

RAREBACK: Make a run for it.

SHYLOCK: A run for what Rareback? The ship? Where is it? The village? where is that?

RAREBACK: He said...a kilometer...*(a pause)* I know...I know...

SHYLOCK: ...What is that?

RAREBACK: On the count of three...Shylock, I'm going where these feet can carry me...one...two...three...

(At the count of three, the dancers stand and assert themselves in a full circle surrounding Shylock and Rareback. The two are frozen.)

RAREBACK: Oh Lord...The spirits have come alive!

SHYLOCK: Looks to me like they've always been alive. Rareback, we've been captured!

(The dancers relax around them, waiting for their next move. Although it is clear they are captured, it is more curiosity than hostility from the Villagers.)

RAREBACK: Try to...say something Shylock...maybe they...will have pity on us. Say something!

SHYLOCK: What...how do...I say it? I don't know no Dahomianese

RAREBACK: I don't know...grunt...make...signs...you seen Tarzan...do what he does.

SHYLOCK: What's the matter with you? These are folks just like our friends at home. *(looking closely)* In fact...if I didn't know better, I'd swear we *were* at home.

RAREBACK: *(Relaxed)* Well, in that case, lets do what we would do at home.

SHYLOCK: What's that?

RAREBACK: Entertain 'em!

(One does a jig: "Happy Jim." The other does "Chocolate Drop.")

SHYLOCK: At least they ain't booing us Rareback...

RAREBACK: No...and ain't nobody thrown nothing yet...

SHYLOCK: C'mon...let's kill 'em with the Cake-walk!

(They do some fancy stepping; with a finish that has flourish. At the end, there are polite smiles of approval.)

SHYLOCK: I don't know man. These people are colder than some of them gigs we had in Cleveland last year.

RAREBACK: Yeah...well everything's cold in Cleveland.

SHYLOCK: Alright...let's give 'em our "piece de resistance."

RAREBACK: What that man?

SHYLOCK: The routine, or course.

RAREBACK: And you call me dumb. How you gonna do a routine for people who don't speak nothing but Dahomian?

SHYLOCK: Well...we can't give up. We gotta try something to make them understand us.

HENRY (HENRI): Try English...

(Shylock and Rareback both nearly fall over. The Dahomian ladies giggle.)

SHYLOCK: Did...you say...English?

ADUKE (ADA): Unless you prefer French?

RAREBACK: ...French?

MANDISA (MINNIE): Or English...which is what you appear to speak.

HENRY (HENRI): Appear is correct. I don't understand anything they're saying...

RAREBACK: Now wait a minute here, Mr. uh...uh.

HENRI: Stamp-Folongolong. Henri Jacques Stamp-Folongolong.

RAREBACK: Gosh, where did you get a name like that?

MANDISA: From the French. That is one of the legacies left us by all the various powers that walked through our continent. And what are your names?

RAREBACK: *(proudly)* `Rareback Pinkerton

SHYLOCK: Shylock Homestead

HENRI: And where did you get those names?

SHYLOCK: ...uh...one of our legacies.

MANDISA (MINNIE): And this is Aduke, I am Mandisa...and this is—

SHYLOCK: Don't tell me...your name is Singh...

MR. SINGH: Yes...yes...how did you know?

RAREBACK: ...I had a hunch.

MR. SINGH: Remarkable! Are you a sorcerer?

SHYLOCK: Why no...we...are entertainers.

ADUKE: Really...have you come here to entertain us? Many do, you know...at least that's what they say at first, then little by little they take things away.

RAREBACK: ...No...no Miss...uh...

ADUKE: Aduke

RAREBACK: We didn't come to take nothing...in fact...we came to find...

SHYLOCK: *(Looks at him)* We came to look...not to find.

HENRI: Oh yes...everyone comes to Africa to look, Mr. Homestead. What is it you look for, gold, diamonds, your roots? What?

SHYLOCK: We came to...entertain sir...we were on the way to Paris...to play the Club Lido...and somewhere the compass on the boat broke...and...

RAREBACK: The Captain navigated by the stars and as he only had one eye, what he thought he saw as a moving star was really a reflection of the moon shivering on the waves which made him turn around and go the wrong way—

SHYLOCK: And we landed up in Africa!

RAREBACK: The French part of course!

HENRI: Wait until The King hears this!

SINGH: Well, you're the Royal messenger, why don't you tell him?

RAREBACK: I thought you looked familiar...do you carry mail too?

HENRI: I beg your pardon...

RAREBACK: Skip it...

SINGH: Go Henri, summon the Royal family.

SHYLOCK: Family? Now that's nice, but we don't need to meet everybody.

SINGH: No...no, The King will be delighted.

RAREBACK: I ain't so sure about that...

MANDISA: You say, you have come to entertain us...

SHYLOCK: Yes...but not the whole town.

SINGH: Then it will be a Royal privilege.

HENRI: And it is also the custom!

SINGH: *(To Henri)* Go now!

SHYLOCK: *(To Singh)* If you don't mind me asking...What do you do?

SINGH: Do? Ah...I'm The Royal shopkeeper. I outfit The Royal Family.

RAREBACK: Oh yeah...do they wear shoes?

SHYLOCK: Shut up man!

(Strains of "The Czar" are heard.)

ADUKE: Look everyone, they are coming!

(All become very solemn and ceremonial as the Royal Three approach. "The Czar" is sung with or without a dance.)

(At the finish King Menuki [Hamilton], Queen Ayat [Cecelia], and daughter Assadou [Rosetta] approach and sit or stand on thrones [or stools someone brings on]. Assadou stands.)

SHYLOCK: *(looking at Princess Assadou)* Rareback, are you thinking what I am thinking?

RAREBACK: I don't know what you are thinking, it's what you're seeing that interests me!...

SHYLOCK: You think maybe we have died and come back somewhere else?

RAREBACK: Seems more like these folks died and came back as somebody else! Somebody else we know!

HENRI: Your Royal Highness King Menuki, these are the intruding visitors we have discovered. They say they have come here to entertain us.

MANDISA: ...*(under her breath)* But...we have our doubts about that...

MENUKI: I see...well, let us first give a just consideration to this before condemnation. *(to Shylock & Rareback)*...Pourquoi vous avez venez ici a Africa? Especialement mon pays, Dahomey?

SHYLOCK & RAREBACK: Huh?

SINGH: They don't speak French, your Highness.

(All look around in amazement)

RAREBACK: But we speak English, your honor.

SHYLOCK: *(to Rareback)* "Your Highness," man.

RAREBACK: I'm sorry, your Holiness.

MENUKI: I see...and what tribe do you belong to?

SHYLOCK: ...uh...The Florida tribe, your Highness. The Colored Florida tribe, with some Seminole Indian mixed in, you know...

SINGH: Indian? INDIAN?

SHYLOCK: Well...not exactly. I mean it's The Seminole Indian kind...mixed with The African...it makes the Colored tribe...*(fading away)*...in Florida.

RAREBACK: U.S.A. Florida...away down at the bottom.

MENUKI: I yes...I remember now...Florida...The Seminole wars...treaties... and African people taken from here on the coast to serve as slave help in America, terrible, terrible!...I study this at The Sorbonne!

RAREBACK: *(Amazed)* That's us!

MENUKI: Then you are our people...we are like...cousins *(pronounced in the French)* of you.

SHYLOCK: *(Amazed)* That's us!

MENUKI: So...you entertain? Sing?

RAREBACK & SHYLOCK: Yes!

MENUKI: Dance?

RAREBACK & SHYLOCK: Yes!

MENUKI: *(Joyfully)* So do I! Listen. This is a dedication to my beautiful Queen Ayat.

(He sings "My Dahomian Queen." As soon as he finishes he says to Rareback & Shylock.)

MENUKI: Now you!

RAREBACK: *(to Shylock)* What is this, a contest?

SHYLOCK: If it is, you'd better win.

RAREBACK: *(to Menuki)* Your honor, I've got a little song I'd like to dedicate to that lovely little lady right there. *(points to Assadou)*

SHYLOCK: Are you crazy?!

MENUKI: *(pleased)* This is my daughter Princess Assadou. She sings too!

ADUKE: *(under her breath)* Very poorly.

AYAT: Menuki, not before commoners!

MENUKI: They are my brothers, Ayat! From across the seas!

AYAT: Yours perhaps, not mine!

SHYLOCK: *(to Rareback)* Are we dreaming or what? Who wants her daughter?

RAREBACK: *(smitten)* I do man…she's…she's beautiful…*(He begins a soulful version of Brownskin Girl, and sings directly to Assadou)*

SHYLOCK: *(Whispering)* You are crazy!

ADUKE: She's doing it again…getting all the attention.

MANDISA: Aduke…you've got to curb your jealousy!

(As the song is sung, it is clear that Assadou is smitten too…Menuki is mildly amused, Shylock and Queen Ayat are horrified.)

(At the end of the song, as Rareback and Assadou slowly start moving towards one another in an almost hypnotic state. Ayat leaps in between them and says:)

AYAT: I won't have it! I don't care what tribe he's from! All those heathen mixtures from across the sea! We are pure blood here…and Royal…Royal and pure…and pure and Royal…pure…pure and besides, he doesn't even speak French!

(Ayat launches into "African Aristocracy" with strong drum line. She is joined by Aduke and Mandisa.)

(As they sing…)

SHYLOCK: I can't believe anything that's happening. Rareback…what in hell are we going to do?

RAREBACK: We are in hell, and I know what I'm going to do, make a run for it!

SHYLOCK: You must be crazy, you don't even know where we are, much less where to go! Where, oh where is that Akanji???

(Just as he speaks, Mutu /Akanji appears dressed as the others.)

MUTU: STOP!

RAREBACK: Akanji! Oh, Thank the Lord brother, you are here!

SHYLOCK: Just in time to save our skins.

RAREBACK: Please…please…tell your father who we are!

MENUKI: What…what…Mutu, you know these Colored Africans?

RAREBACK & SHYLOCK: MUTU???

MUTU: I do Uncle, they are dangerous intruders who come from the infidel land where you sent your son to betray you.

MENUKI: I sent Akanji there to learn animal husbandry!

MUTU: But he went the wicked way and followed the foreign traitors. He has sold his birthright and no longer deserves to rule. These people are his emissaries.

MENUKI: But where is my son? Why does he not reveal himself and speak directly to me? I will listen. Even if I do not like what I hear, I will listen. You are his cousin, Mutu, you were boys together…What has happened between you to cause this terrible breach?

MUTU: He has betrayed you, Uncle!

AYAT: What!

RAREBACK: That boy is lying your honor...lying...he's the one that betrayed your son...that's why we—

SHYLOCK: Careful Rareback!

MUTU: No...no...This not true...your majesty...Uncle, I did not wish to hurt you, but now I must show my cousin Akanji for the traitor he is. He has forgotten us...The Kingdom...you. He has passed this to me...(*Mutu reveals the necklace. As he does Rareback says:*)

RAREBACK: That does it...I'm outta here! (*He bolts away, runs offstage as:*)

SHYLOCK: Rareback...Wait!

MENUKI: Stop! Stop! Mutu...no more of this!

(*One of the Dahomians walks back in with a captured Rareback who hangs his head low.*)

SHYLOCK: Stupid!

MENUKI: I will hear this matter out. The intruders will be imprisoned until further notice. Mutu, you will come with me. Now! The King has spoken!

(*The King and Queen leave with Assadou following. Assadou looks back at Rareback.*)

SHYLOCK: (*As he and Rareback are being taken away*) Can't you keep your big mouth shut?

RAREBACK: But, where is Akanji? You don't think that guy messed over him do you?

SHYLOCK: Who knows what to think? But I advise you to stop right now, cause everytime you think, we get into a peck of trouble!

(*Assadou reappears*)

RAREBACK: (*seeing her*) Bet you don't know what I'm thinking right now....

ASSADOU: (*to Rareback*) Please...have courage...I will come to visit you... tonight...(*she steals away*)

(*The two are led away by the Dahomians who chant "The Caboceers March." Rareback flashes a big smile to the audience as he is led away.*)

End of Act II, Scene I

ACT II
Scene 2

(*The same place—a clearing. The stage is empty. Aduke runs on stage.*)
(*Aduke looks around as Mandisa enters.*)

MANDISA: Aduke...what are you doing out here alone?

ADUKE: I am looking for Mutu.

MANDISA: Still running after that rake? Aduke, he is a poison, and he brings nothing but bad to our village. I hope he has brought no harm to Akanji.

ADUKE: That is why I am looking for him...although I love him I cannot permit him to bring evil to us or the Royal Family...

MANDISA: And what is this affection for The Royal family? Everyone knows you envy Princess Assadou!

ADUKE: Because Mutu can see only her.

MANDISA: It is not also because she sings the leads in our ceremonial pageants?

ADUKE: ...well...that too...But once Mutu hears me sing, he will see no other...listen!

(As she sings Mandisa covers her ears.)

(We hear the voices of Shylock and Rareback offstage. The women exit.)

(Enter Mr. Reeder, hands tied. He is a prisoner. Shylock and Rareback enter, hands tied led by a Dahomian. The women exit the other side of the stage simultaneously.)

ACT II

Scene 3

(The prisoners sit.)

DAHOMIAN GUARD: You will stay here with the other prisoner until further notice.

RAREBACK: *(Calling to guard)* Say Boss, who's gonna notify us?

SHYLOCK: Oh shut up fool, he means we're here till they decide how they're going to kill us.

RAREBACK: Well we gotta be tried first.

SHYLOCK: For what, trespassing? Intruding?

MISSIONARY: Oh...rest assured dear friends, there will be a fair trial... Dahomians are very fair people. By the way, my name is—

RAREBACK: Let me guess...it's Reeder. Mr. George Reeder.

MISSIONARY: *(Amazed)* Well...isn't that remarkable!

SHYLOCK: Almost.

MISSIONARY: Yes, almost! My name is O'Reeder. Father George O'Reeder.

SHYLOCK: From Ireland.

MISSIONARY: ...Ha...Caught my brogue did you? Well you're right, County Cork in fact. But how did you know my name...a gift for clairvoyance? It's rare in men you know.

RAREBACK: I know...nearly scared my mama to death. Say...you don't happen to have any relations in Florida do you? I mean Florida, USA? In the Post Office?

MISSIONARY: ...well let's see...there was...a letter bearer cousin named...

RAREBACK: ...George...

MISSIONARY: ...yes, yes...like me he left Ireland with his parents at a tender age on a journey to the new world...

RAREBACK: And they ended up in Florida...

MISSIONARY: Uncanny, this fellow! *(meaning Rareback)*

SHYLOCK: Ain't he though...But Father...what are you doing here?...And why in prison?

MISSIONARY: ...It's a sad tale really...I was sent by the Church...to save the savages, so to speak...but as it turned out they had already been saved. Though not by us. Why they were even speaking French!...and as I couldn't...it was difficult...

RAREBACK: But they speak English too.

MISSIONARY: Exactly. So I couldn't teach that either, you see. There really was nothing for me to do.

SHYLOCK: How about going home?

MISSIONARY: Too late. Ship already left. They anticipated a long term post, you see. It's all quite embarrassing...

RAREBACK: Say...maybe you can go back with us...it's the long way round of course...but maybe you could drop off and see your cousin George.

MISSIONARY: There's a thought...

SHYLOCK: Rareback, do you know what you're talking about? We are prisoners! And so is he! We may end up calling this place home!

RAREBACK: Hmmm...that may not be so bad Shy. It was home once, and now that I've found Miss Assadou, maybe the missionary here could end up marrying us!

MISSIONARY: *(enthusiastically)* I'd be delighted!

SHYLOCK: Now I'm stuck with two fools instead of one!
(Rareback hums "Brown Skin Baby.")

ASSADOU: *(enters) (whispers)* Mr. Rareback! Mr. Rareback!

RAREBACK: Oh just call me Rareback, Princess, ain't no need to be formal.

ASSADOU: And you may call me Assadou, Rareback..

RAREBACK: *(struggling)* AH-SA...Sweetheart, would you mind if I called you Rosetta?

ASSADOU: But why?

RAREBACK: *(realizing)* Never mind. I'll get it. Just have patience. What's going on? When are we going to get out of here?

ASSADOU: Now you must have patience my love. I bring a message from my brother Akanji, the heir to the Royal throne...he will help you...but he must be very careful.

SHYLOCK: *(overhearing)* Akanji...then he is safe???

ASSADOU: He is alive...but not safe...as long as Mutu wears the chain there is danger...he would not hesitate to kill my brother should he show himself.

MUTU: *(appears)* You are right, my beloved Princess. I will kill him, and your father would never believe that I was the one who did it...even if you said so.

RAREBACK: But you're his daughter...he'd believe you!...

MISSIONARY: No...it's 1903, and a man's world, still.

MUTU: Now my pretty, there is one way still that you can save your brother's life...*(takes her aside)*

(Aduke enters from the other side, unseen.)

RAREBACK: Now wait a minute!

SHYLOCK: *(grabbing him)* Now you wait a minute Rareback...you messing with several lives here...

MUTU: *(shows her the chain)* I would give all this up...let your brother go...and these heathens too...

MISSIONARY: Heathens?

MUTU: If...you would...be mine...

RAREBACK: What?

ASSADOU: But we can't marry, we are royal cousins...

MUTU: Oh yes we can. They do it in Europe all the time.

(Assadou, confused runs off...Aduke, heartbroken, remains on the other side of the stage, listening. Mutu stands for a moment both defiant and dejected, as the three look at him.)

RAREBACK: She don't want you boy, don't you get it?

SHYLOCK: Maybe she'll change her mind, man.

MISSIONARY: Would you like to talk to someone, Son?

MUTU: Silence! All of you! This is none of your affair! You are foreign invaders who have brought only evil to my cousin and my country. For this you shall pay! *(He goes)*

RAREBACK: Ain't he confused about something?

SHYLOCK: I know what's wrong with that boy, he's in love.

(Guard appears)

GUARD: Suivez-moi pour dîner, s'il vous plaît.

(A pause as the three look at each other)

HENRI: *(disgusted)* Follow me for food!

(All exit behind the guard)

(A beat later Assadou runs on from offstage, and Rareback returns quickly. They run into each others arms, embrace passionately. Aduke watches.)

RAREBACK: Mon cheri!

ASSADOU: My darling!

(they quickly separate)

ASSADOU: Who taught you that?

RAREBACK: Father O'Reeder! Who taught you that?

ASSADOU: Akanji!

RAREBACK: How is he? Where is he? Oh Lord Assadou, I think we're in a real mess. Looks like Mutu wants Akanji's Kingdom and his sister too.

ASSADOU: You must understand. These two young men...sons of brothers... alike in so many ways...have been rivals for years...

RAREBACK: Maybe so...but he ought to get his own gal.

ASSADOU: But who? *(Aduke runs off)* Royal blood flows in his veins too...it is decreed that he must wed his own kind. Is it the same in The States United?

RAREBACK:: Oh no, we don't have that sort of stuff... *(softly in the background we hear women voices humming "Colored Aristocracy")* Well...I guess it ain't so different except that you can move up a little faster if the price is right.

ASSADOU: What do you mean?

(Offstage voice...)

GUARD: Prisoner, come to eat!

SHYLOCK: Rareback, food's getting cold!

ASSADOU: Go before someone finds us here. Akanji says he has a scheme... trust him...but do not cross Mutu!

(Rareback leaves blowing kisses as Queen Ayat and Minnie approach still humming [singing] "African Aristocracy.")

ASSADOU: Ah! Mother...I did not hear you coming...why are you out into the night?

AYAT: *(Angry)* I search for my son Akanji who I am told hides for his life in the bush of his own village...I search for his cousin, raised as a son by me, who wanders about, filled with rage towards one who could be his twin...and I search also for my daughter Assadou, who runs away to rendez-vous with Colored Africans who have been imprisoned by my own husband, The King, who sings to me, but tells me nothing!

ASSADOU: Mother...I am sorry...

AYAT: Listen, have I not told you of the strength of our women who so many years ago were forced to lead when the traders took our men away? Doubly cursed by those who sold us and those who bought us, we learned well to do the work of those who left us.

Now that I know that Akanji is near, I will tell you the truth of all this, for even Menuki has forgotten.

(As she tells this story, there should be a stylized pantomime danced by Mandisa with drum underneath.)

AYAT: Assadou, go to your brother Akanji. Aduke, go to your beloved Mutu. Tell each of them this story that AYAT, The Queen now tells you.

AYAT: *(Begins.)* Many years ago, the heir to the throne of This Kingdom fell in love with a beautiful Princess from a tribe in the North. She was a young widow with a small child, and custom would not allow him to marry her because she was from a different tribe and already a mother. Undaunted, the Prince abdicated the throne to his brother. Then the real Prince and his bride fled to the North to live in happiness among her people, and they had a son. Now the Prince's brother, the new King, also had a son, born about the same time. Although they did not know each other they could have been twins, these sons of The Royal brothers. When the boys were in their early years, a terrible plague struck the North and all in the family of the exiled Prince died except the son who was returned to the village of his father to be raised by his uncle The King. King Menuki.

ADUKE: Mutu is that son?

AYAT: Yes. Menuki is the brother of that eldest Prince who was to be King. I am his wife, a peasant woman who became a Queen by default you might say.

(Pantomime ends.)

ASSADOU: Then Akanji is not the rightful heir to the Throne of Tuma?

AYAT: They rule equally. Mutu by Blood, Akanji by decree. Go now. *(She beckons to Mandisa who brings two packages. Ayat gives one to Aduke)*

AYAT: Give this to Mutu. It is a necklace like the one he stole. I was saving it for him. Tell him the story. *(Aduke leaves)* And Aduke...Don't sing! Now Assadou...go to Akanji and give him this...it will help him to escape. *(Assadou goes.)*

(The King rushes in with Mr. Singh close behind.)

MENUKI: Mon Dieu! Mon Dieu!

AYAT: *(innocently)* What is wrong, My King?

MENUKI: Just about everything! And I can't understand any of it! Akanji missing, and Mutu mad!...The villagers are pitted one against the other...

AYAT: Perhaps I can help, your Highness.

MENUKI: What could you do? You are my beautiful Queen, but a woman after all...Singh, why are you fidgeting so?

SINGH: Practicing a dance that the fast American taught me, your Highness... he calls it..."Cake-Jump," I believe...

MENUKI: Well stop it...it makes me nervous...I've got to sort all this out...

SINGH: Yes, your Highness...

MENUKI: *(to Ayat)* Help me my sweet, even if you don't understand...Mutu says I must punish these intruders if I ever want to see Akanji again.

AYAT: Punish?...How?

MENUKI: I don't quite know...we haven't had a crime in years! Quiet now... Singh, Sing!

SINGH: But your Highness...I was prepared to dance.

MENUKI: Sing!

SINGH: *(He sings a song. Perhaps a verse of two of "He's The Czar.")*

(After the song)

MENUKI: Bring in the prisoners!

(They are brought in with The Missionary and the other locals appear, except Aduke.)

MENUKI: After considerable consideration to this matter I have made a decision...

MANDISA: *(to Henri)* It is truly time...

HENRI: Wait...il n'est pas fini.

SHYLOCK: Did he say we're finished?

RAREBACK: I think he said we'll be fine!

MISSIONARY: Hush you two, let The King speak.

MENUKI: That's right you two, hush and let The King speak.

RAREBACK: Sorry. Go ahead King.

MENUKI: After careful deliberation...and consideration...and...

AYAT: Be brief, your Highness.

MENUKI: Yes, yes...After keeping counsel with my nephew Mutu, I have decided that these three shall be punished by—

MUTU: *(bursting in)* Wait, Uncle!

RAREBACK: Oh Lord, what now!

MUTU: With your Highness' most humble pardon, this errant nephew whom you have raised as a son wishes to recant his ways, and dwell once again in a spirit of peace and love.

MENUKI: Well, we all want that, Mutu. But, it was you who said these foreigners had changed all that!

SHYLOCK: We just made a mistake your Highness...

MUTU: The Colored American African is right Uncle! I wish to share all equally with my cousin Akanji and prove it, thusly! *(He produces the necklace)*

RAREBACK: Well there it is Shylock...we sure been through a whole lot for that thing.

SHYLOCK: Damn right! It ought to be ours...

MUTU: And so it shall be! As a token of our sincere appreciation of your coming to Dahomey to aid my cousin Akanji. Here...this will more than pay for your passage home and many mansions when you get there!

SHYLOCK: Hallelujah! Rosetta, set the date and tell the Preacher to dust off his marriage book!

MISSIONARY: I'd be delighted...

MENUKI: But Mutu...my son Akanji...you know where he is?

ASSADOU: *(quickly)* Oh he's on his way now Father...so overjoyed was he about his cousin Mutu's change, he went at once to book passage for his immediate return. He's already late for his University studies you know.

MENUKI: Know? I've already paid fees for one term...but he will come to say goodbye before sailing won't he?

MUTU: Of course, Uncle!

MENUKI: Are you sure? It seems as if he barely got here!

AYAT: He's sure Menuki.

RAREBACK: *(looking at Assadou)* But your honor...I...I can't leave without...I don't want to leave...I mean...

MENUKI: What does he mean?

ASSADOU: Mutu!

MUTU: There is one more thing...two in fact...two new events which are a result of my new enlightenment.

HENRI: I don't think I can stand much more...

MANDISA: What more can there be?

MUTU: I am happy to announce that I will take as my bride, the lovely Aduke, whom I have loved secretly and silently for many years.

MANDISA: Que est que il dis?

RAREBACK: Say what?

MENUKI: This is splendid Mutu, but where is she?

MUTU: Why, off in the bush, where I shall soon join her!

ASSADOU: *(impatiently)* MUTU!

MUTU: Before we part, there will be one more marriage to celebrate, as my dear Uncle, The King has given my cousin Assadou to...Mr. Rareback Pinkerton, Impresario extraordinaire!

MENUKI: I have?

SHYLOCK: What did he call you?

RAREBACK: I don't know, but it sounds good.

MUTU: This means Mr. Pinkerton will return often to help us stage our annual harvest moon festival. He will instruct us in Colored American-African song and dance, fusing it with our own. It will be a..."Broadway in Dahomey" you might say...

MISSIONARY: Why this is even better than conversion!

HENRI: I suppose Mademoiselle Aduke will sing the lead now.

MANDISA: I certainly hope not.

RAREBACK: Well I certainly want to thank both your Holinesses for this supreme honor. Me and my bride will do you proud. And in my absence as "leader of the pageant," I appoint my friend Mr. Singh to rehearse all new material!

(Singh bows to all)

SHYLOCK: Can we please go now, your Highness...

MISSIONARY: Yes, yes, we wouldn't want you to miss your boat.

MENUKI: Of course, of course…everything is happening so fast…but where is Akanji?

MUTU: At the ship…awaiting his friends…and you, Uncle to say goodbye. Come! All! Let us bid adieu!

(They leave with a flourish singing a version of "Emancipation Day" or humming a slow version of "In Dahomey Bye and Bye" as a prelude to the big version of it.)

(All exit stage except Ayat who stands alone. We hear music softly in the background.)

(A beat.)

(Mutu returns quickly.) (He hugs Ayat.)

MUTU: We did it Mother. Thanks for the robe! They really believed me! *(He pulls off the robe. It is Akanji, in his earlier clothes.)*

AYAT: Yes, it was a good show my son, but certainly a lot of trouble, don't you think?

AKANJI: Well it gets Mutu off my back, so I can study in peace, Aduke gets a Prince, Assadou gets an Impresario, and you get a trip to Florida from time to time! And when you tell The King everything, he'll give you his ear.

AYAT: In three months time he will swear it was all his idea.

AKANJI: *(affectionately)* But we shall always have our little secret Mother, and I thank you for that.

AYAT: Study well my son, and return to us one day. Keep an eye on your sister!

AKANJI: *(going)* They will welcome her well and she will bring joy to them. *(He goes.)*

AYAT: *(Standing alone)* Goodbye, Akanji…my son
(The music begins to fade as the lights fade…)

ACT II
Scene 4
(Scene Lights up on the Post Office.)
(Mr. Reeder, Minnie, and Henry are there.)
(Mr. Reeder and Henry are busy sorting things and generally fussing around.)

REEDER: Now Henry, did you stamp all the Midwest mail and put in the green bins?

HENRY: Don't I always? Midwest in green, Northeast in blue, Southeast in red, Northwest in grey…

REEDER: Northeast in grey…I told you! That's why it gets all mixed up.

HENRY: What's the difference, they get it eventually. Anyway I got more important things to do.

REEDER: You certainly have…did you pick up the big "Welcome Home" banner that Hamilton had made over at the sign shop?

HENRY: Ooops! I forgot! But I'll get it when we close down.

REEDER: Can't wait that long...Rareback and Shylock will be here anytime now and Hamilton wants that sign up for everybody to see! Not every little town has a pair of crackerjack detectives who travel to a foreign country to help a Prince re-claim his Kingdom! Eatonville, Florida is in all the papers...even the White ones! I'll bring a few back with me!

(He goes.)

MINNIE: Did you know that Henry? We're in all the newspapers!

HENRY: Of course I know. This is a post office. I'm surrounded by papers.

MINNIE: *(shocked)* Henry, you don't read the mail do you?

HENRY: Not if it's sealed.

(Singh enters as Ada follows—he is carrying a newspaper and she is carrying a small box.)

SINGH: Look, look...we're in all the prints! What a day for our town! Not so much excitement since the alligator escaped from the swamp and run down street last year.

ADA: Its bigger than that Mr. Singh, we made the Pittsburgh Courier!

MINNIE: And some New York papers too...Mr. Reeder's gone out to bring a few back!

HENRY: We've already got one here.

ADA: I've got the welcome sign...Mr. Lightfoot asked me to stop by and pick it up.

MINNIE: Oh, Mr. Reeder just went to get it...

(They start to unfold it and put it up...it reads "Welcome Home Heroes. Shylock Homestead and Rareback Pinkerton.")

SINGH: What a thing! *(Reads)* "Heroes return from Motherland after aiding Prince in pursuit of Kingdom."

MINNIE: Did you read about the award part? Prince Akanji gave them a necklace worth a fortune! They sure won't be poor little entertainers anymore!

HENRY: I didn't believe he was a real Prince.

ADA: *(Dreamingly)* I did. He would be a Prince even if he didn't have a penny.

HENRY: Well!

MINNIE: I hear Miss Cecelia has made a complete turn about since Shylock is rich. Seems she gave Rosetta's hand in marriage before Mr. Lightfoot even knew about it!

HENRY: Well that's nothing! What about Rareback going over there and bringing back a bride-to-be?

MINNIE: And they say he says she puts him to mind of Rosetta, so I guess everybody's happy...

HENRY: I knew that Akanji was mixed up in some kinda black magic!

(All stare at him.)

HENRY: I mean magic.

SINGH: What's keeping Mr. Reeder? And where are the Lightfoots? I wanted to get in one rehearsal before the honorees arrive...

(Hamilton, Lightfoot, Cecelia and Rosetta enter.)

SINGH: There you are...we were waiting...didn't want you to get here before the guests.

LIGHTFOOT: Is the sign here?

ADA: There it is!

LIGHTFOOT: Good...good...Where is Mr. Reeder...he should be here!

HENRY: He'll be here...one way or another.

LIGHTFOOT: Remember the song now...Cecelia my dear, give us a note. *(She does)*

ADA & MINNIE: Here they come!

(Shylock and Rareback enter as the group sings an American version of "Here Comes The Czar.")

(Song finishes and there are general handshakes.)

LIGHTFOOT: It goes without saying how happy we are to welcome you boys back in our midst, humble as it may be...we are proud of your exploits, proud of your conquests, proud of your accomplishments!

CECELIA: Be brief, Hamilton...

HAMILTON: Yes, yes...but I have to say that as a special gift, I wish to offer Mr. Shylock Homestead my own special jewel, my beloved daughter Rosetta, in marriage. And of course my wife, Cecelia joins me in this honor.

(Shylock and Rareback respond with the new song.)

ADA: Where is Mr. Akanji, Shylock...wasn't he to come with the two of you?

SHYLOCK: Precisely...he just stopped to bring a little...surprise with him.

HENRY: I can't stand no more of these!

ROSETTA: Oh, if he brought your bride Rareback, perhaps we could have a double wedding!

RAREBACK: Great idea!

HENRY: Now that *would* be voodoo.

MINNIE: Look, Mr. Akanji is coming!

(Akanji enters with Father O'Reeder)

AKANJI: Hello everyone!! I was just a bit detained...here is Father George O'Reeder! He has come to see his distant relative in America, Mr. Reeder...where is he?

LIGHTFOOT: Gone out to get some newspapers, I believe...

HENRY: *(to audience)* I don't think that's the real reason.

O'REEDER: *(brightly)* Well, no matter...I am delighted to be here amongst all of you dear new friends...my how familiar you all seem...I almost feel that I know each of you...but, aside from being here to meet my cousin, I have a wedding to perform...two weddings perhaps...is not Princess Assadou to be here?

RAREBACK: I thought she was with you. Akanji.

AKANJI: Well she was up until...

HENRY: *(Produces a letter)* Maybe this will explain it...*(Gives it to Rareback)*

RAREBACK: It's from Assadou

SHYLOCK: *(to Henry)* How did you get it, man?

HENRY: This is a post office, remember?

LIGHTFOOT: What does she say, Rareback?

RAREBACK: *(Reading)* "My darling…I am sorry I had to rush off this way but when I realized I had to teach Aduke the solo for the pageant coming up, I took the boat right back without having time to say a proper goodbye! Have no fear, she's a quick study and I'll be on the next boat returning. Then we will go ahead with our wedding. All my love, Assadou.

(All sigh)

ADA: Aduke…what a funny name.

ROSETTA: I don't think so.

LIGHTFOOT: Never mind…we still have one wedding coming up…and I have yet more wonderful news!!

HENRY: Pu-lease!

SINGH: Yes, yes, but Mr. Lightfoot, first I have awful confession to make:

ALL: Yes???

SINGH: One shoe shipment…grave error was made. Men's shoes went to Senegal instead of Dahomey…My French very poor…I'm sorry…better next time…

LIGHTFOOT: It's alright. Singh…there is need there too…And now, my news…while in New York…to meet with Dr. Dubois about our mission, I chanced upon some excellent new, bright—*(O'Reeder exits)* Where is he going?

CECELIA: *(impatiently)* Go on Hamilton.

LIGHTFOOT: Colored showmen who are new in the business of producing their own musicals…they've had quite a few successes already.

HENRY: Are they interested in us??

LIGHTFOOT: Yes. They've not been to Broadway yet however, but when I explained that we had been rehearsing for quite a while here—

HENRY: Have we been rehearsing!…wait till you see…

(Group gets into position for "Broadway Dahomey Bye and Bye.")

ROSETTA: Who are these men, Daddy?

LIGHTFOOT: Oh…just fellows you've never heard of baby…but they've got great promise…Bert Williams…Jesse Shipp, Paul Lawrence Dunbar… George Walker…and let's see…Will Marion Cook and…

HENRY: You're right, ain't nobody ever heard of them or us!

SHYLOCK & RAREBACK: No, but they will!

AND ALL:

(The company begins a rousing "In Dahomey Bye and Bye" as Mr. Reeder runs in breathlessly and joins The Company in performance.)

END

Jeff Stetson

THE MEETING

Crossroads National Education & Arts Center

Jeff Stetson

Mr. Stetson's first play, *The Meeting*, was the recipient of the Louis B. Mayer Award, eight 1987 NAACP Theatre Image Awards, including Best Play and Best Writer, and six New York AUDELCO nominations. The play has had independent productions in more than fifty theatres throughout the country, and was also produced in Canada following a four-month tour throughout the Dutch Netherlands. It was produced in Johannesburg, South Africa, Nigeria, and Kenya. Mr. Stetson adapted the play to critical acclaim for an American Playhouse production televised nationally on PBS in May of 1989.

Mr. Stetson's play, *Fraternity*, was a winner in the 1988 Multi-Cultural Playwrights Festival sponsored by Seattle's Group Theatre Company. *And the Men Shall Also Gather* was one of twelve stage plays selected from among over 1500 submissions as part of the prestigious National Playwrights Conference Eugene O'Neill Theatre Center. The play was developed at their July 1988 Conference and received its world premiere at the Bushfire Theatre in Philadelphia in October 1989. Adapted as a one-hour pilot for FOX Television by Mr. Stetson, *To Find a Man* received critical acclaim during its extended production at the Estelle Harmon Theatre in Los Angeles, June 1988 and was nominated for four NAACP Theatre Image Awards including best play and best writer.

Mr. Stetson's *Fathers . . . and Other Strangers*, was the recipient of the Third Annual Theodore Ward Playwrights' Award sponsored by Columbia College of Chicago. It has received numerous productions throughout the country in the last two years.

Mr. Stetson has written several screenplays including *Out of the Ashes*, a feature film for Steven Spielberg's Amblin Productions in association with Touchstone Pictures; *Divided Soul: The Marvin Gaye Story*; and *Keep the Faith: The Story of Adam Clayton Powell, Jr.* His latest is *The Buffalo Soldiers*, which is to star and be directed by Morgan Freeman. Mr. Stetson has completed *Witness to an Assassination: The Gene Roberts Story* for HBO feature films which focuses on the former New York detective's undercover assignment as bodyguard to Malcolm X.

Mr. Stetson currently is a Professor at the Theatre Arts and Dance Department at California State University, Los Angeles, where he teaches playwriting. He is a proud member of the Los Angeles Black Playwrights; Dramatists Guild; Playwrights' Theatre of Los Angeles; and Writers Guild of America, West.

CROSSROADS NATIONAL EDUCATION AND ARTS CENTER

Crossroads National Education And Arts Center was established in response to an overwhelming need to provide viable arts and education programs in the inner community of Los Angeles. Crossroads is housed within The Vision Complex, located in the Crenshaw-Leimert Park community. Crossroads' commitment to excellence has earned it numerous awards, including the LA Weekly, Dramalogue, New York AUDELCO Award, and 12 NAACP Image Awards. The award-winning television show, "227", began as a play at Crossroads, as well as the Broadway play "Checkmates".

Crossroads National Education and Arts Center seeks to utilize the arts to create avenues for economic development, self-sufficiency, education, and enlightenment while providing a legacy for current and successive generations. Crossroads offers training opportunities for youth (ages 4 to 19), adults, and seniors in the dramatic arts, movement for the actor, entrepreneurship, dance, martial arts, voice, visual/design arts, conflict resolution/mediation, and other areas. Crossroads has helped to launch the careers of several of its students in theatre, film, and television. As Crossroads continues to grow, its potential to utilize the arts as an instrument of peace, healing, and understanding—as well as a vehicle for jobs and economic growth—also grows.

Crossroads was co-founded in 1981 by popular television actress Marla Gibbs ("The Jeffersons" and "227") and Angela Mills, actress, writer, and director.

THE MEETING
by Jeff Stetson

Directed by
JudyAnn Elder

Cast in Order of Appearance

MALCOLM X ....Dick Anthony Williams

RASHAD..Taurean Blacque

DR. MARTIN LUTHER KING, JR ....Felton Perry

TIME: February 14, 1965

PLACE: A hotel room in Harlem

CAST:

RASHAD, bodyguard to Malcolm X. He is in his mid-thirties. Lean but muscular. He is meticulously dressed and bald-headed. A gun is protruding through its holster which he wears just underneath his left shoulder.

MALCOLM X

DR. MARTIN LUTHER KING, JR.

ACT I
SCENE I

It is the front suite of a hotel room. MALCOLM X is asleep on the couch. The room is modestly furnished with a dresser with a mirror, a television, night table, chairs. There is a large window/sliding glass door that opens to a balcony which overlooks all of Harlem. This window/door is a significant part of the room which seems to be the freedom that the confines of the room seeks to deny. MAL-COLM X is wearing a dark grey suit which is in need of an iron. His tie is loos-ened at the neck. This is a restless sleep that results in MALCOLM rising sharply and letting out a groan as if awakened by a nightmare. RASHAD ENTERS quickly with gun drawn. He searches the room as if in looking for an intruder. But he senses that MALCOLM is not in danger this time, but rather has experienced yet another restless sleep. There is a tense moment as the two men look at each other.

MALCOLM: *(Looking at the gun.)* Will you put that away.

RASHAD: *(He puts his gun back into his shoulder holster.)* Was it the same one?

MALCOLM: *(He rises and begins to stretch, ignoring the question. He looks at his watch.)* He should be here soon.

RASHAD: Wonderful.

MALCOLM: I take it you don't approve?

RASHAD: You know I don't. But since when has that made a difference?

MALCOLM: *(He looks at RASHAD and smiles gently.)* Stop pouting.

RASHAD: Malcolm, why are you meeting with him?

MALCOLM: *(Pause.)* Do you remember the first time you made love?

RASHAD: What?

MALCOLM: Do you remember the first time you made love?

RASHAD: Yeah, sort of.

MALCOLM: Why did you do it?

RASHAD: What do you mean, why did I do it?

MALCOLM: Was it planned? Was there a reason behind it? Or did it just happen because it was meant to? Because you knew sooner or later you would...because it was time.

RASHAD: *(He thinks for a moment.)* It was mostly 'cause the woman said I could.

MALCOLM: *(Laughs and shakes his head.)* Rashad, there's nothing romantic about you. If you weren't my bodyguard, I think you'd be alone.

RASHAD: For all you share with me, sometimes I am.

MALCOLM: *(He walks to the dresser and studies himself in the mirror.)* Did I ever tell you about when I met Billie Holiday?

RASHAD: *(Thinks he's about to hear a tall tale.)* Yeah, okay, Malcolm.

MALCOLM: She sang a song for me. Did I ever tell you about that?

RASHAD: *She* sang a song for *you?* Then, Louis Armstrong asked you to play the trumpet.

MALCOLM: *(He moves toward RASHAD.)* No Rashad, I'm serious. She sang it for me. She walked straight up to me, ignored everyone else in the room, then she took the flower out of her hair, and gave it to me. Then, she started to sing. *(He thinks about the moment, after a pause begins to sing softly.)*

YOU DON'T KNOW WHAT LOVE IS
UNTIL YOU'VE LEARNED THE MEANING OF THE BLUES
UNTIL YOU'VE LOVED A LOVE YOU'VE HAD TO LOSE
YOU DON'T KNOW WHAT LOVE IS

(He is swaying back and forth. RASHAD after listening begins to move a bit himself, until he finds himself doing a slow dance and joins MALCOLM for the second verse.)

BOTH:

YOU DON'T KNOW HOW HEARTS YEARN
FOR LOVE THAT CANNOT LIVE YET NEVER DIES

(On the word "dies," MALCOLM seems to become sullen, lost in thought. He goes through with the rest of the song, but there is no movement or life in contrast to RASHAD who is now lost in the song and loving it.)

UNTIL YOU'VE FACED EACH DAWN WITH SLEEPLESS EYES
YOU DON'T KNOW WHAT LOVE IS.

(RASHAD becomes aware of the mood change and looks at MALCOLM who has turned away and after several moments seems to notice the phone and is drawn to it. He takes the phone, dials it, and waits.)

MALCOLM: Hi, it's me...Are you okay?...And the children? *(He smiles, but it is a smile with more that a trace of concern.)* They always could sleep through anything...Just like their mama...*(There is a quiet, painful laugh.)* Betty?...I'm sorry for not being there with you. You know that, don't you?...Next week, when I speak at the Audobon, I want you there with me. I want the whole family there. After that, we'll spend more time together. I promise...Don't get so excited girl, we got enough children. *(HE laughs. It seems more relaxed.)* I've got to go, he should be here soon...Betty?...I love you. *(The words come out slowly, and painfully real.)* Kiss my girls for me. *(He smiles, and it gradually turns to the word, "Goodbye." He cradles the phone for several moments, then places it softly in its rightful place. He bows his head slightly and quickly pounds his fist into the palm of his hand. He does this only once, and it seems to release the tension, at least, momentarily. He begins to relax and picks-up the phone again. RASHAD has been the loyal observer during all of this, wishing to give his friend privacy yet there to help at the first sign. MALCOLM speaks into the phone again.)* If the F.B.I. is still listening, I'm hungry...could you deliver some Chinese food and red soda. *(He starts to hang up, then remembers.)* Oh...and hold the pork.

(Both MALCOLM and RASHAD look at each other and laugh. After several moments, RASHAD walks toward MALCOLM.)

RASHAD: Is everything all right?

MALCOLM: *(Nods yes.)* The children are asleep.

RASHAD: Sister Betty?

MALCOLM: *(There is a painful, bittersweet pause.)* Our house is bombed this morning, and I'm here...I haven't given her much have I, Rashad?

RASHAD: Do you think she will ever feel that?

MALCOLM: She would never be that selfish. But I know. I can hear it in her voice, the fear, for me mostly, but for the family too. I should be with her tonight. I should be with my children as often as possible. *(Pause.)* They should remember their daddy.

RASHAD: The *world* will remember their daddy.

MALCOLM: They won't be remember me. I know that. If I could just be sure that what I represent will be remembered. That's all that's important to me. This country will do what it can to see that that won't happen.

RASHAD: This country has always tried its best to eliminate the black man. It ain't happened yet.

MALCOLM: What can be changed, doesn't need to be eliminated. *(He takes his glasses off, rubs the bridge of his nose, gently.)* I'm tired, Rashad...It seems like I've been a lot of things lately...but whatever else I've been...tired has been in there somewhere. *(Pause.)* It's stuffy in here.

(MALCOLM moves toward the window but RASHAD rushed to stop him.)

RASHAD: Stay away from that window, Malcolm! Please.

MALCOLM: *(He moves back toward the seat, but remains standing. RASHAD cautiously opens the window, making sure that the curtain remains drawn.)* All the forces in this country couldn't protect their own President. You think it makes a difference not to be able to breathe the Harlem air?

RASHAD: It may make a difference *tonight*.

MALCOLM: Those used to be my streets, Rahshad.

RASHAD: They'll always be your streets...They'll just never be safe. *(Pause.)*

MALCOLM: We're in the tallest building in Harlem, Rashad. How high up do I have to be, before I'll finally be safe?

(MALCOLM kicks the chair in disgust or anger. RASHAD moves to pick it up.)

RASHAD: Just give the word, Malcolm, and we can strike back.

MALCOLM: *(Angrily)* Strike back? Do you think I trained them in the art of self defense, so they could protects themselves from *us?*

RASHAD: Did you train them to throw a fire-bomb through your house?

MALCOLM: *(HE moves slowly toward RASHAD.)* I don't think it was them.

RASHAD: *(Frustrated.)* Malcolm!

MALCOLM: No, Rashad. It just doesn't make any sense. Even Elijah doesn't have the power to do some of the things that's happened recently. *(Pause.)* It's gone way beyond that. Next Sunday, at the rally, I'm going to say some things, sone things that might really begin to put the heat on us...I'm going to say that the Muslims didn't act alone.

RASHAD: And who are you going to accuse?

MALCOLM: Who else could it be? Do you think Elijah could get the French government to ban me from France?

RASHAD: You won't even get the letters out of your mouth, Malcolm.

MALCOLM: *(Smiles.)* I'll just have to remember to talk fast.

RASHAD: We can't afford to lose you.

MALCOLM: When I can't go near that window, you already have.

RASHAD: Won't you at least cut back on some of the speaking engagements? There's no way we can manage large crowds anymore. Not when we have to watch out for people who look like *us*.

MALCOLM: Ain't no one out on those streets look like you, Rashad. You got to go *clear* 'cross the ocean, to another land, to find someone as *ugly* as you. Either that, or all the way downtown.

(Both men laugh.)

RASHAD: Please be serious, Malcolm...

MALCOLM: *(Smiles.)* After the Audobon, I'll cut down. Anyway, I told Sister Betty I would be with her more often. It's the first time she laughed in months. *(MALCOLM moves to the coffee table that has a chessboard already set. He picks-up one of the pieces and smiles.)* You want to play a quick game?

RASHAD: No.

MALCOLM: Why not?

RASHAD: Because I always beat you.

MALCOLM: *(Smiles.)* Have I become that predictable?

RASHAD: You play as if the object of the game was to protect the pawns. The pawns are there to protect the king, Malcolm.

MALCOLM: Maybe it's time somone protected the pawns for a change.

RASHAD: Then the game wouldn't be Chess anymore. It would be something else. Something nobody would play.

MALCOLM: Would that be so bad?

RASHAD: It ain't a question of good or bad. It's a question of winnin' or dyin'.

MALCOLM: You can't sacrifice your own people and expect to win. Look at that board, Rashad. What do you see?

RASHAD: *(He looks at it then, with some degree of regret of sadness responds.)* I see a game, Malcolm. A game we didn't invent. *(He reacts to MALCOLM's disappointment.)* You don't like the rules? Fine. Neither do I. But, the only chance we got of winning is to protect the leader. Once the leader gets too far our in front, it's open season. Hell, Malcolm, even the pawns will help to sacrifice you. *(He picks up the king from the chessboard and moves it toward MALCOLM.)* As long as this one piece is free and protected, the games isn't over. Whatever else you say or do, won't change that. *(He touches his friend as if he is giving one final plea.)* As long as this *one* piece had a chance...we *all* do.

MALCOLM: *(Takes the king and places it back on the board.)* Rashad, we're all pawns. When we begin to realize that, maybe the old game will be over, and a new one can begin.

RASHAD: *(Moves toward MALCOLM.)* Malcolm, go home. Be with Betty. Be with your children. You don't need to do this. We've got enough problems with half the people thinking you betrayed Elijah, and the other half thinkin' you're getting soft. All this new talk about white folks not being all bad, now you're meeting with the "King of Love." It ain't right, Malcolm. I can feel it. Nothing good can come of this.

MALCOLM: Something good already has.

RASHAD: What?

MALCOLM: I asked him to come up, and he said yes. And he never asked why. *(Silence.)*

RASHAD: *(RASHAD places his hand gently on MALCOLM's arm.)* Do you trust him? *(MALCOLM smiles, reassuringly touches RASHAD's hand, then walks slowly away.)* Malcolm, do you trust me?

MALCOLM: *(Without turning toward him.)* I don't know that I can trust anyone, any more.

RASHAD: *(Stung by what appears to be an indictment.)* I'd *die* for you!

MALCOLM: *(Looks at him for the first time, then, without emotion.)* People who'd die for me, I trust least of all. *(MALCOLM after a moment seems to realize what he has said and the effect that it has had on RASHAD. He moves toward him.)* I didn't mean that, Rashad. I guess I haven't shaken the nightmare yet. *(Beat. Then, to himself.)* At least it will be over soon.

RASHAD: *(Surprised by that statement and a bit alarmed.)* Why will it be over? Malcolm?

(The two men look at each other in silence for several moments. The silence is interrupted by several loud knocks at the door. RASHAD makes no movement toward the door and appears to be ignoring it. MALCOLM studies him patiently.)

MALCOLM: Don't you think you ought to let him in?

RASHAD: You know what I think.

(RASHAD goes to the door and opens it. He greets DR. KING who enters, holding a small brown bag. He looks at MALCOLM.)

DR. KING: Malcolm.

MALCOLM: Doctor King. *(Pause.)* Rashad, I think you can leave Doctor King and I alone. We'll be all right.

RASHAD: *(He pauses, uncomfortably.)* I need to check Doctor King.

DR. KING: Check? I was "checked" once downstairs.

RASHAD: Not by me.

MALCOLM: *(Smiles.)* Rashad, somehow I think that's unnecessary. I'm sure I'll be safe with Doctor King.

RASHAD: I'm sure you'd be safe with Doctor King, too, but how do I know that's him?

DR. KING: Perhaps I could give a short speech, or an appropriate sermon?

MALCOLM: Oh please, Doctor, not that. *(Both men laugh good-naturedly.)* We'll be okay, Rashad.

RASHAD: Very well, if you say so. *(Pause. He begins to exit then stops.)* Oh, can I take your coat, Doctor?

DR. KING: Why, thank you.

(RASHAD helps DR. KING off with his coat, and manages to get a quick, but obvious frisk or two in as well. MALCOLM gives an embarrassed glance toward DR. KING. He then takes a bag from DR. KING opens in and looks curiously at him, then a quick glance at MALCOLM. He returns the bag to KING and gives him a slow and mistrusting look. RASHAD begins his exit having accomplished what he set out to do, and is satisfied about having done it. He stops near the door.)

RASHAD: I'll be just outside if you need me.

(He exits.)

MALCOLM: I'm sorry about that, these are troubled times.

DR. KING: I understand…I suppose the bombing has unsettled everyone.

MALCOLM: *(Smiles.)* Didn't do much for the price of real estate in my neighborhood…Did anyone see you come in?

DR. KING: No. I followed your instructions. The next time you want me to take the back stairs, I wish you could get a room on a floor lower than the seventh.

MALCOLM: *(Laughs.)* I've seen you on T.V. You could afford to lose a few pounds.

DR. KING: Television makes you look heavier…And, anyway, this stomach is the finest sense of southern tradition and the ministry. Congregations don't warm-up to thin preachers…means the preachin's not good enough to receive sweet potatoe pies in lieu of other donations.

MALCOLM: My congregation sells pies street to street…You might say it keeps them thin and the donations fat. *(Looks at the bag.)* Speaking of pies, is that your lunch in that bag…or perhaps a tape recorder?

DR. KING: And why would I need a tape recorder.

MALCOLM: Maybe you're nervous about coming out of hotel rooms...Mister Hoover does have a way of making people paranoid.

DR. KING: I have never thought that the Lord could have made a mistake...but Hoover does push one's faith beyond reasonable limits.

MALCOLM: Have a seat, Reverend.

(DR. KING *places the bag on the couch and takes a seat near the table.*)

MALCOLM: Don't you want the couch?

DR. KING: This will do just fine, thank you.

MALCOLM: Oh, yes...I forgot; you're used to sit-ins and such.

DR. KING: I find they're generally better for your back.

MALCOLM: Not too good for the head, as I recall. I'm surprised you still have one with all that non-violent *action* you've been involved in.

DR. KING: You'd be amazed how much one can take, when the purpose is clear.

MALCOLM: Perhaps, but I think some folks just naturally have hard heads. (*MALCOLM takes his seat, directly across the table from DR. KING.*) When I was in Selma two weeks ago, I almost paid you a visit.

DR. KING: You should have; plenty of room in the jail.

MALCOLM: I try not to visit jails, voluntarily.

DR. KING: I heard your speech on my behalf was very moving.

MALCOLM: The *younger* people seemed to enjoy it...In fact, if I had spoken any longer, we all would have come by the jail house...except we wouldn't be planning on stayin'...of course, there probably wouldn't have been much jail remainin' after we left.

DR. KING: Then, I should thank you for not speaking too long...Being in jail is unpleasant enough...having it torn down while you're there is not my idea of how to spend a Sunday afternoon.

MALCOLM: Oh, you can thank some of your conference planners for that, if it were up to them, I wouldn't have spoken at all...As it was, they spent several hours after I spoke trying to calm the crowd down.

DR. KING: Maybe they were trying to move them in a different direction.

MALCOLM: Calming them down certainly would have done that.

DR. KING: Well, since you didn't visit me then, I'm visiting you now.

MALCOLM: Yes, I must say, I'm impressed. I didn't think you visited Northern cities too often...I imagine our streets are more difficult to maneuver than those country roads you're accustomed to.

DR. KING: If the road was meant to be traveled, it will be.

MALCOLM: And if it's destroyed?

DR. KING: It will be rebuilt...Or it wasn't the road for us.

MALCOLM: Still the dreamer?

DR. KING: And you're still the revolutionary?

MALCOLM: *(Smiles.)* Thank you.

DR. KING: I hadn't realized I had paid you a compliment.

MALCOLM: Ignorance is sometimes the sincerest form of flattery.

DR. KING: If I didn't know better, I'd think you were trying to upset me.

MALCOLM: *(Smiles.)* A man that allows himself to get hit upside the head, certainly wouldn't get upset at some mere words. *(He smiles again, somewhat more coyly, then politely speaks.)* Care for some water, Martin?

DR. KING: No. Thank you.

MALCOLM: Some tea?

DR. KING: I'm fine.

MALCOLM: *(He moves toward the dresser and takes a drink of water and then takes an apple from a fruit basket. He thinks for a moment. He brings it toward DR. KING.)* I want you to eat this.

DR. KING: No, thank you...I'm not hungry.

MALCOLM: I don't care...I want you to eat it anyway.

DR. KING: I don't want it.

MALCOLM: It's good for you.

DR. KING: That may be, but I still don't want it.

MALCOLM: What if I make you eat it?

DR. KING: And just how would you do that?

MALCOLM: By force, if necessary.

DR. KING: I'd still refuse.

MALCOLM: You mean to tell me, you would refuse to eat this apple, even if I resorted to force?

DR. KING: Yes.

MALCOLM: Even if it's good for you?

DR. KING: Even then.

MALCOLM: You're right, Martin, you can't force people to take something they don't want. Try as hard as you can to make white folks love us, no matter how smooth you make it, the simple fact is, they just won't swallow the truth...even if it's good for them.

(He places the apple back in the basket.)

DR. KING: *(The two men look at each other in silence for a moment.)* Isn't it odd, that you should try to tempt me with an apple?

MALCOLM: *(Smiles.)* You see the apple as a temptation...I see it as a nourishment.

DR. KING: We see what we want to see, I suppose.

MALCOLM: Some of us don't see anything at all, even when it's staring right at us. For example, when you passed by the front of the hotel, did you notice a woman standing outside? She was wearing a short red dress and heavy make-up.

DR. KING: The prostitute?

MALCOLM: *(Nods yes.)* How old would you guess she is?

DR. KING: Thirty to thirty-five?

MALCOLM: *(A painful laugh.)* She's seventeen, Reverend, although after three years on the street age has no real significance...Tomorrow morning she won't know how many men she slept with tonight. She can't even tell from the money she makes. Her pimp collects that right after each trick. *(MALCOLM stands and moves slowly across the room.)* She's part of a larger congregation but you won't find them in any of your churches. They would curse your God if they were alive enough to curse...But they're dead, Martin...They're the living dead. They exist because they're accustomed to it and haven't thought about why they shouldn't. If they weren't used to moving so often...not staying in any one place too long...someone would have swept them away by now.

DR. KING: I take it you have a point to all this?

MALCOLM: I know something of the living dead, young women working the streets, and their pimps. When you're around the same people everyday you don't notice the change right away...Then all of a sudden, you're aware...someone is fat or old...or without hope. The purpose of all this, Martin...is to show you the hopeless and to let you know that the number is growing everyday.

DR. KING: Do you have a solution?

MALCOLM: Unity.

DR. KING: I've never been against that.

MALCOLM: Your unity is sitting around the camp fire while the cross is burning singing, "we shall overcome"...If you're really for unity you'd be singing, "we shall come over!" Everytime there's an injustice, we shall come over. Everytime there's a black woman being frightened by a white face behind a white hood, we shall come over...Everytime and *anytime* there's a need to stop white people from persecuting black people, WE SHALL COME OVER! And we will stay until black people feel safe again.

DR. KING: *(Leans his body slowly in the direction of MALCOLM, and very clearly and deliberately responds.)* We *also* sang, "Ain't gonna let *nobody* turn *us* around."

(The two men stare at each other. MALCOLM breaks the silence.)

MALCOLM: It really doesn't matter what the song was. Nobody ever got their freedom from singing. On the other hand, if you're prepared to do some swinging?

DR. KING: Violence? Revenge? Is that the unity you seek?

MALCOLM: I care about survival, Martin. I care about the quality of that survival. No. I don't seek violence. I seek to stop it and I'll stop it by any means necessary. I have that as a duty.

DR. KING: Violence never stops violence, Malcolm.

MALCOLM: But marches do? All those people gathered together singing songs. What did that bring? A piece of legislation? Did that legislation help those civil rights workers murdered in the south...or the children blown-up in their own church? You got nothing, Martin! Nothing...but some more empty promises, and a piece of paper that betrayed yet another lie in a long list of lies...the American lie...the grand *white* lie. *(Pause.)* You know, I had a dream tonight.

DR. KING: Oh?

MALCOLM: *(Smiles.)* I'm sorry, that's your line.

DR. KING: You may borrow it, if you choose.

MALCOLM: This dream I had...we had been dead for some time...the time it takes to miseducate the average American...Young black men and women didn't know who we were...They knew nothing about the movement...the struggle. It was as if it had never happened. I woke up in a cold sweat, shaking, confused. You know, Martin, I have seen my own death countless nights, but that vision was never as frightening as that dream. *(Pause.)* We will be sold out...you and I. It might happen over a promise for a job...or a deal to be supported as the new leader. It may happen any number of ways...but it will happen, Martin...You might even do it yourself.

DR. KING: And how do you think I will accomplish my own undermining?

MALCOLM: *(He takes a piece of paper from the inside of his jacket. He unfolds it neatly, and begins to read, at first, seriously, then a bit mockingly, then finally, with some degree of anger.)* "We will match your capacity to inflict suffering, with our capacity to endure it. We will meet your pysical force with soul force...Do to us what you will...Threaten our children and we will *still* love you...Come into our homes at the midnight hour of life, take us out on some desolate highway and *beat us* and then leave us there and we will *still love you*...Say that we aren't worthy of integration; that we are too *immoral*; that we are too *low*; that we are too *degraded* and we will still love you...Bomb our homes and go by our churches early in the moring and bomb them if you please...and we will still love you...*(Beat.)* We will wear you down, with *our* capacity to *suffer!*" *(Pause.)* Did you really say that, Martin?

DR. KING: You know I said it. And, furthermore, you know the context.

MALCOLM: The context! The context has to be insanity.

DR. KING: Is love insane?

MALCOLM: No! But we aren't talking about love.

DR. KING: Maybe you need to read it again.

MALCOLM: I try not to inflict suffering on myself more than once...I suppose my *capacity* for that, is not as large as yours.

DR. KING: *(HE leans forward, angrily.)* You are not before any cameras now,

Malcolm! You have an audience of one, and I am not cheering...So, you can stop with the sarcasm and you flippant remarks!

MALCOLM: I don't want any cameras and I don't need any audience!

DR. KING: And I didn't come here to debate you, so you can stop the contest.

MALCOLM: The "contest" is more important than the debate, doctor!

(Both men are leaning toward each other. Their opposite arms are extended, elbows on the table, coming to rest in an arm wrestling position. Their hands touch, by accident or impulse, and they both smile. At first the smile appears to be a sly one, then it turns to a satisfying grin, as they seem to fall naturally into an arm wrestling contest. They struggle briefly, but not strenuously. MAL-COLM wins and the two men stare at each other silently, for several moments.)

DR. KING: *(MALCOLM still has KING's arm pinned to the table, but without force.)* Are you satisfied?

MALCOLM: *(Letting KING's hand go.)* I wish it were that easy, Doctor.

DR. KING: Why is it every time you say the words "Doctor" or "Reverend" I have the distinct impression I should feel insulted?

MALCOLM: *(Laughs.)* I imagine it's my secret accent...Having not had the advantage of university training, my words sometimes appear too harsh.

DR. KING: You're being too modest, Malcolm. It's doubtful that Harvard invites someone to lecture who has difficulty being understood.

MALCOLM: They didn't bring me there to lecture...They brought me there to be embarrassed...But then I don't embarrass easily...And since Harvard didn't have anything I wanted...I never say a reason to apologize for not having it...Of course, there were an ample number of Negroes there who seemed to have an abundance of apologies all saved up for just such an occasion.

DR. KING: Do you see me as that kind of Negro?

MALCOLM: No...But I see you being used by white folks, whether you intend to be or not. Which is why they'll erect monuments to you before you're through.

DR. KING: Oh, I don't know about that...Seems like the mention of your name is likely to cause a great deal of attention...They may even name whole cities after you.

MALCOLM: You got the award, Martin.

DR. KING: Yes...On behalf or all of us...People everywhere who fought against injustice.

MALCOLM: White people gave you the award, Martin...Doesn't it worry you just a little that the people who are doing most of the oppressing are also giving out all the awards? I think you must have impressed them most when you said, "If blood has to flow on the streets...let it be ours"...Hell, every cracker in the South would have chipped in to but you an award for that one!

DR. KING: The award was for *peace*, Malcolm.

MALCOLM: No, Doctor, the award was for getting beaten and not fighting back.

DR. KING: I didn't expect acceptance from you, Malcolm...A little understanding would be sufficient.

MALCOLM: You want me to understand how a black man would ask his people to be the first, last, and only ones to bleed? To give their precious blood, let it spill to the pavements of these cities, or sink into the soil of this nation, the nation we helped build? You want me to *understand* that?

DR. KING: Did it ever occur to you that perhaps you were more responsible for the blood of our people flowing than I? That your speeches are unwittingly causing violence?

MALCOLM: No! Not once! Not ever! Agression in the name of self-defense is not violence...It's honor...We have to begin to *think* for ourselves. To *do* for ourselves...Not let the "man" shape our values for us; 'cause he has some tricky logic. He'll make us think that defending our families is wrong. That defending our communities is violence. When the music is a tango...you tango...Simple as that...If they don't want you to tango, stop playin' the white music and then maybe we can waltz...nice and polite like, with white gloves and black ties.

DR. KING: Don't you think we've made any progress, Malcolm?

MALCOLM: Progress? Martin, you got some consessions because I was the alternative...They threw some legislation, some money, and some cracker controlled programs your way in hopes that non-violence would win out. Except, we were the only ones to remain non-violent. (*Pause.*) If they kill me first, you'll have nothing to negotiate with. If they kill you first, they can't let me live. They'll make you into a martyr, Martin. They'll hold your non-violent methods up to the world as a testament to your courage. If they hold it up long enough, people won't even notice the contradiction, you were *killed* preaching it. We can't learn anything from martyrs anymore, Martin.

DR. KING: Jesus was a martyr.

MALCOLM: Two thousand years ago it was possible to die and not kill a movement...Today it's brought to you in living color...flashed across the big screen and small all with the same clear and unrelenting message, "when you lead, you die." When you lead, you die. How long will we continue teaching that to our children? (*DR. KING walks toward the window and stares outside. MALCOLM, who is now seated, looks silently at the floor. He looks toward KING, and begins to speak again.*) This ain't the country Reverend...They stack families on top of each other our here...black man on top of black man...'til there's no room...'til you can't breath...When you can't breath you either die, or you strike out and someone else dies...And, the women, it can be a curse to be young and attractive out there on those streets...And then, Martin, there's the drugs...You put enough drugs out threre, and they'll dream anything...Why, they'll even believe your dreams, Doctor.

DR. KING: I can't change, Malcolm. I think you know that.

MALCOLM: Everyone can change. That girl in the street changed. Three years ago, she was fourteen, today she...

DR. KING: I *can't* change!

(*MALCOLM takes his glasses off, massages the bridge of his nose and gradually his temple. He puts his glasses back on and looks at DR. KING, who has turned away from the window and moves back toward his seat.*)

DR. KING: (*cont.*) (*Softly.*) Neither can you.

MALCOLM: If you can't change, can you at least get angry?

DR. KING: The first march I ever led...I was surrounded by all kinds of people...Old women, who found it hard to walk across the room, somehow found strength to march for miles...Young men and women carrying their children...Older children holding the hands of their younger brothers and sisters...All of a sudden a bottle was thrown from the middle of a crowd of whites...We shouted "duck"! And all the adults did...But children...children have a need to know what's being done...The bottle struck this young child...It cut the who left side of her face...None of us really had time to be angry then...We rushed to protect her...to console her...to worry about stopping the bleeding...But we marched on. (*KING is speaking with a sense of emotion that makes MALCOLM realize he is reliving that moment, with all the pain and fear that must have existed.*) Then a few moments later, this huge white man...bigger than the truck he must have been driving that night...this man with all his force yelled: "Go home you little NIGGER BASTARD!" He was screaming at this young boy, couldn't have been older than seven or eight... (*Pause.*) I saw the look on this child's face...He was scared...and hurt, and maybe most of all, ashamed. He thought he must have sone something terribly wrong to have all that hate directed toward him... (*Looking directly at MALCOLM.*) Yes, Malcolm, I can get angry...with all the history that makes me a black man...I can get angry...But it's a different kind of anger...An anger that makes you know you can't stop lovin'...can't stop believin'...It's an anger that makes you want to prove hate wrong.

MALCOLM: (*Beat.*) I just want to prove hate less powerful.

DR. KING: We both deal with power, Malocolm. We just do it differently.

MALCOLM: Yes. You see our children bleeding and in tears and you seek to comfort them...I see the man who has he rock in his hand and I seek to stop him...If I can't stop him before he throws it...I'll see to it that he never throws another.

DR. KING: And what will that accomplish, Malcolm? If you stop that one, there will just be another, and another, and another.

MALCOLM: Doctor, it doesn't matter how good a football player you are, when the game is baseball you better get yourself a bat. And if you've got problems swinging it, you ought to stay out of the game.

DR. KING: Somehow, I had hoped that your trips to Mecca had given you a greater vision than that, perhaps even a broader compassion.

MALCOLM: You don't tame the lion and leave the jungle unchanged, Martin. Yes. I saw things outside this country, *outside* this country. Saw things that perhaps my heart wouldn't or couldn't let me see before. I saw whites, who when they talked about color, made it seem incidental; like describing a suit or a sunset. But here, *(Smiles.)* here, it's different. When the "Man" here talks about color, you know what he means. You hear it in his voice, see it in his expression. He means he's on top and you're not. And there's no way he's gonna let that change. It's a simple question of power and privilege. And the one in power, always decides the privilege. *(He touches KING's arm slightly.)* We aren't the ones in power, Martin. And we won't be until we gain control of our own lives, our own thinking.

DR. KING: You want to free blacks, I want to free America. It's the only way any of us can be free, Malcolm.

MALCOLM: *(Frustrated.)* Martin, can't you see what's happening to us? Five years from now, ten at the most, whites won't have anything to us. We'll be doing it ourselves. Some of the brothers who sit peacefully in your demonstrations, and have their heads split open, do you know they go back to their *own* communities and commit violent acts. It's the *rage*, Martin. It's the *hurt* that's all balled-up inside and makes you strike out in the only way you can...the only way that's acceptable. *(Pause.)* I can't free us from that rage...but at least I can try and direct it to the right source.

DR. KING: Don't we really want the same things, Malcolm?

MALCOLM: You want us to be able to but a cup of coffee...I want us to be able to sell it...You want us to integrate the coffe shop...I want us to be able to hire ourselves...No, Martin...We do not want the same things...I'm afraid your quest for integration will be the white man's solution for control...Maybe the only hope we have is that they'll hate us so much that they won't recognize the power they'd have over us, if they just let us in.

DR. KING: And so, those of us who don't agree with your definition of power and control...I suppose we are to be called, "Uncle Tom's"?

MALCOLM: I only refer to the *older* ones as "Uncle"...and I don't call them "Tom" anymore...I call them "Roy" or "Ralph" or "Uncle Whitney."

DR. KING: They don't deserve that from you, Malcolm...They don't deserve that from anyone. Do you think the unity you seek can be achieved through insult and ridicule?

MALCOLM: *(Innocently.)* Have I "ridiculed" you, Reverend?

DR. KING: Do you think I should be flattered at the term, the "Reverend Doctor Chickenleg"?

MALCOLM: It was, "Chickenwing" to be more precise. Would you have found it more flattering if I refered to you as, "De Lawd"?

DR. KING: *(KING begins to roll up his sleeve.)* "The Movement" would have been sufficient.

MALCOLM: *(Smiles, while taking his jacket off.)* Isn't it wonderful how well the two of us are getting along?

DR. KING: I suppose it's time for a rematch.

MALCOLM: So there is an ego to bruise. You should feel fortunate that a rematch is possible...Oh well, my friend, I am prepared to inflict suffering if you are prepared to endure it. *(Both men smile. It's a smile less sly and more respectful than the first contest, but still manifesting a degree of distance. After a brisk encounter, KING emerges the winner.)* Well, it's seems we are even, Reverend.

DR. KING: Yes. I suppose we are. Is that why you invited me?

MALCOLM: Actually, I'm surprised you accepted the invitation.

DR. KING: I came because I wanted to offer my protection.

MALCOLM: *(In disbelief.)* What?

DR. KING: When I heard about this morning, I thought you...

MALCOLM: *(Laughs.)* Protection? You? Offer me...protection? *(Angrily.)* And how are you going to do that, Sir. Are you going to have a mass sit-in and pray? Or perhaps your non-violent *action* movement will frighten the Molotov cocktail throwers so much that...

DR. KING: *(Angrily.)* Any Molotov cocktails that were thrown through you house, were thrown there because of *your* movement, Malcolm, not mine!

MALCOLM: Yes, Doctor King, *my* movement is *flexible*. It considers *all* options! It rules *nothing* out! It's one goal is *freedom*. Absolute. Total. And complete. It doesn't ask. It doesn't beg. It takes. It's willing to pay the price for freedom. Those that aren't willing to pay for it really don't want it.

DR. KING: Don't set yourself up as the authority on freedom, Malcolm!

MALCOLM: Why, I wouldn't think of it, Reverend. "Authorities" are those who study so hard to be white. If they do real good, they get to be "scholars" and if they speak for all Negroes, they get to be called "authorities"!

DR. KING: I came here to offer my help, Malcolm, if you don't want it I can...

MALCOLM: Your help? You're helping to kill me, Doctor!

DR. KING: Am I do be accused for that too?

MALCOLM: Not accused. Indicted. This non-violent movement of yours will get us killed.

DR. KING: Non-violence is the only chance we have, Malcolm. By appealing to the conscience of this country...

MALCOLM: The conscience of this country!? This country has no conscience.

It has no morality, no sense of honor! Hell, Martin, it doesn't even have a memory. It forgets what it doesn't want to remember and what we won't let it forget, it lies about. This country only has a conscience when you agree with it. It doesn't care about right or wrong. It just cares if you agree with it. And if you agree with it, it agrees with you. It calls you a hero when you tell black people to be non-violent here, but it would call you a liar and a traitor of you told those same black people to stop dropping napalm on brown-skinned babies is Vietnam. You think you can appeal to the conscience of a country like that? *(Beat.)* The Jews in Germany were non-violent, Martin. They remained non-violent all the way to the gas ovens. Go ask the victims who survived the concentration camps if non-violence got them their freedom. As for me, I'm going to deal with the victims of the concentration camps, we have in America, except here they're called, New York City, or Detroit, or Philadelphia, or Chicago. *(Pause.)* No, Martin. If you're looking for a conscience, you better look some place else. Anybody who preaches non-violence while they see the man out there building gas ovens, is helping to destroy his own people. And, when black people refuse to fight back, it not only becomes easy for racists to kill us, it becomes justifiable.

DR. KING: And you think I've contributed to that?

MALCOLM: Let's just say, anyone who wants to kill me, anyone who wants to kill any black man, does not have to stop and think about the consequences of their actions. They don't stop to ask: "Now, what would the good Doctor do?" They know what you'll do. Nothing! Which is about what you've accomplished.

DR. KING: *(He looks at MALCOLM, at first with anger, and then with disappointment.)* Don't tell me that we haven't accomplished anything, Malcolm. That people got beaten for nothing. Do you really think that it is easy for me to see our own people beaten? To sit there and risk the lives of my own children? Malcolm, do you think I would risk my own life for nothing? I don't want to die. I don't want my people to die. I don't preach non-violence because I like it! I preach it because it's right. And, because I'm a man. And, because I'm a child of God! *(He moves toward the window.)* You look out over this city, and see neon signs that tell you what to do, and where to go. But I grew up with a different kind of sign. It wasn't a neon light, but if you were black, you had no trouble seeing it. Signs of separation. Signs that burned the words "for colored only" in the psyche of Negro children. Signs that degraded and humiliated those children's parents on a daily and constant and continuing basis. *(He moves toward MALCOLM.)* When those signs came down, the spirit of black people went up, so, don't tell me *nothing* was accomplished. *(Beat.)* I was in a Montgomery church, when the announcement was made that buses in Alabama would no longer be segregated. What was accomplished was written on the faces of those who struggled so long to prove you could take a stand by sitting down. No, Malcolm, the only ones who doubted that we had accomplished anything, were those who never had to get up to give their seat to a white person, or move to the back of the bus, or watch white patrons being served in the comfort of a public restaurant while being forced to take food out into the rain or cold. Don't diminish what was accomplished and don't misunderstand what will be accomplished. Sometimes you got to be able to ride the bus before you can drive it, Malcolm. But don't think that we're not planning to own the whole bus line, one day. (Pause. Then, he moves very close to MALCOLM.) And, Malcolm, don't ever mistake non-violence for non-action. You might do a disservice to those who have been beaten so that you might have the freedom to question their courage.

MALCOLM: (Beat.) I have never questioned their courage, just their judgment.

DR. KING: I'm beginning to question my own for coming here.

MALCOLM: Well, that can easily be corrected, Doctor. The same steps that brought you here, will lead you away.

DR. KING: On that, we can at least agree.

MALCOLM: Yes! Yes, we can! (He moves toward the door.) Rashad! Rashad! (RASHAD ENTERS.) Get a driver for Doctor King. He wishes to leave.

RASHAD: It will be my pleasure.

(He exits.)

MALCOLM: Have a pleasant trip home.

DR. KING: (KING gets his hat and coat.) I shall. Thanks very much for the lecture on unity.

MALCOLM: You're welcome. And before you go, you should know this, my faith teaches me not to embarrass even my own enemies. I let you beat me in arm wrestling the second time.

DR. KING: My faith teaches me to show mercy, especially to my enemies. I let you beat me the first time. It seemed the Christian thing to do.

(KING begins to move toward the door as MALCOLM spots the paper bag and picks it up.)

MALCOLM: You forgot you lunch.

DR. KING: It's not mine. It's a gift.

MALCOLM: (He opens the bag and removes a black doll. He looks at it suspiciously and then says sarcastically) Is this what you brought me for protection? Does it possess some kind of magical powers? Or is the doll non-violent too?

DR. KING: It's not for you. It's for your daughter. My family was watching television when the news bulletin about the bombing appeared. They showed a film report of the damage to your home. You were on the front lawn holding one of your daughters.

MALCOLM: (Softly.) Attallah?

DR. KING: Yes. My daughter wondered if everything in the house had been destroyed. When she learned that I was going to see you tonight she thought Attallah could use a friend. That's her favorite doll. She loves it very much. If it has any "magical powers" I suppose it's because of that.

MALCOLM: *(For the first time, he is unsure and obviously taken back by the kindness as well as his own actions.)* What's her name?

DR. KING: I don't know that she has one.

MALCOLM: *(Smiles.)* I meant your daughters.

DR. KING: *(Chuckles.)* Yolanda.

MALCOLM: How old is she?

DR. KING: Nine.

MALCOLM: Attallah is six. She'll love this. *(Pause.)* Thank your daughter, thank Yolanda, for her...for both of us. *(The two men stare at each other briefly, somewhat awkwardly and yet with a sense of tenderness brought on by the moment. KING nods approval or possibly, good-bye, as he turns to exit. MALCOLM quickly and loudly says:)* Doctor King! *(There is a pause as the two men face each other again.)* Martin, you've been to the mountain top. If you have a moment, I'd like to share mine with you. That could be my gift, to you.

DR. KING: *(Smiles.)* I could hardly refuse an offer like that. *(MALCOLM moves to the balcony, slides the window back, and motions for DR. KING to step out with him.)* The balcony?

MALCOLM: I want you to see, what I see.

DR. KING: From out there?

MALCOLM: What's the matter, Reverend?

DR. KING: I've never been partial to heights.

MALCOLM: You're afraid of high places, Martin?

DR. KING: I didn't say I was afraid. I just said I wasn't partial.

MALCOLM: *(MALCOLM starts to laugh. But it is clearly the type of laughter and teasing that is shared among friends.)* Well, don't that beat all? *(MALCOLM moves onto the balcony and seems relieved to be able to breath.)* The problems all seem smaller from here, Martin, more manageable. *(MALCOLM beckons KING, who moves tentatively toward him. They stand side by side, looking over the streets of Harlem, in silence.)* It may not be the country, Reverend, but there are some things you can love more than the land.

DR. KING: Like the people who live on it?

MALCOLM: Yes, Martin, the people. *(There is a pause, as the two men look at each other. It is a tender look, one of admiration and concern.)* Would you do it again, Martin? *(Beat.)* If you had the choice, would you do it all over again?

DR. KING: do we ever really have a choice, Malcolm?

MALCOLM: You know, it's ironic, you tried to stop whites from hating us, and I tried to stop us from hating ourselves. We'll probably be killed by those we tried so hard to teach.

DR. KING: What makes you think that a black will kill you?

MALCOLM: There won't be any whites who could get close enough. I just
hope it happens from someone I don't know. I would hate to think I
could be that wrong about a friend.

DR. KING: Why did you really want to see me, Malcolm?

MALCOLM: *(Softly.)* I don't know...I suppose I wanted to see if you'd come.

DR. KING: Another test?

MALCOLM: No...Another chance. Another chance. *(Pause.)* Did you really
come here to offer protection?

DR. KING: Maybe I should have said, comfort...the type of comfort one man
can give to another.

MALCOLM: Do you think that people will remember us as "men" and only
"men"?

DR. KING: No. And we can't afford to let them know that that's all we were.
At least, not for awhile.

MALCOLM: Have you ever wondered what type of men we would have been,
had we been born in a different time...You know, a time when race didn't
matter...Where injustice was just a part of a history lesson.

DR. KING: I imagine we would have been quite dull.

MALCOLM: *(Laughs.)* And we would have grown very old.

DR. KING: The dull have a way of outliving the rest of us...Perhaps that's
their greatest punishment.

MALCOLM: Punishment...my father was murdered because he spoke out...my
mother was institiutionalized, because some pain deep inside of her
drowned out the language of the world...I have nothing to leave my own
family, no money, now not even a home...And yet, I still wonder, was
there more I should have done...more of myself I could have give?

DR. KING: My father used to tell me the story of a young Baptist minister who
had gone North to seek his fame and fortune. After he had become very
successful, the pastor of his former small southern church extended an
invitation to return home for a visit and preach before his old congregation. Well, this minister could hardly refuse such an offer, in fact, he was
rather proud at the thought of coming back and showin' the folk how successful he had become. He decided to bring his seven year old son with
him, to teach him a lesson about his history...his roots...When the minister returned to his old church he was moved so much, that he proceeded
to give one of the best sermons of his life...had the congregation rollin'
from one emotion to another. When it was all over the Pastor threw his
arms around the young minister and said: "John, that was a truly moving
and inspirational sermon...I wish we could give you some kind of hono-
rarium, but as you know, our church is not doing so well." *(Both MAL-
COLM and KING laugh.)* John just waved the Pastor off and said that was

fine, it was payment enough simply to return home for a visit. As John and his son were leaving, they passed the church collection box. John stopped and took out a crisp new ten dollar bill and placed it in the box. He and his son then proceeded out of the church to the parking lot. As they were getting into the car all of a sudden the Pastor came running outside calling John's name. As the Pastor caught up to John he said: "I know you don't want any payment, but we just couldn't let you leave without at least a token of our appreciation." The Pastor handed John a crisp new ten dollar bill which John immediately recognized as the one he placed in the collection box, just moments before. He took the money, exchanged final farewells with the Pastor and got into his car. After a moment or two, he looked at his son, smiling proudly and confidently and said: "Son, I hope this teaches you a lesson." His son nodded, looked at his father and said: "Yes dad, it has. If you had given more, you would have gotten more." *(MALCOLM laughs, but DR. KING smiles sadly. He gives a quiet and distant look, then softly to MALCOLM he says:)* We all have to give more, Malcolm...More than we thought we needed to. Even then, sometimes it's not enough.

MALCOLM: We may both give our lives for this thing we call, "freedom." You know that, don't you? *(The two men look at each other, MALCOLM then turns toward his streets having received the only answer he could. DR. KING begins to think of something that brings a faint smile which turns into an amused laugh. MALCOLM seems surprised by this sudden change in mood.)* What's so funny?

DR. KING: I was just wondering what Coretta might think, if she know we spent the night arm wrestling.

MALCOLM: *(He thinks about it then laughs, too.)* I suppose if Betty knew, she's go into early labor.

(They both look at each other and laugh more loudly.)

DR. KING: When is she due?

MALCOLM: *(Shrugs.)* You know about babies, Martin...They come when they want to. Whether you're ready or not. *(There is a tender moment as these two men think of their families.)* Martin, can you keep a secret?

DR. KING: Who, me?

(They both laugh.)

MALCOLM: I'm hoping for a son, this time. *(MALCOLM moves into the room, KING after a beat, follows. MALCOLM picks-up the doll, smiles.)* And a little child shall lead them.

DR. KING: *(Pulls the curtains together.)* And the lion shall dwell with the lamb. *(MALCOLM begins rolling up his sleeves, begins to take some deep breaths, a few stretching exercises, and places the chairs in order. KING watches him curiously.)* What are you doing?

MALCOLM: *(Smiles.)* I suppose we ought to declare a winner.

DR. KING: *(Smiles.)* Yes...I suppose we should. If there can't be a truce, at least there ought to be a winner.

(KING begins to take his coat off, roll up his sleeves, loosens his tie, and begins deep knee bends.)

MALCOLM: We're arm wrestling, Reverend, not racing in the relays.

DR. KING: You warm-up the way you want to, I'll warm-up the way I want to.

(Malcolm studies him for a moment, then decides he too should do some knee bends. MALCOLM is exercising in unison with DR. KING, but out of KING's vision. Both men, when warmed-up move toward the table for final contest, and loosen their ties and shirts to have maximum comfort.)

MALCOLM: Don't take advantage of me, Reverend...Remember, I'm older than you.

DR. KING: The public for some reason continues to think of you as younger.

MALCOLM: They associate militancy *(Spits in his hand.)* with youthfulness.

DR. KING: That's odd, it's rather an *(Spits in his.)* old idea.

(They both lock hands.)

MALCOLM: Some of the best ideas are.

DR. KING: Whoever wins here will not necessarily be the winner outside you know?

MALCOLM: If I thought that, I would have invited you, a long time ago. *(Both men are now seriously into the combat. MALCOLM begins to get a slight advantage.)* Beware, Doctor...The old man is taking charge.

DR. KING: *(Begins to even the contest.)* "HE didn't lead me here only to have me turn around now!"

MALCOLM: Quoting scriptures, won't help you.

(Both men are seesawing to victory.)

DR. KING: *(Straining a bit.)* Can't hurt.

MALCOLM: You should fight this hard when some sheriff tries to put a knot upside your head.

DR. KING: I fight even harder then, you just haven't noticed.

MALCOLM: How long do you think we can continue this?

DR. KING: What?

MALCOLM: I said, how long!?

DR. KING: Not long!

MALCOLM: How long!?

DR. KING: I'm willing to call it a draw, if you are?

MALCOLM: Okay, you stop first.

DR. KING: I'm from the country, Malcolm, but give me some credit.

MALCOLM: All right...All right...I'll count to three.

DR. KING: Are you going to do all the counting?

MALCOLM: *(Still struggling.)* We'll alternate...Does that meet with your approval?

DR. KING: They taught me at school that "three" was an odd number.

MALCOLM: All right, all right! I'll start, you go next, and we'll finish at the same time. Agreed?

DR. KING: Agreed.

MALCOLM: One.

DR. KING: Two.

BOTH: Three.

(They both stop and let out groans of battle. They look at their hands that have gone through much punishment.)

DR. KING: Just imagine what we could have accomplished, if only we had joined hands and pushed in the same direction.

MALCOLM: *(Pause. MALCOLM studies KING, then, softly asks:)* Martin, do you respect me?

DR. KING: I will always be against violence, Malcolm, regardless of the cause.

MALCOLM: *(Almost painfully.)* I asked you if you respected me, and you speak of violence. Is that all you see?

(RASHAD enters, but remains at the door, unnoticed.)

DR. KING: *(He moves slowly toward the window.)* You don't need to ask me that, Malcolm. Just walk out there on those streets. The eyes of the dead come alive in your presence. They believe in you, and because of that they are beginning to believe in themselves. They respect you. And, yes, Malcolm, I respect you. You would have made one fine Baptist preacher!

MALCOLM: *(Smiles warmly.)* I wish my father were alive to hear that. *(Pause.)* I suppose we will not be seeing much of each other?

DR. KING: *(He notices Rashad, for the first time.)* No. I imagine we won't.

RASHAD: Malcolm, is everything all right? We've been waiting for Doctor King.

MALCOLM: I suppose I should be letting you go. It's getting rather late.

DR. KING: Yes. It is.

MALCOLM: Rashad, you want to help Doctor King with his coat.

DR. KING: Oh, no! That's quite all right. I think I can manage myself.

RASHAD: Wonderful.

MALCOLM: *(Laughs.)* Let me help you with that, Martin. *(MALCOLM helps KING with his coat. Hands him his hat.)* Rashad will accompany you downstairs. I have someone with a car, he'll take you where you need to go.

DR. KING: I appreciate that.

(They walk toward the door.)

MALCOLM: We could have made quite a team.

DR. KING: We *do* make quite a team…Most persons just don't realize it.

MALCOLM: *(Smiles.)* May they be ignorant a little while longer.

DR. KING: Amen to that.

MALCOLM: All praise to Allah.

RASHAD: Malcolm, do you want more time together, to exchange prayers with your friend.

MALCOLM: You don't have to be together to exchange prayers, Rashad. *(Beat.)* Particularly, with a friend.

DR. KING: *(Smiles.)* Rashad, I'm ready, if you are.

(They begin to move toward the door, when MALCOLM speaks.)

MALCOLM: I never meant to hurt you with anything I might have said publicly. It's very important to me that you know that.

(KING stops. He turns very slowly toward MALCOLM. He is obviously touched by MALCOLM's words. He proceeds toward MALCOLM.)

DR. KING: It's very important to me that you told me.

(The two men stare at each other in silence, only a few feet apart from one another. They both reached out to shake hands, but suddenly embrace. It is a tender embrace that recognizes the friendship and respect that has occured, but also the reality that they may never see each other again.)

MALCOLM: *(MALCOLM moves to the window and looks out on Harlem. King is near the door and begins to open it. MALCOLM speaks without turning to face KING.)* Martin?…If you're around longer than I am, tell them we climbed one mountain, together.

DR. KING: And, we saw the promised land.

MALCOLM: *(He turns toward KING and smiles.)* Yes. Tell them all.

DR. KING: *(He smiles, warmly.)* Take care of yourself, Malcolm.

(KING exits. RASHAD watches MALCOLM.)

RASHAD: Malcolm, is there anything I can do?

(There is no response as the men look at each other. RASHAD exits.)

MALCOLM: Goodbye, Martin…Goodbye. *(He places in hands in position for prayer.)* Allah…Protect the dreamer.

(He smiles warmly, and then notices the doll. He picks it up and stares at it, sadly at first. Then he shakes his head. He chuckles, then laughs. He moves toward the window and looks out on his beloved Harlem. He studies the doll and begins to sing softly.)

YOU DON'T KNOW WHAT LOVE IS

UNTIL YOU'VE LEARNED THE MEANING OF THE BLUES

UNTIL YOU'VE LOVED A LOVE YOU'VE HAD TO LOSE

YOU DON'T KNOW WHAT LOVE IS

(The lights fade gently on him holding the doll. When the rest of the stage is dark the one light on MALCOLM fades quickly.)

CURTAIN

Talvin Wilks

TOD, THE BOY TOD

Crossroads Theatre

IMMEDIATE THEATRE!
An Interview With Talvin Wilks
by Sydne Mahone

*For while the tale of how we suffer
and how we are delighted, and
how we may triumph is never
new, it always must be heard.
There isn't any other tale to tell,
it's the only light we've got in
all this darkness.... And this tale,
according to that face, that body,
those strong hands on those strings,
has another aspect in every country,
and a new depth in every generation.*
　　*—James Baldwin
　　from "Sonny's Blues" (a story)*

"I wanted to create an 'Immediate Theatre' that could explore political, sociological and psychological issues in a very direct and personal way for performer and audience," says Talvin Wilks, author of *Tod, The Boy, Tod.* The world of theatre, according to Wilks, is one that can respond to newspaper and magazine headlines as well as channel the cries and whispers of the ancestral voices. The central character, Tod, is an assimilated young African American man suffering from cultural schizophrenia. His challenge is to hear the truth and transcend the myths of racism through self-definition as a movement towards wholeness.

"I don't call it a play," says Wilks. "I call it a Dance With Text or A Rap Rock Ritual Dance Theatre piece." For Wilks, definitions are death when imposed from the outside. His challenge to himself is to explore those definitions, to destroy them and to create new ones. As a former actor/director, Wilks refers to himself more as a collaborator than a playwright. He begins with the basic text but relies upon his fellow collaborators to complete the world by bringing their perspectives to the work. In his theatrical universe, all the elements—text, music, myth, poetry, movement, lights—have equal weight. The text is the vehicle for the intricate structuring of the other elements.

The play takes place in the mind of Tod during what Wilks describes as "an electrical brainstorm. It's a war-torn battlefield. His psyche is a battleground on which every point of him is a contradiction and yet he's created a successful persona with all these demons living in him." He undergoes a trial by fire through the revelation of truth which brings clarity to his purpose, journey, battle. Through the books containing the history of racism, he discovers the centuries of denigration and violence perpetrated through false definitions and lies.

Tod, The Boy, Tod came out of a direct response to the "media blitz" in the late 1980's that focused on the problems of the growing black middle class. The great success of the Civil Rights Movement, which established that strong middle class, ironically spawned a new generation of well-educated African Americans who had successfully assimilated into mainstream society, but were frighteningly disconnected from their cultural context.

This new generation had an awareness of racism only through stories of their parents' experience; they had no first-hand experience of overt racism. Their journey through the hallowed halls of Ivy League schools offered a delusion of protection from the poverty and segregation of less fortunate blacks, but subjected them to an even more dangerous, subtle brand of racism that ultimately threatened the psyche, causing a psychic split, an identity crisis.

On the heels of that black middle class media hype came another series of national newsflashes that attempted to establish an underclass. "These two issues were presented back to back, and I began to look upon it a a conspiracy," Wilks says. "I was concerned that there was an acceptance of this notion of the underclass. Many African Americans were following the same route as whites—moving to the suburbs or following the patterns of gentrification, constantly shifting, escaping, but never really addressing the issues."

Wilk's personal experience at Princeton University also contributed to the creation of *Tod*. "I was well on my way to the mainstream and fully assimilated. But as I moved forward, I found myself not fully welcomed, still encountering bits of racism. One moment, you're fully accepted and then in the next moment, an epithet can strip you down to your base nature."

He speaks of the personal epiphany: "One time, going back to Princeton, I was stopped on the street as a suspect for shoplifting. I'd just gotten off the bus and I was walking with a bag. Three policemen stopped me on the street; and this was right across from the Firestone Library, just a year after I'd graduated. This never happened as a student, but once I was away from that institution, suddenly, here I am on the street. And I'm looking at all the faces around me. There isn't a single black face and here I am with police surrounding me. And here, I'd believed I was a part of this institution and protected. Looking in a face and not seeing any support whatsoever, I began to be flooded by what other people were thinking. It was as if they were saying 'Yes, yes. They got him.' I had believed that I was free of this."

"I still can't go into a Woolworth's and walk out without buying something for fear that someone will think I've shoplifted. Now what war is that? Why does it still exist? How do I overcome that? It's come to the point where my walking out of a Woolworth's without buying something is defiance. I feel I've overcome something, but it's a battle every time. So, when did I learn this? How do I break through? For me, in many ways, it had become a personal battle for my own sanity. In direct response to that, I created *Tod*."

"It's hard to resolve because it is in a context of contradiction. It's hard to see life from death, coming to a point of liberation from that great act of despair, this great descent into the abyss of racism and rising from it. But I believe in that."

"It has to do with being free, with having an independent psyche, a wholeness that has nothing to do with an 'other,' negation of . . . It's an identity that stands firm and complete on its own. Tradition, heritage, complete. Timeless centuries, millennia of ancestry that is all in one place."

"The modern day battle is about filling in holes in our history, knowing that, celebrating and putting it in our mission and our drive forward."

Sydne Mahone is the literary manager/resident dramaturgist at Crossroads Theatre Company.**CROSSROADS THEATRE COMPANY**

A history of Crossroads Theatre is supplied on page 300

TOD, THE BOY, TOD
by Talvin Wilks

Directed by
Ken Johnson

CAST

John, the Psychiatrist...JON AVNER

Reverend Joe...................................HELMAR AUGUSTUS COOPER

Tod, The Boy, Tod ....DENNIS GREEN

Committee Executive..MICHAEL GREER

Committee Senior ....MICHAEL HANEY

Committee Junior ....SPIKE McCLURE

Mary Martha ....ESSENE R

**PLACE: IN THE MIND OF TOD
TIME: THE PRESENT**

The horror carries the endorsement of centuries and the entire life span of a
    nation. It is a way of life which reaches back to the beginning of recorded
    time. And all the bestiality, whenever it occurs and however long it has
    been happening, is narrowed, focused and refined to shine into a black
    child's eyes when first he views his world. All that has ever happened to
    black men and women he sees in the victims closest to him, his parents.

A life is an eternity and throughout all that eternity a black child has breathed
    the foul air of cruelty. He has grown up to find that his spirit was crushed
    before he knew there was need of it. His ambition, even in their formings
    showed him to have set his hand against his own. This is the desolation of
    black life in America.

—*BLACK RAGE, Grier & Cobbs*

If we can bring back on ourselves, the absolute pain our people must have felt
    when they came onto this shore, we are more ourselves again, and can
    begin to put history back in our menus, and forget the propaganda of dev-
    ils that they are not devils.

—*THE SYSTEM OF DANTE'S HELL, LeRoi Jones*

Characters

TOD, THE BOY, TOD *African American, Age 27*
MARY MARTHA, THE VIRGIN MOTHER *African American, Age 48*
REVEREND JOE, HIS HOLY FATHER *African American, Age 50*
JOHN, THE PSYCHIATRIST, THE BEARER OF TRUTH *Jewish*
  American, Age 50
THE COMMITTEE OF SOCIAL REFORM *Caucasian (American)*
  COMMITTEE EXECUTIVE, *Age 67*
  COMMITTEE SENIOR, *Age 48*
  COMMITTEE JUNIOR, *Age 27*

Set

The set is an altar in the form of a dream-like exaggeration of JOHN THE PSYCHIATRIST's office. Central to the set is a 4x6 ft. long ebony table that rests on a low sloping rake perpendicular to the stage. The rake is hard polished wood with an oriental rug that runs the length of the table. There is a black leather swivel chair at each side of the table. The four corners represent the hierarchy: down stage center sits TOD, THE BOY, TOD; stage right sits MARY MARTHA, THE VIRGIN MOTHER; stage left sits REVEREND JOE, HIS MOST HOLY FATHER; upstage center sits JOHN THE PSYCHIATRIST, THE BEARER OF TRUTH.

At the back of the rake begins an isolated wooden bookshelf that is the width of the rake and ten feet high. There is a ladder on wheels that rolls on brackets across the bookshelf. The top of the bookshelf serves as a conference table for the COMMITTEE OF SOCIAL REFORM. At each of the three positions there is a black telephone and a working microphone. The set should have the feel of an isolated unit suspended in darkness. The entire back wall is draped with a white cyc which serves as a canvas for mood lighting. The canvas changes colors as the play progresses.

ACT I

PROLOGUE: THE STORY OF TOD

TOD, THE BOY, TOD appears in isolation. THE STORY OF TOD is his incantation. There is a flash of lightning followed by an electrical sound of thunder as the story begins.

TOD: Once upon a time, not so long ago, there was Tod. Now these were the days when Tod was very strong and confident. These were the days when he was very secure in the concept of himself, when he was still innocent, a strong warrior, a child, the pride of his people he left behind.

Now during this time, Tod, our hero, garnered many awards and achievements. He was among the best and the brightest in spite of his slight "handicap" which no one seemed to notice, or if they did, they kept it to themselves. Oh, how Tod thrived in this new found land...

(A black-face minstrel appears in the style of Al Jolson.)

Until one day, Tod was approached by evil, and evil was black, as evil always is. Evil told him that he had become a token of the system, that he shouldn't believe what they say because he wasn't really accepted. Well, this Tod did not believe and he rebuked this first temptation.

(The minstrel exits and then reappears in the guise of a 60s militant.)

But evil approached again with a stronger hand and told him that he had conformed to the system, and had been changed, his voice was different, his thoughts were different. This, Tod, also did not believe.

(The minstrel exits and then reappears as a 90s rapper.)

But evil approached again and told him that because of this change, he could be held accountable for the misdeeds of the system. That he was guilty for their crimes. But why was evil haunting him, reminding him with this temptation to look back upon his shame. So to evil, Tod said, "begone," and closed his mind and his heart, and evil seemed to stay away.

Until that glorious day, not so long ago, the voice of the system bestowed upon Tod a new identity, and they gave him a certificate that said, "yes, Tod, you are special, Tod, you are not like them, Tod, you are one of us." This Tod believed, because wasn't this what they were saying all along. His long lost friends who weren't bussed to the Montessori school, his parents whom he never understood anyway. Wasn't he now finally accepted by the system? Wasn't this what he was sent out to achieve? And wasn't this like the voice of God, speaking to him? And so he listened, and his heart was filled with joy until he noticed that his skin was starting to fade, and his blood was thinning out, and there were no more awards, and he was no longer special because he was one of them. And suddenly he felt alone, and suddenly he felt black, blacker than he had ever felt before. There were faces he did not know, words he did not understand. My mother, I do not know her. My father, I do not know him. No one speaks to me, me, in my language. And this is where the story begins, not once upon a time, but now. Woe is me, woe is Tod, from the moment he believed he was different, his soul was lost, perhaps forever...

SCENE ONE—THE STORM OF SOCIAL ILLS

THE STORM OF SOCIAL ILLS contains the sounds of TOD's mind that lead him to the ritual sacrifice. A radio signal is faintly heard. There is a flash of lightning followed by thunder. The sound of high static is heard. Voices are muffled in the static until they slowly become distinguishable. They are the voices of THE COMMITTEE OF SOCIAL REFORM delivering a newscast. The messages fade in and out with the static. The storm continues...

VOICE COMMITTEE EXECUTIVE: In a related story today the case of Tawanna Brawley...

VOICE COMMITTEE SENIOR: In Forsythe County a parade for freedom has disclosed...

VOICE COMMITTEE JUNIOR: Social order broke down today in the nation's second largest city...

VOICE COMMITTEE EXECUTIVE: ...racism once again has reared its ugly head...

VOICE COMMITTEE SENIOR: ...in a process labeled purification...

VOICE COMMITTEE JUNIOR: ...one dead, two beaten...

VOICE COMMITTEE EXECUTIVE: In Howard Beach...

VOICE COMMITTEE SENIOR: ...with racial epithets smeared in excrement...

VOICE COMMITTEE JUNIOR: ...what do blacks really want...

VOICE COMMITTEE EXECUTIVE: Get out...

VOICE COMMITTEE SENIOR: Acquittal of four white officers...

VOICE COMMITTEE EXECUTIVE: ...and the masses attempt to rise...

VOICE COMMITTEE SENIOR: ...chanting, Rodney, Rodney, Rodney...

VOICE COMMITTEE JUNIOR: ...in the guise of the Black middle class...

VOICE COMMITTEE EXECUTIVE: ...a gunfight broke out this afternoon...

VOICE COMMITTEE JUNIOR: It's no longer about race it's all economics...

VOICE COMMITTEE EXECUTIVE: ...between Korean merchants and a group of black men...

VOICE COMMITTEE JUNIOR: ...as predicted by Moynihan...

VOICE COMMITTEE SENIOR: ...and more and more upwardly mobile blacks...

VOICE COMMITTEE EXECUTIVE: ...struggled to reconcile those images...

VOICE COMMITTEE JUNIOR: ...in a process labeled purification...

(During the storm TOD begins a ritual sacrifice, he holds his wrists out as an offering and slowly cuts them with a razor blade. At the first sight of blood a siren is heard followed by the appearance of his demons, MARY MARTHA, THE VIRGIN MOTHER, REVEREND JOE, HIS HOLY FATHER, and JOHN THE PSYCHIATRIST, THE BEARER OF TRUTH.)

VOICE COMMITTEE SENIOR: ...a rise in teenage pregnancy...

VOICE COMMITTEE EXECUTIVE: ...re gentrification

VOICE COMMITTEE JUNIOR: ...beating a black man...

VOICE COMMITTEE SENIOR: ...and looters roamed the streets...

VOICE COMMITTEE EXECUTIVE: ...and drug dependency...

VOICE COMMITTEE JUNIOR: ...just before 7 p.m.

VOICE COMMITTEE SENIOR: ...two white men...

VOICE COMMITTEE JUNIOR: ...were attacked by a group of 15 black men...

VOICE COMMITTEE EXECUTIVE: ...as racial problems on the nation's campuses...

VOICE COMMITTEE SENIOR: ...struggled yesterday to reconcile those images...

VOICE COMMITTEE EXECUTIVE: ...with societal problems and social backlash...

VOICE COMMITTEE SENIOR: ...acquittal of four white officers...

VOICE COMMITTEE JUNIOR: ...in a process labeled purification...

VOICE COMMITTEE EXECUTIVE: ...cries out from all four corners of the land...

ALL VOICES: ...can we just get along...

(The voices of MARY MARTHA, REVEREND JOE and JOHN THE PSYCHIATRIST become audible as the storm continues. They call TOD's name as if searching through his conscience.)

VOICE COMMITTEE SENIOR: ...we've had enough...

VOICE COMMITTEE JUNIOR: ...can't take no more...

VOICE COMMITTEE EXECUTIVE: ...anger ran far deeper...

MARY MARTHA: Tod!

VOICE COMMITTEE SENIOR: ...than reaction to the acquittal...

VOICE COMMITTEE JUNIOR: ...blacks do not count...

VOICE COMMITTEE SENIOR: ...in this country...

REVEREND JOE: Tod!

VOICE COMMITTEE JUNIOR: ...chanting...

VOICE COMMITTEE SENIOR: ...African...

JOHN: Tod!

VOICE COMMITTEE EXECUTIVE: ...American...

VOICE COMMITTEE SENIOR: ...struggled...

REVEREND JOE: Tod.

VOICE COMMITTEE JUNIOR: …cried out…

VOICE COMMITTEE EXECUTIVE: …looters…

MARY MARTHA: Tod, my son.

VOICE COMMITTEE SENIOR: …in a process…

REVEREND JOE: My son.

VOICE COMMITTEE JUNIOR: …broke down…

VOICE COMMITTEE EXECUTIVE: …labeled…

MARY MARTHA: I don't understand.

VOICE COMMITTEE SENIOR: …gunfight…

VOICE COMMITTEE JUNIOR: …acquittal…

REVEREND JOE: Tod.

VOICE COMMITTEE EXECUTIVE: …horrified…

VOICE COMMITTEE SENIOR: …black…

JOHN: The diagnosis…

VOICE COMMITTEE EXECUTIVE: …beating…

VOICE COMMITTEE SENIOR: …no more…

MARY MARTHA: My son.

VOICE COMMITTEE JUNIOR: …illusion…

VOICE COMMITTEE SENIOR: …backlash…

JOHN: The diagnosis is…

VOICE COMMITTEE JUNIOR: …question…

VOICE COMMITTEE EXECUTIVE: …Serbian…

MARY MARTHA: Suicide?

VOICE COMMITTEE JUNIOR: …officers…

VOICE COMMITTEE EXECUTIVE: …America…

VOICE COMMITTEE SENIOR: …white…

REVEREND JOE: Tod.

VOICE COMMITTEE JUNIOR: …dream…

VOICE COMMITTEE EXECUTIVE: …I had…

MARY MARTHA: What has happened to my son?

VOICE COMMITTEE SENIOR: …excrement…

VOICE COMMITTEE JUNIOR: …purification…

VOICE COMMITTEE EXECUTIVE: …Korean…

REVEREND JOE: Suicide.

VOICE COMMITTEE SENIOR: …one dead…

VOICE COMMITTEE JUNIOR: …process…

VOICE COMMITTEE SENIOR: …two beaten…

JOHN: …difficult.

VOICE COMMITTEE JUNIOR: ...anarchy...

VOICE COMMITTEE EXECUTIVE: ...struggled...

VOICE COMMITTEE SENIOR: ...to reconcile...

VOICE COMMITTEE JUNIOR: ...those images...

MARY MARTHA: Suicide!

REVEREND JOE: Suicide?

JOHN: Suicide.

MARY MARTHA: Suicide!

REVEREND JOE: Suicide?

JOHN: Suicide.

MARY MARTHA: Blacks don't commit suicide.

REVEREND JOE: Blacks don't commit suicide.

JOHN: Blacks don't commit suicide.

MARY MARTHA: So they say.

REVEREND JOE: That's what they used to say.

JOHN: That's what they want to believe.

MARY MARTHA: Suicide.

Blacks don't commit suicide.

So they say.

At least that was what I was always told

I don't know how this happened.

It's been a real shock to us all.

Who would've suspected that he was so unhappy.

REVEREND JOE: Suicide, blacks don't commit suicide. That's what they used to say. But those were the days when the threat of death was always near, and there were enough crackers around waiting to do it for you. So you lived in spite of it all. Death existed already. What need there be of suicide. But today things are different. Death is still at hand. But it's your own hand that's the greatest threat.

JOHN: Suicide? Blacks don't commit suicide, that's what they want to believe. But I don't think all is lost. He survived that's the most important thing. That makes it less of a tragedy. We just have to go through the healing process now.

MARY MARTHA: My son's been brainwashed.

JOHN: I think they've all been a little damaged by everything.

MARY MARTHA: All these years trying to be white.

JOHN: But they could see it coming.

MARY MARTHA: Trying to be white.

JOHN: It's a sign of the times.

MARY MARTHA: Has finally affected his brain. Not only does he sound like them, he has to act like them too? Nothing can be so bad that you have to act this way. It's a conspiracy. It's been a conspiracy all this time. There's still time. Now we know. This will help. He will change. We know what we're dealing with now.

REVEREND JOE: I think it all began when they gave religion back to the niggers...

MARY MARTHA: Things just got a little out of hand.

REVEREND JOE: ...the concept of paradise has never been the same since.

MARY MARTHA: But there's still time.

REVEREND JOE: Oh, I don't believe that the great God of Judgment is going to be some starched white spirit, I believe it's going to be the voice of a million bloated pitch black babies sitting regal on their bones, with their heads barely supported for the weight of their knowledge, speaking with the power of the hungry, casting sinners into eternal darkness.

JOHN: Tod has developed a paranoid response to the delusions of his father and the restrained neglect of his mother. They represent two extremes of black militancy and crisis.

TOD: Suicide, suicide, Blacks don't commit suicide.

MARY MARTHA: There's still time.

REVEREND JOE: Everything becomes clearer and clearer every day.

MARY MARTHA: I saw this coming.

REVEREND JOE: Cheated death...

MARY MARTHA: We're just a little shocked by it all.

REVEREND JOE: ...we've cheated death.

MARY MARTHA: But things will be different...

REVEREND JOE: And now we're alive again.

MARY MARTHA: ...now that we know the truth.

REVEREND JOE: It's all part of a plan.

MARY MARTHA: We know what we're dealing with, right?

REVEREND JOE: It all becomes much clearer.

MARY MARTHA: Yes, of course.

REVEREND JOE: My faith had faltered.

MARY MARTHA: I wasn't aware that he was hurting so much.

REVEREND JOE: I've allowed temptation to steer me away.

MARY MARTHA: This is just a way to get attention.

REVEREND JOE: But now I'm renewed once again.

MARY MARTHA: I don't think there was much of a crisis.

REVEREND JOE: The enemy has shown their evil hand.

MARY MARTHA: I don't think he really meant to do it.

REVEREND JOE: The battle is in Tod.

MARY MARTHA: He's been depressed lately.

REVEREND JOE: The battle is for the mind of Tod.

MARY MARTHA: A lot of hard decisions to make.

REVEREND JOE: I thought they would come for me first.

MARY MARTHA: It's hard to see clearly.

REVEREND JOE: But he is the one...

MARY MARTHA: Clearly...

REVEREND JOE: ...the most vulnerable...

MARY MARTHA: ...for someone like him.

REVEREND JOE: ...the chosen one.

(*The storm ends as lights go out on MARY MARTHA and REVEREND JOE.*)

JOHN: Tod's mother developed a very militant response to a similar pressure. He represents a second generation of compound social crisis, lack of identity, and character conflict due to racial assimilation. He is a perfect example of what the past has created. That's why they're here. He is not what they wanted.

SCENE TWO—TOD IS THE ONE

(*THE COMMITTEE OF SOCIAL REFORM appears for the first time. The committee consists of three white male executives who sit on top of a ten foot high bookshelf, the books on the shelf represent the history of the "Negro problem" in America.*)

COMMITTEE JUNIOR: Then what are we going to do?

JOHN: As of yet, I do not know.

COMMITTEE SENIOR: Such perfection seems to be a terrible thing to waste.

JOHN: I know.

COMMITTEE EXECUTIVE: And this crisis?

COMMITTEE SENIOR: It's a sign

COMMITTEE JUNIOR: A possible identity rejection?

JOHN: I'm not sure.

COMMITTEE SENIOR: We're too close to fail now.

COMMITTEE JUNIOR: He's unstable.

COMMITTEE EXECUTIVE: Always when we get this close they turn. I thought his assimilation was complete.

COMMITTEE JUNIOR: You're the reason we're in this mess in the first place. Sending off your little alarms.

COMMITTEE EXECUTIVE: I can't control the youth of today, it's unnatural.

JOHN: They've caused him to question his purpose.

COMMITTEE SENIOR: Maybe we've miscalculated the times.

COMMITTEE EXECUTIVE: You can't blame this on me. We've tolerated this situation far too long. The system can no longer support a dying race.

COMMITTEE SENIOR: Our crimes were almost forgotten. If you could have held out for at least another decade, this problem would have been solved.

COMMITTEE EXECUTIVE: It's not my fault liberalism is dead.

COMMITTEE JUNIOR: We must become one, it's the only way to battle the global shift. Tod is perfect.

JOHN: There's one more problem.

THE COMMITTEE: What is that?

JOHN: He still believes in God.

THE COMMITTEE: God? How did that happen?

COMMITTEE EXECUTIVE: I thought their belief in God went out in the 60s.

COMMITTEE SENIOR: Whatever happened to those fine militants, I thought they destroyed their belief in God.

JOHN: They are forgotten like all prophets.

COMMITTEE EXECUTIVE: I loved those pseudo Marxists. They were so self-destructive.

JOHN: Tod is pure, he was protected from the beginning. His parents hid him away in private school at an early age.

COMMITTEE SENIOR: He is the first?

COMMITTEE JUNIOR: No, he is the last to know legalized oppression in his lifetime.

JOHN: It's not that he remembers, but it still exists in his subconscious. And can be reclaimed.

COMMITTEE EXECUTIVE: He has a claim to the past?

JOHN: He is a very important link.

COMMITTEE SENIOR: He is dangerous.

JOHN: He is unstable.

COMMITTEE SENIOR: His salvation is still intact, that's far too dangerous. It can cause dissension.

COMMITTEE EXECUTIVE: John, it says here that his mother was a Black Panther.

JOHN: She's a corporate executive now.

COMMITTEE JUNIOR: Minority Affairs?

JOHN: No, International Marketing.

COMMITTEE SENIOR: That's progressive.

JOHN: She's quite a wonder.

COMMITTEE JUNIOR: He must hate her.

JOHN: His father is a Baptist minister.

COMMITTEE SENIOR: Oh, John, this should be easy enough, he must hate them both.

COMMITTEE EXECUTIVE: I'm getting nervous.

COMMITTEE JUNIOR: Calm down.

COMMITTEE EXECUTIVE: I'm anxious, I want this thing over.

COMMITTEE SENIOR: I want it over too, but you can't be irrational like the last time.

COMMITTEE JUNIOR: Don't let your bigotry get in the way of progress.

COMMITTEE EXECUTIVE: You haven't lived with this goddamned black menace as long as I have. Hell, I've been everything. I was a conservative, I was a hip liberal before it was in vogue, I've been a reactionary, an abolitionist, nothing seems to work. I'm tired.

COMMITTEE SENIOR: Give it time.

COMMITTEE EXECUTIVE: There is no more time. Can't you see the signs? Tod is the one. He is the link. With his successful assimilation the past will have no meaning and all will be forgotten like a history lesson. We've waited long enough. I should have known to never trust a Jew.

COMMITTEE SENIOR: Sir! There's a way to handle this diplomatically.

COMMITTEE EXECUTIVE: Yes, of course. I'm sorry, John, but you're not really Jewish anyway, you're one of us. I despise ethnicity, it just gets in the way of efficiency and free enterprise. That's why the goddamned Japanese are on our tails. They have no such problems. Those people work for peanuts. Unions and quotas destroy the system, Affirmative Action is a farce, it all destroys the system. We need efficient blacks not welfare cases.

COMMITTEE JUNIOR: Sir, I believe you've gotten off the subject.

COMMITTEE EXECUTIVE: Yes, yes, of course. I just have so much on my mind. I was almost wiped out today. A billion dollars gone in a flash and then it reappeared. It's a sign my friends. Nothing's certain. I want this problem solved. I don't have time for race, I've got an economic crisis on my hands.

JOHN: Then what is your decision?

COMMITTEE EXECUTIVE: Destroy his belief in God.

COMMITTEE SENIOR AND JUNIOR: Don't be irrational.

COMMITTEE EXECUTIVE: What do you mean? It's the first step, it's what we've done in the past. It worked before, it will work now. It's all very simple. We used to give the niggers religion until those self-righteous mammies turned God against us. We use capitalism now, it's much more effective. Poverty is immediate, starvation is immediate, salvation takes too long. It encourages endurance. Take away his god, and all he has left is the system, and we're the system. It's so clear. I call for a vote, all in favor... (*All three raise their hands.*) Good, none opposed. Tod's belief in God must be destroyed.

JOHN: I'm not sure I can do it.

COMMITTEE EXECUTIVE: Don't worry, we'll be with you. You're an atheist, right? It should be easy.

JOHN: Well, I've been thinking.

THE COMMITTEE: Thinking? Without us? That's not part of the bargain, John.

JOHN: I've been thinking I would like to go home.

COMMITTEE SENIOR: Preparing for Armageddon?

COMMITTEE JUNIOR: What is it that you want?

JOHN: Will you give me back my belief in God?

COMMITTEE JUNIOR: An exchange for an exchange?

COMMITTEE EXECUTIVE: That's one thing I envy about you people, your sense of history. You do nothing for it, yet you still call upon it when you feel betrayed. Yes, we will give you back your Jehovah and your Torah. We're almost through with that anyway, we have no need of your folklore anymore. Just take away our white man's guilt and this great black burden and we'll call it an even trade.

COMMITTEE SENIOR: He's not as perfect as we had hoped.

COMMITTEE EXECUTIVE: But he's close enough. There just isn't any time. The doors of democracy are opening. I want this black problem solved. It's getting in the way of progress. We can't let this follow us into the next century. Either assimilate him or we will be forced to eliminate him. It's the only way.

COMMITTEE JUNIOR: It's all a process for the new age, new life, new freedom, a new deal...Show him the way.

COMMITTEE EXECUTIVE: Bring him into the world.

COMMITTEE SENIOR: Make the way clear for him, the end is near.

THE COMMITTEE: You have been chosen.

JOHN: It shall be done.

THE COMMITTEE: Amen.

(Lights fade out on the COMMITTEE as JOHN prepares to enter his session with TOD.)

JOHN: Amen...And these were the days of darkness that had been prophesied. And I am a lost voice in the wilderness searching for my home. Much has been lost, yes much has been forgotten. Sold. Sold. Sold my soul and no longer know my people or my reason, all to live in this world. Judaism, what do I know of it, its words, its dates, its salvation.

This was my father's prophecy, not my own, the calling was his. "This is right, the fight for Civil Rights, the fight for justice." Every generation was "the" generation, every newborn was the liberator. Denial, denial, denial, could this be the one?

God will think I'm a Christian even if I don't believe.

I lost the way somewhere, a connection, a purpose. But in Tod's eyes I see myself. In his eyes I see my failure. Have we destroyed the days of bigotry, have we overcome?

There's a voice in the wilderness, I am. Tod is a white man like all white men. This he must accept.

SCENE THREE—THE FIRST ENCOUNTER

JOHN: What was college like for you?

TOD: It was in many ways all that I expected. Great buildings, great architecture, history, it was filled with inspiration. But it was very clear that when I arrived something had just died, or was dying.

JOHN: What was that?

TOD: Something had been lost. I could see it on the few black faces who had been there when the spirit was alive. There had been riots there too you know. But there were no signs of that anymore. There was black unity but it seemed forced, well, at least to me it did. I thought, "what's the point, I'm here, right?" You see, I was very naive, I still am. Something was dead and I watched it fade away. I even think I was part of its death. They no longer need to go to the inner city for their quotas. There are enough people like me in their little private schools to fulfill any liberal need that might still exist. And they're all very much like me, terribly insane. We recognize it in each other's faces, me and my white friends, them and theirs.

JOHN: Why do you think it was like that?

TOD: It's very hard to say. From the very first day I was there I was challenged. I remember going down to eat and suddenly stepping into what seemed to be a segregated dining hall. There were whites on one side and blacks on the other. I was confused. I thought, "when did this happen." I thought I had missed something, some special code or instructions.

JOHN: What did you do?

TOD: I sat on the white side like everybody else.

JOHN: And everybody else was white?

TOD: Yes, at the time everybody else was all white. I've never really had any black friends. Do you think that's a sign of some kind of pathology? Maybe I learned something incorrectly somewhere.

JOHN: How did you feel?

TOD: I felt white like everybody else. All the blacks were on the other side. But I kept thinking that I belonged on the other side. I was afraid that I had made some mistake.

JOHN: You made a choice.

TOD: A very ridiculous choice to have to make.

JOHN: Were you angry at the other blacks?

TOD: Why? We all had to make choices for whatever reason. We all had our needs. Whites congregate automatically with other whites and there's no sense of threat. But as soon as you put more than two blacks together there's a rebellion, then your table has turned black and no one white will sit there. And if it's two black men, no one will even consider it. It was all very confusing. I found myself having to defend my race, and to justify how I had gotten to the promised land.

JOHN: Do you worry about not having any black friends?

TOD: Not anymore, now I worry about not having any.

JOHN: What do you mean?

TOD: Something happened somewhere. I can't explain it. I live my life alone now. I am very alone now. My whole world, my whole reason is fading away before my eyes. I have no connection with the people I'm supposed to know. I've lost my sense of purpose. It used to be to succeed. But those games are over now. There are no more written tests. There are no right answers. It's all a lost cause.

(MARY MARTHA and REVEREND JOE slowly enter the scene as JOHN fades out.)

SCENE FOUR—THE CONFLICT

REVEREND JOE: Why are we here?

TOD: It's hard to get a stronghold.

MARY MARTHA: Our son needs help.

REVEREND JOE: Our son needs prayer.

TOD: Everyone is talking about reverse discrimination and even I'm starting to agree.

MARY MARTHA: We've been praying, prayer doesn't stop.

TOD: It's very frightening.

MARY MARTHA: We'll always be praying, I'm getting used to it. I would like a few answers.

TOD: I scream at my parents constantly, they scream back.

REVEREND JOE: Doesn't God give answers? It's in His hands, it's His plan. Wait on the Lord. Don't influence the outcome with your desperation.

TOD: They try to explain, but I don't understand.

MARY MARTHA: And maybe this is part of His plan.

TOD: They want me to be something that they dreamed of long ago.

MARY MARTHA: Prayer doesn't mean you have to sit and wait. You can do. We can move. I thought you would have learned that by now, or maybe you've forgotten.

TOD: They don't want to hear my doubts, they don't want to hear my fears. They want me to be perfect.

REVEREND JOE: Read your Bible.

MARY MARTHA: I'm tired of reading my Bible, all of that "he can't, we can't shit." That's just another damn puzzle. I want some answers.

REVEREND JOE: And this is where you come for answers?

MARY MARTHA: We didn't have much choice.

REVEREND JOE: Be patient.

MARY MARTHA: You drive me crazy.

REVEREND JOE: You need some faith, trust in Him, "He's never failed us yet."

MARY MARTHA: Nigger, don't preach to me. This ain't Sunday, and I am not in the mood.

REVEREND JOE: You want some answers. I've got your answer. Worry about your own soul and let your son take care of his.

MARY MARTHA: That's not an answer, that sounds like some tired old parable. We're talking about more than salvation. When did you become so complacent?

REVEREND JOE: I think it happened while you were sleeping.

MARY MARTHA: We've both been sleeping.

REVEREND JOE: There's a time for everything.

MARY MARTHA: You're full of shit.

REVEREND JOE: A little respect here, please.

MARY MARTHA: Respect for what, some two bit preacher who's lost his cause?

REVEREND JOE: Enough of that.

MARY MARTHA: Who would ever know that you were once a rebel, a renegade? No signs from that middle-age paunch and that conservative brow.

REVEREND JOE: Casting stones, Martha?

MARY MARTHA: Can't you tell I'm frightened man. Don't act like you don't know what I'm talking about. I've seen your failure when our son speaks. You shudder when you hear his thoughts. I see your shame when you hear his ignorance. Who is this stranger in our home. Certainly not the son of one so respected for his fight. It's a tragedy. You're looking at the end. Something died. The words that come out of his mouth sound like they belong to someone else. They sound like words I can't even trust.

REVEREND JOE: That's your son you're talking about.

MARY MARTHA: You're damn right, and I'm not going to lose him without a fight.

REVEREND JOE: Martha, you're not going to lose him, he's exactly what you've made him into...perfect.

MARY MARTHA: So, that's what allows you to sit there so calm, saying it's all my fault. Well, ain't that just like a black Nigger who lost the war long before the battle even started. I guess it's been that way since the beginning. You lost your way the day I met you. There's no need in my feeling sorry for you now. And if he is perfect, I want that shit cured.

TOD: In our lives there has been great absence.

MARY MARTHA: All that is left is talk.

REVEREND JOE: We never talked about the past.

TOD: In our lives there has been unforgivable silence.

MARY MARTHA: Talk, talk, no action.

REVEREND JOE: We never talked about the present.

TOD: In our lives there have been parents who do not talk to their children who do not talk.

MARY MARTHA: No one speaks to me, they say I sold out.

REVEREND JOE: And in our silence, a stranger was born that we fear.

MARY MARTHA: All that I have left is my son.

TOD: History, never taught me, the past, what do I know about the past?

REVEREND JOE: Who is this stranger, my son?

TOD: Are you ashamed of my ignorance?

MARY MARTHA: He is my salvation but somehow I have failed.

TOD: Are you ashamed?

SCENE FIVE—LAMENT

JOHN: You mustn't look upon it as failure.

MARY MARTHA: He's dangerous.

JOHN: More dangerous to himself.

MARY MARTHA: We went wrong somewhere.

JOHN: It's not a question of right or wrong. You made choices.

MARY MARTHA: I feel guilty.

COMMITTEE EXECUTIVE: Does part of this guilt have to do with your failure with the Party?

MARY MARTHA: The party?

COMMITTEE SENIOR: The Black Panther Party, you were once a member weren't you.

MARY MARTHA: How the hell did you find that out?

COMMITTEE JUNIOR: From your file.

MARY MARTHA: My file?

JOHN: Your corporate file.

MARY MARTHA: Oh, I see. You must have access to a whole lot of shit because of the accident.

JOHN: Suicide is a crime.

MARY MARTHA: I see. Well, yes, I was a member of the Party. I still am, in spirit. The fight is just different. In those days I thought I had found the answer. I dug what the brothers were saying and it was my way of breaking out from my half-white inheritance. But you grow numb after awhile. You become a Muslim or you sell barbecue. I mean you freak when you come that close to true power. The movement ended because blacks are afraid of power, it could mean your death. That's why we're always looking for a savior. Give one dude all the power and when he fails you can save your own neck.

JOHN: It must have been very hard for you to enter the corporate world.

MARY MARTHA: No, it was very easy. I made my move when Black was in and we saved the nation just like in slavery. Of course not being black enough had a few drawbacks then, but I hung in there. Now, once again, I'm almost the ideal. But believe me, on the job I am very black, it's been my edge. You take advantage of every angle you can. I make no mistakes and I record everything.

Most people today are unable to see the faults in the system because they view the world in the same way that white men view the world. Poor Tod, doesn't know the difference. He believes everything he's told. Blind faith, that's a curse. He's so damn perfect. I'm going to get that boy to wake up. How the hell did he get that way? My son believes in America and I feel like I've been the butt of some cruel joke. If he were white he wouldn't exist at all.

JOHN: When did things start to change?

MARY MARTHA: I don't know when it started, I only know when I was aware of it. It just happened. I didn't know him, and one day I said it...

JOHN: What?

MARY MARTHA: I didn't mean it.

TOD: I couldn't do it.

MARY MARTHA: We got into a fight.

JOHN: About what?

MARY MARTHA: I didn't mean it.

JOHN: What did you say?

TOD: She wanted me to hire some black man at the office.

MARY MARTHA: He had the opportunity to hire someone black at his office.

JOHN: Well?

MARY MARTHA: Well?

TOD: I couldn't do it.

MARY MARTHA: I'm not surprised.

TOD: I thought long and hard. I just couldn't justify it, it wouldn't have been fair.

MARY MARTHA: Fair? What is fair, Tod?

TOD: He just wasn't the best man for the job.

MARY MARTHA: No?

TOD: No!

MARY MARTHA: Was he qualified?

TOD: I guess.

MARY MARTHA: Was he black?

TOD: Yes.

MARY MARTHA: Was he the only black?

TOD:: Yes.

MARY MARTHA: Then he was the best man for the job.

TOD: That's not fair, Mother. You have to look at things more deeply than that.

MARY MARTHA: I thought that was pretty deep.

TOD: You can't get away with things like that anymore.

MARY MARTHA: Says who? It's what they do all the time.

TOD: Your age is over, things are different now.

MARY MARTHA: That's when I said it.

JOHN: What?

MARY MARTHA: I said, "you talk might bold for someone who'd be out on his black ass if he didn't act so white."

JOHN: You said what?

TOD: She said I was white.

MARY MARTHA: I said he was white.

TOD: What does that mean?

MARY MARTHA: You sound white, you act white, you're starting to smell white...

TOD: Can you believe she said that to me. Do I sound white to you? Don't answer that. I think you're going insane.

MARY MARTHA: Yeah, you're driving me crazy.

TOD: You have white men on the brain.

MARY MARTHA: I have one living in my house.

TOD: That's enough of that!

MARY MARTHA: Enough of what, the truth.

TOD: Don't you ever get tired?

MARY MARTHA: No, I never get tired. That's how I've survived.

TOD: Do we have to go through this again?

MARY MARTHA: Untiring, unyielding, Mary Martha!

TOD: Your fight is over mother.

MARY MARTHA: This shit ain't over, it's just getting started.

TOD: It deserved its death, let it die.

MARY MARTHA: I fought too long and too hard for you to be so goddamned naive.

TOD: I didn't ask you to fight for me.

MARY MARTHA: You didn't have to. Besides, I didn't do it just for you, I did it for our people.

TOD: Well, then leave me alone and go scream at our people. Go scream at the crack heads, and the welfare cases, and the welfare mothers, and the...

MARY MARTHA: Why? You're the biggest case around. You're more dangerous than they are. You have so much to give, Tod, and you're wasting it. It's time to start giving something back.

TOD: What do you want from me?

MARY MARTHA: I want you to fight.

TOD: Fight what? You're living in the past.

MARY MARTHA: This is not the past I'm talking about. We're in a hell of a lot of trouble when everyone's afraid of hiring black people, especially black people.

TOD: I'm here mother. What am I if not a sign of your success? You think you failed because I don't hate white people. You want me to agree with everything you have to say but I can't. Why do you have so much hatred?

MARY MARTHA: I'm a black woman in a racist and sexist society. It doesn't take much. I don't want to fight with you, Tod. I don't want to hurt you. I just want you to understand what's going on. Stop being so trusting.

TOD: You have no faith in me.

MARY MARTHA: That's not true.

TOD: I'm not as naive as you think I am.

MARY MARTHA: You'll see the truth someday. You're not as white as you want to be.

TOD: And I'll never be black enough...she said, "white."

MARY MARTHA: I said, "Tod, it's time you stopped trying to be white."

TOD: How can she say that to me, what does she know about it? How does she know how I feel? My mother doesn't know the first thing about being black. She's like some white-assed liberal looking for a cause. No offense.

JOHN: None taken.

MARY MARTHA: I felt guilty.

TOD: She thinks my life's been perfect. I've been destined for failure from the moment I was sent to private school. I was imperfect, I had to become perfect. I had to become white or else I wouldn't have survived.

JOHN: And that was it.

MARY MARTHA: That was something.

TOD: The beginning. We were separate then. I never knew, I never knew that she felt that way too. I thought she was proud. I thought I was doing what she wanted, but now there was something else. There was something that she expected of me, I didn't know what.

MARY MARTHA: We're not bad parents.

JOHN: I didn't say you were.

MARY MARTHA: We're not bad black parents.

JOHN: What about your husband?

MARY MARTHA: Religion does not always acknowledge the need to continue the fight against racism. It's not that he doesn't understand, my husband was once very militant. Let's just say that he's turned the other cheek so many times, he's lost his sense of direction.

REVEREND JOE: My wife doesn't think that I understand the problem, she thinks that I've given up the cause. But do not be deceived by my silence. We must have patience, patience. There is nothing wrong with my son, he is coming into power. A great war has been waged and Tod is the culmination of that war. Our enemy has trained our generals, they have all the knowledge that they need, but they are lost. They are successful, upwardly mobile and lost. We let them battle too long on their own, without our help, without our guidance. But there was a purpose to that as well. The movement did not fail my friend, but it will have failed if we can't find a way to bring them home again. You see John, we too have children wandering in the wilderness looking for the promised land. We are close, we are very close to coming together. There are still great risks to take, and great sacrifices. This is where you come in. You must teach Tod how to get back home.

JOHN: I don't quite understand what you expect from me. Analysis is not teaching, there are no guarantees that I will be able to help him.

REVEREND JOE: Help him? Who the hell wants your help!

JOHN: Well, that is why most people come to me.

REVEREND JOE: I want you to teach him and your prejudice will do the rest. You don't understand, Tod has led a sheltered existence for a purpose.

JOHN: Have you tried explaining that to him?

REVEREND JOE: He doesn't understand my language, but he will understand you and your liberalism. So don't try to help, it only gets in the way of purity.

JOHN: What do you want from me?

REVEREND JOE: There is nothing wrong with my son.

MARY MARTHA: The American Dream is a white man's dream.

TOD: The issue is definition that is what I want.

JOHN: I'm sure that there's a way to help.

REVEREND JOE: He needs no help only knowledge.

MARY MARTHA: It's as if I'm supposed to forget that segregation took place.

JOHN: It's not a question of forgetting...

REVEREND JOE: He's coming into power.

TOD: Tell me what it means to be black and that's what I'll be.

JOHN: These matters cannot be so easily answered.

MARY MARTHA: Am I supposed to forget that people spat in my face?

REVEREND JOE: I'm allowing him to do this because he needs to know the language of the enemy.

JOHN: I am not the enemy.

TOD: Extract the goodness from what is white and make it black.

REVEREND JOE: The language of temptation.

TOD: And that is what I'll be.

JOHN: I cannot get personally involved.

MARY MARTHA: Am I supposed to forget my childhood?

REVEREND JOE: And with this knowledge he will lead us to the promised land.

TOD: Destroy the whiteness from what is right and that is what I'll be.

JOHN: This is not logical.

REVEREND JOE: You were selected for a purpose.

MARY MARTHA: Am I supposed to forget the reasons not to trust white people?

TOD: This is what I have become.

JOHN: I am not to blame.

REVEREND JOE: Follow your guilt.

TOD: In their absence.

REVEREND JOE: Your profession.

TOD: In their ignorance.

REVEREND JOE: And not your heart.

JOHN: There's a procedure that we must follow.

MARY MARTHA: Racism still exists, time is running out.

TOD: What is black?

REVEREND JOE: Teach Tod and the truth will reveal itself to him.

JOHN: You must follow the rules.

TOD: What is black?

REVEREND JOE: Tod is waking up.

JOHN: I cannot tolerate ignorance of the process.

MARY MARTHA: What happened to my child?

TOD: Tell me who I am?

REVEREND JOE: The awakening had to be violent.

JOHN: You cannot expect me to solve all of your problems.

REVEREND JOE: The awakening had to be bloody.

MARY MARTHA: What happened to my child?

JOHN: You must follow the rules.

TOD: Tell me who I am.

REVEREND JOE: You know what you must do.

THE COMMITTEE: You people need to learn how to help yourselves!

JOHN: No, no, that's not what I mean. You see...you see... *(JOHN removes a book from the shelf and begins reading.)*

I know that you "obstinate ignorance is merely a defense mechanism against my role in the patriarchal structure." No, I mean, well, look it's all very simple, here... *(He reads from another book.)* "Minority groups in particular may have a culturally induced high level of paranoid belief and this belief may be based upon real discrimination..." *(He begins flipping wildly through many books as the COMMITTEE OF SOCIAL REFORM recite quotations from the history of "The Negro Problem.")* No, look...maybe your answer is here...no, maybe here...no, maybe here...no, maybe here...no, maybe here...no, maybe here...

SCENE SIX—THE ASCENSION OF BOOKS

COMMITTEE EXECUTIVE: In the beginning God created the heaven and the earth...

COMMITTEE SENIOR: And he said, "cursed be Canaan, a servant of servants shall he be unto his brethren..."

COMMITTEE JUNIOR: The Negro is the son of Ham, and his inferiority to his white brother is the result of a curse...

COMMITTEE EXECUTIVE: ...in recognizing the Negro as a man and a brother they were compelled to declare man an ape...

COMMITTEE SENIOR: When I am told the human race are all from Adam seed...

COMMITTEE JUNIOR: ...that kinky headed coons and I are from one common breed...

COMMITTEE EXECUTIVE: ...skin color was affected by the bile...

COMMITTEE SENIOR: ...marks the human species degenerate...

COMMITTEE JUNIOR: ...the cerebral cranium less developed than the white...

COMMITTEE SENIOR: ...characterized by a very strong offensive odor...

COMMITTEE EXECUTIVE: ...believed that Negroes were apes...

COMMITTEE SENIOR: ...that ape-Negro copulation might produce fertile offspring...

COMMITTEE JUNIOR: Christianity is the religion of white people.

COMMITTEE EXECUTIVE: Islam is the natural, though false religion of the Negroes

COMMITTEE SENIOR: The Semites do not possess the harmonious equilibrium,…

COMMITTEE JUNIOR: With the passing of the need for black laborers…

COMMITTEE EXECUTIVE: …black people have become useless…

COMMITTEE SENIOR: …the black man occupies a very special sexual role in American society…

COMMITTEE JUNIOR: …if you are ever going to have anything like an equal Negro community…

COMMITTEE SENIOR: You are for the next thirty years going to have to give them unequal treatment.

COMMITTEE EXECUTIVE: That the American Negro has survived at all is extraordinary…

COMMITTEE SENIOR: …Affirmative action is a failure.

COMMITTEE EXECUTIVE: Then you have to wonder if we're ever going to get women and minorities to fit in…

COMMITTEE SENIOR: …as smoothly as white males did…

COMMITTEE JUNIOR: …in a system that contained only white males.

THE COMMITTEE: Hello, John. John, the Psychiatrist, John, looking for an answer and a cause.

COMMITTEE EXECUTIVE: There's something that these people have forgotten.

COMMITTEE SENIOR: They were sent here to learn what they could about us, but it seems they've given up that mission.

COMMITTEE JUNIOR: It's sad. They've grown content. They think we define life.

COMMITTEE EXECUTIVE: They think this is all there is to life.

COMMITTEE SENIOR: They dream the same dreams, they have the same ideals, goals.

THE COMMITTEE: It's a great burden on us.

(The COMMITTEE OF SOCIAL REFORM begin a rap.)

COMMITTEE JUNIOR: They have no hope,
they're filled with dope,
trying to be free.

THE COMMITTEE: They are free,
isn't that a great irony?

COMMITTEE EXECUTIVE: Give them chains
and all they want is freedom.

COMMITTEE SENIOR: Give them freedom
and all they want is equality.

COMMITTEE JUNIOR: Give them equality
   and they cease to exist,
   tsk, tsk, tsk
COMMITTEE SENIOR: You see, they're just poor,
   and now that they're poor,
   they can be forgotten.
COMMITTEE EXECUTIVE: America,
   has no sympathy for the poor.
   How can we?
COMMITTEE SENIOR: They lost their cause
   in their fight for equality,
   we have no sympathy.
   How can we?
COMMITTEE EXECUTIVE: Poverty is the foundation of capitalism,
   everyone knows that.
COMMITTEE SENIOR: It's a shame
   but we can no longer
   carry the strain
   of our white man's guilt.
COMMITTEE JUNIOR: Our greatest defense
   is prove that slavery
   was essential to this country.
COMMITTEE EXECUTIVE: Write it like history,
   make them forget.
COMMITTEE EXECUTIVE: Forget they were slaves,
   make them ashamed to see
   what they once were
   to what they can be.
COMMITTEE JUNIOR: Train their youth,
   make them forget.
COMMITTEE EXECUTIVE: Hell, never teach them.
   They won't teach themselves.
COMMITTEE SENIOR: Create a generation
   that will never know the reason for their oppression
   and we
   will never face a revolution.
COMMITTEE JUNIOR: They will just blame
   their pain on the shame
   of their parents.

THE COMMITTEE: And they'll forget about us.

COMMITTEE EXECUTIVE: We're almost there, John. This generation is the last that has ever known legalized oppression in their lifetime. The Bakke decision was the first sign of the times, the beginning of the end of the myth of racism. We have almost reached the end. Free at last, John, free at last.

THE COMMITTEE: Free at last...

JOHN: I remember the first time that I passed...the first time that I denied my faith. I thought that was the answer. There was no God, there was no faith, for me this was what it meant to be white. I had no identity, I was like everybody else, I belonged. This was freedom. Yes, Tod, this was freedom.

SCENE SEVEN—THE FIRST LESSON

TOD: I have failed somehow. There was something I was working towards. I seem to have forgotten. Maybe I never knew. My parents seem to know but they won't tell me. When I ask they simply turn their heads in shame. There has never been something I didn't know, or know where to look for the answer. But this...

JOHN: What is it?

TOD: I remember the first time I heard the voice. The blacks were there blaming the establishment for not being sensitive to their cause, and I heard someone say, "Then go back where you came from." And it was me...Am I a traitor?

JOHN: What?

TOD: Am I a traitor? I've become the enemy somehow by not doing what I was supposed to do, but I don't know what that is. Do you know? Can you tell me what it is, do you know?

JOHN: Tod, you're just battling your parents expectations.

TOD: No, it's more than that. I shouldn't be this angry.

JOHN: Why are you angry?

TOD: The enemy has eluded me. The face is unclear, but I'm coming closer. I'm getting closer everyday. It's a face I almost recognize. I'm afraid.

JOHN: What are you afraid of.

TOD: I'm afraid of what I have become. I'm afraid they'll find me out.

JOHN: Find out what?

TOD: I'm afraid I've become a white man. They'll think it's a conspiracy and that I'm to blame. Can you help me get back?

JOHN: Get back?

TOD: Get back to what I once was.

JOHN: What was that.

TOD: Black, I once was black. I think?

JOHN: Tod, you're still black.

TOD: Are you sure?

JOHN: You look black.

TOD: Looks can be deceiving. People say that I'm not really black. I don't feel black. Is there a way that I'm supposed to feel? I'm not comfortable around blacks. The true blacks, the ones that everyone talks about, the ones who have a purpose and a cause, the ones who call me names and reject me for sounding white.

"Oh, you're not really black." People actually say this to me, still, today, now even more than in the past. Even my mother says it. "You're not really black." What does it mean? What does any of it mean?

They won't accept me, they don't trust me. They treat me like a white man. My mother says I need to wake up, well maybe she better wake up. I won't be blamed for their weakness. Blacks are despised the whole world over. Even the Japanese are racist. Even Africans hate blacks. The true blacks, the people with a purpose and a cause. The race the Americans invented.

JOHN: Tod, please stop.

TOD: Why, do I sadden your liberal soul? Do I disgust you with my honesty? Isn't it sad to see that this is what we've come to.

JOHN: Tod, you haven't become a white man, you've become a racist.

TOD: I'm not a racist, I'm a neoconservative economist who suffers from white liberal guilt, that's a mental disorder. Can it be cured? No? Well, I guess you suffer from it too. I tried working for this non-profit urban rehabilitation group called PURGE, but that didn't help. I could probably be cured if I went to work for Wall Street. I hear that cures many things. Someone once told me that the best way to cure socialist apathy was to become an investment banker. Is that true?

JOHN: Tod, please...

TOD: This is a trial John. You are the prosecutor, my parents are the victims, and I'm the crime. The creation of Tod was a very dirty crime. He's not a racist, he hates everybody. But he hates himself most of all.

Once Tod believed he had eaten of the tree of knowledge and discovered that he was a Nigger. An angel told him of salvation called assimilation and Tod studied and was faithful and waits for his day. But there are times when he sins, and his sins are black, as all sins are. And he bends his knees and begs forgiveness for being what he is.

MARY MARTHA: Why, Tod?

TOD: At that moment, Tod was sitting on the edge of his oppression, and the tempter came and said,...

REVEREND JOE: You have tried the white man's way, now try the true way.

TOD: And the tempter looked like Tod's father, and he was black like evil. And this was the first time that Tod ever had any doubts. Everything used to be so clear. Had he reached the end of liberty? And his first taste of oppression invaded him like a plague. Was he a Nigger? Where were his white majority friends, and his white majority world, and his white majority liberal arts education when there was no majority acceptance. What did Tod want, sitting on the edge of his oppression...And the tempter said,

REVEREND JOE: Rise up and lead your people to prove that you are chosen.

TOD: But Tod said he would not and overcame temptation, but he was never really sure if he had done the right thing. And it was that uncertainty that grew in him as he waited on the edge for his salvation, but it never came. I just wanted to hear God's voice.

MARY MARTHA: Suicide?

TOD: I just wanted to hear Him say, "Peace be still."

MARY MARTHA: Blacks don't commit suicide.

TOD: I had to free myself. I wanted to walk into the ocean to free my soul. Father, where is the light? Where is the light?

MARY MARTHA: I found him.

TOD: The ancestors cry out from my veins, from my veins.

REVEREND JOE: Come home, Tod, come home.

MARY MARTHA: Forsaken like all Marries. A simple death.

TOD: But I could not answer. I do not speak their language. I look back and there's no recognition. I look forward and there's no light. They do not trust my voice. They say I sound white, sound white, do I sound white to you? Don't answer that. Do I sound white to you? Don't answer that.

MARY MARTHA: Noble in some respect.

TOD: I look forward, the path is dark. Where is the light? Help me find the way. Help me get to the promised land. Hey mister, do you know how to get to the promised land? Do you know the way to the promised land?

MARY MARTHA: He survived a three day coma.

REVEREND JOE: His survival was a perfect sign.

TOD: Father, speak to me. *(TOD removes the bandages from his left wrist.)* Father, speak to me. *(TOD removes the bandages from his right wrist.)* But the voice never came. Forsaken.

MARY MARTHA: Not by grace, but by misfortune.

REVEREND JOE: I knew then that my efforts were not in vain.

MARY MARTHA: You would think that such an event would confirm my faith. No, this was a cruel ungodly joke. I don't believe in grace, I believe in Tod. Your world took God away from me. You stole my virginity and now He'll never speak to me again.

REVEREND JOE: Tod is the chosen one.

TOD: God is a coward, I called His bluff, and He would not come out from hiding.

There is a battle going on inside of me, a consciously implanted warfare I believe, and I have no choice but to fight. I want a freedom moment before I die. I want to know a freedom moment in my lifetime. Teach me.

THE COMMITTEE: Teach him the way you will have him to go,

and he will never stray from it,

like trees

and streams

like slaves...Peace be still...Peace be still.

JOHN: Come, Tod, and I will show you the way.

Come, Tod, and I will help you justify your past.

Come, and I will lead the way.

Come, I have been chosen...

Come and you will see.

Lesson One: God is dead.

COMMITTEE EXECUTIVE: The belief in salvation is what has kept the black masses oppressed for hundreds of years. It is the force which allows them to remain victimized, lost in the illusion of just retribution by a white high holy God.

JOHN: Lesson One: God is dead.

COMMITTEE SENIOR: Religion is an opiate which distracts oppressed people from struggling to change their material circumstances. As long as it remains intact, blacks will always be dependent upon white society for their identity and their salvation.

JOHN: Lesson One: God is dead, repeat...

COMMITTEE JUNIOR: The most effective way to infiltrate and destroy a society is to replace their pagan gods with an image of the conqueror. This will have the most dramatic effect on the generations still to come. In order for them to overcome this oppression they must destroy the God they have come to love.

JOHN: Lesson One: God is dead, repeat...

TOD: God is dead, and my salvation is at hand. Teach me, teach me more...

MARY MARTHA: What must we do now, Joe?

REVEREND JOE: We must pray.

MARY MARTHA: What must we pray for.

REVEREND JOE: Mercy, pray for mercy.

MARY MARTHA: I asked God for a child.

REVEREND JOE: Yes, Martha.

MARY MARTHA: My prayers were answered, weren't they Joe?

REVEREND JOE: Yes, Martha.

MARY MARTHA: We protected our son from the terror, didn't we Joe?

REVEREND JOE: Through sleepless nights.

MARY MARTHA: Watching over this child. Waiting for the morning to come. Watching and waiting. I lived through nights of terror, and now this...

REVEREND JOE: In time, Martha, in time. We will destroy our oppressors and not lose our souls. In time all will be clear. All will not survive, but a few shall, a few shall be whole again.

MARY MARTHA: When I gave birth to Tod, the lightning glistened across the horizon. When I gave birth to truth and light. I had no life before. My life began with his.

COMMITTEE EXECUTIVE: Oh, stop worrying, John. He's just another educated Nigger going insane, you can help prevent the inevitable. You know what happens to insane niggers, the ones who talk of liberation and the war. Don't let things get out of hand this time. We'll be with you. People without gods become apathetic, it's part of the plan. There's nothing we can do about it.

THE COMMITTEE: The final battle has begun, freedom is at hand. Amen.

JOHN: Amen.

REVEREND JOE: And a time will come when your stories will no longer be your own, and your music will be abused, and your soul enslaved, but there is one who will be born of both worlds and he will know, he will know and will lead you, and will suffer greatly, and will prevail. Teach my son, Oh, teach him well...

(There is a flash of lightning. Blackout.)
END OF ACT ONE

ACT TWO
SCENE ONE—LESSON TWO

JOHN: Tod.

MARY MARTHA: Tod?

REVEREND JOE: Tod.

JOHN: Tod you don't know.

MARY MARTHA: Tod, you don't know.

REVEREND JOE: Tod, you don't know.

JOHN, MARY MARTHA, REVEREND JOE: What it means to be black in America.

REVEREND JOE: And that is good.

MARY MARTHA: You know nothing about your past.

JOHN: And that is what your parents are responding to.

MARY MARTHA: You think I'm telling you some fucking fairly tale.

REVEREND JOE: Those who say they know have already been defeated.

MARY MARTHA: This shit happened, the stories I tell you are true, they happened to me.

REVEREND JOE: It means nothing.

JOHN: Your apparent lack of knowledge of your culture and your past history. Do you understand what I'm trying to say? In a sense you're not really "black."

MARY MARTHA: Not really black.

REVEREND JOE: Not really black.

JOHN: You've been able to escape those denigrated aspects of your culture which are the only things that people are able to identify as uniquely black.

REVEREND JOE: Uniquely black.

MARY MARTHA: Uniquely black.

REVEREND JOE: For so long we've fought to bring meaning to our existence here. What's the use. There is no meaning to our existence here.

MARY MARTHA: You look at me as if I'm making this shit up.

REVEREND JOE: That's a lost cause.

MARY MARTHA: You look at me with that liberal arts education and I want to slap it off your face.

REVEREND JOE: That's a lost cause.

MARY MARTHA: You think I'm over-reacting. It happened. Not like in your fantasy books, why do you think I talk so much about it?

JOHN: My experience is very similar. My Jewish heritage has been greatly diminished.

REVEREND JOE: I know history, Tod, I wrote history. We knew the world. We've explored every vast land. We were the discoverers, we knew about the enemy long before they knew about us. We knew of their savagery, their ignorance, their curse. And we denied the truth for fear of taking on their evil ways.

JOHN: Your hindrance is, of course, your black skin, but most people don't even acknowledge that after awhile.

MARY MARTHA: I spent my lifetime fighting.

JOHN: Fighting.

REVEREND JOE: Fighting.

MARY MARTHA: For what you so easily take for granted, as if life has always been like this. As if it will always be this way and never change. As if my life means nothing, has meant nothing.

REVEREND JOE: Nothing.

JOHN: Nothing.

MARY MARTHA: How can I make you understand.

REVEREND JOE: Self righteous idiots, conquering the world, enslaving every spirit they encountered with their bestiality, stealing land that they claimed to have discovered in the face of men who were already there.

JOHN: Your problem seems to be your inability to reconcile this sense of loss. But to be quite honest, I don't believe there was anything there to lose. You're caught up in a black myth. Tod, Lesson Two: there is no black culture. It does not exist, that is why you cannot find it. There is nothing to find. It's all made up from a failed rebellion that has faded away.

MARY MARTHA: White people cannot be trusted.

REVEREND JOE: And we blinded by prophecy, by prophecy, knew they were to come, knew we were to be enslaved, knew the evil that they possessed, yet said nothing, did nothing, devoured ourselves, embellished them with riches, sold our souls because of our cursed curiosity and our acquiescent gods.

MARY MARTHA: White people cannot be trusted.

REVEREND JOE: Armageddon has begun. Armageddon is the battle for the minds of the people. It is no longer a question of whether they can love us or not, that would have been the easy way out. It is now a question of whether they can love.

SCENE TWO—MARY MARTHA'S LAMENT

(In the blackout an African beat begins. It slowly turns into the tempo of "The Battle Hymn of the Republic." COMMITTEE SENIOR begins humming the melody as the lights come up on the COMMITTEE and MARY MARTHA. COMMITTEE JUNIOR is wearing a headset and listening to a reel-to-reel tape recorder. COMMITTEE EXECUTIVE speaks as the voice of God during MARY MARTHA's lament.)

MARY MARTHA: It all seemed to happen in a moment, a black and white moment.

(COMMITTEE SENIOR begins singing "The Battle Hymn of the Republic.")

We were marching in the movement for freedom, all together, black and white.

Everything around me was black and white, the signs were black and white, the monument, the nuns, and there was singing, and there was chanting, and we marched to the beat, and the dogs, even the dogs were black and white, and the police were white and we were marching and shouting for liberty as the world turned white, then black.

(COMMITTEE JUNIOR begins playing Martin Luther King, Jr.'s "I Have a Dream" speech on the reel-to-reel.)

There was a ringing, a ringing, but I could see nothing in this darkness until a voice spoke to me and from the darkness God appeared in a harsh

white light, and He was black, as black as I had though He would be..."Are
you God?

COMMITTEE EXECUTIVE: Yes!

MARY MARTHA: He said, "Yes!" Are you God?

COMMITTEE EXECUTIVE: Yes!

THE COMMITTEE: Yes, yes, He said, "yes."

MARY MARTHA: He said, "Yes!"

    God, I want a freedom moment 'fore I die.

    I want a freedom moment from my black and white life.

    I want a freedom moment in my lifetime,

    free from black and white.

    I can't wait for salvation.

    I can't wait for my Judgment Day.

    And God said, "Yes!"

COMMITTEE EXECUTIVE: Yes, this is that moment.

THE COMMITTEE: Yes, this is that moment, yes, this is that moment...

MARY MARTHA: And he called me "baby."

COMMITTEE EXECUTIVE: Baby, yes, baby.

THE COMMITTEE: Baby, baby, baby, baby...

MARY MARTHA: He said, "Yes!"

    And took me in his arms

    and held me for a moment

    and his love was black.

    And I asked him for freedom,

    he smiled and I saw stars.

    Are you God?

COMMITTEE EXECUTIVE: Yes!

THE COMMITTEE: Yes, he said, yes, he said, yes, he said, yes...

MARY MARTHA: He said, yes, and for a moment there was freedom,

    freedom ringing, sounds so sweet, chanting for some justice,

    crying for redemption,

    marching for freedom in one sweet moment.

    And he said, "There will be a child...

THE COMMITTEE: There will be a child, there will be a child, there will be a
child...

COMMITTEE EXECUTIVE: There will be a child of freedom, oh, baby, this is
freedom, yes, this is freedom...

THE COMMITTEE: Baby, baby, baby...

    This is your freedom, yes,

This is your freedom, yes,
This is your freedom, yes...
MARY MARTHA: A child, a child, a child,
from this moment of freedom
and he smiled.
God seemed so pleased
I believed I had made Him happy for a moment.
And he said, "I've never seen anyone as white as you before..."
COMMITTEE EXECUTIVE: I've never had anyone white before.
This is freedom.
THE COMMITTEE: Yes, this is freedom.
MARY MARTHA: This is freedom.
White.
A sign of my purity.
White as snow.
And he caressed my skin
with his great black hands.
Are you God?
THE COMMITTEE: Yes, I am God.
MARY MARTHA: He said, "Yes, I am."
And freedom was sweet
and painful
freedom was joy,
washed in his blood,
filled with his love   THE COMMITTEE:
as pure as snow,   Like a dream,
freedom was a moment   like a dream,
in my lifetime   like a dream,
like a dream   like a dream...
I once had, forgotten...
have I fallen to temptation,
have I lost my salvation...
and now they come
to seek us out
and destroy my child.   a child
                                              a child
Rape!   a child
I've been raped   a child
forsaken.   a child

My salvation.	yes
My redemption.	yes
My hope.	yes
Tod.	is
Tod.	is
Tod.	is
My salvation cries out in	Mary Martha
MARY MARTHA: (continued)	THE COMMITTEE: (continued)
the wilderness	Mary Martha
and I am helpless,	Mary Martha
helpless to save my	poor
own child.	poor
Yes,	poor
yes,	poor
yes,	poor,
poor,	Mary Martha
poor,	Mary Martha...

SCENE THREE—POWER

REVEREND JOE: My wife had a very traumatic experience during the March, she was raped by a black man who thought she was white.

JOHN: Were there any witnesses?

REVEREND JOE: A few, I believe.

JOHN: And you were there?

REVEREND JOE: I found her.

MARY MARTHA: Are you God?

REVEREND JOE: Yes, I'm God's messenger.

THE COMMITTEE: He said, "yes."

MARY MARTHA: Are you God?

REVEREND JOE: Yes, I'm God's messenger.

THE COMMITTEE: He said, "yes."

MARY MARTHA: Yes.

REVEREND JOE: She was unconscious for awhile. She never seemed to remember anything of what happened.

JOHN: And that was how you met?

REVEREND JOE: Yes.

JOHN: And the marriage followed?

REVEREND JOE: I thought she was the answer.

JOHN: Answer to what?

REVEREND JOE: My prayers, my salvation. I had asked God for a wife, a mate, somehow this seemed...

JOHN: Prophetic...

REVEREND JOE: It was a day of miracles. There was something we were both searching for, why not this, why not love, and from that a son and our salvation? It was my day of judgment.

JOHN: And the voice of God spoke to you...

REVEREND JOE: The voice of God spoke to us all. If you had been there you...

JOHN: I was there.

REVEREND JOE: Then you understand.

JOHN: Yes, I'm beginning to.

REVEREND JOE: Why should I waste my time trying to explain this to you. It's useless.

JOHN: Was it you?

REVEREND JOE: Would it make any difference if I said, yes?

JOHN: Is Tod your son?

REVEREND JOE: I have never had any reason to doubt that Tod was my son.

JOHN: But your wife believes...

REVEREND JOE: What she needs to believe.

JOHN: And you plan to continue to indulge her fantasy?

REVEREND JOE: I plan to continue this journey until the end. I will see that justice prevails.

JOHN: And Tod?

REVEREND JOE: Tod is part of that justice. We all have our part to play.

JOHN: You control your family's lives with these delusions, you're driving them insane with your beliefs. How can you expect Tod to be normal with such expectations, no one should have to live up to your ideals.

REVEREND JOE: The ideology, the ideology is intact. Tod has entered in and will come out clean. He will learn the ways of the enemy and set us free. He is our liberator.

JOHN: You are causing him great turmoil with your beliefs.

REVEREND JOE: No one said it would be easy. Tod is now on the other side. We must work together to bring him back intact...whole.

JOHN: Your son is suffering.

REVEREND JOE: At last my son is suffering, as we all have had to do. Millions have lost their lives. He must understand, suffering is part of survival in the land of the enemy. Suffering is the key to his salvation. And ours.

JOHN: I just don't understand how you can continue to uphold these beliefs, it has almost cost him his life.

REVEREND JOE: But he survived, that was the first sign. I cannot explain to you why I believe what I do. Your heart is cold. You do not want to understand. You want to believe in the white man's world. Tod represents another world, the white man's world cannot accept him, it strives to destroy him. Tod's power lies in his complete knowledge of the enemy. He knows so well the ways of white men. That knowledge will be his salvation, and he shall lead us to the promised land.

MARY MARTHA: I met God one day.

JOHN: There was once an alliance.

REVEREND JOE: Those days are over.

MARY MARTHA: It was at the March on Washington.

JOHN: My father fought long and hard for integration.

REVEREND JOE: The world still hates Niggers.

MARY MARTHA: I asked God for a child.

JOHN: Blacks demanded too much.

REVEREND JOE: Jews demanded too much.

MARY MARTHA: And He said, "yes."

JOHN: You shattered our temples.

REVEREND JOE: You betrayed our trust.

MARY MARTHA: Are you God?

JOHN: You betrayed our trust through your negligence.

REVEREND JOE: Through your arrogance.

MARY MARTHA: And God was black.

JOHN: You failed to teach your history.

REVEREND JOE: You were afraid of our power.

MARY MARTHA: Black as I always thought He would be.

JOHN: We were your greatest allies.

REVEREND JOE: You were white like everybody else.

MARY MARTHA: Poor yellow gal, as black as you're ever going to be.

JOHN: Your revolution destroyed the movement.

REVEREND JOE: You never wanted blacks to have power.

MARY MARTHA: So I married the blackest man I could find.

JOHN: You failed to tell the truth.

REVEREND JOE: "The only way we gonna stop them white men from whipping us is to take over."

MARY MARTHA: And put an end to my half white legacy.

JOHN: Tod doesn't trust you.

REVEREND JOE: "We been sayin' freedom for years and we ain't got nothin'."

MARY MARTHA: Rape.

JOHN: You lied to him.

REVEREND JOE: "What we gonna start sayin now is Black Power."

MARY MARTHA: Rape.

JOHN: Live the results of your silence.

REVEREND JOE: Black Power!

MARY MARTHA: I've been raped.

JOHN: You betrayed yourselves.

REVEREND JOE: Black Power!

MARY MARTHA: By America!

REVEREND JOE: Racism is a great evil that has to be extracted from the heart. It shall be ripped out if it must. We have been forced to eat of the tree of knowledge and we know that we were once naked. Lost innocence, raped, we have been raped. Curse the forgotten mythology, curse the forgotten history, curse the forgotten land that we do not know. We do not know how it feels to walk on peaceful soil, native land. All we have are ourselves, the nation, home, Tod.

SCENE FOUR—AM I BLACK ENOUGH

TOD: What is it?

REVEREND JOE: I want to go home.

TOD: What do they want from me?

REVEREND JOE: Take us there.

TOD: I don't understand what it is I'm supposed to be.

REVEREND JOE: To the promised land.

TOD: I don't understand how I feel.

REVEREND JOE: I want to go back to a time when I was free.

TOD: Am I not black enough for you?

REVEREND JOE: And my language was my own.

TOD: Am I not as black as you think I should be?

REVEREND JOE: My land.

TOD: What do you expect from me.

REVEREND JOE: Take us there.

TOD: I sound white, am I,

REVEREND JOE: We shall remember.

TOD: I sound white, am I?

REVEREND JOE: We must remember.

TOD: I feel it all slipping away.

REVEREND JOE: Do you remember?

TOD: You created me black...

REVEREND JOE: To be black.

TOD: ...and educated.
REVEREND JOE: In America.
TOD: Too black...
REVEREND JOE: Doesn't mean...
TOD: ...and too educated
REVEREND JOE: ...a damn thing.
TOD: ...for you to understand.
REVEREND JOE: That's all you need to learn.
TOD: Is this what you wanted,
    to forget?
    You wanted to forget,
    but you can't forget.
    You wanted to raise
    a generation untouched and
    unscarred by the pain and
    blood of struggle.
    I do not know my oppression
    I do not know my oppression
    Where did you go wrong?
    You created me,
    but I am not what you wanted,
    Am I?
    Am I your enemy?
    Am I your failure?
    Mother, I do not know you.
    Father, I do not know you.
    Speak to me,
    my language...
    my language
    (MARY MARTHA and REVEREND JOE begin a musical minstrel journey
    back to the past.)
MARY MARTHA: Whatever happened to soul?
REVEREND JOE: Whatever happened to soul?
MARY MARTHA: Soul!
REVEREND JOE: Black as coal!
MARY MARTHA: Soul crossed-over, Joe.
REVEREND JOE: Whatever happened to soul?
MARY MARTHA: We sold our soul.
REVEREND JOE: For gold?

MARY MARTHA: No.

REVEREND JOE: We sold our soul.

MARY MARTHA: For knowledge?

REVEREND JOE: No.

MARY MARTHA: For what?

REVEREND JOE: What did we sell it for?

MARY MARTHA: For salvation?

REVEREND JOE: No.

MARY MARTHA: For Freedom?

REVEREND JOE: No.

MARY MARTHA: What did we sell it for?

REVEREND JOE: Acceptance.

MARY MARTHA: Acceptance?

REVEREND JOE: Yes, acceptance.

MARY MARTHA: We got taken.

REVEREND JOE: We got tooked.

MARY MARTHA: We lost our soul?

REVEREND JOE: We sold our soul.

MARY MARTHA: We sold our soul?

REVEREND JOE: Soul crossed over.

MARY MARTHA: Now, it's over sold.

REVEREND JOE: Solid gold.

MARY MARTHA: Solid!

REVEREND JOE: We sold our soul?

MARY MARTHA: We sold ourselves.

REVEREND JOE: For Acceptance?

MARY MARTHA: That's all we got?

REVEREND JOE: Not even that.

MARY MARTHA: Not even that?

REVEREND JOE: Am I still a slave?

MARY MARTHA: Am I still a slave?

REVEREND JOE: Am I still a slave?

MARY MARTHA: Am I still a slave?

TOD: I am your monster,
      you created me.
      But you reject me
      you won't accept me
      Not black enough,
      not black enough,

not black enough
I have become what you wanted
me to become
Adaptable.
I am America!
I am your savior
I am your death!
Tod
No struggle
no fight
no history
no heritage
no cause
no culture
no God
I'm afraid.
I'm afraid of what I might do.
I'm afraid I want to slit your throats
and my options are running out.
I'm trying to be fair, but now I have
discovered something dormant in me
that is rising, something rising in me that has
no fear, speaking to me,
the voice of destruction!

SCENE FIVE—THE TRIAL

JOHN: I'm just not certain?
COMMITTEE EXECUTIVE: Just not certain?
JOHN: It may be too soon.
COMMITTEE SENIOR: It may be too soon?
JOHN: Our timing might be off. He seems so volatile.
COMMITTEE JUNIOR: Sounds like cold feet.
JOHN: This is an unpredictable situation.
COMMITTEE EXECUTIVE: Things go differently everyday.
COMMITTEE JUNIOR: That is a sign of the end.
COMMITTEE SENIOR: Now, sir, I think we should proceed with caution.

COMMITTEE EXECUTIVE: We've always been cautious with the colored, Nigger, Negro peoples of the world, to our disadvantage. We should have wiped them out when they became obsolete.

COMMITTEE JUNIOR: I never realized how old you were.

COMMITTEE EXECUTIVE: Hell, man, I remember the day when you could string up a nigger and that would be the last word on it.

COMMITTEE SENIOR: But you have to give up that memory if we are going to proceed successfully.

COMMITTEE EXECUTIVE: The past is hard to give up.

COMMITTEE JUNIOR: We must make our changes as well. Any sign of your continued bigotry could be detrimental. You've lost Yonkers.

COMMITTEE SENIOR: You lost Forsythe County.

COMMITTEE EXECUTIVE: But I still have Boston.

COMMITTEE JUNIOR: You're losing Atlanta.

COMMITTEE SENIOR: Yes, and your little skin head Nazis running around are not helping either.

COMMITTEE EXECUTIVE: It's hard to keep things in check, it's unnatural, I can't pretend anymore. They are the youth of today, they say, "let's go," and I say, "go!"

JOHN: I think you're going to far. I think we've pushed to hard. We've destroyed him already. We can never get him back now.

COMMITTEE SENIOR: John, John, John, so naive, we haven't destroyed him, he's perfect.

COMMITTEE EXECUTIVE: History repeats itself, history repeats itself.

COMMITTEE JUNIOR: We've just sped up the process.

JOHN: I don't understand.

COMMITTEE EXECUTIVE: John, this is the moment that we've been waiting for. This generation is far too apathetic to come up with any philosophy of its own. Their ideology is something they have stolen from the past, and the past we know how to correct. Tod is now ready.

JOHN: What must I do?

COMMITTEE EXECUTIVE: It's all so simple John, love him.

COMMITTEE SENIOR: Love him.

JOHN: Love him? I can't, it's a lie.

COMMITTEE JUNIOR: You have no choice. How else will you fund your trip to Zion?

COMMITTEE SENIOR: You need us, you can't return without your god.

COMMITTEE EXECUTIVE: John, you are broke, you have no cause.

COMMITTEE JUNIOR: You are us, we are the same.

COMMITTEE EXECUTIVE: You have your own Niggers now.

COMMITTEE SENIOR: The world has no sympathy for you.

COMMITTEE JUNIOR: Yes, John, how do you plan to resolve Palestine.

COMMITTEE SENIOR: Just like us, John. Just like us.

JOHN: I'm not a racist.

COMMITTEE EXECUTIVE: I'm not a racist.

COMMITTEE SENIOR: I'm not a racist.

COMMITTEE JUNIOR: I'm not a racist.

JOHN: I've never assimilated.

THE COMMITTEE: I've never assimilated.

JOHN: I am not a part of your culture.

THE COMMITTEE: I am not a part of your culture.

JOHN: I am separate.

THE COMMITTEE: I am separate.

JOHN: I will persevere.

THE COMMITTEE: I will persevere.

JOHN: It is written.

THE COMMITTEE: It is written.

JOHN: It is prophecy.

THE COMMITTEE: It is prophecy. We are one!

COMMITTEE EXECUTIVE: And Tod to shall be, we shall all be one white one.

COMMITTEE JUNIOR: It's the only way to over come the global shift.

COMMITTEE SENIOR: There was never a revolution and there never shall be. Go fight your own battle. But remember these words, John.

COMMITTEE JUNIOR: Just like us, John. Just like us.

COMMITTEE EXECUTIVE: It was we who were slaves, we who were strangers, and therefore we recall these words as well...

JOHN: Stop it. Stop it.

COMMITTEE JUNIOR: You shall not oppress a stranger, for you know the feelings of the stranger.

JOHN: Stop it. You know nothing about me. You have no right.

COMMITTEE SENIOR: Having yourselves been a stranger in the land of Egypt.

JOHN: This is mine, my heritage. My language.

COMMITTEE JUNIOR: When a stranger resides with you in your land, you shall not wrong him...You shall love him as yourself.

JOHN: This is not your battle. You abuse culture, you steal culture.

COMMITTEE EXECUTIVE: For you were strangers in the land of Egypt. Love him.

JOHN: I want my belief back.

THE COMMITTEE: As we loved Bobby
As we loved Huey
Love him

JOHN: I want to go back, I want to go back.

THE COMMITTEE: As we loved Martin.
As we loved Malcolm.
Love him.

JOHN: To a time when I was free. Free.

THE COMMITTEE: As we loved Marcus.
As we loved William.
As we loved Frederick.
As we loved them all.
As we loved them all.

JOHN: Free.

THE COMMITTEE: As we loved Mary.
As we loved Fannie.
As we loved Angela.
As we learned to love you.

JOHN: When I was free.

THE COMMITTEE: Love him.

JOHN: Am I still a slave?

THE COMMITTEE: At last he has arrived.
You must make him complete
and he shall disappear forever.
And the rest will defeat
themselves.

JOHN: Am I still a slave?

THE COMMITTEE: There is no defense against love,
acquiesce and accept,
it costs us nothing to concede equality,
it's simple and ideal,
no man can make another man equal.

JOHN: Am I still a slave?
I must answer the call.
I must answer the call.

COMMITTEE JUNIOR: The battle is no longer with us.

COMMITTEE SENIOR: The battle is with the weakness in himself.

COMMITTEE EXECUTIVE: Teach him, John. Teach him well.

JOHN: I would like to do this without guilt please.

COMMITTEE EXECUTIVE: Very well, we'll see you on the other side.
COMMITTEE SENIOR: The doors are opening to a free world, a new society.
COMMITTEE JUNIOR: Be a part of it or be lost forever.
    (The COMMITTEE disappears.)
JOHN: On the battlefield, my friends. On the battlefield. Tod!

SCENE SIX—THE FINAL LESSON

TOD: I had a dream once that I was at war.
    The war seemed to have been going on for quite some time
    but I was unaware.
    I just appeared,
    but I didn't have any armor
    and I didn't know what I was fighting for.
    But I began to learn how to survive.
    I found some books
    and they helped a little,
    but there was very little time to read
    and there was very little air.
    Tod, on the edge of oppression, just doesn't care.
JOHN: Come Tod,
    I will give you comfort.
    Come Tod, I will help you understand
    Come Tod, I will explain it all
    It is time for your final lesson.
TOD: Have I learned all there is to know?
JOHN: Almost all.
TOD: What is the final lesson about?
JOHN: Love. The final lesson is always about love.
TOD: Will it be a painful lesson?
JOHN: Love is always painful.
    (JOHN positions TOD in his chair for the final lesson, the rape of mind, body and soul. He slowly removes his belt and walks around TOD's chair cracking it like a whip.)
JOHN: Come, Tod. Trust. Think. You must remember.
    (This phrase is repeated throughout REVEREND JOE and MARY MARTHA's chant. During the chant JOHN removes TOD's belt and lowers his trousers. He takes TOD's belt and fastens it around his neck like a noose. He inspects TOD's body as if he were on the auction block.)

MARY MARTHA, REVEREND JOE: How to reach that moment,
   the selling of ourselves,
   the frantic sacrifice of our hearts
   to merciless savages...
TOD: Are you going to beat me?
JOHN: I'm going to love you.
MARY MARTHA, REVEREND JOE: As we stood and watched with horror,
   devils, devils,
   in their divine right destroy our heritage,
   with a single sleight of hand,
   the pulling of a switch,
   the rape of mind, body and soul,
   the poisonous vapors that overwhelm us,
   the stench of our dying ancestors,
   that haunt us forever...
JOHN: Let us take a journey, Tod,
   and you will see the truth,
   you will know your oppression,
   you will fell the pain,
   you will see...
MARY MARTHA: , REVEREND JOE: History,
   we must remember,
   we must remember,
   and wait for one who shall be all powerful,
   and shall know the evil that dwells among us,
   and shall cast our tormentors away

TOD: And this is knowledge?

JOHN: The purest knowledge.

TOD: And this is power?

JOHN: Power eternal. Do you like it?

TOD: Yes.

JOHN: Why?

TOD: It's the most honest lesson I

MARY MARTHA, REVEREND JOE:
our history
History, our history
they tied him to a tree
they strapped her to a stake
they tied his hands together
they chained their ankles
they locked the shackles
they tied the noose
they gathered kindling
they struck the match
they aimed the rifle
they branded flesh

have learned.

JOHN: Yes?

TOD: Has it always been this way?

JOHN: From the beginning.

TOD: And it is never forgotten?

JOHN: Civilizations have been born
on this knowledge. It's been done for
centuries.

TOD: And what will come of this?

JOHN: I give you my white male
guilty conscience. I give it to you.
freely
I give you knowledge. I give you
truth to liberate my soul.

As it was given to me so many year's.
ago. Face the beast, Tod. Face the
beast and see anew!

they raped the child
they held her down
they cut the flesh
they chopped his foot
they sold the child
they fed the fire
they yanked the rope
the alligator smiled
the children screamed
the man screamed

the woman screamed
the knives fed
the hounds fed
the alligators fed
the fire fed
the ocean fed
the noose fed
the shackles fed

on our flesh
on our flesh
on our flesh
greedily
ravenously
greedily
ravenously
our children as live bait
devoured
a nation
a nation
a nation
fed on spirit
on culture
on flesh
on spirit
on culture
on flesh
on soul

a nation
no nations
on millions
millions
six million
no millions
sixty million
no millions
six hundred million
millions...

(The rape is an exchange of knowledge, the Ascension of Books begins in reverse. TOD and JOHN recite the passages together as the rape continues.)

TOD, JOHN: Then you have to wonder if we're ever going to get women and minorities to fit in...

Affirmative Action is a failure...

THE COMMITTEE: Stop, what are you doing?

Stop, you're unleashing demons.

Stop, it is an abomination.

Stop, you cannot teach them.

Stop, you'll destroy the world...

TOD, JOHN: ...the Negro community has been forced into a matriarchal structure...

That the Negro American has survived at all is extraordinary...

THE COMMITTEE: Stop, they cannot learn. Stop, you cannot teach them, they are inferior...

TOD, JOHN: ...you are for the next thirty years going to have to give them unequal treatment...

...the black man occupies a very special sexual role in American society...

THE COMMITTEE: You are creating a great danger. They cannot learn, you cannot teach them, they are inferior...

TOD, JOHN: ...black people have become useless...

...the semites do not possess the harmonious equilibrium...

...Christianity is the religion of white, white people...

...the pure blood white is the creature whom God, God destined should perform the mental labor...

THE COMMITTEE: You are creating your demise. They will destroy you.

TOD, JOHN: ...lower race of the human species...

...rigorous tradition of Negro-ape affinity...

THE COMMITTEE: Nigger, nigger lover, nigger lover, nigger lover...

(The COMMITTEE continues to chant as they gradually disappear.)

TOD, JOHN: ...the Negro has the cerebral cranium less developed than the white...

...marks the human species degenerate.

...skin color was affected by the bile...

...a people of beastly living without God, law, religion, or common wealth...

TOD: Is this oppression?

Is this oppression?

Is this oppression?

JOHN: Yes, Tod, yes, this is how oppression feels. That pain which you've forgotten, so sweet, the rapes, the lynchings, the sacrifice of life to keep you in your place. A history of hundreds of years of oppression which for you exist as if they occurred in a single moment. Rape, pain, oppression is so safe, secure, the fear.

This I give to you freely, the way it was given to me. My white man's guilt is yours, take it, take it, take it...

TOD: And he said, cursed be Canaan, a servant of servants shall he be unto his brethren...

In the beginning God created the heaven and the earth. And the earth was without form, and void; and darkness was upon the face of the deep, and the Spirit of God moved upon the face of the waters. And God said, "Let there be light: and there was light.

(A darkness envelopes the stage. TOD and JOHN are the only characters lit.)

JOHN: At last I am free. My God, my sovereignty abused and reshapened till I no longer felt divine and God no longer spoke to me. Evil, Tod, the world is ruled by Evil and Hypocrisy, open your eyes and see anew.

TOD: What has happened? It seems so peaceful.

JOHN: Yes, they're gone. Freedom is so peaceful and so transient. They're gone now and I am free for the first time, and see myself for the first time. Tod, I have sacrificed so much to live in this world. Waiting, waiting for the call, the trumpet blast, waiting to go home. I have given you the truth. If the Niggers really knew that the white man never intended to love them, the world would have ended years ago. Live free or die, Tod, live free or die.

I really have to go now. Freedom is just a suspended moment, Tod, such a fleeting moment. Use it while it lives. Never let a man tell you what you are, if you do you will always be a slave. *(JOHN recites as he exits)* Someone is shouting in the desert, get the road ready for him, make a straight path for him to travel. All low places must be filled up, all hills and mountains leveled off. The winding roads must be made straight, all the rough paths made smooth. All mankind will see his destruction.

SCENE SEVEN—STILL A NIGGER

TOD: I am the last revolutionary, the only person with a cause that's running out. Was there a revolution before, shall there be? For you will remember that a concession was made and now a debt has to be paid to save your sense of morality. You denied me my humanity and called me beast. And from this you created a world. But now the beast is rising and the debt shall be collected, for your chance to confess has passed, and you have not changed your ways. And there shall be no salvation for you. I your enemy stand and possess the final jewel that you cannot usurp. I am all that you cannot be, I am all that you cannot see. Now, I know all there is to know about you and you barely know me at all.

(*Three panels of the bookshelf begin to open as the COMMITTEE OF SOCIAL REFORM appears.*)

COMMITTEE EXECUTIVE: Hello, Tod.

COMMITTEE JUNIOR: Hello, Tod.

COMMITTEE SENIOR: Tod, the boy, Tod.

COMMITTEE EXECUTIVE: Tod, the Nigger, Tod.

COMMITTEE JUNIOR: Fighting his way to the 21st Century.

COMMITTEE SENIOR: Who would have thought you would make it this far.

COMMITTEE EXECUTIVE: Tod, the boy, Tod.

COMMITTEE JUNIOR: Tod, the Nigger, Tod.

COMMITTEE SENIOR: Tod, crying cause the system seems so unfair.

THE COMMITTEE: Poor, Tod, the boy, Tod.

COMMITTEE SENIOR: He believes in language.

COMMITTEE JUNIOR: He thinks that words will set him free.

COMMITTEE EXECUTIVE: Bound to an image and a sigh.

TOD: Who are you?

THE COMMITTEE: Why, Tod, we're John's white male guilty conscience. We now belong to you.

TOD: I thought you were gone. I thought I was free.

THE COMMITTEE: This is freedom, Tod.

COMMITTEE SENIOR: Freedom carries a great responsibility.

COMMITTEE JUNIOR: Freedom makes strange allies.

COMMITTEE EXECUTIVE: Freedom is a great burden.

COMMITTEE JUNIOR: A burden.

COMMITTEE SENIOR: A burden.

COMMITTEE EXECUTIVE: Feel it.

COMMITTEE JUNIOR: See it.

COMMITTEE SENIOR: Hear it.

COMMITTEE EXECUTIVE: Taste it.

COMMITTEE JUNIOR: Touch it.

COMMITTEE EXECUTIVE: A burden for eating of the tree of knowledge to liberate your soul.

COMMITTEE SENIOR: The road to freedom is dark narrow.

COMMITTEE JUNIOR: The road to freedom feels something like this...

COMMITTEE EXECUTIVE: Everyone has claims to retributions, Tod, what do you want? We gave you forty acres and a mule. We gave the Japanese $20,000 and a smile, will that do?

COMMITTEE SENIOR: I just don't understand you people. You want us to compensate for the crimes of the past. That wouldn't solve anything.

COMMITTEE JUNIOR: We're smarter than that now. We have a better understanding now. We can now extract what is discriminatory from what is idleness.

COMMITTEE SENIOR: The blacks in our society have every opportunity to achieve.

COMMITTEE JUNIOR: Let's face it, there's no better place to go. There are no Black Utopias except for the ones you create in your dreams and your false memories of what Africa used to be.

COMMITTEE EXECUTIVE: Don't you remember, I was there. Africa was Hell on Earth. It was no paradise. Savage, barren, with jewels you weren't even aware of, riches, you had no idea.

COMMITTEE SENIOR: Oil, uranium, iron, what use did you have for these things. You had no technology, you now have our technology.

COMMITTEE JUNIOR: Make the best of your situation, I have my own life to live.

COMMITTEE EXECUTIVE: We pretend that we're some modern society that can solve everything diplomatically. Oh, but we're beasts, we ravage and shit on everything in our path.

COMMITTEE JUNIOR: We have not become great men, just more efficient savages.

COMMITTEE SENIOR: You laugh and think that we don't know this. We're not trying to fool ourselves, we know this and accept it.

COMMITTEE EXECUTIVE: You laugh when we pretend not to know that you're still oppressed. What fools. Everything you are, everything you're allowed to be is still in our hands.

COMMITTEE SENIOR: Oh, no, not consciously, we just don't know any better.

THE COMMITTEE: And have no reason to change.

COMMITTEE JUNIOR: Hell, what do you want from us, a piece of paper?

(All three open their briefcases and take out a folder.)

COMMITTEE SENIOR: Here, have a guarantee that you are free.

(They hold out a sheet of paper, then snatch it back.)

COMMITTEE EXECUTIVE: My freedom isn't guaranteed. Tod, my boy, I wouldn't expect many social reforms in the 21st century, that budget has been cut drastically. You see, even we have our doubts. Life is not as great as it once was. Everything is so easy. We're all so idle. Life was rich when wars were bloody. But now there's very little blood. Just a lot of talk and bombs. Well, we're not as bad as the HUD, but it's still not good. Did you send that memo? Who does the filing now? Oh, here...no, see, not good at all. I never thought that I would resent paradise. Hopefully, there won't be much more to remember. Almost like Black History, wouldn't you say, Tod. A one week curse that you took in the 7th grade and that's all you know. And I know even less. Ignorance is bliss.

COMMITTEE SENIOR: You see, Tod, we wanted to spare you all of this, but you've eaten of the tree of knowledge, and now you have to be cast out.

COMMITTEE JUNIOR: You see, Tod, oppression is the state of peace. Paradise is slavery, without a care in the world. The oppressed know exactly who and what they are, but we fumble around for meaning each day. I mean what can you expect from me, I spend most of the day just trying to cover my ass.

COMMITTEE EXECUTIVE: I almost lost a billion dollars today, one minute it was there, then gone. I got it back, but you can never be certain. Hell, the issue is no longer about race anymore, race is dead, let it die. It's about power, and it always has been. Why should I give up my advantage over you? We fight for advantage, if you want power, goddamnit, then take it! I'm tired of your apathy, your crying, your welfare. "Am I black?" You better believe your black ass is black, but can you fight, motherfucker?

COMMITTEE JUNIOR: Sir, you're going to ruin everything with your melodrama, calm down.

COMMITTEE EXECUTIVE: I'm tired I told you, I want this black thing over. I almost lost a billion dollars today! I could be the fucking homeless tomorrow. I'm supposed to care about his simple ass.

COMMITTEE SENIOR: We have to keep him appeased.

COMMITTEE EXECUTIVE: You're just a bunch of chicken shits.

COMMITTEE JUNIOR: Sir, please try to remain professional.

COMMITTEE EXECUTIVE: Chicken shits. You're afraid of Niggers, you've always been afraid of Niggers. I'm not, bunch of pansy liberals.

COMMITTEE JUNIOR: This is the same attitude that got us into trouble in Simi Valley, let me handle this.

COMMITTEE EXECUTIVE: You little shit, you're going to get us into more deliberations.

COMMITTEE SENIOR: Let him handle it, you've already alarmed everyone with your little neo-nazis, remember Howard Beach.

COMMITTEE EXECUTIVE: Guilty, guilty, yeah, I'm guilty! Who the fuck cares? Take another four hundred years and figure that one out.

(COMMITTEE JUNIOR walks over to TOD. COMMITTEE SENIOR and COMMITTEE EXECUTIVE remain behind.)

COMMITTEE JUNIOR: Tod, I know what you're going through. I know you, I understand. We went to school together, remember? We lived together for four years. I know your life story.

Look, I'm trying to help you out, Tod, but these two are from the Old School, they believe in the system. They created the system.

Someday we too shall create a system, but there's only so much I can do.

COMMITTEE EXECUTIVE: I'm tired of your apathy, your crying, your welfare. Do something about it. Weak, simple, assimilated, empty, white assed, nigger...

COMMITTEE SENIOR: Sir, please!

COMMITTEE EXECUTIVE: Can he fight? Can he fight?

COMMITTEE JUNIOR: You have to start coming up with some of the answers, the burdens all on you, Babe. Why you're the first to get this far so pure and innocent. We're proud of you, but don't let us down, we're counting on you. We've invested a lot in you. Be confident with these people. You know, Tod, I think I've worked with Black people more than you have, imagine that. We're with you all the way, just don't turn against us.

Tod, the boy, Tod still hates the world. You used to crack me up you were so naive and innocent. Perfect like a dream. You have the potential to be greater than anything I've ever seen. I envy your oppression, Tod. My idealism is just an obsession. There's no need for me to be ideal. I believe that you could have been a savior, but you were led astray. You began to believe in your own perfection.

TOD: Wait, I know you. I know you.

COMMITTEE JUNIOR: Yes, Tod, you created me. I followed you like all of your devoted friends who had never met anyone quite like you before. Why you spoke so well and you were so intelligent. I think we felt betrayed, dumber than a nigger, now that's dumb.

TOD: It was you. I thought you loved me.

COMMITTEE JUNIOR: We all loved you, but did you really think that I could ever vote for you for president. People laughed at us, people called us names as we followed you so perfect and pure. But this is the end, Tod. I'm sorry, but as of now we were never really friends. I can't take the risk of that coming up in some file somewhere. They might think I'm a nigger lover, and then I'd be lost forever. You are the first and the last.

(COMMITTEE JUNIOR calls over the other members.)

Yes, here he is boys, the one I told you about. Tod the boy, Tod, Tod the nigger, Tod, shining black in all his potential. The one who calls himself a savior. The one who performs such miracles. Why one time he even graduated Phi Beta Kappa right before my eyes. I call for the vote. All in favor say, "Aye."

THE COMMITTEE: Aye!

COMMITTEE JUNIOR: Those opposed. Oh, so sorry, Tod. Still a nigger, Tod, in the 21st Century. As I said, I wouldn't expect many social reforms if I were you. What's another four hundred years anyway? You seem to be so good at waiting.

COMMITTEE EXECUTIVE: I'm surprised he even got this far.

COMMITTEE SENIOR: And the book is closed, a tragic chapter in the history of making the American Negro extinct. The anthropologists will say they died from apathy.

COMMITTEE JUNIOR: Sign your name here please.

TOD: I don't remember how.

COMMITTEE JUNIOR: Just make an "X."

COMMITTEE EXECUTIVE: Who's next on the list.

COMMITTEE JUNIOR: Tod Goldstein.

COMMITTEE SENIOR: Sounds like a Jew.

COMMITTEE JUNIOR: No he still can't be a Jew.

COMMITTEE EXECUTIVE: Why not? Check code 517 section 10 under the Tribal Egalitarian Act. We must use the term of "Judaic origin."

COMMITTEE EXECUTIVE: But still a kike!

COMMITTEE JUNIOR: All in favor?

THE COMMITTEE: Aye!

COMMITTEE JUNIOR: None oppose, still a kike.

COMMITTEE EXECUTIVE: Next on the list.

COMMITTEE JUNIOR: Tod Gonzales.

COMMITTEE EXECUTIVE: Come on, what's with you guys, a spic now?

COMMITTEE JUNIOR: But that's our job.

COMMITTEE EXECUTIVE: I hate ethnicity.

COMMITTEE SENIOR: Look here, at least he's from Spain.

COMMITTEE EXECUTIVE: Does Spain still exist?

COMMITTEE JUNIOR: Spain is dead.

COMMITTEE EXECUTIVE: Total reform!

COMMITTEE JUNIOR: All in favor?

THE COMMITTEE: Aye!

THE COMMITTEE: If you turn against us, we will destroy you.

COMMITTEE EXECUTIVE: Next!

COMMITTEE JUNIOR: Tod Gortowski.

THE COMMITTEE: A Pollock!

(The COMMITTEE leaves laughing as the bookshelf closes behind them.)

SCENE EIGHT—RESURRECTION

TOD: My eyes are clearer now. At last I see, the mystery is gone. No veiled promise, no unseen hand. The truth, the truth at last, not free.

You never really intended for me to survive, did you?

You never intended for me to be equal.

But the road has been made ready. All is clear.

Let there be a new language.

Let there be new words.

Elijah said we must have a place to be ourselves, with no contradictions, and no justifications, and no psychological mandates, free to ourselves...

And Malcolm said by any means necessary...

And Martin said let freedom ring...

And Marcus said,

and WEB said,

and Booker T. said,

and Fannie said,

and Angela said,

and Huey said,

and Moses said let my people go...

And Tod says, enough's been said.

All it takes is a leap of faith,

the leap of faith.

Do I believe I'm free?

Do I believe I am free?

Do you believe?

And now I know that every moment

is a freedom moment in an act to survive.

I come to bring truth to the word. Haven't you heard this before. Do you not see it manifest before your eyes.

Live free or die!

(TOD raises a Black Power fist.)

Live free or die!

Live free or die!

(TOD slowly opens up his fist as a blinding light fills the stage. TOD slowly lowers his open hand and offers it to the audience.)

MARY MARTHA: *(sings)* Tod opened his black bound fist and found his salvation there.

Tod opened his black bound fist and found a new world there.

Tod opened up his black bound fist to lead his people there.

Tod opened up his black bound fist and unleashed the power...
Bound was the light.
The blinding light,
for a second
he saw the wonder,
for a second
he saw the future,
for a second
he saw the past.
His hand could bend.
His hand could build.
His hand could take.
His hand could kill.
He was a man.
He has come home.
We all can see,
for a second.

REVEREND JOE: There were no written texts to prophesy his birth. Writing is the way of the oppressor. But you see the signs, can't you see the signs? The day will come when he will rise and the earth shall stand still.

Tod will say, "this is the end," and it will end. Tod will say, "let there be darkness," and the stars will fall from the sky. Tod will say, "enough!" and peace, peace in the morning.

TOD: We did not know who we were.
We did not know our richness.
We did not know our beauty.
Until now.
We had to fight for identity.
We had no identity before.
We had to fight for beauty.
Now we know.
And can go home.
The doors are open.
Won't you come?
Won't you come?
By his hand.
By his hand.
Tod took himself
by his hand and...

MARY MARTHA: Tod?

TOD: Yes.

REVEREND JOE: Tod?

TOD: Yes.

MARY MARTHA: , REVEREND JOE: Tod.

TOD: I'm alive?

MARY MARTHA: Yes.

TOD: I'm alive?

REVEREND JOE: Yes.

TOD: I'm alive.

(TOD takes one single step into darkness. Blackout.)
END OF PLAY

RAIN CITY PROJECTS
ABIGAIL'S ATLAS *Suzanne Maynard*
  Annex Theatre, Seattle
CAPOEIRA *Tania Myren-Zobel*
  Audrey Skirball-Kenis Theatre, LA
CONTENTS UNDER PRESSURE *Deb*
  Parks-Satterfield Alice B. Theatre, Seattle
DEAR MISS ELENA *Ludmilla Razumovskaya*
Seattle Group Theatre
THE FATTY ARBUCKLE SPOOK HOUSE REVUE
Chris Jeffries Annex Theatre, Seattle
GHOSTS *John O'Keefe*
New City Theater, Seattle
GIRL BAR *Phyllis Nagy*
The Loft Theatre, Tampa
GOD IN LITTLE PIECES *Silas Jones*
  Audrey Skirball-Kenis Theatre, LA
HALCYON DAYS *Steven Dietz*
A Contemporary Theatre, Seattle
HIDDEN HISTORY *Drew Emery* Alice B.
  Theatre, Seattle
HIGH STRANGENESS *Todd Alcott* Annex
  Theatre, Seattle
N. DEBEAUBIEN'S HUNCHBACK OF
  NOTRE DAME *Larson, Lee, Wackler, &*
  Kohler Annex Theatre, Seattle
HUNGER *Ki Gottberg* New City Theater, Seattle
IN MY FATHER'S BED *Randa Downs*
  Alice B. Theatre, Seattle
ISMENE & INTRUDERS *Jan Maher* Local
  Access, Seattle
THE LADIES OF THE CAMELLIAS *Lillian*
  Garrett-Groag Oregon Shakespeare Festival
LETTERS TO THE ALIEN *Jonathan*
  Harris Theatre R.A.W., Seattle
LIVING WATER *Mary Victoria*
  Dombrowski Living Water Theater, Bainbridge Island
LOUISIANA PURCHASE *Rick Rankin*
  Alice B. Theatre, Seattle

THE 1992 HOUSE OF DAMES
 ANTHOLOGY *13 Authors* House of
 Dames, Seattle
THE 1992 NEW DRAMATISTS
 SCRIPTSHARE CATALOG New
 Dramatists, NYC
THE 1993 NEW DRAMATISTS
 SCRIPTSHARE CATALOG New
 Dramatists, NYC
PLANET JANET *Bret Fetzer* Angry Red
 Planet, Seattle
REAL WOMEN HAVE CURVES *Josefina*
 Lopez Seattle Group Theatre
THE SNOWFLAKE AVALANCHE *Y York*
 Seattle Group Theatre
TEARS OF RAGE *Doris Baizley* A
 Contemporary Theatre, Seattle
TIMBER *Burke Ormsby & Mary Myrtly*
 Moss (adapt. Bryan Willis) Seattle
 Public Theater
TOD, THE BOY, TOD *Talvin Wilkes*
 Seattle Group Theatre
TRUST *Steven Dietz* A Contemporary
 Theatre, Seattle
THE 20TH CENTURY *10 Playwrights*
 Annex Theatre, Seattle
THE WATER PRINCIPLE *Eliza Anderson*
 Audrey Skirball-Kenis Theatre, LA
WHO CAUSES THE DARKNESS? *Marion*
 Isaac McClinton Seattle Group Theatre
WILLI *John Pielmeier* A Contemporary
 Theatre, Seattle
WISHING ACES *Rosary O'Neill* Southern
 Repertory Theatre, New Orleans
WOLF AT THE DOOR *Erik Ehn* Empty
 Space Theatre, Seattle
THE WOODEN BREEKS *Glen Berger*
 Annex Theatre, Seattle

VOICES OF COLOR

50 SCENES AND MONOLOGUES
BY AFRICAN AMERICAN PLAYWRIGHTS

Edited with an introduction by
Woodie King, Jr.

Voices of Color is the first collection of scenes and monologues by African American playwrights. While scene and monologue books proliferate by and for the dominant culture, there has rarely been signigicant representation of the vibrant literary contributions of African American theatre artists. Until now.

This major omnibus of contemporary American wirting will serve as a primary resource for African American artists in search of their own voice for the stage. Actors and directors will now have access to a much larger spectrum of work in which to shine. Readers will be introduced to a rich medley of work of the human spirirt. And schools, colleges and libraries will, at last, have the book we all need to fully explore America's potnetial for drama.

$9.95 • PAPER • ISBN: 1-55783-174-2

APPLAUSE